# 1 Taking phone calls

→ **Greet customers**
Good morning.
Good afternoon.
Good evening.

→ **Answer the telephone**
Good morning.
Can I help you?

→ **Ask who is calling**
Who's calling?
Who's speaking?

→ **Take messages**
Can I take a message?

## ■ Starter

Look at May Lee, Matthieu, Isobel, and James and
name their job. Look at the picture of reception and
name four pieces of equipment.

## ■ Listening  *Taking phone calls*

1  Listen to the calls and tick (✓) the correct answers.

**Call 1**
1  Caller's name      ☐ Mr Carl      ☐ Mr Phillips

**Call 2**
2  Room number      ☐ 329      ☐ 221

**Call 3**
3  Hotel      ☐ Rio Parc      ☐ Rio Parthenon

**Call 4**
4  Receptionist      ☐ Luke      ☐ James

2  Listen again and complete the sentences from the
receptionists' dialogues. Use these words.

| help | Can | speaking |
|------|-----|----------|
| connect | calling | through |

**Call 1**
1  Good afternoon, New Palace Hotel. May Lee
............[1]. How can I ............[2] you?

**Call 2**
2  One moment, and I'll ............[3] you.

**Call 3**
3  Just one moment. Who's ............[4], please?
Thank you, Mr Falgado. You're ............[5] now.

**Call 4**
4  Yes, sir. ............[6] I have your name, please?

Turn to the Listening script on page 66 and practise the
dialogues with a partner. Take turns to be the caller
and the receptionist.

## ■ Language study

| | |
|---|---|
| *May Lee speaking. How can I help you?* | S |
| *Can I have your name, please?* | S |
| *I'd like to speak to Mrs Bader.* | C |
| *One moment, and I'll connect you.* | S |
| *Who's calling, please?* | S |
| *You're through now.* | S |

C = customer
S = member of staff

Trish Stott & Rod Revell

OXFORD
UNIVERSITY PRESS

# Unit contents chart

| UNIT | COMMUNICATIVE AREA | SITUATIONS/FUNCTIONS | STRUCTURES |
|------|--------------------|----------------------|------------|
| ■ 1 | Taking phone calls | Incoming calls: *James speaking. How can I help?* Making simple requests: *Can/Could I reserve a parking space? I'd like to speak to Mrs Bader.* | Requests with *Can/Could*, *I'd like to* |
| ■ 2 | Giving information | Hotel and restaurant location and facilities: *There are more than 900 bedrooms on eight floors.* Identifying yourself: *My name's Caroline.* | Present Simple of *be*: *Is there?/Are there?, There is/ There are, There isn't/There aren't* |
| ■ 3 | Taking room reservations | Requesting information: *Do you have a double room? Does the hotel have a restaurant?* | *Do, Does* Prepositions of time: *on, at, in, from ... to* |
| ■ 4 | Taking restaurant bookings | Opening and closing times: *When do you close? What time do you serve dinner?* | Dates Adverbs of frequency: *always, often, sometimes, rarely, never* |
| ■ 5 | Giving polite explanations | Turning down requests: *I'm sorry,/ afraid we're fully booked that weekend.* | Present Simple (short forms): *be, do, can* |
| ■ 6 | Receiving guests | Guests arriving at hotel reception or restaurant: *Could you fill in this registration card? Here's your key card.* | Possessive adjectives: *my, your, his, her, our, your, their* |
| ■ 7 | Serving in the bar | In the bar: *What can I get you?* Requests and offers: *Would you like ice and lemon?* | Requests and offers with *Can, Could, Shall, Would you like?* |
| ■ 8 | Instructions | Mixing a cocktail: *How do you make a Margarita?* Giving instructions in sequence: *First, take a cocktail shaker and fill it with crushed ice. Next, pour in one measure of tequila.* | Instructions: *take, fill, pour* Sequence markers: *first, next, then, finally* |
| ■ 9 | Taking a food order | Restaurant staff taking orders for aperitifs, starters, and main courses: *Are you ready to order? Would you like to order some wine?* | *a/an, the* *a/an, some* |
| ■ 10 | Desserts and cheese | Restaurant staff explaining cheese and dessert menus: *I recommend the French apple tart. The lemon tart is very good, too. What kind of cheese is Stilton?* | *some, any* |
| ■ 11 | Talking about wine | Restaurant wine waiter taking orders: *The Sauvignon Blanc is drier than the Riesling.* | Comparisons: *-er than, more ... than, not as ... as* |
| ■ 12 | Dealing with requests | Hotel reception and restaurant staff replying to requests: *I'll get you some more. I'll bring you another.* | Offering help: *I'll get you some/one/another/some more.* |
| ■ 13 | Describing dishes | Waiter explaining menu: *It contains/consists of/is made of pasta.* | Present Simple Passive |
| ■ 14 | Dealing with complaints | Guests complaining in a hotel and restaurant: *We ordered our drinks twenty minutes ago.* | Past Simple |
| ■ 15 | Jobs and workplaces | Hotel reception and kitchen staff explaining responsibilities: *This is Louise. She's responsible for six staff.* | *this/that, these/those, here/there responsible to, responsible for* |

| | | |
|---|---|---|
| book | make a reservation | parking space |
| busy | manager | reserve |
| computer | meeting | tomorrow |
| double room | message | tonight |
| make | | |

➤➤ Wordlist page 97

## Structures to practise

*Can/Could*

**3** Make requests with *Can* or *Could*.

Example  speak to / Mrs Bader
          ***Could** I speak to Mrs Bader, please?*

1  reserve / a parking space
2  help / you
3  make / a room reservation
4  have / your name
5  speak to / Miss Jennifer Diaz
6  book / a double room

➤➤ Language review page 76

*I'd like to*

**4** Match the words and make requests with *I'd like to*.

| | | | |
|---|---|---|---|
| book | make | speak to | reserve |

1  the manager
2  a single room
3  a reservation
4  a parking space

➤➤ Language review page 76

## ■ Listening *Taking messages*

**5** Listen to the dialogue and complete the message. Choose the correct words.

| | | |
|---|---|---|
| 502 | today | ten o'clock |
| tomorrow | 402 | Mr Schmidt |
| meeting | Mr Wollman | two o'clock |

| | |
|---|---|
| **Message for** | |
| **Room number** | |
| **Caller** | |
| **Event** | |
| **Day** | |
| **Time** | |

**6** Listen again and put the dialogue in the correct order. Complete the sentences with the information in exercise 5.

☐ A  Just one moment, and I'll connect you. I'm sorry, there's no answer from room ............[1]. Can I take a message for you?

☐ B  Hello. Could I speak to Mr ............[2] in room ............[3], please?

☐ A  Good morning, Athens Palace Hotel. Angela speaking. How can I help you?

☐ A  Certainly, sir.

☐ B  Yes, please. My name's Hans ............[4]. Please tell him there's a meeting ............[5] at ............[6] o'clock.

Practise the dialogue with a partner. Take turns to be the caller and the receptionist.

## Activity

Work with a partner. Student A's information is here. Student B's information is on page 60.

**A1**  You work at reception in the Hotel Canaria. Read the information and answer the calls.

| | | |
|---|---|---|
| **Mr Luiz** | room 204 | line is busy (take a message?) |
| **Jane Williams** | room 48 | no answer |
| **Mrs Lane** | room 469 | connect the call |

Example  *Good afternoon, Hotel Canaria. How can I help you?*

**A2**  Make three calls to the Hotel Superior. Ask to speak to these people.

| | |
|---|---|
| **Reservations Manager** | leave a message (ask him to call you back on 0778 938471) |
| **Marcello Benito** | room 571 (no answer, you will call back later) |
| **Mrs Franklin** | room 18 |

Example  *Good morning, could I speak to … please?*

## More words to use

| Greetings | Farewells | Titles | |
|---|---|---|---|
| Good morning | Good night | Mrs | Mr |
| Good afternoon | Goodbye | Ms | Dr |
| Good evening | | Miss | sir |
| | | madam | |

# 2 Giving information

⇢ **Identify yourself**
My name's Caroline.
I'm Scott.

⇢ **Ask and answer questions**
Is there air-conditioning?
Are there any shops?
There's a cocktail bar.
There aren't any shops.

⇢ **Talk about numbers**
There are 900 bedrooms.

CUMBERLAND HOTEL

## ■ Starter

Look at the photographs. Tick (✓) what you can see.

café ☐   train ☐   restaurant ☐   waiter ☐
taxi ☐   bus ☐   shop ☐   hotel ☐

## ■ Listening *Where people work*

1 Look at the pictures. Listen and complete the tables.

**Cumberland Hotel**

City: ......................... Number of rooms: .........

Number of floors: .........

Number of shops: .........

**Sydney Tower Restaurant**

City and country: .........................................

.........................................

Number of seats: .........

Type of cuisine:  Italian ......... international .........

Number of bars: .........

2 Listen again and complete the sentences.

**Dialogue 1**
1  The Cumberland Hotel is ............ London.
2  ............ ............ more than 900 bedrooms.
3  The bedrooms are on eight ............ .
4  ............ satellite TV and Internet access in all rooms.
5  ............ ............ a swimming pool?

**Dialogue 2**
6  The tower is ............ metres high.
7  ............ ............ 200 seats in the restaurant.
8  Is ............ a bar in the restaurant?

## ■ Language study

**! Expressions to learn**

| | |
|---|---|
| *Good morning. My name's Caroline.* | S |
| *There's satellite TV in all rooms.* | S |
| *Are there any shops?* | C |
| *Is there a swimming pool?* | C |
| *Hello, I'm Scott.* | S |
| *There are 200 seats in the restaurant.* | S |
| *The Sydney Tower is an à la carte restaurant.* | S |

**! New words to use**

| | |
|---|---|
| air-conditioning | floor |
| at the top of | information |
| bar | international |
| bedroom | Internet access |
| car park | laundry |
| cloakroom | money |
| cuisine | reception |
| disabled facilities | tower |
| exchange bureau | waiter |

➤➤ Wordlist page 97

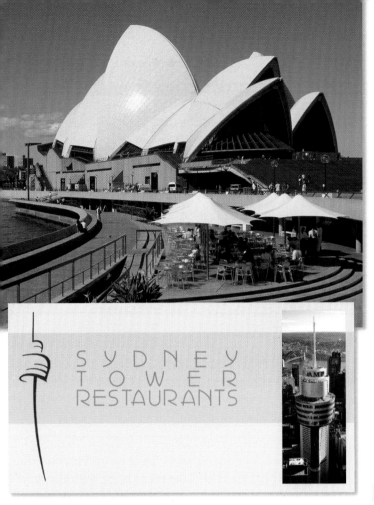

SYDNEY TOWER RESTAURANTS

## Structures to practise

*Is there?/Are there?, There is/There are, There isn't/There aren't*

Look at these examples.

*Is there a TV in the room?*      *Are there any shops?*
*There's a TV in the room.*       *There are three shops.*
*There isn't a TV in the room.*   *There aren't any shops.*

➤ Language review page 76

3 Read the information about the Plaza Hotel. Make six dialogues using *Is there?/Are there?, Yes, there is./No, there isn't. Yes, there are./No, there aren't*. Practise your dialogues with a partner.

### The Plaza Hotel in Chicago.
- There are three shops and two restaurants.
- There's a car park but there isn't a swimming pool.
- There are 300 rooms on eight floors.
- There's satellite TV, air-conditioning, and Internet access in all the rooms.

Example  A  *Is there a swimming pool?*
         B  *Yes, there is./No, there isn't.*
         A  *Are there any shops?*
         B  *Yes, there are./No, there aren't.*

■ **Listening** *What facilities are there?*

4 Match each symbol with the correct facility. Listen to part 1 and check your answers.

1 👫  2 🅿  3 🏊  4 ⓘ  5 ▣  6 ♿
7 🍸  8 💱  9 ▭  10 🖥  11 ❄AC  12 🍴

a ☐ car park            g ☐ cloakroom
b ☐ restaurant          h ☐ swimming pool
c ☐ exchange bureau     i ☐ laundry
d ☐ disabled facilities j ☐ bar
e ☐ Internet access     k ☐ information desk
f ☐ satellite TV        l ☐ air-conditioning

5 Listen to part 2. Note the hotel facilities that are available.
Example  *f*
Turn to the Listening script on page 66 and practise the dialogues with a partner. Take turns to ask and answer the questions.

## Activity

Work with a partner. Student A's information is here. Student B's information is on page 60.

**A1** Ask questions about the Manor Hotel and complete the table. Answer questions about the Hyatt Hotel. Use *Is there?/Are there?, There is/There are, There isn't/There aren't.*

| Hyatt Hotel Barcelona | Manor Hotel Melbourne |
|---|---|
| a restaurant **yes** | a restaurant ...... |
| a swimming pool **no** | a swimming pool ...... |
| any shops **no** | any shops ...... |
| air-conditioning in the rooms **no** | air-conditioning in the rooms ...... |
| Internet access in the rooms **yes** | Internet access in the rooms ...... |
| more than 200 rooms **no** | more than 300 rooms ...... |
| satellite TV in the rooms **yes** | satellite TV in the rooms ...... |

Example  A  *Excuse me, is there a restaurant?*
         B  *Yes, there is./No, there isn't.*

## More words to use

| Numbers | | | | | |
|---|---|---|---|---|---|
| 11 | eleven | 18 | eighteen | 70 | seventy |
| 12 | twelve | 19 | nineteen | 80 | eighty |
| 13 | thirteen | 20 | twenty | 90 | ninety |
| 14 | fourteen | 30 | thirty | 100 | a hundred |
| 15 | fifteen | 40 | forty | 200 | two hundred |
| 16 | sixteen | 50 | fifty | 300 | three hundred |
| 17 | seventeen | 60 | sixty | 1000 | a thousand |

# 3 Taking room reservations

- ➤ **Handle enquiries**
  Does the hotel have a restaurant?
- ➤ **Take a room reservation**
  Yes, we have a double room available.
- ➤ **Take down guest details**
  Do you have a contact number?
- ➤ **Write an email of confirmation**
  We confirm your reservation of a double room.

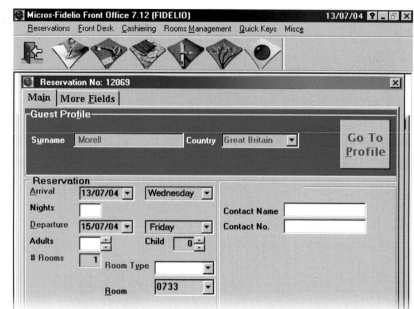

## ■ Starter

Match the words to the pictures.

1 ☐ double room
2 ☐ single room
3 ☐ suite
4 ☐ twin room

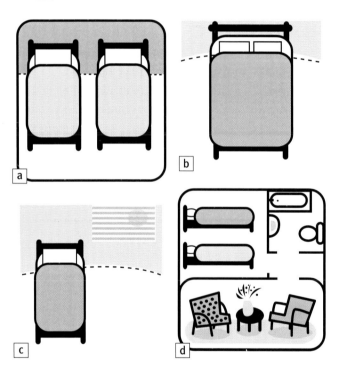

## ■ Listening *Taking a reservation*

1 Listen to the phone call and circle the correct answer.

| | |
|---|---|
| 1 Do Mr and Mrs Morell want to book a room for Tuesday night? | Yes/No |
| 2 Does the room cost 225 euros per night? | Yes/No |
| 3 Does the hotel have a restaurant? | Yes/No |
| 4 Do they want to book a table for seven o'clock? | Yes/No |
| 5 Does Mrs Morell have a mobile phone? | Yes/No |

2 Listen again and complete the five white boxes on the screen.

Turn to the Listening script on page 66 and practise the dialogue with a partner. Take turns to be the caller and the receptionist.

## ■ Language study

### ! Expressions to learn

| | |
|---|---|
| *I'd like to book a room, please.* | C |
| *Do you have a double room for next Wednesday?* | C |
| *How many nights is it for?* | S |
| *Yes, we have a double room available.* | S |
| *Would you like me to book you a table?* | S |
| *Do you have a contact number?* | S |
| *Could you send an email or fax to confirm your reservation?* | S |

### ! New words to use

| | | | |
|---|---|---|---|
| adjoining | breakfast | family | suite |
| arrive | children | husband | twin (room) |
| bath | daughter | sauna | wife |
| booking | departure | single (room) | |

➤➤ Wordlist page 97

### Structures to practise

*Do, Does*

Use *Do* and *Does* to make questions in the Present Simple.

Example   **Do** *you have a parking space?*
          **Does** *the hotel have a sauna?*

Use *do/don't, does/doesn't* in short answers.

Example  *Does the hotel have a sauna?*
           *Yes, it **does**./No, it **doesn't**.*

➤ Language review page 76

**3**  Make questions and short answers using these words.

| Do | serve lunch/dinner/afternoon tea?<br>have a parking space/swimming pool/sauna?<br>have a double room/twin room/single room? |
|---|---|
| Does | the hotel have a sauna/restaurant?<br>the bar open at lunchtime/in the evening? |

Practise the questions and short answers with a partner.

Example  A  *Do you serve dinner?*
         B  *Yes, we do./No, we don't.*

**Prepositions of time**

Look at these examples.

*on Monday, on 1st September,*
*at 8.30, at 15.00, at the weekend, at Christmas,*
*in two weeks, in September, in 2005, in spring,*
*in the evening, from 12.00 to 3.00, from 2001 to 2004*

**4**  Make questions and answers using the correct preposition.

Example  A  *Does the bank close on Mondays?*
            *(Sundays)*
         B  *No, it closes on Sundays.*

1  the restaurant close / Sundays? (Mondays)
2  the exchange bureau open / 9.00? (yes)
3  the shops close / the weekend? (no)
4  the summer season start / July? (June)
5  you serve tea / the afternoon? (yes)
6  the hotel serve dinner / 7.00–11.00? (7.00–10.00)

Practise the questions and answers with a partner.

■ **Listening** *Checking and confirming*

**5**  Listen to the voicemail message. Put the message in the correct order.

☐ Thank you, goodbye.
☐ We arrive in Düsseldorf at 6.00 p.m. on the 18th.
☐ I'd like to make a room reservation for five nights from the 18th to the 22nd of June.
☐ Please reserve us a parking space and a table for four for dinner at 7.30.
☐ Hello. This is Steven Dickson from Edinburgh, UK.
☐ I'd like a double room for me and my wife, and an adjoining twin room for my two daughters.

**6**  Complete the email confirmation. Use these words.

| table | 7.30 | twin |
|---|---|---|
| reserved | confirm | car park |

From    hoteltowers@düsseldorf.de
To:      steven.dickson@aol.com
Subject:  Confirmation

Dear Mr Dickson
We ........... your reservation of a double and adjoining ........... room for five nights from 18 to 22 June. A parking space is ........... in the hotel ........... and a ........... for four is reserved in the restaurant for dinner at ........... .
We look forward to seeing you and your family on Monday 18 June.

Regards
Trudi Fischer
Reservations

**Activity**

Work with a partner. Student A's information is here. Student B's information is on page 60.

**A1**  You work at reception in the Sonotel Hotel. Take this phone reservation. Remember to ask for confirmation in writing.

- all rooms have air-conditioning
- bathrooms have baths not showers
- there is a car park, an exchange bureau, and shops

Example  *Good morning, Sonotel Hotel. Can I help you?*

**A2**  Call the Mercury Hotel. Book a twin room for the night of 27 May for you, and your five-year-old daughter. Find out if the rooms have showers and air-conditioning, and if the hotel has a restaurant. If so, book a table for two at 7.30 p.m. Your name is Francis/Frances Lyon and you will arrive at about 7.00 p.m. Your mobile is 0778 468291.

Example  *Good morning, I'd like to book …*

**More words to use**

| Days of the week | Family members | Email abbreviations | |
|---|---|---|---|
| Monday | brother | as soon as possible | asap |
| Tuesday | children | at | @ |
| Wednesday | daughter | confirm | cfm |
| Thursday | father | for the attention of | attn |
| Friday | husband | please | pls |
| Saturday | mother | regarding | re |
| Sunday | sister | regards | rgds |
| | son | telephone | tel |
| | wife | | |

# 4 Taking restaurant bookings

- **Say opening and closing times**
  What time do you serve dinner?
  We serve dinner from 7.00 to 11.00 p.m.

- **Say what is available**
  I have a table for six on Friday evening.

- **Talk about dates**
  Saturday 24th September.

- **Talk about how often you do things**
  We never open on Mondays.

## Starter

Complete the puzzle and find a type of restaurant.

- you eat pizza here
- you drink coffee here
- you drink alcohol here

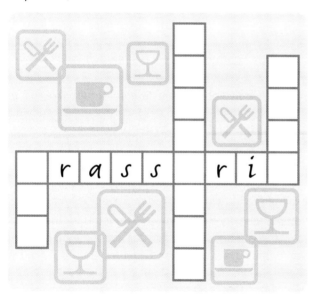

## Listening  *I'd like to book a table*

1 Listen to the phone call. Are the statements true or false?

1 The restaurant closes on Sundays. true/false
2 The restaurant opens for lunch and dinner. true/false
3 The restaurant serves lunch from twelve o'clock to two o'clock. true/false
4 Mrs Kruger wants to book a table for six people. true/false
5 The manager has a table for six at 8.00 on Saturday 24th September. true/false

2 Listen again and complete the answers. Then match them to the questions.

1 ☐ We open ………… ………… to ………… .
2 ☐ We close ………… ………… .
3 ☐ We serve dinner ………… ………… o'clock to ………… p.m.
4 ☐ We serve lunch ………… ………… o'clock to ………… o'clock.
5 ☐ I'm afraid ………… ………… ………… on Saturday 24th.

a When do you close?
b I'd like to book a table for six on Saturday evening, 24th September, please.
c What time do you serve dinner?
d What days do you open?
e What time do you serve lunch?

Practise the questions and answers with a partner. Take turns to be the customer and the restaurant manager.

## Language study

*I'd like to make a reservation, please.*          c
*What days do you open?*                            c
*We open from Tuesday to Sunday.*                   s
*What time do you serve dinner?*                    c
*We sometimes have cancellations.*                  s
*I have a table on the 23rd.*                       s
*Friday the 23rd is fine.*                          c
*We look forward to seeing you.*                    s

| | | |
|---|---|---|
| a.m. (morning) | lunch | open |
| customer | meet | p.m. (afternoon/evening) |
| fully booked | o'clock | train |

➤➤ Wordlist page 97

## Structures to practise

### Dates

3 Complete the sentences using the correct dates.

Example  *(5/8)*  The restaurant is closed on **5th August**.

1  (23/5)  We'd like to book a table for two on ... .
2  (7/11)  The new bar opens on ... .
3  (24/12) Does the restaurant open on ... ?
4  (15/2)  My holiday begins on ... .
5  (30/8)  The train leaves at 9.15 a.m. on ... .
6  (27/5)  Could I reserve a double room on ... ?

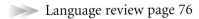 Language review page 76

### Adverbs of frequency

Look at these examples.

*I **always** go to my English classes.*
*I **often** meet friends at the weekend.*
*I **sometimes** eat in a restaurant on Saturday evenings.*
*I **rarely** go to the cinema.*
*I **never** drink alcohol in the morning.*

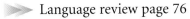 Language review page 76

4 Make a list of some things you *always, often, sometimes, rarely, never* do. Practise exchanging information with a partner.

Example  A  *I **always** have coffee for breakfast. What about you?*
         B  *No, I **rarely** have coffee for breakfast./ Yes, I **always** have coffee, too.*

### ■ Listening  *What time is it?*

5 Listen and match the times to the clocks.

a □        b □        c □        d □

6 Listen to the dialogues and write the times in each sign.

7 Read the notes and make questions and answers.

Example  what / the restaurant serve dinner (7.00 – 10.30)
         *What time does the restaurant serve dinner?*
         *From 7.00 to 10.30.*

1  when / the restaurant open for lunch (12.15 – 3.00)
2  what / my flight leave (18.20)
3  when / the group arrive from Russia (6.45 p.m.)
4  what / the exchange bureau open (8.00 a.m.)
5  what / the train leave (14.50)
6  when / the fitness centre close (10.30 p.m.)

Practise the dialogues with a partner. Take turns to ask and answer the questions.

 Language review page 76

## Activity

Work with a partner. Student A's information is here. Student B's information is on page 65.

A1 Practise taking table reservations with your partner. Use these notes to help you or invent your own responses. Then change roles.

| *Good afternoon/evening ...* | *I have a table for ...* |
|---|---|
| The Bridge Bistro | four at 8.30 |
| The River Brasserie | two at 7.00 |
| The City Restaurant | six at 8.15 |
| *We/We're ...* | *I'm sorry, we're* |
| open from 7.00 to midnight | closed on Sunday |
| open from 7.30 to 11.30 | fully booked on |
| closed on Sunday evenings | Saturday night |
| and all day Monday | *What name is it, please?* |

Example  A  *Good evening, the Bridge Bistro. Can I help you?*
         B  *Yes, please. I'd like to book a table for Saturday evening.*
         A  *Yes, certainly. How many is it for?/I'm sorry, we're fully booked on Saturday.*
         B  *I'd like a table for four, please.*
         A  *Yes, I have a table for four at 8.30.*
         B  *Thank you, 8.30 is fine.*

### More words to use

| Months | | |
|---|---|---|
| January | May | September |
| February | June | October |
| March | July | November |
| April | August | December |

# 5 Giving polite explanations

⋯⟩ **Give polite explanations**
I'm sorry, the hotel's full.
Unfortunately, we're closed on
Sundays.

⋯⟩ **Use verb short forms**
I'm afraid we're fully booked.

⋯⟩ **Give formal written apologies**
We regret that we are unable to …
I regret that I cannot …

## ■ Starter

Look at the pictures. Name the four places.

## ■ Listening *Making apologies*

1 Listen to the dialogues and tick (✓) the correct place.

| | | | |
|---|---|---|---|
| 1 | ☐ hotel | ☐ restaurant |
| 2 | ☐ car park | ☐ restaurant |
| 3 | ☐ restaurant | ☐ hotel |
| 4 | ☐ restaurant | ☐ bar |
| 5 | ☐ car park | ☐ hotel |
| 6 | ☐ restaurant | ☐ bar |
| 7 | ☐ hotel | ☐ car park |
| 8 | ☐ restaurant | ☐ hotel |

2 Listen again and complete the sentences.

1 I'm sorry, the ………… full on Tuesday.
2 Unfortunately, we're ………… on Sundays.
3 I'm afraid we're fully ………… that weekend.
4 I'm …………, we don't have anything left for tomorrow.
5 Unfortunately, the car park's ………… this weekend.
6 I'm sorry, we only ………… in the evenings.
7 I'm ………… there's only a shower.
8 I'm …………, there's no answer from room 345.

Turn to the Listening script on page 67 and practise the dialogues with a partner. Take turns to ask and answer the questions.

## ■ Language study

*I'm sorry, the hotel's full on Tuesday.*     S
*I'd like to reserve a table for Sunday lunch.*     C
*Unfortunately, we're closed on Sundays.*     S
*I'm afraid we're fully booked that weekend.*     S
*I'm sorry, we don't have anything left for tomorrow.*     S
*Does the bathroom have a bath?*     C

accept        Christmas
age           left (remaining)
anything

➤➤ Wordlist page 97

### Structures to practise
### Present Simple (short forms)

We usually use the short form of *be, do,* and *can* in the following ways.

Examples   *He's in the bar.*
         *She **isn't** a receptionist.*
         *We **don't** have anything left.*
         *I'm sorry, I **can't** reserve you a table.*

➤➤ Language review page 77

**3** Rewrite these sentences using the short forms.

1 I am sorry, but we are closed in January.
2 We do not have a reservation for tonight.
3 I am afraid I cannot reserve you a table.
4 He is the hotel manager.
5 They are not open on Mondays.
6 She cannot work today. She is not in town.
7 He does not want a single room.
8 I am sorry, we do not have a table for tomorrow.
9 Here is your room key. You are in room 409.

Practise the short forms with a partner.

**4** Refuse these requests. Give polite explanations and use the short forms.

Example  Can I reserve a table for tomorrow night?
           (no tables)
           *I'm sorry, we **don't have** any tables.*

1 I'd like to book a family room for the Easter weekend. (fully booked)
2 Can I have a parking space, please? (full)
3 Can I reserve a table for four for Tuesday? (closed on Tuesdays)
4 I'd like to speak to Mr Keane in room 248, please. (no answer)
5 I'd like to book a table for Sunday lunch. (only open evenings)

## ■ Listening  *Written apologies*

**5** Read these written apologies. Then listen to the voicemail messages and match each request to one of these apologies.

1 ☐ We regret that we cannot confirm your reservation. Unfortunately, the hotel is fully booked on Saturday.
2 ☐ We regret that we cannot reserve you a table for four on Sunday evening.
3 ☐ I regret that the restaurant is closed all day on Wednesday.
4 ☐ I regret that we cannot reserve you a double room this evening. Unfortunately, we only have single rooms left.
5 ☐ We regret that there aren't any single rooms left on Monday night.

**6** Write an email confirming the following booking. Unfortunately, there are no parking spaces until Wednesday and the bathrooms only have showers.

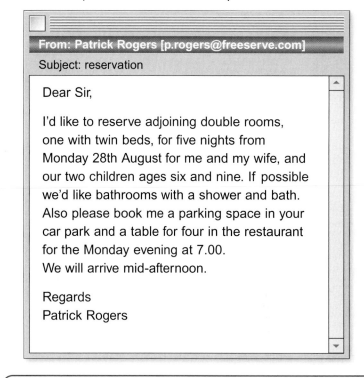

From: Patrick Rogers [p.rogers@freeserve.com]
Subject: reservation

Dear Sir,

I'd like to reserve adjoining double rooms, one with twin beds, for five nights from Monday 28th August for me and my wife, and our two children ages six and nine. If possible we'd like bathrooms with a shower and bath. Also please book me a parking space in your car park and a table for four in the restaurant for the Monday evening at 7.00.
We will arrive mid-afternoon.

Regards
Patrick Rogers

## Activity

Work with a partner. Student A's information is here. Student B's information is on page 62.

**A1**  Your name is Marc/Maria Aston. Call and make these reservations.

**Hotel Palazzo:** Two double rooms for Saturday 29th March with bathrooms with shower, and a car parking space.

**La Giralda restaurant:** Table for three for dinner on Saturday p.m. Table for two for lunch on Sunday. Table for two for lunch on Monday.

Example  *Hello, I'd like to make a reservation, please.*

**A2**  You work in this hotel and restaurant. Reply to the requests.

**Queen's Hotel:** You have double and single rooms available on Sunday 5th April, with baths not showers. All rooms have satellite TV.

**La Rueda restaurant:** Fully booked on Sunday. Open all day Sunday and closed all day Monday.

Example  *Hello, Queen's Hotel. How can I help you?*

### More words to use

| Times of day | | |
|---|---|---|
| mid-afternoon | this afternoon | this morning |
| mid-morning | this evening | |

# 6 Receiving guests

⇢ **Make polite requests**
Could I have your passport, please?

⇢ **Talk about possession**
Is this your luggage?

⇢ **Ask where places are**
Excuse me, where's the bar?
It's on the first floor next to the restaurant.

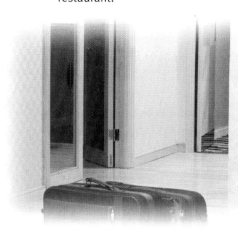

## Starter

Look at the photograph. Tick (✓) what you can see.

| | | | |
|---|---|---|---|
| 1 | receptionist ☐ | 4 | luggage ☐ |
| 2 | reception desk ☐ | 5 | telephone ☐ |
| 3 | computer ☐ | 6 | key card ☐ |

## Listening  *Checking into a hotel*

1 Listen and complete the registration card.

### Registration card

Name  ........................

Address  C/Puente 3°, 1, Madrid..

Passport Number  428329177..........

Arrival date  ........................

Departure date  ........................

Room number  ........................

Signature  C. Rodrigues..........

2 Listen again and complete the sentences.
1 Good ............, sir . Can I ............ you?
2 ............ name's Rodrigues.
3 Could you please ............ in this registration card?
4 Do I fill in ............ home address?
5 And ............ I have ............ passport?
6 The porter will ............ you with ............ luggage.

Turn to the Listening script on page 67 and practise the dialogue with a partner. Take turns to be the receptionist and the guest.

## Language study

### ! Expressions to learn

*I'd like to check in, please.*  C
*Could you please fill in this registration card?*  S
*Your room number's 361. It's on the third floor.*  S
*Here's your key card for your room.*  S
*Would you like to have dinner in the restaurant?*  S
*Can you reserve me a table for two at eight o'clock?*  C

### ! New words to use

hair salon  luggage (US baggage)
home address  night
lounge

➤ Wordlist page 97

## Structures to practise
### Possessive adjectives
singular: *my, your, his, her, its*; plural: *our, your, their*

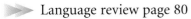 Language review page 80

3 Complete the sentences with the correct possessive form.

1 Could I have dinner in ………… room, please?
2 Would you like some help with ………… luggage?
3 We'd like to have lunch in ………… room.
4 He wants to know where to park ………… car.
5 Ask Ms Lee for ………… passport.
6 Scott and Josh are waiters at the Sydney Tower Restaurant. That's ………… job.

■ **Listening** *Where is it?*

4 Listen to the dialogues. Look at the diagrams and match these places to the rooms on the plan.

1 ☐ bar          4 ☐ hair salon
2 ☐ fitness centre    5 ☐ sauna
3 ☐ lounge

Turn to the Listening script on page 67 and practise the dialogues with a partner.

5 Work with a partner. Practise asking for and giving directions.

Example  A  *Excuse me, where's the florist?*
         B  *It's next to …*

## Activity

Work with a partner. Student A's information is here. Student B's information is on page 60.

**A1** You are a receptionist at the Queen's Hotel. Check in the guests. Remember these things: name, address, passport, key card, registration card.

Example  *Good morning. How can I help you?*

**A2** Read the two data files and check into the Park Hotel.

| | |
|---|---|
| **Name:** | Mr George/Mrs Georgina Wade |
| **Room:** | double, three nights |
| **Address:** | Flat 7A, Connex House, London N2 9PU |
| **Passport No:** | 433800125 |

| | |
|---|---|
| **Name:** | Mr Xiang/Mrs Li Zhu |
| **Room:** | single, two nights |
| **Address:** | 22 Sunland Villas, 688 Quing Xi Road, Shanghai 200336 |
| **Passport No:** | 239347596 |

Example  *Good afternoon. My name's George/Georgina Wade. I'd like to check in, please.*

### More words to use

| Seasons | | Special occasions | |
|---|---|---|---|
| spring | autumn | Christmas | Diwali |
| summer | winter | Easter | Ramadan |
| | | New Year | public holiday |

in

on

next to

opposite

behind

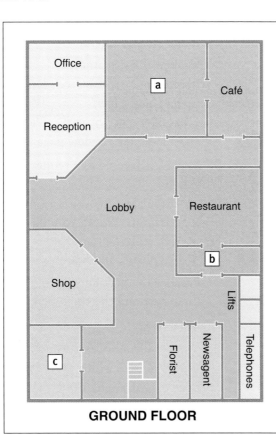

**GROUND FLOOR**

(Office, a, Café, Reception, Lobby, Restaurant, b, Shop, Florist, Newsagent, Telephones, Lifts, c)

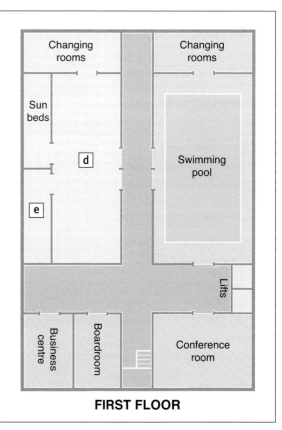

**FIRST FLOOR**

(Changing rooms, Changing rooms, Sun beds, d, Swimming pool, e, Business centre, Boardroom, Conference room, Lifts)

# 7 Serving in the bar

⇢ **Ask what people want**
Good evening. What can I get you?

⇢ **Ask how customers would like their drinks served**
Would you like ice and lemon?

⇢ **Ask how customers want to pay**
Shall I charge this to your room?

■ **Starter**

Divide the drinks in the picture into four categories.
- beer • wine • spirits • soft drinks/mixers

■ **Listening** *What can I get you?*

1 Listen to the customers ordering drinks from the bar. What do they order?

| Margarita | San Miguel | Guinness | gin and tonic |
|-----------|-----------|----------|---------------|

1 Paul     ............
2 Gaby     ...........
3 Michelle     ...........
4 Kurt     ...........

2 Listen again and answer the questions.
1 Where does Paul want to have a drink?
2 What kind of drink is a Margarita?
3 Does Kurt order bottled or draught beer?
4 What does Gaby want in her gin and tonic?
5 How does Paul pay?

■ **Language study**

### ! Expressions to learn

| | |
|---|---|
| *What can I get you?* | S |
| *Would you like draught or bottled beer?* | S |
| *Would you like ice and lemon?* | S |
| *Shall I charge this to your room?* | S |
| *No thanks, I'll pay cash.* | C |

### ! New words to use

| | | |
|---|---|---|
| beer | mineral water | tonic |
| brandy | (sparkling/still) | vodka |
| cocktail | soda | whisky |
| dry (wine) | soft drink (US soda) | wine (red/white) |
| gin | spirit | |
| medium dry (wine) | sweet (wine) | |

➤ Wordlist page 97

**Structures to practise**
**Requests and offers**

Look at these examples.

| Requests | Offers |
|----------|--------|
| *Could I* have a beer? | *Would you like* ice? |
| *Can I* have your key card? | *Shall I* charge this to your room? |

➤ Language review page 80

3 Match each reply to a request or offer in the examples above.
1 Yes, please. My room number's 235.
2 Certainly. Would you like draught or bottled?
3 Certainly. Here it is.
4 Yes please, and lemon.

Practise the dialogues with a partner. Take turns to be the server and the customer.

**Adjectives**

Look at the adjectives we use with different drinks.

| Wine | red, white, dry, medium dry, sweet |
|------|-------------------------------------|
| Beer | draught, bottled, large, small |
| Spirits | large (double), small (single) |
| Water | sparkling, still |

| BAR TARIFF in € (euros) | large | small |
|---|---|---|
| Beer ............................ | 7 | 4 |
| Whisky ........................ | 10 | 6 |
| Gin ............................. | 9 | 5 |
| Vodka .......................... | 9 | 5 |
| Bacardi ...................... | 10 | 6 |
| Cognac ....................... | 14 | 7 |
| Red wine (glass) ........... | 8 | 4 |
| White wine (glass) ......... | 8 | 4 |
| Orange juice ................ | 3 | |
| Tonic .......................... | 3 | |
| Soda water .................. | 3 | |
| Coke ........................... | 3 | |
| Mineral water .............. | 4 | |

**4** Practise asking questions with a partner. Use *Would you like ...?* and the correct adjectives to find out exactly what the customers want.

Example  A  *Hi, Could I have a beer, please?*
           B  *Yes, **would you like** a **large** one or a **small** one?*
           A  *A **large** one, please.*

1 Can I have two whiskies, please?
2 Could I have a mineral water?
3 A glass of white wine, please.
4 A vodka and tonic, please.
5 Could I have a beer?
6 Can I have a brandy, please?

Practise the dialogues with a partner. Take turns to be the server and the customer.

## ■ Listening *How much is that?*

**5** Listen to five people buying drinks. Read the bar tariff. How many euros is each person charged?

**6** Write three short dialogues taking orders for drinks and asking for payment.

Example  A  *What can I get you?*
           B  *A beer and a vodka and tonic, please.*
           A  *A large or a small beer?*
           B  *Small, please.*
           A  *Would you like ice with the vodka?*
           B  *Yes, please. How much is that?*
           A  *Twelve euros.*

Practise the dialogues with a partner. Take turns to be the server and the customer.

## Activity

Work with a partner. Look at the drinks list and practise ordering drinks. Take turns to be the server and the customer.

Example  A  *Could I have a vodka and orange, please?*
           B  *Certainly. Would you a large one or small one?*
           A  *A large one.*
           B  *Would you like ice and lemon?*
           A  *Ice but no lemon, thank you.*

| | |
|---|---|
| vodka and orange | red wine |
| brandy and ginger ale | beer |
| whisky and soda | mineral water |
| bacardi and coke | orange juice |
| gin and tonic | lemonade |
| white wine (sweet, medium dry, dry) | |

## More words to use

| Spirits (US liquor) | Wines (fortified) |
|---|---|
| brandy | madeira |
| pastis | port |
| rum | sherry |
| tequila | vermouth |

| Wines (table) | | |
|---|---|---|
| Barsac | Chardonnay | Riesling |
| Beaujolais | Chianti | Sauvignon Blanc |
| Bordeaux | Frascati | Shiraz |
| Chablis | Merlot | Zinfandel |
| Champagne | Muscadet | |

# 8 Instructions

⸱⸱> **Ask for instructions**
How do you make a Margarita?

⸱⸱> **Explain how to do things**
Pour in one measure of tequila.

⸱⸱> **Put things in order**
First, take a cocktail shaker and fill it with ice.

## ■ Starter

Most bars serve cocktails. What cocktails do you know? What's in them?

## ■ Listening *How do you make a cocktail?*

1 Listen to the instructions and follow the sequence of pictures from 1–9.

2 Match the instructions to the pictures.
- ☐ Shake well, to mix and chill the liquids.
- ☐ Next, pour in one measure of tequila.
- ☐ First, take a cocktail shaker and fill it with crushed ice.
- ☐ Finally, pour the Margarita into the glass and serve.
- ☐ Garnish with a slice of lime.
- ☐ Then squeeze some fresh lemon juice into the shaker.
- ☐ Then pour in a quarter measure of triple sec.
- ☐ Then add a dash of lime juice.
- ☐ Then put some ice cubes into a salt-rimmed glass.

Take turns to practise the instructions and mime the actions with a partner.

## ■ Language study

### ! Expressions to learn

| | |
|---|---|
| *First, take a cocktail shaker.* | S |
| *Fill it with crushed ice.* | S |
| *Next, pour in one measure of tequila.* | S |
| *Then add a dash of lime juice.* | S |
| *Shake well.* | S |
| *Then put some ice cubes into a salt-rimmed glass.* | S |
| *Garnish with a slice of lime.* | S |

### ! New words to use

| | | | |
|---|---|---|---|
| Angostura bitters | chill | liquid | squeeze |
| bar spoon | cocktail glass | mix | stir |
| caster sugar | fresh | olive | strain |
| cherry | half | quarter | triple sec |

➤➤ Wordlist page 97

### Structures to practise

**Instructions and sequence markers**

Make instructions with the base form of the verb, e.g. *take, fill, pour.* Use sequence markers like *first, next, then, finally* to explain the order of actions.

Example    *To make a Bloody Mary, **first, take** a glass. **Next, add** some ice. Pour in two measures of vodka. **Then fill** the glass with tomato juice. **Then add** a dash of Worcester sauce, and Tabasco sauce. **Finally, stir** with a bar spoon and **garnish** with a slice of lemon.*

3 Write instructions using sequence markers.

1 Make a cafetière of coffee:
- put / coffee / cafetiere
- boil / water
- fill / cafetière

2 Send an email:
- write / email address
- write / information
- send

3 Register a guest:
- give / registration card
- ask / guest / fill in
- ask / passport
- give / key card

## ■ Listening  *Can you make these drinks?*

4 What do you need to make a Daiquiri and a Manhattan? Listen and write D or M in the boxes.

- ☐ ice
- ☐ lemon juice
- ☐ crushed ice
- ☐ cherry
- ☐ Canadian whisky
- ☐ caster sugar
- ☐ slice of lemon

- ☐ cocktail shaker
- ☐ large glass
- ☐ Angostura bitters
- ☐ sweet vermouth
- ☐ cocktail glass
- ☐ slice of lemon
- ☐ light rum
- ☐ cocktail glass

5 Listen again and use the words in exercise 4 to complete the instructions for each cocktail.
Take turns to practise giving the instructions with a partner.

## Activity

Work with a partner. Student A's information is here. Student B's information is on page 60.

A1 Ask your partner how to make a cocktail called a Broadway. Take notes on how to make it. Read the notes back to your partner.

A2 Here are the instructions for making a cocktail called a Whisky Sour. Tell your partner how to make it. Ask him/her to take notes and read it back to you.

1 First, take a chilled wine glass from the fridge.
2 Then pour in a measure of whisky.
3 Next, add a dash of sugar syrup.
4 Then add two teaspoons of lemon juice.
5 Stir gently.
6 Finally, garnish with a slice of lemon and a cherry.

### More words to use

| Cocktails | Liqueurs | Fractions |
|---|---|---|
| Americano | Amaretto | $1/4$  a quarter |
| Bloody Mary | Bailey's | $1/2$  a half |
| Cosmopolitan | Cointreau | $3/4$  three quarters |
| Cuba Libre | Drambuie | $1/3$  a third |
| Mai Tai | Grand Marnier | |
| Sea Breeze | Sambuca | |
| Whisky Sour | Southern Comfort | |
| | Tia Maria | |

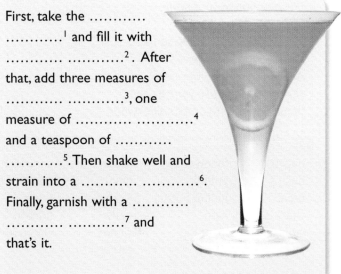

# Daiquiri

First, take the ............ ............¹ and fill it with ............ ............². After that, add three measures of ............ ............³, one measure of ............ ............⁴ and a teaspoon of ............ ............⁵. Then shake well and strain into a ............ ............⁶. Finally, garnish with a ............ ............ ............⁷ and that's it.

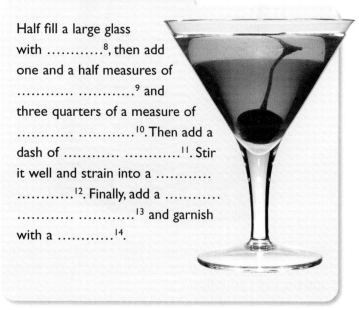

# Manhattan

Half fill a large glass with ............⁸, then add one and a half measures of ............ ............⁹ and three quarters of a measure of ............ ............¹⁰. Then add a dash of ............ ............¹¹. Stir it well and strain into a ............ ............¹². Finally, add a ............ ............ ............¹³ and garnish with a ............¹⁴.

## 9 Taking a food order

> **Look after guests as they arrive**
> Can I take your coats?
> This way, please.

> **Make guests feel welcome**
> Here's the menu.
> Can I get you an aperitif?

> **Take orders**
> Are you ready to order?

### ■ Starter

Read the menu. Which dishes are vegetarian?

### ■ Listening *Taking an order*

1 Listen to the dialogue. Are the statements true or false?

| | | |
|---|---|---|
| 1 | The guests order aperitifs. | true/false |
| 2 | The soup of the day is minestrone. | true/false |
| 3 | They don't order a first course. | true/false |
| 4 | The woman orders fish for her main course. | true/false |
| 5 | They order a bottle of white wine. | true/false |
| 6 | They order a bottle of sparkling mineral water. | true/false |

2 Listen again and complete the server's order pad with the customers' food order.

Turn to the Listening script on page 68 and practise the dialogue in groups of three. Take turns to be the waiter and the two customers.

## À La Carte Menu

**First courses**

Avocado and prawn tart

Mushrooms in garlic

Asparagus with Hollandaise sauce

Chicken liver pâté

Goat's cheese salad

Smoked trout

**Main courses**

Fillet steak

Pork chops with lemon and celery

Lamb cutlets in red wine

Salmon with dill sauce

Grilled aubergines with parmesan

King prawns with chilli and garlic

Red pepper and mushroom tart

### ■ Language study

**! Expressions to learn**

| | |
|---|---|
| *I'll show you to your table.* | S |
| *Can I take your coats?* | S |
| *Here's the menu and wine list.* | S |
| *Can I get you an aperitif?* | S |
| *Are you ready to order now?* | S |
| *How would you like your steak?* | S |
| *Would you like to order some wine?* | S |

**! New words to use**

| | | | |
|---|---|---|---|
| bacon | followed by | medium rare | sandwich |
| basil | grilled | menu | soup |
| bread | half (a bottle) | mushroom | toast |
| chef's salad | ham | ready | tomato |
| croissant | meat | salmon | watercress |
| egg | | | |

➤ Wordlist page 97

### Structures to practise

#### a/an, the

Use *a/an* when you first talk about something. Use *the* when you talk about something for the second time or when it's clear what you're talking about.

Examples  *We have **a** reservation. **The** reservation is for eight o'clock.*
*I'd like **an** aperitif, please.*
*Is this **the** menu?*

➤➤ Language review page 80

**3** Complete the sentences with *a/an* or *the*.

1  Can we have ………… adjoining room?
2  What's ………… dish of the day?
3  Could we have ………… table for four?
4  Put ………… olive on a cocktail stick. Then, put ………… olive in the glass.
5  Yes, the hotel has ………… car park.
6  Put some crushed ice into ………… cocktail shaker. Pour three measures of gin into ………… shaker and stir.

#### a/an, some

Use *a/an* instead of *one* to talk about countable nouns. Use *some* to talk about uncountable nouns.

Examples  *I'd like **a** bottle of wine/**an** aperitif.*
*I'd like **some** bread/**some** water/**some** milk.*

➤➤ Language review page 80

**4** Complete the sentences with *a/an* or *some*.

1  Would you like ………… wine?
2  ………… bottle of Chablis, please.
3  Could we have ………… bread?
4  Would you like ………… aperitif?
5  Could I have ………… ice in my coke?
6  Could you call me ………… taxi?
7  Just ………… glass of red wine, please.
8  I want to change ………… money.

### ■ Listening  *Are you ready to order?*

**5** Listen to the dialogues and complete the orders. Use these words.

| soup | mushroom | tea |
|------|----------|-----|
| salad | bacon | sandwich |

**Dialogue 1**

1  egg and …………
2  pot of …………

**Dialogue 2**

3  basil and tomato …………
4  ………… risotto

**Dialogue 3**

5  cheese and ham …………
6  chef's …………

Listen again and put the food and drink into three menus.

| breakfast | lunch | dinner |
|-----------|-------|--------|
| ………… | ………… | ………… |
| ………… | ………… | ………… |

Take turns to practise taking and making orders from the different menus with a partner.

### Activity

Work with a partner. Create a menu with five first courses and five main courses. Refer to the menu on page 20 to help you. Take turns to practise making orders.

| *Starters* | *Main course* |
|------------|---------------|
| *mushroom pâté* | *chicken casserole* |

### More words to use

| Starters/First courses | Main courses |
|------------------------|--------------|
| crab cakes | fillet/sirloin/T-bone steak |
| duck's liver pâté | poached monkfish/salmon/ |
| moules marinière | halibut |
| red onion tart | pork or lamb chops/cutlets |
| rocket salad | roast beef/lamb/chicken/ |
| smoked salmon terrine | pork |

# 10 Desserts and cheese

⤷ **Present the dessert menu**
Today, we have French apple tart.

⤷ **Give guests a choice**
Would you like it with cream or ice cream?

⤷ **Talk about cheese**
Manchego is a hard cheese from Spain.

## ■ Starter

Look at the dessert menu and specials board.
Which desserts from the menu can you find in
the photographs?

### DESSERT MENU

Profiteroles with chocolate sauce

Lemon tart

Chocolate mousse

Crème brulée

Tiramisu

Ice cream (vanilla, raspberry,
chocolate)

Blackcurrant sorbet

### TODAY'S SPECIALS

– French apple tart

– Summer pudding

– Hazelnut meringue with
summer berries

All desserts served with
cream or ice cream.

## ■ Listening  *What's for dessert?*

1  Listen to the dialogue. Which desserts do the
customers order?

2  Look at the *Expressions to learn*. Practise choosing
desserts from the menu and the specials board with a
partner.

Examples  A  *What do you recommend?*
B  *I recommend the crème brulée. It's
delicious. The lemon tart is very good, too.*

A  *I'll have the summer pudding.*
B  *Would you like it with cream or ice cream?*
A  *Ice cream, please.*

## ■ Language study

| ! Expressions to learn | |
|---|---|
| *I'm glad you enjoyed it.* | S |
| *Would you like the dessert menu?* | S |
| *Do you have any ice cream?* | C |
| *We also have a specials board.* | S |
| *I recommend the French apple tart.* | S |
| *The summer pudding is very good, too.* | S |
| *I think I'll have the French apple tart.* | C |
| *Would you like it with cream or ice cream?* | S |

| ! New words to use | | |
|---|---|---|
| blackcurrant | delicious | raspberry |
| blue | enjoy | soft |
| cheese | hard | sorbet |
| chocolate sauce | meringue | vanilla |

⤸ Wordlist page 97

## Structures to practise

*some, any*

Use *some* in positive statements and in polite offers and requests.

Examples   *I'd like **some** ice cream.*
*Would you like **some** more wine?*
*Can we have **some** bread, please?*

Use *any* in questions and negative statements.

Examples   *Do you have **any** cheese?*
*We don't have **any** wine.*

➤➤ Language review page 80

**3** Complete the sentences with *some* or *any*.

1 Do you have ............ fresh fruit?
2 Could we have ............ water, please?
3 Would you like ............ coffee?
4 I'm sorry, we don't have ............ fresh fish today.
5 Can I get you ............ more drinks?
6 There isn't ............ cheese.

**4** Make questions and answers.

Example   apple pie (cream or ice cream)
A *Can I have **some** apple pie, please?*
B ***Would you like** it **with** cream **or** ice cream?*
A *Ice cream, please.*

1 coffee (milk or without)
2 cheesecake (cream or ice cream)
3 steak (French fries or salad)
4 profiteroles (chocolate sauce or without)
5 salad (French dressing or mayonnaise)

Practise the dialogues with your partner. Take turns to ask and answer the questions.

## ■ Listening  *What about some cheese?*

**5** Listen to the description. Which of the cheeses are soft, hard, or blue? Where are they from? Complete the table.

| Cheddar | *hard* | *Britain* |
|---|---|---|
| **Mozzarella** | | |
| Manchego | | |
| **Gouda** | | |
| Gruyère | | |
| **Camembert** | | |
| Stilton | | |
| **Danish Blue** | | |

**6** Practise describing these cheeses with your partner.

Example  A ***What kind** of cheese is Cheddar?*
B *Cheddar is a **hard** cheese **from** Britain.*

1 Camembert   3 Manchego   5 Mozzarella
2 Stilton      4 Danish Blue  6 Gouda

## Activity

Work with a partner. Student A's information is on page 64. Student B's information is on page 62.

## More words to use

| Desserts | | Cheese |
|---|---|---|
| apple pie | fruit salad | cow's cheese |
| crème caramel | roulade | goat's cheese |
| crêpes | | sheep's cheese |

| Countries and nationalities | |
|---|---|
| America (US)/American | Japan/Japanese |
| Belgium/Belgian | Morocco/Moroccan |
| Brazil/Brazilian | Portugal/Portuguese |
| China/Chinese | Russia/Russian |
| England/English | Thailand/Thai |
| India/Indian | |

# 11 Talking about wine

→ **Compare different wines**
The Frascati is lighter than the Riesling.
The Chilean Merlot isn't as smooth as
the French.

→ **Talk about countries and nationalities**
It comes from Spain.
Chianti is an Italian wine.

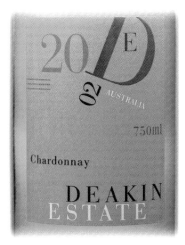

## ■ Starter

What wines can you see in the photographs?

## ■ Listening *Would you like to order some wine?*

1 Listen to the dialogue. Which wines do the customers
choose?

2 Listen again. Are the statements true or false?
1 The Riesling is drier than the
Sauvignon Blanc. true/false
2 The Sauvignon Blanc isn't as dry
as the Pinot Grigio. true/false
3 The Chardonnay is sweeter than
the Sauvignon Blanc. true/false
4 The Chilean Merlot is a full-bodied
wine. true/false
5 The Chilean Merlot is smoother than
the French. true/false
6 The French Merlot is more expensive
than the Chilean. true/false

## ■ Language study

### ! Expressions to learn

*Which is drier, the Riesling or the Sauvignon Blanc?* C
*The Sauvignon Blanc is drier than the Riesling.* S
*It isn't as dry as the Pinot Grigio.* S
*They're both full-bodied wines.* S
*The French Merlot is more expensive than
the Chilean.* S

### ! New words to use

| | | |
|---|---|---|
| become | improve | recommend |
| district | light (wine) | smooth (wine) |
| east | north | south |
| excellent | popular | west |
| fine | produce (v) | |

➤ Wordlist page 97

**Structures to practise**

**Comparisons**

Compare things using *-er than, more … than,
not as … as.*

Examples   *The Italian wine is sweeter than the
New Zealand wine.
The French wine is more expensive than
the Chilean.
The New Zealand wine isn't as dry as
the Portuguese.*

➤ Language review page 82

3 Complete these sentences with the correct comparative
forms.
1 The restaurant is ………… (busy) tonight than
last weekend.
2 The Plaza is ………… (close) to the airport than
the Grand.
3 A suite is ………… (expensive) than a single room.
4 I think the Sauvignon Blanc is ………… (good)
than the Riesling.
5 Mineral water is ………… (cheap) than wine.
6 The Chilean Merlot is ………… (not smooth) as
the French.

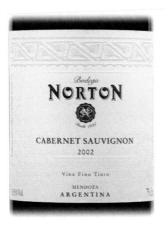

## ■ Listening  *Wines around the world*

**4** Listen and match the wines with a country or region.

| | | | |
|---|---|---|---|
| 1 ☐ Port | a France |
| 2 ☐ Sherry | b New Zealand |
| 3 ☐ Champagne | c Australia |
| 4 ☐ Sauvignon Blanc | d Portugal |
| 5 ☐ Frascati | e California |
| 6 ☐ Zinfandel | f Italy |
| 7 ☐ Chardonnay | g Spain |

**5** Look at these examples. Then listen again and underline the correct alternative.

Examples  *It's **north** of Paris.*
*It's **in the north-west**.*
*It **comes from the south**.*

NORTH
WEST — EAST
SOUTH

1 Champagne comes from a district *east/west* of Paris.
2 Further *south-west/south-east* we have the Médoc, St. Emilion, and Graves wines of the Bordeaux region.
3 Portugal is most famous for port which comes from Oporto in the *north/south*.
4 Rioja comes from an area *west/north* of Madrid.
5 South Africa produces wine in the Stellenbosch and Paarl vineyards in the *south/east* of the country.

**6** Complete the sentences to make a summary of the information in exercise 5.

| | | | |
|---|---|---|---|
| Champagne | Port | France | Bordeaux |
| Italian | Spain | Frascati | |

............¹ is the famous sparkling wine produced east of Paris. St. Emilion is also produced in ............² in the ............³ region. Two ............⁴ wines include Chianti from the Florence region and ............⁵ near Rome. ............⁶ comes from Portugal and sherry from the south of ............⁷.

### Activity

Work with a partner. Look at the webpage on page 65 and take turns to compare the different red and white wines. Discuss where they come from, their quality and their taste. Which ones would you and your partner buy?

Example   A  *Where does Selección del Castillo come from?*
B  *It comes from Spain.*
A  *What's it like?*
B  *It's a light wine and quite fruity, but it isn't as fruity as the Australian Cabernet Sauvignon.*

### More words to use

| Wine terms | Directions |
|---|---|
| cork | north/northern/the north of |
| corked | south/southern/the south of |
| corkscrew | east/eastern/the east of |
| label | west/western/the west of |
| room temperature | |

## 12  Dealing with requests

⟶ **Help guests at reception**
I'll order a taxi right away.

⟶ **Help guests in the restaurant**
Of course. I'll get you some.

⟶ **Follow customer care advice**
Always welcome customers with a smile.

### ■ Starter

Look at the pictures. What are the guests asking for?

### ■ Listening  *I'll get you some now*

1  Listen and complete the requests.

1  ............ you order a taxi for room 145, please?
2  I'd ............ a glass of wine, please.
3  ............ we have some more bread?
4  Can you send ............ ............ up to room 467, please?
5  We'd ............ a table on the terrace.
6  ............ ............ does the exchange bureau open?
7  Excuse me, this ............ is dirty.

2  Match these responses to the requests in exercise 1. Listen again and check your answers.

a  ☐ I'll see if there's one free.
b  ☐ Of course, I'll get you some now.
c  ☐ Yes sir, I'll order you one now.
d  ☐ Certainly. I'll get you one right away.
e  ☐ I'm sorry. I'll bring you another.
f  ☐ I'll send someone up right away.
g  ☐ One moment, I'll check for you.

Work with a partner. Take it in turns to practise the requests and responses.

### ■ Language study

| **!  Expressions to learn** | |
| --- | --- |
| *I'll get you one right away.* | S |
| *I'll see if there's one free.* | S |
| *One moment, I'll check for you.* | S |
| *I'll bring you another.* | S |

| **!  New words to use** | | | |
| --- | --- | --- | --- |
| business traveller | disabled | needs (n) | smile |
| conversation | eye contact | patient | terrace |
| delay | more | ring (n) | women |
| dirty | | | |

⟶ Wordlist page 97

**Structures to practise**
**Offering help**

Use *I'll* + verb to offer to do something. Use *one, some, another, some more* instead of repeating the noun.

Examples  A  *I'd like a map.*
          B  *I'll get (you)* **one.**
          A  *I'd like some bread.*
          B  *I'll bring (you)* **some.**
          A  *This spoon is dirty.*
          B  *I'll get (you)* **another.**
          A  *There isn't any bread left.*
          B  *I'll order (you)* **some more.**

⟶ Language review page 82

b

d

3   Respond to the requests using *one, some, another* or
    *some more*.

    Example   A   Could we have some bread? (get / some)
              B   *Yes. I'll **get** (you) **some**.*

    1   Can I have an orange juice, please? (get / one)
    2   Our water jug is empty. (get / some more)
    3   This bottle of wine is corked. (bring / another)
    4   Is the exchange bureau open? I need some change.
        (get / some)
    5   Could I have a beer, please? (get / one)
    6   My bath towel is very wet. (get / another)
    7   This fork is dirty. (bring / another)
    8   There isn't enough soap in the bathroom.
        (bring / some more)

    Practise the requests and responses with a partner.

■ **Listening** *Customer care*

4   Listen to the dialogue. What should you do in these
    situations?

    1   New customers arrive at reception.
    2   A customer telephones the hotel.
    3   A customer with disabilities arrives at reception.
    4   Reception is busy. Customers want to speak to you.

5   Work with a partner. Write a dialogue between a hotel
    receptionist and a woman business traveller as she
    checks in to the hotel. Use these notes.

    • book a wake-up call
    • dry cleaning (suit)
    • book a taxi
    • Internet access?
    • sauna?

    Practise the dialogue, taking turns to be the
    receptionist and the customer.

## Activity

Work with a partner. Student A's information is here.
Student B's information is on page 61.

A1   Use the notes below to make requests to your partner.

    • room noisy – move to a quieter one?
    • breakfast in my room?
    • bottle of gin and some tonic – room 488
    • more clean towels in the bathroom?
    • soup not hot enough

    Example   *Excuse me, my room is very noisy. Could I move
              to a quieter one?*

A2   Answer your partner's requests using these notes. Choose
    the best alternative.

    • will check for you
    • will send up immediately
    • will call taxi office and find out
    • will deliver to room before 8 a.m.
    • will ask them to be quiet

    Example   *Yes, of course. I'll send some up immediately.*

### More words to use

| Uncountable nouns | |
| --- | --- |
| advice | paper |
| cutlery | time |
| homework | work |
| news | |

# 13 Describing dishes

⟶ **Explain what type of dish it is**
This is a pasta dish.

⟶ **Explain what dishes are made of**
It's made from milk, cream, and eggs.

⟶ **Explain what dishes contain**
It contains mussels, lobster, and king prawns.

**STARTERS**

Asparagus with Hollandaise sauce

Mushroom and red wine pâté

Smoked salmon blinis

**MAIN COURSES**

Pork chops with port wine and plum sauce

Lamb cutlets with rosemary and garlic

Salmon coulibiac

Mixed seafood for two

Penne arrabbiata

Grilled aubergine with red peppers

## ■ Starter

Find two meat dishes, three fish dishes, and four vegetarian dishes on the menu.

## ■ Listening  *What's it made from?*

1 Look at the menu. Listen and tick (✓) three dishes from the menu that you hear.

2 Listen again and complete the sentences.
  1 This is a ............ dish.
  2 It ............ of penne, a type of pasta, in a chilli and tomato sauce.
  3 This is ............ from layers of rice mixed with onions and mushrooms.
  4 It's wrapped in puff pastry and ............ in the oven.
  5 It ............ half a lobster, king prawns, scallops and mussels.
  6 It's ............ warm with a crisp, green salad.

Take turns to describe the dishes with a partner.

## ■ Language study

**! Expressions to learn**

| | |
|---|---|
| *Excuse me, could you explain the menu to us, please?* | C |
| *What's in the penne arrabbiata?* | C |
| *This is a pasta dish.* | S |
| *It consists of penne, a type of pasta.* | S |
| *It's made from chilli, tomato, garlic, and basil.* | S |
| *This is made from layers of rice ...* | S |
| *It contains half a lobster, king prawns ...* | S |
| *It's served warm with a crisp, green salad.* | S |

**! New words to use**

| | | |
|---|---|---|
| baked | hard-boiled egg | puff pastry |
| butter knife | layer | salt (cellar) |
| candle | mussels | scallops |
| dessert fork | napkin | side plate |
| dessert spoon | onion | spicy |
| fish fork | pepper (mill) | spoon |
| fish knife | pine nut | tablecloth |
| flower arrangement | plate | |

⟶ Wordlist page 97

## Structures to practise
### Present Simple Passive

The Passive is often used to describe how things are made or done.

Look at these examples.

The chef makes ice cream from cream, eggs, and sugar.
*Ice cream **is made** from cream, egg, and sugar.*

The chef makes pancakes from eggs, milk, and flour.
*Pancakes **are made** from eggs, milk, and flour.*

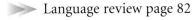 Language review page 82

**3** Change these sentences to the Passive form.

1  We make pasta from flour, eggs and salt.
2  You make a Margarita with tequila.
3  The receptionist tells guests about the hotel facilities.
4  The restaurant serves dinner from 7.30 to 11.00.
5  We make dressing from oil and vinegar.
6  The waitress takes your order at the table.

## ■ Listening  *Do you know how to lay a table?*

**4** Listen and match the items in the place setting.

1  ☐ napkin
2  ☐ side plate
3  ☐ butter knife
4  ☐ main course knife
5  ☐ main course fork
6  ☐ first course knife
7  ☐ first course fork
8  ☐ soup spoon
9  ☐ wine glass
10 ☐ salt and pepper
11 ☐ fish knife and fork
12 ☐ dessert spoon and fork

**5** Make sentences using the correct passive form. Practise the instructions with a partner.

Example  *The table **is laid** in the evening.*

| | | |
|---|---|---|
| table | lay | in the evening |
| tablecloth | place | on the table |
| napkin | fold and place | on the side plate |
| knife and fork | place | each side of the plate |
| wine glass | put | above the soup spoon |
| salt and pepper | put | in the middle of the table |
| main course plate | take away | when the main course is finished |
| dessert spoon and fork | bring | with the dessert menu |
| flower arrangement | place | next to the salt and pepper |

### Activity

Work with a partner. Student A's information is on page 64. Student B's information is on page 62.

### More words to use

| Cooking methods | | Sauces |
|---|---|---|
| bake | grill (US broil) | Aioli |
| barbecue | poach | Bearnaise |
| boil | roast | Béchamel |
| deep fry | steam | Hollandaise |
| fry | stew | Mornay |

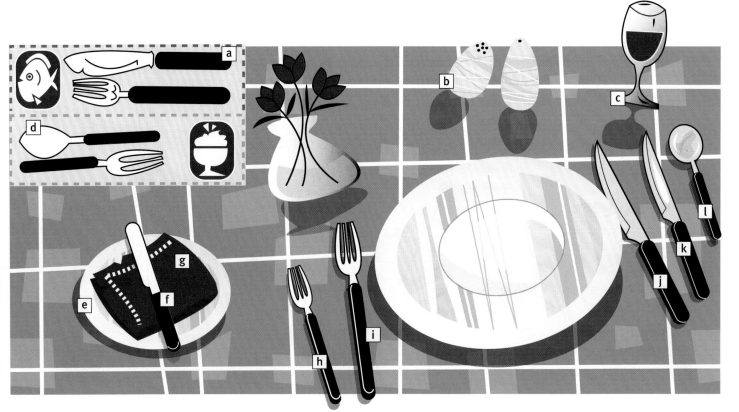

# 14 | Dealing with complaints

⇝ **Accept and apologize for complaints**
I'm sorry. We overbooked the
car park yesterday.

⇝ **Take action to help customers**
I'll speak to the chef.

⇝ **Talk about the past**
I started work three years ago.

## ■ Starter

Look at the pictures and identify five problem situations.

## ■ Listening *What is there to complain about?*

1 Listen to the complaints and match the key words to
the problems.

| 1 ☐ car park | a overcooked |
|---|---|
| 2 ☐ restaurant | b full |
| 3 ☐ rooms | c nobody gave it |
| 4 ☐ steak | d short-staffed |
| 5 ☐ message | e on different floors |

2 Listen again and match the sentences with the replies.

1 ☐ We asked you to reserve a parking space.
2 ☐ We ordered our drinks twenty minutes ago.
3 ☐ We reserved adjoining rooms.
4 ☐ This steak is really overcooked.
5 ☐ A colleague left a message at reception last night.

a I'll check with the wine waiter.
b I'm sorry. I'll change your rooms straightaway.
c I'll reserve you a space for tomorrow.
d I'm so sorry. I'll look into it.
e I'll speak to the chef and bring you another one.

# Language study

## Structures to practise

### Past Simple (Regular verbs)

The Past Simple tense is for completed actions in the past. Look at these examples of regular verbs.

*We **asked** you to reserve a parking space.*
*We **ordered** our drinks twenty minutes ago*

⟫⟫  Language review page 82

3   Use these words to make sentences in the Past Simple.

Example   We / want / buy / new mobile phone
         *We **wanted** to buy a new mobile phone.*

1   they / arrive / hotel / yesterday
2   she / ask for / dessert / without cream
3   chef / cook / wonderful / meal
4   guests / enjoy / their stay
5   he / key in / reservations data
6   waiter / open / bottle of champagne

### Past Simple (Irregular verbs)

Look at these examples of irregular verbs.

*My friend **left** (leave) a message at reception.*
*We **had** (have) lunch at the new bistro in town.*

⟫⟫  Language review page 82

4   Use the irregular verb list on page 111 to complete these sentences in the Past Simple.

1   They ............ (tell) the waiter about the mistake on the bill.
2   He ............ (go) into the kitchen to speak to the chef.
3   The guests from Japan ............ (speak) very good English.
4   Yesterday I ............ (meet) my colleagues in a bar.
5   She ............ (write) an email confirming the reservation.
6   He ............ (eat) his meal and ............ (pay) his bill.

# Listening   *I'll look into it for you*

5   Listen to the complaints and fill in the table.

| Problem | Action |
|---|---|
| 1   *beer flat* | *get you another* |
| 2   ..................... | ..................... |
| 3   ..................... | ..................... |
| 4   ..................... | ..................... |
| 5   ..................... | ..................... |
| 6   ..................... | ..................... |

6   Write the dialogues from your notes in exercise 5 and practise them with a partner.

## Activity

Work with a partner. Student A's information is here. Student B's information is on page 61. Check any words you don't understand in the Wordlist on page 97.

A1   Use these notes to make complaints to your partner. Make notes of their solutions.

| | | |
|---|---|---|
| TV broken | bath dirty | bread stale |
| bed not made | beef too salty | vegetables overcooked |
| soup cold | order late | minibar empty |

Example   *Excuse me, the TV in my room is broken.*

A2   Respond to your partner's complaints. Apologize and say what you will do to put things right.

Example   *I'm sorry. I'll send someone up immediately.*

### More words to use

| Customer complaints | | | |
|---|---|---|---|
| dusty | rude | stringy | tough |
| filthy | salty | tasteless | vinegary |
| late | stained | torn | watery |
| off | stale | | |

# Jobs and workplaces

··> **Show people around**
Here's front office.

··> **Introduce people**
This is Louise, our reception manager.

··> **Talk about people's jobs**
Melanie is responsible to the head chef.
The porters are responsible for taking
out the rubbish.

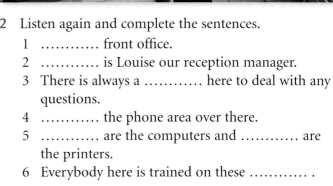

■ **Starter**

Look at the pictures. Name the workplaces and the
people's jobs.

■ **Listening** *Let's start at front office*

1 Listen to the dialogue. Are the sentences true or false?

| | | |
|---|---|---|
| 1 | Louise is responsible for seven staff. | true/false |
| 2 | They handle all the reservations in reception. | true/false |
| 3 | Requests for laundry and dry cleaning go to the kitchen. | true/false |
| 4 | The housekeeper is responsible to the assistant manager. | true/false |
| 5 | The Fidelio system is used for check-ins and payments. | true/false |
| 6 | The Galileo system is used for travel arrangements. | true/false |

2 Listen again and complete the sentences.
1 ............ front office.
2 ............ is Louise our reception manager.
3 There is always a ............ here to deal with any questions.
4 ............ the phone area over there.
5 ............ are the computers and ............ are the printers.
6 Everybody here is trained on these ............ .

■ **Language study**

! **Expressions to learn**

*Here's front office and this is Louise.* S
*Louise is responsible for six staff.* S
*In reception they handle all the reservations.* S
*There is always a receptionist here to deal
with any questions.* S
*She's responsible to the assistant manager.* S

! **New words to use**

| | | |
|---|---|---|
| arrival | in-room services | sharpen |
| cashier | pastry | side order |
| clean | payment | starter |
| dry cleaning | printer | station (work) |
| duty | process (v) | travel arrangement |
| front office | rubbish | vegetable |
| housekeeper | | |

➤➤ Wordlist page 97

## Structures to practise
*this/that, these/those, here/there*

*This is Louise.*

*That's Seth.*

*These guests are checking in.*

*Those guests checked out five minutes ago.*

*Here's the reception desk.*

*There's the reservations office.*

➤ Language review page 82

3 Practise with a partner using objects in the room.

Examples  A  *These are my books. Those are Henri's books.*
          B  *Here is the computer. There are the printers.*

### responsible to, responsible for

Look at these examples.

*The receptionist is **responsible to** the reception manager.* (the reception manager is her boss)

*The receptionist is **responsible for** taking room reservations.* (it's her job)

4 Complete the sentences using *responsible to* or *responsible for*.
  1 The cashiers are ............ the reception manager.
  2 The waiters are ............ taking orders.
  3 The duty manager is ............ all the full time staff.
  4 The porters are ............ taking the guests' luggage to their rooms.
  5 The barman is ............ the bar manager.
  6 The car park attendant is ............ parking the cars.

## ■ Listening ... *and in the kitchen*

5 Listen to the dialogue. Match the staff to their duties.

  1 ☐ Head chef          a  bakes all the bread, rolls, and croissants
  2 ☐ Sous chef          b  are responsible to the sous chef
  3 ☐ Commis chefs       c  prepare the vegetables, sharpen the knives
  4 ☐ Chefs de partie    d  writes the menus
  5 ☐ Pastry chef        e  handle all the cold dishes, the sauces, and mayonnaise
  6 ☐ Kitchen porters    f  prepare all the soups, hot starters, and side orders

6 Listen again and complete the sentences.
  1 He writes the menus and he's responsible for the ............ courses.
  2 She ............ all the soups.
  3 The chefs de partie ............ all the cold ............ .
  4 He ............ all the bread.
  5 The kitchen porters have lots of ............ .
  6 They prepare the vegetables, ............ the knives, and ............ the ovens.

7 Work with a partner. Take it in turns to explain the different jobs and duties in exercise 5.

Example  *The pastry chef bakes all the bread, rolls, and croissants. He's **responsible for** the hot desserts.*

➤ Activity page 65

### More words to use

| Kitchen equipment | Kitchenware |
|---|---|
| blender | baking tin |
| deep fat fryer | flan/tart dish |
| dishwasher | frying pan |
| food processor | mixing bowl |
| heat lamp | roasting tin |
| hob | saucepan |
| refrigerator | soufflé dish |
| toaster | stockpot |

# 16 Explaining and instructing

→ **Explain how to do things**
Put the dirty linen in the laundry bag.

→ **Talk about food preparation**
I'll chop the onions.

→ **Understand hygiene regulations**
You must wash your hands in the
hand basin.

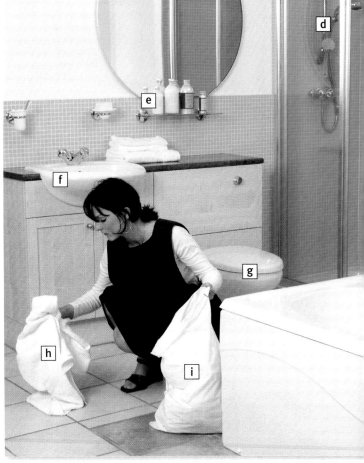

## ■ Starter

Match the words with the items in the pictures.

| | | | |
|---|---|---|---|
| 1 ☐ knife | 4 ☐ toilet | 7 ☐ saucepan |
| 2 ☐ shower | 5 ☐ towels | 8 ☐ toiletries |
| 3 ☐ hand basin | 6 ☐ colander | 9 ☐ laundry bag |

## ■ Listening *How to do it right*

1 Listen to the two dialogues and answer the questions.

**Dialogue 1**

1 What are they preparing?
2 What must they do first?
3 Do they have to scrape the potatoes?

**Dialogue 2**

4 What does Petra have to do first?
5 What does Lyn do?
6 List some of the complimentary toiletries.

2 Listen again and complete the sentences.
1 We ......... ............ prepare the lunch vegetables.
2 First, you ............ wash your hands.
3 ............ them into little sticks.
4 ............ we ............ to scrape them?
5 Then I'll ............ the onions.
6 It ............ cook for long.
7 Put the ............ linen in the laundry bag here.
8 Everything ............ be spotless.

## ■ Language study

➤ Wordlist page 97

### Structures to practise

***must, have to, don't have to, mustn't***

Look at these examples.

*You **must** wash your hands before preparing food.*
*(obligation = the speaker thinks that it's important)*
*You **have to** break the broccoli into florets.*
*(obligation = it's part of the job)*
*We **don't have to** change the towels every day.*
*(no obligation = it's not necessary)*
*You **mustn't** smoke in the kitchen.*
*(prohibition = don't do it!)*

➤ Language review page 84

3 Complete the sentences using *must, have to, don't have to, mustn't*.

1 You ............ have clean hands in the kitchen.
2 We ............ start work at 8.00 a.m.
3 I ............ (not) work on Sundays.
4 We ............ prepare the vegetables before 11.30.
5 The attendants ............ change the beds every day.
6 You ............ leave food on the floor.
7 Guests ............ check out by 12.00 noon.

### ■ Listening *Kitchen hygiene*

4 Listen and match the phrases. Then take it in turns to practise saying the regulations with a partner.

1 ☐ must always wash     a all kitchen work surfaces regularly
2 ☐ mustn't wash     b the bins regularly
3 ☐ must clean     c the floors every day
4 ☐ must sweep and wash     d your hands in the food preparation sinks
5 ☐ have to clean     e the rubbish in the correct bins
6 ☐ must put     f their hands in the hand basin

5 Look at these ideas for customer care. Take turns to practise them using *must* or *mustn't*.

- greet customers with a warm smile
- be polite
- don't keep customers waiting long
- answer the phone quickly
- remember the caller's name and use it
- don't ignore customers while you are on the phone
- smile and make eye contact if customers are waiting
- look after customers with specific needs
- be patient and helpful at all times

Example    *You **must** always greet customers with a warm smile.*

### Activity

Work with a partner. Student A's information is here. Student B's information is on page 61.

A1   Put the instructions for the recipe in the correct order. Explain your recipe to your partner.

**Mulet à la Martegale**

☐ Then pour on some olive oil.
☐ Slice a lemon and place it on top of the fish.
☐ First, wash, clean, and dry the fish.
☐ Season with salt and pepper.
☐ Cook in a moderate oven for 25–30 minutes.
☐ Place the fish in an oiled dish with the tomato and onion.
☐ Slice the tomato and chop the onion.

A2   Listen to your partner's recipe and take notes. Read your notes back to him/her and check them.

### More words to use

| Kitchen utensils | Kitchen skills |
|---|---|
| balloon whisk | beat |
| food mixer | blend |
| garlic crusher | cream |
| ladle | fold |
| rolling pin | stir |
| sieve | whip |
| wooden spoon | whisk |

# Taking telephone requests

-:*: **Give good customer service**
I'll send someone up for them right away.

-:*: **Describe hotel facilities**
The coffee shop is over there behind the lifts.

## ■ Starter

Look at the pictures. Which are to do with room service and which are to do with housekeeping?

## ■ Listening *Room service. Can I help you?*

1 Listen to the four calls. Tick (✓) the words you hear.

1 ☐ champagne      3 ☐ lunch
  ☐ wine             ☐ breakfast
  ☐ glasses          ☐ coffee

2 ☐ washing        4 ☐ button
  ☐ dry cleaning     ☐ zip
  ☐ ironing          ☐ repair
  ☐ cleaning         ☐ pressing

2 Listen again and complete the sentences.

1 We ............ four glasses.
2 My husband's suit ............ dry cleaning.
3 I have a dress that needs ............ .
4 No, you ............ ............ to do that.
5 How ............ will it be?
6 We need ............ ............ in half an hour.
7 I need ............ this afternoon.
8 Do they need ............ ?

## ■ Language study

| ! Expressions to learn | |
| --- | --- |
| *How many glasses do you need?* | S |
| *No, you don't need to do that.* | S |
| *I'll send someone up for them right away.* | S |
| *How long will it be?* | C |
| *Do they need pressing?* | S |

| ! New words to use | |
| --- | --- |
| continental breakfast | lift (US elevator) |
| foyer | trousers |
| haircut | zip |

➤➤ Wordlist page 97

## Structures to practise

### need

Look at these examples.

*He **needs** his **trousers** this afternoon.*

*She **doesn't need** her **jacket** this afternoon.*

Do you **need** a **receipt**? *Yes, I **do**./No I **don't**.*

(***need*** + noun)

*Her dress **needs** ironing.*

(***need*** + -ing)

*We **need to have** them this afternoon.*

(***need*** + full infinitive)

➤ Language review page 84

**3** Complete these sentences with *need(s)* or *don't/doesn't need.*

1 The rooms ............ cleaning after each guest.
2 The room attendants ............ to change the towels every day.
3 Your jacket ............ ironing. It's fine.
4 The guest in room 292 ............ a taxi now.
5 No, thank you. We ............ a porter.
6 You ............ to pay now, sir. I'll put it on your bill.

## ■ Listening *Facilities and services*

**4** Listen to the dialogue and answer the questions.

1 What is the first thing the guest wants to do?
2 Where is the exchange bureau?
3 When is it open?
4 Where is the hair salon?
5 Why does he want a travel agency?
6 Where is the coffee shop?

**5** Work with a partner. Match the words in columns 1 and 2 with the facilities and services in column 3. Practise asking and answering questions.

| 1 | 2 | 3 |
|---|---|---|
| airport | breakfast in bed | car park |
| backache | haircut | dry cleaning service |
| business meeting | masseur | hair salon |
| cinema | parking space | housekeeping |
| early flight | taxi | laundry service |
| feeling ill | theatre tickets | room service |
| headache | wake-up call | fitness centre |
| theatre | stained suit | theatre-booking service |
| tired | car-hire | 24-hour taxi service |

Example A *Excuse me, we're going to the **cinema** and I **need to order a taxi.***

B *Certainly, sir. We have a **24-hour taxi service.***

## Activity

Work with a partner. Student A's information is here. Student B's information is on page 60.

**A1** You are a business traveller. Phone reception and request the things on your list.

Example *Excuse me. I need to send a fax to Argentina.*

- send a fax to Argentina
- trousers / pressing
- massage
- wake-up call (5.00 a.m. tomorrow)
- taxi to airport (6.00 a.m. tomorrow)
- today's newspaper
- ashtray
- whisky for the minibar

**A2** You work in reception. Listen to your partner's requests and make appropriate responses. You may be able to help directly, or need to contact room service or housekeeping.

Example *Yes, of course. I'll contact housekeeping and send some up straightaway. How many towels do you need?*

### More words to use

| Clothes | Snack menu items |
|---|---|
| blouse | beefburger |
| cardigan | chef's salad |
| dinner jacket | coffee – espresso, latte, cappuccino |
| jumper/sweater | French fries |
| shirt | garlic bread |
| skirt | ice cream |
| socks | omelette |
| tie | pastries |
| T-shirt | soft drinks |
| underwear | soup |
| | tea – breakfast, China, Indian, fruit, herb |

# Taking difficult phone calls

⇢ **Ask for clarification over the phone**
I'm sorry, I didn't catch the date.

⇢ **Clarify spelling**
Did you say N for November?

⇢ **Negotiate prices with customers**
I can do a weekend mini-break discount.
We can give you a special weekend rate if
you stay Saturday and Sunday nights.

## ■ Starter

Look at the reservations screen. What information does
the hotel need to make a room reservation?

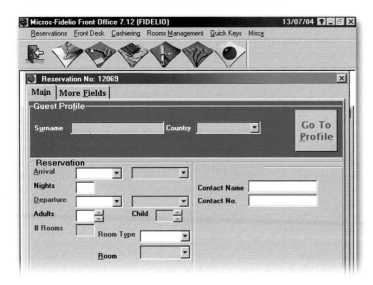

## ■ Listening *Could you repeat that, please?*

1 Listen to the dialogue. Tick (✓) the three pieces of
information Gabriella can't hear.

| | | |
|---|---|---|
| time ☐ | date ☐ | passport number ☐ |
| name ☐ | address ☐ | telephone number ☐ |

2 Listen again and complete the seven white boxes on the
reservations screen.

3 Put the words in the correct order to make phrases
from exercise 1.
1 can / little / you / up / please / speak / a / ?
2 date / the / sorry / I'm / I / didn't / catch
3 you / could / that / spell / me / for / ?
4 N / did / say / for / November / you / ?
5 you / could / that / repeat /please / ?

Turn to the Listening script on page 71. Sit back-to-back
with a partner and practise the phone call.

## ■ Language study

### ! Expressions to learn

| | |
|---|---|
| *The line is very bad.* | S C |
| *Can you speak up a little, please?* | S C |
| *I'm sorry, I didn't catch the date.* | S C |
| *What name is it, please?* | S |
| *Could you spell that for me?* | S C |
| *Did you say N for November?* | S C |
| *Can I have a contact number for you?* | S |
| *Could you repeat that, please?* | S C |

### ! New words to use

| | | |
|---|---|---|
| budget | less | sister hotel |
| country code | mini-break | standard |
| discount | rack rate | still (adv) |
| give | room rate | too much |
| include | | |

➤➤ Wordlist page 97

## Structures to practise

**Past Simple: questions and short answers**

Use *Did* and the base form of the verb to make questions in the Past Simple. Use *did* and *didn't* in short answers.

Examples  **Did** *you* **say** *N for November?*
            *Yes, I* **did.**/*No I* **didn't.**
            **Did** *he* **make** *a reservation?*
            *Yes, he* **did.**/*No, he* **didn't.**

➤ Language review page 84

4  Make questions and short answers.

Example  **Did** *they* **arrive** *last night? (yes)*
            *Yes, they* **did.**

1  They arrived last night. (yes)
2  He reserved two double rooms. (no)
3  You heard what she said. (no)
4  Mr Alimoglu called from Istanbul. (yes)
5  She ordered a cooked breakfast. (yes)
6  You booked a table for one o'clock. (no)

**Past Simple: negative statements**

Use *didn't* to make negative statements in the Past Simple.

Examples  *We* **didn't leave** *the hotel last night.*
           *She* **didn't have** *a contact number.*

➤ Language review page 84

5  Look again at exercise 4. Change the sentences into the negative form.

## ■ Listening *Negotiating room rates*

6  Listen to the dialogue and complete the table.

| | | |
|---|---|---|
| 1 | standard rack rate | € ...... |
| 2 | weekend discount rate (with breakfast) | € ...... |
| 3 | customer's budget | € ...... |
| 4 | weekend mini-break offer (with breakfast) | € ...... |
| 5 | weekend mini-break offer (without breakfast) | € ...... |

7  Listen again. Underline the correct alternative.
1  260 euros. That's for a *single/double* room, with breakfast included.
2  Isn't there some sort of weekend *discount/offer* you can give me?
3  We can *give/offer* you a special weekend rate if you stay Saturday and Sunday nights.
4  That's 200 euros per *day/night* for a double room, including breakfast.
5  I'm afraid that's still *too/very* much.
6  What's your *limit/budget*? Maybe one of our sister hotels can help.
7  We need to find a room for *less/more* than 120 euros a night.
8  Well, I can do you a special *weekday/weekend* mini-break offer of 320 euros.

Turn to the Listening script on page 71 and practise the dialogue with a partner.

## Activity

Work with a partner. Student A's information is here. Student B's information is on page 63. Make bookings and make a note of your partner's bookings.

**A1** Call the Windsor Hotel. You stayed there a year ago. Make a booking for 17–20 November for a double room with a child's bed. Get the best rate you can. Last year you paid €135 for the same type of room. Ask about weekend rates and other discounts for previous guests.

Example  *Hello, I'd like to make a reservation.*

**A2** You work at the Gatehouse Hotel. Take a phone booking, getting all the necessary details. Prices have gone up this year. The rack rate for a double room is €240. Group bookings of eight people or more get a 15% discount. Weekend rates include a 10% discount.

Example  *Good morning. Gatehouse Hotel ...*

## More words to use

| Telephone words | |
|---|---|
| battery | operator |
| cordless phone | payphone |
| dial/key in | phonebox (US callbox) |
| dialling tone | receiver/handset |
| engaged/busy tone | recharge |
| international call | reversed charges (US collect call) |
| local call | touch-tone phone |
| mobile (US cell phone) | |

# Health and safety at work

- **Be aware of health and safety precautions**
  We test the alarms regularly.

- **Find out who is qualified to help**
  Louise is a trained first aider.

- **Follow fire drill procedures**
  The assembly point is in front of the hotel.

## ■ Starter

Look at the pictures. Find six health and safety hazards.

## ■ Listening *Your health and safety is important to us*

1 Listen to the dialogue. Are the sentences true or false?

| | | |
|---|---|---|
| 1 | Health and safety is a very serious subject. | true/false |
| 2 | The hotel has regular fires. | true/false |
| 3 | The hotel tests the fire alarms regularly. | true/false |
| 4 | If staff see an accident, they must phone reception. | true/false |
| 5 | There is a list of first aiders at reception. | true/false |
| 6 | Many cleaning products are poisonous. | true/false |
| 7 | When lifting heavy objects you must bend your back. | true/false |

2 Listen again and complete the phrases with the correct adverb.

| immediately | carefully | clearly | carefully | regularly |
|---|---|---|---|---|

1 test the alarms ............
2 check fire exits ............
3 find a first aider ............
4 read the list ............
5 cleaning products must be marked ............

## ■ Language study

### ! Expressions to learn

| | |
|---|---|
| *Please, listen carefully.* | S |
| *You must keep the fire exits clear.* | S |
| *If you see an accident, find a first aider immediately.* | S |
| *Please, read the list carefully.* | S |
| *These (products) must be marked clearly.* | S |

### ! New words to use

| | | | |
|---|---|---|---|
| announcement | fire alarm | knee | strain (n) |
| assembly point | fire brigade | poisonous | subject |
| back | fire drill | regular/ly | test drill |
| bend (v) | fire extinguisher | roll call | trained |
| emergency | food slicer | serious | trip |
| evacuate | guard | | |

➤➤ Wordlist page 97

### Structures to practise

**Adjectives and adverbs**

Adjectives describe nouns; adverbs describe verbs.

Examples  *Health and safety is a very **serious** subject.*
(adjective)
*We take health and safety very **seriously**.*
(adverb)
*There are **regular** fire drills.* (adjective)
*We have fire drills **regularly**.* (adverb)

Note the irregular adverbs.

*good/**well**, hard/**hard**, fast/**fast**, late/**late***

➤➤ Language review page 84

**5** Read these safety regulations. Listen again and tick (✓) the ones they do.

> ### WHAT TO DO IN THE CASE OF A FIRE
> - Evacuate the guests from the rooms. ☐
> - Shut all the fire doors. ☐
> - Call the fire brigade. ☐
> - If the fire is small, use a fire extinguisher. ☐
> - Make an announcement. ☐
> - Direct the guests to the assembly point. ☐
> - Take a roll call. ☐

Read the Listening script on page 72 and check any words you don't understand in the Wordlist.

---

**Activity**

Work with a partner. Look at these safety hazard signs. Discuss what you think they mean and where you would find them in a hotel. Check your answers on page 91.

Example   *I think sign i means lift things carefully. I think you'd find it in a hotel kitchen.*

---

**3** Complete the sentences with the correct adjective or adverb.

| quiet | hard | expensive | carefully |
|-------|------|-----------|-----------|
| fresh | late | politely | serious |

1 We serve ........... bread and rolls.
2 Please check the safety regulations ............ .
3 That's a ........... problem.
4 I'd like a ........... room next to the garden.
5 She's an excellent commis chef and works ............ .
6 The Regal is a very ........... hotel.
7 The group from Norway arrived very ............ .
8 Front desk staff must speak ........... to guests.

■ **Listening** *Sound the alarm!*

**4** Listen to the dialogue and answer the questions.

1 What's the noise everyone can hear?
2 Where's the fire?
3 What do Tom and Mark use to put out the fire?
4 What does Mary do?
5 Where is the assembly point?
6 What does Mary tell Jo to do?

**More words to use**

| Fire fighting equipment | |
|-------------------------|---|
| fire axe | sand bucket |
| fire blanket | smoke alarm |
| fire door | water sprinkler |

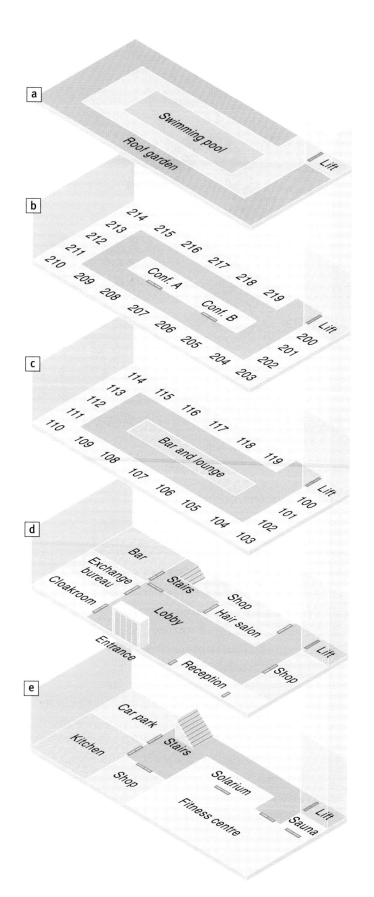

# 20 | Giving directions indoors

⤑ **Direct guests around the hotel**
Take the lift to the third floor.
Walk along the corridor and it's on
the right.

⤑ **Talk about room preparation**
One of the light bulbs isn't working.
Pull the curtains and fold back
the bedspread.

## ■ Starter

Match these parts of the building.

1  ☐ ground floor
2  ☐ 1st floor
3  ☐ 2nd floor
4  ☐ roof
5  ☐ basement

## ■ Listening  *Excuse me, where's the bar?*

1  Listen to the directions and mark the five places on the plan.

2  Listen again and complete the phrases.
1  ............. the lift to the first floor.
2  Walk ............ the corridor and it's ............
the left.
3  Go ............ the lobby and through that doorway.
It's at the ............ of the corridor.
4  It's on the ground floor, ............ ............
the lift.
5  When you come out of the lift, ............ left.
6  Go ............ conference suite B.
7  Go ............ the door ............ the exchange
bureau.
8  And the fitness centre is ............ ............
of you.

## ■ Language study

| ! Expressions to learn | |
|---|---|
| *Take the lift to the first floor.* | S |
| *Turn left/right.* | S |
| *Walk along the corridor.* | S |
| *It's on the left/right.* | S |
| *Go across/past/through the lobby.* | S |
| *It's at the end of/the top of/ the bottom of the corridor.* | S |
| *It's on the ground/first/top floor.* | S |
| *Go past the stairs ...* | S |

42 | **Unit 20** Giving directions indoors

| bedding | drawer | spare |
|---|---|---|
| bedside light | hanger | table lamp |
| bedspread | light bulb | turn-down service |
| cabinet | opposite | wardrobe |
| conference room | pull | welcome folder |
| curtain | roof garden | |

➤ Wordlist page 97

## Structures to practise
### Prepositions of location and direction (1)

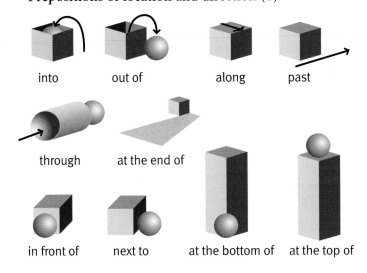

into    out of    along    past

through    at the end of

in front of    next to    at the bottom of    at the top of

3  Study the diagrams and the building plan. Read the sentences and underline the correct alternative.

1  Room 213 is *at the end of/at the top of* the corridor.
2  The roof garden is *at the top of/at the end of* the hotel.
3  From the entrance, walk *out of/past* reception to get to the shop.
4  For the sauna, turn left *at the end of/out of* the lift.
5  The kitchen is *at the top of/at the bottom of* the stairs in the basement.

4  Write directions from reception to these places.

Example  *room 104*

> **Take** *the lift to the first floor.* **Turn left** *out of the lift and room 104 is at the end of the corridor.*

1  room 204
2  the sauna
3  room 118
4  the car park
5  the swimming pool
6  the lounge

## ■ Listening  *Is the room ready?*

5  Listen to the dialogue. Match the words to the pictures.

1  ☐ wardrobe        5  ☐ hangers
2  ☐ light bulb       6  ☐ welcome folder
3  ☐ cabinet         7  ☐ drawers
4  ☐ table lamp       8  ☐ minibar

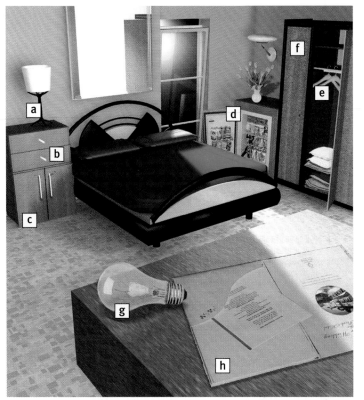

6  Listen again and answer the questions.

1  What did Petra check in the wardrobe?
2  What's wrong with the table lamp?
3  Was the air-conditioning set correctly?
4  What information is in the welcome folder?
5  What's in the minibar?
6  What must Petra do for the turn-down service?

## Activity

Work with a partner. One of you works in reception and the other is a guest. Take turns to ask for and give directions inside the Park Hotel. The plan of the ground floor is on page 63.

### More words to use

| In the hotel room | | In the bathroom | |
|---|---|---|---|
| blanket | mattress | bath | shower |
| carpet | mirror | bath mat | shower cap |
| cupboard | pillow | bidet | wash basin |
| duvet/quilt | shelf | shaver point | |
| heating | trouser press | | |

# Giving directions outside

→ **Ask for directions**
How do I get to the museum?

→ **Give directions**
Turn left outside the hotel and walk towards Rossio square.

→ **Talk about the London underground system**
Take the Victoria line to Green Park.

## ■ Starter

Which of the following places can you find on this tourist map of Lisbon?

| | | |
|---|---|---|
| bus station | hotel | swimming pool |
| café | railway station | theatre |
| cinema | restaurant | underground station |

## ■ Listening *Can you direct me to the theatre?*

1 Listen to the directions from the Hotel International and follow them on the map.

2 Listen again and complete the directions.

**The Dona Maria theatre (Teatro Nacional Dona Maria II)**

1 You can go ............ ............[1]. Turn left outside the hotel and walk ...........[2] Rossio square. The theatre is ...........[3] the other side of the square.

**The Roman museum (Núcleo Arqueológico)**

2 Turn right ...........[4] the hotel. Then ...........[5] the first right down Rua dos Correeiros. Keep ............ ...........[6] down that street for 700 metres. You'll see the museum ...........[7] your right.

**Oceanarium**

3 The best way is to ...........[8] the metro from Rossio. Get a ticket for Oriente. ...........[9] lines at Alameda and then ............ ...........[10] at Oriente.

Work with a partner. Practise asking for and giving directions. Use the map of Lisbon or your own map.

## ■ Language study

| | |
|---|---|
| *It's quite near here.* | S |
| *Turn right/left outside the hotel.* | S |
| *Walk towards the square.* | S |
| *It's on the other side of the square.* | S |
| *Keep straight on down the street.* | S |
| *You can't miss it.* | S |

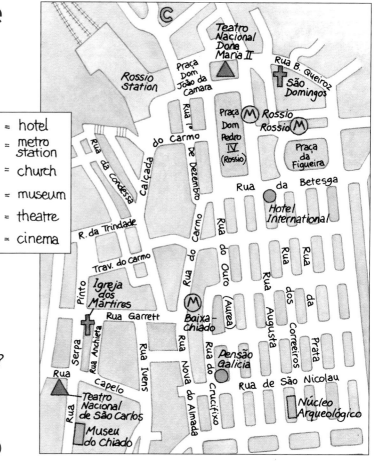

| | |
|---|---|
| ○ | = hotel |
| Ⓜ | = metro station |
| ✝ | = church |
| ▯ | = museum |
| ▲ | = theatre |
| Ⓒ | = cinema |

**! New words to use**

| | | |
|---|---|---|
| cross (v) | museum | stop (n) |
| direct (v) | outside | tube/underground |
| miss (v) | station (train) | (US subway) |

≫ Wordlist page 97

### Structures to practise

**Prepositions of location and direction (2)**

Look at the illustrations.

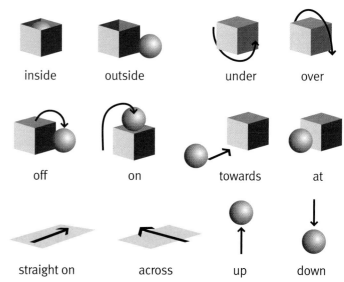

inside    outside    under    over

off    on    towards    at

straight on    across    up    down

**3** Complete these sentences with the correct preposition.

| off | across | up | outside |
|-----|--------|-----|---------|
| straight on | over | on | towards |

1 Turn right and walk ............ the big hotel.
2 Take the second left. Go ............ ............ and then turn right.
3 Go ............ the bridge and ............ the hill.
4 Park the car ............ the bank.
5 You get on the train at Rossio and get ............ at Oriente.
6 Go ............ the road and the cinema is ............ your right.

## ■ Listening  *Travel in the city*

**4** Look at the map of the London Underground (the tube). Listen to the four sets of directions. Find the starting points, and the destinations.

Turn to the Listening script on page 72 and practise asking for and giving directions with a partner.

**5** Work with a partner. Choose different starting points and destinations on the map and practise asking for and giving directions.

Example A *Victoria to Baker Street*
B ***Take*** *the Victoria line to Green Park. Then* ***change onto*** *the Jubilee line and it's two* ***stops*** *to Baker Street.*

### Activity

Work with a partner. Student A's information is on page 64. Student B's information is on page 63.

### More words to use

| Transport | Road signs | Street terms |
|-----------|-----------|--------------|
| by air | Access Only | cycle path |
| by boat | Bus Lane | dual carriageway |
| by bus | Give Way | footpath |
| by car | No Entry | main road |
| on foot | No Parking | motorway |
| by plane | No U-turns | no through road |
| by taxi | One Way | pavement (US sidewalk) |
| by train | Slow | pedestrian street |
| | Stop | |

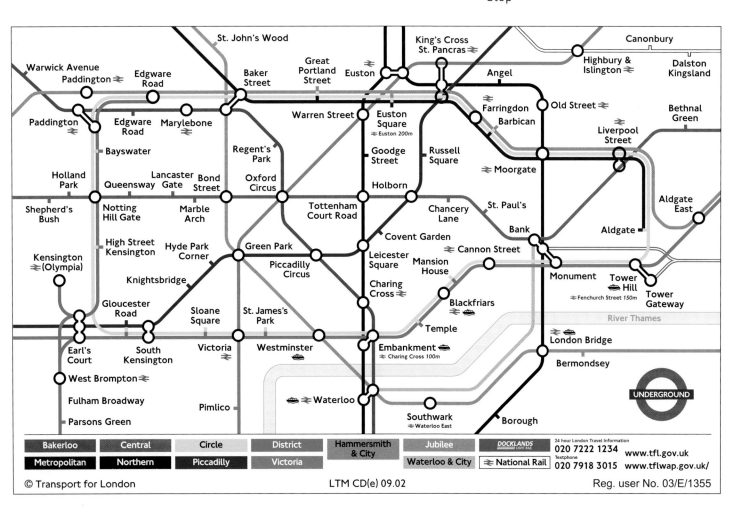

© Transport for London        LTM CD(e) 09.02        Reg. user No. 03/E/1355

# Facilities for the business traveller

⇢ **Explain about room facilities**
The rooms have high-speed
Internet access.

⇢ **Talk about hotel services**
We have 24-hour room service
and a babysitting service.

⇢ **Talk about conference facilities**
There are projectors and screens.

## Starter

Look at the picture and name five pieces of office
equipment.

## Listening *What can you offer the business traveller?*

1 Listen and tick (✓) the facilities or services you hear.
Which ones are mainly for the business traveller?

| | | | |
|---|---|---|---|
| 1 ☐ photocopier | 10 ☐ satellite TV |
| 2 ☐ disabled access | 11 ☐ printer |
| 3 ☐ TV Internet access | 12 ☐ fax |
| 4 ☐ garden | 13 ☐ emails |
| 5 ☐ pay-per-view films | 14 ☐ car hire |
| 6 ☐ multi-line phones | 15 ☐ swimming pool |
| 7 ☐ broadband | 16 ☐ babysitting service |
| 8 ☐ electronic safe | 17 ☐ minibar |
| 9 ☐ 24-hour room service | 18 ☐ laundry service |

2 Listen again and complete the sentences using the
facilities in exercise 1.

1 All rooms have satellite TV with ............-
............-............ facilities.
2 There's Internet access for sending ............ .
3 Both the minibar and the ............ ............ are
standard in all rooms.
4 We have ............-............ room service.
5 The printer, ............, and ............ facilities are
in the business centre.
6 The centre's fully equipped and offers ............
Internet access.

## Language study

*Can you tell me about your in-room facilities?*    C
*Both the minibar and the electronic safe are
standard in all rooms.*    S
*What about facilities for business travellers?*    C
*The centre's fully equipped.*    S

! **New words to use**

| | | |
|---|---|---|
| audio-visual | car hire | PowerPoint |
| babysitting | equipment | projector (digital) |
| banqueting | high-speed | screen |
| boardroom | pay-per-view | venue |
| broadband | play | video conferencing |

⇉ Wordlist page 97

**Structures to practise**
**Linking and contrasting**
*so, both ... and, but*

Look at these sentences.

*All rooms have Internet access. You can send emails.*
*All rooms have Internet access **so** you can send emails.*

*The minibar is standard in all rooms. The electronic safe
is standard in all rooms.*
***Both** the minibar **and** the electronic safe are standard in
all rooms.*

*Internet access is in the rooms. Fax facilities are in the
business centre.*
*Internet access is in the rooms **but** fax facilities are in the
business centre.*

**3** Use *both ... and*, *so*, or *but* to link these pairs of sentences.

1 The hair salon is open during the week. It's closed at weekends.
2 The restaurant is fully booked. We can't take any more bookings.
3 The hotel has a fitness centre. The leisure centre has a fitness centre.
4 The chef is ill. The sous chef is in charge.
5 The table was booked for eight o'clock. The guests didn't arrive until 9.00.
6 Petra finishes her work placement next week. Dirk finishes his next week.

## ■ Listening *We're planning a conference*

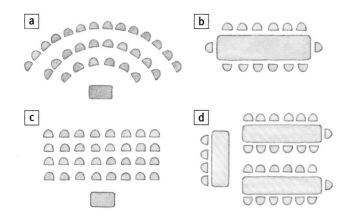

**4** Listen to the dialogue and label the pictures.

1 boardroom-style meeting room ☐
2 theatre-style meeting room ☐
3 banqueting room ☐
4 classroom-style meeting room ☐

**5** Listen again and complete the table.

| Conference facilities | | |
|---|---|---|
| type of rooms | type of audio visual equipment | business services |
| .................... | .................... | .................... |
| .................... | .................... | .................... |
| .................... | .................... | .................... |
| .................... | .................... | |

## Activity

Work with a partner. Student A's information is here. Student B's information is on page 63.

**A1** Call the Hotel Olympia and make a booking for a business conference. Use the following information.

> **Organization** International Tango Teachers' Association
> **Delegates** 150
> **Rooms needed** boardroom or conference room (capacity 150), five classroom-style rooms (capacity 30), ballroom and banqueting room
> **Equipment** digital projectors, flip charts, PowerPoint
> **Accommodation** full board
> **Time** three days from midday 24 November to midday 27 November.

Example    *Hello. I'd like to book a business conference, please.*

**A2** You work at the Skyros Hotel. Take a conference booking. The hotel facilities include:

- banqueting room, ballroom
- theatre style conference room x 2 (capacity 1000)
- boardroom style room x 4 (capacity 90)
- classroom style rooms x 6 (capacity 25)
- Audio visual equipment (flip charts, digital projectors, PowerPoint)
- Video conferencing facilities, high-speed data lines, secretarial services

Example    *Hello. Skyros Hotel. Can I help you?*

### More words to use

| Hotel facilities and services | Business services |
|---|---|
| airport transfer | courier service |
| barber | florist |
| cabaret/floor show | microphone |
| covered garage | photographer |
| excursions | stationery |
| express checkout | |

# Offering help and advice

··▷ **Talk about the recent past**
One of the guests has fallen over.

··▷ **Give advice**
You should see a doctor.
We should call an ambulance.

··▷ **Talk about illness**
My wife has terrible toothache.

## ■ Starter

What has happened to the man in the photographs?

## ■ Listening  *Emergency first aid needed*

**1**  Listen to the dialogue. Are the sentences true or false?

| | |
|---|---|
| 1  Mr Schmidt has a stomach ache. | true/false |
| 2  The porter has called an ambulance. | true/false |
| 3  Mary gives Mr Schmidt a drink of water. | true/false |
| 4  Mr Schmidt ate too much for breakfast. | true/false |
| 5  Mary thinks Mr Schmidt should see a doctor. | true/false |
| 6  Mr Schmidt has cut his hand. | true/false |

**2**  Listen again and complete these sentences.

1  One of the guests ............ ............ ............ over.
2  ............ move him.
3  I ............ ............ lunch yet.
4  You ............ see a doctor.
5  So ............ ............ an ambulance.
6  You've ............ your head.

## ■ Language study

### ! Expressions to learn

| | |
|---|---|
| *One of the guests has just fallen over.* | S C |
| *We should call an ambulance.* | S |
| *Don't move him.* | S |
| *Are you in pain?* | S |
| *How are you feeling now?* | S |
| *You should see a doctor.* | S |

### ! New words to use

| | | |
|---|---|---|
| accident report | emergency | on call (doctor) |
| bleeding | faint | pharmacy |
| burn (v) | hospital | plaster |
| cut (n) | hurt (v) | sick |
| dentist | leg | toothache |

➤➤ Wordlist page 97

## Structures to practise
### Present Perfect

The Present Perfect (*have* + past participle of the verb) is used for actions not yet finished, or only recently finished. Look out for key words *just* and *yet* which often indicate the use of the Present Perfect.

Examples  *One of the guests **has fallen** over.*
*One of the guests **has just fallen** over.* (very recently)
*The doctor **hasn't arrived**.*
*The doctor **hasn't arrived yet**.* (but he will)

➤➤  Language review page 86

**3**  Complete the sentences with the Present Perfect.
1  The Japanese group ............ (just/arrive).
2  I ............ (not finish) my exercise yet.
3  The man ............ (have) a bad fall.
4  They ............ (not eat) lunch yet.
5  We ............ (live) here all our lives.
6  He ............ (not start) work yet.

### Giving advice
*should*

Look at these examples.
*He doesn't feel well. He **should** see a doctor.*
*He has had a bad fall. We **shouldn't** move him.*

**4**  Match these sentences to each other.
1 ☐ It's going to rain.
2 ☐ He has hurt his leg badly.
3 ☐ It's my mother's birthday.
4 ☐ I was late for work yesterday.
5 ☐ She has lost her bag.
6 ☐ Tom has bought a very expensive car.

a  He should see a doctor.
b  You shouldn't be late today.
c  She should contact the police.
d  You should take an umbrella.
e  He shouldn't waste his money.
f  You should buy her a present.

## ■ Listening *Can you call a doctor, please?*

**5**  Listen to the four dialogues and complete the table.

| Problem | Action |
|---|---|
| 1 ........................ | ........................ |
| 2 ........................ | ........................ |
| 3 ........................ | ........................ |
| 4 ........................ | ........................ |

**6**  Turn to the Listening script on page 73 and practise the dialogues with a partner.

## Activity

Work with a partner. There has been an accident. Discuss the following actions and decide which ones you should do and which you shouldn't do. Then put them in order of importance.

A woman has dived into the swimming pool and cut her head badly. She has climbed out and is sitting on the ground.

☐ Call an ambulance.
☐ Call a first aider.
☐ Give her a cognac.
☐ Call a lifeguard.
☐ Cover her in a warm blanket.
☐ Call a taxi.
☐ Move her.
☐ Get her a hot drink.
☐ Ask her to lie down.
☐ Ask her to walk around.
☐ Give her some food.
☐ Massage her head.
☐ Fill out an accident report form.
☐ Give her a painkiller.

### More words to use

| Health problems | Health care personnel | Emergency services |
|---|---|---|
| a cold | dentist | ambulance |
| asthma | doctor | fire brigade |
| diarrhoea | nurse | police |
| earache | optician | |
| flu | osteopath | |
| headache | paramedic | |
| high temperature | pharmacist | |
| stomach ache | physiotherapist | |
| | surgeon | |

# 24 Dealing with problems

⋯→ **Complain about bad service**
My room hasn't been cleaned.

⋯→ **Give an explanation**
This should have been done this morning.

⋯→ **Give solutions**
I'll call the housekeeper straightaway.

a

## ■ Starter

Match the problems with the pictures.

1 ☐ There isn't any hot water.
2 ☐ The air-conditioning isn't working.
3 ☐ The room is smoky.
4 ☐ He doesn't have a clean shirt.
5 ☐ He didn't have a wake-up call.
6 ☐ They haven't serviced the room.

## ■ Listening *Are we service-minded enough?*

1 Listen to the dialogues and match the solutions with the problems in the starter.

a ☐ chase up housekeeping
b ☐ look into it
c ☐ send up a service engineer
d ☐ call maintenance
e ☐ change your room
f ☐ call the housekeeper

b

2 Listen again and complete sentences.

1 I ............ a non-smoking room.
2 Your request should ............ ............ registered.
3 The bed hasn't been ............ .
4 This ............ ............ ............ mended yesterday.
5 You should ............ ............ a call.
6 It ............ ............ fixed yet.

Turn to the Listening script on page 73 and practise the dialogues with a partner.

c

d

e

f

## Language study

**! New words to use**

| | |
|---|---|
| access | sleep (v) |
| ask | smell |
| mend | suitable |
| overnight | wake-up call |
| properly | |

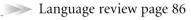 Wordlist page 97

### Structures to practise

*should* + Present Perfect Passive

Look at these examples.

*The room **should have been cleaned**.*

*The shirts **should have been delivered**.*

Language review page 86

3  Look at these complaints. What should have been done?

Example   The phone doesn't work. (check)
     ***It should have been checked.***

1  The light bulb is broken. (replace)
2  Our bath is dirty. (clean)
3  The rubbish bin is full. (empty)
4  These glasses are dirty. (wash)
5  The TV isn't working. (mend)
6  Our taxi hasn't arrived. (order)

4  What would you say to guests in these situations?

Example   The bed isn't made.
     *I'm sorry, it **should have been made**. I'll send
     someone up immediately.*

1  Our bathroom hasn't been cleaned.
2  The minibar is empty.
3  The bathroom doesn't have any new soap or
   shampoo.
4  We asked for a quieter room.
5  There's something wrong with the air-conditioning.
6  We ordered room service twenty minutes ago.

## Listening   *Did you enjoy your stay?*

5  Listen and tick (✓) the correct statements.

1  ☐ Personnel called Mrs White to complain.
   ☐ Personnel called Mrs White about a complaint.
2  ☐ The hotel didn't have disabled access.
   ☐ The hotel had good disabled access.
3  ☐ The first room wasn't on the ground floor.
   ☐ The first room was on the ground floor.
4  ☐ It was too small.
   ☐ It was too noisy.
5  ☐ The second room was quiet and near the
      garden.
   ☐ The second room was quiet and had a balcony.
6  ☐ The manager sent flowers and fruit.
   ☐ The manager sent flowers and champagne.

6  Turn to the Listening script on page 73 and practise the
   dialogue with a partner. Take turns to be the personnel
   officer and the guest.

### Activity

Work with a partner. Read this extract from a letter of
complaint to a hotel. Discuss the letter with your partner
and offer advice and solutions.

> ... when we ordered aperitifs they never arrived.
> The food in the restaurant was awful. The steak was
> overcooked and the glasses were dirty. We
> complained to the restaurant manager but he didnt
> do anything. Our hotel room was very small, the
> shower didnt work and our towels were dirty! We
> phoned reception and asked for more towels but we
> didnt get them until the next day. We asked the
> receptionist to send an engineer to mend the shower
> but nobody came. My husband ordered a wake-up
> call for 6.30 but we didnt get one. So we were late
> for our train ...

Example   *That shouldn't have happened. The drinks
         should have arrived straightaway. The restaurant
         manager should have apologized to them.*

### More words to use

| Stationery | Room extras |
|---|---|
| envelopes | dressing gown (US bathrobe) |
| note pad | sewing kit |
| pen | shoe cleaning kit |
| post cards | slippers |
| writing paper | tissues |

# Paying bills

⋯ **Deal with customer payments**
Your bill's ready for you.

⋯ **Handle different forms of payment**
How would you like to pay?

⋯ **Explain the bill to customers**
The total in euros is just here.

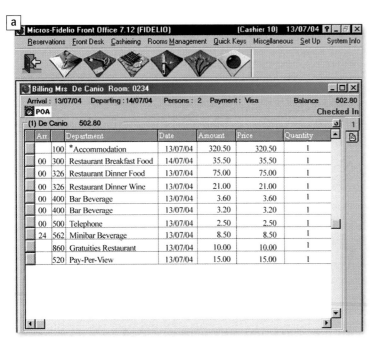

## ■ Starter

Think of some ways in which guests can pay their hotel bills.

## ■ Listening  *Could we have our bill, please?*

1   Listen to the two dialogues and match them to the correct screen.

Dialogue 1 ☐
Dialogue 2 ☐

2   Listen again and answer the questions.

**Dialogue 1**

1   Has reception prepared the bill for room 234 yet?
2   How is Mrs De Canio paying?

**Dialogue 2**

3   When is the restaurant customer leaving?
4   Are the drinks included in the restaurant bill?
5   Is service included in the restaurant bill?
6   How is the customer paying the bill?
7   Does the customer want a VAT receipt?

## ■ Language study

**! Expressions to learn**

| | |
|---|---|
| I asked for my bill to be prepared. | C |
| Your bill's ready for you. | S |
| How would you like to pay? | S |
| Could you sign here, please? | S |
| Is service included? | C |
| How are you paying? | S |
| The total in euros is just here. | S |
| Would you like a VAT receipt? | S |

**! New words to use**

| | | |
|---|---|---|
| card (Visa) | debit card | itemised |
| cash | directly | total |
| change (n) | hope | traveller's cheque |
| company | included | Visa slip |
| copy | invoice | voucher |

➤➤ Wordlist page 97

### Structures to practise
**Present Continuous**

The Present Continuous is used for actions which are happening now.

Look at these examples.

*We're leaving now.*
*I'm paying in cash.*

➤➤ Language review page 86

**3** Answer these questions about what is happening now.

1 What are you doing now?
2 Who are you sitting next to?
3 Where are you studying?
4 What are you wearing?
5 What's your teacher doing?
6 What are your friends doing?

**Object pronouns**

*me, you, him, her, it,* (singular) *you, us, them* (plural)

Look at these examples.
*Could you bring us the bill, please?*
*I've included them here.*

➤ Language review page 86

**4** Complete these sentences with the correct object pronoun.

1 A Where's your bag?
  B I gave ............ to the porter.
2 A Where did you put the pillows?
  B I put ............ in room 201.
3 A Did you tell Mrs Dupont her husband called?
  B Yes. I gave ............ the message.
4 A Where's Franco?
  B I saw ............ a moment ago.
5 A I hope you and your family enjoyed your stay.
  B We did, thank you. You looked after ............ very well.
6 A Goodbye.
  B Goodbye. We hope to see ............ again soon.

■ **Listening** *How would you like to pay?*

**5** Listen to the four dialogues and write the correct methods of payment.

1 ............
2 ............
3 ............
4 ............

**6** Listen again. Are these sentences true or false?

1 Mr Badel is paying for his room and meals only.    true/false
2 The hotel vouchers are for the room and breakfast.    true/false
3 Ms Kohl is paying for her bar bill and hotel bill separately.    true/false
4 Mr Popovic gives the cashier the correct money.    true/false

Turn to the Listening script on page 74 and practise the dialogues with a partner.

## Activity

Work with a partner. Look at the four bills and the extras in brackets. Choose a different method of payment for each situation and the amount (if any) of the service. Practise and change roles.

- restaurant bill (bar bill)
- hotel bill (room service, restaurant, laundry charges)
- bar bill (drinks, snacks)
- parking bill (4 days)
- car-hire (3 days)

Example   A   *Excuse me. Could I have the bill now, please?*
           B   *Yes, it's ready for you. Here you are. It includes your drinks from the bar, one gin and tonic, a vodka and lime …*

**More words to use**

| Credit cards | Debit cards |
|---|---|
| American Express | Delta |
| Diners Club | Switch |
| Eurocard | |
| Mastercard | |
| Visa | |

| Currencies |
|---|
| Baht *Thailand* |
| Dollars *Australia* |
| Hong Kong dollars *Hong Kong* |
| Krona *Sweden* |
| Krone *Norway* |
| Pounds sterling *UK* |
| Rand *South Africa* |
| Ringit *Malaysia* |
| Rouble *Russia* |
| Rupee *India* |
| Yen *Japan* |
| Yuan renminbi *China* |

## 26 Payment queries

→ **Acknowledge customers' queries**
I'm sorry, madam. This isn't your bill.

→ **Provide a solution**
One moment, I'll get the right bill for you.

→ **Handle queries politely**
One moment, I'll just check for you.

a

### ■ Starter

What problems do you think these customers are having with their bills?

### ■ Listening  *I think there's a mistake*

1  Listen to the two dialogues. Are the sentences true or false?

**Dialogue 1**

1  The woman queried the bill because it was too much.            true/false
2  There were a lot of items on the bill.            true/false
3  The waiter gave her the bill for table sixteen by mistake.            true/false

**Dialogue 2**

4  Mr Badouvas's minibar bill is fourteen euros.            true/false
5  Mr Badouvas queried the phone bill.            true/false
6  Mr Badouvas didn't make many calls.            true/false

2  Listen again and complete these sentences.

1  I think there's a ............. .
2  There are a ............ ............ items here.
3  I didn't have ............ wine.
4  How ............ is the minibar bill?
5  How ............ drinks did you have?
6  We ............ make many calls.

b

### ■ Language study

| ! Expressions to learn | |
|---|---|
| *Could we have the bill, please?* | C |
| *I think there's a mistake.* | C |
| *I'm sorry, madam. This isn't your bill.* | S |
| *I'll get the right bill for you.* | S |
| *I'd like to settle my bill.* | C |

| ! New words to use | | |
|---|---|---|
| appear | extra | issue (v) |
| charges (n) | grey | ridiculous |
| click | | |

  Wordlist page 97

**Structures to practise**

*much, many, a lot of*

Look at these examples.

*I don't have **much** money.*
*How **much** time do you have?*
(negative sentences and questions with uncountable nouns)

*There aren't **many** free tables left.*
*How **many** rooms are booked tonight?*
(negative sentences and questions with countable nouns)

*We have **a lot of** guests from Scandinavia.*
*He isn't paid **a lot of** money in his job.*
*Are there **a lot of** guests in the hotel?*
(positive and negative sentences, and questions with countable and uncountable nouns)

  Language review page 88

**3** Complete the sentences with *much*, *many* or *a lot of*. In some cases more than one answer is possible.

1  There aren't ………… people in tonight.
2  There's ………… preparation to do.
3  How ………… single rooms do you have?
4  Is there ………… work to do this morning?
5  There are ………… beds to change.
6  We don't have ………… time.
7  There's ………… information on our website.
8  How ………… money do you have?

## ■ Listening    *Working with Fidelio Suite 7*

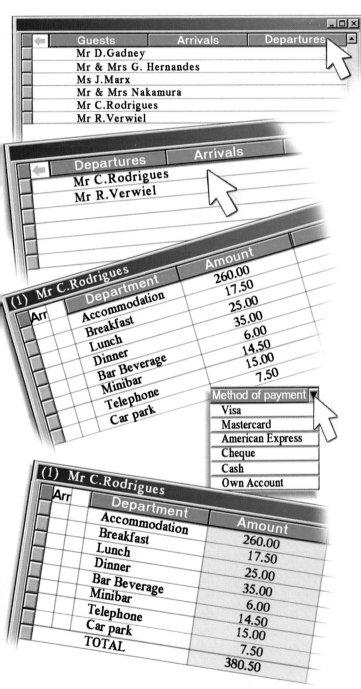

**4** Look at the screens. Listen to the dialogue and answer the questions. Choose the correct alternative.

1  What computer system are they using?
   *Galileo/Fidelio*
2  What are they doing?
   *creating an invoice/creating a guest list*
3  Where are they?
   *at reception/in the restaurant*

**5** Listen again and put the dialogue in the correct order.

- ☐ He's paying by Visa, so click on *Visa*.
- ☐ Then, click on the guest's name, Mr Rodrigues.
- ☐ First, look at the guest list here and click on *Departures*.
- ☐ Now, his charges all appear on the screen in grey. Finally, click and issue an invoice.
- ☐ You've just checked out a guest.
- ☐ All the items for his bill will now appear on the screen.

## Activity

Work with a partner. Student A's information is here. Student B's information is on page 61.

**A1**  Your hotel bill includes these items but the correct information is in brackets. Complain to your partner who works in reception and explain the mistakes.

```
HOTEL BILL
-----------------------------------------------
FULL RACK RATE   (AGREED 10% DISCOUNT ON RACK RATE)
CALLS TO PARIS   (NO INTERNATIONAL CALLS)
TWO DAYS PARKING   (DIDN'T USE CAR PARK)
$17 MINIBAR CHARGES   (DIDN'T DRINK ANY ALCOHOL)
$20 SUIT PRESSING   (TROUSERS WERE PRESSED)
```

Example  *Excuse me, but there's a mistake. When I booked my room we agreed a 10% discount …*

**A2**  You work in a restaurant and have prepared your guest's bill. Listen to your partner's complaints. Apologize and explain.

- wine bill is for a different table (table 4)
- main meal bills are a mistake
- coffees and drinks are correct (one coffee and Armagnac were ordered by the gentleman 20 minutes later)

Example  *One moment. I'll check for you.*

### More words to use

| Payments | | Service |
|---|---|---|
| account | deposit | service charge |
| amount | exchange rate | |
| balance | sub-total | |
| credit | supplement | |
| debit | | |

# Applying for a job

- Write your CV
- **Begin and end letters correctly**
  Dear Sir/Madam, Yours faithfully
  Dear Mrs Ramirez, Yours sincerely
- **Answer a job advertisement**
  I would like to apply for the job of ...

# Curriculum Vitae

| | |
|---|---|
| Name | Caroline Davros |
| Address | 18 rue de Rousseau<br>1205 Geneva<br>Switzerland |
| Tel. no<br>Email | 41 45 67 80<br>caro.davros@yahoo.com |
| Date of birth | 30.09.80 |
| Education | City College<br>Geneva |
| Qualifications | ....................................................................<br>....................................................................<br>.................................................................... |
| Work experience | *Company* ............................................<br>*Position* ..............................................<br><br>*Company* ............................................<br>*Position* ..............................................<br><br>*Company* ............................................<br>*Position* .............................................. |
| Personal qualities | ....................................................................<br>....................................................................<br>.................................................................... |
| References | Mr Schultz<br>*Position* .............................................. |

## ■ Starter

Work with a partner. Brainstorm some things that you could include on your CV.

## ■ Listening  *Writing your CV*

1 Listen to the dialogue and complete Caroline's CV.

2 Work with a partner. Read the completed CV and ask questions. Take turns to be Caroline and the agent.
Example  A  *What school qualifications do you have?*
B  *I have my baccalaureate professionale.*

## ■ Language study

| | |
|---|---|
| *Dear Sir/Madam, Yours faithfully* | A |
| *Dear Mr/Mrs/Miss/Ms, Yours sincerely* | A |
| *I would like to apply for ...* | A |
| *With reference to ...* | A |
| *Would you please send me ...?* | A |
| *I enclose an s.a.e. (stamped addressed envelope)* | A |

A = applicant

| | | |
|---|---|---|
| advert | friendly | qualities |
| advise | hard-working | register |
| apartment | hospitality | responsibility |
| catering college | motorbike | skill |
| driving licence | organized | sociable |
| experience | qualification | tourism |

➤➤ Wordlist page 97

**Structures to practise**

**Formal language for business letters and applications**

For business letters, polite informality is required. Look at *Expressions to learn* for standard forms to use in business letters and applications.

3   Complete this letter using the words and phrases in *Expressions to learn*.

> 18 rue de Rousseau
> 1205 Geneva
>
> Swissotel Metropole
> 34 Quai General Guisan
> 1204 Geneva
>
> 24th May 2003
>
> Dear ............¹
>
> RE: VACANCY FOR RECEPTIONIST
>
> ............² the job of receptionist which you advertised in this month's Hotelkeeper.
>
> ............³ an application form? I ............⁴ an s.a.e.
>
> Yours faithfully
>
> *Caroline Davros*

- ■ **Listening**  *Writing a covering letter*

In addition to a CV, job advertisements often need a covering letter to highlight the applicant's best qualities.

➤   Language review page 88

4   Listen to the biography and complete the information.

> NAME _____  AGE ____
> PROFESSIONAL QUALIFICATIONS
> _____
> _____
>
> WORK EXPERIENCE
> _____
> _____
>
> CURRENT JOB _____
> REASONS FOR ANSWERING ADVERT
> _____
> _____

# JUNIOR SOUS CHEF

Fully trained to Michelin Red M standard, with experience, for busy brasserie kitchen.

Live out. Own transport.
Post available immediately.

**Apply in writing with CV and covering letter to Sebastian Lescaux at headchef@lacroixdor.fr**

5   Read the job advertisement and listen to the biography again. Write a covering letter to go with the speaker's application. Turn to the Language review on page 88 for a covering letter to refer to.

## Activity

Work with a partner. Write a short biography for yourself. Invent some qualifications and work experience. Then take turns to ask each other questions.

Example   A   *What professional qualifications do you have?*
          B   *I have a two-year diploma in hotel management.*
          A   *What was your first job?*
          B   *When I left college I worked in the Grande Hotel in Rouen.*

### More words to use

| Personal details | Abbreviations | |
|---|---|---|
| first name/Christian name | asap | as soon as possible |
| married | CV | curriculum vitae |
| nationality | eg | for example |
| second name/surname | ie | that is |
| single | re | regarding |

# The interview

···➔ **Talk about yourself**
I've lived in Lyon all my life.

···➔ **Talk about your future plans**
I'd like to see more of the world.

···➔ **Respond to interview questions**
I'm enthusiastic, hard-working,
and a good team member.

## ■ Starter

Number each item in order of
importance for good interview
technique.

☐ speak clearly
☐ smile
☐ listen
☐ prepare questions
☐ be confident
☐ be relaxed

## ■ Listening *Presenting yourself at an interview*

1 Listen to the interview and answer the questions.
   1 Where was Michel born?
   2 What qualifications does he have?
   3 Where does he work now?
   4 Why does he want to leave?
   5 How many more candidates is the interviewer seeing tomorrow?
   6 What is the interviewer going to do?

2 Listen again and complete the sentences.
   1 I've ............ in Lyon all my life.
   2 I'd ............ to learn some new menus.
   3 I'm enthusiastic, ............ , and a good team member.
   4 I think I have the right skills and ............ for the job.
   5 I'm ............ three more candidates tomorrow.
   6 I'm ............ ............ ............ a shortlist.
   7 We ............ phone you to arrange a second interview.

Turn to the Listening script on page 75 and practise
reading the interview with a partner.

## ■ Language study

### ! Expressions to learn

| | |
|---|---|
| *Tell me something about yourself.* | I |
| *I was born in Lyon.* | A |
| *I've lived here all my life.* | A |
| *I got my chef's certificate eighteen months ago.* | A |
| *I think I have the right skills and experience for the job.* | A |
| *I'm going to make a shortlist.* | I |
| *We'll phone you to arrange a second interview.* | I |

I = interviewer

### ! New words to use

| | | |
|---|---|---|
| candidate | hotel chain | television series |
| career | team worker | various |
| enthusiastic | | |

➤➤ Wordlist page 97

### Structures to practise
**Talking about the future**

Look at these examples.

*I'm seeing three more candidates tomorrow.*
(arrangement)
*I'm going to make a shortlist.*
(intention)
*I will phone you on Thursday.*
(decision at time of speaking)
*A number of applicants will be disappointed.*
(prediction)

➤➤ Language review page 88

**3** Answer these questions about your future using the above forms.

1 When are you taking your exams?
2 When are you leaving college?
3 What are you going to do after college?
4 How will you find a job?
5 Where will you live?
6 Are you going to travel to other countries?

## ■ Listening *A celebrity chef*

**4** Read the sentences. Listen to the interview with Jamie Oliver and put his responses in the correct order.

☐ I was head pastry chef in a top London restaurant.
☐ After that, I went to France and worked in various kitchens.
☐ I was born in Essex in May 1975.
☐ Definitely. I'm going to be the head chef.
☐ I've made three TV series so far.
☐ When I was sixteen I left school and went to Westminster Catering College.
☐ After that, I worked at the River Café for three and a half years.
☐ It'll be about my restaurant which opened in October 2002.
☐ I've written four books and Hollywood is going to make a film about me!
☐ My dad runs a pub and as a child I helped in the kitchens.

**5** Work with a partner. Take turns to interview each other. Ask your partner questions about his or her past, and hopes and plans for the future.

## Activity

Work with a partner. Student A's information is here. Student B's information is on page 61.

**A1** Your partner is interviewing you for this job. Read your biography and think about why you want this position and what qualities you will bring to it.

**Manager, Front of house, Bristol Hotel, Tinnes**

| | |
|---|---|
| Name | Johan/Johanna Durst |
| Age | 25 |
| Qualifications | One-year Hotel Studies certificate |
| Experience | Two years as junior receptionist, Hotel Aurora, Manchester |
| | Three years as receptionist, Grand Hotel, Nice |
| | Three years as assistant front of house manager, Scala Hotel, Hanover |
| Languages | English, French, German |

Example   *My name's Johan/Johanna Durst and I'm 25 years old.*

**A2** Interview your partner for this job. Discuss age, qualifications, and experience. Ask why they are applying for the position and what qualities they will bring to it.

**Head waiter, Le Tomate, Lubenham**

Example   *Tell me something about yourself.*

## More words to use

| Family | More interview tips |
|---|---|
| aunt | be well informed |
| cousin | concentrate on the questions |
| grandparents | have a firm handshake |
| guardian | have a positive attitude |
| half-brother/sister | have good posture |
| in-laws | look smart |
| nephew | make eye contact |
| niece | use a little humour |
| step-brother/sister | |
| uncle | |

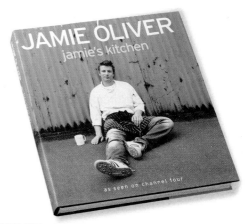

# Activity material

## From Unit 1, page 5

B1 Make three calls to the Hotel Canaria. Ask to speak to these people.

| Mr Luiz | room 204, leave a message (there's a meeting tomorrow at the Hotel at 2.30 p.m.) |
|---|---|
| Jane Williams | room 48 (no answer, you will call back later) |
| Mrs Lane | room 469 |

Example   *Good morning, could I speak to … , please?*

B2 You work at reception in the Hotel Superior. Read the information sheet and answer the calls.

| Reservations manager | line is busy (take a message) |
|---|---|
| Marcello Benito | room 571 (no answer) |
| Mrs Franklin | room 18 (connect the call) |

Example   *Good morning. Hotel Superior. How can I help you?*

## From Unit 2, page 7

B1 Ask questions about the Hyatt hotel and complete the table. Answer questions about the Manor. Use *Is there?/Are there? There is/there are, There isn't/there aren't.*

| Hyatt Hotel Barcelona | Manor Hotel Melbourne |
|---|---|
| a restaurant …… | a restaurant *yes* |
| a swimming pool …… | a swimming pool *yes* |
| any shops …… | any shops? *no* |
| air-conditioning in the rooms …… | air-conditioning in the rooms *yes* |
| Internet access in the rooms …… | Internet access in the rooms *yes* |
| more than 200 rooms …… | more than 300 rooms *no* |
| satellite TV in the rooms …… | satellite TV in the rooms *no* |

Example   B   *Excuse me, is there a restaurant?*
          A   *Yes, there is./No, there isn't.*

## From Unit 3, page 9

B1 Call the Sonotel Hotel. Book a double room for tonight. Find out if the rooms have air-conditioning and a shower or bath in the bathrooms. Find out if the hotel has a swimming pool, an exchange bureau, and a car park. If so, book a parking space. Your name is Mr/Mrs Pappadopolous and your mobile is 0778 569232.

Example   *Good morning, I'd like to book …*

B2 You work at reception in the Mercury Hotel. Take this phone reservation. Remember to ask for confirmation in writing.

• all rooms have air-conditioning, and Internet access
• all bathrooms have baths and showers
• there is a private car park and restaurant

Example   *Good morning, Mercury Hotel. Can I help you?*

## From Unit 6, page 15

B1 Read the two data files and check in to the Queen's Hotel.

| Name: | Mr Lee/Mrs Lucy Foster |
|---|---|
| Room: | twin bed, one night |
| Address: | Appt 2004, Westward Avenue, Portland, 78054 |
| Passport No: | 261501831 |

| Name: | Ms Paula/Mr Ivan Zanardi |
|---|---|
| Room: | double, three nights |
| Address: | via Roma, Firenze, Italy |
| Passport No: | 823934716 |

Example   *Good morning. My name's Lee/Lucy Foster. I'd like to check in, please.*

B2 You are a receptionist at the Park Hotel. Check in the guests. Remember these things: name, address, passport, key card, registration card.

Example   *Good afternoon. How can I help you?*

## From Unit 8, page 19

B1 Here are the instructions for making a cocktail called a Broadway. Tell your partner how to make it. Ask them to take notes and read it back to you.

1  First, half fill a shaker with crushed ice.
2  Then add a measure of gin.
3  Next add half a measure of Italian vermouth.
4  Then add a dash of orange bitters.
5  Shake well.
6  Finally, strain and serve in a small wine glass.

B2 Ask your partner how to make a cocktail called a Whisky Sour. Take notes on how to make it. Read the notes back to your partner.

## From Unit 17, page 37

B1 You work in reception. Listen to your partner's requests and make appropriate responses. You may be able to help directly, or need to contact room service or housekeeping.

Example   *Certainly, sir/madam. You can send a fax from the business centre. Do you need a directory?*

B2 You are part of a family of five and have booked a family room. Phone reception and request the things on your list.

Example    *Excuse me, we need some clean towels, please.*
           *Could you send some up?*

- clean towels
- dinner in hotel room
- babysitting service
- dress / dry cleaning
- more toilet rolls
- fruit juice for the baby
- newspaper

## From Unit 12, page 27

**B1**  Answer your partner's requests using these notes. Choose the best alternative.

- will send room service up
- will replace it
- will send porter to help change rooms
- will call housekeeping and arrange it
- will send it up straight away

Example    *Yes, of course. I'll send a porter to help you*
           *change rooms right away.*

**B2**  Use the notes below to make requests to your partner. Choose the best alternative.

- no red wine in minibar
- people in next room – very noisy
- order a newspaper?
- any messages for me in reception?
- cost of taxi to airport?

Example    *Excuse me, but there's no red wine in the minibar.*
           *Could you please send some up to our room?*

## From Unit 16, page 35

**B1**  Listen to your partner's recipe and take notes. Read your notes back to him/her and check them.

**B2**  Put the instructions for the recipe in the correct order. Explain your recipe to your partner.

**Salsa verde**
- [ ] Add some olive oil to the mixture until smooth.
- [ ] Then chop some anchovies and capers and add to the herbs.
- [ ] First, chop the mint, basil, and parsley.
- [ ] Add salt and pepper and serve.
- [ ] Mix this with some vinegar and mustard.

## From Unit 26, page 55

**B1**  You work in reception and have prepared your guest's bill. Listen to your partner's complaints. Apologize and explain.

- room rate and telephone bill for a different room
- car park fee is a mistake
- minibar charge is correct (for snacks and soft drinks)
- laundry received jacket **and** trousers on one hanger

Example    *I'm sorry, this isn't your bill …*

**B2**  Your restaurant bill includes these items but the correct information is in brackets. Complain and explain the mistakes to your partner who works in the restaurant.

| | |
|---|---|
| THREE BOTTLES SAUVIGNON BLANC | (TWO BOTTLES SAUVIGNON BLANC) |
| FOUR MAIN COURSES | (THREE MAIN COURSES) |
| FOUR DESSERTS | (THREE DESSERTS) |
| THREE COFFEES | (TWO COFFEES) |
| TWO COGNACS AND ONE ARMAGNAC | (TWO COGNACS) |

Example    *Excuse me, but there's a mistake. My bill*
           *includes three bottles of Sauvignon Blanc but*
           *we didn't have so many bottles. We had …*

## From Unit 14, page 31

**B1**  Respond to your partner's complaints. Apologize and say what you will do to put things right.

Example    *I'm sorry. I'll look into it straightaway.*

**B2**  Use these notes to make complaints to your partner. Make notes of their solutions.

- Internet connection doesn't work
- table too noisy
- ordered 30 minutes ago
- fish undercooked
- no snacks minibar
- coffee cold
- biscuits stale
- towels dirty
- bed not made

Example    *Excuse me, the Internet connection doesn't work.*

## From Unit 28, page 59

**B1**  Interview your partner for this job. Discuss age, qualifications, and experience. Ask why they are applying for the position and what qualities they will bring to it.

**Manager, Front of house, Bristol Hotel, Tinnes**

Example    *Tell me something about yourself.*

**B2**  Your partner is interviewing you for this job. Read your biography and think about why you want this position and what qualities you will bring to it.

**Head waiter, Le Tomate, Lubenham**

| | |
|---|---|
| Name | Pascal/Pascale Blanc |
| Age | 24 |
| Qualifications | One-year Restaurant Studies certificate |
| Experience | Two years as junior waiter, NATO Staff restaurant, Brussels |
| | Three years as waiter, Four Seasons Hotel, Cambridge, UK |
| | Two years as senior waiter, Normandy Restaurant, Hong Kong |

Example    *My name's Pascal/Pascale Blanc and I'm*
           *24 years old.*

## From Unit 10, page 23

B1 You are the waiter. These are the cheeses and desserts you have. Describe them to your partner. Recommend the ones you prefer and help them to choose.

**Cheese**
Dolcelatte (soft, blue, Italy)
Emmenthal (hard, Switzerland)
Cambozola (soft, blue, France)
~~Edam~~ (finished) (hard, Netherlands)
Tomme de Savoie (hard, France)

**Desserts**
~~chocolate soufflé~~ (finished)
ice cream (chocolate, vanilla, strawberry)
raspberry tart (with cream or ice cream)
chocolate cake (with cream)

Example
- *Dolcelatte is a soft, blue cheese from Italy.*
- *The ... is finished but we have ...*
- *I recommend the ...*

B2 You don't know what to have after your meal. Ask your partner if there are any of the following cheeses or desserts. Ask your partner to describe some of them to you and/or to recommend something. Then choose.

**Cheese**
Blue Vinney   Lancashire
Gruyère        Tallegio
Chèvre

**Desserts**
strawberry meringue   pear tart
lemon sorbet              chocolate torte

Example
- *Excuse me, what kind of cheese is Blue Vinney? What's it like?*
- *Do you have any strawberry meringue? What do you recommend?*
- *I think I'll have ...*

## From Unit 5, page 13

B1 You work in this hotel and restaurant. Reply to the requests.

**Hotel Palazzo:** You have twin rooms and single rooms but no double rooms for Saturday 29th March. These have bathrooms with baths. The car park has spaces available.

**La Giralda restaurant:** You have four places left on Saturday evening. You are open for lunch on Sunday but closed in the evening and all day Monday.

Example   *Hello, Hotel Palazzo. How can I help you?*

B2 Your name is Frank/Frances Smith. Call and make these reservations.

**Queen's Hotel:** Twin room for Sunday 5th April with bathrooms with shower, and satellite TV.

**La Rueda restaurant:** table for three for dinner on Saturday evening. Table for two for lunch on Sunday. Table for two for dinner on Tuesday.

Example   *Hello, I'd like to make a reservation, please.*

## From Unit 13, page 29

B1 Your partner will ask you about these dishes. Tell them what they consist of or what they are made from, how they are eaten and what they are served with.

|  | Spaghetti Bolognese | Pizza Napolitana | Fish chowder |
|---|---|---|---|
| It consists of ... It's made from ... | minced beef, tomato puree, carrots, celery, onions, oregano, garlic | mozzarella cheese, tomato sauce, black olives, anchovies, capers | sea fish, mussels, prawns, potatoes, garlic, paprika |
| It's eaten ... | hot | hot | hot |
| It's served with ... | spaghetti, parmesan cheese, red wine | green salad, garlic bread, red or white wine | bread, white wine |

B2 Complete the table. Ask your partner what these dishes consist of or what they are made from, how they are eaten and what they are served with.

|  | Paella Valencia | Lasagne | Dolmas (stuffed vine leaves) |
|---|---|---|---|
| It consists of ... It's made from ... | *rice* |  |  |
| It's eaten ... |  |  |  |
| It's served with ... |  |  |  |

## From Unit 21, page 45

**B1** Your partner will ask you for directions. Give directions from Central Square to the five destinations.

Example   *Turn right into ... and then ...*

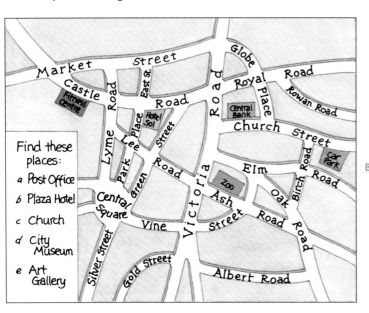

Find these places:
a Post Office
b Plaza Hotel
c Church
d City Museum
e Art Gallery

**B2** Work with a partner. Look at the city street map. Ask your partner for directions from Central Square to the five places listed on the map.

Example   *Excuse me. How do I get to ...*

## From Unit 22, page 47

**B1** You work at the Hotel Olympia. Take a conference booking. The hotel facilities include:

- banqueting room, ballroom
- theatre style conference room x 1 (capacity 500)
- boardroom style room x 3 (capacity 60)
- classroom style rooms x 5 (capacity 30)
- Audio visual equipment (digital projectors, slide projectors, flip charts, Powerpoint)
- Video conferencing facilities, high-speed data lines, secretarial service

Example   *Hello. Hotel Olympia. Can I help you?*

**B2** Call the Skyros Hotel and make a booking for a business conference. Use the following information.

**Organization:** Chiang Medical Foundation
**Delegates:** 80
**Rooms needed:** boardroom (capacity 80), four classroom-style rooms (capacity 20)
**Equipment:** slide projectors, flip charts, PowerPoint
**Office support functions:** photocopying and secretarial services, video conferencing links to Europe and Tokyo
**Accommodation:** full board
**Time:** four days from evening 16 June to midday 20 June

Example   *Hello. I'd like to book a business conference, please.*

## From Unit 18, page 39

**B1** You work at the Windsor Hotel. Take a phone booking, getting all the necessary details. Prices have gone up this year. The rack rate for a double room is €175. Previous guests get a 10% discount. Weekend rates include a 15% discount. A child's bed in the room is €15 per night extra.

Example   *Good morning. Windsor Hotel ...*

**B2** You work for the Solsken Travel Agency in Karlskrona, Sweden. Call the Gatehouse Hotel. Make a booking for a group of six adults for the weekend of 14/15 September. You want three double rooms. Ask about group rates and weekend rates and try and get a discounted rate.

Example   *Hello. I'd like to make a reservation.*

## From Unit 20, page 43

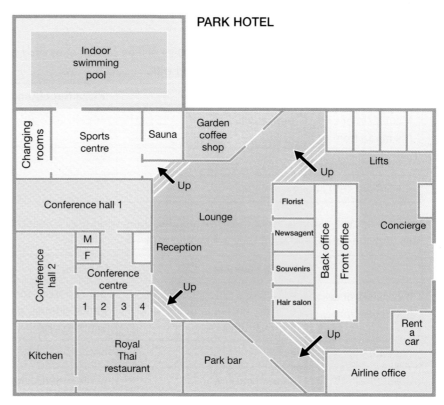

PARK HOTEL

## From Unit 10, page 23

Work with a partner. Student A's information is here. Student B's information is on page 62.

A1 You don't know what to have after your meal. Ask your partner if there are any of the following cheeses or desserts. Ask your partner to describe some of them to you and/or to recommend something. Then choose.

| Cheese | | Desserts |
|---|---|---|
| Dolcelatte | Edam | chocolate soufflé |
| Emmenthal | Tomme de Savoie | ice cream |
| Cambozola | | raspberry tart |
| | | chocolate cake |

Example
- *Excuse me, what kind of cheese is Emmenthal? What's it like?*
- *Do you have any chocolate souffle? What do you recommend?*
- *I think I'll have …*

A2 You are the waiter. These are the cheeses and desserts you have. Describe them to your partner. Recommend the ones you prefer and help them to choose.

| Cheese | Desserts |
|---|---|
| Blue Vinney (hard, blue, Britain) | strawberry meringue (with cream) |
| ~~Gruyère~~ (finished) (hard, Switzerland) | lemon sorbet |
| Chèvre (soft, France) | ~~pear tart~~ (finished) |
| Lancashire (hard, Britain) | chocolate torte (with cream or ice cream) |
| Tallegio (soft, Italy) | |

Example
- *Blue Vinney is a hard, blue cheese from England.*
- *No, we don't have any … but we have strawberry meringue.*
- *I recommend the …*

## From Unit 21, page 45

A1 Work with a partner. Look at the city street map. Ask your partner for directions from Central Square to the five places listed on the map.

Example   *Excuse me. How do I get to …*

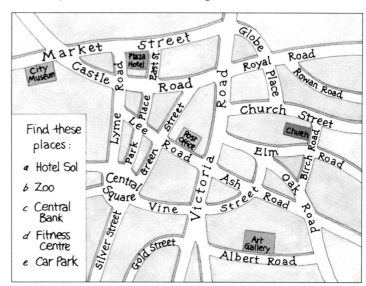

A2 Your partner will ask you for directions. Give directions from Central Square to the five destinations.

Example   *Go down … and turn left into …*

## From Unit 13, page 29

A1 Complete the table. Ask your partner what these dishes consist of or what they are made from, how they are eaten, and what they are served with.

| | Spaghetti Bolognese | Pizza Napolitana | Fish chowder |
|---|---|---|---|
| It consists of … It's made from … | *minced beef* | | |
| It's eaten … | | | |
| It's served with … | | | |

A2 Your partner will ask you about these dishes. Tell them what they consist of or what they are made from, how they are eaten, and what they are served with.

| | Paella Valencia | Lasagne | Dolmas (stuffed vine leaves) |
|---|---|---|---|
| It consists of … It's made from … | rice, garlic, onions, chicken, prawns, mussels, peas, paprika, olive oil | minced beef, tomato puree, garlic, onions, pasta, white sauce | vine leaves, rice, olive oil, lemon juice, herbs |
| It's eaten … | hot | hot | cold |
| It's served with … | bread, white wine | garlic bread, red wine | bread, white wine |

**From Unit 11, page 25**

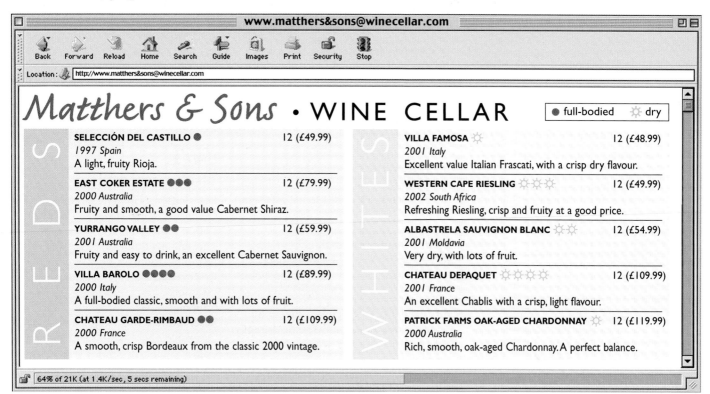

**From Unit 15, page 33**

Work with a partner. Take it in turns to describe these positions to your partner.

Example    *The receptionist is responsible to the reception manager. He's/She's responsible for making reservations.*

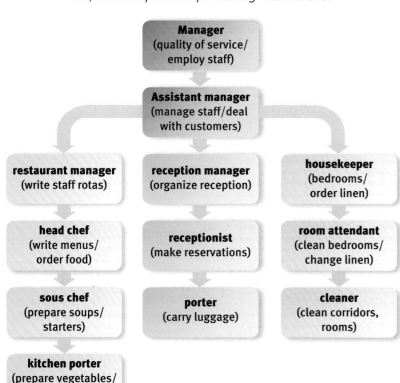

**From Unit 4, page 11**

B1    Practise making table reservations with your partner. Use these notes to help you or invent your own. Then change roles.

*I'd like to book a table for …*

| Friday | Friday at 8.30 | 25th |
| Saturday | Saturday | Friday 31st |
| tomorrow | evening | July 2nd |
| lunch | Sunday | two |
| this evening | lunchtime | three |
| dinner | Saturday 2nd | four |

*What time do you …*

| open | close |
| serve lunch | serve dinner |

*My name's …*

| Mr Johnston | Mme Rochelle | Mrs Horrowitz |

Example    A    *Good evening, the Bridge Bistro. Can I help you?*

B    *Yes, please. I'd like to book a table for Saturday evening.*

A    *Yes, certainly. How many is it for?/ I'm sorry, we're fully booked on Saturday.*

B    *I'd like a table for four, please.*

A    *Yes, I have a table for four at 8.30.*

B    *Thank you, 8.30 is fine.*

# Listening scripts

## UNIT 1
## Taking phone calls

**1**

**Reception:** Good afternoon, New Palace Hotel. May Lee speaking. How can I help you?

**Caller:** Good afternoon. I'd like to make a room reservation for tomorrow night, please.

**Reception:** Yes, sir. Can I have your name, please?

**Caller:** Phillips. Carl Phillips.

**2**

**Reception:** Good morning, Sofitel Nice. Matthieu speaking. Can I help you?

**Caller:** I'd like to speak to Mrs Bader in room 329, please.

**Reception:** One moment, and I'll connect you.

**Caller:** Thank you.

**3**

**Reception:** Rio Parthenon, Isobel speaking. Can I help you?

**Caller:** Could I reserve a parking space for tomorrow, please?

**Reception:** Just one moment. Who's calling, please?

**Caller:** Mr Paolo Falgado.

**Reception:** Thank you, Mr Falgado. You're through now.

**4**

**Reception:** The London Hilton, James speaking. How can I help you?

**Caller:** I'd like to book a double room for tonight, please.

**Reception:** Yes, sir. Can I have your name, please?

**Caller:** Mr Luke Horrowitz.

## Taking messages

**Reception:** Good morning, Athens Palace Hotel. Angela speaking. How can I help you?

**Caller:** Hello. Could I speak to Mr Wollmann in room 502, please?

**Reception:** Just one moment, and I'll connect you. I'm sorry, there's no answer from room 502. Can I take a message for you?

**Caller:** Yes, please. My name's Hans Schmidt. Please tell him there's a meeting tomorrow at ten o'clock.

**Reception:** Certainly, sir.

## UNIT 2
## Where people work

**1**

**Caroline:** Good morning. My name's Caroline. I'm a receptionist at the Cumberland Hotel in London. There are more than 900 bedrooms on eight floors. There's satellite TV and Internet access in all rooms.

**Interviewer:** Are there any shops?

**Caroline:** Yes, there's one shop.

**Interviewer:** Is there a swimming pool?

**Caroline:** No, there isn't a swimming pool.

**2**

**Scott:** Hello, I'm Scott. I'm a waiter at the Sydney Tower Restaurant. The restaurant's at the top of a tower in Sydney, Australia. The tower is 300 metres high. There are 200 seats in the restaurant. The Sydney Tower is an à la carte restaurant with international cuisine.

**Interviewer:** Is there a bar in the restaurant?

**Scott:** Yes, there's a cocktail bar.

## What facilities are there?

**1**

1  cloakroom
2  car park
3  swimming pool
4  information desk
5  laundry
6  disabled facilities
7  bar
8  exchange bureau
9  satellite TV
10  Internet access
11  air-conditioning
12  restaurant

**2**

**Caller:** What facilities are there in the hotel?

**Reception:** Well, all rooms have satellite TV and air-conditioning.

**Caller:** I see. And is there a restaurant?

**Reception:** Yes, there are two restaurants.

**Caller:** Good. And is there a swimming pool?

**Reception:** No, there isn't.

**Caller:** OK. What about money? Can I change money in the hotel?

**Reception:** Yes, there's an exchange bureau in reception.

**Caller:** And is there an information desk?

**Reception:** Yes, it's in reception too.

**Caller:** Good, and can I park my car?

**Reception:** No, there isn't a car park.

## UNIT 3
## Taking a reservation

**Reservations:** Good morning, reservations. Felipe speaking. How can I help you?

**Caller:** Hello. I'd like to book a room for me and my husband, please. Do you have a double room for next Wednesday?

**Reservations:** Yes, we do. How many nights is it for?

**Caller:** Two. Wednesday and Thursday.

**Reservations:** Yes, we have a double room available.

**Caller:** Good. How much is it?

**Reservations:** It's 225 euros per night including breakfast.

**Caller:** Good, that's fine. Does the hotel have a restaurant? You see, we arrive in the evening at about 7.00.

**Reservations:** Yes. Would you like me to book you a table?

**Caller:** Yes, please. Can we have a table for two at 7.30 on Wednesday evening?

**Reservations:** Yes, madam. And your name please?

**Caller:** Mrs Julia Morell.

**Reservations:** Do you have a contact number?

**Caller:** Yes, my mobile number is 07780 161236.

**Reservations:** Thank you, Mrs Morell. Could you send an email or fax to confirm your reservation?

**Caller:** Yes, of course.

**Reservations:** Thank you for calling. Goodbye.

**Caller:** Goodbye.

## Checking and confirming

Hello. This is Steven Dickson from Edinburgh, UK. I'd like to make a room reservation for five nights from the 18th to the 22nd of June. I'd like a double room for me and my wife, and an adjoining twin room for my two daughters. We arrive in Düsseldorf at 6.00 p.m. on the 18th. Please reserve us a parking space and a table for four for dinner at 7.30. Thank you, goodbye.

## UNIT 4
## I'd like to book a table

**Customer:** Good morning. I'd like to make a reservation, please. What days do you open?

**Manager:** We open from Tuesday to Sunday.

**Customer:** When do you close?

**Manager:** We close on Mondays.

**Customer:** I see. And what time do you serve dinner?

**Manager:** We serve dinner from seven o'clock to 11.00 p.m.

**Customer:** And what time do you serve lunch?

**Manager:** We serve lunch from twelve o'clock to three o'clock.

**Customer:** Hmm ... good. Well, I'd like to book a table for six people at eight o'clock on Saturday the 24th of September, please.

**Manager:** We're always busy on Saturdays. We sometimes have cancellations but I'm afraid we're fully booked on Saturday the 24th. Oh ... but I have a table on the 23rd.

**Customer:** OK. Friday the 23rd is fine. Thank you very much.

**Manager:** So ... that's a table for six at 8.00 on Friday the 23rd of September.

**Customer:** Yes.

**Manager:** What name is it, please?

**Customer:** Kruger ... K-R-U-G-E-R.

**Manager:** OK. We look forward to seeing you on Friday the 23rd of September.

## What time is it?

**1**
1 two thirty
2 eight fifteen
3 five o'clock
4 six forty-five

**2**
a
**A:** When does the train leave?
**B:** At five past eleven.
b
**A:** What time does the shop close?
**B:** At five thirty.
c
**A:** When does the swimming pool open?
**B:** At eight forty-five.
d
**A:** What time does the restaurant open?
**B:** At seven fifteen.
e
**A:** What time is lunch?
**B:** At ten past one.
f
**A:** What's the time?
**B:** It's six thirty-five.

## UNIT 5
## Making apologies

**1**
**Customer:** Can I book a double room for Tuesday night?
**Reception:** I'm sorry, the hotel's full on Tuesday.

**2**
**Customer:** I'd like to reserve a table for Sunday lunch.
**Reception:** Unfortunately, we're closed on Sundays.

**3**
**Customer:** Could I book a family room for the Christmas weekend?
**Reception:** I'm afraid we're fully booked that weekend.

**4**
**Customer:** Do you have a table for six tomorrow evening?
**Reception:** I'm sorry, we don't have anything left for tomorrow.

**5**
**Customer:** Can I reserve a parking space for the weekend?
**Reception:** Unfortunately, the car park's full this weekend.

**6**
**Customer:** I'd like to book a table for Monday lunch.
**Reception:** I'm sorry, we only open in the evenings.

**7**
**Customer:** Does the bathroom have a bath?
**Reception:** I'm afraid there's only a shower.

**8**
**Customer:** Can I speak to Mr Rizzo in room 345?
**Reception:** I'm sorry, there's no answer from room 345.

## Written apologies

a
Good afternoon. My name's Steven Rolls. Could I reserve a table for four on Sunday evening at 8.00 p.m., please?

b
Hello, my name's Sylvia Pilotto. I'd like to reserve a single room with bathroom for Monday night.

c
My name's Simon Lewis. I'd like to book a double room for this evening, please.

d
Good morning. My name's Paul Jones. I'd like to book a table for lunch on Wednesday. Do you have a table for four?

e
Hello. My name's Jane Wells. I'd like to reserve a twin room for this Saturday, please.

## UNIT 6
## Checking into a hotel

**Reception:** Good afternoon, sir. Can I help you?

**Mr Rodrigues:** Good afternoon. My name's Rodrigues. I'd like to check in, please. I have a reservation for a double room.

**Reception:** Yes, Mr Rodrigues, let me see. Yes, today and tomorrow, the 10th and 11th of June. Could you please fill in this registration card?

**Mr Rodrigues:** Yes, of course. Do I fill in my home address?

**Reception:** Yes, please. And could I have your passport? Thank you. Your room number's 361. It's on the third floor. And here's your key card for your room. Would you like to have dinner in the restaurant this evening?

**Mr Rodrigues:** Yes, please. Can you reserve me a table for two at eight o'clock?

**Reception:** Certainly. The porter will help you with your luggage. The lift's just ...

## Where is it?

**1**
**A:** Excuse me, where's the bar?
**B:** It's on the ground floor next to the restaurant.

**2**
**A:** Would you like to use the hotel fitness centre?
**B:** Yes, please. How do I get there?
**A:** It's opposite the swimming pool on the first floor.

**3**
**A:** Hello Jane, good to see you. Where's Mike?
**B:** He's waiting for us in the lounge. Come on. It's next to reception.

**4**
**A:** Excuse me, is this the way to the hair salon?
**B:** Yes, it is. It's over there behind the hotel shop.

**5**

**A:** Could you tell me where the hotel sauna is?

**B:** Yes. It's in the fitness centre.

## UNIT 7

## What can I get you?

**Paul:** Let's have a drink in the bar before we go on to the club. Come on, here's a table.

**Gaby:** Good idea, Paul. What're you going to have Michelle?

**Michelle:** Hmm … I think I'll have a cocktail. A Margarita for me. What about you, Gaby?

**Gaby:** I'll have a gin and tonic.

**Waiter:** Good evening. What can I get you?

**Paul:** A Margarita, a gin and tonic, and a large beer for me, please.

**Waiter:** Would you like draught or bottled?

**Paul:** I'll have a large, draught Guinness, please. What about you, Kurt?

**Kurt:** Could I have a bottle of San Miguel?

**Waiter:** Certainly, sir. And would you like ice and lemon in the gin and tonic, madam?

**Gaby:** Yes, please.

**Waiter:** Here you are. Shall I charge this to your room, sir?

**Paul:** No thanks, I'll pay cash.

**Waiter:** OK, so that's …

## How much is that?

**1**

**Server:** Good evening. What can I get you?

**Customer:** A large whisky, please. And a rum and coke.

**2**

**Customer:** Excuse me. Could we have a small beer and a mineral water?

**Server:** Certainly, madam.

**3**

**Server:** What would you like?

**Customer:** A large vodka and orange, a gin and tonic, and a large glass of red wine, please.

**4**

**Customer:** Two large beers, a whisky, and a whisky and soda, please.

**Server:** Right, sir.

**5**

**Server:** What can I get you?

**Customer:** Two cognacs, and a vodka and tonic with ice and lemon. Oh, and an orange juice too, please.

## UNIT 8

## How do you make a cocktail?

**Trainee:** How do you make a Margarita?

**Server:** First, take a cocktail shaker and fill it with crushed ice.

**Trainee:** I see. What next?

**Server:** Next, pour in one measure of tequila. Then pour in a quarter measure of triple sec.

**Trainee:** OK.

**Server:** Then squeeze some fresh lemon juice into the shaker.

**Trainee:** Right.

**Server:** Then add a dash of lime juice. Shake well to mix and chill the liquids.

**Trainee:** OK.

**Server:** Then put some ice cubes into a salt-rimmed glass. Finally, pour the Margarita into the glass, and serve!

**Trainee:** What about garnish?

**Server:** Oh yes. Garnish with a slice of lime.

## Can you make these drinks?

OK. This morning I'm going to show you how to make two cocktails: a Daiquiri and a Manhattan. Let's start with the Daiquiri. First, take the cocktail shaker and fill it with crushed ice. After that, add three measures of light rum, one measure of lemon juice, and a teaspoon of caster sugar. Then shake well and strain into a cocktail glass. Finally, garnish with a slice of lemon, and that's it. Are there any questions?

Let's move on to our next cocktail, the Manhattan. Half fill a large glass with ice, then add one and a half measures of Canadian whisky and three quarters of a measure of sweet vermouth. Then add a dash of Angostura bitters. Stir it well and strain into a cocktail glass. Finally, add a slice of lemon and garnish with a cherry.

## UNIT 9

## Taking an order

**Waiter:** Good evening, sir. A table for two?

**Mr Marquez:** Yes, please. The name's Marquez.

**Waiter:** I'll show you to your table. This way. Can I take your coats?

**Mr/Mrs Marquez:** Thank you.

**Waiter:** Here's the menu and wine list. Can I get you an aperitif?

**Mrs Marquez:** Yes, please. A gin and tonic.

**Mr Marquez:** And the same for me.

**Waiter:** Thank you.

**Waiter:** Here you are. Two gin and tonics. Are you ready to order now?

**Mrs Marquez:** Yes, I think so. What's the soup of the day?

**Waiter:** It's tomato and basil.

**Mrs Marquez:** Hmm … I think I'll have the avocado and prawn tart to start with, followed by the salmon.

**Mr Marquez:** And the goat's cheese salad for me please, followed by the fillet steak.

**Waiter:** How would you like your steak?

**Mr Marquez:** Medium rare, please.

**Waiter:** And would you like to order some wine?

**Mr Marquez:** Yes. What about the Cabernet Sauvignon, Anna?

**Mrs Marquez:** I think I'd prefer white. Why don't you have half a bottle of the Cabernet and I'll have a glass of Chablis. And can we have a bottle of mineral water, please?

**Waiter:** Still or sparkling?

**Mrs Marquez:** Still, please.

## Are you ready to order?

**1**

**Waiter:** What would you like for breakfast, madam?

**Woman:** Just a coffee and a croissant, please.

**Man:** I'll have egg and bacon, and a pot of tea. And some toast, please.

**Waiter:** Thank you, sir. Can I have your room number?

**2**

**Waiter:** Are you ready to order, sir?

**Man:** Yes, please. For a starter I'd like basil and tomato soup. Then to follow I'll have the mushroom risotto.

**Waiter:** Would you like something to drink?

**Man:** A glass of dry white wine and some water, please.

**3**

**Woman:** I just want a light lunch. I'll have mushroom soup and a toasted sandwich. Cheese and ham, please.

**Waiter:** And for you, madam?

**2nd Woman:** Hmm … the chef's salad, please. And some bread.

## UNIT 10

## What's for dessert?

**Woman:** Thank you. That was very nice.

**Waiter:** Good. I'm glad you enjoyed it. Would you like the dessert menu?

**Woman:** Yes, please. Do you have any ice cream?

**Waiter:** Yes, we do. There's vanilla, raspberry, and chocolate, and there's also blackcurrant sorbet. Here are the menus. We also have a specials board. Today we have French apple tart, summer pudding, and hazelnut meringue with summer berries.

**Woman:** Oh, I'll have the blackcurrant sorbet, please.

**Man:** Hmm ... I don't know. What do you recommend?

**Waiter:** I recommend the French apple tart. It's delicious. And the summer pudding is very good, too.

**Man:** I think I'll have the French apple tart.

**Waiter:** Would you like it with cream or ice cream?

**Man:** Ice cream, please.

**Waiter:** Would you like coffee now or after your dessert?

**Man:** After, please.

## What about some cheese?

There are three main types of cheese in Europe. The first of these is the hard type. For example, in the north of Europe there's Cheddar from Britain, and Gouda from the Netherlands. Further south you can find Gruyère and Emmenthal in Switzerland, and Manchego in Spain. And in Italy there's a cheese which is harder than all the others, Parmesan.

The next group is soft cheese. Camembert and Brie are two famous French soft cheeses while Mozzarella and Mascarpone are the best known Italian soft cheeses.

Many countries also have blue cheese. In Britain there's Stilton, and in Denmark there's Danish Blue, while in France there's Roquefort, a soft, creamy blue cheese, and in Italy there's Dolcelatte, which is also soft and creamy.

## UNIT 11
## Would you like to order some wine?

**Waitress:** Would you like to order some wine with your meal?

**Man:** Yes, please. Which is drier, the Riesling or the Sauvignon Blanc?

**Waitress:** The Sauvignon Blanc is drier than the Riesling but it isn't as dry as the Pinot Grigio.

**Man:** Right. I'll have a glass of Sauvignon Blanc then. Nancy, you prefer something sweeter, don't you?

**Woman:** Yes. A glass of Chardonnay, please.

**Man:** Then we'd like a bottle of red to go with our main course. Which is lighter, the French or the Chilean Merlot?

**Waitress:** Well, they're both full-bodied

wines. I recommend the French. It's more expensive that the Chilean, but it's smoother.

**Woman:** OK then, let's have the French.

**Waitress:** Thank you, madam. Would you like some mineral water?

**Woman:** Yes, a bottle of sparkling water, please.

**Waitress:** OK, so that's a glass of Sauvignon Blanc ...

## Wines around the world

The most famous wine from the old world is Champagne. It comes from a district east of Paris. Also from France, there are the Muscadet and Sancerre wines of the Loire Valley. Further south-west, we have the Médoc, St.Emilion, and Graves wines of the Bordeaux region. In the Rhone Valley, we find the Burgundy wines such as Beaujolais and Macon.

Italy produces around 25% of the world's wine. Two famous wines are Chianti from the Florence region, and crisp, white Frascati produced near Rome.

Portugal is most famous for port, which comes from Oporto in the north. Spain is well known for sherry, a fortified wine, from the south. Rioja comes from an area north of Madrid and is very popular too.

New world wines are improving all the time. South Africa produces wine in the Stellenbosch and Paarl vineyards in the south of the country. Australia is now famous for its Chardonnay and Shiraz. New Zealand's Sauvignon Blanc is becoming very popular. California now produces some of the world's finest Cabernet, Merlot, and Zinfandel. The Merlot and Shiraz wines from Chile and Argentina are also very good.

## UNIT 12
## I'll get you some now

**1**

**A:** Can you order a taxi for room 145, please?

**B:** Yes sir, I'll order you one now.

**2**

**A:** I'd like a glass of wine, please.

**B:** Certainly. I'll get you one right away.

**3**

**A:** Could we have some more bread?

**B:** Of course, I'll get you some now.

**4**

**A:** Can you send laundry service up to room 467, please?

**B:** I'll send someone up, right away.

**5**

**A:** We'd like a table on the terrace.

**B:** I'll see if there's one free.

**6**

**A:** What time does the exchange bureau open?

**B:** One moment, I'll check for you.

**7**

**A:** Excuse me, this glass is dirty.

**B:** I'm sorry. I'll bring you another.

## Customer care

**Trainer:** At reception, always welcome customers with a warm smile. Be polite and friendly at all times.

**Trainee:** What do you do when people make a telephone reservation?

**Trainer:** Always answer the call within three rings or apologize for the delay when you answer. When you know the customer's name, use it in conversation.

**Trainee:** Yes. I see.

**Trainer:** Take special care of customers with particular needs, for example, older clients or women business travellers.

**Trainee:** And disabled customers?

**Trainer:** Yes, of course. Find out what they would like and be patient and helpful.

**Trainee:** Sometimes reception is very busy.

**Trainer:** Yes, don't keep people waiting long. Smile at guests while they're waiting but don't keep them waiting long ...

## UNIT 13
## What's it made from?

**Woman:** Excuse me, could you explain the menu to us, please?

**Waiter:** Yes, of course.

**Woman:** What's in the penne arrabbiata?

**Waiter:** Well, this is a pasta dish. It consists of penne, a type of pasta, in a chilli and tomato sauce. It's made from chilli, tomato, garlic, and basil with pine nuts.

**Woman:** Hmm ... sounds good. And what's the salmon coulibiac?

**Waiter:** This is made from layers of rice mixed with onions and mushrooms, fresh salmon, and hard boiled eggs. It's wrapped in puff pastry and baked in the oven.

**Woman:** And what's the seafood dish?

**Waiter:** This is a dish for two people. It contains half a lobster, king prawns, scallops, and mussels. And it's served warm with a crisp, green salad.

## Do you know how to lay a table?

**Instructor:** This morning I want to check that you all know the standard restaurant place setting. So, Tina, can you start, please?

**Tina:** Well, first place a clean tablecloth and napkin on the table, and make sure that the napkin is correctly folded and placed on the side plate to the left of the plate position. Then put the butter knife on top of the napkin. For each cover, work from the inside out. Place a main course knife and fork to the right and left of the plate position, and then a first course knife and fork outside them.

**Instructor:** Good. What else?

**Tina:** Finally, a soup spoon is placed to the right of the first course knife. Oh, and put a wine glass above the soup spoon.

**Instructor:** Good. Is there anything else, Neeta?

**Neeta:** Yes. Don't forget the salt and pepper, a flower arrangement, and if it's the evening, a candle.

**Instructor:** Yes, that's right. Put them in the middle of the table. And what if the customer orders fish, Tomas?

**Tomas:** If the customer orders fish, the main course knife and fork are replaced with a fish knife and fork before you bring the main order.

**Instructor:** Good. Carry on, Tomas. What about the dessert cutlery?

**Tomas:** When the customer finishes the first course, clear the table. Take away the cutlery, dishes, and salt and pepper. Just leave the wine glasses. Then bring the dessert menu, a clean napkin, and a dessert spoon and fork. These are placed on top of the clean napkin, to the right of the plate position.

## UNIT 14
## What is there to complain about?

1

**Guest:** We asked you to reserve a parking space but the car park attendant says the car park's full.

**Reception:** I'm sorry, we overbooked the car park yesterday and today. I'll reserve you a space for tomorrow.

2

**Customer:** Excuse me, we ordered our drinks twenty minutes ago.

**Waiter:** I'm sorry, madam. I'll be with you in a moment. The restaurant is short-staffed tonight. I'll check with the wine waiter.

3

**Guest:** We reserved adjoining rooms but these are on different floors.

**Reception:** I'm sorry. I'll change your rooms straightaway.

4

**Customer:** This steak is really overcooked. I asked for it medium rare.

**Waiter:** I'm sorry, sir. I'll speak to the chef and bring you another one.

5

**Guest:** A colleague left a message for me at reception last night but nobody gave it to me.

**Reception:** I'm so sorry. I'll look into it.

## I'll look into it for you

1

**A:** Excuse me, this beer's flat.

**B:** I'm sorry, sir. I'll get you another.

2

**A:** My room isn't ready.

**B:** I'll send up someone from housekeeping straightaway.

3

**A:** The people in the room next door are making a lot of noise.

**B:** I'm sorry. I'll look into it for you.

4

**A:** Excuse me, this fish is undercooked.

**B:** I'm sorry, madam. I'll talk to the chef and bring you another.

5

**A:** Excuse me, this table is too small. There are six of us.

**B:** I'm sorry. I'll change your table straightaway.

6

**A:** Excuse me, this fork is dirty.

**B:** I'm so sorry. I'll get you a clean one.

## UNIT 15
## Let's start at front office

**Personnel:** Here's front office. This is Louise, our reception manager.

**Trainee 1:** Hello … (Hello … )

**Personnel:** Louise is responsible for six staff: a cashier, two receptionists, a reservations clerk and two porters. In reception they handle all the reservations, arrivals, payments, and departures, and there's always a receptionist here to deal with any questions or requests.

**Trainee 1:** What about phone calls?

**Personnel:** Yes. Phone calls too. That's the phone area over there. If guests want services like laundry or dry cleaning, front office staff tell the housekeeper. She's responsible to the assistant manager.

**Trainee 2:** Is there much computer work?

**Personnel:** Yes. These are the computers and those are the printers over there. All reservations, check-ins, payments, and in-room services are processed on these. We use the Fidelio system.

**Trainee 2:** Oh, I see.

**Personnel:** We also use the Sabre system for travel arrangements as most travel agencies use this system. So everybody here is trained on these systems. Now, if you'd like to come through here …

## … and in the kitchen

**Personnel:** These are the kitchens. Paul's our head chef. He writes the menus and he's responsible for the main courses, all the meat and fish. [<Hello> <Hello>] Melanie is the sous chef and that's her station over there. She prepares all the soups, hot starters, and the side orders like chips and vegetables.

**Trainee:** She has a lot to do.

**Personnel:** Yes. But two commis chefs are responsible to the sous chef, so they help her. The chefs de partie handle all the cold dishes, the sauces, and mayonnaise, things like that. The pastry chef works over there. He bakes all the bread, rolls, and croissants, and he prepares the hot desserts. The kitchen porters have lots of duties. They prepare the vegetables, sharpen the knives, and clean the ovens. And they're responsible for taking out the rubbish. Now, let's go into …

## UNIT 16
## How to do it right

1

**Robbie:** Right. This morning we have to prepare the lunch vegetables, so I'll show you what to do. First, you must wash your hands over there in the hand basin. Let's start with the carrots. Peel them like this.

**Dirk:** Is this OK?

**Robbie:** Fine. Then we have to julienne the carrots. Cut them into little sticks, like this. I'll do that. You sort and wash the new potatoes. Slice the big ones in half.

**Dirk:** Do we have to scrape them?

**Robbie:** No, we don't. We boil them with the skins on.

**Dirk:** Good.

**Robbie:** Then I'll chop the onions and you can do the broccoli. You have to break it into florets and wash it well in cold water.

It mustn't cook for long, only four or five minutes. Then strain it into a colander.
**Dirk:** OK, I'll start ...

**2**

**Lyn:** Hi Petra, my name's Lyn. First, we have to strip the beds – sheets, pillow cases, everything. Put the dirty linen in the laundry bag, here. You do that, and I'll clean the bathroom. Everything must be spotless.
**Petra:** Fine. Do we have to change the towels every day?
**Lyn:** No, only if guests leave them on the floor. But we have to replace the complimentary toiletries every day. They're all on the trolley – soap, shampoo, bath/shower gel, and body lotion.
**Petra:** Hmm ... they look nice.
**Lyn:** Yes. They're really very good ...

## Kitchen hygiene

This morning I would just like to say a few words about kitchen hygiene. Remember that all kitchen staff must always wash their hands in the hand basin. You mustn't wash your hands in the food preparation sinks. You must clean all kitchen work surfaces regularly, and wash and dry all the utensils after use. It's important that the kitchen is clean, so you must sweep and wash the floors every day. The kitchen porters are responsible for the rubbish and they have to clean the bins regularly. So, the chefs don't have to do this, but they must put the rubbish in the correct bins. Food in one, and general rubbish in the other. This is very important ...

## UNIT 17
## Room service. Can I help you?

**1**

**Room Service:** Room service, can I help you?
**Man:** Hello, could I have a bottle of champagne, please?
**Room Service:** Certainly, what room number, please?
**Man:** Room 352.
**Room Service:** And how many glasses do you need?
**Man:** We need four, please.
**Room Service:** Right away, sir.

**2**

**Housekeeping:** Housekeeping. Valerie speaking. Can I help you?
**Woman:** Yes, please. My husband's suit needs dry cleaning and I have a dress that needs ironing. Shall I leave them at reception?

**Housekeeping:** No, you don't need to do that. I'll send someone up for them right away. What's your room number?

**3**

**Room service:** Good morning. Room service.
**Man:** Good morning. Could we have a continental breakfast for two? With orange juice and coffee, please.
**Room service:** Certainly. A continental for two. Which room number, please?
**Man:** 697. How long will it be? We need to leave in half an hour.
**Room service:** It'll be with you in fifteen minutes.
**Man:** Great. Thank you very much.

**4**

**Housekeeping:** Hello, housekeeping. Can I help you?
**Man:** Yes, please. Can you put a new zip in a pair of trousers? I need them this afternoon.
**Housekeeping:** We can do that for you by lunchtime, sir. Do they need pressing?
**Man:** Oh ... yes, please.
**Housekeeping:** I'll send someone up to your room.

## Facilities and services

**Guest:** Hi, can you tell me where I can change some American dollars?
**Reception:** Yes, there's an exchange bureau in the foyer.
**Guest:** Do you know if it's open now?
**Reception:** Yes. It's open from 8.00 a.m. to 11.00 p.m., every day. So you have plenty of time.
**Guest:** Great. And I need a haircut. Is there someplace I can get one?
**Reception:** Yes, sir. The hair salon is on the other side of the foyer and it's open from 9.00 a.m. to 5.00 p.m. every day.
**Guest:** Good ... oh, and I need to change my plane ticket.
**Reception:** There's a travel agent next to the hotel. It's open from 9.00 a.m. to 5.00 p.m.
**Guest:** And I'd like a coffee. Is there a coffee shop around here?
**Reception:** Yes, the coffee shop's over there, behind the lifts. It's open 24 hours a day.
**Guest:** The lifts? You mean the elevators?
**Reception:** Yes, that's right. Behind the elevators.

## UNIT 18
## Could you repeat that, please?

**Reservations:** Park Hotel reservations, Gabriella speaking. Can I help you? Hello? The line is very bad. Can you speak up a little, please?

**Man:** I'd like to make a room reservation.
**Reservations:** When is it for?
**Man:** For three nights from September the ...
**Reservations:** I'm sorry, I didn't catch the date. September ... ?
**Man:** September the 4th. A double room for three nights.
**Reservations:** What name is it, please?
**Man:** Alimoglu. Mr Alimoglu from Istanbul.
**Reservations:** Could you spell that for me?
**Man:** A-L-I-M ...
**Reservations:** Did you say N for November?
**Man:** No, no I didn't. M, M for Mike.
**Reservations:** Right. A-L-I-M ...
**Man:** ... O-G-L-U.
**Reservations:** Thank you, sir. And can I have a contact number for you?
**Man:** The country code is 90. Then 216 8 ...
**Reservations:** Could you repeat that, please?
**Man:** 90 216 877 03 43.
**Reservations:** Thank you very much. I've made that reservation for you. Three nights from the 4th of September. Would you please confirm in writing by fax or email ... ?

## Negotiating room rates

**Reservations:** ... that will be 260 euros. That's for a double room with breakfast included.
**Woman:** Isn't there some sort of weekend discount you can give me?
**Reservations:** Well, madam, the room rate I've given you is the standard rack rate. But we can give you a special weekend rate if you stay Saturday and Sunday nights.
**Woman:** How much is that?
**Reservations:** That's 200 euros per night for a double room, including breakfast.
**Woman:** I'm afraid that's still too much.
**Reservations:** What's your budget? Maybe one of our sister hotels can help.
**Woman:** We need to find a room for less than 120 euros a night.
**Reservations:** Well, I can do you a special weekend mini-break offer of 320 euros.
**Woman:** Hmm ... 160 a night. What if we don't have breakfast?
**Reservations:** That's 280 euros for the two nights.
**Woman:** OK. I'll take it.
**Reservations:** Thank you very much. What name is it, please?

# UNIT 19
## Your health and safety is important to us

I'd like to say a few words on the hotel's health and safety regulations. Now, this is a serious subject, so please listen carefully.

Firstly, fire. The hotel has regular fire drills so please find out where the assembly points are for your area. We test the alarms regularly, and you must keep the fire exits clear at all times so please check them carefully.

Secondly, accidents. We must keep the hotel clean and tidy at all times, as guests could trip on torn carpets or slip on dirty floors. If you see an accident, find a first aider immediately. We have several members of staff who are trained first aiders, and their names are at reception. Please read the list carefully.

Thirdly, the kitchen area. Many cleaning products are poisonous so these must be marked clearly and kept away from food. When lifting heavy objects, bend your knees and don't strain your back. And finally, when using the food slicer all staff must put the guard in place. Now are there any questions? Yes …

## Sound the alarm!

**Mary:** It's the fire alarm. Is it a test drill or is it real?
**Jo:** I don't know … Hello?
**Pat:** Mary, there's a fire in the kitchen. One of the ovens is on fire. Evacuate the guests from the rooms.
**Mary:** Can I send anyone to help you in the kitchen, Pat?
**Pat:** No, it's OK. Tom and Mark are here using the fire extinguishers, and the fire brigade's coming.
**Mary:** Right. I'll make an announcement. This is an announcement. We have an emergency situation in the hotel. Would all guests please leave the building by the nearest exit. Please go to the assembly point, in front of the hotel.
Jo, here's the guest list. Go to the assembly point and take a roll call. Check all the names and room numbers as the guests come out. Take the mobile with you. I'll call in a few minutes with the names of any guests who checked out this morning, or who haven't checked in yet.

# UNIT 20
## Excuse me, where's the bar?

**1**
**Visitor:** Excuse me, how do I find room 102?
**Reception:** Take the lift to the first floor. Turn left when you come out of the lift, walk along the corridor and it's on the left.

**2**
**Guest:** Excuse me. Where's the hair salon?
**Porter:** It's here on the ground floor. Go across the lobby and through that doorway. Turn right and it's at the end of the corridor.

**3**
**Guest:** Where's the hotel shop?
**Attendant:** It's on the ground floor, next to the lift.

**4**
**Guest:** I'm looking for conference suite A.
**Attendant:** Yes, madam. It's on the top floor. When you come out of the lift, turn left and then turn immediately right into the corridor. Go past conference suite B, and conference suite A is on your right.

**5**
**Guest:** Where's the fitness centre, please?
**Reception:** It's in the basement. Go through the door past the exchange bureau and down the stairs. Go along the corridor and turn right. And the fitness centre is in front of you.

## Is the room ready?

**Housekeeper:** Did you check that the hangers and spare bedding were all in place in the wardrobe?
**Petra:** Yes. I did.
**Housekeeper:** And the cabinet. Did you look in all the drawers?
**Petra:** Yes.
**Housekeeper:** Good. So now, light bulbs. Check all the lights and the table lamp.
**Petra:** The bulb in the table lamp isn't working.
**Housekeeper:** Right, here's a new bulb. What about the air-conditioning? See if that's set correctly.
**Petra:** It's fine. Erica said we must check the welcome folder as well.
**Housekeeper:** Yes. It has all the information in it about the hotel. Guests can access all the information on the TV but some people prefer to read the folder. Then, most important of all, the minibar. You must check it every day and replace the snacks and drinks. Check them on this list. Finally, the turn-down service. Pull the curtains and fold back the bedspread like this …

# UNIT 21
## Can you direct me to the theatre?

**1**
**Woman:** Excuse me, can you direct me to the Dona Maria theatre?
**Reception:** Yes. It's quite near here. You can go on foot. Turn left outside the hotel and walk towards Rossio square. The theatre is on the other side of the square.

**2**
**Man:** We want to go and look at the Núcleo Arqueológico this afternoon. Can you tell us how to get there?
**Reception:** Yes, it's easy to find from here. Turn right outside the hotel. Then take the first right down Rua dos Correeiros. Keep straight on down that street for 700 metres. You'll see the museum on your right. You can't miss it.

**3**
**Woman:** Can you tell us how to get to the Oceanarium?
**Reception:** Yes. The best way is to take the metro from Rossio. Get a ticket for Oriente. Change lines at Alameda and then get off at Oriente. The Oceanarium is in the Park of Nations about five minutes on foot from the station.

## Travel in the city

**1**
**Tourist:** Excuse me. Can you tell me how to get to Harrods?
**Londoner:** Yes. Take the tube from here, Oxford Circus, to Knightsbridge. First, take the Victoria line to Green Park. Then change onto the Piccadilly line and it's just two stops to Knightsbridge.

**2**
**Tourist:** Can I get to the Tower of London on the subway from here?
**Londoner:** Yes, take the Northern line to Embankment. It's only two stops. Then take the Circle line or District line east to Tower Hill station. Get off there and it's next to the river.

**3**
**Tourist:** Can you tell me how to get to the National Gallery from here?
**Londoner:** Hmm … yes. The nearest tube station is Charing Cross. Take the Central line from Marble Arch here to Tottenham Court Road. Then change onto the Northern line. That'll take you south to Charing Cross … Get off there and the National Gallery is just across Trafalgar Square from the station.

**4**

**Tourist:** How do I get to King's Cross?

**Londoner:** That's no problem. Take the Central line from here, Bond Street, three stops to Holborn. Then change onto the Piccadilly line. Take the train marked Cockfosters. From there it's only two stops to King's Cross. It'll take you about fifteen minutes ...

## UNIT 22
### What can you offer the business traveller?

**Woman:** Can you tell me about your in-room facilities?

**Reception:** Of course. All rooms have satellite TV with pay-per-view facilities so that you can watch films, play games, and listen to music. There's Internet access for sending emails, accessing websites, and for finding out information about the hotel, for example, services, facilities, and car hire. Both the minibar and the electronic safe are standard in all rooms. We have 24-hour room service and a babysitting service ...

**Woman:** What about facilities for business travellers?

**Reception:** All the rooms have multi-line phones. But the printer, photocopier, and fax facilities are in the business centre just opposite reception. The centre's fully equipped and offers broadband Internet access.

### We're planning a conference

**Woman:** We're planning a conference for one thousand people in Barcelona. Can you tell me a little about your conference facilities?

**Man:** Certainly. The hotel has a total of twenty-eight meeting rooms. The theatre-style room is the largest and holds 1,200 people, then there's the boardroom-style, and finally the classroom-style which is the smallest. The 19th floor has a rooftop banqueting room with panoramic views of the city.

**Woman:** Fine. What about audio-visual equipment?

**Man:** We can organize digital projectors, slide projectors and screens, PowerPoint facilities ...

**Woman:** Good. And what about business services?

**Man:** We have high-speed data lines, and full secretarial services, and we can also arrange video conferencing facilities for you.

**Woman:** Excellent. Can you send me your information pack? I'll contact you next week.

## UNIT 23
### Emergency first aid needed

**Porter:** Anna, one of the guests has just fallen over and cut his head badly. It's Mr Schmidt from room 397.

**Anna:** Right. I'll get the first aid equipment and come straight up. Don't move him. We should call an ambulance.

**Porter:** Yes. I've just called one.

**Anna:** Here, Mr Schmidt. You shouldn't move. Drink some water. I think you fainted in the heat. It's very hot today. Have you eaten anything today?

**Mr Schmidt:** No, no. I haven't had lunch yet. I didn't feel well this morning.

**Anna:** How are you feeling now? Are you in pain?

**Mr Schmidt:** I feel better now but my head ...

**Anna:** You should see a doctor so we've called an ambulance. They'll be here soon.

**Mr Schmidt:** Oh ... yes. Thank you. Thank you.

**Anna:** You've cut your head so I'll put a plaster on it to stop the bleeding ...

### Can you call a doctor, please?

**1**

**Mrs Spiros:** Reception, it's Mrs Spiros in room 542 here. Can you call a doctor please for my little boy? He's very hot and has been sick all morning.

**Reception:** Yes, Mrs Spiros. We have a doctor on call, Doctor Fong. I'll call him immediately.

**2**

**Man:** My wife has terrible toothache. Can you give me the number of an emergency dentist?

**Reception:** Yes, of course. It's 652 3974. There's a pharmacy across the road. I'm sure the pharmacist will give you something for the pain.

**3**

**Porter:** Louise, quick. One of the waiters needs first aid. He's burnt his hand badly on the coffee machine.

**Louise:** Right. Tell him to put his hand in cold water. I'll be right there. Nick, get an accident report form out. Put the date and time on the top of it, please.

**4**

**Porter:** Anna, one of the guests has fallen down the stairs. I think she's broken her arm.

**Anna:** Right. I'll call an ambulance. Tell her she shouldn't move. Then, call Louise in reception. She's a first aider and will know what to do.

## UNIT 24
### Are we service-minded enough?

**1**

**Guest:** Reception, I requested a non-smoking room, but this room really smells of smoke.

**Reception:** I'm very sorry. Your request should have been registered. I'll change your room immediately.

**2**

**Guest:** Excuse me, but my room hasn't been serviced. The bed hasn't been made and the bathroom hasn't been cleaned.

**Reception:** I'm very sorry. It should have been done this morning. I'll call the housekeeper straightaway.

**3**

**Guest:** Reception, there's still no hot water in our room. This should have been mended yesterday.

**Reception:** I'm very sorry. I'll call maintenance right away.

**4**

**Guest:** I didn't have a wake-up call this morning, but I asked for one for 6.30.

**Reception:** Room 152. Yes, you should have had a call. I'm very sorry, I'll look into it.

**5**

**Guest:** I asked for your overnight laundry service but my shirts haven't arrived back yet.

**Reception:** I'll chase up housekeeping right away, sir, to see what's happened to your shirts. They should have been ready before 8.00 a.m.

**6**

**Guest:** Excuse me, we still don't have any air-conditioning in our room. It hasn't been fixed yet. I told you about it yesterday.

**Reception:** I'm sorry, sir. This should have been dealt with. I'll send up a service engineer immediately.

### Did you enjoy your stay?

**Personnel:** Hello, Mrs White. My name's Roger Scales from the personnel department at the Bay Hotel, and I'm just calling you about your recent visit. I know there were problems when you stayed with us and I wanted to check that we dealt with them properly.

**Mrs White:** Oh ... yes ... OK.

**Personnel:** I see there were problems with the disabled facilities.

**Mrs White:** Well, the disabled access in the hotel was very good really. You know, to the bars and the restaurants, but the main lift wasn't working when we arrived. So, that's why we needed a room on the ground floor.

**Personnel:** I see, and did we give you a room on the ground floor?

**Mrs White:** Yes, you did, but the room you gave us was very noisy. That first night, we couldn't sleep at all.

**Personnel:** Oh dear. That shouldn't have happened. Did we give you a different room on the ground floor?

**Mrs White:** Yes, you did. The next day you gave us a beautiful room next to the gardens. It was very quiet, and the manager sent us some flowers and a complimentary bottle of champagne. So, in the end we had a very pleasant stay.

**Personnel:** Good. I'm glad you enjoyed it. Well, we look forward to seeing you again.

**Mrs White:** Yes, thank you very much. Goodbye.

**Personnel:** Goodbye.

## UNIT 25
## Could we have our bill, please?

1

**Mrs De Canio:** Hello. We're checking out now. Could we have the bill for room 234, please? I asked for it to be prepared.

**Reception:** Yes, your bill's ready for you, Mrs De Canio. Here you are. Everything is itemised: your room, meals, telephone calls, pay-per-view, and the minibar. Service and VAT are included. How would you like to pay?

**Mrs De Canio:** With Visa. Here's my card.

**Reception:** Could you sign here, please? Thank you. Here's your receipt and your Visa slip copy. Thank you very much. We hope to see you again.

**Mrs De Canio:** Thank you.

2

**Woman:** Excuse me, we're leaving now. Could you bring us the bill, please?

**Waiter:** Certainly, madam.

**Woman:** Have you included the drinks from the bar?

**Waiter:** Yes. I've included them here.

**Woman:** Ah. And is service included?

**Waiter:** No, madam. How are you paying?

**Woman:** I'm paying in cash. Do you accept euros?

**Waiter:** Yes, we do. The total in euros is just there. Would you like a VAT receipt?

**Woman:** No thanks. This is fine.

## How would you like to pay?

1

**Cashier:** The invoice for your room and meals goes directly to your company.

**Mr Badel:** Yes, that's right.

**Cashier:** So, here's your bill for the extras. How are you paying, Mr Badel?

**Mr Badel:** With Mastercard.

2

**Cashier:** Your hotel vouchers are for room and breakfast, Mr Franks. Your bill for the other meals and drinks comes to 230 dollars. How would you like to pay?

**Mr Franks:** With US dollar traveller's cheques, please.

3

**Ms Kohl:** Can I pay my bar bill separately, please?

**Reception:** Yes, certainly Ms Kohl.

**Ms Kohl:** I'll pay by credit card. Do you take Visa?

**Waiter:** Yes, Visa is fine.

4

**Waiter:** That's £17.50 altogether Mr Popovic. How would you like to pay?

**Mr Popovic:** In cash, please. Here you are, £20.

**Waiter:** One moment, and I'll get your change.

**Mr Popovic:** No, that's alright. Keep the change.

**Waiter:** Thank you very much.

## UNIT 26
## I think there's a mistake

1

**Woman:** Could I have the bill, please?

**Waiter:** Thank you, madam.

**Woman:** Excuse me, I think there's a mistake. There are a lot of items here but I didn't have much wine or any extra dishes. This looks too much.

**Waiter:** I'm sorry, madam. This isn't your bill. It's table seventeen's. One moment, I'll get the right bill for you. Here we are. I'm sorry about that.

**Woman:** Ah. That's better. Here's my Visa card.

**Waiter:** Thank you, madam …

2

**Mr Badouvas:** Hello. I'm in room 532 and I'd like to settle my bill.

**Reception:** 532. Here we are, Mr Badouvas. Are you paying by American Express?

**Mr Badouvas:** Yes, but just a moment. What are all these items? How much is the minibar bill?

**Reception:** Forty euros.

**Mr Badouvas:** Forty euros! Alex, how many drinks did you have?

**Alex:** Oh, just a few … and some snacks …

**Mr Badouvas:** And look at the phone calls! We didn't make many calls. This amount is ridiculous.

**Reception:** One moment, I'll just check for you. No, you didn't make many calls but there was one very expensive call to Athens on Tuesday evening.

**Mr Badouvas:** Tuesday evening? Alex …

## Working with Fidelio Suite 7

We use the Fidelio system for checking out our guests. Let's check out Mr Rodrigues. First, look at the guest list here … and click on *Departures*. Then click on the guest's name: *Mr Rodrigues*. All the items for his bill will now appear on the screen, for example, accommodation, breakfast, and so on. He's paying by Visa, so click on *Visa*. Now, his charges all appear on the screen in grey. Finally, click and issue an invoice. That's it. You've just checked out a guest. See, it's quite easy.

## UNIT 27
## Writing your CV

**Agent:** Hello, thank you for coming in to register with the agency. Can you tell me a little bit about yourself?

**Caroline:** Well, my name's Caroline Davros. I was born in 1980. I'm single. I live in Geneva with my parents. I left school in 1998 with my baccalaureate professionale.

**Agent:** And what professional qualifications do you have?

**Caroline:** I have my BEP certificate in Tourism and Hospitality from City College.

**Agent:** And work experience?

**Caroline:** During my college holidays I worked in the Hotel Central as a receptionist. It's a small hotel in Geneva. I took reservations and ran the reception desk during the daytime. When I left college, I worked in the Sun Hotel which is part of the Triad group. This is where I learnt how to use the Fidelio System. After a year, I applied for a job at a larger hotel in the same group. I'm now a receptionist at the Sofitel.

**Agent:** I see. And what qualities do you bring to your work?

**Caroline:** I love my work. I'm sociable and friendly, and I enjoy helping and advising people. I'm well organized and hard-working.

**Agent:** Do you have any references?

**Caroline:** Yes, Mr Schultz, the manager of the Sofitel.

## Writing a covering letter

My name's Michel Laval. I'm 21 years old and I was born in Lyon, in south-east France. When I finished school, I went to catering college for three years where I got my chef's certificate. While I was at college, I worked in various hotel and restaurant kitchens as a kitchen porter and commis chef. It was very good experience and I learnt a lot about people as well as cooking. Last year I started work at the busy Grand Hotel Mercure in the city centre. It's a good job but I would really like to have more responsibility and use my cooking skills more. I have my own apartment in Lyon and I have a clean driving licence.

## UNIT 28
## Presenting yourself at an interview

**Personnel:** So, Michel, tell me something about yourself.

**Michel:** Well, I'm 21 years old and I was born in Lyon. I've lived in Lyon all my life. I got my chef's certificate eighteen months ago and since then I've worked at the Mercure Hotel.

**Personnel:** Why do you want to leave?

**Michel:** Well, I really like working there but I'd like to learn some new menus and work with a new head chef.

**Personnel:** And what do you know about our company?

**Michel:** You're part of one of the biggest hotel chains in the world with some of the top chefs.

**Personnel:** Why do you want to work for us?

**Michel:** I've spent all my life in Lyons and I'd like to see more of the world. I think I'd learn a lot and it would be good for my career.

**Personnel:** What could you offer us if we gave you a job?

**Michel:** Well, I'm enthusiastic, hard-working, and a good team worker. I learn quickly, and I think I have the right skills and experience for the job ...

**Personnel:** Right. Well, I'm seeing three more candidates tomorrow, Michel. Then I'm going to make a shortlist to discuss with chef. If you're shortlisted, we'll phone you to arrange a second interview ...

## A celebrity chef

**Interviewer:** So Jamie, tell us a little bit about yourself.

**Jamie:** Well, I was born in Essex in May 1975. My dad runs a pub and as a child I helped in the kitchens. I just loved cooking.

**Interviewer:** Were you a good student at school?

**Jamie:** No, not really. But I knew I wanted to be a chef. When I was sixteen, I left school and went to Westminster Catering College. After that, I went to France and worked in various kitchens.

**Interviewer:** What was your first really good job?

**Jamie:** I was head pastry chef in a top London restaurant. I learnt a lot there. The head chef taught me how to make the best pasta and focaccia bread. After that, I worked at the River Café for three and a half years.

**Interviewer:** How many television series have you made?

**Jamie:** I've made three TV series so far but I'll probably make another.

**Interviewer:** And how many books have you written?

**Jamie:** I've written four books and Hollywood is going to make a film about me! It'll be about my restaurant which opened in October 2002.

**Interviewer:** Are you going to work in the restaurant too?

**Jamie:** Definitely, I'm going to be the head chef.

# Language review

- ## Units 1–5

## Can/Could, I'd like to

• Use questions with *Can/Could* to make requests or offers. *Could* is more polite than *Can*.

| | |
|---|---|
| ***Can/Could** I reserve a parking space?* | (request) |
| ***Can** I help you?* | (offer) |
| ***Can/Could** I take your coat?* | (offer) |

• Use *I'd like to/I'd like* to make requests. It is a more polite way of saying *I want*.

| | |
|---|---|
| ***I'd like to** book a room.* | (*I'd like to* + verb) |
| ***I'd like** a coffee, please.* | (*I'd like* + noun) |

## Is there?/Are there?, There is/There are, There isn't/There aren't

• Use *Is there?/Are there?* to ask questions about singular nouns or plural nouns.

| | |
|---|---|
| ***Is there** a TV in the room?* | (singular) |
| ***Are there** any restaurants?* | (plural) |

• Use *There's/There isn't* to give information about singular nouns and uncountable nouns.

| | |
|---|---|
| ***There's** a TV in all the rooms.* | (positive sentence) |
| ***There isn't** any air-conditioning.* | (negative sentence) |

• Use *There are/There aren't* to give information about plural nouns.

| | |
|---|---|
| ***There are** three restaurants.* | (positive sentence) |
| ***There aren't** any disabled facilities.* | (negative sentence) |

## Do/Does

• Use questions in the Present Simple to ask about general situations. Use *Do/Does* + the base form of the verb to make questions for all verbs except *be*. Use *do/does, don't/doesn't* to make short answers.

A: ***Do** you speak English?*
B: *Yes, I **do**./No, I **don't**.*

A: ***Does** the room have air-conditioning?*
B: *Yes, it **does**./No, it **doesn't**.*

## Prepositions of time

• Use the following prepositions when talking about periods of time.

| preposition | time |
|---|---|
| *on* | days, dates |
| *at* | clock times, *the weekend*, *night*, festivals |
| *in* | periods of time, months, a certain year, seasons, parts of the day |
| *from ... to* | clock times, days, dates, months, years |

## Dates

• In British English, write and say the day first, then the month, and finally the year (if necessary).

write:   *21/10/06* or *21 October 2006* or *21st October 2006*
say:     *the twenty-first of October, two thousand and six*

• In American English, write and say the month first, then the day, and finally the year (if necessary).

write:   *10/21/06* or *October 21, 2006* or *October 21st 2006*
say:     *October (the) twenty-first, two thousand (and) six*

## Adverbs of frequency

• Use adverbs of frequency to describe how often you do something. Put them after the verb *be*, but before other verbs.

*She is **sometimes** late for work.*
*I **never** work on Sundays.*

## Times

• Use the 12-hour clock in spoken English and informal written English. In British English, there are two different ways:

| | |
|---|---|
| 6.10 | *six ten* or *ten past six* |
| 8.25 | *eight twenty-five* or *twenty-five past eight* |
| 12.50 | *twelve fifty* or *ten to one* |

• Use *a.m.* after the time to indicate the morning, and *p.m.* to indicate afternoon, evening, or night. Use *quarter past/half past/quarter to* as an alternative to *fifteen/thirty/forty-five*.

| | |
|---|---|
| 6.15 a.m. | ***quarter past** six (in the morning)* |
| 6.30 p.m. | ***half past** six (in the evening)* |
| 10.45 p.m. | ***quarter to** eleven (at night)* |

• Use *o'clock* to describe the hour.

| | |
|---|---|
| 7.00 | *seven* or *seven **o'clock*** |

• Use the 24-hour clock for timetables and schedules, but **not** in spoken English.

*Dinner: 19.00–22.00*

# Present Simple (short forms)

• Use the short forms (in brackets) in spoken English and informal written English.

## be (Irregular verb)
### POSITIVE

| singular | plural |
|---|---|
| I am (I'm) Scott. | We are (We're) the guests. |
| You are (You're) Mr Phillips. | You are (You're) the guests. |
| He is (He's) Matthieu. | They are (They're) the guests. |
| She is (She's) May Lee. | |
| The hotel/It is (It's) expensive. | |

### NEGATIVE

| singular | plural |
|---|---|
| I am not (I'm not) Scott. | We are not (aren't) the guests. |
| You are not (aren't) Caroline. | You are not (aren't) the guests. |
| He is not (isn't) Matthieu. | They are not (aren't) the guests. |
| She is not (isn't) May Lee. | |
| The hotel/It is not (isn't) expensive. | |

### QUESTION

| singular | plural |
|---|---|
| Am I late? | Are we late? |
| Are you Mr Phillips? | Are you the guests? |
| Is he Matthieu? | Are they the guests? |
| Is she May Lee? | |
| Is the hotel/it expensive? | |

## have (Irregular verb)
### POSITIVE

| singular | plural |
|---|---|
| I have a reservation. | We have a reservation. |
| You have a reservation. | You have a reservation. |
| He has a reservation. | They have a reservation. |
| She has a reservation. | |
| The hotel/It has a restaurant. | |

### NEGATIVE

| singular | plural |
|---|---|
| I do not (don't) have a reservation. | We do not (don't) have a reservation. |
| You do not (don't) have a reservation. | You do not (don't) have a reservation. |
| He does not (doesn't) have a reservation. | They do not (don't) have a reservation. |
| She does not (doesn't) have a reservation. | |
| The hotel/It does not (doesn't) have a restaurant. | |

### QUESTION

| singular | plural |
|---|---|
| Do I have a reservation? | Do we have a reservation? |
| Do you have a reservation? | Do you have a reservation? |
| Does he have a reservation? | Do they have a reservation? |
| Does she have a reservation? | |
| Does the hotel/it have a restaurant? | |

## arrive (Regular verb)
### POSITIVE

| singular | plural |
|---|---|
| I arrive at 9.00. | We arrive at 9.00. |
| You arrive at 9.00. | You arrive at 9.00. |
| He arrives at 9.00. | They arrive at 9.00. |
| She arrives at 9.00. | |
| The flight/It arrives at 9.00. | |

### NEGATIVE

| singular | plural |
|---|---|
| I do not (don't) arrive at 9.00. | We do not (don't) arrive at 9.00. |
| You do not (don't) arrive at 9.00. | You do not (don't) arrive at 9.00. |
| He does not (doesn't) arrive at 9.00. | They do not (don't) arrive at 9.00. |
| She does not (doesn't) arrive at 9.00. | |
| The flight/It does not (doesn't) arrive at 9.00. | |

### QUESTION

| singular | plural |
|---|---|
| Do I arrive at 9.00? | Do we arrive at 9.00? |
| Do you arrive at 9.00? | Do you arrive at 9.00? |
| Does he arrive at 9.00? | Do they arrive at 9.00? |
| Does she arrive at 9.00? | |
| Does the flight/it arrive at 9.00? | |

# Test yourself 1

## 1 Rearrange the words to make requests and offers.

1 name / I / your / Could / have / ?      *Could I have your name?*
2 meet / at / like / to / I'd / 6.00 p.m.      .....................................
3 Can / take / you / message / for / I / a / ?      .....................................
4 manager / I'd / to / speak / the / to / like      .....................................
5 help / you / I / Can / ?      .....................................
6 your / have / Can / passport / I / ?      .....................................
7 a / I'd / room / like / double      .....................................
8 me / tell/ you / Could / number / my / room / ?      .....................................

## 2 Correct the sentences.

1 Are there Internet access?      *Is there Internet access?*
2 There aren't a car park.      .....................................
3 There's 300 rooms.      .....................................
4 Is there any disabled facilities?      .....................................
5 There are an exchange bureau.      .....................................
6 Are there a minibar in the room?      .....................................
7 There isn't any shops.      .....................................
8 Is there any cloakrooms?      .....................................

## 3 Make questions and short answers with Do/Does, do/does, don't/doesn't.

1 ....... *Do* ...... you have any luggage?      Yes, I ...... *do* .......
2 ............... the hotel have a laundry?      No, it ...............
3 ............... she want to book a room?      Yes, she ...............
4 ............... you work in reception?      No, I ...............
5 ............... he speak English?      Yes, he ...............
6 ............... we have a parking space?      Yes, you ...............
7 ............... she know the city?      No, she ...............
8 ............... they have any children?      Yes, they ...............

## 4 Complete the sentences with prepositions of time on, at, in, from ... to.

1 Is the bar open ....... *on* ...... Sundays?
2 I work ............... 7.00 a.m. ............... 4.00 p.m.
3 The swimming pool closes ............... the evening.
4 We serve breakfast ............... 8.00 a.m. ............... 9.30 a.m. ............... the weekend.
5 The new hotel opens ............... two months.
6 The autumn season starts ............... September.
7 I'd like to book a table for three ............... 3rd January.
8 Do you close ............... Christmas?

## 5 Write the dates in British English.

1 07/03    *the seventh of March*      5 10/09/08 .....................................
2 23 May    .....................................      6 3 December .....................................
3 08/10    .....................................      7 12/02 .....................................
4 16th January .....................................      8 22nd July .....................................

**6 Now write the dates in American English.**

1 07/03 ................. *July (the) third* .................
2 23 May ...............................................................
3 08/10 ...............................................................
4 16th January...........................................................
5 10/09/08 ...............................................................
6 3 December ...............................................................
7 12/02 ...............................................................
8 22nd July ...............................................................

**7 Complete the sentences with adverbs of frequency.**

1 I ...*sometimes*... (50%) eat lunch at work.
2 The car park is ................ (75%) full.
3 She ............... (0%) works on Wednesday.
4 We ................ (25%) leave a tip.
5 The food is ................ (75%) very good.
6 They ................ (50%) visit Spain.
7 The manager ................ (75%) speaks English.
8 He ................ (100%) stays in the same hotel.

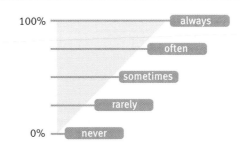

**8 Write the times in the two different ways.**

1 7.20 .....*seven twenty*.... / ..*twenty past seven*..
2 5.55 ...................... / ......................
3 12.10 ...................... / ......................
4 3.45 ...................... / ......................
5 8.30 ...................... / ......................
6 1.00 ...................... / ......................
7 9.15 ...................... / ......................
8 11.40 ...................... / ......................

**9 Complete the sentences with *am*, *is*, or *are*. Use short forms if appropriate.**

1 My name ......*'s*...... Anne.
2 We ................ in a hotel in Bangkok.
3 I ................ a receptionist.
4 ................ you in room 302?
5 John ................ in the restaurant.
6 ................ the room on the ground floor?
7 They ................ in the lounge.
8 ................ they in the restaurant?

**10 Complete the sentences and questions with the correct form of the Present Simple.**

1 The bar .....*opens*..... (open) at 7.00.
2 ............ they often ............ (visit) Chicago?
3 Scott ................ (not work) in Sydney.
4 ................ you ................ (live) in Tokyo?
5 The hotel ................ (have) 250 rooms.
6 ............ the restaurant ............... (seat) 85 people?
7 The restaurant ............ (serve) over 200 customers a day.
8 I ................ (not go) to London every week.

# Language review
■ Units 6–10

## Possessive adjectives

• Use possessive adjectives before a noun. They stay the same if the noun is singular or plural, e.g. *my room, my rooms.*

| singular | plural |
|---|---|
| Here's *my* room. | Here's *our* room. |
| Here's *your* room. | Here's *your* room. |
| Here's *his* room. | Here's *their* room. |
| Here's *her* room. | |
| What's *its* number? | |

## Requests and offers

• Use *Can/Could* to make requests. *Could* is more polite than *Can*. Use *Shall I* and *Would you like* to make offers. *Would you like* is a more polite way of asking *Do you want.*

| | |
|---|---|
| *Can I order?* | (request) |
| *Could I have the beer in a glass?* | (request) |
| *Shall I open the wine?* | (offer) |
| *Would you like another bottle?* | (offer) |

## a/an, the

• Use *a/an* before singular nouns when you first talk about something. Use *an* before words beginning with a vowel.
• Use *the* when you talk about something for the second time, or when it's clear what you're talking about. Use *the* before singular or plural nouns.

A: *I'd like a table for two, please.*
B: *Certainly, sir. Would you like the table near the window?*

## a/an, some

• Use *a/an* instead of *one* to talk about singular countable nouns.
*I'd like a menu.*
*Can I have an aperitif?*

• Use *some* to talk about plural countable nouns and uncountable nouns.
*Can we have some aperitifs, please?*
*I'd like some information.*

## some, any

• Use *some* in positive sentences, and polite offers and requests.

| | |
|---|---|
| *I'd like some wine.* | (positive sentence) |
| *Would you like some wine, sir?* | (offer) |
| *Could I have some coffee, please?* | (request) |

• Use *any* in questions and negative sentences.
A: *Do you have any Australian Chardonnay?* (question)
B: *I'm afraid we don't have any Australian wines.*
(negative sentence)

# Test yourself 2

### 1 Complete the sentences with the correct possessive adjective.

1 Jack Green is the hotel manager. He's in ...... *his* ...... office.
2 We can't help you at the moment because ............... computer system isn't working.
3 I'm afraid I can't find ............... key card. Do you have another?
4 The guests from Japan would like ............... luggage now.
5 What time is ............... train? Do you have the ticket?
6 Mrs Bell would like lunch in ............... room.
7 Can I contact the hotel? Do you have ............... email address?

### 2 Put the words in the correct order to make requests and offers.

1 lemon / you / like / ice / Would / and / ?     *Would you like ice and lemon?*
2 smoke / in / Can / here / I / ?     ...................................
3 reservation / Shall / check / I / your / ?     ...................................
4 menu / I / a / have / Could / ?     ...................................
5 like / more / Would / some / you / ?     ...................................
6 Could / the / pool / I / swimming / use / ?     ...................................

### 3 Complete the sentences with *a/an* or *the*.

1 Is there ...... *an* ...... exchange bureau in the hotel?
2 A: Can I leave ............... message in reception?
   B: Certainly, sir. Is this ............... message?
3 This is ............... bar I like.
4 A: I'd like to have ............... sauna.
   B: Of course. ............... sauna is open from 8.00 a.m. to 8.00 p.m.
5 Would you like ............... aperitif?
6 A: There's ............... key card on the desk.
   B: Yes, but it isn't ............... key card for Mr Nagy's room.

### 4 Complete the sentences with *a/an* or *some*.

1 There's ...... *some* ...... ice in the minibar.
2 Could I have ............... aperitif?
3 We have ............... group from Sweden here at the moment.
4 Can I give you ............... advice?
5 Would you like ............... large whisky or ............... small one?
6 ............... Japanese businessmen are in reception.

### 5 Complete the sentences with *some* or *any*.

1 Would you like ...... *some* ...... wine with your meal?
2 Are there ............... guests from Thailand in the hotel?
3 Table 5 wants ............... water.
4 Excuse me, but there isn't ............... hot water in my room.
5 I'd like ............... dessert, please.
6 Do you have ............... euros?

# Language review
■ Units 11–15

## Comparisons

• Use *-er than, more … than, not as … as* to compare things.

*The Sauvignon Blanc is **drier than** the Riesling.*
*The Sauvignon Blanc is **more expensive than** the Riesling.*
*The Riesling isn't **as dry as** the Sauvignon Blanc.*

| adjective | comparative | spelling |
|---|---|---|
| old | older than | 1 syllable + *-er* |
| cheap | cheaper than | |
| big | bigger than | 1 vowel + 1 consonant = |
| hot | hotter than | double consonant |
| dry | drier than | consonant + *y* = *-ier* |
| heavy | heavier than | |
| tasteless | more tasteless than | 2 or more syllables = |
| expensive | more expensive than | *more* + adjective |
| | not as dry as | 1, 2, or more syllables = |
| | not as tasteless as | *not as* + adjective + *as* |
| | not as expensive as | |
| good | better than | irregular |
| bad | worse than | |

## Offering help
### *I'll … one/some/another/some more*

• Use *I'll* + the base form of the verb to make an offer. Use *one* instead of repeating a singular noun. Use *some* instead of repeating a plural countable noun or an uncountable noun.

A: *I don't have a knife.*
B: *I'll bring you **one**.*

A: *There isn't any milk.*
B: *I'll get you **some**.*

• Use *another* with singular countable nouns. Use *some more* with plural countable nouns or uncountable nouns.

A: *This cup of coffee is cold.*
B: *I'll send up **another**.*

A: *The toilet paper is almost finished.*
B: *I'll see if there's **some more**.*

## Present Simple Passive

• Use the Passive to say how things are made or done. For the Present Simple Passive, use the verb *be* + the past participle of the verb. Go to the irregular verbs list on page 111 for a list of past participles.

active:  *The waiter **opens** the wine at the table.*
passive: *The wine **is opened** at the table.* (singular verb)

active:  *First, the chef **adds** the tomatoes.*
passive: *First, the tomatoes **are added**.*    (plural verb)

## Past Simple

• Use the Past Simple for completed actions in the past. Use the same form of the verb with all pronouns.

### Regular verbs

verb + *-ed*        (verbs ending in a consonant)
visit + *-ed*
*She **visited** New York last month.*

verb + *-d*        (verbs ending in *-e*)
arrive + *-d*
*The guests **arrived** last night.*

### Irregular verbs

Some verbs have irregular Past Simple forms, e.g.

*go / **went***
*have / **had***
*I **went** to Paris last week.*
*I **had** a meeting in the Georges V Hotel.*

## *this/that, these/those, here/there*

• Use *this* or *that* for singular nouns near or at a distance from the speaker. Use *these* or *those* for plural nouns near or at a distance from the speaker.

A: *Is **this** your hotel?*
B: *No, **that's** my hotel across the street.*

A: *Are **these** your friends in reception?*
B: *No, **those** are my friends outside.*

• Use *here* for the place where the speaker is. Use *there* for a place at a distance from the speaker.

***Here's** your key card, sir.*
***There's** your taxi in front of the hotel.*

# Test yourself 3

### 1 Complete the sentences using the comparative form of the adjective in brackets.

1 The chicken is ........*cheaper*....... (cheap) than the fillet steak.
2 The rooms on the second floor are ..................... (comfortable) than those on the ground floor.
3 City hotels are often ..................... (big) than country hotels.
4 Onions have a ..................... (strong) smell than carrots.
5 This room is ..................... (good) for a family than that one.
6 The Chilean Merlot isn't as ..................... (smooth) as the French Merlot.

### 2 Match the requests and complaints with the best answers.

1 [f] There isn't any soap in the bathroom.
2 [ ] Excuse me, I don't have a fork.
3 [ ] I asked for white wine, not red.
4 [ ] Do you have any milk?
5 [ ] We ordered four coffees.
6 [ ] We finished the bread with our starter.

a I'm sorry, I'll get you one.
b Would you like some more with your main course?
c I'll tell the wine waiter to bring you some.
d Four? Of course. I'll get you another.
e Certainly, madam. I'll bring some.
f I'm sorry, I'll send some up straight away.

### 3 Complete the sentences with the Present Simple active or passive of the verbs in brackets.

1 We ......*open*..... (open) the restaurant every day at 12.00.
2 The rooms ..................... (clean) every morning.
3 First, you ..................... (chop) the onions.
4 Champagne ..................... (produce) in France.
5 You ..................... (not cook) smoked salmon.
6 The dish ..................... (not serve) hot. It ..................... (serve) cold.

### 4 Check the Past Simple of the verbs.

prepare    know    take    leave    fill in    order

#### Now complete the sentences with one of the verbs.

1 I ....*filled in*.... the registration card when I checked in.
2 The chef ................ a special meal for the child's birthday.
3 He ................ that something was wrong.
4 Table 24 ................ three bottles of champagne last night.
5 They ................ their bags at reception.
6 The porter ................ the bags up to their room.

### 5 Complete the dialogue between a manager and a new receptionist with *this/that, these/those, here/there*.

A: OK, so ......*here*.....¹ we are in reception. Now, where's Simone? She's the other receptionist. Ah, ................'s ² Simone, outside with the group from Poland. ................'s ³ their bus. Anyway, back to reception.
B: Is ................⁴ my computer?
A: Yes, it is.
B: And are ................⁵ the names of the guests checking out this morning?
A: Yes, they are. Ask me or Simone if you have any problems. My office is over ................, ⁶ through ................⁷ double doors. OK?

# Language review

■ Units 16–20

## must, have to, don't have to, mustn't

• Use *must* or *have to* for talking about an obligation. Use *must* or *have to* + the base form of the verb.

• Use *must* for a situation when the speaker thinks something is important.

*I **must** finish before lunch.*

(I want to because it's important.)

• Use *have to/has to* when there is an obligation from a rule or situation.

*We **have to** check the minibar every day.*

(It's part of the job.)

• Use *don't/doesn't have to* when there **isn't** an obligation from a rule or situation.

*I **don't have to** clean the windows every day.*

(It isn't a rule of the job.)

• Use *mustn't* when there is a negative obligation or prohibition.

*Guests **mustn't** smoke in the non-smoking lounge.*

(Don't do it!)

• Use *had to* (the Past Simple of *have to*) to express an obligation in the past.

*We **had to** work late yesterday.*

## need

• Use *need* in the following ways:

1 as a main verb (*need* + noun)

  A: *When do they **need** their luggage? (need = require)*
  B: *They **need** it as soon as possible.*

2 as an auxiliary verb (*need* + *-ing*)

  A: *I think the room **needs cleaning**.* (passive meaning)
  B: *No, it's OK. It **doesn't need cleaning**.*

3 as an auxiliary verb (*need* + full infinitive)

  A: *Do I **need to show** anything? (need = have to)*
  B: *You **need to show** your passport.*

## Past Simple: questions, short answers and negative statements

• Use *Did* + the base form of the verb to make questions in the Past Simple. Use *didn't* + the base form of the verb to make negative sentences in the Past Simple. Use *did* or *didn't* to make positive or negative short answers.

A: ***Did** they arrive yesterday?*
B: *Yes, they **did**./No, they **didn't**.*

A: ***Did** they check in to a hotel?*
B: *No, they **didn't** have a reservation.*

## Adjectives and adverbs

• Use adjectives to describe nouns, and use adverbs to describe verbs. Most adverbs are made by adding *-ly* to the adjective.

| adjective | adverb |
|---|---|
| slow | slowly |
| quick | quickly |
| polite | politely |

*The waiter was **polite** to the guests.* (adjective)
*The waiter spoke **politely** to the guests.* (adverb)

However, some adjectives and adverbs have the same form.

| adjectives/adverbs | |
|---|---|
| daily | early |
| weekly | late |
| monthly | fast |
| yearly | hard |

*The flight was **early**.* (adjective)
*The flight arrived **early**.* (adverb)

The adjective *good* has a completely different form.

| adjective | adverb |
|---|---|
| good | well |

*She's a **good** receptionist.* (adjective)
*She works **well** in reception.* (adverb)

# Test yourself 4

## 1 Complete the sentences with the correct form of *must* or *have to/has to*.

1 One of the guests is ill. We ........*must*........ call a doctor.
2 Receptionists ..................... dress smartly. It's a hotel rule.
3 The air-conditioning broke down so we ..................... call an electrician.
4 Do you ..................... work in the kitchen?
5 We ..................... remember to say thank you to the manager.
6 Phillipe ..................... clean the tables before breakfast.

## 2 Complete the sentences with the correct form of *mustn't* or *don't/doesn't have to*.

1 I promised to arrive before nine. I .......*mustn't*...... be late.
2 You ..................... change the towels every day. Twice a week is OK.
3 The restaurant was closed at the weekend so we ..................... work on Sunday.
4 You ..................... overcook the vegetables.
5 Akemi ..................... wear her uniform every day.
6 Fabien and Pascal ..................... work behind the bar. That's Adam's job.

## 3 Complete the sentences with the correct form of *need*.

1 She says her jacket ...*needs cleaning*... (need/clean).
2 We ..................... (need/buy) a map of the city centre.
3 The minibar is empty. You ..................... (need/fill) it.
4 The TV ..................... (need/change) in Room 22.
5 My trousers ..................... (need/press).
6 The kitchen ..................... (need/have) the vegetables as soon as possible.
7 Their taxi ..................... (need/order) for 8.00 p.m.
8 Do I ..................... (need/come) to the staff meeting tomorrow?

## 4 Complete the dialogue between two guests using *did/didn't*.

A: ......*Did*......[1] you check in OK this morning?
B: Yes, I ...............[2] ...............[3] you have to fill in a registration card?
A: Yes, I ...............[4]. Actually, my wife filled it in.
B: ...............[5] she leave your passports at reception?
A: No, she ...............[6]. The receptionist took the numbers and gave them back.
...............[7] you get your passport back?
B: No, I ...............[8]. I must remember to pick it up.

## 5 Underline the correct alternative.

1 The night porter always walks *quiet/quietly* along the corridors.
2 The service here is too *slow/slowly*.
3 Make sure you clean the room *careful/carefully*.
4 He works *quick/quickly*.
5 Security in the car park is *important/importantly*.
6 There's a *regular/regularly* test of the fire alarms.
7 The manager speaks English very *good/well*.
8 Bollinger is an *expensive/expensively* Champagne.

# Language review
- Units 21–25

## Present Perfect

• Use the Present Perfect to talk about actions in the past that are **not** completed. Use the Past Simple (see page 82), to talk about actions in the past that are completed.

*He **hasn't finished** his breakfast.*  (not completed)
*He **finished** his breakfast at 10.00 a.m.*  (completed)

• Use *just* with the Present Perfect to show that an action is recently completed.

*The group from New Zealand has **just** arrived. They're in reception.*

• Use *yet* with the Present Perfect to mean *up to now*.

*I **haven't** met the manager **yet**. Maybe tomorrow.*

• Make the Present Perfect with *have/has* + the past participle of the verb. Go to page 111 for the irregular verbs list with past participles. Use the short forms (in brackets) in spoken English and informal written English.

POSITIVE

| singular | plural |
|---|---|
| I have (I've) arrived. | We have (We've) arrived. |
| You have (You've) arrived. | You have (You've) arrived. |
| He has (He's) arrived. | They have (They've) arrived. |
| She has (She's) arrived. | |
| The flight/It has (It's) arrived. | |

NEGATIVE

| singular | plural |
|---|---|
| I have not (haven't) arrived. | We have not (haven't) arrived. |
| You have not (haven't) arrived. | You have not (haven't) arrived. |
| He has not (hasn't) arrived. | They have not (haven't) arrived. |
| She has not (hasn't) arrived. | |
| The flight/it has not (hasn't) arrived. | |

QUESTION

| singular | plural |
|---|---|
| Have I arrived? | Have we arrived? |
| Have you arrived? | Have you arrived? |
| Has he arrived? | Have they arrived? |
| Has she arrived? | |
| Has the flight/it arrived? | |

## *should* + Present Perfect Passive

Use *should* + Present Perfect Passive to apologize and to make explanations. Use *should* + *have been* + the past participle of the verb. Go to page 111 for the irregular verbs list with the past participles.

*I'm sorry. The minibar **should have been refilled**.*

## Present Continuous

• Use the Present Continuous to describe something that is happening at the time of speaking, or for something that is temporary. Use the Present Simple for something that is generally true, or happens regularly, or is permanent (see page 77).

*She's **working** on the computer.*  (at the time of speaking)
*She's **working** from home this week.* (temporary)

*She **works** hard.*  (generally true)
*She often **works** with Pierre.*  (happens regularly)
*She **works** in Paris.*  (permanent)

• Make the Present Continuous with *am/are/is* + *-ing*. Use the short forms (in brackets) in spoken English and informal written English.

POSITIVE

| singular | plural |
|---|---|
| I am (I'm) staying here. | We are (We're) staying here. |
| You are (You're) staying here. | You are (You're) staying here. |
| He is (He's) staying here. | They are (They're) staying here. |
| She is (She's) staying here. | |
| The weather/It is (It's) getting hot. | |

NEGATIVE

| singular | plural |
|---|---|
| I am not (I'm not) staying here. | We are not (aren't) staying here. |
| You are not (aren't) staying here. | You are not (aren't) staying here. |
| He is not (isn't) staying here. | They are not (aren't) staying here. |
| She is not (isn't) staying here. | |
| The weather/It is not (isn't) getting hot. | |

QUESTION

| singular | plural |
|---|---|
| Am I staying here? | Are we staying here? |
| Are you staying here? | Are you staying here? |
| Is he staying here? | Are they staying here? |
| Is she staying here? | |
| Is the weather/it getting hot? | |

## Object pronouns

• Use object pronouns after the verb.

| singular | plural |
|---|---|
| The porter took *me/you/him/her/it* to the room. | The porter took *us/you/them* to the room. |

# Test yourself 5

## 1 Complete the sentences with the Present Perfect of the verbs in brackets. Use short forms if appropriate.

1 I ......'ve...... just ....spoken.... (speak) to Mr Souliman on the phone.
2 They ............... (not see) the new restaurant yet.
3 I ............... (write) the manager a letter. Here it is.
4 Mary ............... just ............... (go) to work.
5 The wine waiter ............... (not take) our order yet.
6 We ............... (not have) lunch yet.

## 2 Complete the sentences with the Present Perfect or Past Simple of the verbs in brackets. Use short forms if appropriate.

1 A: ....Have..... you ....whisked.... (whisk) the cream yet?
  B: Yes, I ............... (whisk) it after I chopped the fruit.
2 A: ............... the Malaysian group ............... (check in) yet?
  B: They ............... (arrive) about an hour ago. They ............... (be) in their rooms for half an hour.
3 A: ............... Mr and Mrs Smith ............... (come) back yet?
  B: No, they ............... (not). They ............... (say) they would be back late.

## 3 Complete the sentences with the correct form of *should* + Present Perfect Passive of the verb in brackets.

1 The sheets .should have been changed. (change).
2 The reservation ............... (cancel).
3 The guests ............... (tell).
4 The passports ............... (put) in the safe.
5 The wine ............... (bring).
6 The fire extinguisher ............... (check).

## 4 Complete the sentences with the Present Continuous or Present Simple of the verbs in brackets. Use short forms if appropriate.

1 Our Front of house manager ......speaks.... (speak) four languages.
2 I usually ............... (work) in housekeeping but this week I ............... (work) in room service.
3 The airport bus is never late. It always ............... (leave) on time.
4 Excuse me. ............... you ............... (work) here?
5 At the moment, the chef ............... (prepare) dinner.
6 ............... you ............... (work) in the restaurant today?

## 5 Complete the sentences with object pronouns.

1 We'd like to pay. Could you bring ......us...... the bill?
2 I'm meeting two colleagues in reception. Have you seen ............... ?
3 A: Has Mrs Bell arrived yet?    B: Yes, that's ............... in the lobby.
4 Good evening, sir. What can I get ............... ?
5 A: Table 8 ordered a bottle of the French Merlot.   B: I've just taken ............... to them.
6 A: Have you met Mr Garcia?    B: Yes, I met ............... yesterday.
7 I'm sorry, did you give ............... my passport back?

# Language review
■ Units 26–28

## much, many, a lot of

• Use *much, many, a lot of* to talk about an amount or number of something.

• Use *much* in negative sentences and questions with uncountable nouns.

*I don't have **much** time.*
*How **much** money do you have?*

• Use *many* in negative sentences and questions with countable nouns.

*There aren't **many** free rooms tonight.*
*How **many** bottles did you order?*

• Use *a lot of* in positive and negative sentences, and questions with uncountable and countable nouns.

*We have **a lot of** time/guests.*
*We don't have **a lot of** time/guests.*
*Do you have **a lot of** time/guests?*

## A covering letter

• Write a covering letter to send with a CV or application form. Use certain key phrases and standard forms as shown in bold. Use the letter to focus on your best qualities.

## Talking about the future

• Use the Present Continuous, or *be going to*, or *will* to talk about the future. Use the Present Simple for timetables.

• Use the Present Continuous for things you have arranged to do or happen.

*I'm meeting my friends after work.*
*The guests **are arriving** at 10.00 tomorrow morning.*

• Use *be going to* + verb for something you have decided to do, or you intend to do but have not yet arranged.

*I'm going to learn French next year.*
*She doesn't enjoy her job. She's going to get a new one.*

• Use *will* when you decide to do something at the time of speaking,

*I'll have a gin and tonic, please.*

or when you forecast or predict something,

*It'll rain this afternoon.*

or when you offer to do something,

*I'll fill in the other parts of the form for you.*

or when you promise or agree to do something.

*I'll send it straight up to your room.*

• Use the Present Simple for timetables or programmes.

*The plane **leaves** at 21.15 and **arrives** at 23.00.*
*The film **begins** at 20.35.*

---

Dear Sir/Madam

**I am writing to apply for** the position of senior receptionist **as advertised in** this month's *Hotel Review*.

**I am a** fully trained receptionist **with a diploma in** Leisure and Tourism Studies, and I have three years' work experience. **I currently work as a** receptionist **at** the Excelsior Hotel **in** Leeds.

**I would like to apply for the position advertised as I feel I have the necessary experience for the job. I have experience using** the Fidelio and Galileo systems and excellent computer skills. **I am** sociable **and** well organized, **and I enjoy** working with people.

**I enclose a copy of my CV and a completed application form. I look forward to hearing from you.**

Yours faithfully

# Test yourself 6

## 1 Underline the correct alternative.

1 I don't have <u>much</u>/*many* work to do today.
2 There are *much*/*a lot of* guests waiting to pay.
3 Is the manager responsible for *much*/*a lot of* staff?
4 We don't have *much*/*many* rooms available.
5 I spent a *many*/*a lot of* money in Madrid.
6 How *much*/*many* time do we have before the taxi arrives?
7 There are *much*/*a lot of* drinks on the menu.
8 How *many*/*a lot of* languages do you speak?

## 2 Correct the *five* mistakes in the covering letter.

Dear Mr Kim

I write to apply for the position of manager as advertised in the November edition of *Hotel & Catering Monthly*.

I am fully trained manager with a diploma in Hotel and Restaurant Management, and I have three years' work experience. I currently worked as assistant manager at Hotel Torre in Pisa.

I would like to apply for the position advertised as I feel I have the necessary experience for the job. I have experience managing a busy hotel with twenty staff. I am sociable and well organized, and I enjoy dealing with customers.

I enclose a copy of my CV and a completed application form. I look forward to hear from you.

Yours faithfully

## 3 Complete the sentences with the correct future form of the verbs in brackets. Use short forms if appropriate.

1 I ..*'m meeting*.. (meet) the head chef tomorrow at 9.00.
2 OK. I ............... (be) there in 15 minutes.
3 Do you think it ............... (rain) tomorrow?
4 The bus to the airport ............... (leave) in ten minutes.
5 I ............... (replace) that bottle immediately, sir.
6 What ............... you ............... (do) this weekend?
7 I want a new job so I ............... (look) for one soon.
8 I ............... (take) your coat for you.

# Test yourself answer key

## Test yourself 1

**1** 2 I'd like to meet at 6.00 p.m.
3 Can I take a message for you?
4 I'd like to speak to the manager.
5 Can I help you?
6 Can I have your passport?
7 I'd like a double room.
8 Could you tell me my room number?

**2** 2 There isn't a car park.
3 There are 300 rooms.
4 Are there any disabled facilities?
5 There's an exchange bureau.
6 Is there a minibar in the room?
7 There aren't any shops.
8 Are there any cloakrooms?

**3** 2 Does, doesn't 3 Does, does 4 Do, don't
5 Does, does 6 Do, do 7 Does, doesn't 8 Do, do

**4** 2 from, to 3 in 4 from, to, at 5 in 6 in 7 on 8 at

**5** 2 the twenty-third of May
3 the eighth of October
4 the sixteenth of January
5 the tenth of September, two thousand and eight
6 the third of December
7 the twelfth of February
8 the twenty-second of July

**6** 2 May (the) twenty-third
3 August (the) tenth
4 January (the) sixteenth
5 October (the) ninth, two thousand (and) eight
6 December (the) third
7 December (the) second
8 July (the) twenty-second

**7** 2 often 3 never 4 rarely 5 often 6 sometimes 7 often 8 always

**8** 2 five fifty-five/five to six
3 twelve ten/ten past twelve
4 three forty-five/quarter to four
5 eight thirty/half past eight
6 one/one o'clock
7 nine fifteen/quarter past nine
8 eleven forty/twenty to twelve

**9** 2 're 3 'm 4 Are 5 's 6 Is 7 're 8 Are

**10** 2 Do, visit 3 doesn't work 4 Do, live 5 has 6 Does, seat
7 serves 8 don't go

## Test yourself 2

**1** 2 our 3 my 4 their 5 your 6 her 7 its

**2** 2 Can I smoke in here?
3 Shall I check your reservation?
4 Could I have a menu?
5 Would you like some more?
6 Could I use the swimming pool?

**3** 2 a, the 3 the 4 a, The 5 an 6 a, the

**4** 2 an 3 a 4 some 5 a, a 6 Some

**5** 2 any 3 some 4 any 5 some 6 any

## Test yourself 3

**1** 2 more comfortable 3 bigger 4 stronger
5 better 6 smooth
**2** 2 a 3 c 4 e 5 d 6 b

**3** 2 are cleaned 3 chop 4 is produced 5 don't cook
6 is not (isn't) served, is ('s) served

**4** 2 prepared 3 knew 4 ordered 5 left 6 took

**5** 2 there 3 That 4 this 5 these 6 there 7 those

## Test yourself 4

**1** 2 have to 3 had to 4 have to 5 must 6 has to

**2** 2 don't have to 3 didn't have to 4 mustn't
5 doesn't have to 6 don't have to

**3** 2 need to buy 3 need to fill 4 needs changing 5 need pressing
6 needs to have 7 needs ordering 8 need to come

**4** 2 did 3 Did 4 did 5 Did 6 didn't 7 Did 8 didn't

**5** 2 slow 3 carefully 4 quickly 5 important 6 regular 7 well
8 expensive

## Test yourself 5

**1** 2 haven't seen 3 've written 4 's just gone
5 hasn't taken 6 haven't had

**2** 1 whisked
2 Have, checked in, arrived, 've been
3 Have, come, haven't, said

**3** 2 should have been cancelled
3 should have been told
4 should have been put
5 should have been brought
6 should have been checked

**4** 2 work, 'm working 3 leaves 4 Do, work 5 's preparing
6 Are, working

**5** 2 them 3 her 4 you 5 it 6 him 7 me

# Test yourself 6

**1** 2 a lot of   3 a lot of   4 many   5 a lot of   6 much
7 a lot of   8 many

**2**

Dear Mr Kim

~~I write~~ I'm writing to apply for the position of manager as advertised in the November edition of *Hotel & Catering Monthly*.

I am **a** fully trained manager with a diploma in Hotel and Restaurant Management and I have three years' work experience. I currently ~~worked~~ work as assistant manager at Hotel Torre in Pisa.

I would like to apply for the position advertised as I feel I have the necessary experience for the job. I have experience managing a busy hotel with twenty staff. I am sociable and well organized and I enjoy dealing with customers.

I enclose a copy of my CV and a completed application form. I look forward to ~~hear~~ hearing from you.

~~Yours faithfully~~ Yours sincerely

**3** 2 'll be   3 'll rain   4 leaves   5 'll replace   6 are, doing
7 'm going to look   8 'll take

## From Unit 19, page 41 (Answers)

# Help yourself 1

This is your chance to personalize the English you have studied.

## Five-star phrases ★ ★ ★ ★ ★

Look back through the book and write the five most useful expressions for front office staff.
Then translate them into your language.

| English | My language |
|---------|-------------|
| 1 ..................................................... | 1 ..................................................... |
| 2 ..................................................... | 2 ..................................................... |
| 3 ..................................................... | 3 ..................................................... |
| 4 ..................................................... | 4 ..................................................... |
| 5 ..................................................... | 5 ..................................................... |

## Key words

Look back through the book and complete the diagram with the most useful words for front office staff.

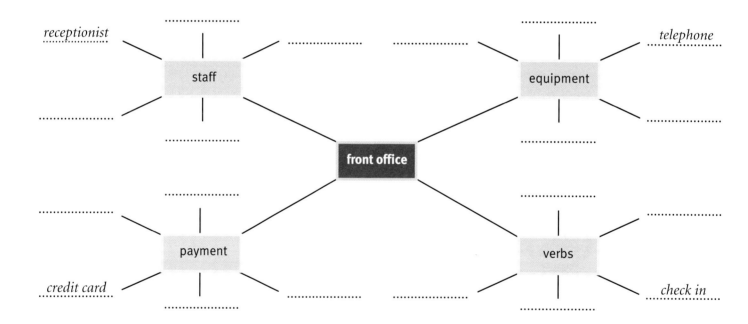

## Extras

Check these extra words in a bilingual dictionary. Then write the translation in your language.

| English | My language |
|---------|-------------|
| availability | ..................................................... |
| cancellation | ..................................................... |
| deluxe | ..................................................... |
| expiry date | ..................................................... |
| signature | ..................................................... |

# Help yourself 2

This is your chance to personalize the English you have studied.

## Five-star phrases ★★★★★

Look back through the book and write the five most useful expressions for bar staff.
Then translate them into your language.

| English | My language |
|---------|-------------|
| 1 ................................................. | 1 ................................................. |
| 2 ................................................. | 2 ................................................. |
| 3 ................................................. | 3 ................................................. |
| 4 ................................................. | 4 ................................................. |
| 5 ................................................. | 5 ................................................. |

## Key words

Look back through the book and complete the diagram with the most useful words for bar staff.

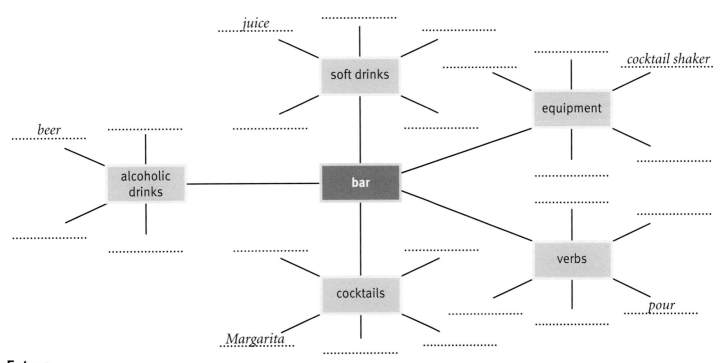

## Extras

Check these extra words in a bilingual dictionary. Then write the translation in your language.

| English | My language |
|---------|-------------|
| barrel | .................................................... |
| coaster | .................................................... |
| drip tray | .................................................... |
| optic | .................................................... |
| pump | .................................................... |

# Help yourself 3

 Kitchen

This is your chance to personalize the English you have studied.

## Five-star phrases ★ ★ ★ ★ ★

Look back through the book and write the five most useful expressions for kitchen staff.
Then translate them into your language.

| English | My language |
|---|---|
| 1 ................................................ | 1 ................................................ |
| 2 ................................................ | 2 ................................................ |
| 3 ................................................ | 3 ................................................ |
| 4 ................................................ | 4 ................................................ |
| 5 ................................................ | 5 ................................................ |

## Key words

Look back through the book and complete the diagram with the most useful words for kitchen staff.

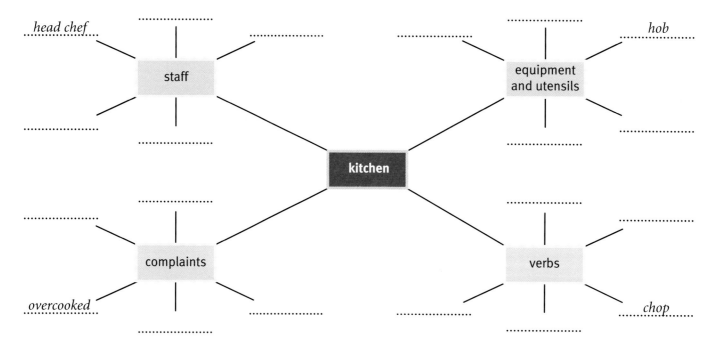

## Extras

Check these extra words in a bilingual dictionary. Then write the translation in your language.

| English | My language |
|---|---|
| chopping board | ................................................ |
| oven gloves | ................................................ |
| stir fry | ................................................ |
| tap (n) | ................................................ |
| uniform | ................................................ |

# Help yourself 4

This is your chance to personalize the English you have studied.

## Five-star phrases ★ ★ ★ ★ ★

Look back through the book and write the five most useful expressions for restaurant staff.
Then translate them into your language.

| English | My language |
|---------|-------------|
| 1 .................................................. | 1 .................................................. |
| 2 .................................................. | 2 .................................................. |
| 3 .................................................. | 3 .................................................. |
| 4 .................................................. | 4 .................................................. |
| 5 .................................................. | 5 .................................................. |

## Key words

Look back through the book and complete the diagram with the most useful words for restaurant staff.

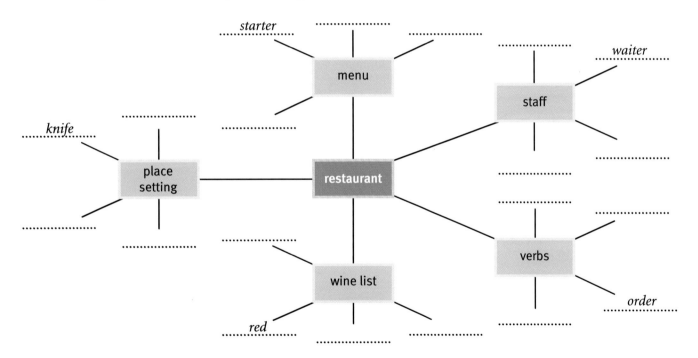

## Extras

Check these extra words in a bilingual dictionary. Then write the translation in your language.

| English | My language |
|---------|-------------|
| bistro | .................................................. |
| chopsticks | .................................................. |
| house wine | .................................................. |
| restroom | .................................................. |
| tip | .................................................. |

# Help yourself 5

This is your chance to personalize the English you have studied.

## Five-star phrases ★★★★★

Look back through the book and write the five most useful expressions for housekeeping staff.
Then translate them into your language.

| English | My language |
|---------|-------------|
| 1 ................................................................ | 1 ................................................................ |
| 2 ................................................................ | 2 ................................................................ |
| 3 ................................................................ | 3 ................................................................ |
| 4 ................................................................ | 4 ................................................................ |
| 5 ................................................................ | 5 ................................................................ |

## Key words

Look back through the book and complete the diagram with the most useful words for housekeeping staff.

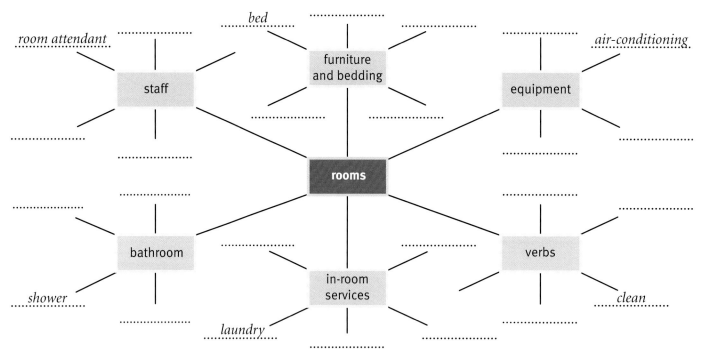

## Extras

Check these extra words in a bilingual dictionary. Then write the translation in your language.

| English | My language |
|---------|-------------|
| balcony | ................................................................ |
| *Do not disturb* | ................................................................ |
| en suite | ................................................................ |
| locked | ................................................................ |
| remote control | ................................................................ |

# Wordlist

| English | French | German | Italian | Spanish | Japanese |
|---|---|---|---|---|---|
| accept 5 | accepter | akzeptieren | accettare | aceptar | 受け取る |
| access 24 | accès | Zugang | accesso | acceso | 通路、アクセス |
| Access Only 21 | Accès réservé aux riverains | Nur für Anlieger | solo accesso | Sólo entrada | 関係車両のみ通行可 |
| accident report 23 | déclaration d'accident | Unfallbericht | verbale dell'incidente | parte de accidente | 事故報告書 |
| account 26 | compte | Konto | conto | cuenta | 会計、勘定 |
| adjoining 3 | voisin | Neben- | attiguo, vicino | contiguo, de al lado | 隣り合った、つながっている |
| advert 27 | annonce | Anzeige | inserzione | anuncio | 広告、募集広告 |
| advice 12 | conseils | Rat | consiglio | consejo | アドバイス |
| advise 27 | conseiller | (be)raten | consigliare, informare | aconsejar | 助言する |
| age 5 | âge | Alter | età | edad | 年齢 |
| air-conditioning 2 | climatisation | Klimaanlage | aria condizionata | aire acondicionado | エアコン（冷暖房装置） |
| airport transfer 22 | navette | Flughafenbus | servizio navetta da e per l'aeroporto | traslados al/desde el aeropuerto | 空港からの乗り継ぎ |
| a.m. 4 (morning) | du matin | morgens | di mattina | por la mañana | 午前 |
| ambulance 23 | ambulance | Krankenwagen | ambulanza | ambulancia | 救急車 |
| amount 26 | montant | Betrag | importo | importe | 総額 |
| Angostura bitters 8 | Angostura amer | Angosturabitter | amaro all'Angostura | bíter de angostura | アンゴストラ・ビター |
| announcement 19 | annonce | Durchsage | annuncio | aviso | アナウンス |
| anything 5 | rien | etwas; (verneint) nichts | niente | nada | 何か、何も |
| apartment 27 | appartement | Wohnung | appartamento | apartamento | マンション |
| appear 26 | apparaître | scheinen | sembrare, apparire | aparecer | 現れる |
| apple pie 10 | tourte aux pommes | Apfelpastete | torta di mela | tarta de manzana | アップルパイ |
| arrival 15 | arrivée | Ankunft | arrivo | llegada | 到着 |
| arrive 3 | arriver | ankommen | arrivare | llegar | 到着する |
| ask 24 | demander | bitten um | chiedere | preguntar | 尋ねる |
| assembly point 19 | lieu de rassemblement | Sammelplatz | punto di raduno | punto de encuentro | 集合場所 |
| asthma 23 | asthme | Asthma | asma | asma | 喘息 |
| at the top of 2 | en haut de | oben auf | in cima a | en la parte de arriba de | ～の一番上にある |
| attendant 14 | gardien | Aufseher(in) | custode | guarda, encargado | 添乗員 |
| attitude 28 | attitude | Einstellung | atteggiamento | actitud | 態度 |
| audio-visual 22 | audio-visuel | audiovisuell | audio-visivo | audiovisual | 視聴覚 |
| aunt 28 | tante | Tante | zia | tía | 叔母 |
| autumn 6 | automne | Herbst | autunno | otoño | 秋 |
| babysitting 22 | baby-sitting | Babysitten | sorveglianza di bambini | guardería, cuidado de niños | 子守り、子供の世話 |
| back 19 | ldos | Rücken | schiena | espalda | 背中 |
| bacon 9 | ard | Speck | pancetta (affumicata) | tocino | ベーコン |
| bake 13 | cuire au four | backen | cuocere al forno | cocer (en el horno) | 焼く |
| baked 13 | cuit au four | gebacken | cotto al forno | cocido (en el horno) | 焼いてある |
| baking tin 15 | plat à four | Backform | teglia | bandeja de horno | 焼き皿 |
| balance 26 | solde | Saldo | saldo | saldo | 差額 |
| balloon whisk 16 | fouet | Schneebesen | frusta | batidora | 泡たて器 |
| banqueting 22 | (salle) des banquets | Bankett- | sala di convivio | de/para banquetes | 宴会場、バンケットルーム |
| bar 2 | bar | Bar | bar | bar | バー |
| bar spoon 8 | cuillère à cocktail | Cocktaillöffel | cucchiaio da cocktail | cuchara para cócteles | バースプーン |
| barbecue 13 | barbecue | Barbecue | barbecue | barbacoa | バーベキュー |
| barber 22 | coiffeur pour hommes | (Herren)friseur | barbiere, parrucchiere | barbero | 床屋 |
| basil 9 | basilic | Basilikum | basilico | albahaca | バジル |
| bath 3 | bain | Bad | bagno | baño | 風呂 |
| bath mat 20 | tapis de bain | Badematte | stuoia da bagno | alfombra de baño | バスマット |
| bath/shower gel 16 | gel de douche | Bade-, Duschgel | doccia schiuma, bagno schiuma | gel de baño/ducha | バス/シャワージェル |
| battery 18 | pile | Batterie | batteria | batería | バッテリー |

| English | French | German | Italian | Spanish | Japanese |
|---|---|---|---|---|---|
| beat 16 | battre | schlagen | battere | batir | かき混ぜる |
| become 11 | devenir | werden | diventare | convertirse en, volverse | 〜の状態になる |
| bedding 20 | literie | Bettzeug | biancheria da letto | ropa de cama | 寝具 |
| bedroom 2 | chambre | Schlafzimmer | camera da letto | dormitorio | 寝室 |
| bedside light 20 | lampe de chevet | Nachttischlampe | lume | lámpara de mesilla | 枕元のライト |
| bedspread 20 | dessus de lit | Tagesdecke | copriletto | colcha | ベッドカバー |
| beef 9 | boeuf | Rindfleisch | manzo | vaca | 牛肉 |
| beefburger 17 | hamburger | Hamburger | hamburger | hamburguesa | ビーフハンバーガー |
| beer 7 | bière | Bier | birra | cerveza | ビール |
| bend 19 | plier | beugen | piegare | doblar, agacharse | 曲げる |
| bidet 20 | bidet | Bidet/Sitzbad | bidet | bidet | ビデ |
| bin 16 | poubelle | Mülleimer | cestino portarifiuti | cubo | ゴミ箱 |
| blackcurrant 10 | cassis | schwarze Johannisbeere | mora | mora negra | クロスグリ、カシス |
| blanket 20 | couverture | Decke | coperta | manta | 毛布 |
| bleeding 23 | saignement | Blutung | emorragia | hemorragia | 出血 |
| blend 16 | mélanger | vermischen | mescolare | mezclar | 混ぜる |
| blender 15 | mixeur | Mixer | frullatore | licuadora | ミキサー |
| blouse 17 | chemisier | Bluse | camicetta | blusa | ブラウス |
| blue 10 | bleu | blau | blu | azul | 青 |
| boardroom 22 | salle du conseil | Sitzungssaal | sala consiglio | sala de juntas | （重役向け）大会議室 |
| boat 21 | bateau | Boot | barca | barco | ボート |
| body lotion 16 | lait corporel | Körperlotion | crema per il corpo | loción corporal | ボディーローション |
| boil 13 | (faire) bouillir | kochen | bollire | hervir | 煮る |
| book 1 | réserver | reservieren | prenotare | reservar | 予約する |
| booking 3 | réservation | Reservierung | prenotazione | reserva | 予約 |
| brandy 7 | cognac | Weinbrand | cognac | coñac | ブランディー |
| bread 9 | pain | Brot | pane | pan | パン |
| break 16 (v) | casser | zerbrechen | rompere | romper | ちぎる、ばらばらにする |
| breakfast 3 | petit déjeuner | Frühstück | prima colazione | desayuno | 朝食 |
| broadband 22 | broadband, haut débit | Breitband | a banda larga | banda ancha, tarifa plana | ブロードバンド |
| brother 3 | frère | Bruder | fratello | hermano | 兄弟 |
| budget 18 | budget | Budget | bilancio | presupuesto | 予算 |
| burn 23 (v) | brûler | sich verbrennen | bruciare | quemar(se) | やけどさせる |
| bus 21 | bus | Bus | autobus | autobús | バス |
| Bus Lane 21 | couloir de bus | Busspur | corsia autobus | carril bus | バス専用車線 |
| business traveller 12 | voyageur d'affaires | Geschäftsmann,-frau | viaggiatore d'affari | viajero de negocios | ビジネス目的の旅行者、出張者 |
| busy 1 | occupé | besetzt | occupato | comunicando | 話し中（電話） |
| butter knife 13 | couteau à beurre | Buttermesser | coltello per il burro | cuchillo para mantequilla | バターナイフ |
| by air 21 | par avion | auf dem Luftweg | via aerea | por vía aérea | 飛行機で |
| cabaret/floor show 22 | spectacle de cabaret | Kabarett, Nachtclub-Show | spettacolo di cabaret | cabaret/espectáculo | キャバレー/フロワーショー |
| cabinet 20 | commode | Schrank | mobiletto, armadietto | armario | 飾り棚、キャビネット |
| candidate 28 | candidat | Bewerber(in) | candidato | candidato/candidata | 候補者 |
| candle 13 | bougie | Kerze | candela | vela | ロウソク |
| car 21 | voiture | Wagen | automobile | coche | 車 |
| card 25 (Visa) | carte (de crédit) | Kreditkarte | carta di credito | tarjeta | クレジットカード |
| car hire 22 | location de voiture | Autovermietung | noleggio auto | alquiler de coches | レンタカー |
| car park 2 | parking | Parkplatz | parcheggio | aparcamiento | 駐車場 |
| cardigan 17 | gilet | Strickjacke | giacca di lana | chaqueta (de punto) | カーディガン |
| career 28 | carrière | berufliche Laufbahn | carriera | carrera profesional | 経歴 |
| carpet 20 | moquette | Teppich | tappeto | alfombra | カーペット |
| cash 25 | liquide | Bargeld | contante | dinero en metálico | 現金 |
| cashier 15 | caissier | Kassierer(in) | cassiere | cajero | 会計 |
| caster sugar 8 | sucre en poudre | Sandzucker | zucchero raffinato | azúcar blanco de grano fino | グラニュー糖 |
| catering college 27 | école de restauration | Hotelfachschule | scuola alberghiera | escuela de cocina | 飲食サービス専門学校、学部 |

| English | French | German | Italian | Spanish | Japanese |
|---|---|---|---|---|---|
| change 25 (n) | petite monnaie | Kleingeld | resto | cambio | お釣 |
| charges 26 (n) | frais | Rechnung | spese | gastos | 手数料 |
| cheese 10 | fromage | Käse | formaggio | queso | チーズ |
| chef's salad 9 | salade composée du chef | Salat des Hauses | insalata dello chef | ensalada del chef | シェフサラダ |
| cherry 8 | cerise | Kirsche | ciliegia | cereza | さくらんぼ |
| chicken 9 | poulet | Hühnchen | pollo | pollo | 鶏肉 |
| children 3 | enfants | Kinder | bambini | niños/niñas | 子供 |
| chill 8 | refroidir | kühlen | raffreddare | enfriar | 冷やす |
| chocolate sauce 10 | sauce au chocolat | Schokoladensoße | crema di cioccolato | salsa de chocolate | チョコレートソース |
| chop 9 (n) | côtelette | Kotelett | braciola | chuleta | 骨付きの切り身、チョップ |
| chop 16 (v) | hacher | klein schneiden | tagliare a pezzetti | cortar/picar | 叩き切る |
| Christmas 5 | Noël | Weihnachten | Natale | Navidad(es) | クリスマス |
| clean 15 | nettoyer | reinigen | pulire | limpiar | きれいな、清潔な |
| click 26 | cliquer | (an)klicken | cliccare | hacer click | クリックする（コンピュータのマウスを） |
| cloakroom 2 | vestiaire | Garderobe | guardaroba | guardarropa | 手荷物預かり所 |
| cocktail 7 | cocktail | Cocktail | cocktail | cóctel | カクテル |
| cocktail glass 8 | verre à cocktail | Cocktailglas | bicchiere da cocktail | copa de cóctel | カクテルグラス |
| coffee 17 | café | Kaffee | caffè | café | コーヒー |
| colander 16 | passoire | Durchschlag | colino | colador | ざる |
| cold 23 (n) | rhume | Erkältung | raffreddore | catarro | 風邪 |
| company 25 | société | Gesellschaft | compagnia | compañía | 会社 |
| complimentary 16 | à titre gracieux, gratuit | Frei- | in omaggio | de regalo | 無料の |
| computer 1 | ordinateur | Computer | computer | ordenador | コンピュータ |
| concentrate 28 | concentrer / se concentrer | sich konzentrieren | concentrare | concentrarse | 集中する |
| conference room 20 | salle de conférences | Konferenzzimmer | sala di convegno | sala de juntas/ reuniones | 会議室 |
| confirm 3 | confirmer | bestätigen | confermare | confirmar | 確認する |
| continental breakfast 17 | petit déjeuner | kleines Frühstück | prima colazione leggera | desayuno continental | コンチネンタルスタイルの朝食 |
| conversation 12 | conversation | Gespräch | conversazione | conversación | 会話 |
| copy 25 | copie | Kopie | copia | copia | コピー |
| cordless phone 18 | téléphone sans fils | schnurloses Telefon | telefono portatile | teléfono inalámbrico | コードレス電話 |
| cork 11 | bouchon | Kork | tappo | corcho | コルク |
| corked 11 | bouchonné | korkig | dal sapore di tappo | que sabe al corcho | コルクの異臭がする |
| corkscrew 11 | tire-bouchon | Korkenzieher | cavatappi | sacacorchos | コルク栓抜き |
| country code 18 | indicatif du pays | Landesvorwahl | prefisso del paese | código del país | 国別コード番号 |
| courier service 22 | coursier / messagerie rapide | Eilbotenservice | servizio di un agente turistico | servicio de mensajería | 宅配便 |
| cousin 28 | cousin | Cousin, Kusine | cugino | primo/prima | いとこ |
| covered garage 22 | garage fermé | überdachte Garage | garage coperto | garaje cubierto | 屋根つき車庫 |
| cow's cheese 10 | fromage de lait de vache | Käse (aus Kuhmilch) | formaggio di mucca | queso de vaca | 牛乳が原料のチーズ |
| crab 9 | crabe | Krabbe | granchio | cangrejo de mar | カニ |
| cream 16 | travailler | cremig rühren | far diventare cremoso, scremare | mezclar con crema | クリーム状にする |
| credit 26 | crédit | Kredit/Guthaben | credito | crédito | 信用貸しをする |
| crème caramel 10 | crème caramel | Karamellcreme | crème caramel | crema catalana | クリームカラメル |
| crêpes 10 | crêpes | dünne Pfannkuchen | crêpe | creps | クレープ |
| croissant 9 | croissant | Hörnchen | croissant | croissant/cruasán | クロワッサン |
| cross 21 (v) | traverser | überqueren | attraversare | cruzar | 横切る |
| cuisine 2 | cuisine, gastronomie | Küche | modo di cucinare, cucina | cocina | 料理 |
| curtain 20 | rideau | Vorhang | tenda | cortina | カーテン |
| customer 4 | client | Kunde, Kundin | cliente | cliente/clienta | 客 |
| cut 23 (n) | coupure | Schnittwunde | taglio | corte / herida | 切り傷 |
| cutlery 12 | couverts | Besteck | posate | cubertería | カトラリ（フォーク、ナイフ、スプーン） |
| cutlet 9 | côtelette | Kotelett | cotoletta | chuletilla | カツレツ |
| CV 27 | CV (curriculum vitae) | Lebenslauf | curriculum vitae | curriculum vitae | 履歴書 |

| English | French | German | Italian | Spanish | Japanese |
|---|---|---|---|---|---|
| cycle path 21 | piste cyclable | Radweg | pista ciclabile | carril bici | 自転車用道路 |
| daughter 3 | fille | Tochter | figlia | hija | 娘 |
| debit 26 | débit | Schuld/Last | debito | débito | 口座引き落としをする |
| debit card 25 | carte bancaire (sans paiement différé) | Debitkarte | carta di addebito | tarjeta de cobro automático / débito | デビットカード |
| deep fry 13 | faire frire | frittieren | friggere | freír | 揚げる |
| deep fat fryer 15 | friteuse | Friteuse | friggitrice | freidora | フライ用の深鍋 |
| delay 12 | retard | Verzögerung | ritardo | retraso | 遅れ、遅延 |
| delicious 10 | délicieux | köstlich | squisito | delicioso | とても美味しい |
| dentist 23 | dentiste | Zahnarzt, -ärztin | dentista | dentista | 歯医者 |
| departure 3 | départ | Abflug | partenza | salida | 出発 |
| deposit 26 | acompte | Anzahlung | acconto | depósito | 保証金、手付金 |
| dessert fork 13 | fourchette à dessert | Dessertgabel | forchetta da dessert | tenedor de postre | デザートフォーク |
| dessert spoon 13 | cuillère à dessert | Dessertlöffel | cucchiaino da dessert | cucharilla de postre | デザートスプーン |
| dial/key in 18 | faire/composer un numéro (de téléphone) | wählen | comporre | marcar | ダイヤルを回す、番号を押す |
| dialling tone 18 | tonalité | Amtszeichen | segnale acustico di linea libera | tono de llamada | 発信音 |
| diarrhoea 23 | diarrhée | Durchfall | diarrea | diarrea | 下痢 |
| digital 22 | numérique | digital | digitale | digital | コンピュータ化された |
| dinner jacket 17 | smoking | Smokingjacke | smoking | smoking | ディナージャケット |
| direct (v) 21 | indiquer le chemin | den Weg zeigen | indicare la strada | indicar cómo ir a un sitio | 道を教える |
| directly 25 | directement | direkt | direttamente | directamente | 直接に、まっすぐに |
| dirty 12 | sale | schmutzig | sporco | sucio | 汚い、不潔 |
| disabled 12 | handicapé | behindert | invalido | discapacitado | 身体障害のある |
| disabled facilities 2 | intallations pour handicapés | Behinderten-einrichtungen | facilitazioni per disabili | servicios para minusválidos | 身体障害者用設備 |
| discount 18 | remise/rabais | Diskont/Rabatt | sconto | descuento | 割引 |
| dishwasher 15 | lave-vaisselle | Geschirrspülmaschine | lavastoviglie | lavavajillas | 食器洗浄機 |
| district 11 | région | Gegend | regione | distrito | 地域 |
| doctor 23 | docteur | Arzt, Ärztin | medico | doctor/doctora | 医者 |
| double room 1 | chambre double | Doppelzimmer | doppia | habitación doble | ダブルベッドの二人用部屋 |
| Dr 1 | docteur | Doktor | dottore | Dr. / Dra. | ～博士 |
| drawer 20 | tiroir | Schublade | cassetto | cajón | 引出し |
| dressing gown 24 (US bathrobe) | robe de chambre | Bademantel | accappatoio | bata | バスローブ |
| driving licence 27 | permis de conduire | Führerschein | patente di guida | permiso de conducir | 運転免許書 |
| dry 7 (wine) | sec | trocken | secco | seco | 辛口の（ワイン） |
| dry cleaning 15 | nettoyage à sec | chemische Reinigung | lavatura a secco | limpieza en seco | ドライクリーニング |
| dual carriageway 21 | route à quatre voies | Schnellstraße | strada a due corsie | vía de dos carriles | 中央分離帯のある幹線道路 |
| duck 9 | canard | Ente | anatra | pato | 鴨 |
| dusty 14 | poussiéreux | staubig | polveroso | polvoriento | ほこりっぽい |
| duty 15 | devoir | Aufgabe | servizio, mansione | tarea / guardia | ほこり |
| duvet/quilt 20 | couette | Daunenbett | piumone | edredón | 羽ぶとん |
| earache 23 | mal à l'oreille | Ohrenschmerzen | mal d'orecchio | dolor de oídos | 耳の痛み |
| east 11 | est | Osten | est | este | 東 |
| eastern 11 | de l'est | östlich | dell'est | del este | 東の |
| egg 9 | oeuf | Ei | uovo | huevo | たまご |
| emergency 19 | urgence | Notfall | emergenza | emergencia | 非常事態 |
| engaged/busy tone 18 | occupé | Besetztzeichen | linea occupata | señal de comunicando | 通話中の音 |
| enjoy 10 | aprécier | genießen | gustare | disfrutar | 楽しむ |
| enthusiastic 28 | enthousiaste | engagiert | entusiasta | entusiasta | 熱心な |
| envelopes 24 | enveloppes | Briefumschläge | buste | sobres | 封筒 |
| equipment 22 | ustensiles (de cuisine) | Küchengeräte | attrezzatura | utensilios | 道具 |
| evacuate 19 | évacuer | evakuieren | evacuare | evacuar | 避難する |
| excellent 11 | excellent | ausgezeichnet | eccellente | exclente | 非常に優れた |
| exchange bureau 2 | bureau de change | Wechselstube | cambio | oficina de cambio | 両替窓口 |

| English | French | German | Italian | Spanish | Japanese |
|---------|--------|--------|---------|---------|----------|
| exchange rate 26 | taux de change | Umtauschrate | tasso di cambio | tipo de cambio de divisas | 通貨両替レート |
| excursions 22 | excursions | Ausflüge | escursioni, gite | excursiones | 小旅行 |
| experience 27 | expérience | Erfahrung | esperienza | experiencia | 経験 |
| express checkout 22 | caisse rapide | Express-Auschecken | cassa veloce | salida exprés | 迅速チェックアウトサービス |
| extra 26 | en supplément | zusätzlich | in più | extra | 割増の、特別の |
| eye contact 12 | échange de regard | Blickkontakt | negli occhi | contacto visual | 目を合わせる |
| faint 23 | s'évanouir | in Ohnmacht fallen | svenire | desmayarse | 失神する |
| family 3 | famille | Familie | famiglia | familia | 家族 |
| father 3 | père | Vater | padre | padre | 父 |
| fillet steak 9 | filet de bœuf | Filetsteak | bistecca di filetto | filete, solomillo de ternera | フィレステーキ |
| filthy 14 | crasseux | schmutzig | sporco | muy sucio | 不潔な |
| fine 11 | excellent | gut | di qualità | de calidad | すばらしい、見事な |
| fire alarm 19 | alarme d'incendie | Feuermelder | allarme antincendio | alarma de incendios | 火災報知器 |
| fire axe 19 | hache d'incendie | Feuerbeil | ascia antincendio | martillo de incendios | 非常用の斧 |
| fire blanket 19 | couverture contre le feu | Feuerdecke | coperta antincendio | manta para apagar incendios | 防火用毛布 |
| fire brigade 19 | pompiers | Feuerwehr | pompiere | bomberos | 消防士 |
| fire door 19 | porte coupe-feu | Feuertür | porta antincendio | puerta contra incendios | 防火扉 |
| fire drill 19 | exercice d'évacuation en cas d'incendie | Probealarm | esercitzione antincendio | simulacro de incendio | 火災避難訓練 |
| fire extinguisher 19 | extincteur d'incendie | Feuerlöscher | estintore | extintor | 消火器 |
| firm 28 | ferme | fest | deciso | firme / fuerte | 固い |
| first name/Christian name 27 | prénom | Vorname | nome | nombre de pila | 名前（苗字でない方） |
| fish fork 13 | fourchette à poisson | Fischgabel | forchetta da pesce | tenedor para pescado | 魚料理用フォーク |
| fish knife 13 | couteau à poisson | Fischmesser | coltello da pesce | cuchillo para pescado | 魚料理用ナイフ |
| flan/tart dish 15 | plat à tarte / à flan | Kuchen-, Tortenblech | timballo | plato para tartas | パイ/タルト用皿 |
| flat 14 (beer) | éventé | schal | stantio | sin gas | 気が抜けた（ビール） |
| floor 2 | étage | Stock/Etage | piano | piso | 階 |
| floret 16 | fleurette | (Broccoli)röschen | cime di broccoli | cogollito | （ブロッコリーの）房 |
| florist 22 | fleuriste | Blumengeschäft | fiorista | floristería | 花屋 |
| flower arrangement 13 | composition florale | Blumengesteck | composizione di fiori, arte di disporre i fiori | centro de flores | フラワーアレンジメント |
| flu 23 | grippe | Grippe | influenza | gripe | 風邪（インフルエンザ） |
| fold 16 | plier | falten | piegare | doblar | 折りたたむ |
| followed by 9 | suivi de | und dann | seguito da | seguido de | 次に～が続く |
| food processor 15 | robot ménager | Küchenmaschine | frullatore | robot de cocina | フードプロセッサー |
| food slicer 19 | éminceur | Küchenschneidemaschine | affettatrice | máquina para cortar o rebanar alimentos | フードスライサー |
| footpath 21 | sentier pédestre | Fußweg | sentiero | sendero | 小道、歩道 |
| foyer 17 | hall | Eingangshalle | atrio | vestíbulo | ロビー |
| French fries 17 (US) | pommes frites | Pommes frites | patate fritte | patatas fritas | フライドポテト |
| fresh 8 | frais | frisch | fresco | fresco | 新鮮な |
| friendly 27 | amical / aimable | freundlich | amichevole | amable | 親しみやすい |
| front office 15 | réception | Empfang | ricezione | zona de recepción | フロント、受付け |
| fruit salad 10 | salade de fruits | Obstsalat | macedonia | macedonia de fruta | フルーツサラダ |
| fry 13 | frire | braten | friggere | freír | 揚げる |
| frying pan 15 | poêle | Bratpfanne | padella | sartén | フライパン |
| fully booked 4 | complet | ausgebucht | al completo | completo | 満室、満席 |
| garlic bread 17 | pain chaud tartiné de beurre et d'ail | Knoblauchbrot | bruschetta | pan con mantequilla y ajo | ガーリックブレッド |
| gin 7 | gin | Gin | gin | ginebra | ジン |
| give 18 | donner | geben | dare | dar | 与える |
| Give Way 21 | Priorité | Vorfahrt | dare la precedenza | Ceda el paso | 対向車優先 |
| goat's cheese 9 | fromage de chèvre | Ziegenkäse | formaggio di capra | queso de cabra | 山羊乳が原料のチーズ |

| English | French | German | Italian | Spanish | Japanese |
|---------|--------|--------|---------|---------|----------|
| good afternoon 1 | bonjour | guten Tag | buon giorno (detto dopo mezzogiorno) | buenas tardes | こんにちは |
| good evening 1 | bonsoir | guten Abend | buona sera | buenas tardes | こんばんは |
| good morning 1 | bonjour | guten Morgen | buon giorno | buenos días | おはようございます |
| good night 1 | bonne nuit | gute Nacht | buona notte | buenas noches | おやすみなさい |
| goodbye 1 | au revoir | auf Wiedersehen | arrivederci/la | adiós | さようなら |
| grandparents 28 | grands-parents | Großeltern | nonni | abuelos (abuela y abuelo) | 祖父母 |
| grey 26 | gris | grau | grigio | gris | 灰色 |
| grill 13 (US broil) | griller | grillen | cuocere alla griglia | asar a la parrilla | 網焼きにする |
| grilled 9 | grillé | gegrillt | alla griglia | a la parrilla | 網焼きの |
| guard 19 | carter | Schutzvorrichtung | schermo di protezione | mampara de seguridad | 保護物、安全装置 |
| guardian 28 | tuteur | Vormund | custode | guarda | 保護者 |
| haircut 17 | coupe de cheveux | Haarschnitt | taglio di capelli | corte de pelo | 散髪 |
| hair salon 6 | salon de coiffure | Friseursalon | parucchiere | (salón de) peluquería | 美容院 |
| half 8 | moitié | klein (Getränke) | mezzo | mitad | 半分 |
| half-brother/half-sister 28 | demi-frère /demi-sœur | Halbbruder,-schwester | fratellastro/sorellastra | hemanastro/ hermanastra | 異父母の兄弟・姉妹 |
| ham 9 | jambon | Schinken | prosciutto | jamón | ハム |
| handshake 28 | poignée de main | Händedruck | stretta di mano | apretón de manos | 握手 |
| hanger 20 | ceintre | Kleiderbügel | gruccia | percha | ハンガー |
| hard 10 | dur | hart | duro | duro | 固い |
| hard-boiled egg 13 | œuf dur | hartgekochtes Ei | uovo sodo | huevo duro | ゆで卵 |
| hard-working 27 | travailleur | fleißig | diligente | trabajador | 勤勉な |
| headache 23 | mal de tête | Kopfschmerzen | mal di testa | dolor de cabeza | 頭痛 |
| heat lamp 15 | lampe chauffante | Heizlampe | lampada che mantiene caldo il cibo | lámpara infrarroja | 調理用バーナー |
| heating 20 | chauffage | Heizung | riscaldamento | calefacción | 暖房装置 |
| high-speed 22 | rapide | Hochgeschwindigkeits- | alta velocità | de alta velocidad | 高速の |
| high temperature 23 | température élevée | hohes Fieber | febbre | fiebre | 高熱がある |
| hob 15 | plaque (chauffante) | Kochfeld | piastra | placa | ガスコンロの天板 |
| home address 6 | adresse personnelle | Heimatadresse | indirizzo | domicilio | 自宅住所 |
| homework 12 | devoirs | Hausaufgaben | compiti per casa | deberes | 宿題 |
| hope 25 | espérer | hoffen | sperare | esperar | 願う、望む |
| hospital 23 | hôpital | Krankenhaus | ospedale | hospital | 病院 |
| hospitality 27 | hospitalité | Gastfreundschaft | ospitalità | hospitalidad | もてなし |
| hotel chain 28 | chaîne d'hôtel | Hotelkette | catena alberghiera | cadena hotelera | ホテルチェーン |
| housekeeper 15 | intendant(e) | Haushälterin | governante | ama de llaves | 家政婦、 ハウスキーパー |
| humour 28 | humour | Humor | senso dell'umorismo | humor | ユーモア |
| hurt 23 (v) | faire mal | (sich) verletzen | fare male | hacer daño | 傷つける |
| husband 3 | mari | Ehemann | marito | marido | 夫 |
| hygiene 16 | hygiène | Hygiene | igiene | higiene | 衛生 |
| ice cream 17 | glace (à manger) | Speiseeis | gelato | helado | アイスクリーム |
| important 14 | important | wichtig | importante | importante | 重要 |
| improve 11 | améliorer | verbessern | migliorare | mejorar | 改良する |
| include 18 | comprendre/inclure | einschließen | comprendere | incluir | 含む |
| included 25 | compris | inbegriffen | compreso | incluido | 含まれた |
| information 2 | renseignement | Informationen | informazioni | información | 案内、情報 |
| in-laws 28 | beaux-parents | Schwiegereltern | parenti acquisiti con il matrimonio | familia política | 義理の、姻戚の |
| in-room services 15 | prestations dans la chambre | Zimmerservice | servizio in camera | servicios dentro de la habitación | ミニバー等客室備え 付けサービス |
| international 2 | international | international | internazionale | internacional | 国際的な |
| international call 18 | appel de l'étranger / international | Auslandsgespräch | chiamata internazionale | conferencia / llamada internacional | 国際電話 |
| Internet access 2 | accès à l'internet | Anschluss ans Internet | accesso a Internet | acceso a Internet | インターネットアク セス |
| invoice 25 | facture | Warenrechnung | fattura | factura | 仕切状、インボイス |
| issue 26 (v) | fournir | ausstellen | dare, consegnare | expedir | 発行する |
| itemized 25 | détaillé | spezifiziert | dettagliato | detallado | 明細が記された |

| English | French | German | Italian | Spanish | Japanese |
|---|---|---|---|---|---|
| julienne 16 | julienne | in feine Streifen schneiden | tagliare a bastoncini | juliana | 千切り |
| jumper/sweater 17 | pull | Pullover | maglione | jersey | セーター |
| knee 19 | genou | Knie | ginocchio | rodilla | ひざ |
| label 11 | étiquette | Etikett/Aufschrift | etichetta | etiqueta | ラベル |
| ladle 16 | louche | Schöpfkelle | mestolo | cucharón | 玉杓子、レードル |
| lamb 9 | agneau | Lamm | agnello | cordero | 子羊 |
| late 14 | en retard | spät | in ritardo | con retraso | 遅い |
| laundry 2 | blanchissage | Wäscherei | lavanderia | lavandería | 洗濯物、洗濯 |
| layer 13 | couche | Schicht | strato | capa | 層、重ね |
| left 5 (remaining) | qui reste, restant | übrig | rimasto | quedar | 残り |
| leg 23 | jambe | Bein | gamba | pierna | 脚 |
| less 18 | moins | weniger | meno | menos | より少ない |
| lift 17 (US elevator) | ascenseur | Fahrstuhl | ascensore | ascensor | エレベーター |
| light 11 (wine) | léger | leicht | leggero | ligero / suave | 軽めの（ワイン） |
| light bulb 20 | ampoule | Glühbirne | lampadina | bombilla | 電球 |
| liquid 8 | liquide | Flüssigkeit | liquido | liquido | 液体 |
| liquor (US) 7 | alcohol | Spirituosen | alcolici | alcohol / bebidas alcohólicas | リキュール、蒸留酒 |
| local call 18 | appel local | Ortsgespräch | chiamata urbana | llamada local/urbana | 市内通話 |
| look 28 | sembler | aussehen | sembrare | parecer | ～に見える |
| lounge 6 | salon | Gesellschaftsraum | salotto | salón | ラウンジ |
| luggage 6 (US baggage) | bagages | Gepäck | bagagli | equipaje | 荷物 |
| lunch 4 | déjeuner | Mittagstisch | pranzo | almuerzo / comida | 昼食 |
| madam 1 | Madame | gnädige Frau | Signora | Señora | ～夫人 |
| madeira 7 | Madère | Madeira | vino di Madeira | vino de Madeira | マデイラ |
| main road 21 | route principale | Hauptstraße | strada principale | carretera principal | 主要道路 |
| make 1 | faire | machen/zubereiten | fare | hacer | 作る |
| manager 1 | directeur | Geschäftsführer (in) | direttore | director | 支配人、マネージャー |
| married 27 | marié | verheiratet | sposato | casado | 既婚の |
| mattress 20 | matelas | Matratze | materasso | colchón | マットレス |
| meat 9 | viande | Fleisch | carne | carne | 肉 |
| medium dry 7 (wine) | demi-sec | halbtrocken | secco | semiseco | 中辛口（ワイン） |
| medium rare 9 | à point | rosa, englisch | al sangue | poco hecho | ミディアムレアー |
| meet 4 | rencontrer | (sich) treffen | incontrare | ver / reunirse con (alguien) | 合う |
| meeting 1 | réunion/rendezvous | Treffen | riunione | reunión | 会合 |
| mend 24 | réparer | reparieren | aggiustare | arreglar | 修理する |
| menu 9 | menu | Menü/Speisekarte | menu | menú | メニュー |
| meringue 10 | meringue | Baiser | meringa | merengue | メレンゲ |
| message 1 | message | Nachricht | messaggio | mensaje | 伝言 |
| microphone 22 | microphone | Mikrofon | microfono | micrófono | マイク |
| mid-afternoon 5 | milieu de l'après-midi | Nachmittag | a metà pomeriggio | a media tarde | 午後3時ンる |
| mid-morning 5 | milieu de la matinée | Vormittag | a metà mattina | a media mañana | 午前11時ンる |
| mineral water 7 | eau minérale | Mineralwasser | acqua minerale | agua mineral | ミネラルウォーター |
| mini-break 18 | cours séjour | Kurzurlaub | vacanza breve | escapada / descanso breve | 短い休暇 |
| mirror 20 | miroir | Spiegel | specchio | espejo | 鏡 |
| Miss 1 | Mademoiselle | Fräulein | Signorina | Señorita | 独身女性の敬称 |
| miss 21 (v) | rater | übersehen | sfuggire | pasar por alto | 見逃す |
| mix 8 | mélanger | mixen | mischiare | mezclar | 混ぜる |
| mixing bowl 15 | bol à mixer | Rührschüssel | terrina | cuenco para mezclar ingredientes | ミキシングボール |
| mobile phone 18 (US cell phone) | téléphone portable | Handy | cellulare | teléfono móvil | 携帯電話 |
| money 2 | argent | Geld | soldi | dinero | お金 |
| monkfish 9 | lotte | Seeteufel | squadro, pesce angelo | rape | アンコウ |
| more 12 | plus | mehr | più | más | より多くの |
| mother 3 | mère | Mutter | madre | madre | 母 |

| English | French | German | Italian | Spanish | Japanese |
|---|---|---|---|---|---|
| motorway 21 | autoroute | Autobahn | autostrada | autopista | 高速道路 |
| Mr 1 | M. | Herr | Signore | Sr. | 男性の敬称 |
| Mrs 1 | Mme | Frau | Signora | Sra. | 既婚女性の敬称 |
| Ms 1 | Mme | Fräulein | Signorina/Signora | Sra. | 女性の敬称 |
| museum 21 | musée | Museum | museo | museo | 博物館 |
| mushroom 9 | champignon | Pilz/Champignon | fungo | champiñón | マッシュルーム |
| mussels 13 | moules | Muscheln | cozze | mejillones | ムール貝 |
| | | | | | |
| napkin 13 | serviette | Serviette | tovagliolo | servilleta | ナプキン |
| nationality 27 | nationalité | Nationalität | nazionalità | nacionalidad | 国籍 |
| needs 12 (n) | besoins | Bedürfnisse | bisogni | necesidades | 必要なもの |
| nephew 28 | neveu | Neffe | nipote | sobrino | 甥 |
| news 12 | nouvelles | Nachrichten | notizie | noticias | ニュース |
| next door 14 | à coté | nebenan | vicino | al lado | 隣 |
| next to 20 | près de | neben | accanto a | junto a | |
| niece 28 | nièce | Nichte | nipote | sobrina | 姪 |
| night 6 | nuit | Nacht | notte | noche | 夜 |
| No Entry 21 | Accès interdit | Keine Einfahrt | vietato l'accesso | Prohibido el paso | 立ち入り禁止 |
| No Parking 21 | Stationnement interdit | Parkverbot | vietato parcheggiare | Prohibido aparcar | 駐車禁止 |
| no through road 21 | voie sans issue | Durchfahrt verboten | strada senza uscita | calle sin salida | 通り抜け不可 |
| No U-turns 21 | Défense de faire demi-tour | Wenden verboten | divieto di inversione | Prohibido girar | Uターン禁止 |
| nobody 14 | personne | niemand | nessuno | nadie | 誰も～ない |
| noise 14 | bruit | Lärm | rumore | ruido | 騒音 |
| north 11 | nord | Norden | nord | norte | 北 |
| northern 11 | du nord | nördlich | a, del nord | del norte | 北の |
| note pad 24 | bloc-notes | Notizblock | blocco degli appunti | libreta | メモ用紙とじ |
| nurse 23 | infirmière | Krankenschwester | infermiera | enfermero(a) | 看護婦 |
| | | | | | |
| o'clock 4 | heure | Uhr(zeit) | l'ora | en punto | ～時 |
| off 14 | pas frais/pourri | schlecht | avariato | malo / pasado | 壊れている、腐っている |
| olive 8 | olive | Olive | oliva | aceituna | オリーブ |
| omelette 17 | omelette | Omelett | frittata, omelette | tortilla | オムレツ |
| on call 23 (doctor) | de garde | in Bereitschaft | in servizio | de guardia (médico) | 待機している |
| One Way 21 | A sens unique | Einbahn | senso unico | Sentido único | 一方通行 |
| on foot 21 | à pied | zu Fuß | a piedi | a pie | 歩いて |
| onion 13 | oignon | Zwiebel | cipolla | cebolla | 玉ねぎ |
| open 4 | ouvert | geöffnet | aperto | abierto | 開店中 |
| operator 18 | standardiste | Vermittlung | centralinista | operadora | 交換手、オペレーター |
| opposite 20 | en face | gegenüber | di fronte a | enfrente de | 向かい側の |
| optician 23 | opticien | Optiker(in) | ottico | óptico | 眼鏡屋 |
| organised 27 | organisé | diszipliniert | organizzato | organizado | 有能な、几帳面な |
| osteopath 23 | ostéopathe | Osteopath(in) | osteologo | osteópata | 整骨医 |
| outside 21 | à l'extérieur | draußen | fuori | fuera | 屋外 |
| overbooked 14 | surréservé | überbucht | prenotati più posti di quanti ne siano disponibili | sobrecontratado | 定員オーバーの予約 |
| overcooked 14 | trop cuit | verkocht | scotto | pasado/demasiado hecho | 焼き過ぎた、煮過ぎた |
| overnight 24 | de nuit | über Nacht | per la notte | de un día para otro | 一晩中 |
| | | | | | |
| paper 12 | papier | Papier | carta | papel | 新聞 |
| paramedic 23 | auxiliaire médical | Sanitäter(in) | paramedico | paramédico/paramédica | 医療補助員 |
| parking space 1 | place où se garer | Parkplatz | parcheggio | plaza de aparcamiento | 駐車スペース |
| pastis 7 | pastis | französischer Anisschnaps | Pernod, liquore al sapore di anice | pastís | パスティス |
| pastries 17 | gâteaux | Gebäck | pasticcini | bollos dulces | 菓子類、ペストリー類 |
| pastry 15 | pâtisserie | Teig/Gebäck | pasta (per pasticceria) | pastelería | ペストリー、ケーキ |
| patient 12 | patient | geduldig | paziente | paciente | 忍耐強い |
| pavement 21 (US sidewalk) | trottoir | Bürgersteig/Gehweg | marciapiede | acera | 歩道 |

| English | French | German | Italian | Spanish | Japanese |
|---|---|---|---|---|---|
| payment 15 | paiement | Bezahlung | pagamento | pago | 支払い |
| pay-per-view 22 | pay per view (paiement par visionnage) | Pay-per-View | visione a pagamento | pago por visión | 有料のテレビ番組 |
| payphone 18 | téléphone publique | Münztelefon | telefono pubblico | teléfono público | 公衆電話 |
| pedestrian street 21 | rue piétonne/ piétonnière | Fußgängerstraße | strada pedonale | calle peatonal | 歩行者通り |
| pen 24 | stylo | Kugelschreiber | penna | bolígrafo | ペン |
| pepper 13 | poivre | Pfeffer | pepe | pimienta | コショウ |
| pepper mill 13 | poivrier | Pfeffermühle | macinapepe | molinillo de pimienta | コショウひき |
| pharmacist 23 | pharmacien | Apotheker(in) | farmacista | farmacéutico(a) | 薬剤師 |
| pharmacy 23 | pharmacie | Apotheke | farmacia | farmacia | 薬局 |
| phonebox (US callbox) 18 | cabine téléphonique | Telefonzelle | cabina telefonica | cabina telefónica | 電話ボックス |
| photographer 22 | photographe | Fotograf(in) | fotografo | fotógrafo/fotógrafa | 写真家 |
| physiotherapist 23 | kinésithérapeute | Physiotherapeut(in) | psicoterapista | fisioterapeuto(a) | 理学療法士 |
| pillow 20 | oreiller | Kissen | guanciale | almohada | 枕 |
| pillow case 16 | taie d'oreiller | Kissenbezug | federa | funda de almohada | 枕カバー |
| pine nut 13 | pignon de pin | Pinienkern | pinoli | piñón | 松の実 |
| plane 21 | avion | Flugzeug | aereo | avión | 飛行機 |
| plaster 23 (first aid) | pansement, sparadrap | Pflaster | cerotto | tirita | ばんそうこう |
| plate 13 | assiette | Teller | piatto | plato | 皿、平皿 |
| play 22 | jouer | spielen | giocare | obra de teatro | 上映する、作動する |
| p.m. 4 (afternoon/ evening) | de l'après-midi/du soir | nachmittags/abends | di pomeriggio o di sera | por la tarde | 午後 |
| poach 13 | pocher | dünsten/pochieren | cuocere 'in camicia' | escalfar | ゆでる |
| poisonous 19 | toxique | giftig | velenoso | venenoso | 有毒な |
| police 23 | police | Polizei | polizia | policía | 警察 |
| popular 11 | qui a du succès | beliebt | popolare | popular | 人気のある、評判のよい |
| pork 9 | porc | Schweinefleisch | carne di maiale | cerdo | 豚肉 |
| port 7 (wine) | porto | Portwein | Porto | vino de Oporto | ポートワイン |
| positive 28 | positif | positiv | affermativo | positivo | 積極的な、前向きな |
| post cards 24 | cartes postales | Ansichtskarten | cartoline | tarjetas postales | 絵葉書 |
| posture 28 | posture | Haltung | posa, posizione | postura | 姿勢、状態 |
| prepare 16 | préparer | vorbereiten | preparare | preparar | 準備する |
| printer 15 | imprimante | Drucker | stampante | impresora | プリンター |
| process 15 | traiter | bearbeiten | inoltrare | procesar | 処理する |
| produce 11 | produire | produzieren | presentare, mostrare | producir | 生産する |
| projector 22 (digital) | projecteur | Projektor | proiettore | proyector | プロジェクター |
| properly 24 | convenablement | zufriedenstellend | bene, correttamente | debidamente | きちんと、完全に |
| public holiday 6 | jour férié | Feiertag | festa nazionale | fiesta oficial | 祝日 |
| puff pastry 13 | pâte feuilletée | Blätterteig | pasta sfoglia | pastel de hojaldre | パイ生地、パフペースト |
| pull 20 | tirer | zuziehen | tirare | abrir/cerrar, correr/ descorrer | 引く |
| qualification 27 | qualification | Qualifikation | qualifica | títulos, preparación | 資格 |
| qualities 27 | qualités | Eigenschaften | qualità | cualidades | 品質 |
| quarter 8 | quart | Viertel | quarto | cuarto | 4分の1 |
| questions 28 | questions | Fragen | domande | preguntas | 質問 |
| rack rate 18 | tarif standard | Zimmerpreis | tariffa media giornaliera | precio normal | 通常の室料 |
| raspberry 10 | framboise | Himbeere | lampone | frambuesa | ラズベリー |
| ready 9 | prêt | bereit | pronto | preparado | 準備が整って |
| receipt 25 | reçu | Quittung | ricevuta | recibo | 領収書 |
| receiver/handset 18 | combiné | Hörer | ricevitore | auricular | 受話器 |
| reception 2 | réception | Empfang | banco dell'hotel | recepción | 受付、レセプション |
| recharge 18 | recharger | aufladen | caricare | recargar | 充電、リチャージ |
| recommend 11 | recommander | empfehlen | consigliare | recomendar | 勧める |
| red 7 | rouge | rot | rosso | rojo | 赤 |
| refrigerator 15 | réfrigérateur, frigo | Kühlschrank | frigorifero | frigorífico | 冷蔵庫 |
| register 27 | enregistrer | (sich) anmelden | dare il proprio nome | registrar(se) | 登録する |

| English | French | German | Italian | Spanish | Japanese |
|---|---|---|---|---|---|
| regularly 19 | régulièrement | regelmäßig | regolarmente | con regularidad | 定期的に、いつも |
| reservation 1 | réservation | Reservierung | prenotazione | reserva | 予約 |
| reserve 1 | réserver | reservieren | riservare | reservar | 予約する |
| responsibility 27 | responsabilité | Verantwortung | responsabilità | responsabilidad | 責任 |
| reversed charges 18 (US collect call) | en pcv | R-Gespräch | telefonata addebitata al ricevente | (a) cobro revertido | コレクトコール、 受信人払い |
| ridiculous 26 | ridicule | lächerlich | assurdo | ridículo | ばかばかしい、 途方もない |
| ring 12 (n) | sonnerie | Klingeln | suonare | llamada | （電話の）鳴る音 |
| roast 9 | rôtir | braten | arrostire | asar | オーブンで焼く |
| roasting tin 15 | plat à rôtir | Bräter | teglia per arrosti | fuente de horno | ロースト用の型 |
| rocket salad 9 | roquette | Rucola Salat | insalata a base di rucola | ensalada de lechuga | ルッコラのサラダ |
| roll call 19 | appel | Namensaufruf | appello | (pasar) lista | 点呼 |
| rolling pin 16 | rouleau à pâtisserie | Teigrolle | matterello | rodillo | 綿棒 |
| roof garden 20 | jardin aménagé sur le toit | Dachgarten | giardino pensile | jardín en la azotea | 屋上庭園 |
| room rate 18 | prix de la chambre | Zimmerpreis | costo della stanza | precio por habitación | 部屋料金 |
| room temperature 11 | température ambiante | Zimmertemperatur | temperatura ambiente | temperatura ambiente | 室温 |
| roulade 10 | roulade | Roulade | rotolo | rollito (comida) | ルーラード（料理名） |
| rubbish 15 | ordures | Müll | spazzatura | basura | ゴミ |
| rude 14 | malpoli | unhöflich | scortese, maleducato | maleducado | 無礼な、無作法な |
| rum 7 | rhum | Rum | rum, liquore | ron | ラム |
| salmon 9 | saumon | Lachs | salmone | salmón | サーモン |
| salt 13 | sel | Salz | sale | sal | 塩 |
| salt cellar 13 | salière | Salzfässchen | saliera | salero | 塩入れ |
| salty 14 | salé | salzig | salato | salado | 塩っぱい |
| sand bucket 19 | seau de sable | Sandeimer | secchiello | cubo de arena | 非常用の砂バケツ |
| sandwich 9 | sandwich | Sandwich/Butterbrot | tramezzino | bocadillo/sandwich | サンドイッチ |
| saucepan 15 | casserole | Kochtopf | pentola | cazuela | シチュー鍋、深鍋 |
| sauna 3 | sauna | Sauna | sauna | sauna | サウナ |
| scallops 13 | coquilles Saint-Jacques | Kammmuscheln | cappe sante | vieiras | ホタテガイ |
| scrape 16 | gratter | schaben | raschiare | limpiar | こする、こすり取る |
| screen 22 | écran | Schirm | schermo | pantalla | スクリーン、画面 |
| second name/ surname 27 | nom de famille | Familienname | cognome | apellido | 姓、苗字 |
| serious 19 | grave | ernst | serio | grave | 重大な、 容易ならない |
| service charge 26 | service | Bedienung | servizio | servicio | サービス料金 |
| sewing kit 24 | nécessaire à couture | Näh-Set | il necessario per cucire | costurero | 裁縫道具 |
| sharpen 15 | éguiser | schärfen | affilare | afilar | 研ぐ、鋭くする |
| shaver point 20 | prise rasoir | Steckdose für Rasierapparate | presa per il rasoio | enchufe para máquina de afeitar | 電気かみそり用 ソケット |
| sheep's cheese 10 | fromage de lait de brebis | Schafskäse | formaggio di pecora | queso de oveja | 羊乳が原料のチーズ |
| sheet 16 | drap | Laken | lenzuolo | sábana | シーツ |
| shelf 20 | rayonnage/étagère | Regal | ripiano | estante | 棚 |
| sherry 7 | sherry/xérès | Sherry | sherry | jerez | シェリー |
| shirt 17 | chemise | Hemd | camicia | camisa | ワイシャツ |
| shoe cleaning kit 24 | trousse de cirage à chaussures | Schuhputzzeug | occorrente per lucidare le scarpe | kit de limpieza de calzado | 靴磨きセット |
| short-staffed 14 | à court de personnel | knapp an Arbeitskräften | a corto di personale | corto de personal | 従業員不足 |
| shower 20 | douche | Dusche | doccia | ducha | シャワー |
| shower cap 20 | bonnet de douche | Duschkappe | cuffia per la doccia | gorro de baño/ducha | シャワーキャップ |
| sick 23 | malade | krank | malato | enfermo | 病気 |
| side order 15 | plat d'accompagnement | Beilage | contorno | guarnición | 付け合せ料理の注文 |
| side plate 13 | petite assiette | Nebengedeck | piattino per il pane | plato del pan | 添え皿 |
| sieve 16 | tamis/passoire | Sieb | colino | tamiz | こしき、ふるい |
| single 3 (room) | pour une personne | Einzel- | singola | soltero(a) | 1人部屋 |
| single 27 (person) | célibataire | ledig | celibe (M), nubile (F) | individual | 独身 |

| English | French | German | Italian | Spanish | Japanese |
|---|---|---|---|---|---|
| sir 1 | Monsieur | (mein) Herr | Signor | Señor | 男性の敬称 |
| sirloin 9 | aloyau | Lendenfilet | lombo di manzo, filetto | carne de vaca | サーロイン |
| sister 3 | sœur | Schwester | sorella | hermana | 姉妹 |
| sister hotel 18 | hôtel sœur | Schwesterhotel | albergo gemello | hotel asociado | 姉妹店 |
| skill 27 | compétence | Fertigkeit | abilità | capacidad / habilidad | 技能、腕前 |
| skin 16 | peau | Schale | buccia | piel | 皮 |
| skirt 17 | jupe | Rock | gonna | falda | スカート |
| sleep 24 (v) | dormir | schlafen | dormire | dormir | 眠る |
| slice 16 | couper en tranches | schneiden | affettare | cortar en rodajas | 薄切りにする |
| slippers 24 | chaussons | Hausschuhe | pantofole | zapatillas de casa | スリッパ |
| smart 28 | élégant | gepflegt | elegante | elegante | 洗練された、きちんとした |
| smell 24 | sentir | riechen | sentire odore di | oler | 臭う |
| smile 12 | sourire | lächeln | sorridere | sonrisa | 笑う |
| smoke alarm 19 | détecteur de fumée | Rauchmelder | allarme antifumo | detector de humo | 煙報知器 |
| smoked 9 | fumé | geräuchert | affumicato | ahumado | 燻製にした、いぶした |
| smooth 11 (wine) | moelleux | lieblich | vellutato | suave | 滑らかな（ワイン） |
| Slow 21 | Ralentissez | Langsam | rallentare | Despacio | 徐行運転 |
| soap 16 | savon | Seife | sapone | jabón | 石鹸 |
| sociable 27 | sociable | umgänglich | socievole | sociable | 社交的な |
| socks 17 | chaussettes | Socken | calzini | calcetines | ソックス |
| soda 7 | eau de seltz | Sodawasser | acqua di seltz | agua de seltz | ソーダー |
| soft 10 | à pâte molle | weich | morbido | blando | 柔らかい |
| soft drink 7 (US soda) | boisson non alcoolisée | alkoholfreies Getränk | bevande non alcoliche | refresco | ソフトドリンク、清涼飲料 |
| son 3 | fils | Sohn | figlio | hijo | 息子 |
| sorbet 10 | sorbet | Fruchteis | sorbetto | sorbete | シャーベット |
| soufflé dish 15 | plat à soufflé | Souffléschüssel | pirofila per soufflé | plato para suflé | スフレ用皿 |
| soup 9 | soupe | Suppe | zuppa, minestra | sopa | スープ |
| south 11 | sud | Süden | sud | sur | 南 |
| southern 11 | du sud | südlich | a, del sud | del sur | 南の |
| spare 20 | de rechange | überzählig | d'avanzo, disponibile | sobrante / de repuesto | 予備の |
| sparkling 7 (water) | gazéifiée | kohlensäurehaltig | gassata | con gas | 発泡性の（水） |
| spicy 13 | épicé/piquant | würzig | piccante | picante | スパイシー、香料のきいた |
| spirit 7 | spiritueux | Branntwein | superalcoolico | licor | 蒸留酒 |
| spoon 13 | cuillère | Löffel | cucchiaio | cuchara | スプーン |
| spotless 16 | impeccable | blitzsauber | pulito | impecable / limpísimo | しみのない、清潔な |
| spring 6 | printemps | Frühling | primavera | primavera | 春 |
| squeeze 8 | presser | pressen | spremere, schiacciare | exprimir | 搾る |
| stained 14 | taché | schmutzig | macchiato | manchado | 汚れている |
| stale 14 | qui n'est pas frais | schal/alt | stantio | pasado/revenido | 新鮮でない |
| standard 18 | standard | Standard- | normale | estándar / normal | 標準 |
| starter 15 | entrée | Vorspeise | antipasto | entrante/primer plato | 前菜 |
| station 21 (train) | gare | Bahnhof | stazione ferroviaria | estación | 駅 |
| station 15 (work) | poste | Arbeitsplatz | posto | lugar / puesto | 部署 |
| stationery 22 | papeterie | Briefpapier | articoli di cartoleria | papelería | 文房具 |
| steam 13 | cuire à la vapeur | ausdünsten | cuocere a vapore | cocer al vapor | 蒸す、ふかす |
| step-brother/step-sister 28 | beau-frère / belle-sœur | Stiefbruder, -schwester | sorellastra/fratellastro | hermanastro/hermanastra | 異父母の兄弟/姉妹 |
| stew 13 | ragoût | Eintopfgericht | spezzatino | guiso | 煮込む |
| still 7 (water) | non gazeuse | ohne Kohlensäure | non gassato | sin gas | 発泡性でない（水） |
| still 18 (adv) | toujours, encore | noch immer | ancora | aún / todavía | まだ、相変わらず |
| stir 8 | remuer | rühren | rimescolare | dar vueltas/revolver | かき混ぜる |
| stockpot 15 | marmite à bouillon | Suppentopf | marmitta | olla | ソース鍋 |
| stomach ache 23 | mal de ventre | Magenschmerzen | mal di stomaco | dolor de estómago | 腹痛 |
| stop 21 (n) | arrêt | Haltestelle | fermata | parada | 駅 |
| Stop 21 | Stop | Stoppschild | stop | Stop | 止まれ |
| straightaway 14 | tout de suite | sofort | subito | en seguida | 直ちに |
| strain 8 (v) | passer | abgießen | scolare | colar | こす |
| strain 19 (n) | muscle froissé | Zerrung | slogatura | esguince | 捻挫、筋違い |
| stringy 14 | filandreux | zäh | filamentoso | con hebras | 筋の多い |
| subject 19 | sujet | Thema | argomento | tema | 主題、テーマ |

| English | French | German | Italian | Spanish | Japanese |
|---|---|---|---|---|---|
| sub-total 26 | sous-total | Teilsumme | totale parziale | total parcial | 小計 |
| suitable 24 | approprié | geeignet | adatto | adecuado | ふさわしい、適した |
| suite 3 | suite | Hotelsuite | suite | suite | スィートルーム |
| summer 6 | été | Sommer | estate | verano | 夏 |
| supplement 26 | supplément | Ergänzung/Nachtrag | supplemento | suplemento | 追加料金 |
| surgeon 23 | chirurgien | Chirurg(in) | chirurgo | cirujano/cirujana | 外科医 |
| sweep 16 | balayer | kehren | spazzare | barrer | 掃く |
| sweet 7 (wine) | doux | süß | dolce | dulce | 甘口の（ワイン） |
| | | | | | |
| tablecloth 13 | nappe | Tischtuch | tovaglia | mantel | テーブルクロス |
| table lamp 20 | lampe de table | Tischlampe | lume | lamparita | テーブルランプ |
| tart 9 | tarte | (Obst)kuchen | torta, crostata | tarta / tartaleta | タルト |
| tasteless 14 | insipide | geschmacklos | insipido | soso/insípido | まずい |
| taxi 21 | taxi | Taxi | tassì | taxi | タクシー |
| T-bone steak 9 | steak américain | T-bone-Steak | fiorentina | chuleta de vaca | ティーボーンステーキ |
| tea 17 | thé | Tee | tè | té | 紅茶 |
| team worker 28 | travailleur d'équipe | Teamarbeiter(in) | operario che lavora in squadra | miembro de un grupo de trabajo | チームワーク、共同作業 |
| telephone 3 | téléphone | Telefon | telefono | teléfono | 電話 |
| television series 28 | feuilleton | Fernsehserie | serie televisiva | teleserie | テレビシリーズ |
| tequila 7 | tequila | Tequila | tequila | tequila | テキーラ |
| terrace 12 | terrasse | Terrasse | terrazza | terraza | テラス |
| test drill 19 | exercice d'évacuation en cas d'incendie | Probealarm | prova di esercitazione | simulacro de incendio | 避難訓練 |
| (a) third 8 | troisième | (ein) Drittel | un terzo | (un) tercio | 3分の1 |
| this afternoon 5 | cet après-midi | heute Nachmittag | questo pomeriggio | esta tarde | 今日の午後 |
| this evening 5 | ce soir | heute Abend | questa sera | esta tarde-noche | 今晩 |
| this morning 5 | ce matin | heute Morgen | questa mattina | esta mañana | 今朝 |
| three quarters 8 | trois quarts | drei Viertel | tre quarti | tres cuartos | 4分の3 |
| tie 17 | cravate | Krawatte | cravatta | corbata | ネクタイ |
| time 12 | temps | Zeit | tempo | hora / tiempo | 時間 |
| tissues 24 | mouchoirs en papier | Papiertaschentücher | fazzoletti di carta | pañuelos de papel | ティッシュ |
| toast 9 | toast | Toast | pane tostato | tostada(s) | トースト |
| toaster 15 | grille-pain | Toaster | tostapane | tostadora | トースター |
| tomato 9 | tomate | Tomate | pomodoro | tomate | トマト |
| tomorrow 1 | demain | morgen | domani | mañana | 明日 |
| tonic 7 | tonique | Tonic | tonico | tónica | トニックウォーター |
| tonight 1 | ce soir | heute Abend | stasera | esta noche | 今夜 |
| too much 18 | trop | zu viel | troppo | demasiado | 多すぎる |
| toothache 23 | mal de dent | Zahnschmerzen | mal di denti | dolor de muelas | 歯痛 |
| torn 14 | déchiré | zerrissen | strappato | roto | 裂けている、破れている |
| total 25 | total | Gesamtsumme | totale | total | 合計、総計 |
| touch-tone phone 18 | téléphone à touches | Tonwahltelefon | telefono a toni | teléfono de sistema electrónico | プッシュホン式電話 |
| tough 14 | dur (viande) | zäh | duro | duro | 固い |
| tourism 27 | tourisme | Tourismus | turismo | turismo | 観光産業 |
| tower 2 | tour | Hochhaus | torre | torre | 塔、タワー |
| train 4 (n) | train | Zug | treno | tren | 電車 |
| trained 19 | qualifié | ausgebildet | preparato professionalmente | preparado / formado | 訓練された、練達された |
| travel arrangement 15 | préparatifs de voyage | Organisation, Buchung etc. einer Reise | piano, disposizione di viaggio | planes de viaje | 旅行の手配 |
| traveller's cheque 25 | chèque de voyage | Reisescheck | travellers cheque | cheques de viaje | トラベラーズチェック |
| trip 19 | voyage | Reise | viaggio | viaje | 旅行 |
| triple sec 8 | triple sec | Triple Sec | secco | triple seco | トリプル・セック |
| trouser press 20 | presse-pantalon | Hosenpresse | stiracalzoni | prensa plancha-pantalones | ズボンプレッサー |
| trousers 17 | pantalon | Hose | pantaloni | pantalones | ズボン |
| T-shirt 17 | T-shirt | T-Shirt | maglietta | camiseta | ティーシャツ |
| tube/underground 21 (US subway) | métro | U-Bahn | metropolitana | metro | 地下鉄 |

| English | French | German | Italian | Spanish | Japanese |
|---|---|---|---|---|---|
| twin 3 (room) | (chambre) pour deux personnes à deux lits | Doppel (-zimmer) | doppia con due letti | habitación doble (dos camas) | ツインベッドの 二人用部屋 |
| uncle 28 | oncle | Onkel | zio | tío | 叔父 |
| undercooked 14 | pas assez cuit | nicht gar | poco cotto | poco hecho/sin hacer | 生煮えの、生焼けの |
| underwear 17 | sous-vêtement | Unterwäsche | biancheria intima | ropa interior | 下着 |
| utensil 16 | utensile | Gerät | utensile | utensilio | 台所用具 |
| vanilla 10 | vanille | Vanille | vaniglia | vainilla | バニラ |
| various 28 | varié | verschiedene | svariato, diverso | diversos | さまざまな |
| vegetable 15 | légume | Gemüse | verdura | verdura | 野菜 |
| venue 22 | lieu | Veranstaltungsort | luogo per un appuntamento | lugar / local | 開催地 |
| vermouth 7 | vermouth | Wermut | vermut | vermut | ベルモット |
| video conferencing 22 | vidéoconférence | Video-Konferenzschaltung | videoconferenza | videoconferencia | テレビ会議 |
| vinegary 14 | acide/qui a un goût de vinaigre | wie Essig | che sa di aceto | avinagrado | 酸っぱい |
| Visa slip 25 | reçu de carte de crédit | Quittung | ricevuta di pagamento con Visa | recibo de la Visa | （ビザカードの） レシート、控え |
| vodka 7 | vodka | Wodka | vodka | vodka | ウォッカ |
| voucher 25 | bon | Gutschein | tagliando | vale | クーポン券 |
| waiter 2 | serveur | Kellner(in) | cameriere | camarero | ウエイター |
| wake-up call 24 | reveil par téléphone | Weckruf | servizio sveglia | llamada para despertar a un huésped | モーニングコール |
| wardrobe 20 | armoire | Kleiderschrank | armadio | guardarropa | 衣装戸棚、衣裳部屋 |
| wash 16 | laver | waschen | lavare | lavar(se) | 洗う |
| wash basin 20 | lavabo | Waschbecken | lavabo | lavabo | 洗面台 |
| watercress 9 | cresson | Brunnenkresse | crescione | berros | クレソン |
| water sprinkler 19 | système d'extinction automatique à eau, type sprinkleur | Sprinkler | spruzzatore | aspersor de agua | スプリンクラー |
| watery 14 | plein d'eau | wässerig | annacquato | aguado | 水っぽい |
| welcome folder 20 | dossier d'accueil | Informationsmappe | cartella /opuscolo di benvenuto | carpeta de bienvenida | 部屋備え付けの宿泊 案内帖 |
| well informed 28 | bien informé | gut informiert | ben informato | bien informado | 見聞の広い、 精通している |
| west 11 | ouest | Westen | ovest | oeste | 西 |
| western 11 | de l'ouest | westlich | occidentale | occidental | 西の |
| wheelchair 24 | fauteuil roulant | Rollstuhl | sedia a rotelle | silla de ruedas | 車椅子 |
| whip 16 | fouetter | schlagen | montare, sbattere | batir (claras) | クリーム状に泡立てる |
| whisk 16 | battre | verquirlen | sbattere con il frullino | batir | 泡立てる |
| whisky 7 | whisky | Whisky | whisky | whisky | ウイスキー |
| white 7 | blanc | weiß | bianco | blanco | 白 |
| wife 3 | femme | Ehefrau | moglie | mujer / esposa | 妻 |
| wine 7 | vin | Wein | vino | vino | ワイン |
| winter 6 | hiver | Winter | inverno | invierno | 冬 |
| women 12 | femmes | Frauen | donne | mujeres | 女性 |
| work 12 | travail | Arbeit | lavoro | trabajo | 仕事 |
| writing paper 24 | papier à lettres | Schreibpapier | carta da lettere | papel de carta | 便箋、筆記用紙 |
| zip 17 | fermeture éclair | Reißverschluss | cerniera | cremallera | ジッパー |

# Useful vocabulary

## Food

### Meat

beef
chicken
duck
goose
lamb
pork
turkey

### Fish

cod
haddock
monkfish
octopus
plaice
salmon
sardine
shark
sole
squid
swordfish
trout
tuna
turbot

### Shellfish

crab
crayfish
king prawn
langoustine
lobster
mussels
oysters
scallops
shrimps

### Game

grouse
guinea fowl
partridge
pheasant
quail
rabbit
venison

### Fruit

apple
apricot
avocado
banana
blackcurrants
blueberries
cherries
cranberries
fig
grapefruit
grapes
kiwi
lemon
lime
mango
melon
olives
orange
peach
pear
pineapple
plums
raspberries
redcurrants
strawberries

### Vegetables

artichoke
asparagus
aubergine
beans
broccoli
Brussels sprouts
cabbage
carrot
cauliflower
celery
courgette
cucumber
fennel
garlic
green beans
leek
lentils
lettuce
mushrooms
onion
parsnip
peas
pepper
potato
radishes
spinach
sweetcorn
tomato
watercress

## Ordinal numbers

| | |
|---|---|
| 1st | first |
| 2nd | second |
| 3rd | third |
| 4th | fourth |
| 5th | fifth |
| 6th | sixth |
| 7th | seventh |
| 8th | eighth |
| 9th | ninth |
| 10th | tenth |
| 11th | eleventh |
| 12th | twelfth |
| 13th | thirteenth |
| 14th | fourteenth |
| 15th | fifteenth |
| 16th | sixteenth |
| 17th | seventeenth |
| 18th | eighteenth |
| 19th | nineteenth |
| 20th | twentieth |
| 21st | twenty-first |
| 22nd | twenty-second |
| 23rd | twenty-third |
| 24th | twenty-fourth |
| 25th | twenty-fifth |
| 30th | thirtieth |
| 31st | thirty-first |

## Telephone alphabet

| | |
|---|---|
| A | Alpha |
| B | Bravo |
| C | Charlie |
| D | Delta |
| E | Echo |
| F | Foxtrot |
| G | Golf |
| H | Hotel |
| I | India |
| J | Juliet |
| K | Kilo |
| L | Lima |
| M | Mike |
| N | November |
| O | Oscar |
| P | Papa |
| Q | Quebec |
| R | Romeo |
| S | Sierra |
| T | Tango |
| U | Uniform |
| V | Victor |
| W | Whisky |
| X | X-ray |
| Y | Yankee |
| Z | Zulu |

# Irregular verbs

| Infinitive | Past tense | Past participle |
| --- | --- | --- |
| be | was/were | been |
| beat | beat | beaten |
| become | became | become |
| begin | began | begun |
| bend | bent | bent |
| bite | bit | bitten |
| blow | blew | blown |
| break | broke | broken |
| bring | brought | brought |
| build | built | built |
| burn | burnt | burnt |
| buy | bought | bought |
| catch | caught | caught |
| choose | chose | chosen |
| come | came | come |
| cost | cost | cost |
| cut | cut | cut |
| dig | dug | dug |
| do | did | done |
| draw | drew | drawn |
| dream | dreamt | dreamt |
| drink | drank | drunk |
| drive | drove | driven |
| eat | ate | eaten |
| fall | fell | fallen |
| feed | fed | fed |
| feel | felt | felt |
| fight | fought | fought |
| find | found | found |
| fly | flew | flown |
| forget | forgot | forgotten |
| freeze | froze | frozen |
| get | got | got |
| give | gave | given |
| go | went | gone |
| hang | hung | hung |
| have | had | had |
| hear | heard | heard |
| hide | hid | hidden |
| hit | hit | hit |
| hold | held | held |
| hurt | hurt | hurt |
| keep | kept | kept |
| know | knew | known |
| lay | laid | laid |
| lead | led | led |
| lean | leant | leant |
| learn | learnt | learnt |
| leave | left | left |

| Infinitive | Past tense | Past participle |
| --- | --- | --- |
| lend | lent | lent |
| let | let | let |
| lie | lay | lain |
| light | lit | lit |
| lose | lost | lost |
| make | made | made |
| mean | meant | meant |
| meet | met | met |
| pay | paid | paid |
| put | put | put |
| read | read | read |
| ride | rode | ridden |
| ring | rang | rung |
| rise | rose | risen |
| run | ran | run |
| say | said | said |
| see | saw | seen |
| sell | sold | sold |
| send | sent | sent |
| set | set | set |
| shake | shook | shaken |
| shine | shone | shone |
| shoot | shot | shot |
| shut | shut | shut |
| sing | sang | sung |
| sink | sank | sunk |
| sit | sat | sat |
| sleep | slept | slept |
| slide | slid | slid |
| smell | smelt | smelt |
| speak | spoke | spoken |
| spend | spent | spent |
| stand | stood | stood |
| steal | stole | stolen |
| stick | stuck | stuck |
| strike | struck | struck |
| swear | swore | sworn |
| swim | swam | swum |
| take | took | taken |
| teach | taught | taught |
| tear | tore | torn |
| tell | told | told |
| think | thought | thought |
| throw | threw | thrown |
| understand | understood | understood |
| wake | woke | woken |
| wear | wore | worn |
| win | won | won |
| write | wrote | written |

# OXFORD
UNIVERSITY PRESS

Great Clarendon Street, Oxford OX2 6DP

Oxford University Press is a department of the University of Oxford.
It furthers the University's objective of excellence in research, scholarship,
and education by publishing worldwide in

Oxford  New York

Auckland  Bangkok  Buenos Aires  Cape Town  Chennai
Dar es Salaam  Delhi  Hong Kong  Istanbul  Karachi  Kolkata
Kuala Lumpur  Madrid  Melbourne  Mexico City  Mumbai
Nairobi  São Paulo  Shanghai  Taipei  Tokyo  Toronto

OXFORD and OXFORD ENGLISH are registered trade marks of
Oxford University Press in the UK and in certain other countries

© Oxford University Press 2004

The moral rights of the author have been asserted

Database right Oxford University Press (maker)

First published 2004

2008 2007 2006 2005 2004
10 9 8 7 6 5 4 3 2 1

ISBN 0 19 457463 6

Printed in China

ACKNOWLEDGEMENTS

*Illustrations by*: Emma Dodd pp 26, 30, 33, 36; Mark Duffin pp 4, 8 (Fidelio), 11,
20, 38, 41, 43, 46–47, 52, 55; Martha Gavin p 18; Joanna Kerr pp 8, 29; Claire
Littlejohn pp 44, 47, 63, 64; Peter Bull pp 15, 23, 42, 63; Harry Venning pp
40–41, 54, 50

*Commissioned photography by*: Gareth Boden pp 14, 32, 34, 48; MM Studios pp
16–17, 24–25, 59

*The authors and publisher are grateful to those who have given permission to reproduce
the following photographs*: Alamy p 19 (Sauce Guides/Daiquiri); Anthony Blake
Picture Library pp 10 (Maximilian), 12 (D.Dibbs/restaurant), 22 (J.Lee/lemon
tart), (S.Lee/chocolate mousse), (R.Stowell/ice cream), (J.Lee/apple tart), 28
(J.Murphy/asparagus), (T.Imrie/smoked salmon blinis), (Eaglemoss Consumer
Publications/pork chops), (Oceania/lamb cutlets), (G.Glynn Smith/salmon in
pastry), (G. Kirk/penne), (M.Brigdale/aubergine), 57 (A.Blake); Transport for
London p 45; Cephas p 19 (D.Johnson/ Manhattan), p 23 (Stock Food/Brie,
Cheddar, Stilton); Collections p 6 (A.Greeley/Big Ben); Corbis pp 4 (J.L.Pelaez
Inc/May Lee top left), 7 (P.Thompson/Sydney Opera House), 12 (E.K.K.Yu/hotel
reception), (M.L.Stephenson/bathroom), 21 (© A.Perlstein/Sygma), 28 (M.Boys/
mushroom pate); by courtesy of The Cumberland Hotel p 6 (hotel); Getty
Images royalty-free cover (Digital Vision/receptionist), pp 4 (Digital Vision),
12 (PhotoDisc Green/car park), 38 (Photodisc Blue); Getty Images rights
managed: cover (D.Oliver/cooks), pp 4 (Matthieu top right), (B.Yee/Isobel
bottom left), 28 (R.MacDougall/mixed seafood), 39 (G.&M-D de Lossy), 56
(S.Shauer), 58 (C.Hawkins); PA Photos p 59 (K.Myung); proudly supplied by
Sydney Tower Restaurants p 7

*The authors and publisher are grateful to those who have given permission to reproduce
the following extracts and adaptations of copyright material*:

pp 8, 38, 52, 55 Images and information from Micros Fidelio Suite 7.
Reproduced by permission of Micros-Fidelio UK Ltd

p 59 Information about Jamie Oliver from www.jamieoliver.co.uk.
Reproduced by permission of Deborah McKenna Limited

*The authors and publisher would like to thank the many teachers, schools, and
institutions who assisted in the development of this new edition, and in particular the
following*:

Maria Segarra Bonet, Niki Lemonnier, Nicholas Mettelet, Arthur Swortfiguer

Special thanks are due to Barbara Mackay

Thanks are also due to Idoia Noble, Virginie Renard, Roberta Sacrato, Mika
Wade, and Christa Wiseman for translating the wordlist

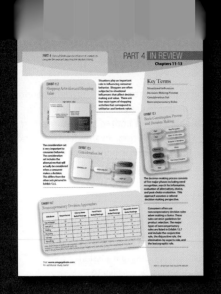

**Chapter-In-Review Cards** in the back of the Student Edition provide students all of the pertinent information for each chapter, while **Part In Review Cards** help students grasp the big picture.

# THE
**CB** Are you in?
# SOLUTION

**CB3**

**Barry J. Babin,** Louisiana Tech University
**Eric G. Harris,** Pittsburg State University

Executive Vice President and Publisher,
Business & Computers: Jonathan Hulbert

Vice President of Editorial, Business:
Jack W. Calhoun

Director, 4LTR Press: Neil Marquardt

Product Development Manager, 4LTR Press:
Steven E. Joos

Executive Editor: Mike Roche

Developmental Editor: Julie Klooster

Editorial Assistant: Megan Fischer

Executive Marketing Manager, 4LTR Press:
Robin Lucas

Marketing Manager: Gretchen Swann

Marketing Coordinator:  Leigh T. Smith

Sr. Marketing Communications Manager: Jim
Overly

Sr. Content Project Manager: Martha Conway

Media Editor: John Rich

Print Buyer: Miranda Klapper

Production House: Bill Smith Studio

Sr. Art Director: Stacy Jenkins Shirley

Internal & Cover Designer: Ke Design, Mason,
Ohio

Cover Images: Veer- image 100 and PhotoAlto/
iStock Photo- © Lisa Marzano and ©
Tomasz Wojnarowicz

Sr. Image Acquisitions Specialist: Deanna
Ettinger

Photo Researcher: Charlotte Goldman

Sr. Rights Acquisitions Specialist: Mardell
Glinski Schultz

Text Permissions Researcher: Elaine Kosta

Inside Front Cover Images: chair and gears © C
Squared Studios/Photodisc/Getty Images;
microscope © Siede Preis/Photodisc/Getty
Images; dartboard and binoculars © Photo-
disc/Getty Images

Back Cover Image: © René Mansi/
iStockphoto.com

Title Page Image: © iStockphoto.com/CostinT

Page iii Images: © Uppercut Images/Getty Im-
ages; © iStockphoto.Com/Robert Churchill;
© Ton Koene/Alamy; © Chuck Savage/
Corbis; © Bobby Bank/Getty Images

> For product information and technology assistance, contact us at
> **Cengage Learning Customer & Sales Support, 1-800-354-9706**
>
> For permission to use material from this text or product,
> submit all requests online at  **cengage.com/permissions**
> Further permissions questions can be emailed to
> **permissionrequest@cengage.com**

The names of all products mentioned herein are used for identification
purposes only and may be trademarks or registered trademarks of their
respective owners. South-Western disclaims any affiliation, association,
connection with, sponsorship, or endorsement by such owners.

Library of Congress Control Number: 2010935347

Student Edition ISBN-13: 978-0-8400-5852-2
Student Edition ISBN-10: 0-8400-5852-7

Student Edition with CourseMate ISBN 13: 978-0-8400-5851-5
Student Edition with CourseMate ISBN 10: 0-8400-5851-9

**South-Western**
5191 Natorp Boulevard
Mason, OH 45040
USA

Cengage Learning is a leading provider of customized learning solutions with
office locations around the globe, including Singapore, the United Kingdom,
Australia, Mexico, Brazil, and Japan. Locate your local office at:
**international.cengage.com/region**

Cengage Learning products are represented in Canada by Nelson Education, Ltd.

To learn more about 4LTR Press, visit **www.cengage.com/4ltrpress**

Purchase any of our products at your local college store or at our preferred
online store **www.cengagebrain.com**

Printed in the United States of America
1 2 3 4 5 6 7  14 13 12 11

# BRIEF CONTENTS

# CONTENTS

© JUICE/JUICE IMAGES/JUPITERIMAGES

## PART TWO  INTERNAL INFLUENCES

## 3 Consumer Learning Starts Here: Perception

## 4 Comprehension, Memory, and Cognitive Learning

# 5 Motivation and Emotion: Driving Consumer Behavior

© ISTOCKPHOTO.COM/STEVE HARMON

# PART THREE EXTERNAL INFLUENCES

## 8 Consumer Culture

© PETER HORREE/ALAMY

## 9 Microcultures

# 10 Group and Interpersonal Influence

# PART FOUR SITUATIONS AND DECISION MAKING

# 11 Consumers in Situations

© ISTOCKPHOTO.COM/PHIL DATE

# 12 Decision Making I: Need Recognition and Search

# 13 Decision Making II: Alternative Evaluation and Choice

# PART FIVE CONSUMPTION AND BEYOND

# 14 Consumption to Satisfaction

© ICP/ALAMY

# 15 Consumer Relationships

# 16 Consumer and Marketing Misbehavior

For my family and my mentors, especially Bill and Joe.
—Barry Babin


To my family, Tara, Christian, and Sydney.
—Eric Harris

## The marketer who

understands consumers will be able to design products that provide more value and, through this process, enhance the well-being of both the company and its customers.

## what do you think?

**In any business, the customer is truly the most important person.**

STRONGLY DISAGREE      STRONGLY AGREE

**①**   **②**   **③**   **④**   **⑤**   **⑥**   **⑦**

Visit CourseMate at
www.cengagebrain.com.

# 1

# What Is CB, and Why Should I Care?

## Introduction

how many times a day does the typical college student act like a consumer? If we stop to think about it, we find that the entire day is filled with consumption and consumption decisions. What should I wear? What will I eat for breakfast? What music should I listen to? Will I go to class today? What am I going to do this weekend? Many questions like these are routinely answered within the first few moments of every day, with the answers ultimately turning the wheels of the economy and shaping the quality of life for the individual consumer.

How can simple decisions be so important to society? The answer to this question is one of the key points of this chapter and of this text. Indeed, the consumer answers these questions by choosing the options that offer the most value. Thus, consumer behavior is really all about value.

As long as time keeps moving, things happen. In the same way, as long as people keep consuming, things happen. The economic downturn experienced recently in the U.S. is linked strongly to a drop in housing sales.[1] When consumers stop buying houses, there are implications throughout the economy. Fewer house sales mean fewer appliance and furniture purchases, and fewer requests for services. Eventually, all home-related industries suffer and people lose jobs. Analysts continue to express concerns about the economy based on falling housing starts in mid-2010.[2]

When consumers buy things a chain reaction is set in motion that has the potential to enhance value for many people, both directly and indirectly. When a consumer purchases an electronic device like an Apple® iPad™, the store will have to replace the item in inventory. The manufacturer will have to replenish the stock. This means that the manufacturer purchases raw materials from suppliers. The raw materials and finished products all need to be shipped by companies such as UPS or DHL. But that isn't all. The consumer will need a new service plan to take advantage of the device, and companies like AT&T will kindly oblige with 3G or

After studying this chapter, the student should be able to:

**LO1** Understand the meaning of *consumption* and *consumer behavior*.

**LO2** Describe how consumers get treated differently in various types of exchange environments.

**LO3** Explain the role of consumer behavior in business and society.

**LO4** Be familiar with basic approaches to studying consumer behavior.

**LO5** Describe why consumer behavior is so dynamic and how recent trends affect consumers.

4G service. The chain doesn't stop here as the consumer has yet to accessorize the iPad or add apps to keep the product entertaining. Just think of how something like an iPad can be so meaningful for so many people. Most importantly, assuming all goes well, the consumer improves his or her quality of life!

Although some may call a course like this one "buyer behavior," the iPad example illustrates that there is much more to *consuming* than simply *buying*. This does not diminish the importance of getting someone to buy something. But, consumption goes on long after purchase, and the story of consumption ultimately determines how much value is created.

As you can see, our behavior as consumers is critically important not just to ourselves, but to many other people. This is why so many people are interested in learning about consumer behavior. The marketer who understands consumers will be able to design products that provide more value and, through this process, en-

hance the well-being of both the company and its customers. Policy makers who understand consumer behavior can make more effective public policy decisions. Last but not least, consumers who understand consumer behavior can make better decisions concerning how they allocate scarce resources. Thus, an understanding of consumer behavior can mean better business for companies, better public policy for governments, and a better life for individuals and households.

# LO1 Consumption and Consumer Behavior

Consumer behavior can be defined from two different perspectives. This is because the term refers to both

1. human thought and action, and
2. a field of study (human inquiry) that is developing an accumulated body of knowledge.

If we think of a consumer considering the purchase of a new phone, consumer behavior can be thought of as the actions, reactions, and consequences that take place as the consumer goes through a decision-making process, reaches a decision, and then puts the product to use. Alternatively, if we consider the body of knowledge that researchers accumulate as they attempt to explain these actions, reactions, and consequences, we are approaching consumer behavior as a field of study. Thus, rather than choosing between the two alternative approaches, an understanding of the way the term *consumer behavior* is used is best gained by considering both approaches.

## CONSUMER BEHAVIOR AS HUMAN BEHAVIOR

First, **consumer behavior** is the set of value-seeking activities that take place as people go about addressing realized needs. In other words, when a consumer comes to realize that something is needed, a chain reaction begins as the consumer sets out to find desirable ways to fill this need. The chain reaction involves multiple psychological processes, including thoughts, feelings, and behavior, and the entire process culminates in value.

Consumers are the key driver of the economy. Purchases like this stimulate other purchases that drive economic activity.

AP IMAGES/FRANK FRANKLIN II

## The Basic CB Process

Exhibit 1.1 illustrates the basic consumption process. Each step is discussed in detail in later chapters. However, the process is briefly illustrated here in the context of a new phone purchase. At some point, the consumer realizes a need for better communication with other people and access to outside media, including the Internet. This realization may be motivated by a desire to do better on the job or to have better access to friends and family. A **want** is simply a specific desire that spells out a way a consumer can go about addressing a recognized need. A consumer feels a need to belong and socialize, and this creates a desire for communication devices.

After weighing some options, the consumer decides to visit an AT&T store where communications devices are sold. After looking at several alternative devices, the consumer chooses a BlackBerry Bold. Next, the consumer participates in an exchange in which he or she gives up economic resources in return for receiving the product. An **exchange** is the acting out of a decision to give something up in return for something of greater value. Here, the consumer decides the phone will be worth at least the price of the product and the service plan needed to make the device functional.

The consumer then uses the product and experiences all the associated benefits and costs. **Costs** are the negative results of consumption. The costs involve more than just the price of the product. Consumers spend time both shopping for and learning how to use a phone. Physical effort also is needed if consumers visit retail stores during the process. The time, money, and effort spent acquiring a phone cannot be allocated toward other activities or processes, resulting in high opportunity costs for the consumer. **Benefits** are positive results of consumption. The

benefits are multifaceted, ranging from better job performance to more entertainment from the MP3 feature.

Over time, the consumer evaluates the costs and benefits and reacts to the purchase in some way. These reactions involve thoughts and feelings. The thoughts may involve reactions to features such as the ease of use. The feelings may sometimes include frustration if the features do not work correctly or conveniently. Ultimately, the process results in a perception of value. We will discuss value in more detail in Chapter 2.

> **want** way a consumer goes about addressing a recognized need
>
> **exchange** acting out of the decision to give something up in return for something of greater value
>
> **costs** negative results of consumption
>
> **benefits** positive results of consumption
>
> **consumption** process by which goods, services, or ideas are used and transformed into value

> Consumption represents the process by which goods, services, or ideas are used and transformed into value.

## Consumption

Another way to look at the basic consumer behavior process is to consider the steps that occur when consumption takes place. Obviously, a consumer consumes! Interestingly, very few consumer behavior books define consumption itself. **Consumption** represents the process by which goods, services, or ideas are used and transformed into value. Thus, the actions involved in acquiring and using a mobile communications device like a BlackBerry Bold create value for a consumer. If the product performs well, a great deal of value may result. If the consumer is unhappy with the product, very little value or even a negative amount of value may result. Eventually, this outcome affects consumer well-being by affecting quality of life.

**EXHIBIT 1.1**
**The Basic Consumption Process**

- Need
- Want
- Exchange
- Costs and Benefits
- Reaction
- Value

© ANTOINE ANTONIOL/BLOOMBERG VIA GETTY IMAGES

# CONSUMER BEHAVIOR AS A FIELD OF STUDY

**Consumer behavior as a field of study** represents the study of consumers as they go about the consumption process. In this sense, consumer behavior is the science of studying how consumers seek value in an effort to address real needs. This book represents a collection of knowledge resulting as consumer behavior researchers go about studying consumers.

Consumer behavior, as a field of study, is a very young field. The first books that discuss consumer behavior or buyer behavior date from the 1960s.[3] Thus, compared with older disciplines, researchers have had less time to develop the body of knowledge. Therefore, each decade the accumulated body of knowledge grows significantly. Clearly, however, much uncertainty remains, and the body of theory that is accepted by researchers and practitioners is relatively small. This is one reason consumer behavior is so exciting to study. Consumer behavior research is quickly expanding the knowledge base.

Like other disciplines, consumer behavior has family roots in other disciplines. Exhibit 1.2 lists some related disciplines.

## Economics and Consumer Behavior

**Economics** is often defined as the study of production and consumption.[4] Accordingly, it is easy to see that marketing has its origins in economics, particularly with respect to the production and distribution of goods. As the definition implies, economics also involves consumption. Therefore, consumer behavior and economics also have much in common. However, the economist's focus on consumer behavior is generally a broad, or macro, perspective. For example, economics studies often involve things like commodity consumption of nations over time. This may even involve tracking changes in consumption, with different price levels enabling price elasticity to be determined. The economist finds data for a study like this in historical sales records. No individual consumers are interviewed, and the data may only count the number of purchases.

To illustrate a macro perspective, we note that researchers and marketing managers are very interested in emerging markets like China and India. Although these places may seem like very distant lands with little relevance to most business students, nothing could be further from the truth. Within a decade, estimates sug-

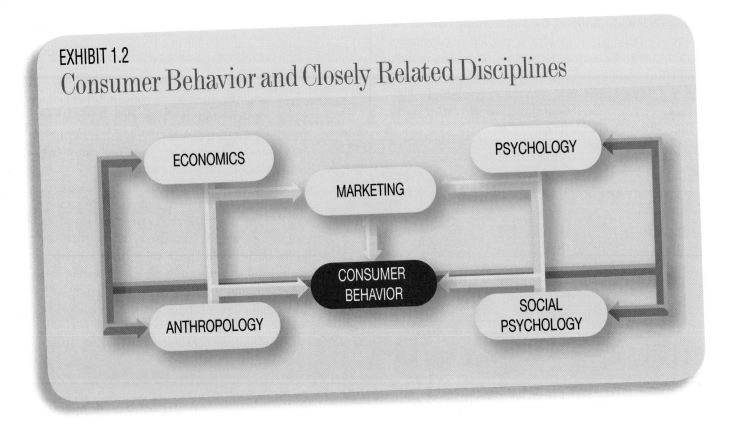

**EXHIBIT 1.2**
## Consumer Behavior and Closely Related Disciplines

ECONOMICS

PSYCHOLOGY

MARKETING

CONSUMER BEHAVIOR

ANTHROPOLOGY

SOCIAL PSYCHOLOGY

gest that China will surpass the United States as the leading country in terms of total consumer purchasing power. Thus, economists might be very interested in estimating the demand for consumer products like alcoholic beverages in an emerging market like China. One study shows that Chinese consumers display greater price elasticity for wine coolers and wine than they do for beer.[5] In other words, changes in price do not affect overall beer consumption as much as they do consumption of wine or wine coolers. This pattern suggests beer is more of a staple good to Chinese consumers; thus, beer consumption should remain relatively stable compared to other beverages.

In contrast, consumer behavior researchers generally study consumer behavior at a more micro level, often focusing on individual consumer behavior. As such, consumer research often involves experiments or interviews involving responses from individual consumers. For example, consumer researchers examined the extent to which exposure to advertisements promoting alcoholic drink specials influences college student drinking. The study was based on responses to such ads from individual consumers. Results suggest that students had a more positive attitude toward the bar running the specials and intended to buy more because of the specials when exposed to the ad.[6]

## Psychology and Social Psychology

**Psychology** is the study of human reactions to their environment including behavior and mental processes.[7] Psychologists seek to explain the thoughts, feelings, and behaviors that represent human reaction. Psychology itself can be divided into several subdisciplines. Social psychology and cognitive psychology, in particular, are highly relevant to consumer behavior.[8] **Social psychology** focuses on the thoughts, feelings, and behaviors that people have as they interact with other people (group behavior). Consumer behavior most often takes place in some type of social setting; thus, social psychology and consumer behavior overlap significantly. **Cognitive psychology** deals with the intricacies of mental reactions involved in information processing. Every time a consumer evaluates a product, sees an advertisement, or reacts to product consumption, information is processed. Thus, cognitive psychology is also very relevant to consumer behavior.

## Marketing

One doesn't have to look very hard to find different definitions of marketing.[9] Many of the older definitions focused heavily on physical products and profitability. Even though

products and profits are very important aspects of marketing, these definitions are relatively narrow. **Marketing** involves the multitude of value-producing seller activities that facilitate *exchanges* between buyers and sellers. These activities include the production, promotion, pricing, distribution, and retailing of goods, services, ideas, and experiences that provide value for consumers and other stakeholders.

Consumer behavior and marketing are very closely related. Exchange is intimately involved in marketing and as can be seen from Exhibit 1.1, exchange is central to consumer behavior too. In fact, in some ways, consumer behavior involves "inverse" marketing as consumers operate at the other end of the exchange. Marketing actions are targeted at and affect consumers while consumer actions affect marketers. A marketer without customers won't be a marketer very long! In fact, without consumers, marketing is unnecessary.

> **psychology** study of human reactions to environments including behavior and mental processes
>
> **social psychology** study that focuses on the thoughts, feelings, and behaviors that people have as they interact with other people
>
> **cognitive psychology** study of the intricacies of mental reactions involved in information processing
>
> **marketing** multitude of value-producing seller activities that facilitate exchanges between buyers and sellers

PRNEWSFOTO/KRAFT FOODS INC.; STOVE TOP, AYNSLEY FLOYD

*Marketing activities are aimed at creating value.*

**sociology** the study of groups of people within a society, with relevance for consumer behavior because a great deal of consumption takes place within group settings or is affected by group behavior

**anthropology** study in which researchers interpret relationships between consumers and the things they purchase, the products they own, and the activities in which they participate

## Consumer Behavior and Other Disciplines

Marketing, as a recognized discipline, grew out of economics and psychology. Commerce increased tremendously with the industrial revolution and the coinciding political changes that fostered economic freedom in many countries. Businesses looked to the new field of marketing for practical advice initially about distribution and later about pricing, packaging, advertising, and communication. Eventually, what some have called the "subdiscipline" of consumer behavior emerged as competition focused marketers on how consumers made decisions.[10] Thus, although marketing may have originally shared more in common with economics, the turn toward consumer research brought numerous psychologists into the field. Many of these psychologists became the first consumer researchers.

Today, consumer behavior and marketing remain closely tied. Consumer behavior research and marketing research overlap with each other more than they do with any other discipline. Thus, the double-headed arrow connecting the two disciplines in Exhibit 1.2 represents the fact that marketing and consumer research contribute strongly to each other. After marketing, consumer behavior research is most closely intertwined with psychology research.[11] Consumer research is based largely on psychology, and to some extent, psychology draws from consumer behavior research.

Other disciplines share things in common with consumer behavior. **Sociology** focuses on the study of groups of people within a society. This has relevance for consumer behavior because consumption often takes place within group settings or is in one way or another affected by group behavior.

**Anthropology** has contributed to consumer behavior research by allowing researchers to interpret the relationships between consumers and the things they purchase, the products they own, and the activities in which they participate. Other disciplines such as geography and the medical sciences overlap with consumer behavior in that they draw from some of the same theories and/or research approaches. Consumer behavior shares the strongest interdisciplinary connections with economics, psychology (and social psychology), marketing, and anthropology.[12]

# LO2 The Ways in Which Consumers Are Treated

the customer isn't always "king." Look at this list of familiar service environments:

- A typical driver's license bureau
- The registrar's office at a state university
- The line for cashing a check at a bank
- A university health clinic
- Cable television service
- A hair salon
- A New York City fine dining establishment

Think about the following questions: Does a consumer receive the same amount of service at each of these places? What is the waiting environment like at each of these places? Is there a clean, comfortable waiting area with pleasant music? How dedicated are the employees to delivering a high-quality service experience? How likely are employees to view the customer as a nuisance? If you don't see the point of these questions yet, contrast the waiting area at a driver's license bureau with the elaborate lounge where customers wait while sipping a cocktail or aperitif before dining in a fine dining establishment in New York City.

Some organizations can survive while treating customers little better than dirt, and others need to pamper customers just to have a chance of surviving. Consider these two questions in order to understand how important serving customers well should be to any given organization:

1. How competitive is the marketing environment?

2. How dependent is the marketer on repeat business?

## COMPETITION AND CONSUMER ORIENTATION

Where do consumers go if they don't like the service at the driver's license bureau? If the choice comes down to visiting the bureau or not driving, nearly all consumers will put up with the less-than-immaculate surroundings, long waits, and poor service that all too typically go along with getting a driver's license. Put yourself into the shoes of the service providers at the bureau. Is there any concern about doing something that would make a customer want to return to do business again? Is there any real incentive to provide a pleasant and valuable experience?

In essence, the driver's license bureau typifies a service organization that operates in a market with little or no competition and a captive audience. No matter how poor the service is, they know consumers will return to do more business when the term on their license expires. The incentive for better customer treatment remains small.

Contrast this with the restaurant. A dining consumer in New York City has over 6,000 full-service restaurants from which to choose. Customers do not have to tolerate poor treatment. They can simply go next door. With few exceptions, a highly competitive marketplace in which consumers have many alternatives ensures good customer service.

Why do you get treated better in some environments than in others? Perhaps competition is a clue.

Unfortunately, public services provided by government institutions can often be notorious for poor service.[13] Unlike a restaurant, Department of Motor Vehicles (DMV) management may not be compelled to adjust workloads to demand. DMV *customers* can face long lines (sometimes over 100 people in some areas) and wait times counted in hours, not minutes. As state budgets have become increasingly tight with the bad economy, wait times have increased and DMV offices have cut hours—some even operating only four days a week.[14] However, a few states have turned to technology and private outsourcing to improve service. Drivers can renew licenses online in some states or go to a company that has been authorized to provide licensing services. These companies generally provide consumers with better service, and states end up with better and more accurate information about drivers.[15]

The realization that competition is important to protecting consumers is recognized by government. In the United States, many federal laws regulate the market to ensure business competition. The Robinson-Patman Act, the Sherman Act, and the Clayton Act are examples of such legislation. Practices such as price fixing, secret rebates, and customer coercion are governed by these acts.

Competition eventually drives companies toward a high degree of consumer orientation. **Consumer (customer) orientation** is a way of doing business in which the actions and decision making of the institution prioritize consumer value and satisfaction above all other concerns. A consumer orientation is a key component of a firm with a market-oriented culture. **Market orientation** is an organizational culture that embodies the importance of creating value for customers among all employees. In addition to understanding customers, a market orientation stresses the need to monitor and understand competitor actions in the marketplace and the need to communicate information about customers and competitors throughout the organization.[16] Profitable firms are usually market oriented, with a few exceptions that will be discussed later.[17]

## RELATIONSHIP MARKETING AND CONSUMER BEHAVIOR

Let's go back to the list of service environments. Certainly, banks and restaurants are generally in very intense competition with rival businesses. Businesses

> **consumer (customer) orientation** way of doing business in which the actions and decision making of the institution prioritize consumer value and satisfaction above all other concerns
>
> **market orientation** organizational culture that embodies the importance of creating value for customers among all employees

**relationship marketing** activities based on the belief that the firm's performance is enhanced through repeat business

**touchpoints** direct contacts between the firm and a customer

are challenged to get consumers to repeatedly purchase the goods or services offered. Even in a city with a population as great as that of New York, without repeat business, each restaurant would have fewer than ten customers per night. In addition, repeat customers are considered less costly to serve.[18] For instance, while a lot of advertising may be needed for every new customer to learn about a restaurant, old customers already know the place.

Thus, **relationship marketing** is based on the belief that firm performance is enhanced through repeat business. Relationship marketing is the recognition that customer desires are recurring and that a single purchase act may be only one touchpoint in an ongoing series of interactions with a customer. **Touchpoints** are direct contacts between the firm and a customer. Increasingly, multiple channels, or ways of making this contact, including phone, email, text messaging, and face-to-face contact.[19] Every touchpoint, no matter the channel, should be considered as an opportunity to create value for the customer. Like any type of relationship, a customer–marketer relationship will continue only as long as both parties see the partnership as valuable.

Marketers are increasingly realizing the value of relationship marketing. Wait staff sometimes provide business cards to customers. These

*Every touchpoint is a way to build a relationship with a customer in a competitive environment.*

© ANDREA CHU/DIGITAL VISION/JUPITERIMAGES

customers can use the card to ask for this waiter again on the next visit or to recommend the restaurant and server to a friend. Notice that with relationship marketing, the firm and its employees are very motivated to provide an outstanding overall experience. In sum, both a competitive marketplace and a relationship marketing orientation create exchange environments where firms truly treat customers as "king."

## LO3 Consumer Behavior's Role in Business and Society

hy study consumer behavior? Many students find studying consumer behavior interesting relative to other college courses. Why might consumer behavior be more interesting than calculus? The answer lies in the student's ability to relate to the content. After all, everyone reading this book has years and years of experience as a consumer. Thus, students should come into the course with a better sense of familiarity and an ability to relate to the subject matter. Not only is the subject interesting, but consumer behavior is also an important topic to understand from multiple perspectives. Consumer behavior (CB) is important in at least three ways:

1. CB provides an input to business/marketing strategy.

2. CB provides a force that shapes society.

3. CB provides an input to making responsible decisions as a consumer.

## CONSUMER BEHAVIOR AND MARKETING STRATEGY

The ultimate hallmark of success for a business is long-term survival. One hundred years is not a long time in the course of history. But very few companies have survived for 100 years. Exhibit 1.3 lists some famous international companies, the products they are known for, and their age.

None of these companies are 100 years old! All of these companies have beaten the odds, and even though we may think about them as lasting forever, chances are some of these "giants" will not be around 100 years from now. So, surviving is not a trivial goal, and the companies that do survive long term do so by obtaining resources from consumers in return for the value they create. This is a basic tenet of **resource advantage theory**, a theory that helps explain why companies succeed or fail.[20] Companies succeed by acquiring more resources from consumers and in turn using those resources to gain advantages in physical and intellectual capital. Consumer research is needed to understand what makes a consumer give up scarce resources. Ultimately, consumers give up resources in the pursuit of value.

In contrast to the companies listed in Exhibit 1.3, consider Curtis Mathes Corporation. Curtis Mathes produced and sold high-quality televisions from 1957 until the 1990s. For much of that time, the Texas-based firm was the leading name in high-quality televisions in the United States. Yet, factors in the external environment made it difficult for them to maintain sales relative to increasingly high-quality imported electronics. Consumers were much more likely to purchase competitor products whose quality was acceptable and whose prices were lower. Eventually, the resource drain caused Curtis Mathes to file for bankruptcy, and the company exists only as a shell of what it once was, with no production capacity.

get? Well, the tangibles include mostly plastic and some integrated circuitry. These are the parts that make up the product. No reasonable consumer would trade any significant sum of money for plastic and circuitry. A consumer isn't really buying **attributes**, or the physical parts of a product. However, the plastic enables the product to be small and light, and the integrated circuitry enables this small, light product to function as an electronic reader. Once again, we can ask, is this really what the consumer wants? The fact is, this function enables the consumer to enjoy the benefits of information availability in a very convenient package. Outcomes like these are valuable and what the customer is ultimately buying.

Marketing firms often implement poor strategies when they don't understand what a product truly is because they don't understand exactly what they are selling. A **product** is a potentially valuable bundle of benefits. Theodore Levitt, one of the most famous marketing researchers, understood this. He emphasized the importance of the value a customer receives from a product, rather than the product itself.

One consumer researcher studied why people bought milk shakes. In contrast to expectation, the largest share of milk shakes purchased in the study was bought before noon, many before 10 A.M., and many were consumed in a car. After studying many milk shake drinkers, one theme emerged. A milk shake is a good solution for consumers with long commutes. They satisfy one's hunger, they are neat, they can be consumed while using one hand, and they take about 20 minutes to finish—the better portion of the commute. The value provided by the

**resource-advantage theory** theory that explains why companies succeed or fail; the firm goes about obtaining resources from consumers in return for the value the resources create

**attribute** a product feature that delivers a desired consumer benefit

**product** potentially valuable bundle of benefits

## EXHIBIT 1.3
## How Old Are These Companies?

| COMPANY[21] | CORE PRODUCTS | YEAR OF "BIRTH" | PLACE |
|---|---|---|---|
| Apple | Computers, Communication Devices | 1976 | California |
| Home Depot | Building Supply and Retailing | 1979 | Georgia |
| Walmart | Mass Merchandising | 1962 | Arkansas |
| Microsoft | Computer Software | 1975 | California |
| Tesco | Food Retailing | 1919 | London, UK |
| Samsung | Electronics | 1969 | Seoul, South Korea |
| McDonald's | Fast Food | 1956 | Illinois |
| Toyota | Motor Cars | 1937 | Japan |

## What Do People Buy?

When a consumer buys something, he or she gives up resources in the form of time, money, and energy in return for what ever is being sold. Consider a customer who purchases a Kindle. What does he or she really

milk shake is partly dealing with hunger but also partly dealing with boredom. Thus, the researcher suggested making shakes even thicker so they took even longer to finish as a way of improving the "product."[22]

Ultimately, companies need to understand why people buy their products in order to understand what business they are in. This is also how they identify their competitors. Let's look at the companies that produced buggies (horse-drawn carriages from 100 years ago) and slide rules (rulers used to do calculations). They did not go out of business because their products were flawed. The companies that did well producing those products went out of business because they failed to innovate and because they didn't understand that they were actually competing with Ford automobiles and Texas Instruments calculators, respectively. Products like VHS players, CD players, and tape recorders are all fast on the road to obsolescence as the technologies that provide the benefits of musical or video entertainment change. Thus, in this sense, technologies don't provide value directly; the activities and benefits associated with the technologies do.

## Ways of Doing Business

Much of the discussion thus far presumes that a company is market oriented. That is, the presumption is that a company has prioritized understanding consumers, as would be the case if in a consumer-oriented corporate culture. This isn't always the case. Each company adopts a way of doing business that is epitomized in their corporate culture. Corporate cultures fall roughly into one of several categories representing different ways of doing business. Exhibit 1.4 summarizes different business orientations. These orientations often guide a firm's market segmentation practices.

In **undifferentiated marketing**, the same basic product is offered to all customers. Mass merchandisers typify undifferentiated marketers in that they rely on selling high volume to be successful. As such, they focus on serving very large segments in which consumers do not have specific desires (are not picky). Undifferentiated marketers generally adopt a **production orientation**, wherein innovation is geared primarily toward making the production process

# Make-Up or Hope?

**T**heodore Levitt was a leader in the cause of getting managers to not allow their companies to become *myopic*. A myopic business view defines the business in terms of products that are sold and not in terms of the value that consumers receive. For instance, the National Radio Company was defined as a—guess what?—radio company! Up until the 1960s, the company was one of the leading names in the business and produced some of the finest radio receivers and transmitters. However, there is a good reason why you've probably never heard of this company! Things change!

Here are some examples of better ways to look at products.

| CONSUMERS DO NOT WANT: | CONSUMERS DO WANT: |
| --- | --- |
| ¼ inch B&D drill bits | ¼ inch holes so they can hang things |
| Kodak film | Recorded memories |
| Lawn mowers | Pride that comes with a great-looking lawn |
| Roach spray | Dead roaches |
| Dry-cleaning service | Clothes that do not stink |

What about a customer buying make-up or cosmetics? What is really being purchased? Charles Revson, founder of Revlon, said, "In the factory Revlon manufactures cosmetics, but in the store we sell hope." Revlon considers itself in the hope business! Thus, in Revlon's eyes, the "hope" helps provide the value as much as the cosmetics. Revlon's understanding of the way value is actually provided makes them see 20/20.

Sources, "Needful Things" *Branding Ad Vice (October 13, 2004),* "Needful Things," October 13, **http://brandingadvice.typepad.com/my_weblog/2004/10/index.html,** accessed January 14, 2007; Christenson, C. M., S. Cook, and T. Hall (2005), "Marketing Malpractice: The Cause and the Cure," *Harvard Business Review* 83, 74–83; Kellog, D. (2006), "Hope and Agility: The Revlon Test," Mark Logic CEO Blog, **http://marklogic.blogspot.com/2006/07/hope-and-agility-revlon-test.html,** accessed December 7, 2007.

© ISTOCKPHOTO.COM/RAINFORESTAUSTRALIA

## EXHIBIT 1.4
# Different Ways of Doing Business

as efficient and economic as possible. In other words, the emphasis is on serving customers while incurring minimum costs. Walmart typifies this approach with their Supercenters and their state-of-the-art distribution network, which ships massive quantities of products to stores around the world at the lowest possible cost.

**Differentiated marketers** serve multiple market segments each with a unique product offering. A market orientation usually serves a differentiated marketer well. The emphasis here is on matching a product with a segment.

Toyota, for example, has three business units each targeted toward a different automotive segment. Scion appeals to consumers interested in economy cars with a unique sense of style. Toyota operates under the Toyota name itself of course, offering a more conservative line of autos for consumers seeking a blend of performance and reliability. Finally, Lexus provides luxury cars to those who want the most in performance, style, comfort, and reliability. Taking differentiated marketing even further, each Toyota line offers coupes, sedans, and SUVs. Thus, a Toyota product exists for practically any automobile consumer's taste. Without an understanding of consumers, Toyota would have a difficult time matching products to segments.

Marketers can take differentiated marketing to the extreme with a practice known as **one-to-one marketing**. Here, the company offers a unique product to each in-dividual customer and thereby treats each customer as a segment of one. Computer-aided information processing, design, and production have helped make this a reality on a large scale. Many casinos, for example, develop promotional packages for individual customers based on information collected and stored about that customer's preferences.

**Niche marketing** is practiced by firms that specialize in serving one market segment with particularly unique demand characteristics. Firms that practice niche marketing may be consumer oriented. However, some niche marketers are product oriented and produce a product that has unique appeal within a segment. Stride Rite is a shoe retailer that offers shoes for children. They don't have a women's fashion section or a golf shoe section because these are segments they choose not to serve. Stride Rite stays in touch with its market with a considerable amount of consumer research. Moreau et fils is a producer of high-quality Chablis (white wine from the northern Burgundy region of France). Moreau does little consumer research because they produce fine Chablis. They have little interest in changing the product because a change would mean marketing something other than Chablis. Moreau wines are more expensive than mass-produced wines or high-production wines from companies like Chateau St. Michelle (which better typifies a differentiated marketer).

## CONSUMER BEHAVIOR AND SOCIETY

The things that people buy and consume end up determining the type of society in which we live. Things like customs, manners, and rituals all involve consumption—value-producing activities. Certainly, not every society around the world is the same. Just think about the ways we eat and the types of food consumed around the world. Additionally, when governments create laws that govern the way we buy and consume products, consumer behavior is involved. Thus, consumer behavior creates the society in which we live and serves as an important source of input to public policy in a free society.

For example, how does U.S. society treat smoking today? Interestingly, popular culture used to glamorize smoking as a valued behavior. On the famous TV classic *The Andy Griffith Show*, produced in the 1960s, the likable Sheriff Andy Taylor casually smoked cigarettes in his living room while talking to his young son, Opie. Cigarette advertisements made up a large chunk of all TV advertising before a federal ban took effect on January 2, 1971. In the theater, James Bond smoked, and his image was certainly not harmed by the behavior. At home, practically every room in the house included at least one ashtray. "No smoking" sections did not exist, and on airlines, flight attendants (or stewardesses) walked the aisles of the plane offering passengers "coffee, tea, or cigarettes."

My, how things have changed! Smoking has become nearly taboo in the United States. Smoking inside any public building is practically impossible either due to laws restricting smoking or rules created by building owners prohibiting smoking. "No smoking" sections in restaurants are now also seen in many parts of Europe and in most cosmopolitan cities around the world. Increasingly, consumers look upon smoking as a non–value-producing activity. Furthermore, politicians realize political advantage in creating more restrictions as consumer opinion continues to turn against the behavior. Policy makers should make such decisions with a thorough understanding of the consumer behavior issues involved.

As this billboard shows, attitudes toward smoking have certainly changed over the last few decades. Smoking isn't so cool.

Another current public policy issue concerns the use of mobile phones. Consider how much consumers' widespread adoption of the mobile phone has changed, and continues to change, society. In Europe and North America alone, consumers account for over 1 billion— that's 1,000 million—mobile phones! Consumers in Asia and Africa are adopting mobile phones at an even faster rate so that today, just about one half of all consumers in the world have a mobile phone.[22a] This means a total of over 4 billion mobile phones! That's not bad for a product that did not exist as we know it 25 years ago. Certainly, the mobile phone has been a discontinuous innovation and has altered our behaviors and communications in many significant ways.

## CONSUMER BEHAVIOR AND PERSONAL GROWTH

We face many important decisions as consumers. Among these include choices that will affect our professional careers, our quality of life, and the very fiber of our families. By this point in your life, you have already experienced many of these decisions. Some decisions are good; some are not. All consumers make dumb decisions occasionally. For instance, modern consumers often carry incredibly high debt relative to our ancestors. Total American consumer debt exceeded $2 trillion in 2010. That's over $15,000 per family.[23] American consumers are not alone. In the United Kingdom, the typical young consumer (18–24 years of age) also has credit card debt totaling nearly $10,000 USD.[24] College students are prime targets for credit cards and as can be seen on many college campuses, students are quite willing to apply for cards in exchange for something as mundane as a new t-shirt. Many consumers continue to have negative net worth years into their professional life because of the debt accumulated in early adulthood.[25]

The decisions that lead to high levels of debt do not seem to be wise as bankruptcy, financial stress, and lower self-esteem often result. Although often overlooked, decisions about budget allocation are very relevant aspects of consumer behavior. There are many other avenues that can lead consumers to make poor decisions.

Thus, when consumers study consumer behavior, they should come to make better decisions.

Several topics can be particularly helpful in enlightening consumers, including:

1. Consequences associated with poor budget allocation
2. The role of emotions in consumer decision making
3. Avenues for seeking redress for unsatisfactory purchases
4. Social influences on decision making, including peer pressure
5. The effect of the environment on consumer behavior

# LO4 Different Approaches to Studying Consumer Behavior

Consumer researchers have many tools and approaches with which to study consumer behavior, and researchers don't always agree on which approach is best. In reality, the consumer researcher should realize that no single best way of studying consumer behavior exists. Rather, different types of research settings

© ISTOCKPHOTO.COM/JACK HOLLINGSWORTH

# Hold the Phone! Consumers and Their Phones

Even though "car phones" have provided value to consumers for many years, the mobile phone that we know today really traces back to the Motorola "Brick" of the 1980s. We can safely say that practically all readers of this book own a mobile phone of some type. In fact, the most popular "handy," as mobiles are known in parts of Europe, now provides high-speed Internet access, serves as an MP3 player, functions as a camera, and contains many cool apps that do countless things, including real-time tracking of the World Cup and other events.

In the United States, 60% of tweens (children 10–14 years of age) have their own cell phone and over one third of teens say they couldn't live without their phone. A recent study in the United Kingdom suggested that 80% of children have a mobile phone, including over one million kids under the age of 10. As a result, the British government is encouraging public schools to create rules governing mobile phone usage in school.

Restrictions on the use of mobile phones in cars are also being enacted or considered in the interest of public safety. However, will we see greater restrictions such as "no phone" sections in restaurants? Consider the following list. In your opinion, do any of these behaviors violate acceptable mobile phone etiquette?

1. Having a mobile phone conversation at the dinner table
2. Using the mobile phone while seated on an airplane
3. Using profanity on the phone
4. Using the phone in a movie theater
5. Using the phone in a public bathroom toilet stall
6. Speaking so loudly that your phone conversation is easily heard by others 10 feet or more away from you
7. Browsing or texting while involved in a conversation with someone else
8. Using a loud and annoying ring tone

The majority of Americans consider mobile phone users to be rude. This is interesting considering that the vast majority of Americans are mobile phone users! Should public restrictions on mobile phone usage be created that govern when, where, and how a phone can be used? Studies of consumer behavior help provide input into public policy decisions on issues like these.

Sources: Krotz, J.L. (2010), "Cell Phone Etiquette: Dos and Don'ts," http://www.microsoft.com/smallbusiness/resources/ArticleReader/website/default.aspx?Print=1&ArticleId=Cellphoneetiquette dosanddonts, accessed June 19, 2010. Cairns, W. (2006), "Child Culture; Kid Consumers and Growing Pains," Brand Strategy (December 18), 46; cmch mentors for parents and children, http://www.cmch.tv/mentors/hottopic.asp?id=70, accessed June 19, 2010.

**What's the best way to study consumer behavior?**

may call for different approaches and the use of different tools. Thus, we provide a brief overview of two basic approaches for studying consumer behavior. The purpose is to provide the reader with an idea of how the knowledge found in this book was obtained. For a more detailed view of the different research approaches, the reader is referred elsewhere.[26]

# INTERPRETIVE RESEARCH

One consumer's music is just noise to another consumer. What creates value in the musical experience? What does music mean and how much does the meaning shape the value of the experience? These are questions that evoke very abstract comments and thoughts from consumers. They are questions that lend themselves well to interpretive research.[27] **Interpretive research** seeks to explain the inner meanings and motivations associated with specific consumption experiences. Consumer researchers interpret these meanings through the words that consumers use to describe events or through observation of social interactions. With this approach, researchers interpret meaning rather than analyze data.

Interpretive research generally falls into the broader category of qualitative research. **Qualitative research tools** include things such as case analyses, clinical interviews, focus group interviews, and other tools in which data are gathered in a relatively unstructured

way. In other words, consumer respondents are usually free to respond in their own words or simply through their own behavior. Data of this type requires that the researcher interprets its meaning. Such results are considered **researcher dependent** because the interpretation is a matter of opinion until corroborated by other findings.

The roots of interpretive consumer research go back over 50 years to the earliest days of consumer research. The focus was on identifying the motivations that lie behind all manners of consumer behavior, including mundane things such as coffee drinking or taking an aspirin, to more elaborate issues such as what "drives" one to buy a Ford versus a Chevy.[28] The motivational research era in consumer research, which lasted through the early 1960s, generally proved disappointing in providing satisfying explanations for consumer behavior on a large scale. Unfortunately, many interpretive research tools were scarcely applied for years afterwards. However, these approaches have made a recent comeback and are now commonly applied to many aspects of the field.

Interpretive researchers adopt one of several orientations. Two common interpretive orientations are phenomenology and ethnography. **Phenomenology** represents the study of consumption as a "lived experience." The phenomenological researcher relies on casual interviews with consumers from whom the researcher has won confidence and trust. This may be supplemented with various other ways that the consumer can tell a story. **Ethnography** has roots in anthropology and often involves analyzing the artifacts associated with consumption. An ethnographer may decide to go through trash or ask to see the inside of a consumer's refrigerator in an effort to learn about the consumer. These approaches represent viable options for consumer researchers.

© ISTOCKPHOTO.COM/COGAL

## QUANTITATIVE CONSUMER RESEARCH

Which consumer group is most likely to listen to rap music? Statistical models can be applied to retail sales data to identify clusters of music consumers based on their likelihood of buying specific types of music.[29] For example, these tools can be used to help explain how a 45-year-old consumer who buys Bob Seger music belongs to a segment that is also likely to buy a Faith Hill recording. Similarly, another segment of consumers likes the music of Nirvana and Green Day. These two segments may be differentiated on factors such as age, income, and possibly even education.

Rather than tracking buying trends, a researcher might ask which consumers are most likely to pirate music via the Internet.[30] This issue illustrates the interplay between ethics and consumer behavior. The researcher can design a questionnaire and ask consumers to respond to questions using 10-point scales. The questions seek answers to things like the risk of being prosecuted, the extent to which music stars are idolized by the consumer, and the perceived social acceptability of music pirating. Responses can be used to explain how likely a consumer is to illegally pirate music. The researcher may find that one segment of music consumers is more likely to pirate than another segment.

These studies typify quantitative research. **Quantitative research** addresses questions about consumer behavior using numerical measurement and analysis tools. The measurement is usually structured, meaning that the consumer will simply choose a response from among alternatives supplied by the researcher. In other words, structured questionnaires typically involve multiple-choice-type questions. Alternatively, quantitative research might analyze sales data tracked via the Internet or with point-of-sale scanners.

Unlike qualitative research, the data are not researcher dependent. This is because the numbers are the same no matter who the researcher may be. Typically, quantitative research better enables researchers to test hypotheses as compared to interpretive research. Similarly, quantitative research is more likely to stand on its own and does not require deep interpretation. For example, if consumers have an average attitude score of 50 for brand A and 75 for

brand B, we can objectively say that consumers tend to prefer brand B. Exhibit 1.5 summarizes some key differences between quantitative and qualitative research.[31]

**quantitative research** approach that addresses questions about consumer behavior using numerical measurement and analysis tools

## LO5 Consumer Behavior Is Dynamic

All one has to do is examine the differences in standards of living between today's consumers and the consumers living just 40, 80, or 100 years ago to gain an appreciation of how consumer behavior has changed over time. As an overall statement, we can say that consumers are never completely satisfied. Actually, this is a good thing because as companies strive to meet consumer demands, increasingly innovative products are offered, and companies grow in response to increased sales. As a result, they hire more people and raise the income levels throughout the economy.

The way marketers respond to consumers is changing dramatically. Marketers have historically used advances in technology to provide consumers with greater

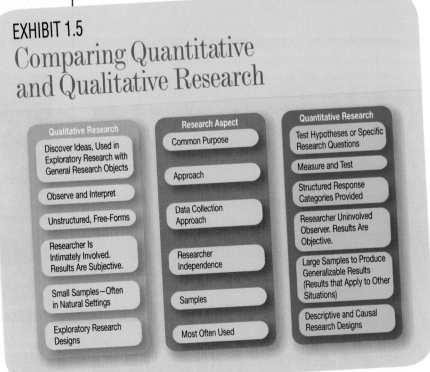

**EXHIBIT 1.5**
### Comparing Quantitative and Qualitative Research

| Qualitative Research | Research Aspect | Quantitative Research |
|---|---|---|
| Discover Ideas, Used in Exploratory Research with General Research Objects | Common Purpose | Test Hypotheses or Specific Research Questions |
| Observe and Interpret | Approach | Measure and Test |
| Unstructured, Free-Forms | Data Collection Approach | Structured Response Categories Provided |
| Researcher Is Intimately Involved. Results Are Subjective. | Researcher Independence | Researcher Uninvolved Observer. Results Are Objective. |
| Small Samples—Often in Natural Settings | Samples | Large Samples to Produce Generalizable Results (Results that Apply to Other Situations) |
| Exploratory Research Designs | Most Often Used | Descriptive and Causal Research Designs |

# The Face of the Consumer? Do You "Like" It?

**P**erhaps no consumer trend is changing consumer behavior and marketing more than consumers' widespread adoption of Internet social networking sites. Social networking is a global phenomenon and goes beyond Facebook.com, the U.S. and European favorite, to sites such as Gupshup (a Twitter-type site popular in India) and Mixi.jp (social networking Japanese-style). Marketers have utilized advancements in social networking technology to reach out to consumers. One company, 33Across, specializes in tracking consumers' interactions with one another via posts and shared messages on social networking sites. 33Across content analyzes millions of communications. This research is extremely powerful because we discuss so many of our purchases with friends and acquaintances, including Facebook friends, before and after the purchase. In addition, companies can track consumer activity at Twitter and Facebook with the help of the cookies that are essentially footprints of your online activity. As a result, advertisers can carefully target messages to consumers who should be most receptive to the message. Have you ever wondered why you see the ads that you do when browsing the Internet? Now you may have a clue why so many marketers have a big "like" for Facebook.

Sources: Steel, E. (2010), "Marketers Watch as Friends Interact Online," *The Wall Street Journal*, (April 15), B1. Patel, K. (2010), "Profiling the Facebooks of the World," *Advertising Age*, (June 14), 6. Trusov, M., R.E. Bucklin, and K. Pauwels (2009), "Effects of Word-of-Mouth Versus Traditional Marketing: Findings from an Internet Social Networking Site", *Journal of Marketing*, 73 (September), 90–102.

jara, Mexico; Seoul, South Korea; London, England; Shanghai, China; Nantes, France; or Ruston, Louisiana, he or she can relax at a Starbucks. Almost anywhere the modern consumer travels, he or she can find a familiar place to eat or drink. An Outback Steakhouse, a Pizza Hut, or a McDonald's never seems far away!

Although these chains can be found worldwide, consumers are not alike everywhere these firms operate. An Outback Steakhouse in Seoul will offer kimchi (fermented cabbage) on the menu, something neither American nor Australian. Companies must therefore deal with geographical distances as well as cultural distances. The international focus of today's modern company places a greater demand on consumer behavior research. Every culture's people will interpret products and behaviors

opportunities to communicate with companies. Today, billions of consumers around the world have 24-hour, seven-day-a-week access to markets via the Internet. Consumers do not need to wait to go to a retail store to purchase music. They can download their favorite new tunes and apps while walking down the street. Here are some of the trends that are shaping the value received by consumers today.

## INTERNATIONALIZATION

When Starbucks opened its first store in 1971, the thought may not have occurred that the concept could spread to other parts of the state of Washington or even other parts of the United States. In 1996, Starbucks opened its first store outside the United States in Tokyo, Japan. Today, consumers around the world can order up a latte at one of over 16,000 Starbucks locations in over 50 countries.[32] Whether one is on business in Guadala-

*Obviously, the success of Starbucks shows that visiting a Starbucks provides many consumers with a high-value experience no matter what country they are in.*

differently. The meanings these consumers perceive will determine the success or failure of the product being offered.

## TECHNOLOGICAL CHANGES

It is no secret that we are living in an age of ever-increasing technological advances. These advances seem to be coming at a faster pace all the time. Upon reflection, we may realize that technology has influenced business practices since the advent of industry. Certainly, many retailers felt threatened by mail-order technology that was practiced through the Sears Roebuck catalog and the telephone. In 1895, the Sears catalog contained 532 pages of products that enabled rural consumers to obtain things that would have been otherwise difficult to get.[33] Why would people go to a store when they could simply telephone and have products delivered to their door?

In the mid–20th century, television revolutionized consumer behavior. Not only did TV change advertising forever, but true home shopping became a possibility. Now, the consumer could actually see a product in use on television and then make a purchase either by picking up the phone or punching buttons on a cable remote. Why would someone go to a store?

A consumer now has 24/7 access to purchasing almost any type of product. The Internet has made geographical distance almost a nonissue. Additionally, the consumer can truly shop on his or her own schedule, not on a schedule determined by store hours. Communication technology has also advanced tremendously. Mobile communication devices continue to get smaller, and now one can access stores via the Internet using a Razr that is smaller than most wallets. The entire world is now truly the market for consumers in free countries. With this being said, total U.S. Internet retailing still accounts for less than 5% of all retailing. Internet retail sales continue to grow, but using projections from the first quarter of 2010 these sales account for only about $150 billion of the almost $3.9 trillion in 2010 U.S. sales.[34]

What types and amounts of value do consumers seek when shopping online? When a consumer needs an airline ticket, he or she is seeking a solution to a real problem. Buying an airline ticket isn't generally a fun thing to do. Thus, the consumer is primarily seeking "utilitarian" value. We discuss different types of value in the next chapter.

Although technology continues to change, the basic consumer desire for value hasn't changed. In fact, the dot.com failures of the late 1990s illustrated that companies that do not enhance the value consumers receive from the current ways of doing things fail.

Today, retailers look at Web technologies more as complementing traditional retailing than competing with the bricks-and-mortar option. A pure play (Internet-only) retailer has a difficult time competing with a shopping adventure to Harrods of London because of the gratification offered by the experience itself.

Shopping online can be a valuable experience, but are virtual shopping and "real" shopping gratifying in the same way?

> Why would people go to a store when they could simply telephone and have products delivered to their door?

## CHANGING COMMUNICATIONS

As technology has changed, so have the ways that people communicate with each other. Once upon a time, consumers' favorite form of communication was face-to-face. Today, many consumers now rank the telephone as a preferred communication method. However, the preference for voice communication over SMS messages (text messaging) varies. In fact, depending on one's age, both of those may take a back seat to social networking communications. Middle-aged consumers use email for the majority of their communications as email has replaced a large portion of phone calls. Consumers in their late 20s to 30s prefer text messaging to email. Younger consumers, including teens, prefer to communicate via Facebook or Twitter. In fact, **www.facebook.com** is second only to **www.google.com** in total page views. One in three of all Internet users in the world use Facebook each day, and the 18–24 year old demographic represents the largest user group for sites like Facebook, MySpace, and Xanga.[35] Marketers are fast learning how to use these tools to communicate with consumers.

## CHANGING DEMOGRAPHICS

In most of the Western world, notable demographic trends have shaped consumer behavior patterns greatly over the past quarter century or so. First, households increasingly include two primary income providers. In contrast to the stereotypical working dad and stay-at-home mom, families today often include two parents with a career orientation. Second, family size is decreasing throughout the United States and Europe. In Europe, families are averaging less than one child per family. As a result, the relative importance of countries as consumer markets are changing. Marketers around the world find it hard to ignore the nearly 2 billion consumers in China or the 1 billion in India. We'll discuss demographic trends more in a later chapter.

## CHANGING ECONOMY

Recent years have seen a downturn in the economy in much of the developed world. With the current high unemployment rate in the United States, consumers have less money to spend. In 2010, the U.S. unemployment rate was approximately 10 percent. As recently as 2008, U.S. unemployment was under 5 percent.[36] Additionally, other consumers are underemployed. Moreover, turmoil in financial markets around the world contributes to an economic picture that leaves consumers uneasy. As a result, consumer spending has changed in several ways. Consumers are more cautious about spending money and react more favorably to price-cutting policies. Private label brands (such as retail store brands like Walmart's Sam's Choice) become more attractive alternatives as a way of saving money. Further, consumers perceive themselves as having less discretionary income and one consequence of this is a decrease in charitable giving.[37] If the bad economy continues, consumers will likely continue to be more cautious about spending.

# 1
## Study Tools

**Located at back of the textbook**
- ❏ Rip-Out Chapter-in-Review Card

**Located at www.cengagebrain.com**
- ❏ Review Key Terms Flashcards (Print or Online)
- ❏ Download audio summaries to review on the go
- ❏ Complete practice quizzes to prepare for tests
- ❏ Play "Beat the Clock" and "Quizbowl" to master concepts
- ❏ Watch Video on ReadyMade for a real company example

# what others have thought...

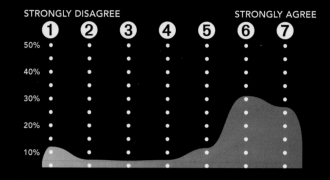

**In any business, the customer is truly the most important person.**

Most respondents tend toward agreement with this statement. Nearly 60 percent of all respondents chose *agree* or *strongly agree* with the belief that the customer is the most important person in any business. Interestingly, just over 10 percent of respondents chose *strongly disagree*. Might a student's major influence his/her response?

**Consumers are sometimes** willing to sacrifice quality and even satisfaction, but consumers never willingly sacrifice value.

## what do you think?

I get a lot out of shopping even when I don't buy anything.

STRONGLY DISAGREE (1) (2) (3) (4) (5) (6) (7) STRONGLY AGREE

Visit CourseMate at www.cengagebrain.com.

© TOOGA/THE IMAGE BANK/GETTY IMAGES

# 2

# Value and the Consumer Behavior Value Framework

After studying this chapter, the student should be able to:

**LO1** Describe the consumer value framework, including its basic components.

**LO2** Define consumer value and compare and contrast two key types of value.

**LO3** Apply the concepts of marketing strategy and marketing tactics to describe the way firms go about creating value for consumers.

**LO4** Explain the way market characteristics like market segmentation and product differentiation affect marketing strategy.

**LO5** Analyze consumer markets using elementary perceptual maps.

**LO6** Justify consumers' lifetime value as an effective focus for long-term business success.

# Introduction

Putting together a band is one thing; making a living by making music is another! Several college buddies, each majoring in business, are exploring a career in the music industry by starting and managing a band. Although they initially think the business courses they are taking are far removed from the music business, they eventually realize that many issues discussed in their marketing classes are very relevant to managing their band. After this realization, they ask several questions about the market. One key question is what makes a consumer willing to pay to hear a band or buy a tune. They all agree that probably more than anything else they can think of, one consumer can absolutely love a song that another consumer absolutely hates. They want to play emo, but is there money in emo? Katy Perry's song "California Gurls" is not exactly their style, but it was number one on the Billboard chart, so she must be doing something right!

They come across the following data showing consumer preferences for different types of music in a newspaper story:[1]

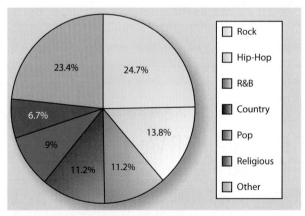

*What is your favorite type of music?*

Why do some consumers love one type of music and loathe another? The band cannot answer this question. Nevertheless, they wonder whether they should let the preferences of consumers shape the music they play. Would being consumer oriented in this way be

**Consumer Value Framework (CVF)** consumer behavior theory that illustrates factors that shape consumption-related behaviors and ultimately determine the value associated with consumption

**Customer Relationship Management (CRM)** systematic management information system that collects, maintains, and reports detailed information about customers to enable a more customer-oriented managerial approach

EXHIBIT 2.1
The Consumer Value Framework (CVF)

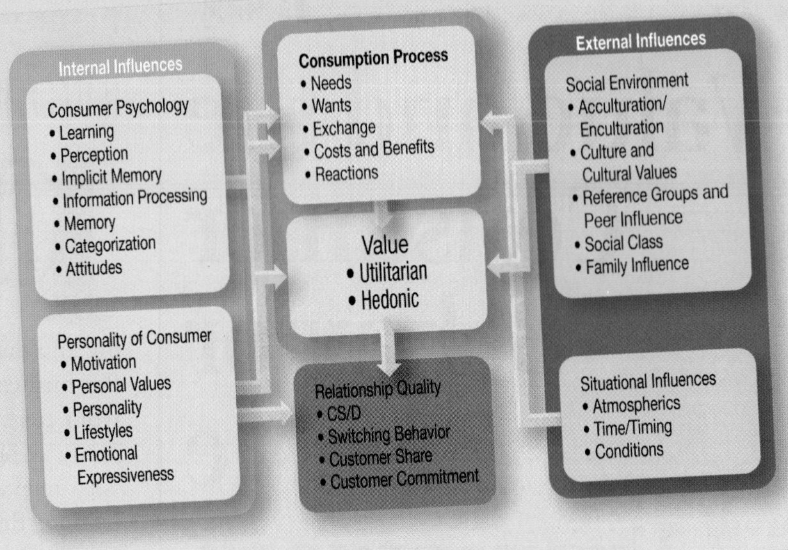


a wise business decision? Are some customers worth more than others? These are all basic consumer behavior issues that ultimately tie back to value! Can they make music that some market finds value in?

# LO1 The Consumer Value Framework and Its Components

Consumer behavior is multifaceted. Not only does the study of consumer behavior involve multiple disciplines, but anyone who has ever made a major purchase like a house, an automobile, or an apartment knows that many factors can affect both the purchase decision and the way one feels after the purchase. This book covers many of these factors.

## THE CONSUMER VALUE FRAMEWORK

Given the potential complexity involved in explaining consumption, a framework for studying consumer behavior is useful. Exhibit 2.1 displays the framework used in this book. The **Consumer Value Framework (CVF)** represents consumer behavior theory illustrating factors that shape consumption-related behaviors and ultimately determine the value associated with consumption. The different components shown with different colors roughly correspond to the different parts of this book. However, the student of consumer behavior must recognize and accept the fact that each aspect of the CVF is related in some way to other components of the model. The arrows connecting the different components typify these connections.

## VALUE AND THE CVF COMPONENTS

Value is at the heart of experiencing and understanding consumer behavior. Thus, we will never get too far from value in any chapter of this book. We'll expand more on value later in this chapter and throughout the book. In the rest of this section, we present the basic components of the CVF that either contribute to or are outcomes of value.

### Relationship Quality

Over the past two decades or so, **Customer Relationship Management (CRM)** has become a popular catchphrase, not just in marketing but in all of business. A basic CRM premise is that customers form relationships with companies as opposed to companies conducting individual transactions with customers. A CRM system tracks detailed information about customers so marketers can make more customer-oriented decisions that hopefully lead to longer-lasting relationships.

# The Grocery Game

relationship quality
degree of connectedness between a consumer and a retailer, brand, or service provider

**T**he heart of the CVF is value. Consumers around the United States are finding a lot of value by playing the Grocery Game (**www.grocerygame.com**). The game is really a process that allows consumers who are willing to put in the time and effort to stock up on groceries at dramatically discounted prices. Manufacturer coupons are one of the key game pieces. Select coupons can be tied to select retailer discounts to allow common grocery items to be purchased for less. "Green items" are free using the Grocery Game. Consumers then compete to see who can save the most money. Although buying groceries may not seem very glamorous, a lot of Grocery Game players get really excited about saving potentially hundreds of dollars each month.

The Grocery Game is not for everyone. Only consumers with a specific lifestyle orientation around thrift are strongly motivated to save money on grocery items this way. A family-oriented consumer with high monthly grocery expenses is more likely to play than is a single consumer living in a small flat. The Grocery Game clearly offers both utilitarian and hedonic value.

Source: **http://www.thegrocerygame.com/con__WhatIsTheGroceryGame.cfm**, accessed August 22, 2010.

actions with customers as a way of gathering additional information about consumers. Along the way, CVS realized that time-starved female consumers made up a large bulk of its business. Armed with information about this segment, CVS designs services aimed at creating value by making health-related services, including getting prescriptions filled, easier to accomplish. Now, rather than advertising heavily to attract new customers, CVS relies more on the same customers to seek health-related services from CVS time and time again. International companies like Dell and Home Depot have also found success in developing high relationship quality.[4]

A CRM orientation means each customer represents a potential stream of resources rather than just a single sale. **Relationship quality** reflects the connectedness between a consumer and a retailer, brand, or service provider.[2] In practice, a strong, or high-quality, relationship is typified by a consumer who buys the same brand each time a need for that product arises. Businesses see loyal customers as being more profitable than customers who are prone to switch providers each time they make a purchase.

When a consumer realizes high value from an exchange with a company, relationship quality improves. Over time, a consumer who experiences high value with one company may well become a loyal, committed customer. CVS, a large U.S.-based drugstore chain, successfully implemented a customer loyalty program founded on increased knowledge of the customer.[3] Caremark, as the program is known, offers more than just prescription drugs. Caremark extends service to a wide assortment of health management services and uses the resulting inter-

## Consumption Process

Consumers must decide to do something before they can receive value. This process involves deciding what is needed and what options for exchange are available, and includes the inevitable reaction to consumption. The consumption process can involve a great deal of decision making and thus represents a consumer decision-making process. Many factors influence this process, and these factors can be divided into two categories, internal and external influences.

## Internal Influences: The Psychology and Personality of the Consumer

**The Psychology of the Consumer.** "It's a small world after all! It's a small world. . . " Sorry! But, now that this song *is* likely stuck in your head, why *is* the song stuck in your head? Further, is getting a song stuck in someone's head a good idea if you want to sell something? Will consumers react the same way to an increase in a price

**internal influences** things that go on inside of the mind and heart of the consumer

**cognition** thinking or mental processes that go on as we process and store things that can become knowledge

**affect** feelings associated with objects or experienced during events

**individual differences** characteristic traits of individuals, including personality and lifestyle

from $80 to $100 as they would to a price decrease for the same product? Is there a good reason to sell a product for $69.99 rather than $70? All these questions involve the psychology of the consumer. In other words, these things are **internal influences**, things that are processed inside the mind of the consumer or that can be thought of as part of the consumer.

The psychology of the consumer involves both cognitive and affective processes. The term **cognition** refers to the thinking or mental processes that go on as we process and store things that can become knowledge. A child hears parents talk about smoking as a *nasty* thing to do. Smoking becomes associated with nastiness, and the child may develop a dislike of smoking. **Affect** refers to the feelings that are experienced during consumption activities or that are associated with specific objects. If the child continues to receive negative information about smoking, the belief about its being nasty may result in feelings of disgust.

Many people think of these types of things when they think of consumer behavior. Certainly, our perceptions help shape the desirability of products, which can influence decision processes and the value perceived from consumption. Recall that value is a subjective assessment. Therefore, value is very much a matter of perception.

## Stuck on Me!

Consumer research has suggested some songs that are most likely to get "stuck in your head." Once you hear one of these songs, perhaps even just a small part of the song, you can expect to have it with you, at least mentally, for some time. Nearly all consumers admit to experiencing this phenomenon. Professor James Kellaris, a faculty member at the University of Cincinnati, believes this happens because there is something that the brain perceives as inconsistent in the song, so one is motivated to replay the song in an effort to satisfy the resulting curiosity. Yes, "It's a Small World" is one such song. Think about it—*small* and *world* are inconsistent terms. Here is a list of some songs that may be stuck in your head after reading this; notice that several are songs created for an advertisement.

"It's a Small World After All" by Disney

"We Will Rock You" by Queen

"Yellow Submarine" by the Beatles

"YMCA" by the Village People

Meow Mix jingle (Meow meow meow meow, meow meow meow, …)

"Whoomp! (There It Is)" by Tag Team

"Macarena" by Los del Rio

"Bohemian Rhapsody" by Queen (…easy come, easy go, a little high, little low, anyway the wind blows…)

Free Credit Report.com (commercial jingle)

Sometimes, psychology can be difficult to explain.

Sources: Hoffman, Carey (2001), "Songs That Cause The Brain To 'Itch': UC Professor Investigating Why Certain Tunes Get Stuck in Our Heads," *UC News* (April 4), **http://www.uc.edu/news/kellaris.htm,** accessed January 10, 2007; "10 Songs Most Likely to Get Stuck in Your Head," *Advertising Age* 75 (December 20, 2004), 12; **http://www.popculturemadness.com/Music/Head-Songs.html,** accessed June 29, 2010.

**The Personality of the Consumer.** Every consumer has certain characteristics and traits that help define him or her as an individual. We refer to these traits generally as **individual differences**. Individual differences, which include personality and lifestyle, help determine consumer behavior. For example, a consumer with a lifestyle oriented toward spending time outdoors may be more likely than someone who is happier indoors to desire a convertible automobile.

Companies have spent vast amounts of money and time trying to harness individual differences in a way that would allow them to predict consumer choices. Individual differences like these include basic human motivations, which trigger consumer desires, and are thus related to product and brand preferences. Also, individual differences shape the value experienced by consumers and the reaction consumers have to consumption.

## External Influences

Why do some consumers like foods such as sushi or habañero peppers while others wouldn't consider eating these things, preferring a hot dog? Why do consumers in different parts of the world have such different tastes for food? In Korea, a typical breakfast often includes a fish soup of some type. In Australia, one might smear a bit of vegemite (a yeast extract paste resembling peanut butter in texture, but not in taste) onto toast in the morning. In the United States, a bowl of frosted flakes with cold milk poured over the top is a common way to start the day. Each of these dishes might be disgusting as a breakfast food to people in certain parts of the world. Even a simple thing like breakfast can cause quite different reactions in different consumers in different places.

*© JORGEN SCHYTTE/STILL PICTURES/PHOTOLIBRARY*

*External influences determine the value of many things, including what's for breakfast.*

These types of events typify external influences on consumers. **External influences** include the social and cultural aspects of life as a consumer. They directly impact the value of activities although the influence comes from sources outside of the consumer. External influences are critical to a thorough understanding of consumer behavior.

**Social Environment.** Consumers learn a culture, including important things like rules about what types of food are appropriate for breakfast and how to greet people. In addition, any time a consumer chooses to do something to please or appeal to another consumer, he or she has been influenced by the **social environment**. The social environment includes the people and groups who help shape a consumer's everyday experiences. Reference group influence is one mechanism through which social influences work. A child's tastes for breakfast foods are shaped very much by what he or she learns from parents, and by an innate desire to conform to their wishes.

## Situational Influences

External influences also include situational influences. **Situational influences** are unique to a time or place that can affect consumer decision making and the value received from consumption. Situational influences include the effect that the physical environment has on consumer behavior. For example, the presence of music in an environment may shape consumer behavior and even change buying patterns. Similarly, music can affect one's feelings when awaiting service. A market for music that creates positive effects on consumers exists. Other characteristics such as the economic condition at a given time also affect the value of things. Factors like these are discussed further later.

Much of the remainder of the book will be organized around the Customer Value Framework. Because it connects the different theoretical areas of consumer behavior, the CVF will be a valuable study aid. Additionally, the CVF is a good analysis tool for solving consumer behavior business problems. Lastly, the CVF is a valuable tool for businesses that are trying to understand the way consumers respond to their product offerings. Thus, the CVF is useful in developing and implementing marketing strategy.

**external influences** social and cultural aspects of life as a consumer

**social environment** elements that specifically deal with the way other people influence consumer decision making and value

**situational influences** things unique to a time or place that can affect consumer decision making and the value received from consumption

**value** a personal assessment of the net worth obtained from an activity

# LO2 Value and Two Basic Types of Value

the heart of the Consumer Value Framework, and *the* core concept of consumer behavior, is value. **Value** is a personal assessment of the *net worth* obtained from an activity. Value is what consumers ultimately pursue because valuable actions address motivations that manifest themselves in needs and desires.

In this sense, value captures how much gratification a consumer receives from consumption.

Across all types of restaurants, fast-food restaurants do not typically offer the highest food quality. When a consumer chooses a fast-food restaurant, chances are lower prices, greater convenience, or faster service are factors that outweigh a need for high food quality. Consumers in fact will repeat behavior for which they have previously experienced low satisfaction. Walmart stores do not have a relatively high consumer satisfaction index, yet many customers repeatedly visit Walmart. Walmart delivers value, as we will see in a later chapter. In contrast to these examples, contriving a situation where consumers are not seeking value is virtually impossible. In fact, everything we do in life is done in the pursuit of value.

Consumers develop value perceptions from consumption after considering all costs and benefits associated with the particular activity. In the everyday vernacular, people sometimes use *value* as a synonym for *price,* particularly *low price,* but this view is narrow-minded. We do use price to try to reflect value; however, price is in many ways a very poor proxy for value. What kinds of things are of high value to you? How easily can one put a "price" on these most valued things?

## THE VALUE EQUATION

Exhibit 2.2 reflects some important components of value and how a consumer might put these together to determine the overall worth of something—or its value! Worth to a consumer is actually a function of much more than price. Value can be modeled by playing the "what you get" from dealing with a company against the "what you have to give" to get the product. The "what you get" includes benefits or the positive consequences of consumption. The "what you give" includes sacrifices or the negative consequences of consumption. Nearly all the components in the value equation come into play when a consumer buys a product like a car that requires multiple considerations.

Later in the book a chapter is devoted to further describing value and other related concepts, including expectations, satisfaction, and quality. However, because value is an essential part of consumer behavior, a basic overview is provided in this chapter.

Value can be understood better by looking at its types. While theoretically one could probably break down value into many very specific types, a very useful value typology can be developed using only two types. Thus, we distinguish utilitarian value from hedonic value.

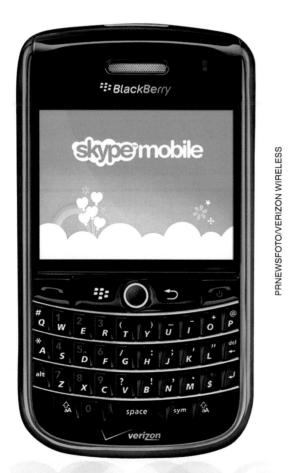

*This image shows how different technologies can be used to provide value by delivering the same benefits—in this case, communication!*

PRNEWSFOTO/VERIZON WIRELESS

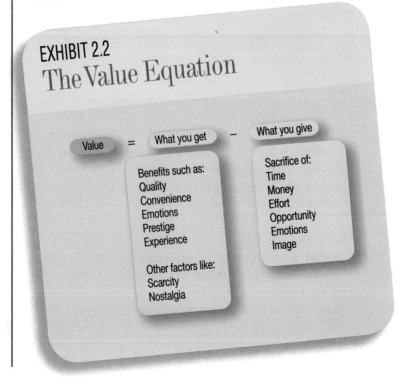

**EXHIBIT 2.2**
The Value Equation

Value = What you get − What you give

Benefits such as:
Quality
Convenience
Emotions
Prestige
Experience

Other factors like:
Scarcity
Nostalgia

Sacrifice of:
Time
Money
Effort
Opportunity
Emotions
Image

## UTILITARIAN VALUE

Activities and objects that lead to high utilitarian value do so because they help the consumer accomplish some task. **Utilitarian value** is derived from a product that helps the consumer solve problems and accomplish tasks. Consumers usually offer a rational explanation of why something is purchased when utilitarian value is the primary motivation. For instance, when a consumer buys Clorox bleach, he or she undoubtedly will be cleaning something. Quite simply, the bleach enables something to become clean. Having something clean is gratifying to the consumer even if the actual process of cleaning is not. In this sense, one can think of utilitarian value as a means to an end.[5] Value is provided because the object or activity allows something else to happen or be accomplished.

## HEDONIC VALUE

The second type of value is referred to in the consumer behavior literature as hedonic value. **Hedonic value** is the immediate gratification that comes from experiencing some activity. Seldom does one go to a horror film, ride Disney's Space Mountain, or read fiction in an effort to get a job done. With hedonic value, the value is provided entirely by the actual experience and emotions associated with consumption, not because some other end is or will be accomplished.

Conceptually, hedonic value differs from utilitarian value in several ways. First, hedonic value is an end in and of itself rather than a means to an end. Second, hedonic value is very emotional and subjective in nature. Third, when a consumer does something to obtain hedonic value, the action can sometimes be very difficult to explain objectively.

Rather than being viewed as opposites, utilitarian and hedonic value are not mutually exclusive. In other words, the same act of consumption can provide both utilitarian value and hedonic value. Dining in a place like Hard Rock Café is an event. One doesn't have to go to a Hard Rock Café to eat, but dining there is a lot of fun—an experience! However, a Hard Rock Café consumer also accomplishes the task of having something to eat—getting nourished. In fact, the very best consumer experiences are those that provide both high utilitarian value and high hedonic value.

PRNEWSFOTO/PANINI AMERICA

**utilitarian value** value derived from a product that helps the consumer with some task

**hedonic value** value derived from the immediate gratification that comes from some activity

Why is *Toy Story 3* such a huge marketing success? Parents can take the kids to the movie and accomplish the job of keeping the kids happy while at the same time enjoying the movie themselves. In this way, Disney's created a product that provides high value and the value has translated into success.

Exhibit 2.3 illustrates the value possibilities associated with consumption. A marketer that provides low

> The very best consumer experiences are those that provide both high utilitarian value and high hedonic value.

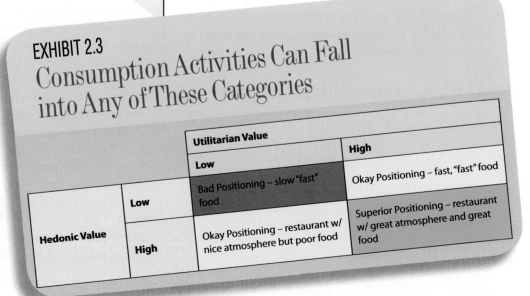

**EXHIBIT 2.3**
## Consumption Activities Can Fall into Any of These Categories

|  |  | Utilitarian Value | |
| --- | --- | --- | --- |
|  |  | **Low** | **High** |
| **Hedonic Value** | **Low** | Bad Positioning – slow "fast" food | Okay Positioning – fast, "fast" food |
|  | **High** | Okay Positioning – restaurant w/ nice atmosphere but poor food | Superior Positioning – restaurant w/ great atmosphere and great food |

levels of both values is not likely to survive very long. Generally, a consumer goes to a fast-food restaurant to accomplish the task of getting something to eat, and doing this as quickly as possible. Food quality may take a back seat to convenience. When the fast-food experience becomes slow, the consumer receives little value of either type.

In contrast, restaurants can survive by specializing in providing one type of value or the other, as would be the case in a place with a great atmosphere but perhaps less than the best food or service quality. As mentioned earlier, the best experience comes when a restaurant can put everything together—high-quality food and impeccable service all packed in a memorable place with a great atmosphere. These are the types of experiences a consumer is most likely to want to repeat.

# LO3 Marketing Strategy and Consumer Value

One way that a company can enhance the chance of long-term survival is to have an effective marketing strategy. To an army general, a strategy provides a way of winning a military conflict. Generally, a **strategy** is a planned way of doing something to accomplish some goal.

With hedonic value, the value is provided entirely by the actual experience and emotions associated with consumption, not because some other end is or will be accomplished.

## MARKETING STRATEGY

In a business environment, a **marketing strategy** is the way a company goes about creating value for customers. The strategy should provide an effective way of dealing with both competition and eventual technological obsolescence by making sure that value is delivered in a way that is not easily duplicated by other companies and not defined only in terms of the tangible product offered.

A complete understanding of the value consumers seek is needed to effectively develop and implement a strategy. AT&T may compete directly with Sprint, but AT&T also competes with companies like Skype, which provides local, long-distance, and even international calling via the Internet, all for prices much lower than traditional telephone services. The consumer who uses Internet calling services like Skype no longer needs a telephone to receive the benefits of talking to friends and family who are far away, and computer-to-computer calls are free. If AT&T laid out a marketing strategy that depended on people buying and owning "phones," technological obsolescence would represent a real threat. A better strategic orientation would focus on providing value by enabling and facilitating communication. Verizon, another AT&T competitor, makes Skype calls available through select mobile phones. All of these companies have to focus on the core benefits they provide, in this case all derived from electronic communication. Without this focus, companies run the risk of developing **marketing myopia**, defined as a company that views itself in a product business, rather than in a value, or benefits producing, business.[6] Thus, when technology makes the product obsolete, the myopic business goes out of business. In contrast, the company that focuses on value creation builds solutions around the need, not the physical product.

Strategies exist at several different levels. Exhibit 2.4 demonstrates this point. Basically, **corporate strategy** deals with how the firm will be defined and sets general goals. This strategy is usually associated with a specific corporate culture, which provides an operating orientation for the company. Marketing strategy then follows. Different business units within the firm may have different marketing strategies. In describing how value is created, the strategies tell why customers will choose to buy things from the company.

Strategies must eventually be implemented. Implementation deals with operational management. In marketing, this level includes activities known as tactics. **Marketing tactics**, which involve price, promotion, product, and distribution decisions, are ways marketing management is implemented. Together, marketing

## EXHIBIT 2.4
# Business Strategy Exists at Different Levels

**Corporate Culture**

CORPORATE STRATEGY

↓

MARKETING STRATEGY

↓

TACTICS

strategy and marketing tactics should maximize the total value received by a company's customers.

# TOTAL VALUE CONCEPT

Products are multifaceted and can provide value in many ways. Even a simple product like a soft drink offers consumers more than a cold drink that addresses one's desire to quench a thirst. If a soft drink were a product that provided value only as a thirst quencher, the market share statistics for soft drink brands would certainly be different than they are today. Exhibit 2.5 shows U.S. soft drink market share data. Global data also shows Coke and Pepsi as the leading players.[7]

As can be seen, Coca-Cola accounts for just less than half of all soft drinks sold. Taken together, the big-name companies represent nearly 90% of all soft drink sales. A quick visit to the supermarket will verify that Coke is far from a bargain product as soft drinks go. Brands such as Faygo and Shasta offer soft drinks at prices far lower on average than Coke. And often, consumers do not have a palate accurate enough to select their favorite brand in a blind taste test. Yet brands like Faygo and Shasta have a fraction of the market share that Coke enjoys. The fact of the matter is that Coke is more than colored, carbonated, flavored water. As ads have proclaimed, "Coke adds life!" It may be just as accurate to say Coke is a "way of life." One

can look back to the 1980s and see what happened when "old" Coke was pulled from the market in favor of "new" Coke. Consumers revolted and demanded that Coke be restored, even though the "new" Coke was supported by millions of dollars of research that focused on flavor. But flavor explains only one small part of the total value offered by a *Coke*.

Some products require installation or other types of service before one can enjoy any benefits. The Apple iPad is a technological marvel. However, without a service plan the technology offers practically no benefits and, therefore, no value. Additionally, the owner will want at least some of the over 200,000 apps offered by Apple—each offering some new benefit ranging from gaming to scanning bar codes. The term **augmented product** means the original product plus

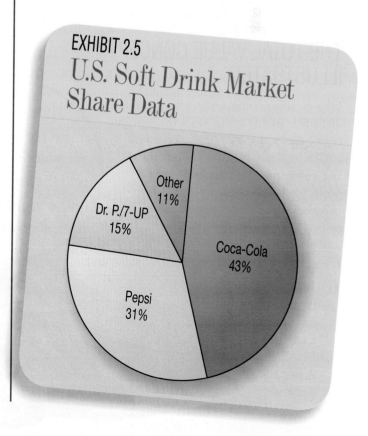

## EXHIBIT 2.5
# U.S. Soft Drink Market Share Data

- Other 11%
- Dr. P./7-UP 15%
- Coca-Cola 43%
- Pepsi 31%

the extra things needed to increase the value for consumption.

Thus, every product's value is made up of the basic benefits, plus the augmented product, plus the "feel" benefits. A company must try to understand all the ways a product offers value to its customers. The **total value concept** is practiced when companies operate with the understanding that products provide value in multiple ways. Many products and brands, for instance, provide some benefits that produce utilitarian value and some that provide hedonic value. This value, in turn, helps provide a brand with meaning in the consumer psyche.

> Every product's value is made up of the basic benefits, plus the augmented product, plus the "feel" benefits. A company must try to understand all the ways a product offers value to its customers.

## THE TOTAL VALUE CONCEPT ILLUSTRATED

Let's consider a consumer who purchases a 2011 Ferrari 458 Italia. Does the consumer buy the car for its 570 horsepower V-8 engine, carbon-filament doors, bright red color, or dual-clutch 7-speed gear box? No, the consumer buys the car because of the total value offered. How does the Ferrari Italia offer value?[8] The answer may not be the same for all consumers, but here are some likely value factors:

1. **Transportation.** The Ferrari solves the job of getting a consumer from point A to point B. This is

*How does the Ferrari provide value? If you understand this, you understand the total value concept.*

one way the Ferrari provides value—utilitarian value in this case.

2. **The Ferrari service plan.** A Ferrari needs TLC. Ferrari offers a 3-year warranty, which means for at least 3 years, the problem of repairing the Ferrari is solved—utilitarian value added.

3. **The feelings associated with driving the car.** The car is very fast and handles well. It has a top speed of just over 200 mph. Of course Ferrari owners always obey the speed limit—right?! The excitement that is the Ferrari driving experience provides hedonic value.

4. **The positive feelings that go along with ownership.** The Ferrari owner will certainly take pride in the car. A Ferrari jacket and cap help make the statement, "I'm a Ferrari owner." He or she can impress friends with a drive on PCH1. He or she may believe that increased social status is a benefit of being a Ferrari owner. The realization of ownership provides hedonic value.

5. **The negative feelings that go along with ownership.** Hopefully, our Ferrari owner is independently wealthy. At a price tag of over $200,000 USD, the car loan could be the size of a modest mortgage—not including insurance. In addition, the Ferrari requires expensive service upkeep. If the Ferrari is a financial strain, then worry will result when the owner thinks about the car. Friends may have also suggested that Ferraris are unreliable. All of these feelings may distract from the hedonic value offered by the car.

Altogether, most readers would certainly like to own the Ferrari but probably not care to pay the high price. Thus, the Ferrari does not offer enough benefits for us to make the necessary sacrifice. A Honda Civic may do the trick, although the hedonic to utilitarian value ratio may not be the same as with a Ferrari.

Automobile marketers sometimes miss the total value equation for their product. In 2005, General Motors began to offer consumers a "total value promise." They hoped this would convey the value of extended

IMAGINECHINA VIA AP IMAGES

warranties, more standard equipment, and lower sticker prices to consumers. Was GM missing something if they believed total value is confined to these tangible aspects?

A few years ago, GM created a discount program in which consumers received the employee discount on new car purchases. This program was wildly successfully in producing sales. Among other factors, GM's plan was increase the value equation in the consumer's favor both by lowering the price and creating positive feelings during the buying process. Consumers perceived themselves as getting a great deal and thus the program added hedonic value.[9] But by 2009, GM had gone through bankruptcy and survived only with drastic government intervention. The reasons for their poor performance are many, but some claim that once the drastic discounting began, consumers felt no need to accept any GM products at premium "non-employee" prices, and the company increasingly lost money. This illustrates a danger of deep discounting. It's easy to cut prices to gain a little business, but the gain in business comes at a drop in margin that proves very difficult to get back. That is, as consumers learned the price at which to buy a GM product, GM could no longer obtain a gross margin from purchases sufficient to sustain profitability.

Innovation is necessary to provide consumers with high value. When a firm practices the total value concept, a full understanding of how value can be created from a product is necessary. In the future, Ferrari might consider rolling routine service into the warranty plan as a way of enhancing value—particularly given the reliability of competitors. Total value is also affected by the technologies and infrastructures that exist. For instance, is Ferrari researching a way to provide value if gasoline-powered engines or high-speed highways become obsolete? What value would a Ferrari offer if you couldn't drive it?[10]

## VALUE IS CO-CREATED

A marketer can only propose a way of creating value to consumers. In other words, a marketer alone cannot create value.[11] Rather, the consumer adds resources in the form of knowledge and skills to do his or her own part in the consumption process. Value is not created solely by the marketer's offering; consumption involves **value co-creation**. Rosetta Stone can offer language instruction to consumers via their specialized software. However, the consumer can only realize value from the offer by purchasing the product and applying effort and skills. In many instances, a bad consumption experience is not entirely the fault of the business. The consumer plays a role in the value equation as well.

# LO4 Market Characteristics: Market Segments and Product Differentiation

marketing management involves managing the marketing mix and deciding to whom a marketing effort will be directed. The **marketing mix** is simply the combination of product, pricing, promotion, and distribution strategies used to position some product or brand in the marketplace. The marketing mix represents the way a marketing strategy is implemented within a given market or exchange environment. Marketers often use the term **target market** to signify which market segment a company will serve with a specific marketing mix. Thus, target marketing requires that managers identify and understand market segments. But, what exactly is market segmentation?

## MARKET SEGMENTATION

**Market segmentation** is the separation of a market into groups based on the different demand curves associated with each group. Market segmentation is a marketplace condition; numerous segments exist in some markets, but very few segments may exist in others. We can think of the total quantity of a product sold as a simple mathematical function ($f$) like this:[12]

$$Q = f(p, w, x, ...z)$$

where $Q$ = total quantity sold, $p$ = price, and $w, x,$ and $z$ are other characteristics of the particular product. The function means that as price and the other characteristics are varied, the quantity demands changes.

For example, as the price of HDTVs decreases, the quantity sold increases; in other words, there is a negative relationship between price and quantity sold.

This type of relationship represents the typical price–quantity relationship commonly depicted in basic economics courses. As the length of the warranty increases ($w$ in this case), more HDTVs are sold. Thus, if we limit the demand equation to two characteristics (price $p$ and warranty $w$ in this case), the equation representing demand for HDTVs overall might be

$$Q = -3p + 2w$$

The numbers, or coefficients, preceding $p$ and $w$, respectively, for each group represent the sensitivity of each segment to each characteristic. The greater the magnitude (absolute value) of the number, the more sensitive a group is to a change in that characteristic. In economics, **elasticity** is a term used to represent market sensitivity to changes in price or other characteristics.[13] This equation suggests that consumers are more sensitive to price than warranty, as indicated by the respective coefficients, –3 for price and +2 for warranty in this case.

However, this overall demand "curve" may not accurately reflect any one particular consumer. Instead, the market may really consist of two groups of consumers that produce this particular demand curve when aggregated. In other words, the two groups may be of equal size and be represented by equations that look something like this:

$$q_1 = -1p + 3w$$

$$q_2 = -5p + 1w$$

In this case, $q_1$ and $q_2$ represent the quantity that would be sold in groups one and two, respectively. Group one is more sensitive to the warranty ($|3| > |1|$), and group two is more sensitive to price ($|-5| > |1|$). If we put all the segments together, we get total demand once again:

$$Q = q_1 + q_2$$

Thus, a market for any product is really the sum of the demand existing in individual groups or segments of consumers. The fast-food market may consist of many segments, including a group most interested in low price, a group most interested in food quality, a group most interested in convenience, and perhaps a group that is not extremely sensitive to any of these characteristics. Market segmentation is not really a marketing tactic because the segments are created by consumers through their unique preferences. Market segmentation is critically important to

effective marketing though, and part of the marketing researcher's job is identifying segments and describing the segment's members based on characteristics such as age, income, geography, and lifestyle.

Exhibit 2.6 depicts the market segmentation process. For simplicity, we consider the quantity sold as a function of only price. The frame on the left depicts overall quantity demanded. Typically, as price goes up (moves right on the x-axis), the quantity sold goes down, meaning price is negatively related to quantity. The frame on the right breaks this market into three segments:

1. The orange line depicts a segment that is highly sensitive to price. Changes in price correspond to relatively large changes in sales. In this particular case, price increases reduce the quantity demanded.

2. The green line represents a segment also sensitive to price so that higher prices are demanded less, but this segment is not nearly as sensitive as the first segment. Changes in price are not associated with as large of a change in quantity sold.

3. The violet line turns out to be perhaps most interesting. Here, when price goes up, the quantity sold actually goes up, too. Thus, the group is sensitive to price but actually buys more at a higher price than at a lower price.

Actually, although a positive relationship between price and quantity may seem unusual, *backward sloping demand*, a term used in economics to refer to this situation, is hardly rare. When one considers product

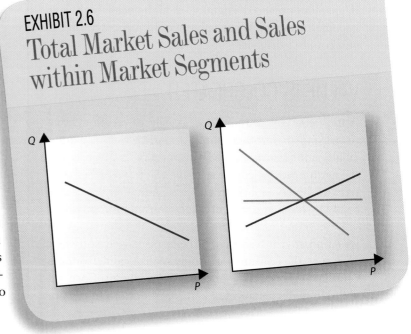

**EXHIBIT 2.6**
**Total Market Sales and Sales within Market Segments**

category demand, a market segment for many products will feature a positive price–quantity demand relationship. For instance, how much perfume with a brand name Trés Cher could be sold in a gallon container for $2? Probably not very much! However, Chanel No. 5 is highly demanded at about $250 an ounce!

Earlier, we discussed the soft drink market in the context of the total value concept, and how higher-priced brands were the best sellers. If we think of the change in price as the difference in price between the bargain brands and Coke, most consumers seem to prefer higher-priced sodas. At the very least, soft drink consumers are insensitive to price. Although this may seem inconsistent with "rational" economics, consumer behavior theory offers an explanation. Name-brand soft drinks like Coke simply are worth more, meaning they are more valuable, than bargain soft drinks. This is a very important point to understand. Ultimately, consumer segments exist because different consumers do not value different alternatives the same way.[14]

Market segments are associated with unique value equations just as they are associated with unique demand equations. Thus, if each segment is offered a product that closely matches its particular sensitivities, all segments can receive high value. This brings us to product differentiation.

# PRODUCT DIFFERENTIATION

**Product differentiation** is a marketplace condition in which consumers do not view all competing products as identical to one another. We refer to commodities very often as products that are indistinguishable across brands and/or manufacturers—that is, no matter who produced them or where they were produced. Regular gasoline approaches a commodity status, but even here, a few consumers will regard certain brands as unique. In contrast, consumers do not all consider Internet retailers the same way. Some purchasers consider a third-party seller like eBay inconvenient and only visit if there is something there that they cannot find easily elsewhere. Conversely, other consumers view the eBay shopping and buying process as intrinsically entertaining and a source of high hedonic value. In this case, market segments can be identified based on the way different consumers view Internet shopping and their differing sensitivities to characteristics of Internet transactions. Fortunately, these segments often align with consumer characteristics like age or generation that enable marketers to reach, communicate with, and serve the segments more efficiently.[15]

**product differentiation** marketplace condition in which consumers do not view all competing products as identical to one another

**product positioning** way a product is perceived by a consumer

**perceptual map** tool used to depict graphically the positioning of competing products

# LO5 Analyzing Markets with Perceptual Maps

**P**roduct differentiation becomes the basis for **product positioning**. Positioning refers to the way a product is perceived by a consumer and can be represented by the number and types of characteristics that consumers perceive. A standard marketing tool is a perceptual map.

## PERCEPTUAL MAPS

A **perceptual map** is used to depict graphically the positioning of competing products. When marketing analysts examine perceptual maps, they can identify competitors, identify opportunities for doing more business, and diagnose potential problems in the marketing mix. For instance, the analyst may realize that by changing the amount of some product characteristic, they can "move"

**ideal points** combination of product characteristics that provide the most value to an individual consumer or market segment

closer to some segment's ideal point and thus increase the competitiveness of the product. Alternatively, a new business may choose to position a product in a way that leaves it facing little direct competition. This can be done by "locating" the product as far away from other brands as possible.

# ILLUSTRATING A PERCEPTUAL MAP

Exhibit 2.7 illustrates a perceptual map. Perceptual mapping is used throughout this book as a way to link differences in consumer behavior to changes in marketing strategy or tactics. In this case, the perceptual map has been generated by a consulting firm exploring the possibility of a new radio station in the Springdale market.

The researcher has collected data on nine radio stations and on the **ideal points**—the combination of characteristics providing the most value—of six Springdale radio consumer segments. These ideal points are indicated by stars. The *x*- and *y*-axes of this perceptual map are dimensions used to separate competitors on a specific characteristic. Here, the *x*-axis separates radio stations based on the era of music they feature. Stations feature music from the 1960s through today. The *y*-axis separates radio stations based on how much the format features news and talk versus music.[16] The analyst can draw several conclusions from the perceptual map including:

1. Stations playing contemporary music with very

little news and talk experience the most intense competition. WEAK, WAKY, WOBL, and WYME all offer "late-model" music with very little news and talk. Thus, they compete rather directly.

2. The blue segment (indicated by the blue star) finds the most value in "late-model" music with little news and talk. Currently, WAKY has the highest share of this segment (the ideal point is very close to WAKY's location).

3. WATE, which plays 1980s music mixed with news and talk, appeals very strongly to the orange segment. This could be a very loyal market segment for WATE.

4. WXPC does not have a format similar to any ideal point.

5. The purple segment appears practically unserved.

After analyzing the perceptual map, the analyst draws several conclusions:

1. Because the station is a start-up without massive resources, an "oldies" format with nearly all music is recommended in an attempt to capitalize on the purple segment.

2. The highest demand quadrant appears to be quadrant 1, with contemporary music and little news/talk. A lot of resources would be required to start here because of the entrenched competition. Thus, option 1 appears preferable.

3. A potential threat exists if WXPC were to decrease the amount of news and talk, thus moving them toward the purple ideal point; however, this appears unlikely. If WXPC were to undergo a format change, a move to more news and talk to try to capitalize on the red segment's ideal point appears easier because of the relative proximity.

# USING CONSUMER BEHAVIOR THEORY IN MARKETING STRATEGY

Businesses are constantly using consumer behavior to make better strategic and operational marketing decisions. We will focus on using consumer behavior in business decision making many times throughout this book. Students, and practicing managers for that matter, sometimes struggle with the application aspect of consumer behavior. Essentially, this comes down to effective decision making. Checklists can be a useful aid to decision making as a way to effectively develop marketing strategy and tactics. Exhibit 2.8 displays

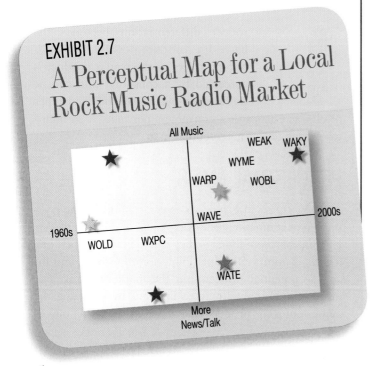

**EXHIBIT 2.7**
A Perceptual Map for a Local Rock Music Radio Market

EXHIBIT 2.8

# The CB Idea Checklist

| Question | Idea |
|---|---|
| What specific consumer needs and desires are involved?<br>• Is a specific product(s) involved in this situation?<br>• Can something else provide the same value or address the same need or desire? | |
| How is the product positioned (types and amounts of value intended)?<br>How is our position superior to competitors?<br>• How can we move closer to desirable ideal points? How is our position inferior to competitors?<br>• How can we isolate ourselves from competition? | |
| How does the consumer actually receive value from this company?<br>• In the current situation,<br>Has value been diminished?<br>Can value be enhanced?<br>• Can the product be modified to enhance value?<br>• Can the company introduce a new product to enhance value?<br>• Can the company add services to improve value for consumers?<br>• Can communication be improved?<br>• Is a competitor in a better position to provide superior value?<br>• If so, how? | |
| Where is this product consumed?<br>• Can value be enhanced by changing the consumption setting? | |
| Who?<br>• Is buying the product?<br>1. Individual Consumers<br>2. Groups of Consumers (Families)<br>3. Business Consumers<br>• Is not buying the product? | |
| Why should a consumer?<br>• Buy this product?<br>• Avoid this product? | |
| When do consumers?<br>• Find the product most valuable?<br>• Find the product least valuable? | |
| What are the key CVF elements involved in understanding the consumption process in this case? | |
| Is additional consumer research needed?<br>• Will the information be worth what it would cost to obtain it?<br>• What type of research would be required? | |

a consumer behavior analysis checklist—the CB idea checklist.

**Customer Lifetime Value (CLV)** approximate worth of a customer to a company in economic terms; overall profitability of an individual consumer

# LO6 Value Today and Tomorrow— Customer Lifetime Value

**W**e defined marketing earlier as value-producing activities that facilitate exchange. In other words, marketing makes exchange more likely. Exchange is far from a one-way street. Both consumers and companies enter exchanges seeking value. The value a company receives from exchange may be slightly easier to explain than the value a consumer receives. Obviously, when a consumer spends money for a product, the company receives economic resources in the form of revenue, which the company can use to pay employees, cover costs, and help the firm grow. The company may also receive additional benefits if the consumer becomes a loyal customer who is an advocate for the firm's products.

Not every customer is equally valuable to a firm. Firms increasingly want to know the customer lifetime value associated with a customer or customer segment.[17] **Customer Lifetime Value (CLV)** represents the approximate worth of a customer to a company in economic terms. Put another way, CLV is the overall, long-term profitability of an individual consumer. Although there is no generally accepted formula for the CLV, the basic idea is simple and can be represented as follows:

$$CLV = npv \text{ (sales} - \text{costs)} + npv \text{ (equity)}$$

The customer lifetime value is equal to the net present value (*npv*) of the stream of profits over a customer's lifetime plus the worth attributed to the equity a good customer can bring in the form of positive referrals and word of mouth. Consider a consumer shopping twice weekly at IKEA (see **www.ikea.com**). On average, this IKEA customer spends $200 per week, or $10,400 per year. If we assume a 5% operating margin, this customer yields IKEA a *net* $520 per year. Even if any potential positive word of mouth is not considered, the consumer is worth about $9,000 to

**Consumers see IKEA as a value provider; in return, each regular customer is highly valuable to IKEA.**

IKEA today assuming a 30-year life span and a 4% annual interest rate. Interestingly, until recently Walmart did not record customer-level data. Thus, out of over 500 terabytes of data, they had no data on CLV.[18] In contrast, other firms, from convenience stores to Harrah's Casinos, have elaborate systems for tracking individual customer behavior and targeting these consumers with individualized promotions and products. This allows them to practice one-to-one marketing in a real sense and to identify segments of consumers containing a high proportion of very valuable customers. For instance, one retailer found that high CLV customers tend to have the following characteristics:[19]

- Female
- 30–50 years of age
- Married
- $90,000 income
- Loyalty card holder

In contrast, the low CLV customers tend to have quite different characteristics:

- Male
- 24–44 years of age
- Single
- Less than $70,000 income
- Single channel shopper (meaning only Internet or only stores)

Thus, marketers can maximize the value they receive from exchange by concentrating their marketing efforts on consumers with high CLVs.

# Is It the Real Cheese? Does Anyone Care?

I s it just blue cheese? Well, to some consumers cheese is cheese and, especially, blue cheese is blue cheese. If you are in the cheese business, though, you realize that some consumers recognize the real cheese from the pretenders. When it comes to blue cheese, consumers who find value in, and are therefore sensitive to, the authenticity of cheese, are willing to spend more for Stilton cheese. Governments, including the European Union (E.U.), recognize the uniqueness of certain products with geographical identification, such as Champagne, Parma hams, Dijon mustard, and Stilton cheese, by protecting their names by law. Thus, only the blue-veined cheese produced in three counties in England can legally be called Stilton. Curiously, cheese makers from the town of Stilton, England, cannot call their cheese Stilton. The town lies outside the three-county region legally recognized as producing authentic Stilton cheese. The E.U. protects over 800 products with specific regional authenticity. True Champagne comes from the Champagne region of France. A wine producer from any other area that calls its wine Champagne risks legal problems and is potentially misleading customers because their products are not authentic. Authenticity is a potential product characteristic that creates product differentiation. There are segments of consumers sensitive to authenticity and others that are not. Which segment are you in?

Sources: Miller, J.W. (2009), "English Village Tries to Milk a Connection to Its Cheesy Past," *The Wall Street Journal*, (12/8), A1. Beverland, M. B., F. Farrelly and P. G. Quester (2010), "Authentic Subcultural Membership: Antecedents and Consequences of Authenticating Acts and Authoritative Performances," *Psychology & Marketing*, 27 (July), 698-716.

# 2 Study Tools

**Located at back of the textbook**

☐ Rip-Out Chapter-in-Review Card

**Located at www.cengagebrain.com**

☐ Review Key Terms Flashcards (Print or Online)

☐ Download audio summaries to review on the go

☐ Complete practice quizzes to prepare for tests

☐ Play "Beat the Clock" and "Quizbowl" to master concepts

☐ Watch Video on Evo for a real company example

## what others have thought...

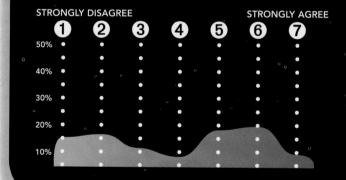

STRONGLY DISAGREE  ① ② ③ ④ ⑤  STRONGLY AGREE ⑥ ⑦

50% 40% 30% 20% 10%

**I get a lot out of shopping even when I don't buy anything.**

They have thought about everything! Responses are almost equally distributed across all seven responses from *strongly disagree* to *strongly agree*. Imagine how different the consumption orientations for those who strongly disagree must be from those who strongly agree!

## Case 1-1

### Total Marketing Strategy: You Won't Come Back by Chance

*Written by Adilson Borges, Ph.D., Reims Management School*

On February 9, 2000, the European Commission accepted a merger between the two biggest French oil companies, Totalfina and Elf Aquitaine, to become The Total Group. The Total Group became the sixth largest oil company in the world.[1] Operating in more than 130 countries, Total has activities in all aspects of the oil industry: exploration, refining and distribution petroleum, and petrochemical products. The consolidation between the two companies was particularly challenging for the company's retail division because many Total and Elf outlets, each offering gas/diesel and a convenience store, are located within a common trade zone.

Moreover, certain aspects of consumer behavior make the marketing strategy decisions resulting from the merger even more complex. For instance, consumer motivations and decision making for convenience products like those offered by the Total Group are very much based on getting high utilitarian value. Most consumers choose using only two simple thoughts: which place is closest, and which place has the lowest prices? With the central product being a commodity, competition in the convenience store industry is extremely fierce and comes not only from other convenience stores, but from other retail formats as well. Hypermarkets like Carrefour pursue a very aggressive price policy and offer gas at particularly low prices as a way of luring customers. This was the context in which Total operates its challenging fusion in its retail stores. With all this in mind, Total made some key marketing strategy decisions.

First, to reduce the risk of cannibalization, Total closed relatively low performing stores within trade areas. In this way, a single store might be left to serve the same trade area where two stores had existed before.

Second, Total used consumer research to identify two primary market segments with differing perceptions and sensitivities to convenience store attributes. The research distinguished these segments based on whether they represent urban or rural consumers. For the rural segment, where competition is less dense, the company created the Elan brand, which by 2009 had 1,800 stores. In the urban area, the company used a segmentation strategy based on two key consumer benefits used by consumers when choosing a gas station: price and convenience. For the price sensitive segment, the company repositioned the Elf brand. The company reduced the service level to cut costs and cut prices, particularly for gas. The Elf brand competes particularly with the hypermarkets. Many Elf stores operate in highly competitive trade zones. In 2009, the company operated 300 Elf stations. Beyond price, Total looked to capitalize on convenience oriented consumers. The Total Group positioned their gas station "Total" for this segment, having gas prices slightly over the average prices found in the market. Total operates over 2,400 gas stations in France as of 2009. Total offers increased service levels and a greater product assortment in the "Bonjour" convenience store found at every Total location. As a result of these strategies, Elf stores are primarily situated in suburban areas where more hypermarkets are situated and Total stores are primarily situated inside the cities, where wealthier and more time conscious consumers reside. Total also developed a loyalty program to reward its best customers.

The *Bonjour* stores create some issues for Total and some potential value for consumers. The increase in the number of SKUs (stock keep unit – each product has a unique SKU) makes distribution an issue. Total, realizing distribution of general merchandise is not a core competency, decided to partner with a French grocery retailer (Casino) and have them supply general merchandise to the *Bonjour* stores. The partnership has been a win-win situation. For Total it reduced the logistics costs associated with the stores, as well as increasing the quality of the overall assortment. Total consumers could now find more than 3,000 different products in the *Bonjour* stores, including fruits and vegetables. Total also redesigned the store layout to increase the feelings of spaciousness, allow more natural light and hopefully, increase hedonic shopping value. Total offers a full range of car services (engine oil exchange, car washing, etc.) in contrast to Elf or the hypermarkets who offer no additional services.

Total uses the tag line, "Total: you won't come back by chance," in all its advertising. You can find some Total ads at YouTube or other video archive sites. The advertising always stresses the kindness of the store employees and the concern that all Total employees put the customer above all.

### Exhibit 1: Sales (volume per gas station)

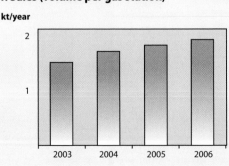

kt/year

2003  2004  2005  2006

*Reprinted with permission from the author

Exhibit 1 shows sales results for the first four years following the merger. Kt/year means thousands of metric tons of product per year. The results look impressive. The sales in volume have increased significantly from 2000 through 2003. Since the market is very competitive and always moving, it becomes complicated to compare the results after that period. However, the company is still today focusing on quality and differentiation in its Total stores. One of the last moves of the company is its new type of gas, developed by Total R&D. This gas is assumed to have a high performance with engines and it is sold in the Total stores.

Total is proving that understanding consumer behavior can help tailor better and more efficient marketing strategies.

## Questions

1. What is the perceptual map for the gas station companies in France (Elan, Elf, Total, and the hypermarkets)? What would be the two dimensions you would use to best describe the portfolio of brands that Total Group has in its market?

2. Based on the perceptual map, propose a set of marketing actions, beyond those that have been mentioned, that should be used by Total brand. Use the 4Ps framework to propose these actions and link each action to the CVF framework.

3. What are the things that may build utilitarian and hedonic value when consumers go for a gas station? Describe how an Elf store might increase value in consumers' shopping experience.

4. What are the marketing segments that each store is trying to cover? What are the fundamental benefits that consumers in each of those segments are seeking when choosing a gas station? Do you think Total Group has done a good job identifying market segments and appealing to these segments? Are some segments left unserved by Total?

## Case 1-2

### Not Buying Organic? Why Not?

*Written by Nancy Artz, Ph.D., University of Southern Maine and Dudley Greeley, USM Sustainability Coordinator*

Like many consumers, Jill would like to buy organic food, but as a college student she doesn't feel she can afford it. Oh, she'll treat herself to Newman's Own® organic cookies when studying for finals, but she normally buys conventional foods when grocery shopping.

When Jill gets a good-paying job, she expects to be like her aunt who shops at Whole Foods, a retailer selling premium-priced natural and organic foods. Jill's aunt is part of the LOHAS segment, which stands for Lifestyles of Health and Sustainability. According to the Natural Marketing Institute, the LOHAS segment represents 19% of the U.S. adult population. LOHAS consumers are dedicated to personal and planetary health, and are more likely than other consumers to buy "green" products.[1]

The organic food market has grown rapidly, but still represents less than 4% of all food products sold in the U.S.[2] Why is organic's share of the market so much smaller than the size of the LOHAS segment? "Organic shoppers" tend to buy organic in a limited range of product categories, and even in those product categories they switch back and forth between organic and nonorganic purchases.

Have you ever wondered why organic garners a higher share of the food market than the apparel market? Jill and her aunt want to protect the environment, but they particularly value the perceived health benefit they associate with organic food. They don't see a health benefit from organic clothes, so that may explain why the product attribute of "organic" drives food sales more than clothing sales. Alternatively, the price differential for organic may be greater for clothes than food. Either way, purchasing is clearly driven by consumer perception of value: consumers choose organic when the benefits of organic exceed the costs.

Jill will be surprised to learn in her green marketing class that scientific research is equivocal about the health benefits of organic food. Some studies suggest a range of possible health benefits,[3] while a comprehensive review of the literature concludes that organic food is not appreciably healthier.[4] There is, however, clear evidence that organic farming is substantially better for farm workers and the environment. Tens of thousands of farm workers die each year from workplace exposure to agricultural pesticides, worldwide.[5] Organic farming also provides the benefits of fostering biodiversity and reducing soil erosion, water use, water contamination, and carbon dioxide emissions that contribute to climate change.[6]

Will Jill's new understanding change her or her aunt's consumption of organic food? Possibly. Green products are generally more successful when the benefits of green attributes are experienced directly by the purchaser, rather than spread across society. Energy-efficient light bulbs and appliances, for example, sell relatively well because the higher initial price is more than offset by lower utility bills – a direct benefit for the purchaser. In contrast, green electricity from renewable energy sources has a low market share because the higher purchase price is not offset by long-term energy savings – the environmental benefits are distributed across society rather than going to the specific purchaser.

*Reprinted by permission of the authors.

Understanding how green attributes and price affect perceived value is no easy task for a marketer. Surveys have long reported that large numbers of consumers say they are willing to pay more for environmentally-friendly products. But what consumers say in a survey doesn't necessarily reflect what they actually do in the marketplace. While a small niche of environmentalists will pay more for green products, the majority of consumers won't pay more or give up other product benefits to buy green. Instead, consumers use green attributes to break a tie between otherwise comparable products.[7] Consumers even hesitate to pay more or invest in energy efficiency when a 25% return on investment is expected! Why? Consumers are extremely sensitive to the price they have to pay now, while undervaluing future benefits.

Finally, consider Jill's claim that she would buy organic foods more often if she could afford the higher price. How would Jill react if a friend points out that Jill routinely pays more for other discretionary product attributes? Jill won't pay $1.50/pound for organic carrots, but she happily pays $1.79/pound for prewashed, mini-carrots. Her frequent purchases of frozen dinners and processed packaged foods cost much more than the same food made with fresh organic produce, such as organic pasta bought in bulk. Jill also buys $1.50 bottled water for lunch, when "free" tap water in her community is renowned for its purity and taste.

Welcome to the field of consumer behavior in which consumer actions are rarely as straightforward as consumers realize!

## Questions

1. The Consumer Value Framework (Exhibit 2.1) lists consumer psychology, consumer personality, the social environment, and situation as internal and external influences on consumption. How have these influenced the consumer behavior mentioned in this case study? How does organic food provide utilitarian and hedonic value to Jill and her aunt?

2. What is Jill's Value Equation (Exhibit 2.2) for regular carrots? How do changes in the value equation explain Jill's purchase of mini-carrots over organic carrots? What is an example of your own consumption in which you gave up something to get something else?

3. How is product differentiation and/or relationship marketing used – by farmers, food companies, or retailers -- to add value for consumers and thus increase repeat sales in the organic food industry?

4. What kind of information could a researcher find out by engaging in a) quantitative research and b) interpretive research? Are you surprised that survey reports are biased in that consumers say they are willing to pay a higher price for organic food than they actually are?

# Case 1-3
## Learning About CB: Is Your Coke OK?

*Written by Paul J. Costanzo, Ph.D., Western New England College*

Randy is a typical student and he is about to learn that he is a very typical consumer. In the buyer behavior class Randy has registered for he will learn that studying his daily activities as a student and a shopper could help him better understand the field of consumer behavior. Randy has an affinity for a select group of products, dislikes some, and is indifferent to others. For example, Randy prefers Coca-Cola over all other soft drinks and he would classify himself as a brand loyal Coca-Cola drinker.

As Randy flipped through the pages of his newly purchased textbook he began to ask himself the following questions: "What exactly is consumer behavior? Why should I study consumer behavior? How does consumer behavior affect me?"

*Reproduced by permission from the author.*

Randy reminisced about a favorite class back in high school. The class was a basic chemistry class and Randy recalled feeling apprehensive before starting that class. At the time, he wasn't interested in chemistry and he remembered asking himself the same questions that he is now. On the first day of his chemistry class his teacher asked each of the students to explain why they had chosen the class. When it was his turn to explain, his response was clear: "I don't know why I am taking this course. I just need a science course. Chemistry doesn't affect me." Randy remembered several of his high school classmates laughed at his candid response. The teacher responded by simply telling the class that the easiest way to learn any subject was to apply the subject matter to your own life.

Was learning about consumer behavior going to be similar to Randy's experience with chemistry? Chemistry (as Randy later learned) is the study of the composition of all substances. It is, after all, the science that explores the components of all physical matter in this world, including Randy. Was this a case of déjà vu? Could Randy learn more about consumer behavior by applying it to himself and his own behaviors?

After reading the definition of consumer behavior, Randy began to think of the definition in terms of his life experiences. Consumer behavior is the study of all of us as we engage in purchase decisions or exchanges, such as purchasing a product, service, or the adoption of an idea.

As he headed back to his apartment, Randy stopped at the campus bookstore and purchased his favorite soft drink, a Coca-Cola. As he raised the can to his mouth and took a drink, he began to think that maybe his actions as a consumer are part of a bigger picture. He began to realize that his choice to buy Coca-Cola, like so many other consumers, is inextricably linked to the success or failure of a brand. Randy's choice to be a brand loyal consumer of Coca-Cola is related to the study of consumer behavior.

*"Today we are the world's largest beverage company selling nearly 570 billion servings a year, which equates to more than 18,000 per second."* … *"Consumers associate happiness with our brand. In fact, Coca-Cola means 'Delicious Happiness' in Mandarin."*[1]

On April 23, 1985, the chairman and CEO of Coca-Cola, Roberto C. Goizueta, announced that after 99 years, Coca-Cola was to replace its revered Coke brand with its Merchandise 7XX formula, a new, sweeter formula known as *New Coke*. How could Mr. Goizueta have known that his decision, some twenty-five years later, would be referred to by Advertising Age as "one of the biggest blunders in marketing and the sixth biggest moment in 75 years of advertising"?[2] (Certainly this is not the notoriety any CEO would want.)

Coca-Cola's decision to replace their cash cow brand was in part a response to Coke's eroding market share. Major competition from Pepsi was at that time, more than ever, becoming a serious threat. The growing popularity of Pepsi was a direct result of positive consumer response to the "Pepsi Generation" and "Pepsi Challenge" advertising campaigns. Coca-Cola was outspending Pepsi in advertising yet their market share continued to decline. Top Coca-Cola executives were faced with a dilemma. What could they do to regain lost market share? What more could they learn about the consumer behavior of cola drinkers?[3]

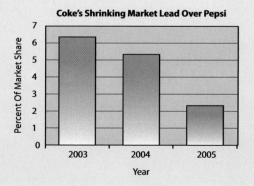

**Coke's Shrinking Market Lead Over Pepsi**

Within three months of Mr. Goizueta's infamous announcement, the decision to discontinue the original Coke brand was reversed. The reversal was the driven by the dissatisfaction of brand loyal consumers. Consumer outrage about the decision to remove the original Coke was substantial. The news media fanned the flames of discontent, with numerous reports featuring unhappy consumers. Outspoken celebrities, politicians, and sports figures publicly chastised Coca-Cola and demanded the return of their beloved soft drink.

Interpreting consumer behavior data is not a pure science as top Coca-Cola marketing executive Zergio Zyman found out. Mr. Zyman was a key figure not only in the decision to introduce New Coke and discontinue Coke, but later, in 1993, he helped introduce another Coca-Cola brand he thought would be embraced by younger consumers. This product was known as OK Soda. OK Soda, like New Coke, was not well received. The OK name was adopted because test marketing found it to be the most recognized word worldwide. The OK Soda brand was quickly discontinued and was never distributed nationwide because it did not meet its expectation to capture 4% of the U.S. beverage market.[4]

To view an OK Soda commercial aimed at the younger consumer market, search **YouTube.com**.

## Questions

1. Define marketing and consumer behavior. Provide your own definition (not the textbook definition) of consumer behavior. How can consumer behavior be applied to your life experiences?

2. Compare/contrast human behavior and consumer behavior. Why do marketers study consumer behavior? What activities of Randy would you identify as being examples of consumer behavior and why?

3. What factors do you think contributed to the failure of New Coke and OK Soda? Do you think these products could be successfully re-marketed today?

4. Keep a log of your daily activities for three days. List and describe those activities which you would categorize as consumer behavior. How might your activities be studied by a consumer behavior researcher?

*Reprinted with permission from the author

## The communication

of value relies on consumer perception and learning.

## What do you think?

**My perceptions of advertisements are usually accurate.**

STRONGLY DISAGREE  STRONGLY AGREE
**1** **2** **3** **4** **5** **6** **7**

Visit CourseMate at
www.cengagebrain.com.

# 3

# Consumer Learning Starts Here: Perception

## Introduction

**m**arketing strategy represents the way a firm goes about creating a unique and valuable bundle of benefits for the consumer. As such, marketing strategy focuses on value creation. Unfortunately, many firms never fully understand the value they create, and this can lead to major problems. For example, the firm Webvan started amid the dot-com boom in the late 1990s. Webvan.com delivered groceries directly to consumers, seemingly a great way to create value for consumers. Webvan attracted tremendous interest among investors but went out of business in 2001, a few years after its creation. Ultimately, Webvan failed to get enough consumers to perceive the value offered by their service. Of course, if a consumer doesn't *think* that a product will deliver the value desired or doesn't understand a product in the intended way, why purchase the product? Today, Amazon owns the Webvan name and offers grocery delivery in just one city, Seattle, through its AmazonFresh website.

After studying this chapter, the student should be able to:

**LO1** Define learning and perception and how the two are connected.

**LO2** List and define phases of the consumer perception process.

**LO3** Apply the concept of the JND.

**LO4** Contrast the concepts of implicit and explicit memory.

**LO5** Know ways to help get a consumer's attention.

**LO6** Understand key differences between intentional and unintentional learning.

## LO1 Defining Learning and Perception

**v**alue cannot be communicated without involving consumer learning and perception. **Learning** refers to a change in behavior resulting from the interaction between a person and a stimulus. **Perception** refers to a consumer's awareness and interpretation of reality. Accordingly, perception serves as a foundation upon which consumer learning takes place. Stated simply, value involves learning, and consumer perception plays a key role in learning because consumers change behavior based on what

> **learning** change in behavior resulting from some interaction between a person and a stimulus
>
> **perception** consumer's awareness and interpretation of reality

**exposure** process of bringing some stimulus within proximity of a consumer so that the consumer can sense it with one of the five human senses

**sensation** consumer's immediate response to a stimulus

**attention** purposeful allocation of information-processing capacity toward developing an understanding of some stimulus

they perceive. Sometimes, consumers set out to *intentionally* learn marketing-related information. Other times, consumers learn *unintentionally* (or incidentally) by simply being exposed to stimuli and by forming some kind of response to it. Both types of learning rely, to greater or lesser degrees, on perceptual processes.

This chapter focuses on issues that are central to understanding the learning process. Specifically, the chapter details the earliest phases of perception along with a number of issues related to unintentional learning. The chapter closes with a discussion of *conditioning*, which represents a well-known approach to unintentional learning. Intentional learning and the cognitive processes associated with it are discussed in a later chapter.

## CONSUMER PERCEPTION

What's more important, perception or reality? This probably seems like a typical "academic" question, but the issue is very important to consumer researchers. Consumer researchers expend a great deal of effort trying to understand consumer perception because the way a consumer perceives something greatly influences learning.

Perception and reality are distinct concepts because the perceptions that consumers develop do not always match the real world. For example, we've probably all listened to a fanatical sports fan boast about his or her favorite team. The cliché "rose-colored glasses" might apply if the favored team is not as good as the fan makes it out to be. Perception simply doesn't always match reality. Perception can also be ambiguous. Exhibit 3.1 illustrates this point.

We treat perception as a consumer's awareness and interpretation of reality. Perception represents a *subjective* reality whereas what actually exists in the environment determines objective reality. For example, at a restaurant, the objective reality is that a certain amount of food is served on a plate. A chef can weigh the food so that he knows the actual amount. However, equally hungry consumers may disagree that it is enough. How can this be? The answer to this question illustrates the concept of subjective reality. In this case, subjective and objective reality may differ because the size of the plate affects the quantity of food a consumer perceives.

Exhibit 3.2 illustrates this effect by showing the same amount of food on three different plates. Placing food on a smaller plate can actually increase the chance that diners are satisfied, not because they have actually had more food, but because they perceive that they are getting more![1] The same amount of food on a larger plate tends to leave a diner wanting more.

## EXPOSURE, ATTENTION, AND COMPREHENSION

During the perceptual process, consumers are *exposed* to stimuli, devote *attention* to stimuli, and attempt to *comprehend* stimuli. **Exposure** refers to the process of bringing some stimulus within the proximity of a consumer so that it can be sensed by one of the five human senses (sight, smell, taste, touch, or sound). The term **sensation** describes a consumer's immediate response to this information.

McDonald's delivers the message "four bucks is **dumb**" on billboards, exposing consumers to a not-so-subtle message about coffee. Marketers can expose consumers to messages like this, but that does not guarantee that the consumer will pay attention. **Attention**

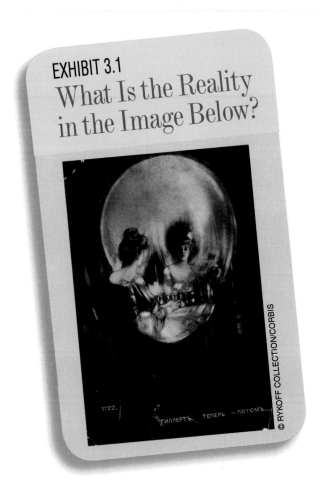

EXHIBIT 3.1
What Is the Reality in the Image Below?

## EXHIBIT 3.2

# Objective and Subjective Reality Don't Always Match

Enough to Eat? May look like more than 500 grams

500 grams of food

Not Enough to Eat? May look like less than 500 grams

is the purposeful allocation of information-processing capacity toward developing an understanding of some stimulus. Many times, consumers simply cannot pay attention to all the stimuli to which they are exposed. As such, consumers are selective in the information to which they pay attention. Quite simply, there is just too much stimulation in the environment for consumers to pay attention to everything!

*When consumers go by a billboard, they are provided with an opportunity to pay attention to the message.*

Comprehension occurs when consumers attempt to derive meaning from information they receive. Of course, marketers hope that consumers comprehend and interpret information in the intended way, but this is not always the case. As a simple example, a receptionist tells patients there will be a *short* wait. Will all patients think the wait is short? For example, two consumers that wait 20 minutes may perceive the wait differently. What is short to one may not be so short to another. A professional taking an hour away from their busy day may react differently than a retired person without a hectic daily schedule. A patient's previous experiences will also affect what length of time they associate with *short*. Furthermore, can something be done to change perceptions of the wait time? The receptionist might update the patient every few minutes explaining what is going on and why the wait is continuing. Alternatively, there could be pleasant music played in the waiting room. In either case, the patient may comprehend a shorter wait than if simply left quietly alone. However, the same patient may also react more negatively to the wait than if left quietly alone.[2]

# LO2 Consumer Perception Process

If a friend were to ask, "Do I look good in this outfit?" you would immediately draw upon your perceptions to determine how to respond to the question. (Whether or not you voice your true opinion is an entirely different subject!) As we have stated, in its most basic form, perception describes how consumers become aware of and interpret the environment. Accordingly, we can view consumer perception as including three phases. These phases include *sensing*, *organizing*, and *reacting*. This is shown in Exhibit 3.3.

Notice that the phases of perception overlap with the concepts of exposure, attention, and comprehension. That is, we sense the many stimuli to which we are exposed, we organize the stimuli as we attend and comprehend them, then we react to various stimuli by developing responses.

## SENSING

A consumer senses stimuli to which he/she is exposed. Sensing is an *immediate* response to stimuli that have come into contact with one of the consumer's five senses (sight, smell, touch, taste, or sound). Thus, when a consumer enters a store, browses on eBay, reads a Tweet, tastes food, encounters an advertisement, or tries on some clothes, the perceptual process goes into action. However, sensing alone does not allow a consumer to make *sense* out of something. This leads to the second stage of the perceptual process.

## ORGANIZING

Imagine being blindfolded and handed an unknown small object. How would you determine what the object might be? Of course, you can feel the object. Is it rough or smooth? Is it soft or hard? These answers may help you decide. A consumer's brain addresses questions like these every time something is sensed. This process takes place literally thousands of times each day. In fact, organization takes place so quickly in most cases that we are unaware of the process.

When we speak of **cognitive organization**, we refer to the process by which the human brain assembles the sensory evidence into something recognizable. This is an important part of perception. Exhibit 3.4 may help you visualize this process. The organization that takes place in your brain is

EXHIBIT 3.3
Sensing, Organizing, and Reacting

What will everyone else think?

Does this fit?

SENSING

ORGANIZING

REACTING

© DAVID STUART/DIGITAL VISION/GETTY IMAGES

# What's the Best Time to Buy?

There is a best time to buy. That time is 10:10! Shop for luxury watches online and you'll start to notice something that seems peculiar at first. Practically all the watches are set to 10:10—that is, 10 minutes after 10. Is this a coincidence? Hardly! The conventional wisdom is that when a consumer senses (sees) a watch showing 10:10, the image is organized in the consumer's mind as a smile (1:50 would smile too). In contrast, a consumer might see a watch showing 8:20 and perceive a frown. According to this theory, when consumers perceive that a product is smiling, it is preferred. Research indicates that, under certain conditions, consumers do indeed demonstrate a preference for smiling products. The effect goes beyond watches and includes cars with a front grill that smiles, or fabrics with certain patterns, among other things. A preference effect occurs particularly when a product can be given some human-like characteristic. A watch smiling at you says "buy me," right?

Sources: Aggarwal, P. and A.L. McGill (2007), "Is that Car Smiling at Me? Schema Congruity as a Basis for Evaluating Anthropomorphized Products," *Journal of Consumer Research* 14 (December), 468-479. Labroo, A. A. (2006), "Do Products Smile? When Fluency Confers Liking and Enhances Purchase Intent," *Advances in Consumer Research* 33, 558-561.

PHOTOS: © ISTOCKPHOTO.COM/DENIS BEYELER

EXHIBIT 3.4
# A Visual Image of the Organization Process

**assimilation** state that results when a stimulus has characteristics such that consumers readily recognize it as belonging to some specific category

**accommodation** state that results when a stimulus shares some but not all of the characteristics that would lead it to fit neatly in an existing category, and consumers must process exceptions to rules about the category

analogous to someone performing a sorting task—such as sorting mail. When an object is first handled, the sorter hasn't a clue what slot the object belongs in. However, information allows the sorter to place the object into progressively more specific categories.

When someone tries to decide if an outfit looks right, the perceptual process goes to work. Consider the clothing pictured in Exhibit 3.3. Is this outfit appropriate for Emilia, a professional consultant? At first, we perceive that the outfit is obviously a woman's dress. However, does the outfit represent proper business attire? If Emilia's brain organizes the outfit into this category, then she becomes likely to buy it and wear it to work as a consultant. Her clients may perceive the outfit differently and react differently. Again, we see the subjectivity of perception.

Consumers develop an interpretation during this stage of the perceptual process and begin to *comprehend* what the stimulus is. This interpretation provides an initial cognitive and affective meaning. The term *cognitive* refers to a mental or thinking process. A reader of this book almost instantly converts a word into meaning as long as the word on the page matches a known English language word. Sometimes marketers need to know how consumers will react to unknown words when creating the name for a new product or new company. In fact, the actual sound of a name (that is otherwise

nonsense) can evoke different meanings and feelings. Consider the following two sounds (say them each aloud):

Sepfut

Sepsop

Which would make a better name for a new ice cream brand? Actually, when consumers sampled the same new ice cream described with one of these two names, Sepsop was the preferred ice cream. The researchers theorized that consumers evaluate sounds with a repetitive pattern (like sep-sop) more favorably, and prefer things associated with it, than sounds with no repetition.[3] Consumers' moods can even be affected by sending sounds that produce a favorably evaluation.[4]

Consumers cannot organize everything they sense so easily. When a consumer encounters a stimulus that is difficult to categorize, the brain instinctively continues processing as a way of reconciling inconsistencies. When even this extra effort leaves a consumer uncertain, he or she will generally avoid the stimulus.

In general, depending on the extent to which a stimulus can be categorized, three possible reactions may occur.

1. **Assimilation.** Assimilation occurs when a stimulus has characteristics such that individuals readily recognize it as an example of a specific category. A light brown, slightly sticky, sweet, round food with a hole in the middle is easily recognized as a doughnut in nearly every part of the world.

2. **Accommodation.** Accommodation occurs when a stimulus shares some, but not all, of the characteristics that allow it to fit neatly in an existing category. At this point, the consumer will begin processing, which allows exceptions to rules

about the category. For example, in New Orleans, a tourist may encounter a *beignet*, which is a French doughnut. Because the beignet does not have a hole, the tourist's perceptual process may have to make an exception to the rule that all doughnuts have holes. Curiously, research indicates that novel stimuli that are mildly incongruent with expectations are actually preferred.[5] Thus, new products that consumers can categorize through accommodation may produce favorable reactions.

3. **Contrast.** **Contrast** occurs when a stimulus does not share enough in common with existing categories to allow categorization. For example, consumers in Kyrgyzstan routinely enjoy fermented mountain mare's milk, known as *koumis*. The only similarity to the milk that most Western consumers know is the color. When a Westerner tastes the milk, particularly if the taster doesn't know what is being consumed, contrast is a nearly certain outcome. People tend to not like things that are so completely unknown. Therefore, contrast is usually associated with negative feelings.

Categorization is discussed in more detail in Chapter 4.

# REACTING

The perceptual process ends with a reaction. If an object is successfully recognized, chances are some nearly automatic reaction takes place. For example, when a driver notices that the car in front of him/her has its brake lights on, the learned response is to apply brakes as well. Here, the reaction occurs as a response or behavior. Note that reactions can include both physical and mental responses to the stimuli encountered.

## Applications to Consumer Behavior

The perceptual process has many implications for consumer behavior. For example, think about how the music playing in a store can affect one's perceptions of and reactions to the store. Would a fine watch be perceived the same way with AC/DC or Mozart in the background?[6] Recall Emilia's questions about her outfit. Online retailers often use technology to allow for more realistic visual depictions of clothing in an attempt to improve consumer perceptions and retail performance.[7] If consumers perceive that a piece of clothing will look good and be a good fit, they will be more likely to purchase it.

# SELECTIVE PERCEPTION

Consumers encounter thousands of stimuli each day. If all stimuli were consciously processed, they would truly be overloaded. Rather than processing all stimuli, consumers practice selective perception. *Selective perception* includes selective exposure, selective attention, and selective distortion. That is, consumers are selective in what they expose themselves to, what they attend to, and what (and how) they comprehend. **Selective exposure** involves screening out most stimuli and exposing oneself to only a small portion of stimuli. **Selective attention** involves paying attention to only certain stimuli.

Consider a tourist walking through downtown Seoul, South Korea. How can he or she possibly pay attention to all of this information? Marketers use the term *clutter* to describe the idea that consumers often are bombarded with too much information in their daily lives. Consumers can't possibly pay attention to all of this. Instead, they will choose something that stands out, or is personally relevant, and devote attention to that object.

What would you pay attention to if you saw this?

© ED FREEMAN/THE IMAGE BANK/GETTY IMAGES

**Selective distortion** is a process by which consumers interpret information in ways that are biased by their previously held beliefs. This process can be the result of either a conscious or unconscious effort. For example, consumers with strong beliefs about a brand tend to comprehend messages about the brand either positively or negatively, depending on their preexisting attitudes. Sports fans provide good examples of selective distortion. Fans from one team may be enraged when a "bad call" goes against his or her team. Fans for the other team are unlikely to comprehend the controversial play in the same way. Both fans observe the same thing but comprehend and react differently.

We now discuss the exposure, attention, and comprehension concepts of perception in more detail.

## Exposure

Exposure occurs when some stimulus is brought within the proximity of a consumer so that it can be sensed. Obviously, marketers who want to inform consumers about their products must first expose them to information. As such, exposure represents a first step to learning. In fact, exposure is a vital component of both intentional and unintentional learning.

Of course, consumers cannot be expected to learn from information to which they've never been exposed. If someone asked you, "Have you seen the new Power Gig™ video game?" and you replied "No," then perhaps you haven't been exposed to it! Next, we discuss issues that pertain to exposure, including subliminal processing, the absolute threshold, the just noticeable difference, and the mere exposure effect.

## SUBLIMINAL PROCESSING

**Subliminal processing** refers to the way in which the human brain senses low-strength stimuli, that is, stimuli that occur below the level of conscious awareness. Such stimuli have a strength that is lower than the **absolute threshold** of perception, the minimum strength needed for a consumer to perceive a stimulus. This type of "learning" is unintentional, because the stimuli fall below the absolute threshold. To illustrate effects below the absolute threshold, consider what often happens when a mosquito lands on one's arm. Chances are the mosquito is so small that the person will not consciously aware of the

sensation without seeing it. Likewise, sounds often occur that are below the threshold. Images also can be displayed for such a short period of time, or at such a low level of intensity, that the brain cannot organize the image and develop a meaning.

**Subliminal persuasion** is behavior change induced or brought about based on subliminally processing a message. Popular conceptions about subliminal persuasion have fueled interest in it for many years. For instance, many people believe that:

- Marketers can somehow induce consumers to purchase products by using subliminal advertising.
- Marketers can subliminally alter products or packages to make them more appealing to consumers.
- Sexual imagery can be "hidden" in a product itself, the product packaging, or in product advertising.
- People's sense of well-being can be enhanced by listening to subliminally embedded tapes of nature sounds and/or music.[8]

The belief is that communication can influence consumers through mere exposure to subliminal stimuli. The most famous example of subliminal persuasion involves a researcher for an ad firm who claimed that he had embedded subliminal frames within the movie *Picnic* in a New Jersey movie theater several years ago. Exhibit 3.5 illustrates the way this process

> **selective distortion**
> process by which consumers interpret information in ways that are biased by their previously held beliefs
>
> **subliminal processing**
> way that the human brain deals with very low-strength stimuli, so low that the person has no conscious awareness
>
> **absolute threshold** minimum strength of a stimulus that can be perceived
>
> **subliminal persuasion** behavior change induced by subliminal processing

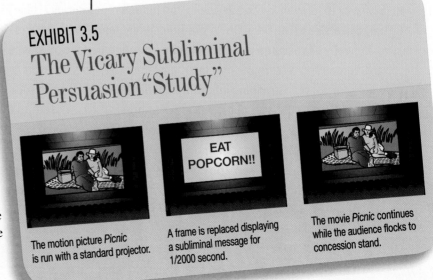

## EXHIBIT 3.5
## The Vicary Subliminal Persuasion "Study"

The motion picture *Picnic* is run with a standard projector.

EAT POPCORN!!
A frame is replaced displaying a subliminal message for 1/2000 second.

The movie *Picnic* continues while the audience flocks to concession stand.

reportedly took place. Very brief embeds of the phrase "Drink Coke" and "Eat Popcorn" were supposedly placed in the movie. The researcher claimed that popcorn sales rose nearly 60 percent as a result and that Coke sales rose nearly 20 percent. This experiment is often called the "Vicary experiment."

This story grew in such popularity that researchers attempted to replicate the study. Interestingly, these scientific replications failed to produce any increase in desire for popcorn or Coke. Consumer researchers also conducted experiments testing the effectiveness of sexual embeds involving air-brushed genitalia, the word *sex*, or provocative nudity in advertisements. Results of these experiments generally indicate that these practices do nothing that would make a consumer more likely to buy the advertised product.[9]

As a general statement, the research examining subliminal processing is conclusive: Subliminal persuasion is ineffective as a marketing tool.[10] This is not to dismiss subliminal processing as having no impact whatsoever on what consumers might learn or how they might behave. But any effects appear to not significantly influence consumer attitude or choice.

Despite evidence that subliminal advertising is ineffective, consumers are generally willing to believe that such powerful influences exist.[11] Estimates suggest that over 60 percent of Americans believe that advertisers can exert subliminal influences strong enough to cause

> Estimates suggest that over 60 percent of Americans believe that advertisers can exert subliminal influences strong enough to cause purchase behavior.

## Subliminal Groovin'?

Is the devil really hidden in the grooves of old rock LPs? Many rock artists have been accused of subliminally embedding messages within their music. According to the accusers, if the music is played backwards, the messages can be heard. Here are some examples from songs you may have heard:

- In "Another One Bites the Dust" by Queen, there is a hidden message that says: "It's fun to smoke marijuana!"
- On the Judas Priest album *Stained Class*, the repeated subliminal message "do it" occurs in an effort to encourage suicide.
- In "Stairway to Heaven" by Led Zeppelin, the hidden messages are "I live for Satan" and "Here's to my sweet Satan."
- Britney Spears's "Hit Me Baby One More Time" really sends the message "Sleep with me, I'm not too young."

In nearly all cases, no good support for intentional maliciousness exists. On occasion, when a song is played backward, something discernible may be interpreted. These occurrences are more likely the result of phonetic accidents (accidental sounds) than anything intentional. Judas Priest, the British rock band, was sued in association with the suicide of one fan and the attempted suicide of another. The case went to trial in the 1990s, but the band was acquitted based on a ruling that subliminal effects could not induce this type of behavior.

In the early 1980s, the rock band Styx included a "warning" sticker on the album *Kilroy Was Here* indicating that hidden messages were contained. The band was poking fun at the idea of subliminal messages *hidden* in the music grooves. Think about it though: if somebody does actually have the ability to play the songs backward and listens to them, would any effect on this particular person be subliminal?

Sources: Henry, W. A., and E. Pappa (1990), "Did the Music Say Do It?" *Time*, 136, 65; Moore, T. (1996), "Scientific Consensus and Expert Testimony: Lessons from the Judas Priest Trial," *Skeptical Inquirer* 20 (November/December), 5-30. **http://www.secretsyoushouldknow.com/music.htm**, accessed July 3, 2010.

© COMSTOCK IMAGES/JUPITER IMAGES

purchase behavior.[12] Over the years, books have fueled the controversy by promoting the idea that advertisers know about, and use, certain "hidden persuaders" to create an irresistible urge to buy.[13]

Consumers are often willing to attribute their own behavior to some kind of "uncontrollable influence," especially when the consumption involves products like cigarettes or alcoholic beverages.[14] Consumers' willingness to believe that subliminal persuasion tricks them into buying these products may simply be an attempt to downplay their own role in decision making.

The truth is that the Vicary experiment was a *hoax*. Vicary himself never conducted the experiment. Rather, he fabricated the story in an effort to create positive publicity for the advertising firm.[15] Marketers sometimes make light of subliminal persuasion by presenting images in advertisements that they know consumers will see!

# LO3 Applying the JND Concept

We have discussed the concept of the absolute threshold as representing a level over which the strength of a stimulus must be greater to activate the perceptual process. A closely related concept deals with changes in the *strength* of stimuli. The **JND** (just noticeable difference) represents how much stronger one stimulus has to be relative to another so that someone can notice that the two are not the same.

The JND concept may be best explained in terms of a physical example. How do people pick out one sound over another? For example, for consumers to be able to physically discern two sounds that originate from the same source, the two sounds must be separated by at least 0.3 second. Separating the sounds by only 0.1 second is likely to produce the perception of one sound. Separating them by 0.3 second or more likely produces the perception of two different sounds.[16]

In general, the ability to detect differences between two levels of a stimulus is affected by the original intensity of the stimulus. This is known as **Weber's Law.** The law states that as the intensity of the initial stimulus increases, a consumer's ability to detect differences between two levels of the stimulus decreases.[17] For example, if the decibel level at a rock concert decreases from 120 to 115 dB, the change likely won't be noticeable.

Marketers need to understand that change made a little at a time may be unnoticed by a consumer; change a lot at once and it will be noticed. The JND has numerous implications for marketers who attempt to provide value for consumers, including:

- **Pricing.** Consumers do not perceive very small differences in price as truly different.[18] A price of $19.95 is generally not perceived as being different from a price of $19.99. Thus, marketers may consider increasing prices in small increments to avoid a negative backlash from consumers. Conversely, a price reduction needs to be large enough so that consumers truly perceive the new price as representing significant savings.[19]

- **Quantity.** Small differences in quantity are often not perceived as being different. For instance, if a toilet paper roll is reduced from 412 to 407 sheets, consumers are not likely to perceive a difference.

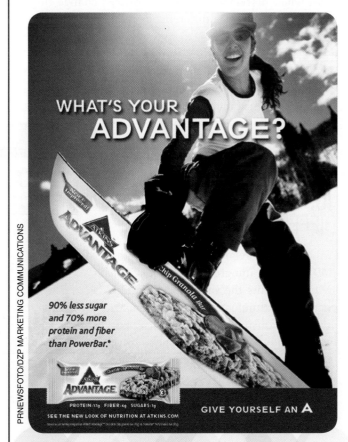

PRNEWSFOTO/D2P MARKETING COMMUNICATIONS

*Does this product offer a big enough advantage over the competition to be noticed?*

- **Quality.** Small improvements in quality may not have any impact on consumers. Thus, if a service provider promotes an improvement such as faster service or better food quality, the difference must be large enough to create a true perceptual difference.

- **Add-on Purchases.** A small additional purchase tacked onto a large purchase may not create the perception of increased spending. For instance, a consumer buying a $145 pair of athletic shoes may be receptive to the suggestion of adding a pair of $8 socks to the order. The total for the shoes is not perceived as being really different than the total for the shoes and socks together.

In general, these examples highlight an important idea: when marketers make a "positive" change they should make sure the difference is large enough to be perceived by consumers. Conversely, when they make a "negative" change, they should think about implementing the change in small increments so that each difference is not distinguished from what existed previously. However, marketers should make sure that changes are not perceived as being deceptive. Deliberately deceptive actions are unethical.

## JUST MEANINGFUL DIFFERENCE

A topic closely related to the JND is the **JMD** (just meaningful difference). The JMD represents the smallest amount of change in a stimulus that would influence consumer consumption and choice. For instance, how much of a change in price is really needed to *influence* consumer behavior and learning? A consumer can surely "notice" an advertisement stating a price drop of a Rolex from $19,999 to $19,499. Clearly, this is a $500.00 difference. However, is this price drop really meaningful? Retailers generally follow a rule that states that effective price drops need to be at least 20 percent.[20]

## LO4 Implicit and Explicit Memory

**n**ormally, we associate learning with educational experiences. When we think about learning, we think of people studying and paying close attention, like when you read this book! The knowledge one obtains from this type of experience is stored in **explicit memory**, that is, memory for information one is exposed to, attends to, and applies effort to remember. However, this is not the only kind of memory we develop. **Implicit memory** represents stored information concerning stimuli one is exposed to but does not pay attention to. Implicit memory creates **preattentive effects**, learning that is developed in the absence of attention. The following example illustrates the contrast between implicit and explicit memory.

How effective are banner ads like the ones you see on practically every web page? If a consumer clicks a banner ad to an advertiser's site, that consumer may absorb the resulting advertisement content and develop some explicit memory of the information. However, click-through rates on banner ads are extraordinarily low and continue to decline. Consumers click through fewer than 1 in 100 banners ads to which they are exposed. Do Web advertisers waste their resources

*Where's Elmo? Can you count the banner ads in this website? Even "unclicked" banner ads may create implicit memory.*

on the other 99 plus consumers? Perhaps not. It turns out that consumers' implicit memory system addresses these ads. Even when consumers pay no attention to a banner ad on a crowded computer screen, implicit memory for the brand develops. This implicit memory creates more favorable attitudes toward the brand that increase the likelihood that the consumer would consider buying something associated with the brand.[21] Interestingly, unlike explicit memory, implicit memory becomes stronger the more distracted one is from attending to the stimulus.

# MERE EXPOSURE EFFECT

The **mere exposure effect** represents another way that consumers can learn unintentionally.[22] The mere exposure effect is the idea that consumers will prefer stimuli they have been previously exposed to over stimuli which they have not. This effect occurs even when there is no recall of the previous stimulus!

Exhibit 3.6 illustrates a classical approach to studying the mere exposure effect. Experiments in mere exposure effect expose subjects to something they do not know. In this case, a group of consumers were shown a list of Norwegian words. Among these words, two were target terms representing potential name brands for a new energy food. Some of the words even contain letters that do not exist in the English alphabet.

## EXHIBIT 3.6
## The Mere Exposure Effect Illustrated

| January 10 | May 10 |
|---|---|
| Agentur | baadsmand |
| Forfølgelse | Prestegård |
| alderdomssvakhet | prosti |
| Overvære | tidsperiode |
| Prestegård | anmerkning |
| brændevinsbrænderi | bryggeri |
| Amme | tjueseks |
| Nittiende | mindreårig |
| Disktriktslege | Forfølgelse |
| Bagermester | badedrakten |

On January 10, subjects were exposed to the list of words on the left. Then, on May 10, the same subjects were exposed to the list on the right. If you look closely, you'll notice that two of the words on the May 10 list were also on the January 10 list.

The results of this type of experiment generally show that the two "familiar" words will be preferred even though subjects have no recall of having ever seen them before. Consumers not only develop preferences for words, but they learn them as well. In fact, the learning process facilitates positive feelings that become associated with the stimuli.[23] The mere exposure effect therefore has applications in both consumer learning and attitude formation.

The mere exposure effect is very resilient. The effect is true for practically any type of content. If the Norwegian words are replaced with faces, names, Chinese characters, brand logos, web pages, or musical samples, the mere exposure effect still holds.[24] Theoretically, an explanation for the increased preference involves familiarity. Even though consumers can't "remember" seeing the stimuli, some degree of familiarity is created.

### Familiarity

All things equal, consumers prefer the familiar to the unfamiliar. Once exposed to an object, a consumer exhibits a preference for the familiar object over something unfamiliar. An interesting application involves political campaigns. Modern technology allows advertisers to morph one individual's characteristics onto a photograph of another. For instance, a photograph of a political candidate can be modified so that subtle physical characteristics of a particular voter are morphed onto the candidate's appearance. In such a case, the particular voter will express a greater liking of the candidate, even if the changes are too subtle to be noticed.[25] The rationale is that the addition of characteristics, even below the JND, increases the perceived familiarity between the voter and the candidate. Familiarity plays a big role in understanding the way preattentive processes can improve attitudes, and the mere exposure effect highlights this.

Several relevant points can be made about the mere exposure effect.

- The mere exposure effect is created in the absence of attention. For this reason, the effect is considered preattentive.

**product placements**
products that have been placed conspicuously in movies or television shows

- Preferences associated with the mere exposure effect are easy to elicit. Thus, marketers can use this effect to improve attitudes marginally.
- The mere exposure effect has the greatest effect on novel (previously unfamiliar) objects.
- The size of the effect (increased liking) is not very strong relative to an effect created by a strong cohesive argument. For example, a Notre Dame football fan might develop a preference for a face to which he's repeatedly been exposed, but if he finds that the face belongs to a USC fan, the preference will likely go away based on the strong information!
- The mere exposure effect works best when the consumer has a low involvement in processing the object, and indeed when a consumer is distracted from processing the focal stimulus. For example, if a small brand logo is displayed on a magazine page across from an involving story, a greater increase in liking would be found than if the consumer were less distracted from the stimulus.

## Note on Subliminal and Mere Exposure Effects

Before moving on, we should distinguish the mere exposure effect from subliminal effects. A subliminal message is one presented below the threshold of perception. In other words, if you are aware of the stimulus or message, then the process is not subliminal. With the mere exposure effect, the stimulus is evident and someone could pay attention to it if they wanted to. As with the Norwegian words, no attempt is made to keep someone from seeing them. The stimuli are presented with strength above the threshold of perception.

# Ethical Dilemmas in Mere Exposure

Generally speaking, we think of preattentive processing, as illustrated by the mere exposure effect, in terms of its effect on consumer purchasing behavior. However, the mere exposure effect can help explain why a consumer might steal something. Research suggests that once a consumer is merely exposed to something unethical, he or she becomes more tolerant of that behavior. A consumer, for instance, may hear coworkers in the next cubicle talking about how to pirate music. Even though the consumer is not paying close attention to the discussion, exposure to it may make him or her more tolerant of music pirating, and ultimately more likely to practice the behavior.

Source: Weeks, W. A., J. Longenecker, J. A. McKinney, and C.W. Moore (2005), "The Role of Mere Exposure Effect on Ethical Tolerance: A Two-Study Approach," *Journal of Business Ethics* 38, 281–294.

## Product Placements

An interesting application of implicit memory and mere exposure involves brand placements in video games. Video games, quite simply, can be very captivating! The person playing a game will likely not be paying attention to things like embedded brand logos. In a manner similar to the way banner ads are processed, implicit memory is created when the logos are executed within a game and an attitude toward the brand develops.[26] As with other preattentive effects, the effect is stronger as the game is more involving!

**Product placements** represent another way that promotions can impart implicit memory among consumers. Product placements involve branded products placed conspicuously in movies or television shows. These placements can result in implicit memory formation. For instance, researchers in the United Kingdom once demonstrated implicit memory learning by exposing children to the movie *Home Alone*. Half of the children saw the movie with a scene in which the actors consumed unbranded drinks. The other half saw the identical scene but with the drinks changed to Pepsi cans. After the movie, the children were given their choice of soft drink. Those who saw the unbranded drink scene chose Coke and Pepsi in similar proportion

© ISTOCKPHOTO.COM/DAN BRANDENBURG

a protective behavior. When consumers pay attention to something, is it more often voluntary or involuntary?

**involuntary attention** attention that is beyond the conscious control of a consumer

**orientation reflex** natural reflex that occurs as a response to something threatening

# LO5 Enhancing Consumers' Attention

Consumers face a difficult challenge in penetrating the clutter to pay attention to an intended message. What's more, consumers today have so many information and entertainment sources (iPods, PCs, cell phones), creating an entire other layer of clutter. Getting a consumer's attention, voluntarily or involuntarily, is even more difficult in today's multi-tasking society, but that is the job of effective marketing communication.

*Getting a consumer's attention is even more difficult in today's multi-tasking society.*

## FACTORS THAT GET ATTENTION

These factors can help create attention:

- **Intensity of Stimuli.** All things equal, a consumer is more likely to pay attention to stronger stimuli than to weaker stimuli. For example, vivid colors can be used to capture a consumer's attention. Loud sounds capture more attention than quieter sounds. A television commercial with a louder volume than the rest of the programming tends to get consumers' attention.

- **Contrast.** Contrasting stimuli are extremely effective in getting attention. Contrast occurs in several ways. In days past, a color photo in a newspaper was extremely effective in getting attention. However, today's newspapers are often filled with color, so a color advertisement is less prominent. A black-and-white image in a magazine filled with color, however, can stand out. A period of silence in an otherwise noisy environment can attract attention.[28] Like loud television commercials, silent commercials also usually work in gaining consumer attention. Nonconformity can also create attention because of the contrast with social norms.[29] Marketers often

to the U.K. market share. However, those who saw the "branded" scene chose Pepsi over Coke by a wide margin.[27]

## ATTENTION

From the discussion above, it's clear that attention plays a key role in distinguishing implicit and explicit memory. Attention is the purposeful allocation of cognitive capacity toward understanding some stimulus. Intentional learning depends on attentive consumers. However, we don't pay attention only to things we wish to. **Involuntary attention** is attention that is beyond the conscious control of the consumer and that occurs as the result of exposure to surprising or novel stimuli. For example, if you were to cut your finger, you would automatically direct attention to the injury due to its pain. When attention is devoted to a stimulus in this way, an orientation reflex is said to occur. An **orientation reflex** is a natural reflex that occurs as a response to a threat from the environment. In this way, the orientation reflex represents

show consumers who "stand out from the crowd" as a means of capturing attention for an ad.

- **Movement.** With electronic billboards or electronic retail shelf tags, marketers attempt to capture consumer attention by the principle of movement. Items in movement simply gain attention. Flashing lights and "pointing" signage are particularly effective tools for gaining consumer attention.

- **Surprising Stimuli.** Unexpected stimuli gain consumers' attention. Infomercials often contain surprising scenes. Recent infomercials showed a car running over a man's hand and the strength of Mighty Putty pulling a "fully loaded 18-wheeler."

- **Size of Stimuli.** All else equal, larger items garner more attention than smaller ones. Marketers therefore often attempt to have brands appear large in advertisements. This is a reason advertising copy usually features large headlines.

- **Involvement.** Involvement refers to the personal relevance a consumer feels toward a particular product. In general, the more personally relevant (and thus more involving) an object, the greater the chance that the object will be attended to. We discuss involvement in more detail in the cognitive learning chapter.

Gaining consumer attention is an important task for any marketer. Of course, paying attention can be beneficial for consumers as well. Consumers should devote cognitive capacity to comprehend choices that offer the most value for them.

## COMPREHENSION

As stated previously, consumers organize and understand information through comprehension. Comprehension is the interpretation or understanding that a consumer develops about an attended stimulus. Comprehension is an especially important topic for marketers because it allows consumers to interpret messages

in the intended way. It is during comprehension that biases enter into perception. A fan of Dodge trucks may comprehend a message from Chevy very differently than would a die-hard Chevy fan. Furthermore, personal factors such as intelligence and motivation affect comprehension. Comprehension is discussed further in the next chapter, focusing on cognitive learning.

## LO6 The Difference between Intentional and Unintentional Learning

**b**efore moving on to cognitive learning and information processing, let's detail the distinction between the two types of consumer learning—intentional and unintentional learning. Both types of learning concern what cognitive psychologists refer to as perceptual processes; however, with **unintentional learning**, consumers simply sense and react (or respond) to the environment. Here, consumers "learn" without trying to learn. They do not attempt to comprehend the information presented. They are exposed to stimuli and respond in some way. With **intentional learning**, consumers set out to specifically learn information devoted to a certain subject. To better explain intentional and unintentional learning, we examine two major theories in the psychology of learning.

## BEHAVIORISM AND COGNITIVE LEARNING THEORIES

Recall that perception and learning are closely related topics. As the preeminent behavioral psychologist B. F. Skinner once wrote: "In order to respond effectively to the world around us, we must see, hear, smell, taste and feel it."[30]

Psychologists generally follow one of two basic theories of learning. One theory focuses on changes in behavior occurring as conditioned responses to stimuli, without concern for the cognitive mechanics of the process. The other theory focuses on how changes in thought and knowledge precipitate behavioral changes. Those in the first camp follow a **behaviorist approach to learning** (also referred to as the behavioral learning perspective). This approach suggests that because the brain is a "black box," the focus of inquiry should be on the behavior itself. In fact, Skinner argued that no description of what happens inside the human body can adequately explain human behavior. [31] Thus, the brain is a black box, and we can't look inside.

From the behaviorist perspective, consumers are exposed to stimuli and directly respond in some way. Thus, the argument is that the marketing focus should be on "stimulus and response." Behaviorists do not deny the existence of mental processes; rather, they consider these processes to be behaviors themselves. For example, thinking is an activity in the same way that walking is; psychological processes are viewed as actions.[32] Note that the term "conditioning" is used in behavioral learning, as behavior becomes conditioned in some way by the external environment.

The second theory of learning involves an **information processing (or cognitive) perspective**. With this approach, the focus is on the cognitive processes associated with comprehension, including that leading to consumer learning. The information processing perspective considers the mind as acting much like a computer. Bits of knowledge are processed electronically to form meaning.

Traditionally, the behavioral learning and cognitive perspectives have competed against one another for theoretical dominance. However, we avoid such debate because on closer inspection, the two theories really share much in common. At the very least, both perspectives focus on changes in behavior as a person interacts with his or her environment. We adopt an orientation more directly applicable to consumer learning by separating learning mechanisms into the intentional and unintentional groups that we have presented. The next section discusses unintentional learning and how consumers respond to stimuli to which they are exposed.

# UNINTENTIONAL LEARNING

Unintentional learning occurs when behavior is modified through a consumer–stimulus interaction without a cognitive effort to understand a stimulus. With this type of learning, consumers respond to stimuli to which they are exposed without thinking about the information. The focus is on *reacting*, not cognitive processing.

Unintentional learning can be approached from the behavioral learning perspective. Two major approaches found in behavioral learning theory are *classical conditioning* and *instrumental conditioning*.

## Classical Conditioning

**Classical conditioning** refers to a change in behavior that occurs simply through associating some stimulus with another stimulus that naturally causes a reaction. The most famous classical conditioning experiment was performed by the behavioral psychologist Ivan Pavlov. Pavlov conducted experiments using dogs, meat powder (an **unconditioned stimulus** that naturally led to a salivation response), and a bell (a **conditioned stimulus** that did not lead to the response before it was paired with the powder).[33] The experiment reveals that the bell eventually evokes the same behavior that the meat powder naturally caused.

**information processing perspective** approach that focuses on changes in thought and knowledge and how these precipitate behavioral changes

**classical conditioning** change in behavior that occurs simply through associating some stimulus with another stimulus that naturally causes some reaction; a type of unintentional learning

**unconditioned stimulus** stimulus with which a behavioral response is already associated

**conditioned stimulus** object or event that does not cause the desired response naturally but that can be conditioned to do so by pairing with an unconditioned stimulus

**unconditioned response** response that occurs naturally as a result of exposure to an unconditioned stimulus

For behaviorists, perception itself is an activity, not a mental process.

In the experiment, Pavlov began ringing the bell every time meat powder was provided to the dogs. Thus, the bell became associated with the meat powder. Eventually, Pavlov rang the bell without providing the meat powder. As predicted, the bell proved enough to increase the amount of saliva the dogs produced. Originally, the dogs would salivate from being exposed to the unconditioned stimulus. The salivation was called an **unconditioned response**, which occurred naturally as a result of exposure to the unconditioned stimulus (the meat powder). The dogs eventually would respond in the same way to the exposure to the bell.

**conditioned response**
response that results from exposure to a conditioned stimulus that was originally associated with the unconditioned stimulus

**instrumental conditioning** type of learning in which a behavioral response can be conditioned through reinforcement—either punishment or rewards associated with undesirable or desirable behavior

**positive reinforcers**
reinforcers that take the form of a reward

**discriminative stimuli**
stimuli that occur solely in the presence of a reinforcer

This response became known as a **conditioned response**. The response became conditioned by the consistent pairing of the unconditioned and conditioned stimuli. Dogs do not cognitively process in the way we usually think that humans do. So, the dogs learned this response without trying to do so.

To be effective, the conditioned stimulus is presented before the unconditioned stimulus, and the pairing of the two should be done consistently (and with repetition). The advertisement at the left illustrates a popular use of unintentional learning through classical conditioning—the use of sexual, or intimate, imagery.

## Instrumental Conditioning

Much of what we know about instrumental (or operant) conditioning comes from the work of Skinner. With **instrumental conditioning**, behavior is conditioned through reinforcement. Reinforcers are stimuli that strengthen a desired response. The focus is on behavior and behavioral change—not on mental processes that lead to learning. With instrumental conditioning, the likelihood that a behavior will increase is influenced by the reinforcers (consequences) of the behavior. The reinforcers are presented after the initial behavior occurs.

As an example of instrumental conditioning, consider childhood development. When a parent is "potty training" a child, he or she is more concerned with getting the desired result than with teaching the child the benefits of using a toilet over a diaper. All parents know that it is very difficult to rationalize with young children. Therefore, attempting to get them to think about the various reasons to become trained is almost useless. The focus is on changing the behavior through reinforcement. When a child performs the desired behavior, he or she receives rewards in the form of hugs, kisses, toys, etc. These rewards reinforce the desired behavior.

**Positive reinforcers** come in many forms in the consumer environment and often take the form of some type of reward. The effects can be seen in marketing efforts that encourage repeat purchase behavior. For example, many casinos have players' cards that accumulate points the more a customer plays. The casino keeps tracks of these points. As the points accumulate, various offers are provided to the consumer, including free hotel rooms, meals, and other things that could otherwise be expensive. In this case, the points are used to elicit a desired response—repeat purchase behavior.

**Discriminative Stimuli, Reinforcement, and Shaping.** **Discriminative stimuli** are stimuli that are differentiated from other stimuli because they signal the presence of a reinforcer. These stimuli essentially signal that a type of reward will occur if a behavior is performed. Advertisements that feature special promotions represent marketing examples of discriminative stimuli. Here the ad informs consumers that they will receive some type of reward (for example, 10 percent

## DOCKERS
### SAN FRANCISCO

DRESS TO LIVE
DOCKERS.COM

PRNEWSFOTO/DOCKERS

*Advertisers try to "condition" brands by pairing branded products with arousing images such as this.*

off a purchase) if they perform the desirable behavior (for example, shop at a store). The stimulus serves as a signal presented before the behavior occurs, and the behavior must occur in order for the reinforcement to be delivered. Brand names can be discriminative stimuli because they signal potential customer satisfaction and value. For example, consumers realize that by using Federal Express, they can receive overnight delivery with outstanding quality. The reinforcer occurs after the behavior has been performed. Exhibit 3.7 presents this process. Again we see the importance of exposure to the discriminative stimuli, further highlighting the relationship between perception and behavioral learning.

## Shaping Behavior

**Shaping** is a process through which the desired behavior is altered over time, in small increments. Here, the focus is on rewarding "small" behaviors that lead to the "big" behavior ultimately desired. For example, a motorcycle shop manager might offer free hot dogs and soft drinks to consumers on a special promotional day. When the consumers come in to the store and receive the food and drinks, the manager may offer them a coupon for free pizza simply for test-driving an ATV. Finally, the manager may offer the consumer a $200 rebate on the purchase of a new ATV. Notice that the behavior that is ultimately desired is the purchase of an ATV. The small rewards along the way help shape the desired behavior.

Not all reinforcement is positive. **Punishers** represent stimuli that decrease the likelihood that a behavior will occur again. When children misbehave, they get punished. The hope is that the behavior will not occur again. In the same way, when consumers make poor decisions and purchase products that deliver less value than expected, they are punished. Chances are they won't buy those same products again! **Negative reinforcement**, on the other hand, refers to the *removal* of bad stimuli as a way of encouraging behavior.

Punishers and negative reinforcers are commonly confused. The concepts are not the same. A punisher is the presence of bad stimuli after an undesirable behavior has occurred, whereas a negative reinforcer represents the removal of undesirable events. Companies frequently use negative reinforcement techniques. For example, advertisements that focus on the bad outcomes associated with *not* using a company's products utilize this technique. The message is essentially "If only you would have tried us, this bad thing wouldn't have happened!"

Behaviors often cease when reinforcers are no longer present. This represents the concept of **extinction**. For example, consumers may become accustomed to receiving free doughnuts and coffee at a local service station every time they get their oil changed. If the station decides to stop offering the free food and drink, the consumers may take their business elsewhere.

## Final Thought on Behavioral Conditioning

Conditioning represents a type of learning because it focuses on behavioral change that occurs through a consumer's interaction with the environment. For behaviorists, perception itself is an activity, not a mental process. Through the behavioral approach, consumers are exposed to stimuli and react in some way. Consumer learning through behavioral conditioning occurs without a conscious attempt to learn anything new.

> **shaping** process through which a desired behavior is altered over time, in small increments
>
> **punishers** stimuli that decrease the likelihood that a behavior will persist
>
> **negative reinforcement** removal of harmful stimuli as a way of encouraging behavior
>
> **extinction** process through which behaviors cease because of lack of reinforcement

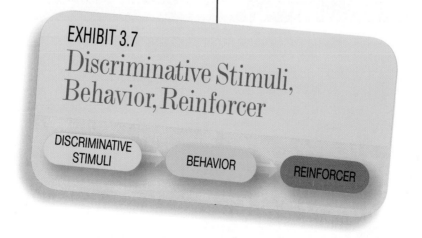

**EXHIBIT 3.7**
## Discriminative Stimuli, Behavior, Reinforcer

DISCRIMINATIVE STIMULI — BEHAVIOR — REINFORCER

# 3 Study Tools

**Located at back of the textbook**

☐ Rip-Out Chapter-in-Review Card

**Located at www.cengagebrain.com**

☐ Review Key Terms Flashcards (Print or Online)

☐ Download audio summaries to review on the go

☐ Complete practice quizzes to prepare for tests

☐ Play "Beat the Clock" and "Quizbowl" to master concepts

☐ Watch Video on Ogden Publications for a real company example

## what others have thought...

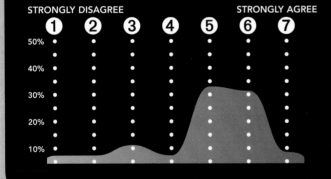

STRONGLY DISAGREE  STRONGLY AGREE

① ② ③ ④ ⑤ ⑥ ⑦

50%
40%
30%
20%
10%

### My perceptions of advertisements are usually accurate.

Readers tend to agree with this statement, but the level of agreement falls short of strong agreement. Sixty-four percent of respondents either somewhat agree or agree. Only 8 percent strongly agree. Overall, the results suggest that readers have some confidence that they accurately perceive advertising messages. Do you?

# LEARN YOUR WAY!

**SHE DID**

We know that no two students are alike. You come from different walks of life and with many different preferences. You need to study just about anytime and anywhere. **CB3** was developed to help you learn Consumer Behavior in a way that works for you.

Not only is the format fresh and contemporary, it's also concise and focused. And, **CB3** is loaded with a variety of study tools, like in-text review cards, printable flashcards, and more.

**Go to CourseMate for CB3 to find plenty of resources to help you study—no matter what learning style you like best! Access at www.cengagebrain.com.**

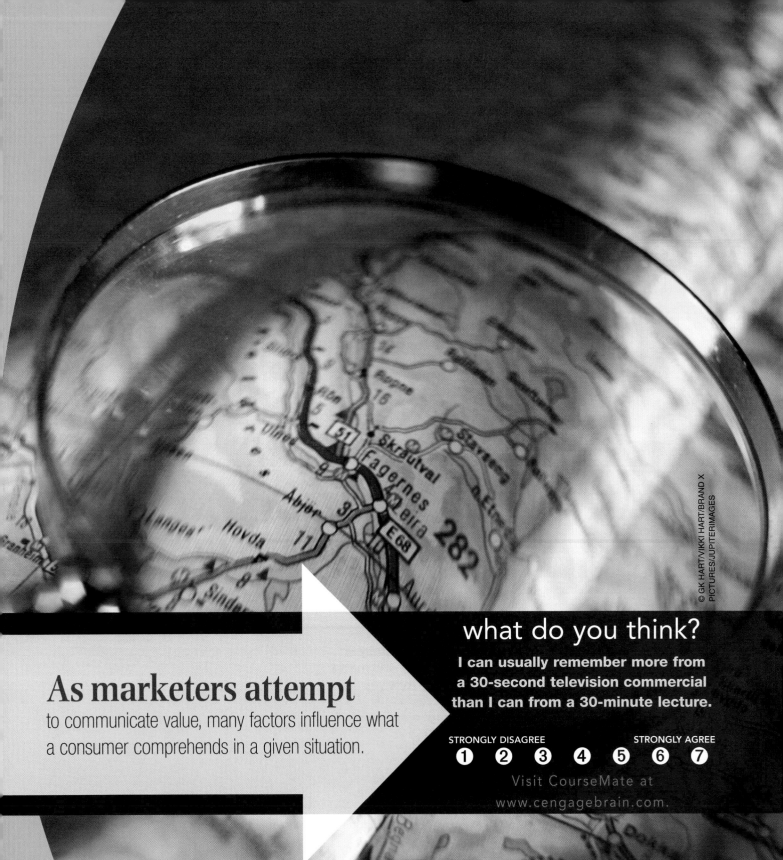

**As marketers attempt** to communicate value, many factors influence what a consumer comprehends in a given situation.

## what do you think?

**I can usually remember more from a 30-second television commercial than I can from a 30-minute lecture.**

STRONGLY DISAGREE    STRONGLY AGREE
① ② ③ ④ ⑤ ⑥ ⑦

Visit CourseMate at www.cengagebrain.com.

# 4

# Comprehension, Memory, and Cognitive Learning

## Introduction

t he previous chapter discussed the preliminary stages of perception and consumer learning. We defined learning as a change in behavior resulting from interaction between a person and a stimulus. We also described the behaviorist approach to learning, which focuses on behaviors rather than inner, mental processes. Cognitive learning focuses on *mental* processes occurring as consumers comprehend and elaborate upon information received. The cognitive perspective views learning as an active, mental process wherein information is processed, associations are made, and knowledge is gained.

Cognitive learning takes place through information processing. Exhibit 4.1 shows the basic components of information processing. We have already discussed several of the concepts presented in the exhibit, including exposure, attention, and comprehension. In the current chapter, we look more closely at comprehension and other issues related to cognitive learning, including memory and elaboration.

Consumers are exposed to thousands of stimuli each day. The chances are slim that any one message will be attended to, comprehended, and elaborated upon in a way that will enable the consumer to accurately encode the message in memory. As a result, consumers rarely gain meaningful knowledge from any particular marketing communication in a way they actually can use. In the same way, students also find studying a challenge because one only can pay attention to, comprehend, elaborate upon, and meaningfully encode so much information.

After studying this chapter, the student should be able to:

**LO1** Identify factors that influence consumer comprehension.

**LO2** Explain how knowledge, meaning, and value are inseparable, using the multiple stores memory theory.

**LO3** Understand how the mental associations that consumers develop are a key to learning.

**LO4** Use the concept of associative networks to map relevant consumer knowledge.

**LO5** Apply the cognitive schema concept in understanding how consumers react to products, brands, and marketing agents.

# LO1 What Influences Comprehension?

Consumers can't realize value without knowing the meaning of the things consumed. **Comprehension** refers to the interpretation or understanding a consumer develops about some attended stimulus based on the way meaning is assigned. What happens when a consumer sees a "some assembly required" sticker on a product? Of course, this means that the consumer will likely have to master a set of detailed instructions before consumption can begin. An easy-to-comprehend set of instructions would certainly contribute to the total value equation for the product. However, we all know how frustrating these instructions can be! In this and in many other ways, marketers must teach us things so that we realize the most value from consumption.

Other products contain warning labels that signal specific associated risks. Consider a typical cigarette package. A warning label will be effective only if consumers comprehend the intended message. Consumers, however, don't always comprehend messages as intended. A consumer might even see a cigarette warning label as authoritarian and ignoring it or challenging it as something contributing to smoking's appeal as "rebellion." Other times, consumers may actually overestimate the dangers associated with smoking when they read a warning of "rare" side effects.[1] Cigarette warning labels actually have only a small effect on consumer behavior.[2] Thus, warnings are only moderately successful in teaching consumers about potentially dangerous consumer behaviors.

Getting consumers to comprehend messages accurately can be difficult. Here are three important issues regarding comprehension:

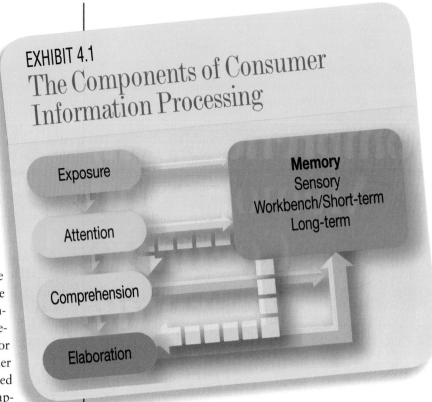

EXHIBIT 4.1
The Components of Consumer Information Processing

- Internal factors within the consumer powerfully influence the comprehension process. Recall from a previous chapter that factors influencing consumer behavior often interact with each other. Numerous components in the Consumer Value Framework alter comprehension.

- Comprehension includes both *cognitive* and *affective* elements. That is, the process of comprehension involves both thoughts and feelings. As such, comprehension applies not only to consumer learning but to consumers' attitudes as well. A number of topics in this chapter apply equally to consumer attitude formation and persuasion (a later chapter is devoted to these topics).

- Every message sends signals. **Signal theory** tells us that communications provide information in ways beyond the explicit or obvious content. A retailer promises to match competitors' prices (a price-matching guarantee) as a signal to consumers that prices are indeed low.[3] Consumers don't always comprehend messages or get the desired signal, and to this extent, consumer comprehension is not always "correct." After all, perception is subjective reality, which may or may not equal objective reality! Quite simply, consumers sometimes just don't get *it*; however, they act on what they get.

# FACTORS AFFECTING CONSUMER COMPREHENSION

Meaning and value are inseparable, and consumers must comprehend marketing messages in order to learn the intended value of a product. As marketers attempt to communicate value, many factors influence what a consumer comprehends in a given situation. While consumer researchers still have a great deal to learn about the factors that influence comprehension, Exhibit 4.2 lists things we do know regarding these factors. These factors can be divided into three categories:

- Characteristics of the message
- Characteristics of the message receiver
- Characteristics of the environment (information-processing situation)

# CHARACTERISTICS OF THE MESSAGE

Marketers believe that they can affect consumer learning by carefully planning the execution of marketing communications. If you flip through any popular magazine, you will see advertisements with many different execution styles. Here are a few tools marketers use to potentially influence comprehension and control what consumers learn.

## Physical Characteristics

The **physical characteristics** of a message refer to the elements of a message that one senses directly. These parts come together to execute a communication of some type. While these elements affect comprehension, you may note that some of these characteristics also affect the likelihood that consumers pay attention. Here are just a few physical characteristics that can contribute to effective communication.

> Meaning and value are inseparable, and consumers must comprehend marketing messages to learn the intended value of a product.

**Intensity.** Generally speaking, the greater the movement, the larger the picture, or the louder the sound, the more likely a consumer is to attend and comprehend something from a message. Signage with large numerals communicates the notion of low prices to consumers.

**Color.** Color affects the likelihood of gaining a consumer's attention, but it can also have an impact on comprehension. Gold signals quality. Some colors mean different things in different cultures. Black is often seen as a somber color in Western cultures, while white signals sad occasions in Eastern cultures. Color can directly influence how one comprehends a message.

**Font.** Consumers derive meaning from both the actual text of a message and the visual presentation of the message. Font styles send meaningful signals. The same brand or store name presented in a block font such as Courier may take on a different

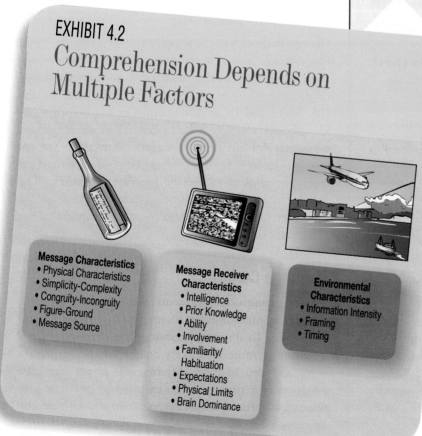

**EXHIBIT 4.2**

## Comprehension Depends on Multiple Factors

**Message Characteristics**
- Physical Characteristics
- Simplicity-Complexity
- Congruity-Incongruity
- Figure-Ground
- Message Source

**Message Receiver Characteristics**
- Intelligence
- Prior Knowledge
- Ability
- Involvement
- Familiarity/ Habituation
- Expectations
- Physical Limits
- Brain Dominance

**Environmental Characteristics**
- Information Intensity
- Framing
- Timing

*The Super 8 image signals low price. Originally, Super 8 hotel rooms were $8.88 per night.*

© JONATHAN LARSEN/DIADEM IMAGES/ALAMY

meaning if presented in a script font. For instance, research suggests that different fonts signal masculinity, femininity, activity, elegance, softness, tradition, just to name a few. Consider the two examples below:

ACME BRICK COMPANY
## ACME BRICK COMPANY

Which sends the better message for a brick company? One can easily see that the signal the font sends should be consistent with the type of service offered.[4]

**Numbers.** In the 1980s, many discos around the world independently adopted the same name. They were called, in one way or another, 2001! In the 20th century, something with a year indicating the 21st century seemed progressive. Now, we would have to try a name like 3003 to create the same effect.

Many automobile companies use seemingly nonsensical combinations of letters and numbers when creating names for new car models. For example, makes and models include: Lexus GS, Acura TL 3.2, Mercedes CLS-550, Honda S2000, and Mazda RX-8. Compare these names with something like Volkswagen Rabbit or Dodge Ram. A consumer expects a car named after a rabbit to possess rabbit-like qualities, which can be both good and bad. In contrast, combinations of numbers and letters have little specific meaning. This gives marketers a better opportunity to shape the intended meaning of a brand. Names with letters and numbers used in combination do tend to signal a "technologically advanced" meaning.

**Spacing.** All types of communicators, from salespeople to advertisers to teachers, repeat messages as a way of increasing comprehension. If a communicator is going to repeat a message multiple times, is it better to repeat it in sequence or to break up the repetition? Actually, consumers display greater recall of an intended message when information is presented in intervals rather than in sequence.[5] For instance, in media advertising, three 30-second ads spread over three hours achieve better consumer recall of information than a single 90-second advertisement.

## Simplicity–Complexity

Generally speaking, the simpler the message, the more likely a consumer develops meaningful comprehension, which, of course, relies on a consumer's ability to process information. For example, research by the U.S. Food and Drug Administration has helped them identify the simplest way to communicate important consumer information. Summary terms like *fat-free* and *low-fat* have replaced more complicated terms that were once linked to specific product attributes.[6] The Food and Drug Administration believes the new terminology better allows consumers to comprehend the desired messages.

## Message Congruity

**Message congruity** represents the extent to which a message is internally consistent and fits surrounding information. To illustrate, consider the question: "Does a consumer more effectively comprehend information when exposed to three different ads about hair care products in a row, or when exposed to one hair care product ad preceded by a detergent ad and followed by an automobile ad?"

# Keep Your Eyes on the Road!

**W**ho pays attention to billboards? Typically, the radio, a companion, or a whole lot of other billboards are competing for your attention on the road. Selective perception allows the consumer to deal with all of this, and billboards can easily lose out. Although many creative approaches are used in billboard advertisement, research suggests that some simple rules can be employed to get a consumer's attention. Two key factors are (1) make the message clear and concise. Don't get cute—just convey a clear message; and (2) locate the billboard near the point of exchange (retail location). Put the billboard close to the action and tell consumers how to get there. Simple rules like these can help marketers communicate with billboards from Atlanta, Georgia, to Tbilisi, Georgia (the country).

Sources: Taylor, C.R., G. Franke, and H.K. Bang (2006), "Use and Effectiveness of Billboards," *Journal of Advertising* 35 (Winter), 21-34. Riza, A. A., E. Kaynak and S. Yalcin (2007), "Foreign Product Purchase Behavior in Transition Economies: An Empirical Analysis of Product Information Sources Among Georgian Consumers," *Journal of Promotion Management* 13 (3), 321–337.

The conventional wisdom is that congruent content would lead to improved comprehension. However, this may not always be the case. Think about a typical television advertisement that contains background music. The ad designer can choose music that is either highly consistent or inconsistent with message content. Consider an advertisement encouraging vacations to China. Oriental music could be included in an effort to be consistent with the message content, whereas some type of Western music could be used in an "inconsistent" way. In a situation such as this, consumers may actually comprehend more from the message with inconsistent background music.[7] The reason is that the incongruity motivates deeper processing than when everything in a message is highly congruent. The result is improved comprehension.

This doesn't mean that incongruent information is always better.[8] An ad with inconsistent background music, such as an ad for China that includes Western music, will generally be liked less than an ad with consistent music. Therefore, the decision to use highly consistent message content depends on the marketing goal. If the primary goal is conveying meaningful information explicitly, some degree of incongruity is a good idea. If the primary goal is to create a favorable attitude, then markers should minimize incongruity.

The incongruity of a message with surrounding messages works in much the same way.[9] In fact, consumers will comprehend and remember more from an ad that is presented with incongruent material surrounding it. Returning to the hair care example, the consumer will comprehend and remember more when presented with only one hair care advertisement in the three-ad sequence (see Exhibit 4.3).

## Figure and Ground

Every message is presented with background, although sometimes the background becomes the message. A photographer usually concentrates on capturing a focal image in a photo

**EXHIBIT 4.3**

## Congruent or Incongruent Message Sequences?

**Congruent Messages**

Consumer comprehends less about L'Oréal

**Incongruent Messages**

Consumer comprehends more about L'Oréal

**figure** object that is intended to capture a person's attention; the focal part of any message

**ground** background in a message

**figure–ground distinction** notion that each message can be separated into the focal point (figure) and the background (ground)

**expertise** amount of knowledge that a source is perceived to have about a subject

**trustworthiness** how honest and unbiased the source is perceived to be

**credibility** extent to which a source is considered to be both an expert in a given area and trustworthy

**counterarguments** thoughts that contradict a message

**support arguments** thoughts that further support a message

frame. The focal image, or the object intended to capture a person's attention, is much the same as a **figure** in a message. In a message, everything besides the figure should be less important and simply represent the **ground** (or background) relative to the central message. The contrast between the two represents the psychological **figure–ground distinction**.

One reason consumers do not always comprehend a message as the sender intended is because the product intended to be the figure becomes the ground. Exhibit 4.4 illustrates how this occurs psychologically. What is this a picture of? If a consumer focuses on the outer rings, it looks something like a funnel. However, focus on the dot in the center and the rings can actually begin to disappear. What one consumer interprets as the figure may be the background to another.

## Message Source

The source of a message also can influence comprehension. Message sources include a famous celebrity in an advertisement, a salesperson in a sales context, a family member giving advice, a Facebook friend, or even a computer-animated avatar. A source influences comprehension to varying degrees based upon characteristics like these:[10]

1. Likeability
2. Attractiveness
3. Expertise
4. Trustworthiness

A likeable source can change the interpretation of a stimulus. For years, consumers have enjoyed the M&M's characters as the most liked spokes-characters for any product. However, younger generations express a preference for the Aflac Duck and the Geico Gecko.[11] Most people would find it difficult to argue with the claim, "15 minutes can save you 15% or more on car insurance" when voiced by the Gecko. In contrast, the Geico Cavemen were not so liked, and if one of them stated the same claim, a consumer may be compelled to disagree. Consumers react much the same way to a source perceived as attractive. The Geico Cavemen lose out here, too.

**Expertise** refers to the amount of knowledge that a source is perceived to have about a subject. **Trustworthiness** refers to how honest and unbiased a source is perceived to be. Consumers associate expertise and trustworthiness with **credibility**. Like likeability, credible sources tend to lower the chances that consumers will develop **counterarguments** toward a message. Counterarguments are thoughts that contradict a message. **Support arguments** are thoughts that further support a message. Brand managers should especially rely on a likeable, attractive, and credible source. BP Chief Executive Tony Hayward may not have been the best face for messages related to the 2010 oil spill disaster off the coast of Louisiana. His expertise alone proved insufficient to prevent counterarguments to practically anything he said.

In summary, we can say that desirable source characteristics can help to convey the desired message

**EXHIBIT 4.4**
**The Figure and Ground Distinction**

through cognitive processes. However, sources can influence consumers in other more subtle ways. In a later chapter, we focus on how sources affect attitude change.

# MESSAGE RECEIVER CHARACTERISTICS

## Intelligence/Ability

As a general statement, intelligent, well-educated consumers are more likely to accurately comprehend a message than are less-intelligent or less-educated consumers. With this being said, we offer two caveats. First, a great deal of knowledge is specific to particular product categories. Therefore, a consumer who does not have a high IQ may be able to comprehend certain product information more readily than another consumer with a high IQ. Second, even a highly intelligent consumer would understand a simpler message better than a more complex message. Marketers should communicate information pertaining to product warnings, usage instructions, or assembly directions in a way that those with relatively low intelligence can understand it.[12]

*The Gecko has proved an effective source for Geico.*

## Prior Knowledge

The human brain matches incoming information with pre-existing knowledge. This pre-existing, or prior, knowledge provides resources, or a way through which other stimuli can be comprehended. Even consumers of very high intelligence may lack prior knowledge to comprehend certain consumer messages. This is why parents sometimes need their children to operate the television remote control. Even young kids have more knowledge of handheld electronic devices than many adults—particularly college professors. Consumers display a preference for things that are consistent with their prior knowledge.

Consider the role that superstition can play in comprehending value propositions. Lucky in Love? Ritz-Carlton and Walmart each offered promotions encouraging consumers to get married on 7/7/07. Consumers could get a 7-night honeymoon stay at the Ritz for $77,777.[13] The same promotion offered on a Friday the 13th in 2013 would not likely be so successful. Going beyond lucky and unlucky numbers, consumers in some cultures associate certain colors with good or bad fortune, and some associate certain foods with good fortune. Even marketers who are not superstitious would be wise to acknowledge the meanings that such beliefs, examples of prior knowledge, can convey to products.

## Involvement

Consumers are not equally involved with every message sent their way. As discussed in Chapter 3, highly involved consumers tend to pay more attention to messages. They also exert more effort in comprehending messages.[14] As a result, these consumers show better recall than consumers with lower levels of involvement.[15] Consider the consumer who views a website describing a new product. The highly involved consumer will click through more hyperlinks, explore more pages, and comprehend more information than a less-involved consumer.

Returning to the FDA labeling/instructions issue, marketers face the challenge of designing messages that either highly involved or uninvolved consumers will comprehend. In 1990, the U.S. Congress passed the Nutrition Labeling and Education Act (NLEA), to ensure that consumers would understand product warnings and nutrition labels regardless of their level of involvement. As a result of this act, marketers began to use simpler summary information on their labels. However, evidence suggests that even though this type of information is preferred, highly involved consumers still comprehend more from the labels than consumers with lower levels of involvement.[16]

## Familiarity/Habituation

Consumers tend to like the familiar. However, in terms of comprehension, familiarity can *lower* a consumer's motivation to process a message. While some degree of familiarity may improve consumer attitude, high levels of familiarity may actually reduce comprehension.[17]

Consumer habituation is a concept resulting from familiarity. **Habituation** is the process by which continuous exposure to a stimulus affects the comprehension of and response to some stimulus. Consider the following psychological experiment. Subjects in one treatment group immerse their arms in extremely cold water (5°C) for 60 seconds. Obviously, this is an unpleasant task. Another group of subjects is asked to do the very same thing, except after the first immersion, they are asked to immediately immerse their arms into slightly less frigid (10°C) water for 30 additional seconds. At the end of the procedure, both groups rated the task hedonically. Surprisingly, the group that immersed their arms for 90 seconds rated the task more favorably than did the group that immersed their arms for only 60 seconds.

Habituation theory explains this result. The first 60 seconds of exposure to the extremely cold water habituated the subjects and created an **adaptation level**. As a result, when the second group was exposed to water that was still unpleasant, but slightly warmer than the first, a more favorable evaluation was obtained because the entire experience was framed by the relatively more valuable (less painful) last 30 seconds.

To illustrate habituation in a consumer setting, consider that consumers in the United States, Canada, Australia, and throughout Western Europe have long been habituated to fairly pleasant shopping experiences in which many goods and services are readily available. This hardly compares with many parts of the world,

# Healthiness can be bad for your brain?

Comprehending the consequences of consuming various foods is difficult. Just wanting to eat healthy food isn't enough to allow consumers to know what's best. Foods that experts say are healthy today may not be considered so tomorrow. Eggs, for instance, have repeatedly come in and out of vogue as a healthy food. College consumers today frequently down an energy bar as a quick alternative to a full lunch. Are they good for you? Some contain trans fat. They can also be very high in calories. At the same time, they contain vitamins, protein, and fiber. Do health-conscious consumers always make better decisions about their diet? Sometimes they make mistakes. Two reasons for this are that the consumer lacks the ability to process health-related information or, even when knowledgeable, prior beliefs strongly influence their comprehension. Once a consumer believes a certain food is healthy, he/she may discount information that contradicts that belief to maintain consistency in knowledge. What about an energy drink before class? Read the label. Is it a healthy choice?

Sources: E. Howlett, S. Burton, J. Kozup (2008), "How Modification of the Nutrition Fats Panel Influences Consumers at Risk for Heart Disease: The Case of Trans-Fats," *Journal of Public Policy and Marketing*, 27 (Spring), 83-97. R.W. Naylor, C.M. Droms and K.L. Haws (2009), "Eating with a Purpose: Consumer Response to Functional Food Health Claims in Conflicting Versus Complementary Information Environments," *Journal of Public Policy and Marketing* 28 (Fall), 221-233.

© ISTOCKPHOTO.COM/JILL FROMER

including third world nations, where shopping as we know it hardly exists. A decade after the breakup of the Soviet Union, consumer researchers measured the hedonic and utilitarian shopping value Russian consumers experienced trying to obtain everyday goods and services.[18] The capitalist reforms had been slow to spread throughout Russia and these consumers still faced shops with empty shelves and long lines to buy things like boots or jackets. A Russian word to describe this experience is **dostats,** which roughly means "acquiring things with great difficulty." The surprising result of the research was that the Russian consumers reported similar amounts of shopping value compared to American shoppers. What is the explanation for this outcome? Even though shopping in Russia was certainly worse than shopping in America, shopping was still framed by their life experiences beyond the familiar reality of *dostats*. These life experiences provided a frame of reference in which shopping was *less* unpleasant than were many other routine activities.

## Expectations

**Expectations** are beliefs of what will happen in a future situation. They play an important role in many consumer behavior settings and can impact comprehension. We discuss expectations in more detail later when satisfaction becomes the focus. For now, note that what consumers expect to experience has an impact on their comprehension of the environment.

To illustrate, consider how packaging influences consumers' comprehension of products. Beverage marketers have realized for decades that packaging plays a major role in how beverages are perceived. In fact, studies indicate that consumers cannot even identify their "favorite" brand of beer without the package/label.[19] Removing the label affects consumers' expectations, which affects their comprehension, by blocking brand-specific thoughts.

## Physical Limits

A consumer's physical limitations can also influence comprehension. For example, we all have limits in our ability to hear, see, smell, taste, and think. Obviously, if someone can't hear, then they can't comprehend information in an audio message. Also, consumers who are color blind will have difficulty comprehending information related to color. For instance, if a caution or warning label is colored red to signal risk, a color-blind consumer will not likely comprehend this aspect of the message.[20]

## Brain Dominance

Brain dominance refers to the phenomenon of *hemispheric lateralization*. Some people tend to be either right-brain or left-brain dominant. This, of course, does not mean that some consumers use *only* the left or right parts of their brains! Right-brain-dominant consumers tend to be visual processors (tend to favor images for communication), whereas left-brain-dominant consumers tend to deal better with verbal processing (words).

# ENVIRONMENTAL CHARACTERISTICS

## Information Intensity

**Information intensity** refers to the amount of information available for a consumer to process within a given environment. When consumers are overloaded, the overload not only affects their attention but also their comprehension and eventual reaction. For example,

evidence suggests that the amount of information presented to consumers participating in online auctions affects their bidding behavior, with highly intense information environments being associated with lower price sensitivity.[21]

## Framing

**Framing** is a phenomenon in which the meaning of something is influenced (perceived differently) by the information environment. Thus, the same event can produce multiple meanings depending on how the information is presented. For example, what does a driver comprehend when the gas gauge shows only a quarter of a tank of gas remaining? If she is driving through the suburbs of her hometown, she probably does not comprehend this as very significant. However, if she is driving through a sparsely populated desert, that same information may result in an entirely different comprehension and reaction. The environment has framed the information.

**Prospect theory** hypothesizes that the way in which information is framed differentially affects risks assessments and associated consumer decisions. For example, a consumer may read a message like "save 50 percent" or "you pay half price!" Or, a beef label might read "95% lean" or "5% fat." Which one is better? Are they saying the same thing?

To illustrate prospect theory, consider what you have likely heard about risks associated with prolonged exposure to the sun. The following are two methods of presenting information about those risks:[22]

- Failing to use sunscreen leaves one vulnerable to skin cancer.
- Using sunscreen helps avoid skin cancer.

The first statement is negatively framed. Use this product or get skin cancer! The second statement is positively framed. Use this product and stay healthy!

**Priming** refers to a cognitive process in which active concepts frame thoughts and therefore affect both value and meaning. Negatively framed information primes

**expectations** beliefs of what will happen in some future situation

**information intensity** amount of information available for a consumer to process within a given environment

**framing** a phenomenon in which the meaning of something is influenced (perceived differently) by the information environment

**prospect theory** theory that suggests that a decision, or argument, can be framed in different ways and that the framing affects risk assessments consumers make

**priming** cognitive process in which context or environment activates concepts and frames thoughts and therefore both value and meaning losses, which consumers wish to avoid, and encourages consumers to be more willing to take a chance on a product and in this case spend some money on the sunscreen. Also, negatively framed information generally has a greater impact on consumers, and so the perceived value of the sunscreen in the above example may be increased by framing the information negatively. The greater impact of negative information is a key aspect of prospect theory. Exhibit 4.5 illustrates this aspect of framing.

**EXHIBIT 4.5**
## An Illustration of Framing — What Would You Do?

Choose one of the two options below:
1. You lose $200.
2. You have a 20% chance of losing $1,000 and an 80 percent chance of losing nothing.

Choose one of the two options below:
1. You win $200.
2. You have a 20% chance of winning $1,000 and an 80 percent chance of winning nothing.

© ISTOCKPHOTO.COM/STEVE LUKER
© ISTOCKPHOTO.COM/JUSTIN HORROCKS

Most consumers faced with the first choice set in the exhibit will choose option 2. Notice that the frame is negative.[23] In the second choice set, consumers tend to choose option 1. In the second set, the frame is positive (priming gains—saving life instead of losing life). This happens even though the expected value ($E(v)$) for each choice is the same ($200). Presenting a negative frame primes thoughts that lead to a consumer being more willing to take risks. In terms of prospect theory, we say that losses weigh more heavily than gains. Losing $200 is certainly a loss and hurts hedonic value more than winning $200 helps create hedonic value.[24] As such, consumers faced with the first choice set are more willing to take a risk.

Priming occurs in many subtle ways beyond positive and negative frames. Brand names and logos can serve as primes, for instance. A recent experiment suggested that the Apple logo primed greater creativity among problem solvers exposed to the logo compared to other problem solvers.[25] The expectations of a bargain can be primed by other prices in the shopping environment. For instance, a consumer may think $200 is a good price for a watch in a counter filled with watches selling for $1,000 or more. Conversely, the same watch at $200 may not seem like a good deal when it is the most expensive watch in the case.[26]

## Timing

Timing also affects comprehension. For our purposes, timing refers to both the *amount of time* a consumer has to process a message and *the point in time* at which the consumer receives the message. For example, consumers who have only a couple of seconds to process a message, such as when driving by a billboard advertisement, cannot possibly comprehend a message in as much depth as a consumer who is not facing a timing issue.

The time of day can also affect the meaning and value of a product. For many consumers, coffee is a morning beverage. Consumers comprehend an advertisement for a brand of coffee quite differently based on the time of day. Most consumers will respond to a coffee advertisement in the morning far more enthusiastically than to the same ad shown before bedtime, because of habituation effects associating hot coffee with morning consumption.

As you can see, many factors influence how we comprehend marketing messages. Now, we turn our focus to the other major concept in cognitive learning, memory.

# LO2 Multiple Store Theory of Acquiring, Storing, and Using Knowledge

**m**emory is the psychological process by which knowledge is recorded. As shown in Exhibit 4.1, all of the elements of the information-processing model are related to memory. In our chapter on perception, we discussed the topics of implicit and explicit memory. Here, we discuss memory from the cognitive learning perspective—the multiple store theory of memory.

# MULTIPLE STORE THEORY OF MEMORY

The **multiple store theory of memory** views the memory process as utilizing three different storage areas within the human brain. The three areas are sensory memory, workbench (or short-term) memory, and long-term memory. Exhibit 4.6 illustrates this approach.

## Sensory Memory

**Sensory memory** is the area in memory where we store what we encounter with our five human senses. When we hear something, sensory memory is responsible for storing the sounds. The consumer walking through a movie theater lobby encounters many sounds, smells, and sights. Sensory memory picks these things out and stores them even though the consumer has not yet allocated attention to any of these sensations. As such, this portion of memory is considered to be preattentive.

Sensory memory is truly remarkable. For one thing, it has unlimited capacity. Sensory memory stores everything one is exposed to, taking an exact record of what is encountered. Our sensory memory uses multiple distinctive mechanisms. **Iconic storage** is the storage of visual information as an exact representation of the scene. **Echoic storage** is the storage of auditory information as an exact representation of the sound. All sights, sounds, smells, tactile sensations, and tastes are recorded as exact replicas in the mind of the consumer.

If this is the case, then why can we recall only a fraction of what we encounter? Another remarkable aspect of sensory memory concerns duration. Sensory memory is very perishable and lasts only a very short time. In most cases, sensory memory begins to fade immediately after the sensation is recorded and lasts less than a second. Thus, the strength of sensory memory is capacity, but the weakness is duration.

Sensory memory can easily be illustrated. Take a quick look at an object and then close your eyes. What happens in the fractions of a second immediately after you shut your eyes? In most instances, your brain will hold the image immediately after you close your eyes—that is, you will be able to see the image mentally. However, very quickly things will start to fall out of the mental picture until eventually only the most central features can be pictured. If you are familiar with a strobe light, you may have noticed that when the light speeds up, images look continuous. This is because sensory memory is able to "hold" the image through the dark portion of the strobe, that is, until the next image is physically sensed.

Although sensory memory is important, its usefulness is limited because images are lost very quickly. Fortunately, sensory memory works in conjunction with other memory functions, allowing a consumer to gain information and knowledge.

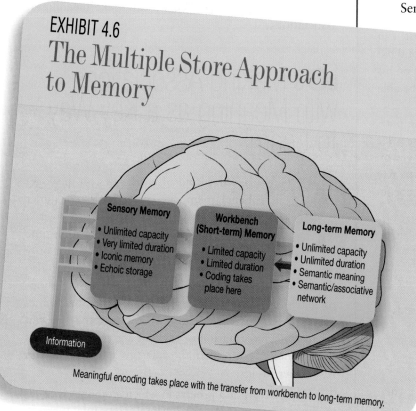

**EXHIBIT 4.6**

## The Multiple Store Approach to Memory

**Sensory Memory**
- Unlimited capacity
- Very limited duration
- Iconic memory
- Echoic storage

**Workbench (Short-term) Memory**
- Limited capacity
- Limited duration
- Coding takes place here

**Long-term Memory**
- Unlimited capacity
- Unlimited duration
- Semantic meaning
- Semantic/associative network

Information

Meaningful encoding takes place with the transfer from workbench to long-term memory.

**workbench memory**
storage area in the memory system where information is stored while it is being processed and encoded for later recall

**encoding** process by which information is transferred from workbench memory to long-term memory for permanent storage

**retrieval** process by which information is transferred back into workbench memory for additional processing when needed

## Workbench Memory

**Workbench memory** is the storage area in the memory system where information is stored and encoded for placement in long-term memory and, eventually, retrieved for future use. As we will see, workbench memory works very closely with long-term memory. **Encoding** is the process by which information is transferred from workbench memory to long-term memory for permanent storage. **Retrieval** is the process by which information is transferred back into workbench memory for additional processing when needed.

To illustrate workbench memory, imagine a consumer who is walking the aisles of an Auchan hypermart in France. The consumer places several produce items into the cart, including some Camembert, paté de canard, Morbier, and multiple household items including paper towels, storage bags, bleach, and toilet tissue. How much do you think all of this is going to cost the consumer? If he doesn't physically write down each item's cost, can we expect that he will be able to know what the total bill will be? To some extent, his accuracy will depend on his ability to hold prices in memory long enough to be able to compute a total upon checkout.

Let's consider a single item. He picks up the paté, checks the price, and puts the item in the cart. The price quickly enters his sensory memory and then moves on to his workbench memory because he is trying to pay attention to the price. The relevancy of duration, capacity, and involvement quickly come into play.

- **Duration.** The term *short-term* is often used when describing workbench memory because this memory storage area, like sensory memory, has limited duration. The duration is not nearly as limited as sensory memory, but stimuli that enter short-term memory may stay there approximately 30 seconds or so without some intervention. Therefore, our consumer can hardly be expected to remember the prices for all items in his cart by the time the checkout counter is reached.

- **Capacity.** Unlike sensory memory, workbench memory has limited capacity. Generally, the capacity limit for workbench memory is between three and seven units of information. Think of a physical workbench. If the bench is almost full, we cannot expect to put additional items on it. Some items must be removed first. Thus, our consumer cannot be expected to remember all the prices of all items in a shopping cart, especially if he is buying several products. In fact, working memory is even taxed further if the prices contain more syllables. A price of $13.37 is harder to remember than $12.10 because it contains more sounds.[27]

- **Involvement.** The capacity of workbench memory expands and contracts based on the level of a consumer's involvement. The more involved a consumer is with a message, the greater will be the capacity of his workbench memory. When involvement is very low, workbench memory capacity contracts to a minimum.

To test your own workbench memory, try to do the following: Without looking back, name all the items purchased by our French consumer. How many can you remember? Don't feel bad if you can't remember them all. In fact, most people would not be able to recall all of the items. However, most consumers would be able to recall at least two items. For instance, many would recall that toilet tissue was one item. Unless a consumer has some knowledge of French cheeses, the Camembert and Morbier are not likely to be recalled. We recall things better when we can make meaningful associations.

# LO3 Making Associations with Meaning as a Key Way to Learn

So, what kind of work goes on in workbench memory? The task of a consumer may be to recall things, both over a short time period and over a long time period. The consumer should not only recall prices while in the store, but also during the days and even weeks following the shopping trip.[28] When we use the term "remember something," we often are referring to the fact that we can recall some information or make it active in our minds intentionally. Four mental processes help consumers remember things:

1. **Repetition** is a process in which a thought is held in short-term memory by mentally repeating the thought.

2. **Dual Coding** is a process in which two different sensory "traces" are available to remember something. As we shall see, a *trace* is a mental path by which some thought becomes active.

3. **Meaningful Encoding** is a process that occurs when preexisting knowledge is used to assist in storing new information.

4. **Chunking** is a process of grouping stimuli by meaning so that multiple stimuli can become a single memory unit.

Meaningful encoding and chunking rely heavily on making associations between new information and meaning that is stored in long-term memory.

**Repetition.** Repetition is a commonly employed way of trying to remember something. Picture someone trying to remember the license plate number:

TT867-53-09

One way to remember this number is by thinking it repeatedly. This process is known as *rehearsal*. However, one major problem with this approach is **cognitive interference**. Cognitive interference simply means that other things are vying for processing capacity when a consumer rehearses information. To illustrate, try to count backwards from 1,000 by 3. This seems like an easy task. But, if you try to do this while someone is calling out random numbers at the same time, the task becomes much more difficult. All things equal, repetition is the weakest form of learning.

**Dual Coding.** Dual coding can be more effective than repetition. To illustrate dual-coding effects, consider Exhibit 4.7. This exhibit illustrates the way a scent can improve recall.[29] Researchers tested the extent to which product feature recall might be enhanced by dual encoding using scents. Consumers in the experiment showed greater recall for product features, even a product as innocuous as a pencil, when the product was infused with a scent. In a similar way, associating products with music helps consumers remember information. Why is this? A consumer is able to retrieve the information in two ways—by the content of the message and by the sound of the music. Jingles have lost favor recently in favor of recycled pop songs.[30] However, most readers can probably easily fill in the product name that completes this jingle:

> Give me a break, give me a break, break me off a piece of that _____.

Images also can assist with dual coding.[31] Chick-fil-A employs a logo that turns the C into a chicken. Thus, consumers can easily remember Chick-fil-A and the types of products it sells.

**Meaningful Encoding.** Meaningful encoding involves the association of active information in short-term memory with other information recalled from long-term memory. By this process, new information is coded with meaning.

To illustrate meaningful encoding, let's return to the license plate example. Consumers often find it difficult to associate anything meaningful with a number. However, a fan of 1980s pop rock would recognize the sequence of digits as the title of a famous hit by the rock artist Tommy Tutone. (The letters *TT* on the plate support this.) If a consumer can retrieve memory of this song and attach it to the license plate, the plate's number would be much easier to remember. In a way, this example involves both dual and meaningful encoding because the music (also stored in memory) serves as a memory aid itself. For a consumer who knows 1980s music, the numbers

**repetition** simple mechanism in which a thought is kept alive in short-term memory by mentally repeating the thought

**cognitive interference** notion that everything else that the consumer is exposed to while trying to remember something is also vying for processing capacity and thus interfering with memory and comprehension

**dual coding** coding that occurs when two different sensory traces are available to remember something

**meaningful encoding** coding that occurs when information from long-term memory is placed on the workbench and attached to the information on the workbench in a way that the information can be recalled and used later

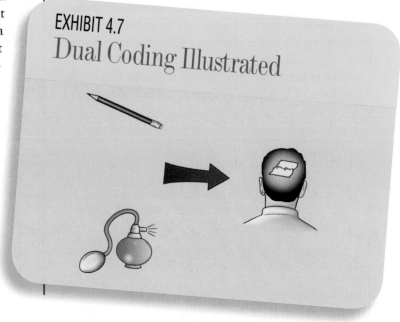

EXHIBIT 4.7
Dual Coding Illustrated

**chunking** process of grouping stimuli by meaning so that multiple stimuli can become one memory unit

**response generation** reconstruction of memory traces into a formed recollection of information

867–5309 can only mean Tommy Tutone. (If you know the song, it's probably going to be stuck in your head now.)

**Chunking.** Chunking is the process of grouping stimuli by *meaning* so that multiple stimuli can become one memory unit. Remember that the capacity of workbench memory is rarely more than 7 chunks of information. A chunk is a single memory unit. Here's a simple experiment that helps demonstrate what is meant by a chunk of memory. Show someone the following list of numbers for only a few seconds:

1 4 9 2 1 7 7 6 1 9 4 5

After taking the list away, engage them in conversation for a couple of minutes. Then, ask the person to recall the list. Why is this task so difficult? When someone treats each numeral as a distinct chunk of information, his or her memory capacity is exceeded. After all, 12 numerals, or chunks, are included in the list.

Now, look at the list in this way:

1 4 9 2    1 7 7 6    1 9 4 5

If the person did well in American history class, the task should be considerably easier. A history student should recognize that these are all important dates in U.S. history. The set of 12 numbers can now be stored and recalled as only three pieces of information instead of 12!

Marketers can also use humor to encourage chunking. Consider a coffee advertisement using the following lines spoken by two cartoon-type characters:[32] The first character says, "Other coffee tastes like mud"; then the other character says, "That's because they're ground every morning!" A tagline for the ad could be either "The Taste of Well-balanced Coffee" or "The Taste of Exquisitely Ground Coffee." The second

> Chunking is an important mental activity because better chunking leads to improved recall.

*PRNEWSFOTO/CHICK-FIL-A, INC., STANLEY LEARY*

*Cows or chickens? Chick-fil-A is easy to remember.*

tagline plays on the idea of ground coffee, related to the ad's humor. Therefore, the second tagline would lead to better encoding and recall. Humor helps to facilitate the process of encoding the message into a meaningful chunk. Marketers designing advertisements or websites, for example, should be careful to group information by meaning in order to assist consumers in encoding chunks of information.

**Retrieval and Workbench Memory.** As we have discussed, a task of workbench memory is the retrieval of information from long-term memory. When a consumer retrieves information from long-term memory, it is processed once again in workbench memory. As a part of this process, long-term memory is scanned for relevant information. Through a process of **response generation**, consumers reconstruct memory traces into a formed recollection of the information they are trying to remember.

Marketers can help this process by ensuring that information placed in marketing messages is also placed on in-store promotions, and perhaps product packaging. One way of doing this is by using *integrated marketing communications* to ensure that a unified promotional message is sent across all consumer contacts.

Clearly, meaning and knowledge are the keys to effective coding and cognitive learning. To illustrate, consider the following list of words:

- Weep  Sheep  Deep  Keep  Peep

Suppose a subject is asked to look at this list and the next day asked if the word *sleep* was on the list. Would there be many false recalls (indicating the word was on the list when it was not or vice versa)?

Now consider another list:

- Night  Rest  Awake  Tired  Dream

Would this list produce fewer false memories? The answer is yes. The key is that the second list enables more meaningful encoding and thus better memory.[33]

## Long-Term Memory

A consumer's long-term memory plays a very important role in learning. **Long-term memory** is a repository for all information that a person has encountered. This portion of memory has unlimited capacity and unlimited duration. Barring some physical incapacity, long-term memory represents permanent information storage. Information stored in long-term memory is coded with **semantic coding**, which means the stimuli are converted to meaning that can be expressed verbally.

Why can't consumers always recall information when needed if storage is permanent? The problem is not a storage issue as much as it is a retrieval issue. To illustrate, consider that even things consumers process at very low levels leave some memory trace. A **memory trace** is the mental path by which some thought becomes active. For example, the childhood Christmas memories of French consumers generally include a bûche de Noel. The memory traces from Christmas to the bûche de Noel also spread to branded products associated with these products, such as Hershey's cocoa and Domino powdered sugar.

Psychologically, a memory trace shows how cognitive activation spreads from one concept to another. This process is known as **spreading activation**. Marketers want their brand names to cause cognitive activation to spread to favorable, rather than unfavorable, thoughts. For example, consider the following brands:

- Tabasco

- KFC

Tabasco is most often associated with "hot." Generally, hot things are good. Hot music is good, hot fashions are good, and hot food is good. Therefore, consumers are willing to purchase Tabasco brand clothing (ties, shirts, etc.).

**Mental Tagging.** Let's look again at Exhibit 4.1. In psychological terms, a **tag** is a small piece of coded information that helps that particular piece of knowledge get retrieved. The tags function much like the bar-coded information on checked luggage. When everything works right, the information on the tag allows the luggage to be located. However, we all realize that not everything always goes right and luggage sometimes ends up in the wrong place. Similarly, if consumers do not tag information in a meaningful way, the encoding process results in errors.

As adults, most people have recalled some innocuous childhood memory for seemingly no apparent reason. These types of memories illustrate how long-term memory is permanent and how events that were poorly tagged during encoding can emerge at practically any time. Stimuli that consumers pay attention to but do not really comprehend or elaborate upon tend to be poorly tagged.

**Rumination.** **Rumination** refers to unintentional but recurrent memory of long-ago events that are not triggered by anything in the environment.[34] These thoughts frequently include consumption-related activities. Brand meaning can be

**long-term memory** repository for all information that a person has encountered

**semantic coding** type of coding wherein stimuli are converted to meaning that can be expressed verbally

**memory trace** mental path by which some thought becomes active

**spreading activation** way cognitive activation spreads from one concept (or node) to another

**tag** small piece of coded information that helps with the retrieval of knowledge

**rumination** unintentional but recurrent memory of long-ago events that are spontaneously (not evoked by the environment) triggered

PRNEWSFOTO/MCILHENNY COMPANY

**nostalgia** a mental yearning to relive the past associated with emotions related to longing

**associative network** network of mental pathways linking all knowledge within memory; sometimes referred to as a semantic network

**declarative knowledge** cognitive components that represent facts

**nodes** concepts found in an associative network

**paths** representations of the association between nodes in an associative network

clouded by bad feelings that accompany rumination. Not all rumination is bad, however, and nostalgic rumination may include positive associations with brands. **Nostalgia**, a mental yearning to relive the past, produces emotions of longing. Often nostalgic memories are tagged with product and brand associations. Cracker Barrel stores are filled with products like Mallo Cups, Moon Pies, and Pixy Stix, which seem to assimilate well with memories of childhood and childhood vacations.

# LO4 Associative Networks and Consumer Knowledge

## ASSOCIATIVE NETWORKS

Knowledge in long-term memory is stored in an associative network. An **associative network**, sometimes referred to as a semantic network, is a network of mental pathways linking knowledge within memory. These networks are similar to family trees, as they represent known linkages between objects.

## ASSOCIATIVE NETWORK GRAPHICS

Exhibit 4.8 illustrates the concept by showing a portion of a consumer's associative network that shows spreading activation from the Mercedes Benz brand. This illustrates the knowledge that can help identify a Mercedes Benz within a consumer's long-term memory. The network illustration also shows where cognitive activation flows after the Mercedes concept becomes active.

## DECLARATIVE KNOWLEDGE

**Declarative knowledge** is a term used in psychology to refer to cognitive components that represent facts. Declarative knowledge is represented in an associative network when two nodes are linked by a path. **Nodes** simply represent concepts in the network, while **paths** show the association between nodes in the network. A consumer's declarative knowledge may not always be correct, but they do act upon the beliefs this knowledge represents. The following are examples of declarative knowledge based on the associative network in Exhibit 4.8:

A Mercedes is an automobile. A Mercedes is expensive. A Mercedes is luxurious. A Mercedes is silver. A Mercedes is a sedan. A sedan is an automobile. A Mercedes is German. Germans drink beer.

In everyday experiences, a consumer compares all of these bits of knowledge with reality. Every time a consumer encounters a supportive instance of declarative knowledge, that knowledge becomes stronger. Consider: "A Mercedes is silver." Not every Mercedes is silver. But, when consumers are asked to name the first color that comes to mind when they think of Mercedes, they are most likely to say silver (with black coming in

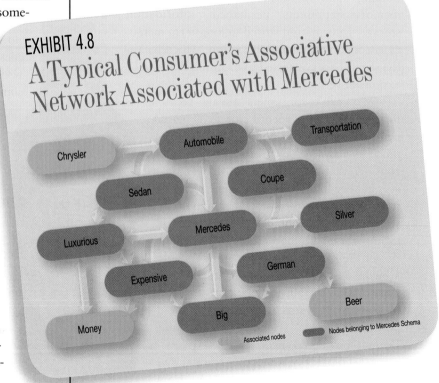

**EXHIBIT 4.8**
**A Typical Consumer's Associative Network Associated with Mercedes**

Chrysler · Automobile · Transportation · Sedan · Coupe · Silver · Luxurious · Mercedes · Expensive · German · Beer · Money · Big

Associated nodes · Nodes belonging to Mercedes Schema

second). Every time a consumer sees a silver Mercedes, this belief becomes stronger, and so the association between Mercedes and silver becomes stronger. When a consumer sees a white or blue Mercedes, the rule may diminish slightly in strength. Associative networks contain rules that become more likely to be used as they get stronger. Now consider: "Germans drink beer." If consumers hold this declarative knowledge, they will expect to encounter more Germans who are beer drinkers than, say, Germans who enjoy sipping a Cabernet Sauvignon.

Amazingly, every concept within a consumer's associative network is linked to every other concept. Consider the following request:

> List at least 10 snack foods in 60 seconds or less.

A typical consumer would list things like potato chips, an energy bar, a Twinkie, and a candy bar. Few would argue that these are indeed snack foods. All are linked to the snack concept and distinct from other food categories—like dinner entrees. A glass of milk may also be a snack, but the association between milk and snack food must first pass through several nodes. By that time, the association is weak. Selling milk as a snack, therefore, would be difficult. However, if a dairy packages milk in a small container reminiscent of a snack food's plastic wrapper, the likelihood that consumers would view milk as a snack will increase, and the rule that milk can be a snack would subsequently increase in strength.

# LO5 Product and Brand Schemas

a consumer's knowledge for a brand or product is contained in a **schema**. A schema is a type of associative network that works as a cognitive representation of a phenomenon that provides meaning to that entity. Exhibit 4.9 illustrates a product schema—snack food—while Exhibit 4.8 illustrates a brand schema—Mercedes Benz. A brand schema is the smaller part within one's total associative network responsible for defining a particular marketing entity. Each time a consumer encounters something that could be a Mercedes Benz, the mind quickly compares all the associations in the schema to see if indeed the thought is correct. Several types of schemata (plural for schema) exist.

**schema** cognitive representation of a phenomenon that provides meaning to that entity

**exemplar** concept within a schema that is the single best representative of some category; schema for something that really exists

## EXEMPLARS

An **exemplar** is a concept within a schema that is the single best representative of some category. Exemplars can be different for different people. In a snack food schema, potato chips may be the exemplar. Katy Perry may be the category exemplar for a female pop singer. Disney World may be the exemplar for a vacation destination. Other examples in a category are compared to the exemplar. When a consumer encounters a carrot, the association with chips as the exemplar of a snack food may not be close. But, if the retailer offers small bite-sized carrots enclosed in a small plastic bag, they may be associated with a bag of chips and fit into the snack food category. Exhibit 4.10 illustrates other possible category exemplars.

## PROTOTYPES

Some categories are not well represented by an exemplar. For instance, a "car salesman" category likely does not evoke a specific person who best

**EXHIBIT 4.9**
## The Knowledge for Snack Foods

Small
Snack Food
Plastic Wrapper
Savory
Sweet
Crackers
Chips
Twinkie
Cheap
Cookies
Money
Greasy
Milk

**prototype** schema that is the best representative of some category but that is not represented by an existing entity; conglomeration of the most associated characteristics of a category

**script** schema representing an event

represents that category. However, an image is associated in one's mind with the category. The image contains the characteristics most associated with a car salesperson. Several characteristics may come to mind. This type of schema is known as a **prototype**. Whether represented by a prototype or an exemplar, consumers compare new and unknown examples to the standard by comparing features with those found in the schema.

## REACTION TO NEW PRODUCTS/BRANDS

When consumers encounter new products or brands, they react to them by comparing them to the existing schema. Europeans are used to small cars. Thus, when Mercedes introduced the "Smart" car in 1998, Europeans were more likely to accept it than American consumers. In the U.S., the Smart car most resembles a golf cart! American consumers don't necessarily fit the Smart car in the auto category. To the extent that a new product or brand can share the same "nodes," or characteristics, with an existing brand, consumers will more easily understand the product. Not many consumers know that *Smart* is a name combining the Swatch and Mercedes brand. Mercedes, perhaps wisely, did not introduce the car under the Mercedes brand.

*Is it a car?*

© OLEKSIY MAKSYMENKO/ IMAGEBROKER.NET/PHOTOLIBRARY

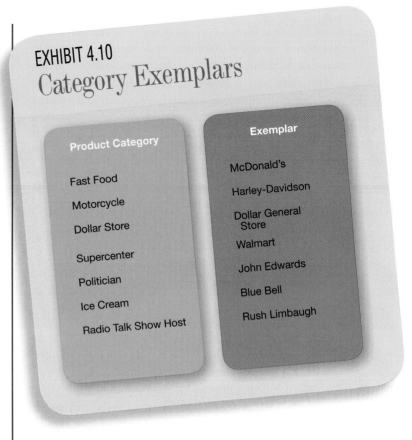

**EXHIBIT 4.10**
## Category Exemplars

| Product Category | Exemplar |
|---|---|
| Fast Food | McDonald's |
| Motorcycle | Harley-Davidson |
| Dollar Store | Dollar General Store |
| Supercenter | Walmart |
| Politician | John Edwards |
| Ice Cream | Blue Bell |
| Radio Talk Show Host | Rush Limbaugh |

## SCRIPT

A **script** is a schema representing an event. Consumers derive expectations for service encounters from these scripts. For instance, when a consumer dines in a nice Italian restaurant, the script probably contains things such as valet parking, a greeting by a maitre d' in a nice suit, a table covered with a tablecloth, etc. Since the script is positive (fine Italian dining is a good experience), restaurant managers try to not vary too much from expectations or risk confusing, and even frustrating, consumers.

Students can probably relate to the concept of a script every time an instructor returns a graded test. For example, students have developed rules about how instructors return tests. Many students believe that if an instructor calls their name early, then the test result is generally good. If this script exists, the longer the student waits to get the test back the more anxious he is about the prospects of a poor grade.

## EPISODIC MEMORY

Closely related to the concept of a script is **episodic memory**. Episodic memory refers to the memory for past events, or episodes, in one's life. A consumer may have fond memories of childhood holiday celebrations. Another consumer may remember graduating from college or getting a first job. Both of these are episodes and they involve products and brands. Brands associated with positive events stored in episodic memory receive something of a halo, and tend to be preferred by consumers.[35] Episodic memories and scripts both can include knowledge necessary for consumers to use products. Young consumers can probably *facebook* or *tweet* each other with little problem, while other consumers may not have this script stored in memory and ready for use.

## SOCIAL SCHEMATA

A **social schema** is the cognitive representation that gives a specific type of person meaning. Another word for social schema is **social stereotype**. The stereotype captures the role expectations of a person of a specific type. For instance, consumers generally like when a service provider matches an existing stereotype. Consumers are comforted by a surgeon that looks like a surgeon and acts like a surgeon. However, consumer behavior may be altered when a service provider does not fit a social schema. A waitress that does not match the stereotype, in this case by being over or underweight, may cause a consumer to eat more or less than they might otherwise![36]

Consumers also realize that, as consumers, they belong to certain categories of person types. This phenomenon falls under the general heading of *social identity*. Many consumers will try to match the characteristics associated with a stereotype. For instance, male consumers often exhibit characteristics that confirm their fit with the male stereotype. Male consumers' reactions to feminine-based advertising may be less positive when viewed in the presence of another male consumer. This may be the result of trying to protect their male identity.[37] A male consumer may sometimes seek out products that allow him to fit better into this category.

A social schema can be based on practically any characteristic that can describe a person, including occupation, age, sex, ethnicity, religion, and even product ownership. For example, what type of person drives a VW Beetle? Chances are most consumers' descriptions of a VW Beetle owner would overlap, and VW even plays this up in their advertising. If the list stopped at energetic and interesting, the stigma would not be present. Even children associate certain types of person, like a "cool kid," with specific types of brands and products

(e.g., A&F clothing).[38]

Also, attempts to demarket a product can be implemented by stigmatizing consumption with a negative stereotype. Perhaps no better example exists than the stigmatization of smoking. A "smoker," as opposed to a nonsmoker, is more likely to be attributed with the following characteristics: *energetic, interesting, disgusting, offending,* and *unkempt.* Additionally, a person described as a smoker is liked less than a similar person described as a nonsmoker, and interestingly, even smokers are more likely to describe a fellow smoker as disgusting and offensive.[39] Thus, the stereotype seems pervasive. Obviously, a product associated with increasing the belief that a consumer is disgusting and offensive is more difficult to sell. To the extent that anti-smoking public policy messages have tried to stigmatize smokers, the messages have been effective.

IMAGE COURTESY OF THE ADVERTISING ARCHIVES

*Here, Stetson relies on the cowboy social schema to provide the brand with meaning.*

**elaboration** extent to which a consumer continues processing a message even after an initial understanding is achieved

**personal elaboration** process by which a person imagines himself or herself somehow associating with a stimulus that is being processed

# ELABORATION

**Elaboration** refers to the extent to which one continues processing a message even after he/she develops an initial understanding in the comprehension stage.[40] With elaboration, increased information is retrieved from long-term memory and attached to the new information and understanding. This means more and richer tags and a better chance of recall. In particular, **personal elaboration**, in which a person imagines himself or herself associating with a stimulus being processed, provides the deepest comprehension and greatest chance of accurate recall.

In Exhibit 4.1, notice that the information-processing steps linked to memory get more pronounced from exposure through elaboration. The darker and more pronounced lines linking comprehension and elaboration to memory represent the strength with which incoming information is tagged. Remember, our brains tag information so that we can understand it. Consumers who reach the elaboration stage are most likely to meaningfully encode information so that intentional retrieval is possible later. In a marketing context, therefore, appeals to a consumer to associate aspects of their own lives are likely to lead to deeper comprehension and better recall.[41] When an advertisement says, "Have you ever been in this situation?" or, "Imagine yourself in a new Porsche Cayenne," these primes can trigger personal elaboration in a consumer, resulting in better recall. Personal elaboration is highly desirable when influence is expected to take place through cognitive reasoning.

## Value Is Meaning: The Small and Big of It!

The associations we have with brands and activities shape the value we expect and actually receive from these brands and activities. Each time we go to a ballpark and see a brand banner, a memory trace is formed. Race for the Cure® is a successful social marketing effort and a brand in itself in the fight against breast cancer. LPGA fans are sure to see Race for the Cure banners at a women's professional golf tournament. The association connects the two in memory and helps build brand equity. Topics in the news also leave memory traces. In late 2009 and early 2010, the Toyota brand was assailed in the media for auto safety problems that supposedly placed drivers at risk. Because the Toyota brand is associated with reliability, consumer rules (built-in memory) made it difficult for many consumers to assimilate the new knowledge. By mid 2010, stories surfaced that Toyota's problems with unintended acceleration were often due to driver error. Thus, consumers in general, and Toyota owners in particular, generally maintain a very positive schema for Toyota, and owners enjoy continued value from their ownership experience.

Sources: Lacey, R., A. G. Close and R. Z. Finney (2010), "The Pivotal Roles of Product Knowledge and Corporate Social Responsibility in Event Sponsorship Effectiveness," *Journal of Business Research*, in press. Freeman, D., S. Shapiro and M. Brucks (2009), "Memory Issues Pertaining to Social Marketing Messages about Behavior Enactment versus Non-Enactment," *Journal of Consumer Psychology* 29, 629-642. Ramsey, M. and K. Linebaugh (2010), "Crash Data Suggest Driver Error in Toyota Accidents," *The Wall Street Journal*, **http://online.wsj.com/article/SB10001424052748703834604575364871534435744.html?mod=WSJ_hps_LEFTTopStories**, accessed July 13, 2010.

© ISTOCKPHOTO.COM/ART-4-ART

# 4 Study Tools

**Located at back of the textbook**

☐ Rip-Out Chapter-in-Review Card

**Located at www.cengagebrain.com**

☐ Review Key Terms Flashcards (Print or Online)

☐ Download audio summaries to review on the go

☐ Complete practice quizzes to prepare for tests

☐ Play "Beat the Clock" and "Quizbowl" to master concepts

☐ Watch Video on Cold Stone Creamery for a real company example

# what others have thought...

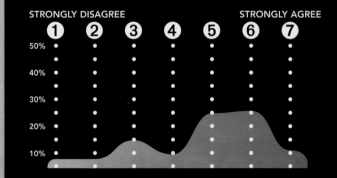

STRONGLY DISAGREE        STRONGLY AGREE

① ② ③ ④ ⑤ ⑥ ⑦

50%
40%
30%
20%
10%

**I can usually remember more from a 30-second television commercial than I can from a 30-minute lecture.**

Results from this question may be somewhat depressing for instructors. More than sixty percent of respondents expressed at least some agreement with this statement, and only 11 percent disagree or strongly disagree. Can professors teach in 30-second jingles?

# Marketing success

is determined by emotions, because actions bring value to a consumer to the extent that desirable emotional states can be created.

## what do you think?

**I do not allow emotions to control my behavior.**

STRONGLY DISAGREE       STRONGLY AGREE

① ② ③ ④ ⑤ ⑥ ⑦

Visit CourseMate at www.cengagebrain.com.

# 5
# Motivation and Emotion: Driving Consumer Behavior

After studying this chapter, the student should be able to:

**LO1** Understand what initiates human behavior.

**LO2** Classify basic consumer motivations.

**LO3** Describe consumer emotions and demonstrate how they help shape value.

**LO4** Apply different approaches to measuring consumer emotions.

**LO5** Understand how different consumers express emotions in different ways.

**LO6** Define and apply the concepts of schema-based affect and emotional contagion.

## LO1 What Drives Human Behavior?

how many times do people ask, "Why did I do that?" Sometimes the reason is simple. A consumer might ask, "Why did I eat two whole Big Macs?" The reason may be as simple as "I was hungry." Many consumers may also relate to another familiar question, "Why did I drink so much?" People usually ask this question the morning after a long night out. The reason here may not be as simple or obvious as "I was hungry" or "I was thirsty." But ultimately, excessive drinking, like all acts, does indeed have an explanation.

The basic consumption process (recall from Chapter 1) is a central component of the CVF and includes consumer needs as the first component. Consumer needs start the process because they kick-start or "motivate" subsequent thoughts, feelings, and behavior. Simply put, **motivations** are the inner reasons or driving forces behind human actions and drive consumers to address real needs. As the CVF indicates, motivations do not completely determine behavior. Other sources, including situational factors like the physical environment, influence behavior. However, motivations do much to provide the intended reason for a consumer's actions.

> **motivations** inner reasons or driving forces behind human actions as consumers are driven to address real needs
>
> **homeostasis** state of equilibrium wherein the body naturally reacts in a way so as to maintain a constant, normal bloodstream

## HOMEOSTASIS

Human motivations are oriented around two key groups of behavior. The first is behavior aimed at maintaining one in a current acceptable state. **Homeostasis** refers to the fact that the body naturally reacts in a way so as to maintain a constant, normal bloodstream. Shivering motivates consumers to wear coats to keep their blood from becoming too cold. When one's blood sugar falls below an acceptable state, the physiological reaction is hunger. Hunger then motivates a consumer to eat something and restore the body to an acceptable state. In this way, a consumer comes to want a Big Mac or some other way of restoring a normal state. Thus, consumers act to maintain things the way they are and their wants are a function of the need driven by homeostasis.

## SELF-IMPROVEMENT

The second group of behavior results from **self-improvement motivation**. These behaviors are aimed at changing one's current state to a level that is more ideal—not simply maintaining the current state of existence. Consider why one exercises. Beyond some level, consumers exercise not to maintain themselves but to improve their health and well-being. In much the same way, when a consumer upgrades from a Touchup handbag to a Prada handbag, she is not acting out a decision to maintain herself, but she sees Prada as a way of improving her status in life. Self-improvement leads consumers to perform acts that cause emotions that help create hedonic value.

Basic motivations are relatively simple to understand. As with many psychological concepts, motives can be classified in several ways. We turn now to two related classification schemes—one a general motivational classification, and another aimed more specifically at consumer behavior.

## LO2 A General Hierarchy of Motivation

Perhaps the most popular theory of human motivation in consumer and organizational behavior is **Maslow's hierarchy of needs**. This theory describes consumers as addressing a finite set of prioritized needs. The following list displays the set of needs starting with the most basic need.

- **Physiological.** Basic survival (food, drink, shelter, etc.)
- **Safety and security.** The need to be secure and protected
- **Belongingness and love.** The need to feel like a member of a family or community
- **Esteem.** The need to be recognized as a person of worth
- **Self-actualization.** The need for personal fulfillment

According to Maslow's theory, consumers first seek value by satisfying the most basic needs. Thus, a starving consumer will risk safety to get something to eat. A consumer whose survival is in doubt would find little value in things that might provide esteem or self-actualization. In contrast, when a successful businessperson retires, he or she may indeed find the most value in things that do not bring esteem, love, or safety, but instead provide self-fulfillment. Several financial firms run advertisements showing retirees leaving high-paying careers to travel to far-off places or go off and work in a mission. This appeal typifies how consumer behavior can provide value by addressing the self-actualization need.

Further, consider how Maslow's hierarchy may operate differently around the world. In war-torn areas of the world, consumers may indeed risk their lives to buy basic necessities. Clearly, this type of shopping is providing only utilitarian value. In the United States, consumers may find esteem through performing well on the job and owning a large house. In Japan, however, space is so scarce that very few people own large

© COURTESY OF MASTERCARD WORLDWIDE

*"For everything else there is Mastercard!" And the "everything else" can lead to self-actualization.*

homes. Therefore, esteem may manifest itself more in owning a nice car or in one's manner of dress.

Similarly, the things that address self-actualization needs are likely to vary in different places around the world. Motivations can determine what type and amounts of value that consumers seek. Generally, the most basic needs are addressed with utilitarian value, and as needs become more elaborate, hedonic value is often needed to satiate the need state. Exhibit 5.1 illustrates the hierarchical aspect of needs and includes an example of a consumer behavior that goes with each need.

## SIMPLER CLASSIFICATION OF CONSUMER MOTIVATIONS

The preceding discussion suggests an even simpler classification of consumer motivations. Not surprisingly, the types of motivations match up with the types of needs. A simple but very useful way to understand consumer behavior is to classify motives based on whether a consumer need can best address a particular need by realizing utilitarian or hedonic value.[1]

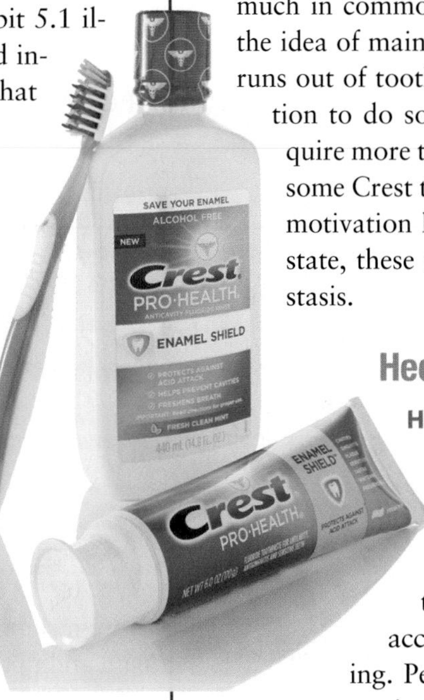

SAVE YOUR ENAMEL
ALCOHOL FREE
NEW
Crest
PRO-HEALTH
ENAMEL SHIELD
Crest
PRO-HEALTH
ENAMEL SHIELD

PRNEWSFOTO/CREST, DYLAN CROSS

EXHIBIT 5.1

An Illustration of Consumer Motivations According to Maslow's Hierarchy

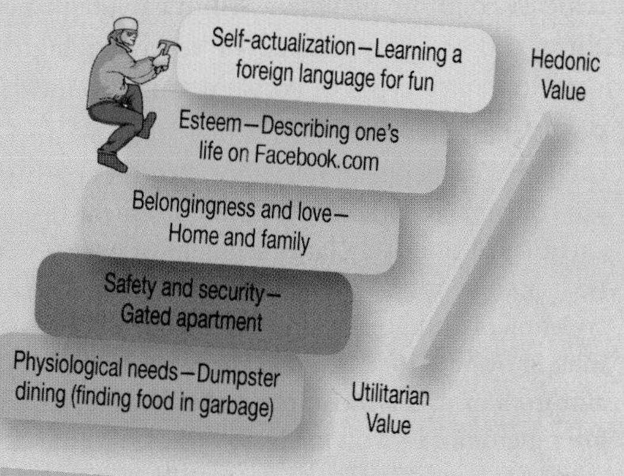

Self-actualization—Learning a foreign language for fun
Esteem—Describing one's life on Facebook.com
Belongingness and love—Home and family
Safety and security—Gated apartment
Physiological needs—Dumpster dining (finding food in garbage)
Hedonic Value
Utilitarian Value

### Utilitarian Motivation

**utilitarian motivation** drive to acquire products that can be used to accomplish something

**hedonic motivation** drive to experience something emotionally gratifying

**Utilitarian motivation** is a drive to acquire products that consumers can use to accomplish things. Utilitarian motivation bears much in common with the idea of maintaining behavior. When the consumer runs out of toothpaste, there will be a strong motivation to do something about this problem and acquire more toothpaste. He or she may want to buy some Crest toothpaste. In the sense that utilitarian motivation helps a consumer maintain his or her state, these motivations work much like homeostasis.

### Hedonic Motivation

**Hedonic motivation** involves a drive to experience something personally gratifying. These behaviors are usually emotionally satisfying. Interestingly, although sales via the Internet continue to grow, they account for less than 5% of all retailing. Perhaps part of the reason is that the process itself is not very rewarding. For people who really love to shop, the Internet may not provide the multisensory experience that a rich shopping environment can deliver. For these consumers, the Internet may be fine for acquiring things but disappointing as a rewarding shopping experience. Exhibit 5.2 illustrates some typical behaviors that are motivated by utilitarian or hedonic shopping motives.

## CONSUMER INVOLVEMENT

Two American tourists are seated in a restaurant in Strasbourg, France. A waiter arrives at the table, provides them with English menus, and asks if anyone would like the special "entrée du jour": fois gras d'oie avec marmalade (in a French restaurant, an "entrée" is a starter dish/appetizer). One customer responds by saying he isn't ready for his entrée, while the other says, "Why yes, that would be a terrific starter, and please serve it with crusty toast points, sweet pickles and a bit of Cadillac." How are these consumers different? Well, many differences may exist, but one big difference is obviously the level of involvement each consumer has in the food category.

## EXHIBIT 5.2
## Utilitarian and Hedonic Motivations Lead to Consumer Behaviors

| Utilitarian Motivations Lead to | Hedonic Motivations Lead to |
|---|---|
| Choosing the most convenient place to have lunch | Going out to a trendy, new restaurant for dinner |
| Buying a tank of gas for the car | Driving the car fast on a curvy road even when not rushed |
| Choosing to shop with retailers that are seen as useful and easy to use | Choosing to shop with retailers that are seen as fun and exciting |
| Using air freshener to cover up a strange smell in the apartment | Using air freshener because one really enjoys the smell |
| Going gift shopping out of a sense of obligation to give a gift | Giving a gift to enjoy the giving process and the joy the recipient experiences when opening the gift |

Involvement is synonymous with motivation in the sense that a highly involved consumer is strongly motivated to expend effort and resources in consuming that particular thing.[2] **Consumer involvement** represents the degree of personal relevance a consumer finds in pursuing value from a given category of consumption. Thus, when a consumer is highly involved, there is a greater chance that relatively high value can be achieved, as long as things go as expected.

## Consumer Involvement as a Moderator

Consumer researchers often consider involvement a key moderating variable. A **moderating variable** is one that changes the nature of a relationship between two other variables. For example, consider the relationship between the number of alternative brands of a product, perhaps running shoes, and the amount of time and effort a consumer spends choosing a pair of shoes. Logically, one might expect that the larger the selection, the greater the time needed to make a decision. However, would this be the case for all consumers?

A highly involved consumer is likely to take more time because he or she recognizes a greater number of attractive alternatives. He or she is willing (motivated) to spend time evaluating multiple pairs of shoes, trying them on, and comparing their attributes. Value is closely tied to making the right choice. On the other hand, a consumer who lacks motivation to study shoes is quickly overwhelmed by a large selection and falls back to some simple choice decision like "pick the cutest."

A consumer needs some degree of involvement to have an ability to evaluate multiple brands effectively. A consumer with low involvement will not spend more time just because there are more types of shoes. A consumer with high involvement, though, is likely to spend more time making a decision as there are more alternatives from which to choose.

## Different Types of Involvement

Involvement can mean different things to different people. However, one way to bring different perspectives together is to realize that there are different types of involvement. In each case, high involvement still means high personal relevance and the importance of receiving high value. Here are some key types of consumer involvement:

- **Product involvement** means that some product category has personal relevance. **Product enthusiasts** are consumers with very high involvement in some category. A relatively large segment of product enthusiasts can be found in the fashion market. These consumers find great value in learning about fashions, shopping for fashions, and wearing fashionable clothes. For every consumer, some product categories are much more involving than others. Exhibit 5.3 contrasts products that are generally associated with low and high consumer product involvement.

© SEAN GALLUP/GETTY IMAGES

*Consumers with high enduring involvement sometimes even earn labels, such as soccer hooligan or clothes horse!*

- **Shopping involvement** represents the personal relevance of shopping activities. This relevance enhances personal shopping value. From a utilitarian value perspective, highly involved shoppers are more likely to process information about deals and are more likely to react to price reductions and limited offers that create better deals.[3]

- **Situational involvement** represents the temporary involvement associated with some imminent purchase situation. Situational involvement often comes about when consumers are shopping for something with relatively low involvement but a relatively high price. Things like household and kitchen appliances usually fit this category. For instance, few consumers are highly involved with air conditioners. However, when a consumer is about to purchase an air conditioner, he or she may temporarily learn a lot about air conditioners to avoid paying too much or choosing an inappropriate unit.

- **Enduring involvement** is not temporary but rather represents a continuing interest in some product or activity. The consumer is always searching for opportunities to consume the product or participate in the activity. Enduring involvement is associated with hedonic value because learning about, shopping for, or consuming a product for which a consumer has high enduring involvement is personally gratifying.

- **Emotional involvement** represents how emotional a consumer gets during some specific consumption activity. Emotional involvement is closely related to enduring involvement because the things that consumers care most about will eventually create high emotional involvement. Sports fans typify consumers with high emotional involvement, and as we know, sports fans can be rowdy and do wild and crazy things.

> **shopping involvement** personal relevance of shopping activities
>
> **situational involvement** temporary interest in some imminent purchase situation
>
> **enduring involvement** ongoing interest in some product or opportunity
>
> **emotional involvement** type of deep personal interest that evokes strongly felt feelings simply from the thoughts or behavior associated with some object or activity

## EXHIBIT 5.3
## Typical High and Low Product Involvement

| High Product Involvement | Low Product Involvement |
|---|---|
| Dresses | Detergents |
| Televisions | Facial soap |
| Champagne | Toothpaste |
| Bras | Yogurt |

## LO3 Consumer Emotions and Value

### EMOTION

What is *emotion*? Emotion is a difficult term to define. In fact, some refer to emotion as a "fuzzy" concept, believing that no exact definition exists. According to this view, the best that one can do is list examples of emotions. Love, for example, is a primary example of an

**emotion** a specific psycho-biological reaction to a human appraisal

**psychobiological** a response involving both psychological and physical human responses

**visceral responses** certain feeling states that are tied to physical reactions/behavior in a very direct way

**cognitive appraisal theory** school of thought proposing that specific types of appraisal thoughts can be linked to specific types of emotions

emotion, and all readers can relate to the experience of love. Yet, how is *love* defined?

Ask someone to put love into words and people will usually provide examples or types of love such as romantic love, brotherly love, maternal love, or love for one's school. Although quite different from love, anger is also a typical emotion and shares something in common with love. Both love and anger are controlling emotions, in that they tend to shape one's behavior strongly.

While emotions seem a bit "fuzzy," we can offer a simple definition. **Emotions** are specific psychobiological reactions to appraisals. Thus, when a consumer receives bad service in a restaurant, he or she appraises the situation and then reacts emotionally. When a

*Love illustrates the controlling nature of emotion. Love can motivate otherwise strange behaviors.*

consumer is contemplating vacation, he or she appraises different sites and thinks about the total vacation experience.[4] A consumer reacts differently to Las Vegas than say, Pigeon Forge, TN. Emotions are considered **psychobiological** because they involve both psychological processing and physical responses.[5] Indeed, emotions create **visceral responses**, meaning that certain feeling states are tied to behavior in a very direct way. Exhibit 5.4 lists some typical visceral responses to emotions.

Emotions are extremely important to consumer behavior and marketing because consumers react most immediately to their feelings. Notice that the word *motivation* and the word *emotion* both contain "motion" as a root. The fact that emotions are hard-wired to behavior has been explained as follows:

> *"[Emotions are] fuels for drives, for all motion, every performance, and any behavioral act."*[6]

Behaviors are closely tied to emotion, creating close links between emotions, consumer behavior, and value. Thus, to this extent, marketing success is determined by emotions because actions bring value to a consumer to the extent that desirable emotional states can be created.[7] One of the secrets to Starbucks's success is an environment that creates relaxing feelings. These emotions end up contributing to the overall value of the Starbucks experience. Price discounts also create emotions that drive consumer behavior. A $200 discount on a $20,000 automobile may not create a lot of emotion, but a $200 discount on a $500 suit creates emotion that can cause consumers to drive out of their way to buy the product.[8]

> Both love and anger are controlling emotions in that they tend to shape one's behavior strongly.

## COGNITIVE APPRAISAL THEORY

What gives rise to consumer emotions? Psychologists have debated the different sources of emotions for decades, but **cognitive appraisal theory** represents an increasingly popular school of thought. Cognitive appraisal theory describes how specific types of thoughts can serve as a basis for specific emotions. When a consumer makes an appraisal, he or she is assessing some

## EXHIBIT 5.4
# Visceral Responses to Emotions by Consumers

| Type of Appraisal / Situation | Emotion | Behavioral Reaction |
|---|---|---|
| Anticipation appraisal— Consumer waits while doctor examines X-rays | Worry | Grim face with turned-down eyebrows and cheeks. Hands likely near face. Consumer would rather avoid situation. |
| Outcome appraisal— Consumer wins a contest | Joy | Genuine smile including turned-up cheeks and eyebrows and open hands. The consumer approaches the situation. |
| Equity appraisal—Consumer sees one customer receive faster and better service than he or she receives | Anger | Turned-down cheeks and eyebrows with clenched fists and hunched back. The consumer seeks to approach an agent of the company. |
| Agency appraisal—Consumer sees a waiter sneeze near a food preparation area | Disgust | Pinched-in facial expression and turned head. The body naturally withdraws (avoids) the situation. |
| Outcome appraisal— Consumer shows up at an important party inappropriately dressed | Embarrassment | Face blushes (turns red and feels hot), head cowers, and a strong desire to flee is experienced. |

past, present, or future situation. Four types of cognitive appraisals are especially relevant for consumer behavior.[9]

1. **Anticipation appraisals.** Focuses on the future and can elicit emotions like hopefulness or anxiety

2. **Agency appraisals.** Reviews responsibility for events and can evoke gratefulness, frustration, guilt, or sadness

3. **Equity appraisal.** Considers how fair some event is and can evoke emotions like warmth or anger

4. **Outcomes appraisal.** Considers how something turned out relative to one's goals and can evoke emotions like joyfulness, satisfaction, sadness, or pride

Exhibit 5.4 illustrates each of these appraisal types. A basic behavioral response is to either approach or avoid. Marketers generally benefit from approach responses and thus, they would like to create appraisals leading to emotions evoking approach behaviors, and avoid appraisals and emotions evoking avoidance.

Appraisals are often complicated enough to involve more than one type of appraisal and sometimes conflicting behavioral responses. Anticipatory appraisals can involve emotions such as hope. A consumer may appraise an ad for a charitable cause in manner that evokes hope and he or she may become more willing to consider donation to that cause. However, the same ad could cause a consumer to feel guilty if he or she makes an agency appraisal and ends up feeling a sense of responsibility for the problem that the charity addresses. Guilt may be less effective than hope in gaining compliance to an appeal.[10] Consumers also make equity appraisals such as the perception of very unfair treatment. They end up feeling angry and may cope with the anger by seeking revenge.[11] Health services often create situations involving both anticipation and outcome appraisals. A consumer visiting the dentist may be worried about having cavities but feel joyful when the dentist provides a clean bill of health.

# EMOTION TERMINOLOGY
## Mood

Moods can be distinguished from the broader concept of emotion based on specificity and time. Consumer **mood** can be thought of as a transient (temporary and changing) and general feeling state often characterized with simple descriptors such as a "good mood," "bad mood," or even a "funky mood." Moods are generally considered less intense than many other emotional experiences; nevertheless, moods can influence consumer behavior. Consumers

**mood-congruent judgments** evaluations in which the value of a target is influenced in a consistent way by one's mood

**consumer affect** feelings a consumer has about a particular product or activity

**autonomic measures** responses that are automatically recorded based on either automatic visceral reactions or neurological brain activity

in good moods tend to make decisions faster and to outspend their bad-mood counterparts. In addition, consumer mood affects satisfaction, with a bad mood being particularly detrimental to consumer satisfaction.[12] In this sense, marketers do not have complete control of the satisfaction they deliver.

Employees' moods can also affect consumption outcomes as they interact with consumer mood. A salesperson in a bad mood can negatively affect a consumer's overall attitude and willingness to buy. Perhaps curiously, consumers who enter a situation in a bad mood react better to service providers who are also in a bad mood than they do to service providers in a good mood. Exhibit 5.5 provides an overview of results from a study investigating this phenomenon. Consumers seem to be most receptive to an employee with a matching mood rather than to an employee who always has a positive mood.[13]

A consumer's mood can serve as a type of frame that can transfer into product value judgments. For example, when consumers are evaluating alternative vacation sites, they tend to rate sites more favorably when they evaluate them in a good mood as opposed to when they are in a bad mood.[14] Consumers make **mood-congruent judgments**, an evaluation in which the value of a target is influenced in a consistent way by one's mood. As a result, marketers should prefer consumers to buy and consume their products when they are in a good mood. This has some implications for designing the purchase and service environment, as we will see in a later chapter.

Sometimes, consumers act to change their moods. Consumers may purchase a gift for themselves, for instance, as a way of improving their mood. In much the same way, research shows that consumers who are in bad moods can be more likely to be generous to others. The rationale is based on the hedonic value produced when one is generous.[15]

## Affect

Affect is another term used to represent the feelings a consumer experiences during the consumption process. At times, affect is used as a general term encompassing both emotion and mood. However, in consumer behavior, **consumer affect** is more often used to represent the feelings a consumer has about a particular product or

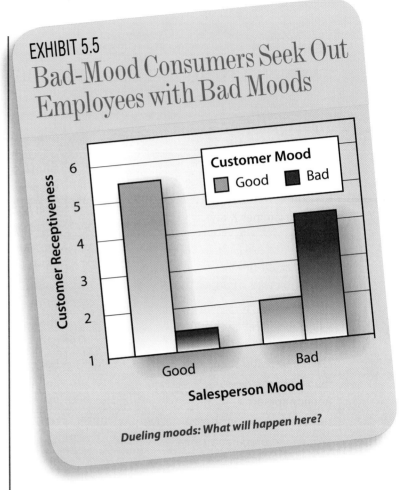

EXHIBIT 5.5

## Bad-Mood Consumers Seek Out Employees with Bad Moods

*Dueling moods: What will happen here?*

activity.[16] Thus, when consumers like Marlboro more than Winston, they are expressing their affect toward the Marlboro brand.

# LO4 Measuring Emotion

marketing and consumer researchers place a great deal of emphasis on properly measuring consumer emotion because emotions play such a key role in shaping value. However, there is no consensus on the best way to measure consumer emotions. Two issues that regularly arise are whether consumers have introspection (can express verbally) connected to their emotions, and how to best categorize these emotions if they can be communicated.

## AUTONOMIC MEASURES

Perhaps autonomic measures offer the greatest validity in representing consumer emotions. **Autonomic measures** are those responses that are automatically

# Charged Up!

WE'VE TAKEN THE Pesticide-Free PLEDGE

© ISTOCKPHOTO.COM/FRANK LEUNG

**C**onsumer research shows how emotion causes behavior and thereby influences value (both utilitarian and hedonic). Some actions require some type of charge to get things started. In particular, behaviors with an ethical angle often need a charge to get started.

What kinds of consumer behavior involve potential ethical angles? At a very simple level, some consumers may judge the actions of others based on whether or not they consider ethical factors in selecting brands. For instance, does a consumer consider the labor practices of competing companies before choosing a brand? Green consumers may react emotionally when they see other consumers behaving in ways that are inconsistent with their beliefs, such as using plastic bags at the supermarket. Interestingly, when consumers are judged by others they are more often viewed less favorably for not purchasing "ethical" products than they are viewed positively for purchasing ethical products.

In the extreme, consumers practice unethical behaviors like shoplifting. Consumer emotions help explain why adolescents steal from retailers. An emotional charge provides a brief thrill, overrides thoughts, and produces unethical behavior. So, a good lesson is to mind one's emotions!

Sources: Iwin, J.R. and R.W. Naylor (2009), "Ethical Decisions and Response Mode Compatibility: Weighting of Ethical Attributes in Consideration Sets Formed by Excluding Versus Including Product Alternatives," *Journal of Marketing Research* 46 (April), 234–246. Jiang, Y. and J. L. Wang (2006), "The Impact of Affect on Service Quality and Satisfaction: The Moderation of Service Contexts," *Journal of Services Marketing* 20 (4), 211–218. Babin, B.J., M. Griffin and J.S. Boles (2004), "Buyer Reactions to Ethical Beliefs in the Retail Environment," *Journal of Business Research* 57 (October), 1155–1163.

created by the measuring device. Interestingly however, research suggests that these autonomic responses generally correspond fairly well to introspective self-reports of emotional experience.[18]

## SELF-REPORT MEASURES

Self-report measures are generally less obtrusive than biological measures because they don't involve physical contraptions. Self-report affect measures usually require consumers to recall their affect state from a recent experience, or to state the affect they are feeling at a given point in time. These paper-and-pencil tests usually involve a questionnaire; the process is not perfect, but generally results are valid enough to be useful to consumer and marketing researchers. However, many different options exist for applying self-report measures, and each option is usually based on a somewhat different perspective of emotion theory.

recorded based on either automatic visceral reactions or neurological brain activity. These include facial reactions, physiological responses such as sweating in a GSR (galvanic skin response) or lie detector test, heart rate monitoring, and brain imaging, which can document activity in areas of the brain responsible for certain specific emotions.[17]

While these measurement approaches have the advantage of assessing emotional activity without requiring a volitional response from the consumer, they have the drawback of being intrusive. The researcher must attach some type of device to the consumer. Imagine a consumer wearing a net stocking cap attached to a computer by wires, in a lab, while a researcher tells him or her to watch some ads and act naturally, as if in her own living room. This would be very difficult to do. So, the disadvantage of this approach is the obtrusiveness

### PANAS

One of the most commonly applied ways to assess one's emotional state is by using the PANAS. PANAS stands for positive-affect-negative-affect scale and allows respondents to self-report the extent to which they feel one of 20 emotional adjectives. Exhibit 5.6 shows an example.

Researchers generally apply the PANAS to capture the relative amount of positive and negative emotion experienced by a consumer at a given point in time. However, this raises several questions about the nature of emotion, including whether or not positive and negative emotions can coexist.

Look at the items making up the PANAS. Each item represents either a good or a bad feeling. Thus, one might wonder why "inspired" and "upset" would both need to be measured. If a new product inspired a consumer,

## EXHIBIT 5.6
# A Short-Form PANAS Application

The scale below lists words that describe the feelings or emotions that you may have experienced while shopping at Hometown Bathshop today. Please use the items to record the way you felt while shopping by indicating the extent to which you felt each of the feelings described. The scale ranges from 1= very slightly or not at all to 5 = extremely.

| | Very Slightly or Not at All | A Little | Moderately | Quite a Bit | Extremely |
|---|---|---|---|---|---|
| Upset | ☐ | ☐ | ☐ | ☐ | ☐ |
| Hostile | ☐ | ☐ | ☐ | ☐ | ☐ |
| Alert | ☐ | ☐ | ☐ | ☐ | ☐ |
| Ashamed | ☐ | ☐ | ☐ | ☐ | ☐ |
| Inspired | ☐ | ☐ | ☐ | ☐ | ☐ |
| Nervous | ☐ | ☐ | ☐ | ☐ | ☐ |
| Determined | ☐ | ☐ | ☐ | ☐ | ☐ |
| Attentive | ☐ | ☐ | ☐ | ☐ | ☐ |
| Afraid | ☐ | ☐ | ☐ | ☐ | ☐ |
| Active | ☐ | ☐ | ☐ | ☐ | ☐ |

Source: Thompson, E.R. (2007), "Development and Validation of an Internationally Reliable Short-Form of the Positive and Negative Affect Schedule (PANAS)," *Journal of Cross-Cultural Psychology*; 38; 227.

it would seem that the consumer could not be upset at the same time. If feeling good excludes feeling bad, then wouldn't a researcher need only measure positive terms or negative terms to account for a consumer's feelings?

This might be an interesting academic question, but the issue also has practical implications if consumers react differently to equal amounts of positive and negative emotions. Does a mad consumer or a glad consumer react more strongly? Considerable attention in psychology and marketing research addresses this question and the evidence isn't crystal clear. The best we can say in addressing whether feeling bad is more influential than feeling good is "sometimes." Take a look at the following situations:

- A consumer rating the feelings experienced when a pop-up box shows up on an electronics retailer website.
- A consumer rating the feelings experienced when planning a wedding.

The first situation is quite simple. In situations like these, positive and negative emotions tend to be opposites. If people have bad feelings during the experience, they are unlikely to have any good feelings. The second situation is more complex and extends over a longer period. In situations such as these, bad and good feelings do not cancel each other out completely, and people can indeed experience some levels of both.

Thus, when consumer researchers are studying highly complex situations, a scale like that of the PANAS allows them to capture both positive and negative dimensions of emotional experience. The possibility exists that each dimension might explain somewhat unique experiences. For example, positive affect is highly related to increased spending, but negative emotion is not. The more good feelings a consumer has, the more he or she buys. A consumer experiencing negative emotions may still complete the shopping task, but he or she may also be more likely to look for another place to shop next time.

## PAD

**PAD** is an acronym that stands for pleasure–arousal–dominance. This scale asks consumers to rate their feelings using a number of semantic differential (bipolar opposites) items that capture emotions in these three dimensions. The theory behind PAD, unlike PANAS, is that pleasure—the evaluative dimension of emotion—is **bipolar**, meaning that if one feels joyful, one cannot also experience sadness.[19] Arousal, which is the degree to which one feels energized, excited, or interested, is also seen as bipolar, in that a consumer is either aroused or bored. Likewise, dominance, the degree that one feels in control of a situation, is also bipolar. Thus, researchers have combined the PAD and PANAS approaches and applied adjectives taken from the PAD scale and put them in a format similar to that in Exhibit 5.6, rather than a semantic differential.

> Marketing and consumer researchers place a great deal of emphasis on properly measuring consumer emotion.

Many researchers use the PAD or a modified PAD approach to study retail atmospherics across many environments including museums and parks, and even in advertising contexts.[20] Because the scale captures arousal separately, the approach is advantageous when the degree of activation or excitement is of particular interest. For example, when consumers go to a movie, they may feel pleased but not excited. Similarly, the PAD approach allows a separate accounting for feelings of dominance, sometimes known as control. When consumers feel lower control, situational influences play a greater role in shaping their behavior.

## LO5 Differences in Emotional Behavior

not all consumers react emotionally or show their emotions to the same extent or in the same way.[21] Two consumers, for instance, may receive the same poor service from a crowded retail store. One might complain furiously to store management, while the other simply walks away to find a more quiet shopping environment. Emotions, as discussed earlier, are deeply tied to personal motivations and traits. Thus, personality characteristics can affect the way consumers respond or demonstrate their emotions. For instance, neuroticism, an important personality trait, is positively related with the amount of negative affect a consumer reports in various service settings.[22]

## EMOTIONAL INVOLVEMENT

Motivation and involvement are closely related, as we discussed earlier in the chapter. The things that tap our deepest emotions have the ability to evoke the greatest value. This brings us to emotional involvement, meaning the type of deep personal interest that evokes strongly felt feelings associated with some object or activity. Emotional involvement drives one to consume generally through relatively strong hedonic motivations. Often, emotional involvement can make a consumer appear irrational. Consider the amount of money and time a college alumnus and football fan will spend following his or her team. Some spend hundreds of thousands of dollars on motor homes used only on football weekends for tailgating. The consumer is deeply and emotionally involved with the team and in many ways becomes one with the team.

Other consumers may experience deeply held feelings over certain fashion products, automobiles, music, wine or even over social networking via the Internet. A consumer experiencing a fantastic dinner with a fantastic bottle of

AP IMAGES/CALEB JONES

*In situations like this, one consumer may become angry and another may become sad. This customer appears to be angry!*

wine is achieving a total customer experience, a maximum value experience, through a combination of high emotional involvement and products that served as expected or better than expected.[23]

Emotional involvement can be increased by receiving something extra with products purchased. For instance, if someone buys a nice leather backpack, the company might consider adding a premium, which may include a phone holster, calculator, or gift certificate to a local pub. In this way, the consumer may develop an emotional attachment or become emotionally involved with the product and with the brand.[24]

Perhaps there is no better example of how different consumers react emotionally than the responses different consumers get when involved with a motion picture. Some consumers have difficulty getting through any heart-touching scene without tears coming to their eyes – which generally means they like the movie. Other consumers see the same scene and are bored. They would rather be watching a classic slapstick movie like *Caddyshack* or *Dumb and Dumber*, which may bring them to tears through laughter.

> One question asked by many who study emotions is whether or not women are more emotional than men.

## Flow

All consumers can probably relate to the experience of enjoying a good book or movie so much that one loses awareness of time passing. When this occurs, a consumer has achieved a state of **flow**, meaning extremely high emotional involvement in which a consumer is engrossed in an activity.

A great deal of the work on flow deals with computer-related activities. For instance, consumers can become so involved in video games or social networking that they have little physical awareness of their surroundings.[25] When a parent calls a child for dinner and the child seems to be ignoring him or her, the child may be so caught up in gaming that there is no conscious awareness of being called. In the extreme, consumers can become

addicted to video game consumption.[26] Similarly, more and more consumers face Facebook addiction. Consumers can become addicted when their level of obsession with an activity becomes too high. Here are a few signs that might indicate Facebook addiction:[27]

- Spending more than 1 hour a day on Facebook
- Ignoring work to stay on Facebook
- Feeling more attached to the Facebook world than the real world
- Replacing sleep with time on Facebook
- Becoming nervous when facing an extended period away from Facebook (more than a day)

*The state of flow is value enhancing, but can it facilitate addiction—such as Facebook addiction?*

Addictions like this are driven in part by a desire to achieve the state of flow where one escapes the real world and realizes high hedonic value.[28]

Highly involved shoppers sometimes achieve a flow experience. When this occurs, the consumer is more likely to spend time browsing, spend more money, make repeat purchases, and be more prone to impulse purchasing.[29] Online consumers can pursue a flow state while shopping; however, interruptions in Internet service, poor navigational clues, or slow page load times can inhibit the flow experience and lower both utilitarian and hedonic shopping value.[30] If the consumer achieves hedonic value, positive outcomes can result for both the consumer and the marketer. However, the consumer must be able to maintain control of the situation to avoid compulsive or addictive behaviors.

## EMOTIONAL EXPRESSIVENESS

Not all consumers express their emotions as obviously as others. **Emotional expressiveness** represents the extent to which a consumer shows outward behavioral signs and otherwise reacts obviously to emotional experiences. The consumer with relatively high emotional expressiveness is likely to react in some way to outcomes that are unexpected. A bad poker player, for example, is unable to hide emotions from other players, and, as such, his/her reaction displays high emotional expressiveness.

Many who study emotions ask whether women are more emotional than men. Researchers do not provide a clear answer to this question. For instance, psychologists interested in studying the human experience of, and reaction to, disgust have conducted experiments in which subjects are exposed to films depicting either an actual amputation or a man being swarmed by cockroaches.[31] Male and female subjects report on average the same level of disgust while viewing the films. However, female respondents are more likely than males to react to the disgusting experience by leaving the room before the film is finished. Studies show similar emotional expression by females for other emotions beside disgust, both positive and negative.[32] Research suggests that when male and female consumers react with similar emotions, women express the emotions more noticeably.[33] Because of this, to the extent that a marketer can judge a consumer's emotional reaction, female consumers may prove more valuable in signaling poor or outstanding service than would male consumers.

## EMOTIONAL INTELLIGENCE

Emotions can be useful in determining the most appropriate reaction to events. **Emotional intelligence** is a term used to capture one's awareness of the emotions experienced in a situation, and an ability to control reactions to these emotions. This includes awareness of the emotions experienced by the individual as well as an awareness and sympathy for the emotions experienced by others. Emotional intelligence (EI) is a multifaceted concept, and Exhibit 5.7 illustrates EI components. High EI consumers are able to use awareness of emotions in decision making and are better able to manage their own emotions and exhibit self-control.[34]

In a marketing context, salespeople with high emotional intelligence are more effective in closing sales with consumers than are salespeople with low emotional intelligence.[35] Sales companies are increasingly realizing the benefits of employees with high EI. EI training is becoming commonplace as marketers attempt to get consumers to buy more and to be more satisfied with the things they buy.[36]

**emotional intelligence** awareness of the emotions experienced in a given situation and the ability to control reactions to these emotions

## LO6 Emotion, Meaning, and Schema-Based Affect

What is the relation between cognition and emotion? Intuitively, emotion and cognition seem so different that one can easily presume they are completely independent of each other. However, emotion and cognition are actually quite closely related, and this is seen clearly in the role that affect, mood, and emotion can play in signaling and developing meaning. This section focuses on the interplay between emotion and cognitive learning.

## SEMANTIC WIRING

In a previous chapter, we learned that in our memory, a network connects all concepts to other concepts. A concept such as a "toaster" is closely linked with a concept like "breakfast," but very remotely linked with another concept like "hurricane." A consumer's ability to remember things about brands and products can be explained using theory developed around the principles of *semantic or associative* networks. Remember, all concepts are linked to all other concepts but some are linked strongly and others very weakly. It's difficult to put weak concepts together.

### EXHIBIT 5.7
# Emotional Intelligence Consists of Multiple Elements

Self-control—ability to control one's emotions

Emotional empathy—ability to read and understand others' emotions

Emotional Intelligence

Upbeat—ability to maintain a generally upbeat and optimistic outlook

Productive—ability to turn emotions into value through better problem solving

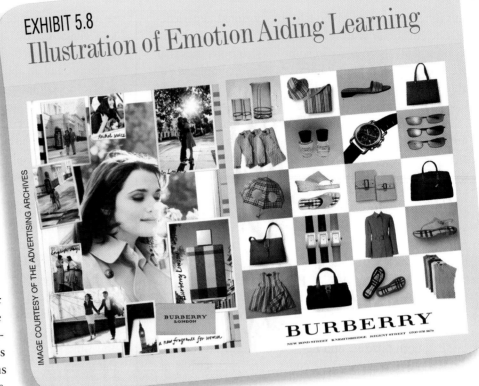

**EXHIBIT 5.8**
### Illustration of Emotion Aiding Learning

IMAGE COURTESY OF THE ADVERTISING ARCHIVES

Although the term *semantic* is more closely tied to cognitive thought processes, the active processing and storage of knowledge is significantly influenced by emotions in several ways. The general expression "**emotional effect on memory**" refers to relatively superior recall for information presented with mild affective content compared to similar information presented in an affectively neutral way.[37]

The implications for marketing are fairly direct. Marketing communications that present product information in a way that evokes mild levels of emotions will tend to be more effective in producing recall than communications that are affectively neutral.[38] Caution is needed in executing such communications because intense emotions are more complicated to deal with and can sometimes even distract consumers from the task of actually processing information. But clearly, emotion and cognition can become closely linked semantically in the mind of a consumer. Exhibit 5.8 illustrates this point.

## MOOD-CONGRUENT RECALL

Many consumers can remember their first day of school, first airplane trip, or first visit to a theme park. In each case, products and brands are associated with the experience. Likewise, in each case, each event is associated with a fairly specific mood. For many consumers, the first day of school is filled with apprehension, the first airplane ride may be a blend of fear and excitement, and a visit to a theme park is associated with joy.

**Autobiographical memories** are memories of previous, meaningful events in one's life. Consumers are more likely to recall autobiographical memories characterized by specific moods when the same mood occurs again in the future.[39] Simply put, moods tend to match memories.

**Mood-congruent recall** means that to the extent that a consumer's mood can be controlled, their memories and evaluations can be influenced. Music is one tool useful in inducing moods. When music sets a mood, consumers will recall products associated with that mood more readily. In addition, consumers in good moods tend to evaluate products positively compared to consumers in bad moods, and vice versa.[40]

## NOSTALGIA

Nostalgia affects consumers in a manner similar to that of mood-congruent recall and autobiographical memory. Recall that we introduced nostalgia in an earlier chapter as a yearning for the past motivated by the belief that previous times were somehow more pleasant. Nostalgia can motivate product purchases as consumers attempt to relive the pleasant feelings of the past. Music, toys, magazines, and movies are products that consumers report commonly buying in association with feelings of nostalgia.[41] The large number of advertisements that include popular "oldies" songs illustrates attempts at evoking nostalgic feelings. Further, consumers become more willing to make purchases when a nostalgic ad evokes or recaptures a childhood mood.

*The little red wagon can evoke a yearning for the past and the purchase of one for a child can allow a consumer to experience the past again in some small way.*

## SCHEMA-BASED AFFECT

As we know from consumer information processing theory, knowledge of familiar things becomes organized in a cognitive unit of meaning known as a schema. A schema contains the knowledge of a brand, a product, or any concept. However, a schema is not a purely cognitive entity. Schemata are developed and reinforced through actual experience. For instance, we come to perceive what a car salesperson truly is based on our total experience with that category. Experience involves more than cognition. When we encounter a car salesperson or hear stories that involve car salespeople, we also experience some type of affect or emotion. These emotions become part of the meaning for a category in the form of **schema-based affect**.

Schema-based affect helps provide meaning and thus is another example of how affect and cognition are wired together. However, a consumer can actually experience schema-based affect once a schema becomes active. For example, a consumer who fears going to a dentist can actually experience true nervousness and apprehension simply by thinking about a visit to the dentist. This makes the dentist visit schema active.

Exhibit 5.9 displays a typical schema for a car salesperson including the schema-based affect.[42] The exhibit displays schema-based affect in yellow. When managers realize that a category is associated with negative affect, as in this case, they may be wise either to change the characteristic attributes (in this case of the car salesperson) to prevent the schema from becoming or remaining active, or to activate an entirely different schema (i.e., team-member). Further, negative schema-based emotions of this type can interfere with the consumer's

> **schema-based affect**
> emotions that become stored as part of the meaning for a category (a schema)

## Bad Hair Days – Bad Times!

**P**rocter and Gamble (P&G) probably won't win a Nobel Peace Prize for their research, but some consumers may feel they deserve one for their efforts to stamp out bad hair days. Bad hair days can really bring a consumer down. P&G research relies on the PANAS scale to help identify just how bad bad hair can make a girl feel. Bad hair days make women feel more hostile, ashamed, nervous and even guilty! Many of these feelings fall into the category of self-conscious emotions. These feelings have a moral element when a consumer perceives that he or she has violated some personal or societal norm; "I shouldn't be seen with hair like this! It's embarrassing!!" P&G's Pantene brand offers help by designing shampoos aimed at keeping hair healthy. When they feel good about their hair, consumers can face the day feeling excited, proud and confident, instead of angry, embarrassed or ashamed. That's good for the consumer and everyone around her! Consumers will act to avoid negative feelings, but negative feelings also motivate a consumer to find a solution. Think about the ways negative feelings cause you to realize the need to act!

Sources: Byron, E. (2010), "Wash Away Bad Hair Days," Wall Street Journal, 255 (June 30), D1 – D3. Honea, H. (2005), "Investigating the Impact of Negative Self-Conscious Emotions on Consumer Memory, Processing and Purchase," Advances in Consumer Research 32, 189–192. Chun, H., V.M. Patrick and D.J. MacInnis (2007), "Making Prudent vs. Impulsive Choices: The Role of Anticipated Shame and Guilt on Consumer Self-Control," Advances in Consumer Research 34, 715–719.

ability to process information about the product. In recent years, many car dealerships have changed the appearance of their salespeople to avoid activating this schema. More females perform the job and the staff attire is more casual, generally sporting a brand logo.

Exhibit 5.10 displays examples of schema-based affect that can influence consumers' reactions to consumption experiences.

## Aesthetic Labor

**Aesthetic labor** deals specifically with employees who most carefully manage their own personal appearance as a requisite to performing their job well, and fitting what managers see as the stereotype for their particular company's service. Many service employees perform aesthetic labor, including cosmetic representatives, fashion models, and flight attendants and table servers for such companies as Air Korea and Hooters. The belief is that a specific appearance is needed to generate the appropriate emotional reaction in the consumer. These emotions promote behavior that can ultimately lead to loyalty.

### EXHIBIT 5.9
## A Typical Car Salesperson Schema

Tie too short · Bad Tie · "Cheesy" · Overweight · Helpless · Male · Smiles · Flicks Butt Away · Smokes · Apprehensive · Pushy · Loud · Skeptical

### EXHIBIT 5.10
## Examples of Schema-Based Affect

| Schema | Affect | Typical Consumer Reaction |
|---|---|---|
| Disney | Joyfulness, fun | Consumers have increased brand equity and lower price sensitivity for Disney products. |
| Individual countries (United Kingdom, France, United States, Japan, Israel, China) | Consumers may have slightly different affect associated with each country | Consumers are less favorable toward products manufactured in countries for which that consumer's schema evokes negative affect. |
| Telemarketing | Aggravation | Consumers often hang up quickly as a built-in avoidance response. |
| Baby | Tenderness, warmth | Products associated with babies are viewed more favorably. |
| Sports star | Excitement | Consumers may generalize excitement to products and services endorsed by the star. |
| Stereotypes | Each stereotype evokes slightly different affect | The affect associated with the stereotype can cause consumers to be more or less willing to approach and may alter information processing. |

*Many ads evoke negative self-conscious emotions. This powerful anti-smoking ad's tag line says: "If this is how a child feels when they lose you for a minute, just imagine how he'd feel if he lost you for life".*

## SELF-CONSCIOUS EMOTIONS

Face it, getting laughed at can be painful. Marketers sometimes execute communications designed to take advantage of consumers' natural tendency to avoid ridicule. Apple introduced a campaign in the late 2000s in which a *cool dude* using an Apple product pokes fun at a *nerdy dude* using a Windows product. Other brands emphasize how embarrassed one should feel for having less than pearly-white teeth, body odor (BO), bad hair, a less than beautiful golf swing, too big a waist, cankles, and on and on. These appeals work because they cause consumers to appraise themselves in some way and play on any resulting negative self-conscious emotions.[43] Self-conscious emotions result from some evaluation or reflection of one's own behavior – which can include both actions and failures to act. **Self-conscious emotions** include pride, embarrassment, guilt, regret, shame and hope. Consumers experiencing negative self-conscious emotions can perceive not only the need to rectify some problem, but also the need to restore their self-esteem.

## EMOTIONAL CONTAGION

Are emotions contagious? This is the idea behind **emotional contagion**, which represents the extent to which an emotional display by one person influences the emotional state of a bystander. Consumers who perceive other consumers or employees surrounding them as either happy or sad may experience a corresponding change in actual happiness or sadness themselves. Emotional contagion means marketing managers who have a mantra of "service with a smile" may have a good reason to do so. When service providers maintain an expression signaling positive affect (service with a smile), consumers report higher incidences of positive affect themselves.[44]

### Emotional Labor

Emotional contagion is closely related to another topic, emotional labor. **Emotional labor** is performed by service

> **self-conscious emotions** specific emotions that result from some evaluation or reflection of one's own behavior, including pride, shame, guilt, and embarrassment
>
> **emotional contagion** extent to which an emotional display by one person influences the emotional state of a bystander
>
> **emotional labor** effort put forth by service workers who have to overtly manage their own emotional displays as part of the requirements of the job

# The Golden Shape Is as Good as Gold!

**S**chema-based affect can be evoked from practically any type of knowledge. For instance, even something as simple as a shape can be associated with specific affect.

A fundamental principle of design that has survived for millennia is that people react favorably to rectangular shapes that have a ratio of width to height of about 1.6. The Parthenon, the famous fifth-century Greek temple, exhibits this dimension. All things equal, consumers will prefer products designed with these dimensions.

Similarly, consumers may react differently to package shapes depending on their knowledge. A uniquely shaped bottle, for instance, will evoke negative affect among highly involved consumers, but positive affect among those who are not as involved. So, shapes matter in part because shapes evoke affect.

Sources: Bloch, P. H. (1995), "Seeking the Ideal Form: Product Design and Consumer Response," *Journal of Marketing* 59 (July), 16–29; Bloch, Peter H., F. F. Brunel, and T. J. Arnold (2003), "Individual Differences in the Centrality of Visual Product Aesthetics: Concept and Measurement," *Journal of Consumer Research* 29, 551–565; Rocchi, B., and S. Gianlucca (2006), "Consumers' Perception of Wine Packaging: A Case Study," *International Journal of Wine Marketing* 18, 33–44.

workers who must overtly manage their own emotional displays as part of the requirements of the job. As an example, when airline flight attendants themselves feel angry, the requirements of their job ask them to hide their true feelings and express more positive emotions. While practically all service employees must perform emotional labor, including professional service providers such as physicians, the long-term impact on their psychological well-being may not be positive, unless the employees learn how to cope with the emotional conflict.

## Product Contamination

Picture this. A consumer sees a price reduction on a shirt he has wanted for a long time. He buys it, but when he gets home and begins to put it on, he realizes it no longer has the pins and cardboard backing that should come with a new shirt. "Has somebody already purchased this and returned it?" he asks himself. All of a sudden, the value in wearing the new shirt is diminished because the idea that someone else may have worn the shirt creates uneasiness. **Product contamination** refers to the fact that consumers feel uneasy about buying things that others have previously touched. Supermarket consumers can be seen searching the back of the shelf for an untouched package or avoiding produce that they have seen others handling. However, in an interesting twist, some research shows that through a type of emotional contagion process, a product's value is actually enhanced when a consumer observes an attractive member of the opposite sex handling a product.[45] Instead of avoiding that product, the consumer will actually seek out the one that has been handled by an attractive person.

# 5

# Study Tools

**Located at the back of the textbook**

☐ Rip-out Chapter-in-Review Card

**Located at www.cengagebrain.com**

☐ Review Key Terms Flashcards (Print or Online)

☐ Download audio summaries to review on the go

☐ Complete practice quizzes to prepare for tests

☐ Play "Beat the Clock" and "Quizbowl" to master concepts

☐ Watch Video on jetBlue for a real company example

## what others have thought...

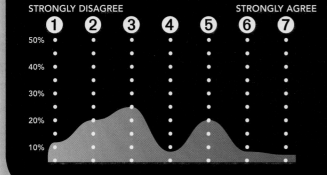

**I do not allow emotions to control my behavior.**

A majority of consumers recognize that emotions do influence their behavior. Nearly six in ten respondents disagree with the statement. Emotions are part of behavior and not all of the influence is a bad thing. So, enjoy them in moderation!

**Although all consumers** ultimately seek value, some are more highly focused on value than others.

what do you think?

My personality can easily be seen in the products that I buy.

STRONGLY DISAGREE
① ② ③ ④ ⑤ ⑥ ⑦
STRONGLY AGREE

Visit CourseMate at www.cengagebrain.com.

# 6

# Personality, Lifestyles, and the Self-Concept

After studying this chapter, the student should be able to:

**LO1** Define personality and know how various approaches to studying personality can be applied to consumer behavior.

**LO2** Discuss major traits that have been examined in consumer research.

**LO3** Understand why lifestyles and psychographics are important to the study of consumer behavior.

**LO4** Comprehend the role of the self-concept in consumer behavior.

**LO5** Understand the concept of self-congruency and how it applies to consumer behavior issues.

# Introduction

his chapter focuses on consumer personality, lifestyles, and self-concept. As such, the chapter deals with what are known as **individual difference variables**, which are descriptions of how individual consumers differ according to specific traits or patterns of behavior.[1] These concepts have several applications to both consumer research and marketing practice. Marketing managers are especially interested in identifying consumer characteristics that are associated with the likelihood of purchasing products. Concepts like personality, lifestyle, and self-concept help to describe these differences.

> **individual difference variables** descriptions of how individual consumers differ according to specific trait patterns of behavior

> **personality** totality of thoughts, emotions, intentions, and behaviors that a person exhibits consistently as he or she adapts to the environment

# LO1 Personality and Consumer Behavior

ersonality has been studied for many years, and the term has been defined in a number of different ways. We define **personality** as the totality of thoughts, emotions, intentions, and behaviors that a person exhibits consistently as he or she adapts to his or her environment.[2] This definition highlights the *cognitive* (thoughts), *affective* (emotions), *motivational* (intentions), and *behavioral* (behaviors) aspects that are central to the study of personality. Personality is but one characteristic that helps explain why a particular behavior, for example listening to the band The Black Eyed Peas, provides great value to one consumer but none to another.

Personality exhibits a number of distinct qualities, including:

1. *Personality is unique to an individual.* Personality helps distinguish consumers based on the specific characteristics each exhibits. Consumers differ in personalities, although some characteristics, or traits, may be shared across individuals.

2. *Personality can be conceptualized as a combination of specific traits or characteristics.* Like all consumers, your overall personality is really a combination of many stable characteristics, or traits. In fact, for many psychologists, personality psychology deals exclusively with the study of human traits.[3]

3. *Personality traits are relatively stable and interact with situations to influence behavior.* Personality traits are expected to remain consistent across situations. However, consumer researchers realize the importance of situational influencers, and the combined influence of situations and traits greatly influences specific behaviors (this is referred to as an *interaction* between the person and the situation).[4] To Illustrate, imagine how an impatient person acts in a crowded restaurant.

4. *Specific behaviors can vary across time.* One major issue in personality research is that simply knowing a consumer possesses a specific trait does not allow us to predict a specific behavior. For example, knowing that a consumer is "materialistic" does not allow the researcher to predict the exact type of product the person may buy. For this reason, personality researchers often advocate an **aggregation approach** in which behaviors are measured over time, rather than relying on a single measure of behavior at one point in time.

As we have mentioned, marketing managers are particularly interested in how consumers differ according to their personalities. Consistent patterns of thoughts, emotions, intentions, and behaviors can signal the need for individualized marketing campaigns, and today's marketers are becoming quite adept at individualizing messages. To understand how personalities differ across consumers, it is important to begin with a description of the various approaches to studying the concept. There are a number of ways to explore the human personality; however, here we focus on two popular approaches: the psychoanalytic approach and the trait approach. These approaches have received considerable consumer research attention.

> Consistent patterns of thoughts, emotions, intentions, and behaviors can signal the need for individualized marketing campaigns.

## PSYCHOANALYTIC APPROACH TO PERSONALITY

According to the famous psychologist Sigmund Freud, human behavior is influenced by an inner struggle between various systems within the personality system.[5] His approach, commonly referred to as the **psychoanalytic approach to personality**, is applicable to both motivation and personality inquiry. Freud's approach highlights the importance of unconscious mental processes in influencing behavior.

For Freud, the human personality consists of three important components: the *id*, the *superego*, and the *ego*. The **id** focuses on pleasure-seeking and immediate gratification. It operates on a **pleasure principle** that motivates a person to focus on maximizing pleasure and minimizing pain. One's id, therefore, focuses on hedonic value. Indeed, a key concept in the id is the *libido*. The libido represents a drive for sexual pleasure, although some researchers view it in slightly different ways. The **superego** works against the id by motivating behavior that matches societal norms and expectations. The superego can be conceptualized as being similar to a consumer's conscience. The **ego** focuses on resolving the conflicts between the id and the superego. The ego works largely in accordance with the **reality principle**. Under this principle, the ego seeks to satisfy the id within the constraints of society. As such, the ego attempts to balance the desires of the id with the constraints of, and expectations found in, the superego.

## Psychoanalytic Approach and Motivation Research

In the early days of consumer research, researchers applied psychoanalytic tools to try to identify explanations for behavior. This was known as the **motivational research era**. Consumer researchers in this era utilized tools such as *depth interviews* and *focus groups* to improve their understanding of inner motives and needs.[6] Researchers applying depth interviews try to explore deep-seated motivations by asking consumers to describe an activity through a series of probing questions. As discussed in our motivation chapter, motivations are the reasons or driving forces behind actions.

Suppose a researcher is studying a consumer who has a strong preference for rhythm and blues music. The researcher might ask the following probing questions:

- "How do you feel when you hear R&B?"
- "What does it mean to you to feel this way?"
- "What kinds of things do you think about when you listen to R&B?"
- "What would you do if you could no longer listen to R&B?"

Although motivational research has been popular, in general, the motivational research era proved disappointing because it did not spawn any compelling, practical consumer behavior theories or guidelines for marketing actions. Nonetheless, Freud clearly influenced the study of personality and consumer behavior.[7] To this day, for instance, consumer researchers remain interested in discovering consumer motivations below the level of conscious awareness.

As an example of the influence of deeply held motivations influencing behavior, consider the id. Although the use of sexual imagery in advertising is often criticized, overtly sexual advertisements are rather common. In fact, the old adage that "Sex sells!" may be directly tied to the Freudian approach. The use of phallic and ovarian symbols in advertising may be traced to a belief that such messages appeal to, and provide value for, the id.

## TRAIT APPROACH TO PERSONALITY

While the psychoanalytic approach helped set the groundwork for much of consumer personality research, the **trait approach to personality** has received significant attention over the past few decades. A **trait** is defined as a distinguishable characteristic that describes one's tendency to act in a relatively consistent manner.

Not surprisingly, there are multiple approaches available for consumer researchers. Here, we discuss the differences between nomothetic and idiographic approaches, and between single- versus multi-trait approaches.

**superego** component in psychoanalytic theory that works against the id by motivating behavior that matches the expectations and norms of society

**ego** component in psychoanalytic theory that attempts to balance the struggle between the superego and the id

**reality principle** the principle in psychoanalytic theory under which the ego attempts to satisfy the id within societal constraints

**motivational research era** era in consumer research that focused heavily on psychoanalytic approaches

**trait approach to personality** approaches in personality research that focus on specific consumer traits as motivators of various consumer behaviors

**trait** distinguishable characteristic that describes one's tendency to act in a relatively consistent manner

AP IMAGES/KIICHIRO SATO

***Does this ad appeal to some deeply held motivation?***

## Nomothetic versus Idiographic Approaches

The nomothetic perspective and the idiographic perspective can be distinguished as follows.[8] The **nomothetic perspective** is a "variable-centered" approach that focuses on particular variables, or traits, that exist across a number of consumers. The goal of this perspective is to find common personality traits that can be studied across people.

An example helps to explain the nomothetic approach. Consider college student, Tia. Tia's friends notice that she is very conscientious with her work. That is, she's very organized, efficient, and precise in everything that she does. Of course, many other people can be described in this way. Here, the focus is on the conscientiousness trait, and it is used to help describe the characteristics of a number of consumers.

The **idiographic perspective** focuses on the total person and the uniqueness of his or her psychological makeup. Attention is not placed on individual traits or how they can be studied across multiple consumers. Rather, the focus is on understanding the complexity of each individual consumer.

The trait approach takes a nomothetic approach to personality. That is, the trait approach assumes that the human personality can be described as a combination of traits that can be studied across consumers. From this perspective, individuals can be described by using various trait descriptors.

### Single-Trait and Multiple-Trait Approaches

We can further distinguish between single-trait and multi-trait approaches to consumer research. With the **single-trait approach**, the focus of the researcher is on one particular trait. Here, researchers can learn more about the trait and how it affects behavior. For example, a researcher may want to investigate the competitiveness trait and how

Athletic consumers are often very competitive.

© ROBIN NELSON/PHOTOEDIT

it impacts the selection of athletic wear. Perhaps highly competitive consumers will prefer one brand of athletic clothing over another.

With the **multiple-trait approach**, combinations of traits are examined and the total effect of the collection of traits is considered. Here, the researcher is interested in trait scores on numerous traits as potential predictors of consumer behavior. The prediction of individual behavior tends to be stronger with the multiple-trait approach.[9] However, both the single- and multiple-trait approaches have been used extensively in consumer research.

# LO2 Specific Traits Examined in Consumer Research

To say that there are many traits that can be studied would be a serious understatement! To illustrate, researchers Gordon Allport and Henry Odbert identified nearly 18,000 names for human characteristics found in Webster's Dictionary. And that was in 1936![10] Although numerous traits have received attention, we will discuss only a handful of important traits found in consumer research, including value consciousness, materialism, innovativeness, complaint proneness, and competitiveness.

## Value Consciousness

As we have stated throughout this text, value is at the heart of consumer behavior. Although all consumers ultimately seek value, some consumers are more highly focused on value than are others. As such, value consciousness is often studied as a trait. **Value consciousness** represents the tendency for consumers to focus on maximizing what is received from a transaction as compared to what is given.

Research reveals that value consciousness is an important concept in consumer behavior. For example, value consciousness underlies tendencies to perform behaviors like redeeming coupons.[11] Value-conscious consumers can be expected to pay close attention to the resources that they devote to transactions and to the benefits that they receive. In today's turbulent economy, value consciousness is an important trait to study.

## Materialism

**Materialism** refers to the extent to which material goods are important in a consumer's life. Most western cultures, including the U.S. culture, are generally thought of as being relatively materialistic. However, within each culture, the degree to which each individual is materialistic varies. Studying this trait has been very popular among consumer researchers, and numerous studies have examined the impact of materialism on various consumer behaviors.

Materialism is seen as consisting of three separate dimensions:[12]

- *Possessiveness.* A tendency to retain control and ownership over possessions

- *Nongenerosity.* An unwillingness to share with others

- *Envy.* Resentment that arises as a result of another's belongings and a desire to acquire similar possessions

Highly materialistic consumers tend to be possessive, nongenerous, and envious of other's possessions. Not surprisingly, these consumers view possessions as a means of achieving happiness and they tend to hold onto possessions as long as possible.[13] What's more, research even indicates that materialistic people establish strong bonds with products in order to ease fears regarding their own mortality![14] Products can be a real source of comfort for materialistic consumers.

Interestingly, consumers today commonly bring many of their favorite material possessions into the workplace. Personal possessions in the workplace can produce calm feelings and stabilize an employee's sense of self.[15] In this way, terial possessions play an important part in self-expression. That is, material possessions help consumers express who they think they are, and even who they would like to be.[16] These issues are discussed later in the chapter.

Materialism tends to differ among generations, with lower materialism scores typically found among older consumers.[17] Indeed, younger consumers have long been thought of as relatively materialistic. A change in the prevalence of materialism does appear to be occurring, however. Although the U.S. culture is widely viewed as materialistic, research suggests that consumers are beginning to "downshift." Downshifting refers to a conscious decision to reduce one's material consumption. This may be a positive development as high levels of materialism can adversely affect debt levels and personal relationships.[18] The recent economic downturn has contributed to a growth in consumer *frugality*, or the extent to which consumers exhibit restraint when purchasing and using material goods.[19]

## Innovativeness

Consumer **innovativeness** refers to the degree to which a consumer is open to new ideas and quick to adopt buying new products, services, or experiences early in their introduction.[20] Innovative consumers are generally dynamic and curious, and they are often young, educated, and relatively affluent.[21] Obviously, consumer innovativeness is an important trait for marketers to consider when introducing new products.

Although researchers do not necessarily agree on the extent to which innovativeness is exhibited across product categories, a consumer with a strong degree of innovativeness may be expected to be innovative in a number of situations. For example, innovativeness has been shown to relate to a number of behaviors including new product adoption, novelty seeking, information seeking, and online shopping.[22]

## Need for Cognition

**Need for cognition** refers to the degree to which consumers tend to engage in effortful cognitive information processing.[23] Consumers who have a high degree of this trait tend to think carefully about products, problems, and even marketing messages. For example, research has shown that consumers with a high need for cognition tend to be influenced heavily by the quality of the arguments in an advertisement. Conversely, consumers with a low need for cognition tend to be more influenced by things like an endorser's physical attractiveness and other cues that are not central to a message.[24]

Research also indicates that the effect of humorous advertising is impacted by need for cognition.

**materialism** extent to which material goods have importance in a consumer's life

**innovativeness** degree to which an individual is open to new ideas and tends to be relatively early in adopting new products, services, or experiences

**need for cognition** refers to the degree to which consumers enjoy engaging in effortful cognitive information processing

**competitiveness** enduring tendency to strive to be better than others

Humorous ads tend to lead to more positive consumer attitudes and purchase intentions for consumers who have a low degree of need for cognition.[25] Studies also indicate that the need for cognition trait influences consumers' reactions to ads with sexual content. For example, consumers with a low degree of need for cognition have exhibited more positive attitudes and purchase intentions towards brands that are advertised using sexual imagery than consumers with a high degree of need for cognition.[26]

## Competitiveness

The **competitiveness** trait may be defined as an enduring tendency to strive to be better than others. The predominance of competitiveness in consumer society is easy to see, and the use of competitive themes in marketing messages is widespread.

A competitive person is generally easy to identify, and research reveals that the trait often emerges in the following ways:[27]

- When a consumer is directly competing with others. Thanks to the Internet, many sports and games are now "played" online. A great example is fantasy sports leagues. The sports network ESPN has even promoted fantasy football, baseball, basketball, and hockey contests with the winners receiving valuable prizes. The growth of online video gaming highlights consumer competitiveness in a technologically advanced environment.

- When a consumer enjoys winning vicariously through the efforts of others (as when we enjoy seeing "our team" win). Sports fans often *bask in reflected glory* (BIRG) when "their" team wins. This

# Trait Superstition

**D**o you feel uneasy if a black cat crosses your path? Do you avoid walking under ladders or opening umbrellas indoors? Have you ever noticed baseball players jump over the foul line rather than step on it? Although a lot of people laugh off superstitions and superstitious rituals, to other people they are very real. Being superstitious can be thought of as a trait because it represents a consumer's tendency to act in relatively consistent ways.

Although consumer research in the area is relatively scarce, some interesting findings have been revealed. For instance, the superstition trait has been shown to influence decisions to gamble, to participate in sweepstakes, to forward emails, and to invest in the stock market. Superstitious consumers have also been shown to be risk averse when negative cues are present.

Decisions based on superstition can have significant effects on business. An example of this was found in the dramatic jump in weddings on the date 07/07/07. The number of weddings on that day nearly tripled due to consumer belief in the lucky 7s. The industry was busy that day!! While 07/07/07 was important for these consumers, dates like 10/10/10 and 11/11/11 hold significance as well. Even though the origins of many superstitions are difficult to determine, it is clear that trait superstition is a relevant topic for consumer researchers.

Sources: Based on online content retrieved at **http://www.time.com/time/business/article/0,8599,1630320,00.html,** accessed May 24, 2010, also Mowen, John C. and Brad D. Carlson (2003), "Exploring the Antecedents and Consumer Behavior Consequences of the Trait of Superstition," *Psychology & Marketing* 20 (12), 1045–1065; Carlson, Brad D., John C. Mowen, and Xiang Fang (2009), "Trait Superstition and Consumer Behavior: Re-Conceptualization, Measurement, and Initial Investigations," *Psychology & Marketing* 26 (8), 689–713; Kramer, Thomas and Lauren Block (2008), "Conscious and Nonconscious Components of Superstitious Beliefs in Judgment and Decision Making," *Journal of Consumer Research* 34 (6), 783–793.

means that they will wear team apparel and display team merchandise when their team is successful. By attempting to show an association between themselves and the team, consumers vicariously live through their team and proclaim things like "We're number one!" (As researchers point out, you hardly ever hear them say things like "They're number one!"[28]) BIRGing has been tied directly to consumer ego and self-esteem. Interestingly, fans may also CORF. That is, they *cut off reflected failure* by hiding their association with losing teams. These fans are often called "fair-weather" fans. Obviously, sports marketers love fan BIRGing behavior and hope to minimize CORFing.[29]

- When a consumer attempts to display superiority over others by openly flaunting exclusive products (as when we flaunt a nice car in front of others). The term *conspicuous consumption* describes a tendency of the wealthy to flaunt their material possessions as a way of displaying their social class. Numerous product categories, ranging from automobiles to jewelry, help to signal a consumer's status and can be used to convey images of consumer "superiority." By buying and displaying the correct products, consumers often feel that they can send the "I'm better than you are!" message.

## Other Traits Found in Consumer Research

It should be emphasized that the preceding traits represent only a small fraction of the many traits that have been investigated in consumer research. Exhibit 6.1

**EXHIBIT 6.1**

# Examples of Other Traits in Consumer Research

**Frugality** The tendency of a consumer to exhibit restraint when facing purchases and using resources.

**Impulsiveness** The tendency for consumers to make impulsive, unintended purchases.

**Trait Anxiety** A tendency to respond with anxiety when facing threatening events.

**Bargaining Proneness** The tendency for a consumer to engage in bargaining behaviors when making purchases.

**Trait Vanity** The tendency for consumers to take excessive pride in themselves, including their appearance and accomplishments.

highlights other traits that are often studied. Again, we emphasize that there are many more!

## The Five-Factor Model Approach

One of the most popular multiple-trait approaches found in both personality psychology and consumer research is the **five-factor model** (FFM) approach.[30] Numerous studies have examined the influence of the traits in the FFM on a wide range of behaviors, both inside and outside of the field of consumer research. The FFM proposes that five dominant traits are found in the human personality, including:

1. Extroversion
2. Agreeableness

3. Openness to Experience (also referred to as "creativity")
4. Stability (or Instability; sometimes referred to clinically as "neuroticism")
5. Conscientiousness

> **five-factor model**
> multiple-trait perspective that proposes that the human personality consists of five traits: agreeableness, extroversion, openness to experience (or creativity), conscientiousness, and neuroticism (or stability)

Extroverted consumers are outgoing and talkative with others. Agreeable consumers are kind-hearted to others and sympathetic. Creative consumers are imaginative and enjoy new ideas. Stable consumers tend to be able to control their emotions and avoid mood swings. Conscientious consumers are careful, orderly, and precise. These traits are presented in Exhibit 6.2.

As we have stated, the FFM approach is a multiple-trait approach, meaning that a consumer's personality is conceptualized as a *combination* of these traits and that each consumer will vary on the respective traits. For example, Corbin might possess relatively strong degrees of extroversion, agreeableness, and openness, but he may not be very stable or conscientious. By examining consumers across the five dimensions of the FFM, we gain an expanded view of how multiple traits influence specific consumer behaviors.

The FFM approach is indeed popular with consumer researchers, and the traits found in the FFM have been shown to impact consumer behaviors such as complaining,

**EXHIBIT 6.2**

# Five-Factor Model

| Personality Trait | Description |
|---|---|
| Extroversion | Talkative, outgoing |
| Agreeableness | Kindhearted, sympathetic |
| Openness to Experience | Creative, open to new ideas, imaginative |
| Stability | Even-keeled, avoids mood swings |
| Conscientiousness | Precise, efficient, organized |

Source: Based on McCrae, R. R., and P. T. Costa (2005), *Personality in Adulthood: A Five-Factor Theory Perspective*, 2nd ed., New York, Guilford.

bargaining, banking, compulsive shopping, mass media consumption, and commitment to buying environmentally friendly products.[31]

Even though the FFM has proved useful for presenting an integrative approach to personality, the model is not universally accepted by all researchers. In fact, there have been some lively debates regarding its usefulness.

## Hierarchical Approaches to Personality Traits

If you are beginning to think that there are so many different approaches to trait psychology theory that it is hard to keep them all straight, you are not alone! Organizing all of these traits is one of the goals of what are known as **hierarchical approaches to personality**.

Hierarchical approaches begin with the assumption that personality traits exist at varying levels of abstraction. That is, some traits are specific (bargaining proneness), and others are more broad (extroversion). Specific traits refer to tendencies to behave in very well-defined situations. For example, a bargaining-prone consumer will bargain when shopping for products. Here, the situation is very specific. Broad traits refer to tendencies to behave across many different situations. For example, an extroverted consumer may be very outgoing when with friends, when in a restaurant, or when discussing a group project with classmates. As a general statement, specific traits tend to be better predictors of individual behaviors than broad traits. A number of researchers have argued for the existence of these hierarchies, with many suggesting that abstract traits influence more specific traits in a hierarchical fashion.[32]

## Final Thoughts on the Trait Approach

The trait approach in consumer research is very popular today in large part due to its ability to objectively assign a personality trait score, from a survey for example, to a consumer. In this way, the approach has an advantage over the psychoanalytic approach in which personality dimensions are assigned

based on the psychologist's subjective interpretation. We should emphasize, however, that the trait approach is not without criticism. Exhibit 6.3 reveals a number of criticisms that have been leveled against trait research.[33]

## EXHIBIT 6.3
### Criticisms of the Trait Approach

- Personality traits have not traditionally been shown to be strong predictors of consumer behavior relative to other explanatory variables.
- So many personality traits exist that researchers often select traits for study without any logical theoretical basis.
- Personality traits are sometimes hard to measure, and researchers often use measures with questionable validity.
- Personality inventories used to measure traits are often meant for use on specific populations, but they are frequently applied to practically any consumer group.
- Researchers often measure and use traits in ways not originally intended.
- Consumer traits generally do not predict specific brand selections.

## Personology

We discussed previously that personality and motivation are closely related topics. A relatively new approach to researching consumers, which combines personality theory and motivation, is the "personology" approach. This approach allows consumer researchers to better understand the uniqueness of the individual consumer by combining information on traits, goals, and even consumer life stories, in order to gain a better understanding of the complexities of the human personality.[34]

As you can see, many ways to view the human personality exist, and several different approaches to exploring the influence of personality on consumer behavior have been used. Personality inquiry, while controversial and not without limitations, continues to be a fruitful avenue of research for consumer researchers.

# BRAND PERSONALITY

Do brands have personalities? Does your favorite brand of soft drink have a personality? Does the personality of the drink match your personality? These questions may sound a bit strange at first, but upon reflection, consumers do describe brands with human-like qualities. How would you describe the personality of MTV? What qualities are associated with Fox apparel? How is PacSun different from Sears?

Marketing managers and consumer researchers alike are very interested in the "personalities" of products. **Brand personality** refers to human characteristics that can be associated with a brand.[35] Brand personalities can be described across five dimensions including competence, excitement, ruggedness, sincerity, and sophistication. These dimensions are described in Exhibit 6.4.

**brand personality** collection of human characteristics that can be associated with a brand

Brand personalities represent opportunities for companies to differentiate their products. Accordingly, a brand's personality may be viewed as a part of its overall image.[36] Brand personalities also provide marketers with opportunities to build strong brand relationships with consumers, especially when they have an understanding of their customer's personality.[37] A well-known LG marketing campaign says "Life's Good", signifying how their products relate to this overall belief. Hallmark cards are seen as sincere and trustworthy. Guess is considered to be sophisticated clothing compared with Wrangler.[38]

## Formation of Brand Personality

Many factors contribute to the development of a brand's personality.[39] A product's category can infer certain qualities. For example, if you hear the name *Sampson, Whitten, and Taylor* and find out that it is a law firm, you may develop an idea that the firm is serious, professional, and competent. If, however, you hear of a new brand of athletic wear called *Activesport*, you

**FASHION SYMBOLS**

*Don't get caught in the wrong outfit*

**Top 10 brands that make you look exciting**
(out of 196 brands tested)

9.1% of hits

Downtown Joey | Bare Essentials | Loopy Guess | High Horse | Pumpkin Primrose | Bxlen Echandia | Roots | South Pole | No Fear

**How it works:** The data are obtained using the yahoo search engine. % of hits is the percentage of web pages that contain 'exciting' out of all web pages that contain the brand.

*Companies pay close attention to brand personality.*

## EXHIBIT 6.4
## Brand Personality Dimensions

| Personality Trait | Description | Example |
|---|---|---|
| Competence | Responsible, reliable, dependable | Maytag—"Depend on Us" |
| Excitement | Daring, spirited | Mountain Dew—"Do the Dew!" |
| Ruggedness | Tough, strong | Ford Trucks—"Built Ford Tough" |
| Sincerity | Honest, genuine | Wrangler Jeans—"Genuine. Wrangler" |
| Sophistication | Glamorous, charming | Cartier jewelry—"Brilliance, Elegance, Exuberance" |

Source: Based on Aaker, Jennifer (1997), "Dimensions of Brand Personality," *Journal of Marketing Research* (August), 347–356.

might expect the brand to be adventurous and outdoorsy. Other factors that contribute to the development of a brand's personality include packaging, price, sponsorships, symbols, and celebrity endorsements.

## Personality and Brand Relationships

The brand personality concept is especially important when one considers that consumers, to a certain extent, have relationships with brands, and that personality traits are important in the formation and maintenance of these relationships.[40] To illustrate, Coca-Cola's sincere and traditional personality enables the Coca-Cola Company to easily remind consumers that the brand has always been and will always be a part of their life. In fact, "Always Coca-Cola" is one of Coke's best-known advertising campaigns.

The concept of consumer–brand relationships has received considerable research attention, and several factors help indicate the level of relationship between a consumer and a brand. Consumer researcher Susan Fournier proposes that the overall quality of the relationship between consumer and brand can be described in terms of the following:[41]

- **Love and Passion.** A consumer may have such strong feelings about a brand that they actually describe it with the term *love*. A consumer may say, "I love my Dell Mini 10" or "I love Axe cologne."

- **Self-Connection.** Brands may help to express some central component of a consumer's identity. Research indicates that the correct match between a

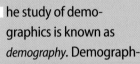

# Demographics Today

The study of demographics is known as *demography*. Demographic variables include age, ethnicity, income, family size, and occupation.

- **Age.** Age is important not only because of its descriptive nature, but also because consumers who experience significant life events at approximately the same age are influenced greatly by the events. This is the "cohort effect." Groups such as "Generation Y" or "Millennials" (born between 1981 and 1995), "Generation X" (born between 1966 and 1980), and "Baby Boomers" (born between 1946 and 1965) and "The Greatest Generation" (born prior to 1946) are identifiable segments. Baby Boomers receive a lot of attention because of the group's size and spending power. Younger consumers, like pre-teens also receive attention.

- **Ethnicity.** Diversity is growing in the United States. Minority groups (such as Hispanics, African-Americans, and Asian-Americans) are expected to grow considerably in the years to come. In fact, projections reveal that by 2050, the "minority" segment will exceed more than half of the total population!

- **Income.** Income is another important variable. "Engel's Law" states that as income increases, a smaller percentage of expenditure is devoted to food, and the percentage devoted to consumption rises slower than the rise in income.

Demographics can be used to help locate and understand lifestyle segments. This is why demographic information is often combined with psychographics. Failing to consider psychographic measures leads to the trap of assuming that all consumers of a certain demographic have the exact same tastes. An example is found in the concept of "psychological age." A person's actual age and his or her psychological age can be very different. As some have said, "today's sixty is yesterday's forty." The demographics topic is discussed again in a later chapter.

Sources: "An Older and More Diverse Nation By Midcentury," *U.S. Census Bureau News*, Washington, D.C., online content found at **http://www.census.gov/population/www/projections/index.html**, accessed March 20, 2009.

customer's personality and a perceived brand personality leads to higher overall satisfaction.[42]

- **Commitment.** In a strong consumer–brand relationship, consumers are very committed to their brands and feel very loyal to them. Harley-Davidson owners are well-known for their commitment to their bikes. In fact, the Harley Owners Group® (H.O.G.) is the largest factory-sponsored group in the world, with more than one million members![43]

- **Interdependence.** Consumer-brand relationships may be marked by interdependence between the product and the consumer. This can be described in terms of the frequency of use, the diversity of brand-related situations, and the intensity of product usage. For example, consumers are often reminded that "Like a good neighbor, State Farm is there."

- **Intimacy.** Strong relationships between consumers and brands can be described as intimate. Deep-seated needs and desires of consumers can be tied directly to specific brands. For example, a need for intimacy and passion can be directly tied to a specific brand of perfume, like Obsession. A need for excitement or status can be related to a sporty automobile, like Porsche.

- **Brand Partner Quality.** In general, brands that are perceived to be of high quality contribute to the formation of consumer–brand relationships. In this sense, consumers develop feelings of trust regarding specific brands, and these feelings of trust foster consumer–brand relationships. Research reveals that brand personality traits also affect customer–brand relationship quality when service problems occur, with sincere brands suffering more than exciting brands when service breakdowns occur.[44]

Purchase patterns are often influenced by consumer lifestyles, and numerous lifestyle categories can be identified. It shouldn't be surprising, therefore, that marketers often target consumers based on lifestyles. For example, Pepsi's Code Red has been aimed at active, young male consumers, while Dasani water appeals to the more health-conscious

**lifestyles** distinctive modes of living, including how people spend their time and money

**psychographics** quantitative investigation of consumer lifestyles

**demographics** observable, statistical aspects of populations such as age, gender, or income

**AIO statements** activity, interest, and opinion statements that are used in lifestyle studies

## Consumer segments very often contain consumers with similar lifestyles.

# LO3 Consumer Lifestyles and Psychographics

t he term *lifestyle* is used commonly in everyday life. For example, we often speak of "healthy lifestyles," "unhealthy lifestyles," "alternative lifestyles," and even "dangerous lifestyles." The word has also been used in many ways in consumer research. Stated simply, consumer **lifestyles** refer to the ways consumers live and spend their time and money.

Personality and lifestyles are closely related topics. In fact, lifestyles have been referred to as context-specific personality traits.[45] This has implications for how the concepts are measured. That is, instead of asking a consumer if he/she is an "outdoor type," a lifestyle approach will ask the consumer about the amount of time she spends outdoors and what she does when she is outdoors. Importantly, lifestyles aren't completely determined by personality. Instead, they emerge from the influence of culture, groups, and individual processes, including personality.[46] Not surprisingly, consumer lifestyles vary considerably across cultures.

Lifestyles have proved extremely valuable to marketers and others interested in predicting behavior.

consumer. Because lifestyle can be directly tied to product purchase and consumption, consumer lifestyles are considered an important manifestation of social stratification.[47] In other words, they are very useful in identifying viable market segments. Appealing to a consumer's lifestyle is so important that it's not uncommon to see advertisements focusing as much on lifestyle as on the actual product itself.

## PSYCHOGRAPHICS

The term **psychographics** refers to the way consumer lifestyles are measured. Psychographic techniques use quantitative methods that can be used in developing lifestyle profiles. Notice that this is not the same thing as demographics. **Demographics** refers to observable, statistical aspects of populations including such factors as age, gender, or income. Lifestyles, although also observable, refer to how consumers live.

Although psychographic research has been used to investigate lifestyles for many years, advances in technology have helped psychographics become even more popular with consumer researchers and marketing managers today. Psychographic analysis involves surveying consumers using **AIO statements**, which are used to

**VALS** popular psychographic method in consumer research that divides consumers into groups based on resources and consumer behavior motivations

gain an understanding of consumers' activities, interests, and opinions. These measurements can be narrowly defined (as relating to a specific product or product category) or broadly defined (as pertaining to general activities that the consumer enjoys).

Consumer segments very often contain consumers with similar lifestyles. Although the categorization of segments is rarely based on consumer behavior theory, the process can be very helpful in identifying marketing opportunities. As an example, one recent effort to identify segments in the European tourism industry resulted in the following lifestyle segment profiles:[48]

- **Home Loving.** Fundamentally focused on the family, this segment values product quality. These consumers enjoy cultural activities such as visiting art exhibits and monuments. The home-loving group takes the greatest number of long, family-oriented travel vacations.

- **Idealistic.** These responsible consumers believe that the road to success is based on bettering the world. They enjoy classical music and theater. Travel destinations for this group are primarily rural locations and country villages.

- **Autonomous.** These independent- thinking consumers strive to be upwardly mobile. They enjoy the nightlife and read few newspapers. This segment enjoys weekend travel.

- **Hedonistic.** The hedonistic segment values human relationships and work. They are interested in new product offerings and enjoy listening to music. These consumers enjoy visiting large cities.

- **Conservative.** Like the home-loving segment, this segment focuses largely on the family. These consumers tend to view success simply in terms of their work careers. This group dislikes nightlife and modern music and instead focuses on issues related to religion, law, and order. These consumers take few weekend trips, but they do enjoy visiting seaside destinations.

Psychographic profiles of various other consumer groups have resulted in lifestyle segments identified for Harley-Davidson owners (including "cocky misfits" and "classy capitalists"),[49] wine drinkers (including "conservatives," "experimenters," and "image oriented"),[50] and Porsche owners (including "top guns," "elitists," and "fantasists"),[51] and health, wellness, and sustainability

*Lifestyle segments explain vacation preferences.*

© ISTOCKPHOTO.COM/ROBERT CHURCHILL

focused consumers (including "lifestyle of health and sustainability").[52] As you can see from these examples, there are numerous ways in which to segment consumers based on lifestyles.

## Specificity of Lifestyle Segments

The lifestyle approaches that we have discussed here can be categorized in terms of specificity—either narrowly defined or more broadly defined. Generally, lifestyles are indeed quite specific. The magazine industry is particularly efficient at identifying consumer lifestyles and developing products around lifestyle segments. For example, consumers who skateboard can read magazines such as *Thrasher*, while those who enjoy paintball can read *PaintballX3*. Exhibit 6.5 presents sample measures used for psychographic analysis for the leisure bowling segment.

# VALS

When using lifestyle segmentation, a marketer can either identify his or her own segments or use established methods that are already available. One popular method in consumer research is the VALS™ approach.[53] Developed and marketed by Strategic Business Insights, VALS is a very successful segmentation approach that has been adopted by several companies. **VALS** stands for "Values and Lifestyles." The current approach, known as VALS 2, classifies consumers into eight distinct segments based on resources available to the consumer (including financial,

## EXHIBIT 6.5
## Sample Psychographic Items for Segmenting the Bowling Market

| TYPE OF ITEM | EXAMPLE | Strongly Disagree | Disagree | Neutral | Agree | Strongly Agree |
|---|---|---|---|---|---|---|
| Activity | I spend much of my free time bowling. | ☐ | ☐ | ☐ | ☐ | ☐ |
| Interest | I am very interested in the latest developments in bowling ball technology. | ☐ | ☐ | ☐ | ☐ | ☐ |
| Opinion | Bowling is truly "America's favorite sport." | ☐ | ☐ | ☐ | ☐ | ☐ |

educational, and intellectual resources), as well as three primary motivations (ideals motivation, achievement motivation, and self-expression motivation).

VALS 2 includes eight groups:

- **Innovators.** Innovators are successful, sophisticated people who have high self-esteem. They are motivated by achievement, ideals, and self-expression. Image is important to these consumers.

- **Thinkers.** Thinkers are ideal motivated. They are mature, reflective people who value order and knowledge. They have relatively high income and are conservative, practical consumers.

- **Achievers.** Achievers have an achievement motivation and are politically conservative. Their lives largely center around church, family, and career. Image is important to this group, and they prefer to purchase prestige products.

- **Experiencers.** Experiencers are self-expressive consumers who tend to be young, impulsive, and enthusiastic. These consumers value novelty and excitement.

- **Believers.** In some ways, believers are like thinkers. They are ideal motivated and conservative. They

follow routines, and their lives largely center around home, family, and church. They do not have the amount of resources that thinkers have, however.

- **Strivers.** Strivers are achievement motivated, but they do not have the amount of resources that are available to achievers. For strivers, shopping is a way to demonstrate to others their ability to buy.

- **Makers.** Makers are like experiencers in that they are motivated by self-expression. They have fewer resources than experiencers. They tend to express themselves through their activities such as raising children, fixing cars, and building houses.

- **Survivors.** Survivors are very low on resources and are constricted by this lack of resources. They tend to be elderly consumers who are concerned with health issues and who believe that the world is changing too quickly. They are not active in the marketplace, as their primary concerns center around safety, family, and security.

## PRIZM

Another popular tool for lifestyle analysis is a geodemographic procedure known as PRIZM®.[54]

**geodemographic techniques** techniques that combine data on consumer expenditures and socioeconomic variables with geographic information in order to identify commonalities in consumption patterns of households in various regions

**PRIZM** popular geodemographic technique that stands for Potential Ratings Index by ZIP Market

**self-concept** totality of thoughts and feelings that an individual has about himself or herself

**symbolic interactionism** perspective that proposes that consumers live in a symbolic environment and interpret the myriad of symbols around them, and that members of a society agree on the meanings of symbols

**semiotics** study of symbols and their meanings

Geodemographic techniques combine data on consumer expenditures and socioeconomic variables with geographic information in order to identify commonalities in consumption patterns of households in various regions. PRIZM is a popular lifestyle analysis technique that was developed by Nielsen Claritas. PRIZM, which stands for Potential Ratings Index by ZIP Market, is based on the premise that people with similar backgrounds and means tend to live close to one another and emulate each other's behaviors and lifestyles.

PRIZM combines demographic and behavioral information in a manner that enables marketers to better understand and target their customers. The technique uses 66 different segments as descriptors of individual households, which are ranked according to socioeconomic variables. Segments found using the PRIZM technique include "Movers and Shakers," "Money and Brains," "Red, White and Blues," and "Back Country Folks." There are other geodemographic techniques available as well, including ESRI's GIS and Mapping Software (**http://www.esri.com**).

*You can explore PRIZM segments at the Claritas website. Check out your favorite U.S. ZIP Code!*

# LO4 The Role of Self-Concept in Consumer Behavior

The self-concept is another important topic in consumer behavior. The term **self-concept** refers to the totality of thoughts and feelings that an individual has about him- or herself. Self-concept can also be thought of as the way a person defines or gives meaning to his or her own identity, as in a type of self-schema.

Consumers are motivated to act in accordance with their self-concepts. As such, consumers often use products as ways of revealing their self-concepts to others. According to a **symbolic interactionism** perspective, consumers agree on the shared meaning of products and symbols.[55] These symbols can become part of the self-concept if the consumer identifies with them strongly.

An important field of study that relates to the symbolic interactionism approach is semiotics. **Semiotics** refers to the study of symbols and their meanings. As we have stated, consumers use products as symbols to convey their self-concepts to others. In this sense, products are an essential part of self-expression.[56] Popular websites like MySpace, Facebook, and Twitter, give consumers easy ways of expressing their selves.[57]

Let's first explore various dimensions of the "self" before examining how a consumer's self-concept influences various behaviors. First, we note that a consumer will have a number of "concepts" about him- or herself that may emerge over time and surface in different social situations.[58] A few of the different "self-concepts" that may emerge include the actual self, the ideal self, the social self, the ideal social self, the possible self, and the extended self.[59]

The *actual self* refers to how a consumer currently perceives him- or herself (that is, who I am). The *ideal self* refers to how a consumer would like to perceive himself (that is, who I would like to be in the future). The *social self* refers to the beliefs that a consumer has about how he or she is seen by others. The social self is also called the "looking-glass" self because it denotes the image that a consumer has when he or she looks into the mirror and imagines how others see him or her. The *ideal social self* represents the image that a consumer would like others to have about him or her. The *possible self*, much like the ideal self, presents an image of what the consumer could become, whereas the *extended self*

# The Cyber Self

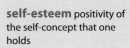

I t will probably come as no surprise that estimates indicate that nearly three-quarters of on-line teens and young adults use social networking sites, with millions of young consumers updating their profiles several times per day. Popular websites such as Facebook, MySpace, and Twitter allow users to post various aspects of their lives and present themselves in almost limitless ways. Connecting with your peeps is, of course, very important.

Unfortunately, some social website users feel that almost any detail of their life is fair game. In many cases, improper information is posted to websites. Young consumers seem to think that posting explicit information related to sexual behavior, drugs, or violence is not a problem, often because they feel in some way distinct from their cyberpersonalities. Of course, the downside is when too much information is given out and bad things happen. This is becoming all too common. From employers reviewing online profiles to websites like "pleaserobme .com," highlighting the dangers of revealing when consumers are, and are not, at home, the implications of social networking are far-reaching. This brings a whole new perspective to the ideal social self! Although the Internet allows consumers to post all kinds of material about themselves, common sense should still apply.

Sources: Based on Gordon, Serena (2009), "Teens Divulge Risky Behavior on Social Networking Sites," *Washington Post*, January 6, online content retrieved at **http://www.washingtonpost.com/wp-dyn/content/article/2009/01/05/AR2009010502588.html,** accessed May 25, 2010. Lenhart, Amanda, Kristen Purcell, Aaron Smith, and Kathryn Zickuh (2010), "Social Media and Young Adults," Pew Internet & American Life Project, online content retrieved at http://pewinternet.org/Reports/2010/Social-Media-and-Young-Adults.aspx, accessed May 25, 2010.; Fletcher, Dan (2010), "Please Rob Me: The Dangers of Online Oversharing," *Time*, February 18, online content retrieved at **http://www.time.com/time/business/article/0,8599,1964873,00.html,** accessed May 25, 2010.

**self-esteem** positivity of the self-concept that one holds

products that purport-edly help improve one's self-image. The term **self-esteem** refers to the posi-tivity of an individual's self-concept. The effect of advertising on consumers' self-esteem is an impor-tant topic in this area.

The fashion indus-try is constantly under fire for promoting overly thin models and body types. In fact, research confirms that con-sumers compare their bodies with those of models found in adver-tisements, and that these comparisons often have harmful effects. This is particularly the case for young females.[62]

In response to grow-ing public concern regard-ing this issue, the Council of Fashion Designers of America (CFDA) updated guidelines to encourage

represents the various possessions that a consumer owns that helps him form perceptions about himself.

The relationship between consumer self-concept and product consumption is a two-way street. That is, consumers express their self-concepts by purchasing and displaying various products, while products help to define how the consumer sees himself or herself.[60] Note that the relationship between the self-concept and consumption is not limited to adult consumers only, as consumer–brand connections have been shown to form as early as childhood![61]

## SELF-CONCEPT AND BODY PRESENTATION

The issue of self-concept in consumer behavior has sev-eral practical implications. For example, the cosmetics and weight-loss industries are well-known for offering

*Unrealistic body images affect consumers' self esteem.*

healthy eating habits and to discourage the use of overly thin models in advertisements. "The fashion business should be sensitive to the fact that we do have a responsibility in affecting young girls and their self-image," CFDA president Diane von Furstenberg commented.[63] The problem is not solely for women, however, as evidence suggests that male consumers are also affected by unrealistic body imagery in advertising.[64] Although the industry has received much negative publicity, note that not all model effects are negative. Consumers can sometimes feel better about themselves when they find similarities between their bodies and those of models.[65]

Unilever Corp. recently addressed the issue of unrealistic body types with their Real Beauty campaign for the brand Dove. The campaign seeks to provide more realistic views of beauty and to improve the self-esteem of both women and young girls.

## Cosmetic Surgery and Body Modification

Because of the many ways in which consumers compare themselves to others, it is easy to understand why many medical procedures that promise to improve a consumer's perception of his or her body are now being offered. According to the American Society for Aesthetic Plastic Surgery, nearly 10 million cosmetic procedures were performed in the United States in the year 2009, despite the economic turndown. This represented only a 2% decrease in procedures during the recession. It seems that even in times of economic uncertainty, people are still willing to pay for cosmetic surgery. Breast augmentation, lipoplasty, and eyelid surgery were common procedures for female patients, while liposuction and rhinoplasty were popular among men. The majority of procedures were found among consumers aged 35–50.[66]

## Body Piercings and Tattoos

Body piercings and other forms of body decorations, such as tattoos, represent other methods of promoting one's self-concept. The growth of piercing among college-aged students is particularly noteworthy. Estimates vary widely, with one recent study revealing that as many as 51% of teenagers and young adults have some form of body piercing. The same estimates reveal that up to 14% of the general population has body piercings. Interestingly, piercings tend to be more popular with female consumers than male consumers.[67] The growth in popularity of body art suggests that new attitudes about the body and its role in self-presentation are emerging.[68]

While body piercings are popular forms of self-expression and are frequently used as innocent methods of self-expression, research also indicates that the use of piercings can sometimes be associated with increased levels of drug and alcohol use, unprotected sexual activity, trait anxiety, and depression.[69] Consumers also form impressions of employees who have tattoos and piercings, and these perceptions may impact how they view organizations with such employees.[70] For consumers, body piercings and tattoos have become more popular than ever.

# LO5 Self-Congruency Theory and Consumer Behavior

reference group members share similar symbolic meanings. This is an important assumption of **self-congruency theory**. This theory proposes that much of consumer behavior can be explained by the congruence (match) between a consumer's self-concept and the image of typical users of a focal product.[71] For example, one study found that store loyalty is largely influenced by the degree of congruency between self-image and store image.[72] How would you describe shoppers of a popular store like PacSun? Hollister? American Eagle? Do you possess any of these characteristics?

## SEGMENTATION AND SELF-CONGRUENCY

Marketers can use congruency theory by segmenting markets into groups of consumers who perceive high self-concept congruence with product-user image. Imagine a consumer who sees himself as being a stylish person. If he believes that people who drive Corvettes are stylish, then he will be motivated to drive a Corvette. In this way, brands become vehicles for self-expression.[73]

As discussed earlier, there are several types of self-concepts, and different products may relate to each concept. That is, one product may relate quite well to the actual self-concept, but not as strongly to the ideal self-concept. One study found that the purchase of privately consumable items (such as frozen dinners or suntan lotion) is heavily influenced by the actual self-concept, while the purchase of publicly visible products (like clothing) is more strongly related to the ideal self-concept.[74]

*Matching the image of a user to the image of a product is a popular marketing tactic.*

A recent advertising campaign for Ford trucks illustrates the role of self-congruency theory in marketing. The successful ad campaign, which centers on the "Built Ford Tough" theme, sends the message that if you are a hardworking man you need a hardworking truck like Ford. Rolex has a long history of positioning its watches as the watch for the successful consumer who pursues excellence. Rolex is well-known for being the watch for people who have either "arrived" or who soon will be "arriving."

### Final Thought on Personality, Lifestyles, and the Self-Concept

Personality, lifestyles, and the self-concept are all important topics in the study of consumer behavior. Consumers differ across each of these concepts, and these differences help signal the need for targeted marketing communications. As technological advancements continue to develop, it can be expected that marketing managers and consumer researchers alike will continue to be interested in these topics.

## 6 Study Tools

**Located at back of the textbook**
- [ ] Rip-Out Chapter-in-Review Card

**Located at www.cengagebrain.com**
- [ ] Review Key Terms Flashcards (Print or Online)
- [ ] Download audio summaries to review on the go
- [ ] Complete practice quizzes to prepare for tests
- [ ] Play "Beat the Clock" and "Quizbowl" to master concepts
- [ ] Watch Video on Wheelworks for a real company example

## what others have thought...

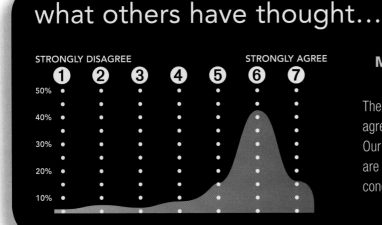

**My personality can easily be seen in the products that I buy.**

The vast majority of students, 75%, at least somewhat agree with this statement, with 43% indicating "agree." Our personalities and the products that we buy usually are closely related. This is a central theme in self-congruency theory.

In general, consumers have positive attitudes toward products that deliver value.

## what do you think?

It's pretty hard to change my attitude about products that I dislike.

STRONGLY DISAGREE ① ② ③ ④ ⑤ ⑥ ⑦ STRONGLY AGREE

Visit CourseMate at www.cengagebrain.com.

# 7

# Attitudes and Attitude Change

## Introduction

**k**eiton recently bought a new Apple iPad. He always liked his iPhone and he figured that the iPad would be the next logical purchase. As it turns out, he really likes it a lot and he thinks it is well worth the price that he paid. He even joined an iPad fan page on Facebook and follows tweets about the iPad on Twitter.

Getting consumers to feel strongly about a product is something that marketers constantly try to achieve. When consumers have positive attitudes toward products, they often promote them to others. This is a win–win situation for both the customer and the company. Conversely, negative attitudes can have a profound impact as well. Some people become so upset with a company and its products that they boycott everything the company sells — and tell others that they should do the same.

Understanding the factors that influence consumer attitudes is very important for marketers. This may seem obvious for companies, but the importance of consumer attitudes is found in nontraditional settings as well. For example, politicians want to know how voters *feel* about candidates. City managers want to know if citizens will *approve* of some new construction project. Musicians want to know if consumers will *like* their new songs. In each of these examples, consumer attitudes are very important.

**attitudes** relatively enduring overall evaluations of objects, products, services, issues, or people

After studying this chapter, the student should be able to:

**LO1** Define attitudes and describe attitude components.

**LO2** Describe the functions of attitudes.

**LO3** Understand how the hierarchy of effects concept applies to attitude theory.

**LO4** Comprehend the major consumer attitude models.

**LO5** Describe attitude change theories and their role in persuasion.

**LO6** Understand how message and source effects influence persuasion.

## LO1 Attitudes and Attitude Components

**t**he term *attitude* has been used in many ways. **Attitudes** are relatively enduring overall evaluations of objects, products, services, issues, or people.[1] Attitudes play a critical role in consumer behavior, and they are especially important because

**ABC approach to attitudes** approach that suggests that attitudes encompass one's affect, behavior, and cognitions (or "beliefs") toward an object

**functional theory of attitudes** theory of attitudes that suggests that attitudes perform four basic functions

**utilitarian function of attitudes** function of attitudes in which consumers use attitudes as ways to maximize rewards and minimize punishment

**knowledge function of attitudes** function of attitudes whereby attitudes allow consumers to simplify decision-making processes

they motivate people to behave in relatively consistent ways. It is therefore not surprising that the attitude concept is one of the most researched topics in the entire field of consumer research. In fact, attitude is one of the most popular concepts in all of the social sciences.

Attitudes and value are closely related. Recall from our opening example that Keiton is very pleased with the value that his iPad provides. In general, consumers have positive attitudes toward products that deliver value. Likewise, when products deliver poor value, consumer attitudes are usually negative. In order to appreciate how attitudes influence consumer behavior, we need to distinguish between the various components of attitudes and the functions that attitudes perform.

## COMPONENTS OF ATTITUDE

According to the **ABC approach to attitudes**, attitudes possess three important components: *a*ffect, *b*ehavior, and *c*ognitions (or beliefs). To understand these components, consider the following statements:

- "I really like my new iPad."
- "I always buy Apple products."
- "My iPad helps me study."

These statements reflect the three components of a consumer's attitude found in the ABC approach. "I really like my new iPad" is a statement of affect because the feelings, or affection, a consumer has about the product is captured in the concept of liking. "I always buy Apple products" refers to one's behavior regarding Apple products. "My iPad helps me study" is a cognitive statement that expresses the owner's belief about the usefulness of the new product.

## LO2 Functions of Attitudes

Knowing that attitudes represent relatively enduring evaluations of products, and that attitudes can be broken into three components, is valuable. But what's the big deal about attitudes? What do they do for the consumer? Understanding the answer to these questions gives marketers an opportunity to develop better promotional messages.

According to the **functional theory of attitudes**, attitudes perform four functions.[2] The four functions are the *utilitarian* function, the *knowledge* function, the *value-expressive* function, and the *ego-defensive* function. These functions are summarized in Exhibit 7.1.

### Utilitarian Function

The **utilitarian function of attitudes** is based on the concept of reward and punishment. This means that consumers learn to use attitudes as ways to maximize rewards and minimize punishment. Buying, and liking, a product because it delivers a specific benefit is one example of the utilitarian function of attitudes. The consumer is rewarded through a desired product benefit. For example, the iPhone delivers many benefits in the form of apps, and millions of consumers enjoy the apps. These consumers therefore develop positive attitudes towards the iPhone. Another way in which consumers maximize rewards through expressing attitudes is by gaining acceptance from others. Consumers often express their attitudes in order to develop and maintain relationships. A study of college sports fans presents an example. In the study, football fans revealed that one of the many reasons they wear their team's apparel is to help fans make and enjoy connections with new friends.[3] In other words, the outward behavior of wearing the apparel leads to the desired consequence of making friends and having fun.

### Knowledge Function

The **knowledge function of attitudes** allows consumers to simplify decision-making processes. For instance, if the telephone rings during dinner and the caller I.D. says

## EXHIBIT 7.1
# Functions of Consumer Attitudes

| Attitude Function | Description | Example |
|---|---|---|
| Utilitarian | Attitudes are used as a method to obtain rewards and to minimize punishment. | Fraternity brothers express attitude to enjoy a sense of belonging to the group. |
| Knowledge | The knowledge function of attitudes allows consumers to simplify their decision-making processes. | Consumers may not like to listen to telemarketers and will therefore avoid calls from them. |
| Value-expressive | This function of attitudes enables consumers to express their core values, self-concept, and beliefs to others. | Consumers commonly attach bumper stickers to their cars to express their attitudes about products and social issues. |
| Ego-defensive | The ego-defensive function of attitudes works as a defense mechanism for consumers to avoid facts or to defend themselves from their own low self-concept. | Smokers use their positive feelings about smoking to filter out incoming information suggesting the behavior is bad for their health. |

**value-expressive function of attitudes** function of attitudes whereby attitudes allow consumers to express their core values, self-concept, and beliefs to others

**ego-defensive function of attitudes** function of attitudes whereby attitudes work as a defense mechanism for consumers

that guide behavior. You may recall that comprehension includes affective and cognitive elements. Here, one can see that attitudes are related to both comprehension and knowledge.

## Value-Expressive Function

The **value-expressive function of attitudes** is found in a number of consumer settings. This function enables a consumer to express his or her core values, self-concept, and beliefs to others. Accordingly, this function of attitude provides a positive expression of the type of person a consumer perceives himself or herself to be. Satisfaction comes from the expression of attitudes which reflect the self-image. For example, consumers who believe in the protection of animals and animal rights may join and promote the actions of a group like People for the Ethical Treatment of Animals (PETA). The behavior of joining the group allows the consumer to express core dimensions of his self-image. Another setting where the value-expressive function is products such as bumper stickers, posters, or t-shirts. Joining specific groups on Facebook is another example of the value-expressive function of attitudes at work.

Ultimately, the expression of attitudes becomes a mechanism by which consumers can make statements about closely held values.

## Ego-Defensive Function

Finally, the **ego-defensive function of attitudes** works as a defense mechanism for consumers. There

"unavailable," a consumer might think "I hate telemarketers!" and decide not to answer the phone. Or, a consumer might see a salesperson approaching him from a mall kiosk and remember that he doesn't like dealing with pushy salespeople, and decide to walk the other way. In each case, the decision-making process of the consumer is simplified. Attitudes therefore perform the important function of helping consumers avoid undesirable situations and approach more desirable situations. Consumers also become loyal to specific brands, in part, to simplify their decision processes. The knowledge function of attitudes is at work here as well. It is usually much easier to buy a product that you know you like than it is to try a new one.

Attitude components become stored in the associative network in consumers' long-term memory, and become linked together to form rules

**hierarchy of effects**
attitude approach that suggests that affect, behavior, and cognitions form in a sequential order

are a couple of ways in which this function works. First, the ego-defensive function enables a consumer to protect himself or herself from information that may be threatening. For example, people who like to smoke may discount any evidence that smoking is bad for their health. In this case, the attitude works as a defense mechanism that protects the individual from the reality that smoking isn't healthy.

Another example of the ego-defensive function is when a consumer develops positive attitudes toward products that enhance his or her self-image. Consider college freshman, April. April likes to wear expensive brand name clothing because she is concerned about how people perceive her physical attractiveness. April's positive attitude toward expensive brands helps her to project a positive image and compensate for her own feelings of insecurity.

# LO3 Hierarchy of Effects

s discussed earlier, the ABC approach to consumer attitudes suggests that there are three components to attitudes: affect, behavior, and cognition. Research indicates that these components may be formed in a sequential pattern. This attitude formation process is known as the **hierarchy of effects** approach.[4] According to this approach, affect, behavior, and cognitions form by following one of the four following hierarchies:

1. High-involvement (or standard learning) hierarchy
2. Low-involvement hierarchy
3. Experiential hierarchy
4. Behavioral influence hierarchy

These hierarchies are discussed in the next section and are presented in Exhibit 7.2.

## HIGH-INVOLVEMENT HIERARCHY

The high-involvement, or standard learning, hierarchy of effects occurs when a consumer faces a high involvement decision. High-involvement decisions are important to a consumer and often contain significant risk. In this hierarchy, beliefs about products are formed first. The consumer carefully considers various

## EXHIBIT 7.2
## Hierarchy of Effects

| Purchase Context | Hierarchy of Effects |
| --- | --- |
| High involvement | Belief–affect–behavior |
| Low involvement | Belief–behavior–affect |
| Experiential | Affect–behavior–belief |
| Behavioral Influence | Behavior–belief–affect |

product features and develops cognitions (beliefs) about each feature. Next, feelings, or evaluations, about the product are formed. The consumer may begin to think the product is good and will suit his or her needs based on the beliefs that have been formed. Finally, after beliefs and feelings are formed, the consumer decides to act in some way toward the product. Here, a purchase decision is made. The consumer may decide to buy (or not buy) the product.

Imagine the process that Matt went through when he bought a new gaming system. Matt knew that it would be a significant purchase, and he was therefore careful about his selection. He first considered the various attributes of each system and began to develop favorable evaluations toward a few of the brands. Realizing that he felt best about the Xbox 360™ Elite, he decided that this would be the one to buy.

## LOW-INVOLVEMENT HIERARCHY

The standard learning approach was once considered the best approach to take in order to understand consumer attitude formation. Marketers began to realize, however, that consumer purchases are often neither risky nor involving. In fact, many purchases are routine and boring.[5]

When low-involvement purchases are made, consumers often have some basic beliefs about products without necessarily having strong feelings toward them. Javan, a self-proclaimed hardcore videogamer, may not carefully consider the feelings that he has toward a brand of paper towels. In fact, he probably doesn't think much about paper towels at all. He may just think, "Brawny is a popular brand, so I'll buy it." Only after he buys and uses the product will he develop any type of feeling, or evaluation, of the towel. At first, he thinks "Brawny is popular" (cognition) and he decides

## I Like this Store!

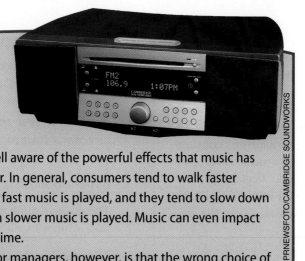

PRNEWSFOTO/CAMBRIDGE SOUNDWORKS

**R**etail managers are well aware of the powerful effects that music has on consumer behavior. In general, consumers tend to walk faster through a store when fast music is played, and they tend to slow down (and buy more!) when slower music is played. Music can even impact consumers' perceptions of wait time.

What is equally important for managers, however, is that the wrong choice of music may actually drive customers away. Of course, different segments of consumers like different types of music, and consumers can become quickly turned off if the wrong kind of music is played. In fact, companies like DMX Music and Muzak know that the tendency to leave a store if unappealing music is played cuts across demographic segments. Quite simply, no one likes to be bombarded with bad music! The right choice of background music can be a critical factor in retail success. Managers should pay close attention. Background music is very, very important!

Sources: Online content retrieved at DMX website, **www.dmx.com**, accessed May 28, 2010; Online content retrieved at Muzak website, **www.muzak.com**, accessed May 28, 2010; Ebenkamp, Becky (2004), "Songs in the Key of Flee," *Brandweek* (February 16), 17; Morrison, Michael, and Michael Beverland (2003), "In Search of the Right In-Store Music," *Business Horizons* 46 (November–December), 77; Milliman, R.E. (1986), "Using Background Music to Affect the Behavior of Supermarket Shoppers," *Journal of Marketing* 46, 86–91.

---

to buy it (behavior). Only later does he say "I like Brawny" (affect). Chances are, however, that he would carefully consider videogame features first, develop an overall like or dislike for each brand, and then buy one type of game or another. As such, it is easy to see that the purchase of an expensive gaming system is much more involving for Javan than a $2 roll of paper towels.

## EXPERIENTIAL HIERARCHY

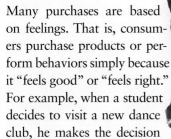

© MARK ANDERSEN/RUBBERBALL/JUPITERIMAGES

Many purchases are based on feelings. That is, consumers purchase products or perform behaviors simply because it "feels good" or "feels right." For example, when a student decides to visit a new dance club, he makes the decision simply because it sounds like a fun thing to do.

Impulse purchases can be explained from the experiential perspective. These purchases are often motivated by feelings. Impulse purchasing means that

a consumer buys a product spontaneously and with little concern for consequences. Dessert items are often purchased on impulse. When the waiter brings the tray by, the chocoholic feels strongly about one of the desserts and simply buys it on impulse. Here, he or she feels strongly and acts on those feelings. A great deal of research focuses on the experiential perspective, exploring the feelings and pleasures that accompany consumer purchases and behaviors.[6]

## BEHAVIORAL INFLUENCE HIERARCHY

The behavioral influence hierarchy suggests that some behaviors occur without either beliefs or affect being strongly formed beforehand. Strong environmental pressures lead to behaviors without belief or affect formation. An example of this may be found when a consumer eats at a restaurant playing soft, slow music. Restaurant managers know that one way to get people to relax and order more drinks is to play soft, soothing music. Consumers have been conditioned to slow down and relax when slow music is played. As such, behavior is influenced by environmental cues. This means that there are times when behaviors may be performed in the absence of strong beliefs or feelings.

## LO4 Consumer Attitude Models

**a**s you can see, understanding consumer attitudes is very important for understanding consumer behavior. This leads to the question of how to measure attitudes. As noted earlier, the study of attitudes has a long-established research tradition. It shouldn't be surprising, therefore, that several methods for measuring attitudes have been used. In this section, some of the major approaches to measuring consumer attitudes are presented, beginning with a well-known approach advanced by Martin Fishbein and Icek Azjen, the attitude-toward-the-object model.[7]

# ATTITUDE-TOWARD-THE-OBJECT MODEL

The **attitude-toward-the-object (ATO) model** (sometimes simply referred to as the *Fishbein model)* proposes that three key elements must be assessed to understand and predict a consumer's attitude. The first element consists of the *beliefs* a consumer has about a salient attribute, or feature, that the consumer thinks the product should possess. The second element is the *strength of the belief* that a certain brand does indeed have the feature. The third element is an *evaluation of the attribute* in question. These elements are combined to form the overall attitude toward the object (referred to as $A_o$, or attitude toward the object). This approach is known as a *multiattribute* approach because consumers consider a number of attributes when forming attitudes in this way. The formula for predicting attitudes with this approach is

$$A_o = \sum_{I=1}^{N} (b_i)(e_i)$$

where $A_o$ = attitude toward the object in question (or $A_{brand}$), $b_i$ = strength of belief that the object possesses attribute $i$, $e_i$ = evaluation of the attractiveness or goodness of attribute $i$, and $N$ = number of attributes and beliefs.

The formula states that belief (*b*) and evaluative ratings (*e*) for product attributes are combined (multiplied) and the resulting product terms are added together to give a numerical expression of a consumer's attitude toward a product. This model can be used both for predicting a consumer's attitude and for understanding how salient attributes, beliefs, and evaluations influence attitude formation.

## Using the ATO Approach

To understand this model, first consider how the various elements are measured. To begin, note that belief ratings can be measured on a 10-point scale such as:

*How likely is it that the Sony television will give you a clear picture?*

| 1 | 2 | 3 | 4 | 5 | 6 | 7 | 8 | 9 | 10 |
|---|---|---|---|---|---|---|---|---|---|
| *Extremely unlikely* | | | | | | | *Extremely likely* | | |

The evaluative *(e)* rating can then be measured on a −3 to +3 scale such as:

*How bad/good is it that a television has a clear picture?*

| −3 | −2 | −1 | 0 | +1 | +2 | +3 |
|---|---|---|---|---|---|---|
| *Very bad* | | | | | *Very good* | |

The consumer would rate the Sony television and any other brand being considered, say Samsung, on every relevant attribute. They would also consider their evaluations of the attributes, and they would ultimately combine the information.

An example may help to clarify the use of this formula. Think of the situation that Brooke faces selecting a fitness center. How could we predict her attitude? This information is presented in Exhibit 7.3.

Brooke is thinking of joining one of the following fitness centers: Lifestyles Family Fitness, Curves for Women, or Shapes. She first considers the attributes that come to mind when she thinks of fitness centers. She considers the availability of circuit training, the variety of workout classes, the amenities (such as showers and lockers), the fees associated with joining, and the physical proximity of the centers to her apartment.

EXHIBIT 7.3

# Attitude-Toward-the-Object Model Applied to Fitness Center Choice

| Attribute | e | Lifestyles b | Lifestyles (b)(e) | Curves b | Curves (b)(e) | Shapes b | Shapes (b)(e) |
|---|---|---|---|---|---|---|---|
| Circuit training | −1 | 1 | −1 | 10 | −10 | 9 | −9 |
| Class variety | 2 | 10 | 20 | 2 | 4 | 3 | 6 |
| Amenities | 1 | 9 | 9 | 5 | 5 | 5 | 5 |
| Fees | −3 | 6 | −18 | 4 | −12 | 5 | −15 |
| Location | 3 | 6 | 18 | 8 | 24 | 9 | 27 |
| $A_o$ | | | 28 | | 11 | | 14 |

Note: "e" = evaluative ratings. These ratings are generally scaled from −3 to +3, with −3 being very negative and +3 being very positive. "b" = strength of belief that the object possesses the attribute in question. Beliefs are generally scaled from 1 to 10, with 1 meaning "highly unlikely" and 10 meaning "highly likely." "(b)(e)" is the product term that is derived by multiplying the evaluative ratings (e) by belief strength (b). $A_o$ is the overall attitude toward the object. This is determined by adding the (b)(e) product terms for each object.

This example shows what Brooke's overall attitudes are toward each center and how belief and evaluations are combined to arrive at these attitudes.

After identifying the relevant attributes, Brooke thinks of how well each gym performs on the attributes, or how likely it is that the centers have these attributes. Brooke would be answering questions such as:

*How likely is it that "CENTER X" offers a variety of classes?*

1   2   3   4   5   6   7   8   9   10
*Extremely unlikely        Extremely likely*

Brooke rates each center across all relevant attributes. Brooke's belief (*b*) ratings for the centers are shown in Exhibit 7.3. From her belief ratings, we can see that Brooke thinks that Lifestyles Family Fitness performs better than other centers on the variety of classes (10).

Next, Brooke considers how she *feels* about the relevant attributes, or how good (or bad) the attributes are. A sample question would be:

*How good/bad is it that a fitness center offers a variety of classes?*

−3   −2   −1   0   +1   +2   +3
*Very bad        Very good*

Brooke isn't too focused on the variety of classes, but she does think variety is nice. She therefore gives this attribute an evaluative rating of 2.

*It is important to emphasize that the evaluation ratings (e) do not vary across the brands under consideration while the belief ratings do.*

Using this model, Brooke's attitude would be calculated by multiplying each belief rating (*b*) by the corresponding evaluation (*e*). For example, the belief rating of 10 (for Curves for Women, circuit training) would be multiplied by the evaluation of −1 for circuit training to arrive at −10. Similarly, the belief rating of 9 for Lifestyles, amenities, would be multiplied by the evaluation of 1 to arrive at 9. This is performed for all belief ratings and evaluations. Finally, the product terms are added together to arrive at a predicted attitude score. From Exhibit 7.3, we see that Brooke's most positive attitude is toward Lifestyles ($A_o$ = 28), followed by Shapes ($A_o$ = 14), and finally Curves ($A_o$ = 11).

What was it that led to the higher attitude toward Lifestyles versus the other two centers? An examination of Exhibit 7.3 reveals that Lifestyles was rated much higher than the other two centers on the variety of classes attribute. Note also that Curves and Shapes were both rated highly on circuit training. Brooke evaluated that attribute rather poorly (*e* = −1).

An examination of the table also reveals that Lifestyles received the highest attitude rating even though it scored highest on the attribute that Brooke rated most poorly, high fees. It can be said that the higher ratings on other attributes (such as variety of classes) compensated for the belief that Lifestyles has higher fees than the other centers. Accordingly, the ATO approach is known as a **compensatory model**. With compensatory models, attitudes are formed holistically across a number of attributes with poor ratings on one attribute being compensated for by higher ratings on another attribute.

## Implications of the ATO Approach

Information obtained from this model has important marketing implications. First, we note that attitude research is most often performed on entire market segments rather than on individuals. For example, marketing researchers would generally want to understand how an entire segment of consumers feels about the various fitness centers. Information would be gathered from a sample of several women in the segment. An important marketing issue would be developing an understanding of what women think about each of the relevant product attributes. What do members of our target segment think about the amenities that are offered in health clubs? What do they think about circuit training? What do they think about variety in class offerings?

An equally important issue for managers would be an understanding of the extent to which women believe that their specific centers offer the relevant attributes. Does our target segment know that we offer variety in our classes? Do they think that we have high fees? If managers were to find out that the target segment does not know that there is plenty of variety offered in the club, this would be something that they should emphasize in advertising campaigns. This would particularly be the case if the attribute was highly valued by the consumers. Therefore, both belief (*b*) and evaluative (*e*) ratings have important implications.

Consumers think about relevant features of products, how much they value the features, and how each product rates on the features.

As a general statement, it would be easier for managers to convince the target segment that they do offer a lot of variety (in other words, to change a belief rating) than it would be to attempt to convince the segment that variety is a bad thing (or to change an evaluation). Accordingly, marketers need to perform extensive research up front to gain clear understandings of attributes that are highly valued, and then develop their products and services around these features.

A couple of questions commonly arise regarding this approach. "Do consumers really form attitudes in this way?" Most consumer researchers would respond "Yes." Think of a person considering the purchase of a new cell phone. Chances are that they will first think of the features that are relevant. Next, they will rate each brand on how well it performs on those features. They will also consider how they feel about each of the features. Finally, they will combine their beliefs with the evaluations and make a decision. Granted, *they may not sit down and follow this exact formula*, but consumers think about relevant features of products, how much they value the features, and how each product rates on the features.

The next question that is commonly asked is: "Do consumer researchers really do this?" Again, the answer is "Yes." Researchers are very interested in how consumer attitudes are formed and the approach presented here can easily be performed through consumer surveys. This information can have a significant impact on marketing strategy. As the fitness center example reveals, this type of research can affect both product development and promotional strategy. For example, a manager could decide that he or she should improve features that are desired by the targeted segment. Or, the manager could focus on improving customer awareness that the center has features that the targeted consumers want. Of course, the manager could also do both of these things.

Overall, the attitude toward the object model has value from both an academic and practical viewpoint. We do note, however, that one difficulty with the model is that the weights that are associated with the various attributes do not necessarily remain constant over time, and the list of relevant attributes may indeed change. For this reason, managers should try to stay current on these issues.

## Do Attitudes Always Predict Behavior?

Marketing managers and researchers alike realize that just because a consumer has a positive attitude towards a product, this doesn't mean that he or she will always purchase the product. In fact, there would be little need for sales promotion if this were the case. **Attitude–behavior consistency** refers to the extent to which a strong relationship exists between attitudes and actual behavior. A number of situations may keep a consumer from selecting a product to which a positive attitude is held.[8] In general, attitudes are stronger predictors of behavior when the decision to be made is classified as high involvement, when situational factors do not impede the product selection (for example, the product is out of stock or the consumer doesn't have enough money), and when attitudes toward the product are very strong. Because attitudes don't always predict behavior, other approaches, including the behavioral intentions model, have been developed to improve upon the ATO approach.

# BEHAVIORAL INTENTIONS MODEL

The **behavioral intentions model**, sometimes referred to as the *theory of reasoned action*, has been offered as an improvement over the attitude-toward-the-object model. This model differs from the attitude-toward-the-object model in a number of important ways.[9] First, rather than focusing explicitly on attitudes, the model focuses on intentions to act in some way. Second, the model adds a component that assesses the consumer's perceptions of what other people think they should do. This is referred to as the *subjective norm*. Finally, the model explicitly focuses on the consumer's attitude toward the behavior of buying rather than the attitude toward the object.

The formula for the behavioral intentions model is as follows:[10]

$$B \approx BI = w_1 (A_{behavior}) + w_2 (SN)$$

where $B$ = behavior, $BI$ = behavioral intention, $A_{behavior}$ = attitude toward performing the behavior (or, $A_{act}$), $SN$ = subjective norm, and $w_1, w_2$ = empirical weights.

This model states that a consumer's behavior is influenced by the intention to perform that behavior ($BI$), and that this intention is determined by the attitude toward performing the behavior ($A_{behavior}$) and *subjective norms (SN)*.

From our fitness center example, the $A_{behavior}$ component includes the belief that the behavior will lead to a consequence (for example, "I'll lose a lot of weight if I go there") and an evaluation of the consequence (for example, "Losing weight is a good thing."). The *SN* component includes a consumer's belief that a reference group thinks that he or she should (or should not) perform the behavior (for example, Brooke's friends think she should choose Lifestyles) and the extent to which the consumer wants to comply with the suggestions of others (for example, does Brooke want to do what her friends say?).

The aspects of the behavioral intentions model are presented in Exhibit 7.4.

The behavioral intentions model was introduced as an improvement to the ATO model. Again, two major differences are found in the attitude toward the behavior and subjective norm components. For marketers, a clear understanding of the perceived consequences of product selection is crucial. Researchers must determine the consequences that are highly

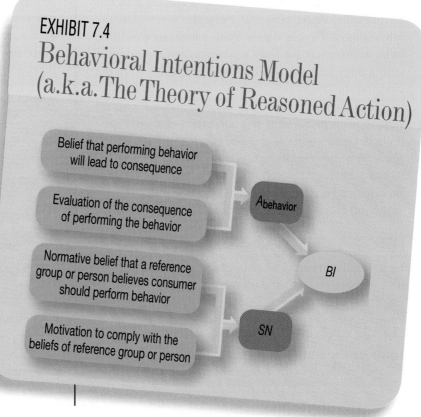

EXHIBIT 7.4
Behavioral Intentions Model (a.k.a. The Theory of Reasoned Action)

Belief that performing behavior will lead to consequence

Evaluation of the consequence of performing the behavior

Normative belief that a reference group or person believes consumer should perform behavior

Motivation to comply with the beliefs of reference group or person

$A_{behavior}$

$SN$

$BI$

valued by their targeted consumer segments. Consumers don't always select products for the most predictable reason. Losing weight isn't the only reason people join a fitness center. Consumers may join simply to meet people and make friends.

Marketing managers should also pay close attention to the subjective norm component of the model. Word-of-mouth communications are becoming critical for marketers. What do referent others think that the consumer should do? To what extent are they motivated to comply with the input of these people? The answers to these questions are quite valuable.

## Factors That Weaken Attitude–Behavior Relationship

Although consumer attitude models are very popular in consumer research, researchers note that a number of factors can detract from the accuracy of this approach. For example, as the length of time between attitude measurement and overt behavior grows, the predictive ability of attitudinal models weakens. The specificity with which attitudes are measured also has an impact on accuracy. For example, measuring the intentions of buying a new Sony television would be more appropriate for Sony managers than would measuring one's intentions to buy a new "television" in the next month.

Strong environmental pressures can also keep consumers from performing intended behaviors. For example, when consumers feel rushed, decisions are often made in haste. Finally, attitude–behavior models tend to not perform very well in impulse-buying situations. As discussed earlier, these behaviors are quite common in a number of consumer contexts.

## Alternative Approaches to Attitude

One small variation of this theory is the **theory of planned action**, which expands upon the behavioral intentions model by including a *perceived control* component. This component assesses the difficulty involved in performing the behavior and the extent to which the consumer perceives that he or she is in control of the product selection.[11] Products can be difficult to purchase, especially if they are in short supply.

## Expanding the Attitude Object

The definition of attitudes presented earlier states that attitudes are relatively enduring evaluations of objects, products, services, issues, or people. For this reason, consumer researchers often study attitudes toward several different entities, not just brands or products.

One area that has received considerable consumer research attention is *attitude toward the advertisement*. Research has shown that there is generally a positive relationship between a consumer's attitude towards an advertisement and his or her attitude towards a particular product.[12] We note, however, that several factors have been shown to affect this relationship, including the overall liking of the television program in which the ad is embedded, the vividness of the imagery in the ad, the ad context, and the mood of the consumer.[13]

A growing area of research interest has also focused on attitude toward the company. What consumers know or believe about a company (sometimes referred to as *corporate associations*) can influence the attitude they have toward its products.[14] The study of consumer beliefs toward companies is therefore gaining considerable attention from consumer researchers. Of particular importance for many consumers is the question of how responsible companies are with their business practices. In general, consumers who feel positively about a company's business practices are likely to react more favorably toward the brands that the company markets.[15]

## Attitude Tracking

Assessing one's attitude toward a specific product, brand, purchase act, advertisement, or company at only one specific point in time can also limit the accuracy of attitudinal models. Researchers therefore track how attitudes change over time. Because attitudes toward a brand can be influenced by several things, including attitude toward advertisements and companies, it is especially important to study changes in consumer attitudes. **Attitude tracking** refers to the extent to which a company actively monitors its customers' attitudes over time. What is important to understand is that even though attitudes are relatively enduring evaluations of objects, products, services, issues, or people, these attitudes should be monitored over time to gauge changes that may occur.

# "*It's Not Worth It"

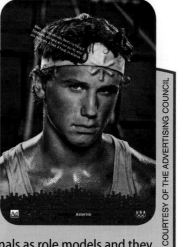

**S**teroid use is a serious problem for both professional and amateur athletes. Recent incidents in professional baseball highlight the problem, with several players being accused of using performance-enhancing steroids. Obviously, millions of young athletes look to professionals as role models and they can learn dangerous behaviors, like steroid abuse, when they do so. Coupled with the perceived pressure to win in their sport, the temptation can become intense.

A recent public service announcement ad campaign by the Advertising Council attempted to change the attitudes of athletes who choose to use steroids. Sponsored by the U.S. Olympic Committee and Johnson & Johnson, with the creative help of volunteer ad agency TBWA/Chiat/Day, the campaign warns athletes to not be an "asterisk" and it also highlights the medical complications that can occur from steroid use. As you may know, an asterisk is often placed next to the names of athlete record holders (or champions) who are found to have cheated in some way. The campaign serves the valuable purpose of teaching athletes that it's just not worth it to use steroids.

Sources: Based on: online content retrieved at Team USA website, **http://www.teamusa.org/news/2008/12/01/don-t-be-an-asterisk-anti-steroids-public-awareness-campaign-awarded-ad-council-s-2008-silver-bell-award-for-creative-excellence/8185**, accessed June 1, 2010; online content retrieved at Advertising Council website, **http://www.adcouncil.org/default.aspx?id=520**, accessed June 1, 2010; online content retrieved at Coloribus Advertising Archive website, **http://www.coloribus.com/adsarchive/tv-commercials/united-states-olympic-committee-dont-be-an-asterisk-513194/**, accessed June 1, 2010.

## LO5 Attitude Change Theories and Persuasion

**a**n important issue in the study of consumer behavior is how attitudes are changed. Marketers frequently want to change consumer attitudes about their products, and they focus their efforts on developing persuasive messages. Advertising obviously plays a major role in this effort. The term **persuasion** refers to specific attempts to change attitudes. Usually, the hope is that by changing beliefs or feelings, marketers can also change behavior.

There are many different persuasive techniques, and the following discussion presents the theoretical mechanisms through which persuasion may occur. These

**persuasion** attempt to change attitudes

include the ato approach, the behavioral influence approach, the schema-based affect approach, the elaboration likelihood model, the balance theory approach, and the social judgment theory approach.

## ATTITUDE-TOWARD-THE-OBJECT APPROACH

According to the ATO model, both beliefs about product attributes and evaluations of those attributes play important roles in attitude formation. By focusing on these components, the ATO approach presents marketers with a number of alternatives for changing consumer attitudes. To change attitudes according to this approach, marketers can attempt to change beliefs, create new beliefs about product features, or change evaluations of product attributes.

### Changing Beliefs

As discussed in our fitness center example, marketers may attempt to change consumers' beliefs. Again consider our example. If consumers do not believe that Shapes offers a variety of classes, then the center could increase the actual number of classes offered and promote this change to its consumers. Or, let's assume that the center actually does offer a number of classes and consumers simply don't realize that they do. In this case, the center would need to advertise its variety of classes to its targeted consumers. With each effort, the focus is on improving the belief rating for an attribute that is evaluated positively (here, variety of classes).

Another approach would be to focus on decreasing the strength of belief regarding a negatively evaluated attribute. For example, since price is evaluated quite negatively (−3), the center might decide to promote the overall value that comes from club membership or the relatively low price of the center as compared to the competition. Here, the focus is on decreasing the belief rating of a negatively evaluated attribute. As we have discussed throughout this text, communicating value is an important marketing task.

### Adding Beliefs about New Attributes

Another strategy for changing attitudes under the ATO approach is adding a salient attribute to the product or service. Like the changing beliefs approach, this may require a physical change to the product itself. For example, a fitness center might add a supervised "play room" for children so that parents can use the facilities without having to make other arrangements for their kids. Here, a new attribute that is likely to be evaluated positively by consumers is added. When a valued attribute that was not previously considered is added, the overall attitude toward the fitness center may be improved, and the fitness center may become the preferred option for targeted consumers.

At other times, the new beliefs may not be exactly tied to a "new" attribute. Rather, they may simply emphasize something that consumers had previously not considered. To illustrate, consider what has happened with the marketing of red wine. In the 1980s, Robert Mondavi Winery added labeling to its wines that referred to the health benefits of drinking wine. Initially, the FDA stopped this practice, based on the notion that the label was misleading and detrimental to consumers. However, after years of research, the health-giving properties of wine are widely accepted. Red wine is associated with a reduced risk of heart disease and cancer, and this information has now been widely promoted. Thus, although the health-related benefits of red wine are nothing new, only in the last few years has the belief become prominently known and accepted. By adding a new belief, wine marketers have increased the market share of wine relative to beer and spirits.

A votre santé! The belief that wine is healthy can lead people to like it even more.

Changing a retail store's design or atmospherics can have a direct influence on behavior.

### Changing Evaluations

As noted earlier, marketers may also attempt to change the evaluation of an attribute. Here, the marketer would try to convince consumers that an attribute is not as positive (or negative) as they may think. For example, a fitness center may attempt to convince consumers that location is not always a positive thing. They may advertise to their customers that any gym can be around the corner, but a good gym is worth the drive. Or, the center may attempt to change evaluations of circuit training by emphasizing that circuit training leads to quicker weight loss and muscle development.

Changing evaluations of an attribute is more difficult than changing the strength of a belief regarding that attribute. Quite simply, consumers know what they like, and they make selections accordingly.

## BEHAVIORAL INFLUENCE APPROACH

Another strategy commonly applied by marketers is directly changing behaviors without first attempting to change either beliefs or feelings. According to the behavioral influence hierarchy, behavior change can precede belief and attitude change. Changing a retail store's design or atmospherics can have a direct influence on behavior. In fact, an entire industry called scent marketing (using scents to influence behavior) is emerging.

You may remember from our discussion on conditioning in an earlier chapter that behavioral conditioning can be very effective. Consumers respond to marketing stimuli in certain ways, and behaviors frequently result without either beliefs or affect occurring prior.

# The 2010 Census — Moving Forward

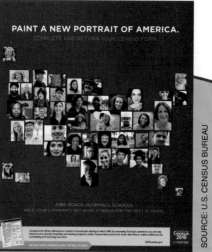

PAINT A NEW PORTRAIT OF AMERICA.
COMPLETE AND RETURN YOUR CENSUS FORM.

SOURCE: U.S. CENSUS BUREAU

**T**he 2010 Census was an important effort for the U.S. government. As stated in the Constitution, an annual census of all residents in the United States is required to take place every 10 years. The effort is very important and is enforced by law. For example, fines can be imposed on residents who refuse to participate, or who knowingly provide false information on the census.

Although participation in the census is required by law, it is still important to get consumer buy-in. This is one reason why the Census Bureau focused on creating positive consumer attitudes toward the 2010 effort. Many of their efforts focused on social networking and Internet sites such as Twitter, Facebook, Youtube, and Flickr. Using the campaign slogan "We Can't Move Forward Until You Mail it Back," the Census Bureau worked hard on consumer attitudes by explaining the ramifications of census data. For example, the Bureau informed consumers that the number of seats in the U.S. House of Representatives is directly impacted by census data, as are billions of dollars of federal funding. The Bureau also explained that several other important causes use census data in their marketing campaigns. Creating more positive consumer attitudes towards the census was an important first step in collecting the information.

Sources: Based on online content retrieved at 2010 Census website: **http://2010.census.gov/2010census/**, accessed June 1, 2010; online content retrieved at USA Today website: **www.usatoday.com/news/nation/census/2008-10-08-Census_N.htm**, accessed June 1, 2010; Longley, R. "Census Answers Are Required by Law," online content retrieved at **www.usgovinfo.about.com/od/censusandstatistics/a/answersrequired.htm**, accessed June 1, 2010.

## CHANGING SCHEMA-BASED AFFECT

We introduced the notion of schema-based affect in a previous chapter. From an attitude perspective, schema-based affect refers to the idea that schemas contain affective and emotional meanings. If the affect found in a schema can be changed, then the attitude toward a brand or product will change as well.

To illustrate, consider what happened when Domino's Pizza first entered Japan. Initially, the company had to deal with a commonly held belief that tomatoes were unhealthy, and that delivery food was not clean. Rather than trying to change these beliefs directly, Domino's created funny delivery carts and advertisements that attempted to attach positive feelings to the product schema and their brand. Thus, a posi-

tive attitude was shaped by this feeling found within the schema. This attitude-change technique can be effective if performed properly.

## THE ELABORATION LIKELIHOOD MODEL

Another popular approach for conceptualizing attitude change is found in the **elaboration likelihood model**.[16] The elaboration likelihood model (or ELM for short) illustrates how attitudes are changed based on differing levels of consumer involvement. Numerous research studies have examined the usefulness of the ELM in explaining the attitude change process. This model is shown in Exhibit 7.5.

According to the ELM, a consumer begins to process a message as soon as it is received. Depending on the level of involvement and a consumer's ability and motivation to process a message, the persuasion process then follows one of two routes: a *central route* or a *peripheral route*.[17]

### The Central Route

If the consumer finds that the incoming message is particularly relevant to his or her situation (and thus highly involved), then he or she will likely expend considerable effort in comprehending the message. In this case, high-involvement processing occurs, and the **central route to persuasion**

**central cues** information presented in a message about the product itself, its attributes, or the consequences of its use

**peripheral route to persuasion** path to persuasion found in ELM where the consumer has low involvement, motivation, and/or ability to process a message

**peripheral cues** non-product related information presented in a message

is activated. Here, the consumer develops a number of thoughts (or cognitive responses) regarding the incoming message that may either support or contradict the information. Contradicting thoughts are known as counterarguments. Thoughts that support the main argument presented are known as support arguments.

In the central route, the consumer relies on **central cues**. Central cues refer specifically to information found in the message that pertains directly to the product, its attributes, its advantages, or the consequences of its use.

To illustrate this process, imagine an experienced photographer who sees an advertisement for Sony cameras. Because he knows a lot about cameras and is highly interested in them, he will likely think carefully about the message he sees and the arguments presented as to why Sony cameras are the best cameras on the market. The arguments presented in the ad are critical. The photographer will consider the arguments and compare them to his current beliefs. He may even form counterarguments against the ad. For example, he may think "Canons are better." Or, he may think, "Sony cameras really are better than Canons after all." (It is important to note that responses can be either negative or positive.)

If the consumer's beliefs are changed as a result of message exposure, attitude and behavior change will follow. Because the consumer is highly involved, and because he has made an effort to carefully attend to the message, it is likely that the attitude change will be relatively enduring. This is an important aspect of the central route to persuasion: *Attitude change tends to be relatively enduring when it occurs in the central route.*

## The Peripheral Route

If a consumer is not involved with a message or lacks either the motivation or ability to process information, the **peripheral route to persuasion** will be followed. In this route, the consumer is unlikely to develop cognitive responses to the message (either supporting arguments or counterarguments), and he is more likely to pay attention to things like the attractiveness of the person delivering the message, the number of arguments presented, the expertise of the spokesperson, and the imagery or music presented along with the message. These elements of the message (that is, non-product related information) are referred to as **peripheral cues**.

If the consumer is influenced more by peripheral cues than central cues, any resulting belief or attitude change will likely be only temporary. That is, because the consumer is not highly engaged in the process, it is unlikely that attitude change will be enduring.

A popular ad campaign for Corona beer illustrates peripheral processing. The campaign includes a series of advertisements that show a man and woman relaxing on a beach. In the ads, there is no ad copy at all, other than the tag-line "Corona—Miles from Ordinary." While there is little ad copy, the ads are full of peripheral cues—from the soothing sound of the waves hitting the sand, to the beautiful imagery of the ocean. These cues play a major role in persuasion even if the consumer isn't presented with a list of reasons of why they should buy Corona, or why Corona is the best beer available on the market.

## Low-Involvement Processing in the Consumer Environment

It is important to note that the vast majority of advertisements to which consumers are exposed are processed with low-involvement processing. Consumers are simply not motivated to carefully attend to the

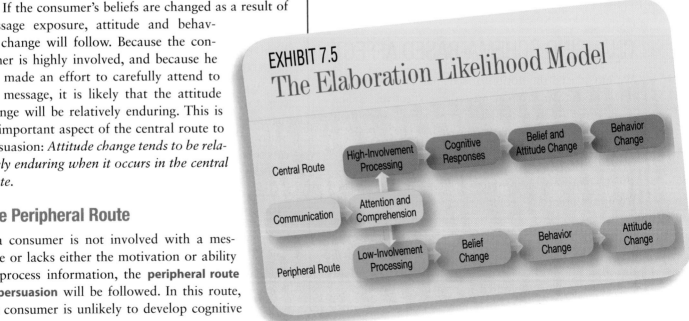

**EXHIBIT 7.5**
**The Elaboration Likelihood Model**

Navigate *life*™

**The use of beautiful scenery represents peripheral cues.**

thousands of ads that they are exposed to each day! Therefore, advertisers tend to rely heavily on the use of peripheral cues—attractive models, enticing imagery, upbeat music—when developing advertisements.

# BALANCE THEORY

Another way to conceptualize attitude change processes is through balance theory. The **balance theory** approach was introduced by social psychologist Fritz Heider.[18] The basic premise of balance theory is that consumers are motivated to maintain perceived consistency in the relations found in mental systems. Accordingly, this approach is based on the **consistency principle**. This principle states that human beings prefer consistency among their beliefs, attitudes, and behaviors.

Balance theory focuses on the associations, or relations, that are perceived between a person (or observer), another person, and an attitudinal object. The relations between these elements may be perceived as being either positive or negative. An example is shown in Exhibit 7.6.

Note that the system (composed of observer, person, and object) is referred to as a *triad* because it consists of a set of three elements. The relations between the elements are referred to either as sentiment relations or unit relations. *Sentiment relations* are the relations between the observer (consumer) and the other elements in the system. In Exhibit 7.6, the observer–person relation and the observer–object relation are referred to as sentiment relations. The object–person relation is referred to as a *unit relation*. Unit relations are based on the idea that two elements are in some way connected to one another.

Again, the basic premise of balance theory is that consumers are motivated to maintain perceived consistency in the relations found in the triad. Importantly, the perceived relations between the cognitive elements in the balance theory system may be changed when inconsistency occurs.

To illustrate, look carefully at Exhibit 7.6. Assume that Derek, a big NASCAR fan, really likes his favorite driver, Dale Earnhardt, Jr. That is, there is a positive (+) sentiment connection between Derek and the star. If Derek sees that Dale is endorsing a service like Nationwide Insurance (an attitudinal object), he would perceive a positive unit relation (+) between Dale and Nationwide. That is, Derek assumes that Dale endorses Nationwide because he really likes it. How would Derek feel about Nationwide? Well, in order to maintain balance in this triad, he would develop positive feelings toward Nationwide, resulting in a positive sentiment connection between himself and the brand.

This example illustrates a key premise of balance theory: *Consistency in the triad is maintained when the multiplication of the signs in the sentiment and unit relations result in a positive value.* When the resulting value is negative, consumers are motivated to change the

**balance theory** theory that states that consumers are motivated to maintain perceived consistency in the relations found in a system

**consistency principle** principle that states that human beings prefer consistency among their beliefs, attitudes, and behaviors

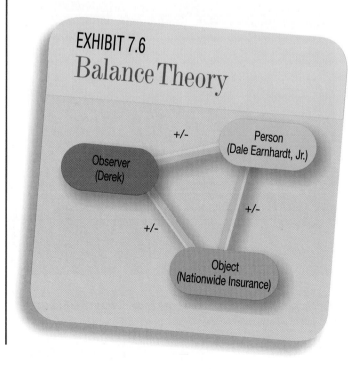

**EXHIBIT 7.6**
**Balance Theory**

**social judgment theory**
theory that proposes that consumers compare incoming information to their existing attitudes about a particular object or issue and that attitude change depends upon how consistent the information is with the initial attitude

signs (feelings) associated with one of the relations.

Suppose Derek doesn't like Dale Earnhardt, Jr. That is, suppose there is a negative (−) sentiment relation between Derek and the star. Because he perceives a positive unit relation between Dale and Nationwide, he will be motivated to form a negative sentiment relation between himself and the brand (note that [−] × [+] × [−] = +). According to the theory, weak perceived relations are generally changed, while stronger relations remain unchanged. Here, Derek would be turned off by the advertisement and would develop a negative sentiment relation between himself and the brand. We

*Balance theory influences celebrity endorsement decisions.*

© JOHN HARRELSON/GETTY IMAGES

note that while balance theory is often used to explain endorser effectiveness, the theory has also been applied in several other contexts, including product placements in television shows,[19] goal-oriented behavior,[20] and consumer–brand relationships.[21]

It should also be noted that marketers who rely on this approach should be careful to monitor any changes that occur in how a target market perceives an endorser. As we have seen, public attitudes toward celebrities can change nearly overnight. In this case, the sentiment connection between the endorser and the consumer can become negative, leading to trouble for the brand advertised!

## SOCIAL JUDGMENT THEORY

**Social judgment theory** is yet another theory for explaining attitude change.[22] This theory proposes that consumers compare incoming information to their existing attitudes about a particular object or issue. The initial attitude acts as a frame of reference, or standard, against which the incoming message is compared. Around these initial reference points are *latitudes of acceptance* and *latitudes of rejection*. For a message to fall within the latitude of acceptance, the information presented must be perceived as being close to the original attitude position. A message that is perceived as being far away from, or opposed to, the original attitude position will fall within the latitude of rejection. These aspects of the theory are presented in Exhibit 7.7.

According to the theory, when an incoming message falls within the latitude of acceptance, *assimilation* occurs. This means that the message is viewed as being congruent with the initial attitudinal position, and the message is received favorably. In fact, the message may be viewed as being even more congruent with the initial attitudinal position than it really is. As a result, the consumer is likely to agree with the content of a message falling within the latitude of acceptance, and the attitude would change in the direction of the message.

If the message is perceived as falling in the latitude of rejection, an opposite effect occurs. In fact, the message will be viewed as being even more opposed to the original attitude than it really is, and the message will be rejected. In this way, a *contrast effect* is said to occur.

The implication for marketers is that messages should be constructed so that they fall within the latitude of acceptance of the targeted consumer. An important finding in this line of research is that when the original

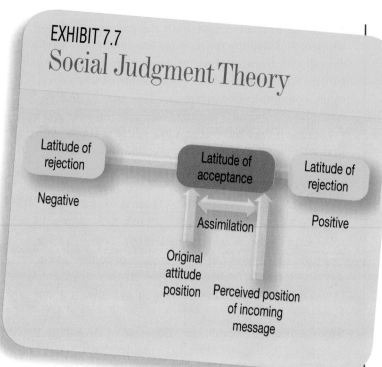

## EXHIBIT 7.7
## Social Judgment Theory

Latitude of rejection

Negative

Latitude of acceptance

Latitude of rejection

Positive

Assimilation

Original attitude position

Perceived position of incoming message

attitude is held with much conviction (either positive or negative), the latitude of acceptance is quite small and the latitude of rejection is large. On the contrary, when the original attitude is weak (either positive or negative), the latitude of acceptance is large and the latitude of rejection is small. This finding helps to explain why it is difficult to change a person's attitude when his or her attitude is very strong.

## LO6 Message and Source Effects and Persuasion

an important part of understanding persuasion is comprehending the many ways in which communication occurs. Marketing messages come to consumers in a variety of ways. As we have discussed, consumers are exposed to literally thousands of messages every day. Many of these messages come directly from marketers. Other messages come from other consumers. In both cases, the message being sent and the source delivering the message influence persuasiveness. For this reason, it is important to consider the roles of message effects and source effects in persuasion.

Message effects is a term that is used to describe how the appeal of a message and its construction affect persuasion. Source effects refer to the characteristics of the person or character delivering a message that influence persuasion. To understand how message and source effects work, we must begin by introducing a simple communication model. A basic communication model is shown in Exhibit 7.8.

According to this model, a source encodes a message and delivers the message through some medium. The medium could be personal (for example, when one consumer talks to another, or when a salesperson speaks with a customer) or impersonal (for example, when a company places an ad on television, radio, or on a web page). The receiver (consumer) decodes the message and responds to it in some way. Feedback consists of the responses that the receiver sends back to the source. For example, a consumer might voice an objection to a sales pitch or decide to call a 1-800 number to receive additional product information.

The *noise* concept is very important to this model. Noise represents all the stimuli in the environment that disrupt the communication process. In today's environment, noise comes in many different forms. For example, the popularity of online pop-up blockers is evidence of the number of distractions found on the Web. From a traditional advertising perspective, the

**message effects** how the appeal of a message and its construction affects persuasiveness

**source effects** characteristics of a source that impact the persuasiveness of a message

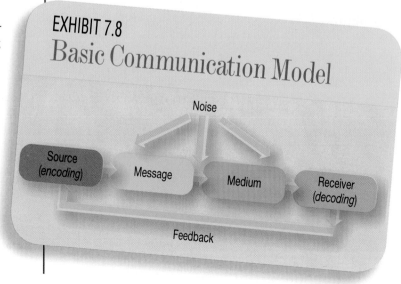

## EXHIBIT 7.8
## Basic Communication Model

Noise

Source (encoding)

Message

Medium

Receiver (decoding)

Feedback

basic communication model is referred to as a "one-to-many" approach, because it illustrates how a marketer may attempt to communicate with numerous consumers.[23]

# INTERACTIVE COMMUNICATIONS

The one-to-many communications model works well when examining personal communications or traditional advertising media such as television, newspapers, or radio. However, interactive communications (including the Internet and cell phones) have radically changed the communication paradigm. In fact, recent estimates reveal that 27% of the world's population now uses the Internet (more than 1.8 billion consumers) and literally trillions of text messages are sent every year.[24] Due to the rapid adoption of the Internet and cell phones as major communication tools, it is necessary to consider how these changes have affected the communication process.

Importantly, information flow is no longer considered a "one-way street," in which consumers passively receive messages from marketers. Rather, communication is seen as an interactive process that enables a flow of information among consumers and/or firms in what might be referred to as a many-to-many approach.[25] Senders can place content (web pages, blogs, photos, videos) into a medium and communicate directly with receivers through IM's, social networking sites (such as Facebook or Twitter), or through text messages. This dramatically changes the communication model, with a newer conceptualization being presented in Exhibit 7.9.

## EXHIBIT 7.9
### Communication in a Computer-Mediated Environment

Source: Adapted from: Hoffman, Donna L., and Thomas P. Novak (1996), "Marketing in Hypermedia Computer-Mediated Environments: Conceptual Foundations," *Journal of Marketing*, 60 (3), 50–68.

As we have discussed, both the message itself and the person delivering the message have an impact on the overall effectiveness of an advertisement. For this reason, marketers must consider both elements when developing communication strategies. This section discusses a number of findings regarding message and source effects. As you may remember, some of these topics were first introduced in our chapter on comprehension.

# MESSAGE APPEAL

There are several ways to conceptualize how a message may impact the persuasiveness of an advertisement. Here, we focus on the appeal (or general content) of an advertisement. A number of appeals are used by advertisers, including sex appeals, humor appeals, and fear appeals.

**Sex Appeals.** A popular saying in marketing is that "sex sells!" Using sexual imagery in advertisements certainly is popular in many parts of the world. In fact, European media usually contain stronger and more explicit sexual appeals than do American media. As we discussed in our personality chapter, the rationale for this approach is found within the psychoanalytic approach, which assumes that behavior is influenced by deep-seated desires for pleasure.

Interestingly, consumers often find sexually appealing ads to be persuasive, even when they consider them to be exploitative or offensive![26] However, consumers' reactions to the strategy depend on a number of factors. Moderate levels of nudity appear to be most preferred, as highly explicit content tends to direct attention away from the product.

Gender plays a role in advertising effectiveness regarding nudity. For example, one study found that women react negatively to the use of female nudity in advertising, but that men respond favorably toward the practice.[27] Conversely, a later study revealed men react negatively toward the use of male nudity in ads, and that women responded favorably. The type of product being advertised also plays an important role. That is, the use of nudity is most effective for products that have some level of intimate appeal.[28]

Finally, research also reveals that including a romantic theme (rather than focusing on the explicit pleasure of sex) may have positive benefits for marketers. This is good news for fragrance marketers, who often focus their ads on romantic situations and settings.[29]

**Humor Appeals.** Marketers also frequently use humorous ads. In today's age of intense advertising clutter, ads that are humorous can be effective. One recent study confirmed that humorous ads can attract attention, create a positive mood, and enhance both attitude towards a brand and purchases intentions. However, humor appeals can also decrease the credibility of a message source.[30] Research also suggests that the use of humor should relate to the product being advertised.[31]

The overall effectiveness of a humorous ad depends, in part, on the characteristics of both the individual consumer and the advertisement. As discussed in another chapter, research indicates that humor is more effective when a consumer's need for cognition is low rather than high,[32] and also when a consumer has a high need for humor.[33] Furthermore, the initial attitude that a consumer has regarding the product plays an important role, as humorous ads appear to be most effective when the consumer's attitudes are initially positive rather than negative.[34]

The amount of humor to place in an advertisement is another issue. High levels of humor can cause consumers to fail to pay attention to the product being advertised, and high levels can also limit information processing.[35] Obviously, marketers don't want to spend millions of dollars on ad campaigns simply for entertainment purposes.

**Fear Appeals.** In addition to using sexual and humor appeals, advertisers also frequently attempt to evoke some level of fear in their target audiences, as a means of changing attitudes and behaviors. These ads often rely on the relationship between a threat (an undesirable consequence of behavior) and fear (an emotional response).[36] The product being advertised is often promoted as a type of "hero" that will remove the threat.

For example, an insurance company might try to evoke fear in consumers by suggesting that their loved ones may fall into financial hardship if the consumer doesn't carry enough life insurance. Public service announcements may attempt to evoke fear in consumers by highlighting the tragic consequences of unsafe sexual practices (for example, HIV). Security monitoring services may use fear appeals to draw attention to the frightening consequences of home invasions.

Numerous research studies have addressed the effectiveness of fear appeals in marketing. As a general statement, research suggests that the use of fear appeals can be effective. However, the level of fear that results is very important. Overly high levels of fear may lead consumers to focus on the threat so much that they lose focus on the proposed solution.[37] Also, different consumers are likely to react in different ways to the exact same fear appeal, complicating the issue further.[38] As a result, it is very difficult to predict how an individual consumer will react to any fear appeal. The context in which fear appeals are placed can also influence their effectiveness. For example, attitudes toward a fear-inducing ad have been found to be less positive when the ad is embedded in a sad television program than when the ad is placed in a happy (comedic) program.[39]

As an overall statement, fear appeals appear to be effective when they (1) introduce the severity of a threat, (2) present the probability of occurrence, (3) explain the effectiveness of a coping strategy, and (4) show how easy it is to implement the desired response.[40]

Although the use of fear appeals is popular among advertisers, it is important to note that there is an ethical question regarding their use. Critics often argue that the use of fear appeals in advertising is essentially a means of unfair manipulation.[41]

*Humorous ads can attract attention and create a positive mood.*

# MESSAGE CONSTRUCTION

The way that the message is constructed also impacts its persuasiveness. Advertisers must consider a number of issues when constructing a message. Here, we present a number of questions that marketers must answer.

- *Should an ad present a conclusion or should the consumer be allowed to reach his own conclusion?*

  Advertisements that allow consumers to arrive at their own conclusions tend to be more persuasive when the audience has a high level of involvement with the product. Conversely, when the audience is not engaged with the message, it is generally better to draw the conclusion for consumers.[42]

- *Should comparative ads that directly compare one brand against another be developed?*

  Advertisers generally have three alternatives when developing an ad. First, they can promote their brands without mentioning competing brands. Second, advertisers can promote their brands and compare them generically to "the competition." Third, they can actively compare their products against specific competitors by explicitly naming the competing brands in the advertisement.

  Directly comparing one brand against specific competitors can be effective—especially when the brand being promoted is not already the market leader.[43]

Promoting a brand as being "superior to all competition" can also be very persuasive when a firm hopes to court users away from all competing brands.[44]

- *Where should important information be placed?*

  The placement of information in a specific message at the beginning, middle, or end of the message impacts the recall of the information. This is a basic tenet of what is known as the **serial position effect**.[45] When material presented early in a message is most influential, a **primacy effect** is said to occur. When material presented later in the message has the most impact, a **recency effect** is said to occur.[46]

  Research suggests that primacy effects are likely to occur when the audience is highly engaged (highly involved) and when verbal (versus pictorial) content is present.[47] If marketers are attempting to reach a highly involved audience, important information should be placed early in the message. Marketers can also attempt to gain the consumer's attention as early as possible, and encourage careful processing of information by using statements such as "an important message" or "listen carefully." For audiences with lower levels of involvement, important information can be placed late in the message. These effects also occur in series of messages, and can impact the recall of commercials placed in any particular block of commercials. For example, research has revealed that primacy effects prevail for the recall of Super Bowl commercials. That is, commercials placed at the beginning of a block resulted in higher levels of consumer recall.[48]

- *Should the message be straightforward and simple, or complex?*

  In general, complex ads take more effort on the part of the consumer and require deep information processing. Overly complex messages can cause frustration within consumers and lead to unfavorable reactions. As presented earlier in the section on the ELM, the number of arguments presented in an ad is considered a peripheral cue. Highly involved consumers are more motivated to attend to a larger number of arguments than are less motivated consumers.

  As you can see, a marketer must consider numerous message-related issues.

# SOURCE EFFECTS

Another important issue in the study of persuasion is how the source of a message (a

> Advertisers must consider both message and source effects.

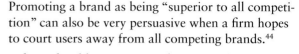

© UPPERCUT IMAGES / ALAMY

spokesperson or model, for example) influences consumers' attitudes. Source effects include issues such as credibility, attractiveness, likeability, and meaningfulness.

**Source Credibility.** Source credibility plays an important role in advertising effectiveness. In general, credible sources tend to be more persuasive than less credible sources. This effect tends to be highest when consumers lack the ability or motivation to expend effort attending to the details of an ad (low involvement).[49] However, credible sources also influence highly involved consumers, especially if their credentials are clearly communicated early in a message.[50] The credibility of sources also impacts the certainty with which consumer attitudes are held, with lower levels of credibility leading to higher levels of certainty.[51]

As we discussed in our comprehension chapter, credibility consists of two elements: expertise and trustworthiness. *Expertise* refers to the amount of knowledge that a spokesperson is perceived to have about the product or issue in question. You may remember from our presentation on the ELM that source expertise represents a peripheral cue in advertising. Expertise can be an important quality for a spokesperson to possess. In fact, a major review of source effects has revealed that source expertise has the biggest influence of all source effects on consumer responses to advertisements.[52]

*Trustworthiness* refers to a perception of the extent to which a spokesperson is presenting a message that he or she truly believes, with no reason to present false information. Interestingly, expertise and trustworthiness can independently influence persuasion. That is, trustworthy sources can be persuasive even if they're not experts, and expert sources can be persuasive even if they're perceived as being untrustworthy.[53]

Finally, we note that source credibility, although generally conceptualized as pertaining to a spokesperson or model, also applies to the sponsoring company. In fact, research reveals that the credibility of both the spokesperson and the company influences the effectiveness of an advertisement, with the credibility of the spokesperson having a stronger influence than the credibility of the company.[54]

**Source Attractiveness.** Source attractiveness is another quality that has received a great deal of attention. Attractive models are often thought to possess desirable qualities and personalities. They also tend to be more persuasive than unattractive spokespeople.[55] However,

the type of product plays an important role in the process. Much like the research regarding the use of sex appeals, research into attractiveness reveals that attractive models are more effective when promoting products that have an intimate appeal, whereas unattractive models are more effective when promoting products that have no intimate appeal.[56] This is particularly the case when consumers have the ability and motivation to process the message being presented.[57]

**Source Likeability.** Source likeability also affects a spokesperson's effectiveness. Likeable sources tend to be persuasive. Of course, individuals differ in terms of which celebrities they like and dislike, and marketers are very interested in finding the best possible spokesperson for a given market segment. The advertising industry relies heavily on a Q-score rating provided by Marketing Evaluations, Inc., as an indication of the overall appeal of celebrities.[58] Interestingly, it has been found that source likeability affects persuasion more for consumers with low need for cognition than for those with a high degree of this trait. This again highlights the importance of individual difference variables in persuasion.[59]

**Source Meaningfulness.** Celebrities have images and cultural meanings that resonate with consumers. For example, a famous athlete like LeBron James embodies the image of hard work and success. Pairing LeBron with athletic apparel or footwear simply makes sense. You should recall that research on the use of sexual imagery and source attractiveness suggests that these characteristics should be matched with the type of product being advertised. This is true for source meaningfulness as well. That is, the dominant characteristics of a source should match the characteristics of the product. This is a key concept that is found in the **matchup hypothesis**, which states that a source feature is most effective when it is matched with relevant products.[60] As such, we should expect LeBron James to be an effective spokesperson for footwear and less effective when promoting a product that has no athletic qualities at all.

As you can see, marketers face a number of decisions when constructing campaigns that are aimed at changing consumer attitudes.

**matchup hypothesis**
hypothesis that states that a source feature is most effective when it is matched with relevant products

## 7 Study Tools

**Located at back of the textbook**

- ☐ Rip-out Chapter-in-Review Card

**Located at www.cengagebrain.com**

- ☐ Review Key Terms Flashcards (Print or Online)
- ☐ Download audio summaries to review on the go
- ☐ Complete practice quizzes to prepare for tests
- ☐ Play "Beat the Clock" and "Quizbowl" to master concepts
- ☐ Watch Video on Numi Tea for a real company example

## what others have thought...

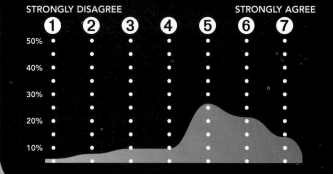

STRONGLY DISAGREE ① ② ③ ④ ⑤ ⑥ ⑦ STRONGLY AGREE

50% 40% 30% 20% 10%

### It's pretty hard to change my attitude about products that I like.

Most students agree with this statement. Social judgment theory is at play here. The more strongly held an attitude is, the more difficult it is to change. We know what we like, and it can be challenging to a marketer who is trying to change our mind.

## Case 2-1

## Are Three Wheels Better than Two? The Can-Am Spyder

*Written by Tia Quinlan-Wilder, University of Denver\**

In late 2007 Jay Leno, the host of TV's venerable "The Tonight Show," became the proud owner of a new 3-wheel on-road vehicle from Canada's BRP. In fact, he became the <u>first</u> owner of the vehicle, having received the very first unit that rolled off the assembly line.[1] Leno is an avid collector of both cars and motorcycles and he has a penchant for era-defining vehicles, so his interest makes sense. But just what would the rest of the world think of the new Can-Am Spyder?

Bombardier Recreational Products is a world leader in design and production of motorized recreational vehicles, and counts Ski-Doo® snowmobiles and Sea-Doo® watercraft among its brands. In February of 2007 Bombardier unveiled the Can-Am Spyder, representing a first foray into the on-road vehicle market. Some automobile experts believe the Spyder will create an entirely new product category. Its innovative design includes two wheels in front and one in the rear, in what has been dubbed "Y-architecture." The design is noted for enhanced stability and obviously departs from traditional three-wheeled motorcycles, which usually include two rear wheels resulting in the nickname "trikes." The Spyder also has several unique safety features, including anti-lock brakes and a computerized stability control system.[2] The car-like setup assists riders who are wary of leaning into turns or hard braking. BRS describes the Spyder as offering "the performance of a traditional motorcycle with the peace-of-mind of a convertible sports car."[3]

Not everyone loves this product, though. Reviewers note that the Spyder is too wide to drive between lanes of traffic (though that is not legal everywhere anyway) and the Y-shaped design makes it hard to miss debris and potholes on the road. Others mention its lack of fuel efficiency too.[4] And some lament that it simply looks like a Ski-Doo on wheels or a swanky golf cart![5]

BRS cites its target market for the Spyder as the 35-45 year old male who already owns a powersports vehicle, perhaps a motorcycle but maybe a snowmobile, all-terrain vehicle, or personal watercraft instead.[6] Some describe the target as a "weekend warrior," enjoying his grown-up toys in his free time. However, the vehicle has obvious appeal to older men and even women, for whom riding a traditional bike (or even holding one in the upright position) may be difficult or intimidating. The Spyder is sleek and modern in its styling, is easy to ride, and eases the fear of tipping, increasing its appeal among young and novice riders, too.[7] With about a $15,000 price tag, there is likely some component of wealth among customers as well.

Whatever the make-up of actual customers, BRS reports that sales of the Spyder have been brisk, saying that response has exceeded expectations, and the bike is "a resounding market success." By late 2008, the company had expanded its sales force to 35 states and 50 countries, and a passionate owners' community has formed. In 2009, the company added a touring model to its line-up to complement the original "roadster sport" vehicle.[8]

Attempting to create an entirely new product class is a risky venture, but signs seem to be positive so far for BRS. Only the future will tell if this new type of vehicle will be permanently embraced by consumers, or if it has simply been the initial buzz of a new concept that has carried sales thus far.

## Questions

1. Describe the motivations that may lead to a Spyder purchase. Do purchasers of the Can-Am Spyder have utilitarian motivations? Hedonic motivations? Both?

2. BRS states that it delivers "paradigm-shifting vehicles that push the envelope."[9] Considering a prospective customer's existing product schema for a motorbike, discuss the implications for cognitive organization, comprehension and acceptance of this vehicle by motorcycle enthusiasts.

3. At introduction of this vehicle, would an attitude-change strategy be necessary to convert the curious into customers? If so, what might be effective?

4. Visit the website **spyder.brp.com** as if you were a potential customer for this product. Is the typical site visitor likely to learn about the product intentionally or unintentionally? Do you think the Web site has been created to maximize the learning that can occur there?

---

## Case 2-2

### Shanghai Advertisements

*Written by Aubrey R. Fowler III, Valdosta State University**

**M**ei Li walks through the busy streets of Shanghai, her school backpack slung across her shoulders, thinking about today's lessons. She sees the familiar skyline along the Huangpu River. Her favorite building is the TV Tower, which she thinks looks like a space ship preparing to blast off into space, always reminding her that she wants to be an engineer when she's finished with college. She looks around at the storefronts that she passes as she makes her way home. Among them, she sees several restaurants that stand out from the crowd: McDonald's, Taco Bell, and—her favorite—KFC. Everywhere she looks, she also sees ads for a variety of Western brands like Omega, Gucci, Lancôme, Dior, Armani, and hundreds of others. A Pepsi billboard up ahead features a young, smiling, Western face, and another ad on a construction façade extols her to "Be the Icon." Mei Li tries her best to ignore the ads as her father tells her to do, believing that, as he says, they will corrupt her education and her responsibility to her friends and family. But it is hard to ignore something that makes her feel as good as the face that smiles down at her. Happy, she turns down a side street that leads to her family's apartment.

Throughout Chinese cities like Shanghai, Beijing, Shenzhen, and Guiyang, students like Mei Li are inundated with advertising that features not only Western brands, but models that have a distinct Western look to them. Like a smiling army, brand icons like Ronald McDonald, Mickey Mouse, and the Aflac duck are crossing international borders in country after country.[1] China is no different. With advertising and brands leading the way, the progress of globalization is spreading not only throughout China but in many other countries as well. Many of these ads feature Chinese citizens celebrating life, family, and unique elements of Chinese life, but many of the Western ads also promote Western images and ideals, seemingly directly from American magazines or TV programs. What effect does this have on the people of China and, especially, on the children of China?

As in the United States, many Chinese citizens are turning to plastic surgery to take more control of their appearance and to help deal with self-concept issues. This would not seem all that abnormal, except for the popularity of one particular type of

plastic surgery. The most popular form of plastic surgery among Chinese citizens is the double eye-lid surgery. This surgery effectively widens the eyes, removing what some might call a distinctive Chinese physical characteristic in favor of something more Western.[2] Often, the patients bring an advertisement ripped from a Chinese version of *Elle, Cosmopolitan,* or *Self* magazine, featuring a Western model. They tell the surgeon, "This is what I want to look like." It seems obvious that these advertisements are having an influence on how Chinese individuals perceive who they are and who they want to be.

Chinese citizens use Western brands and advertising to help them form identities, both of their individual self, and of the nation.[3] Chinese youth, in particular, are enamored with Western brands, and luxury brands in particular.[4] Western ads and brands may be used to form the building blocks of how students like Mei Li think of themselves. They do so by presenting the possibility of who one can be if one just tries the brand in question. But many students like Mei Li do not focus on the brand, but on the ad itself. As they are urged to "Be the Icon" or "Treat Yourself" or "You're the One," they imagine themselves looking like the models in the ads. Considering that China is a collective nation, this is truly an interesting phenomenon.

Mei Li can't seem to help herself from doing just that—being herself—as she leaves her apartment to meet up with friends at the local Pizza Hut. She sees one ad in particular that stands out from the clutter of ads decorating a street near her home. It shows a glamorous woman wearing an evening dress looking over her shoulder at a really cute guy who is "checking her out." Mei Li, at fourteen years old, understands the appeal of being "checked out," and wants to be the center of attention, just like the Western woman in the advertisement. Her mother won't let her wear make-up just yet, but when she reaches her fifteenth birthday in a few months, she plans on buying the brand of makeup the ad is trying to sell. She thinks the woman in the ad looks glamorous and sophisticated, and the makeup will make her look that way as well. Smiling, she races off to meet her friends.

## Questions

1. What function or functions are evident in Mei Li's attitude toward the advertisements that line the streets around her?

2. Using the psychoanalytic approach to motivation, explain how Mei Li deals with the advertisements that surround her?

3. What effect do these Western ads appear to be having on the self-concept of Chinese consumers?

4. What part does the perception process play in Mei Li's reaction to the make-up advertisement?

*Reproduced with permission from the author.

## Case 2-3

### Thrill-Seekers Unite

*Written by Paul Costanzo, Western New England College\**

Thrill-seekers of all ages unite! Bob and Mary-ann represent an emergence of a new wave of empty nesters. Their children have moved out of their house to assume the responsibilities of adulthood. The couple now has more time and money to spend on leisure activities that remind them of their youth. They have always been the ones who, in their younger years, friends affectionately called "the thrill-seekers" or "adrenaline junkies." They now pride themselves on telling their grandchildren that they—Baby Boomers—would be categorized as low on a risk-aversion scale. Bob and Maryann are part of a growing segment of older American consumers who participate in activities that are focused on stimulating their hedonic side. Baby Boomers and older thrill-seeking consumers are active participants in extreme sports, including but not limited to: sky diving (former President George H.W. Bush marked his 85th birthday, in 2009, by skydiving[1]), BASE jumping, cycling, road racing, mountain climbing, and attending NASCAR events.

Partially fueled by their desire to stay healthy, more and more older consumers have adopted an active, extreme sports lifestyle. Engaging in thrill-seeking adventures such as extreme sports is one way older adults can feel energized and revitalized. The "thrill of the hunt" has taken on new meaning with these older consumers. Financial security, along with a quest for excitement, has enabled them to pursue activities usually associated with consumers half their age.

Older extreme thrill-seekers have been around for quite some time. For example, in 2001, the 71-year old director of The Area Agency on Aging of Broward County, in Florida, participated in a billboard advertising campaign, posing on a black Harley-Davidson Wide Glide®. Other participants in the ad campaign included an "86-year-old extreme sports addict who skis barefoot at Cypress Gardens, and a 74-year-old blacksmith and cowboy who competes in rodeo roping."[2]

Unlike their younger thrill-seeking counterparts, this older, thrill-seeking segment has effectively planned an active retirement

*\*Reproduced by permission from the author.*

lifestyle. This is possible partly because many of them have freed themselves of the typical financial burdens and responsibilities of younger Americans. These older thrill-seeking consumers can afford many of the expenses usually associated with extreme sports because their home mortgages are usually paid off, they have ownership of their automobile titles, and child expenses are a thing of the past. Another unique opportunity available to older consumers, which enables them to pay for many of their thrill-seeking adventures, is the use of home equity in a reverse home mortgage.[3] A reverse home mortgage is an attractive option to older consumers because it allows them access to funds they otherwise might not have available to them. They may receive monthly payments from their mortgage lender with the stipulation that the lender will eventually take title of the home.

Home owners 62 years and older have access to the equity of their property with very flexible terms either in the form of a lump sum, monthly payments, line of credit, or combination thereof.[4]

Relying on funds made available to them by a reverse home mortgage, more and more older adults are now able to spend their retirement years enjoying themselves at exotic beach resorts, where an array of extreme sports are readily available.[5]

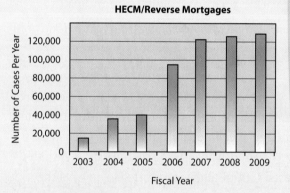

**HECM/Reverse Mortgages**

Traditionally, extreme sports have generally attracted younger consumers. Attendance at mixed martial arts (MMA) competitions is on the rise for both younger and older thrill-seeking consumers. These events provide a form of shock value for the consumer not usually experienced at traditional sporting events.

"Mixed martial arts may be today's fastest-growing spectator sport, with amateur or pro bouts legal in 40 states and many countries."[6]

The popularity of extreme sports is partially attributed to the effective media coverage and marketing of events. Sports such as snowboarding, skateboarding, and the extreme motor sports provide excitement and value to the consumer who seeks a unique entertainment experience. With the help of athletes like Shaun White, who has rapidly attained celebrity status, and events such as the ESPN Summer and Winter X Games, extreme sports are becoming more and more popular.

Several Winter X-Games events, which at one time drew only modest ticket sales, have been accepted as Olympic sports. Some of these sports were the most watched of the 2010 Winter Olympic Games.

Participation in extreme sports will most likely increase in the next decade for young and older consumer alike. By studying the dynamic customer profile of high-risk seeking consumers of all ages, marketers have been successful in providing viable opportunities by which they can satisfy their thrill-seeking need for adventure and excitement.

## Questions

1. Develop a psychographic profile of a consumer who identifies himself/herself as a "thrill seeker." Identify three personality traits that you think would be associated with a consumer attending the ESPN Summer or Winter X Games. How might consumers with differing levels of thrill seeking (very low versus very high) have different attitudes about a reverse mortgage?

2. Choose an extreme sports event and describe its brand personality.

3. Describe three ways you think the personality of an extreme sports consumer affects their shopping decisions. How does your personality have an impact on the product/services you purchase?

## Case 2-4

### Do Zipped Commercials Influence You?

*Written by Robert Rouwenhorst, University of Iowa**

Since the dawn of television, broadcasters and their affiliates have had near total control over how commercials are viewed. The invention of the videocassette recorder (VCR) and remote control were revolutionary in that viewers began to control how much advertising they watched. With this increased control, audiences started to do what they could to avoid commercials. The invention of the digital video recorder (DVR) has enabled audiences to have a greater choice of what to watch and when to watch it. The greatest threat to advertisers is the DVR's ability to quickly fast-forward, or "zip," through advertising. There are approximately 36.7 million DVR customers in the United States.[1] TiVo states that 77 percent of customers who record a show and watch it later fast-forward through the commercials. CBS found that 64 percent of DVR owners zipped all commercials.[2]

A viewer must engage in an active process and make a conscious effort to avoid watching commercials. If a viewer elects to zip

through advertising, he or she must pay close attention to the television to ensure they do not unintentionally zip into the desired program. Thus, attention level and consequently memory for zipped commercials may be greater than those viewed at normal speed. Through internal market research, Procter & Gamble discovered that viewers retain fast-forwarded commercials at about the same rate as those watched in normal speed.[3]

Researchers have looked at zipping speeds of 300, 1800, and 6000 percent real-time (speeds utilized by a popular DVR manufacturer, TiVo). At 300 percent zipping speed, it was demonstrated that recall for advertised brand names actually increased over normal viewing.[4] Although this initially appears counterintuitive, remember that a viewer zipping commercials must pay attention to the commercials to locate the start of his desired program. Research has also shown that a silent segment in a commercial increases attention and recall of the commercial.[5] Using a DVR to fast-forward induces silence on all commercials zipped; hence, possible audio distractions are eliminated. Faster zipping speeds of 1800 and 6000 percent hindered recall of advertised brand names as it became increasingly difficult for viewers to process, let alone recall, what was occurring in a highly accelerated advertisement.

Although explicit recall of a commercial is hindered at high zipping speeds, can a zipped commercial still have an impact on viewers even if they do not recall seeing the commercial? Explicit memory measures, such as recognition and recall, are often used in judging advertising effectiveness. However, there

*Reprinted with permission from the author.

may be other forces at work in shaping consumers' decisions to buy products. One such mechanism is unconscious or implicit memory. This type of memory does not rely on consumers thinking back to prior experiences and memories the way explicit memory retrieval works. Instead, implicit memory is demonstrated by changes in task performance due to exposure to certain information, but without a deliberate attempt to recall the information.[6, 7]

Much implicit memory research centers on the phenomenon of priming. Priming can be thought of as an unconscious form of memory.[8] The typical priming experiment involves two stages. First, participants are exposed to some stimulus object or information (e.g., a list of words). After a delay or a task unrelated to the experiment, participants are given incomplete information about the object (e.g., word stems) and are asked to complete the information. Implicit memory or priming is said to have occurred if one completes the second task (word stems) with information (words) one was exposed to in the first stage.

There have been many interesting experiments involving priming. For instance, researchers have flashed photos of people on a computer screen so fast participants do not recall them. Later in the experiment they interact with people, some of whom they saw a photo of before.[9] Participants preferred those individuals whose photo they had been exposed to. It has also been found that the more frequently a banner ad appeared advertising a camera, the more viewers liked the camera even when they could not recall what the banner ad displayed.[10] Other researchers have found that priming people with an Apple logo caused them to behave more creatively than those exposed to an IBM logo.[11]

As for zipped commercials, viewers' brand preferences can significantly shift toward brands for which they saw zipped commercials during a television program, compared with a control group who made similar brand purchase decisions after watching an identical television program without commercials. The brand choice change was relatively small, 10 percent (viewers exposed to the zipped commercials selected the advertised brands in a later implicit memory test 61 percent of the time versus the control group which chose the brands 51 percent of the time). However, in 10 of the 12 categories where viewers made choices between two brands, there was a preference shift toward the brand that was advertised.[12] For instance, more people said they preferred Subway over Quizno's if they had been exposed to a zipped commercial for Subway than viewers who were not exposed to any commercials.

Small changes in market share can often equate to billions of dollars in sales. While marketers and advertisers are rightly concerned about the impact DVRs will have on television commercials' effectiveness, it is important to note that highly zipped ads still have some influence. As DVR penetration continues to grow, brand managers and advertisers need to better understand how zipping influences viewers' memories, attitudes, and subsequent behaviors. While explicit measures such as recall and recognition have traditionally been used to judge the effectiveness of television commercials, additional measures may be more appropriate in the age of zipping.

## Questions

1. Why do you think zipped commercials can still impact a viewer?

2. How should one judge the effectiveness of television commercials? Is recognition and recall of the brand name enough? What other measures would you suggest?

3. What are ways advertisers could counteract the effects of zipping? How could you encourage consumers to watch commercials in real time?

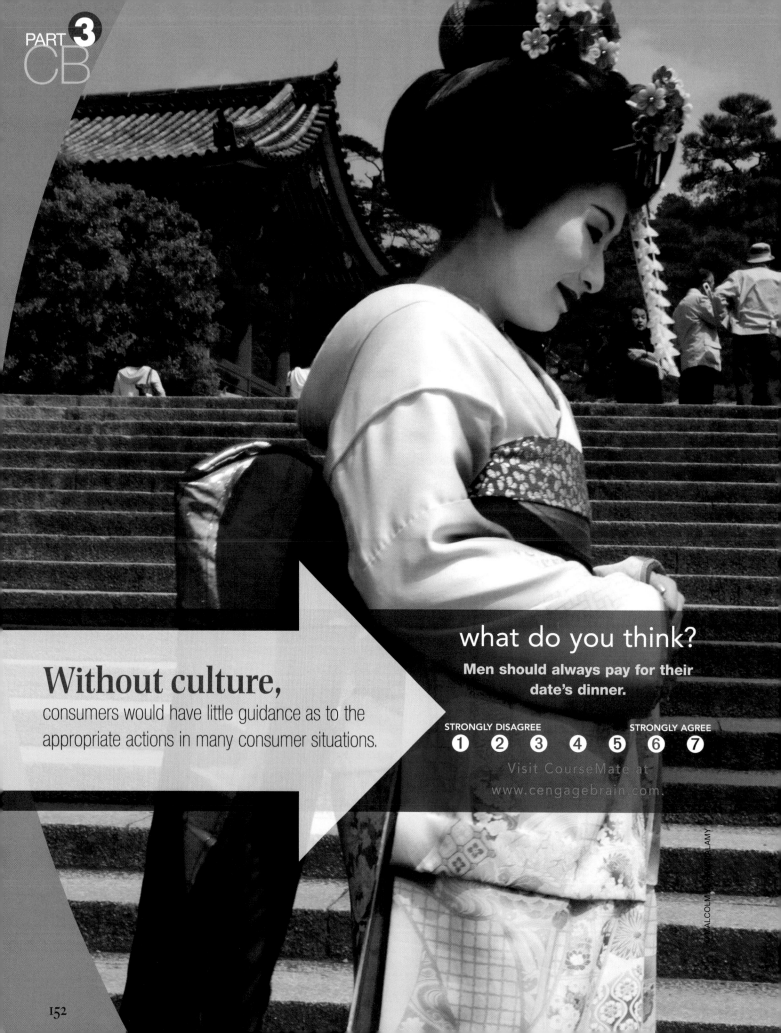

# Without culture,

consumers would have little guidance as to the appropriate actions in many consumer situations.

## what do you think?

**Men should always pay for their date's dinner.**

STRONGLY DISAGREE ① ② ③ ④ ⑤ ⑥ ⑦ STRONGLY AGREE

Visit CourseMate at www.cengagebrain.com.

# 8

# Consumer Culture

## LO1 Culture and Meaning Are Inseparable

grande doppio latte, please! What language is this? A consumer can use this expression in 50 countries and get exactly what he or she wants, with no translation. The popularity of Starbucks, clearly a company with American roots, has led to a universal language describing coffee consumption.

Americans do not really have a deep history as gourmet coffee lovers. In fact, prior to the last few years, the typical American coffee was cheap, weak, and, outside of Seattle and New Orleans, nondescript at best. In America, coffee is and remains the first choice for a morning beverage. In much of Europe, consumers drink coffee not only in the morning but in the afternoon and evening as well. In parts of Asia, coffee consumption is relatively rare, as tea is viewed as the beverage of choice in the morning and throughout the day.

With all these different coffee-drinking habits and orientations, how could a single coffee company succeed, with the same basic formula, in so many different places around the world? In fact, the feature "The World *Is* Their Cup" describes how Starbucks defied the odds in expanding in new and different cultures, like China. In the United States, a $2 cup of coffee may seem relatively high compared to traditional convenience store prices, but $2 is within reach of nearly all Americans. However, consider how a $2 price tag might compare in countries like Poland, Mexico, or China. For Starbucks to succeed, they have to offer an experience that adds value to consumers who come from many different backgrounds and many different orientations. Thus, Starbucks's success depends on being accepted by culture and somehow creating a meaning that conveys value in the coffee shop experience.

## WHAT IS CULTURE?

Consumers make very simple decisions involving things like coffee drinking, and very important and meaningful

### After studying this chapter, the student should be able to:

**LO1** Understand how culture provides the true meaning of objects and activities.

**LO2** Use the key dimensions of core societal values to apply the concept of cultural distance.

**LO3** Define acculturation and enculturation.

**LO4** List fundamental elements of verbal and nonverbal communication.

**LO5** Discuss current emerging consumer markets and scan for opportunities.

decisions involving things like religious affiliations. In all cases, what a person consumes helps determine how accepted one is by other consumers in society. Likewise, the consumption act itself generally has no absolute meaning, only meaning relative to the environment in which the act takes place. Culture, therefore, embodies meaning.

**Consumer culture** can be thought of as commonly held societal beliefs that define what is socially gratifying. Culture shapes value by framing everyday life in terms of these commonly held beliefs. The fact that the average price for a cup of coffee in the United States has risen indicates that in America, the beliefs that people have about the coffee-drinking experience have certainly changed, and define a more valuable experience than in decades past. Culture ultimately determines what consumption behaviors are acceptable.

Although American adults enjoy coffee, some consumers believe that providing coffee to a child is unacceptable. In other areas, however, consumers may see this behavior as quite normal. Culture shapes the value of beverages, just as it does with other products. Exhibit 8.1 lists some consumption behaviors that vary in meaning, value, and acceptability from culture to culture.

## CULTURE, MEANING, AND VALUE

The focus of this chapter is on culture. This focus acknowledges that the marketplace today truly is global. Modern technology has greatly reduced the geographic barriers that prevented consumers from doing business with marketers in other parts of the world. Without

## The World *Is* Their Cup!

Starbucks has over 16,000 stores in practically every corner of the world. Starbucks has even been successful in places like Paris, where "experts" told them the concept was too American, and inconsistent with the Parisian idea of a coffeehouse. However, can Starbucks succeed in a place where consumers associate drinking coffee with the parched sensation of a Saharan desert?

This is the challenge that faces Starbucks. China is a tea-drinking country, and one where a $4 grande latte is truly a luxury. The average income in this area is under $4,000 per year. Starbucks's strategy in China is to capitalize on the stores as a gathering place. So, the stores are generally bigger with larger sitting areas than in a typical U.S. Starbucks. The ambiance is clearly Starbucks. Additionally, an emphasis on sweeter products, more food items, and fresh-brewed tea, is the recipe they will follow. Starbucks hopes to deliver a high-hedonic-value experience and one that will lead to success for most of its more than 400 stores across China.

Sources: Adamy, J. (2006), "Eyeing a Billion Tea Drinkers, Starbucks Pours it on in China," *The Wall Street Journal* (November 29), A1; Chao, L. (2006), "Starbucks Raises Stake in Beijing, Tianjin Stores," *The Wall Street Journal* online (November 25), **http:online.wsj.com/article/SB116167895560901902.cb.html**, accessed November 25, 2006; Adamy, J. (2007), "Starbucks Chairman Says Trouble May Be Brewing," *The Wall Street Journal* (February 24), A4.

© ISTOCKPHOTO.COM/SAPANDR

culture, consumers would have little guidance as to the appropriate actions in many common consumer situations. Thus, culture performs important functions for consumers. These functions shape the value of consumer activities and include:

1. **Giving meaning to objects.** Consider how much culture defines the meaning of food, religious objects, and everyday items like furniture. For instance, in Japan, refrigerators are tiny by most Western standards.

2. **Giving meaning to activities.** Consider, for example, the role of things as simple as recreational activities and even washing (hygiene). A daily shower is not a universally accepted norm.

3. **Facilitating communication.** The shared meaning of things facilitates communication. When strangers meet, culture indicates whether a handshake, hug, or kiss is most appropriate. Things as simple as making eye contact can take on dramatically different meanings from one culture to another.

## EXHIBIT 8.1
# Culture, Meaning, and Value

| Behavior | Meaning in United States | Alternate Meaning |
|---|---|---|
| Consumer age 14–18 consuming beer or wine in a restaurant | Unacceptable or even illegal in most areas. | Wine is part of a nice family meal in other areas, including much of western Europe. |
| People gathering to eat barbecue pork ribs | This menu is part of a pleasant social event. | Pork is not an acceptable food item among Jews and Muslims. |
| Supervisors and employees socializing together | Supervisors and coworkers can be friendly with each other. | Employees and supervisors should keep their distance away from work. An employee who acts too casually with a "senior" could incur a sanction. |
| Kissing | Purely a family or romantic activity. | In many nations, kissing is common when making a new acquaintance or greeting a friend. |

**cultural norm** rule that specifies the appropriate consumer behavior in a given situation within a specific culture

**cultural sanction** penalty associated with performing a nongratifying or culturally inconsistent behavior

## CULTURAL NORMS

Culture, meaning, and value are very closely intertwined. For this reason, culture determines things that are socially rewarding (valuable) or socially unrewarding (not valuable). A consumer who acts inconsistently with cultural expectations risks being socially ostracized. The term **cultural norm** refers to a rule that specifies the appropriate behavior in a given situation within a specific culture. Most, but not all, cultural norms are unwritten and simply understood by members of a cultural group.

In Korea, for example, a consumer is not expected to pour a drink for himself or herself when out in a bar or restaurant with friends or family. The cultural norm is that one pours a drink for friends and family. Thus, by pouring drinks for others and waiting for someone else to pour a drink for him or her,

*Does Lady Gaga set any cultural norms?*

the consumer has performed a socially rewarding (valuable) act consistent with the norms of that society.

## CULTURAL SANCTIONS

So, what happens to a consumer who performs an act inconsistent with cultural norms? Unfortunately, the consumer is likely to experience a cultural sanction. A **cultural sanction** refers to the penalties associated with performing a nongratifying or culturally inconsistent behavior. Cultural sanctions often are relatively innocuous. For instance, if one were to pour her own drink in Korea, he is likely to get only a curious look or suffer some innocent teasing from members of the group. In other instances however, a consumer performing a culturally inconsistent act may be shunned or suffer banishment from a group.

Many societies still have strong cultural norms about marrying outside of one's social class, religion, or ethnic group. Violation of this norm can result in isolation from family or worse. Physically or socially harming a family member for fraternizing beyond one's cultural group represents a fairly strong cultural sanction.

### Popular Culture

Popular culture captures cultural trends and shapes norms and sanctions within society. A few decades ago, a male American college student might routinely wear platform shoes, silk shirts, sideburns, and maybe even an Afro hairstyle. For a student in the 1970s, all of these consumer behaviors

GARY MOYES/BRAVO/NBCUPB VIA AP IMAGES

**role expectations** the specific expectations that are associated with each type of person within a culture or society

would be consistent with popular culture. A student who showed up at class in this fashion today would certainly stand out from his or her classmates and might face at the least one or two curious glances. Pop icons such as Lady Gaga or Taio Cruz help determine acceptable style for many groups of admirers who desire to fit in with today's popular culture.

## Role Expectations

Every consumer plays various roles within society. Culture expects people to play these roles in a culturally rewarding fashion. In other words, when a consumer interacts with another person, any characteristic upon which that person can be categorized activates certain behavioral expectations. Recall that in a previous chapter we described how social schema (stereotypes) help consumers organize knowledge about people. **Role expectations** are the specific expectations that are associated with each type of person. One's sex, one's occupation, one's social class, and one's age all are relevant bases for forming societal role expectations. Role expectations become a primary basis for cultural norms and sanctions. They define not only the way one should act to play the role, but also the types of products that are appropriate for a person within a role. When a consumer travels to a foreign country, he or she may well find that expectations for a given role are different from at home. As a result, the consumption activities associated with roles can also vary from culture to culture.

In most parts of the United States for example, a typical service employee in a restaurant, department store, or even in a hotel, plays their societal role well by speaking English only. However, in much of Scandinavia, for instance Norway, a consumer expects that a service employee can respond in at least two languages, if not more. A service employee in Norway would generally be somewhat surprised even to be asked if he or

**EXHIBIT 8.2**
## Societal Role Expectations Vary

| Role | Role-Expectations USA | Role-Expectations Outside of USA |
|---|---|---|
| Service Employee | Treat customers promptly, courteously, and as a priority | Russia: Customers not treated quite so promptly or courteously–the worker is prioritized over the customer |
| College Student | Attentive in class, do assigned work on time, buy the assigned text, and do not eat in class | Europe: Talking with classmates more accepted, the syllabus is more a suggestion, and eating in class is common |
| Motorcycle Driver | Dress down and generally follow the same driving rules as automobile drivers | Italy: Dressed up (often going to the office) and generally ignore the rules for automobiles—particularly traffic lanes |

she can speak English, because it is very much expected of them within their role. Exhibit 8.2 provides some other examples of cultural role expectations. In the next chapter, we focus more specifically on societal roles tied to demographic characteristics.

# LO2 Using Core Societal Values

## WHERE DOES CULTURE COME FROM?

Consumer researchers commonly use culture to explain and predict consumer behavior.[1] Estimates suggest that out of all academic explanations of consumer behavior, more than 10% of all explanations include culture as a key factor.[2] Cultural beliefs define what religion is acceptable, what types of art and recreation are preferred, what manners are considered polite, the roles for different types of individuals, including expectations for men and women in a society, and much more. Distinguishing the unique effects of culture on these more specific things is extremely difficult since as part of culture, these things tend to function together. There is, however, little doubt that culture causes differences in the value consumers perceive from different products and experiences.[3]

How do people in one nation end up with a culture distinct from that of people in another? In other words, what causes culture? The answer to this question involves two important components.

First, ecological factors cause differences in culture because they change the relative value of objects. **Ecological factors** are the physical characteristics that describe the physical environment and habitat of a particular place. Thus, for example, consumers from groups that have traditionally lived in desert areas place a great value on water relative to consumers from areas filled with freshwater lakes. As a result, consumers from a desert area may have different habits when it comes to hygiene, including the frequency and duration of baths or showers. This can affect sales of beauty products, soaps, and toilet water, and also things like hotel room and building design.

Second, over time, tradition develops among groups of peoples, and these traditions carry forward to structure society. **Tradition** in this sense refers to the customs and accepted ways of structuring society. Traditions include things like the family, and political structures of a society. In the United States, Australia, Canada, and much of Europe, families traditionally consist of two generations (parents and children) living in a household, in which a husband and wife share decision making. In other cultures, India for instance, more than two generations (grandparents, parents, and children) may share a household, and the key decision maker is the oldest male living in the house. Thus, consumer advertising may need to differ based on the traditional family decision-making style associated with a culture. While tradition can be thought of as influencing culture, one can safely say that, in the long run, culture also defines tradition.

Religious traditions shape consumption experiences.

> **ecological factors** physical characteristics that describe the physical environment and habitat of a particular place
>
> **tradition** customs and accepted ways of everyday behavior in a given culture

> While tradition can be thought of as influencing culture, one can safely say that, in the long run, culture also defines tradition.

Exhibit 8.3 illustrates how tradition and ecology come together to influence culture, with each culture described by different amounts of core societal values (discussed later in this chapter), and these values driving differences in consumer behaviors and the value derived from them. Over time, traditions become embedded in culture and become relatively stable. However, while stable, they do slowly change, as illustrated by the changes in places where people could traditionally smoke without fear of sanctions. In this sense, not only are the choices and behaviors of consumers influenced by culture, but, in the end, subtle changes in these choices and behaviors also influence culture.

## DIMENSIONS OF CULTURAL VALUES

Although conflicting views exist on what exactly are the best dimensions to describe differences in cultural values, the most widely applied dimensions are those developed by Geert Hofstede.[4] This theory of value-based differences in cultures is based on five key dimensions, with each dimension representing a core societal

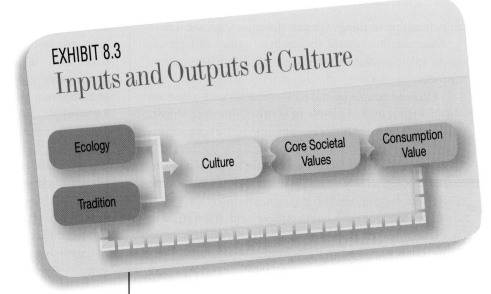

**EXHIBIT 8.3**
## Inputs and Outputs of Culture

Ecology → Tradition → Culture → Core Societal Values → Consumption Value

value. **Core societal values (CSV)**, or **cultural values**, represent a commonly agreed-upon consensus about the most preferable ways of living within a society. Even though not all members of a culture may share precisely the same values to the same degree, a specific cultural group will tend to have common worldviews along these dimensions. Exhibit 8.3 illustrates how core societal values serve as the mechanism by which culture affects value. Cultural values can be classified using multiple dimensions. In some cases, the dimensions overlap with each other or relate to one another.

## Individualism

The first CSV dimension contrasts cultures based on relative amounts of individualism and collectivism.[5] **Individualism** as a CSV means the extent to which people expect each other to take responsibility for themselves and their immediate family. Highly individualistic societies place high value on self-reliance, individual initiative, and personal achievement. In contrast, nations with low individualism are seen as high in **collectivism**, which refers to the extent to which an individual's life is intertwined with a large, cohesive group. Highly collectivistic societies tend to live in extended families, take their identity from the groups to which they belong, and be very loyal to these groups.

Clearly, this dimension has important implications for the way consumers make decisions and the way that consumers extract value from consumption (see the CVF in Chapter 2 for an illustration). In the United States, marketers often communicate the value of various products by illustrating the extent to which they help one achieve personal freedom. American consumers often see important purchases as an extension of themselves. Advertisements for cigarettes,

jeans, ATVs, and even laptop computers commonly use adjectives such as *rugged*, *tough*, and *dependable*.[6] In contrast, an advertisement for a collective culture may rely more on adjectives such as *honest* or *friendly*.

Generally, Western societies tend to be more individualistic, whereas Eastern nations tend to be more collectivistic. Collectivist societies tend to be more compliant with requests from group members. American consumers, for instance, once they have made a

*A typical advertisement appealing to individualism as a CSV.*

IMAGE COURTESY OF THE ADVERTISING ARCHIVES

choice, are more likely to repeat that choice a second time because its value is enhanced by virtue of having been selected originally. In contrast, consumers from Asia do not increase the value of something they chose previously, and are more susceptible to make a choice that someone in their group has chosen previously.[7] This generality is just that—a generality! There are exceptions to this rule. Later, we'll discuss specific scores on all dimensions across many countries.

## Masculinity

The **masculinity** CSV dimension captures distinctions existing in societies based on mannerisms typically associated with Western male traits, such as valuing assertiveness and control, over traditional feminine traits such as caring, conciliation, and community. **Femininity** represents the opposite of masculinity, but in this case, the masculinity-femininity distinction does not refer to a political or social movement, or to the prominence that men and women have within a society. In fact, women's traits tend to vary less from nation to nation than do those of men, so femininity is most clearly obvious within a masculine culture. In other words, in a culture with low masculinity, men also tend to share some *feminine* traits.[8]

Advertisements for laptop computers in a highly masculine nation, such as Japan, may emphasize the computer's ability to help one get ahead. A newer, faster computer with more features can help one assert himself in the workplace or at school. In contrast, in a more feminine country such as Mexico, an advertisement for the same laptop computer might emphasize the benefit of being able to stay in touch with family and friends through email and web-based communication.

## Power Distance

**Power distance** is the extent to which authority and privilege are divided among different groups within society and the extent to which people accept these divisions as facts of life within the society. Social class distinctions become a very real issue among consumers in high-power-distance nations. However, the distinctions go beyond just social class and affect relationships between supervisory and subordinate employees, and even between students and teachers.

Low-power-distance nations tend to be more egalitarian. First names are commonly used among people of different social classes, and even between employees and supervisors. In high-power-distance nations, those with less status must show deference to those with greater status; therefore, the lower-status person would not likely call a person of higher status by first name.

In many Asian nations, where power distance is relatively high compared to that in the United States, the terms *senior* and *junior* are often used to capture status distinctions. A student might be junior to a faculty supervisor or to another student who preceded him or her through a program of study. When one is unclear about whether or not he or she is junior or senior to another, he or she might well ask the other person, "How old are you?" Age would be a tiebreaker, with older people having more status than younger people. Senior and junior status can affect simple things such as seating arrangements and whether or not one carries his or her own briefcase. Juniors may need to be careful in what they buy and do so as not to seem superior in any substantive way to a senior. A consumer violating a custom and acting more "senior" than appropriate may well face cultural sanctions for the behavior.

In high-power-distance nations, certain consumer behaviors are designated exclusively to individuals by class or status. For example, in high-power-distance nations, golf is seen as an activity only for those with very high status. Additionally, authority appeals in marketing are more effective when power distance is high.[9]

## Uncertainty Avoidance

**Uncertainty avoidance** is just what the term implies. A culture high in uncertainty avoidance is uncomfortable with things that are ambiguous or unknown. Consumers high in uncertainty avoidance prefer the known, avoid taking risks, and like life to be structured and routine. Uncertainty avoidance has important implications for consumer behavior because marketing success and improved quality of life often depend on obtaining value from something innovative and, therefore, somewhat unfamiliar. The task becomes making the unfamiliar seem familiar in appealing to consumers high in uncertainty avoidance.

Nations that are high in uncertainty avoidance will be slower to adopt product innovations. Additionally, nations that are relatively high in uncertainty

**masculinity** role distinction within a group that values assertiveness and control; CSV opposite of femininity

**femininity** sex role distinction within a group that emphasizes the prioritization of relational variables such as caring, conciliation, and community; CSV opposite of masculinity

**power distance** extent to which authority and privileges are divided among different groups within society and the extent to which these facts of life are accepted by the people within the society

**uncertainty avoidance** extent to which a culture is uncomfortable with things that are ambiguous or unknown

avoidance, such as France, will react differently to basic CB generalizations. For instance, one such generalization is that scarcity affects the perceived value of products. A scarce product is worth more, and consumers are more likely to purchase a product perceived to be scarce. The extent to which scarcity drives actual purchase intentions is more pronounced among cultures high in uncertainty avoidance.[10] In other words, consumers in high-uncertainty-avoidance cultures are quicker to buy something because of perceived scarcity.

*Astrological charts are important ways to predict the future in some cultures high in uncertainty avoidance. Can astrology reduce uncertainty avoidance?*

Uncertainty avoidance has important implications for consumer behavior, because marketing success and improved quality of life often depend on obtaining value from something innovative and, therefore, somewhat unfamiliar.

Basic consumer principles such as the price-quality relationship are also affected by differing CSV. For instance, the price-quality relationship is not as strong among cultures with high uncertainty avoidance. These consumers are more skeptical and likely to discern individual features of products separately. Such is the case with Chinese consumers, who are more likely to perceive a price-risk relationship than a price-quality relationship. In other words, higher price means higher risk in conditions of uncertainty.[11] Superstitions and myths also play a bigger role among cultures high in uncertainty avoidance.[12] Consumers in these cultures may even use astrological charts to help plan visits to casinos. Thus, the casinos in these cultures can somewhat predict peak periods of traffic based on these types of beliefs.

Consumers in high-uncertainty-avoidance cultures also demand greater amounts of product information and explanation. Bosch automotive industries, based in

Germany, designs different packages for products sold in Europe and products sold in the United States. For example, a packet containing replacement windshield wipers might be sold in a simple cellophane package in the United States. In Europe, the same product might require a box, not because the products differ in size but because the box allows more room to include product information about the wipers, and how to install them, than does a plastic wrapper. As a result, the European customers find more value and experience greater job satisfaction with these products.

## Long-Term Orientation

The final CSV dimension is long-term orientation. **Long-term orientation** reflects values consistent with Confucian philosophy and a prioritization of future rewards over short-term benefits. As such, high long-term orientation means that a consumer values thriftiness and perseverance as well as the maintenance of long-term relationships.[13] Relationships need time to develop and are intended to last for a lifetime. As a result, negotiations between suppliers and buyers are more likely to consider long-term effects for both parties in a high long-term orientation culture such as Japan.[14] At the other end of the spectrum, a short-term orientation is associated more with immediate payoffs and face saving.[15]

*Guanxi* (pronounced gawn-shi) is the Chinese term for a way of doing business in which parties must first invest time and resources in getting to know one another, and becoming comfortable with one another, before consummating any important deal. *Guanxi* is a common mode of operation among cultures with high long-term orientation—as in many nations in the Far East.[16] Western consumers depend on credit cards for everyday purchases, and even in many cases as instant financing for luxury items. Thus, American consumers often have multiple credit cards, each from a different bank or credit company. As the Chinese economy develops, the principles of *guanxi* and long-term orientation present barriers for credit card companies.[17] The Chinese consumers are loath to take a card from a company they do not know or fully understand. Also, the idea of financing consumer products remains foreign.

*Renquing* is another phenomenon associated with long-term orientation. **Renquing** is the idea that when someone does a good deed for you, you are expected to return that good deed. The reciprocation need not be immediate however. In fact, the expectation of reciprocation at some point in the future fosters long-term relationships, as individuals are forever trying to balance the *renquing* score with one other.[18] Thus, a consumer and personal service provider may end up in a long-term relationship facilitated in part by *renquing*.

## THE CSV SCOREBOARD

A CSV scoreboard can be put together using historical CSV dimension scores found in many resources,

including the Hofstede website **www.geert-hof-stede.com**. How does your country stack up on the CSV scoreboard? The CSV scores for a given country can be essential information for marketers wishing to appeal to consumers in another country. The more similar the CSV scores, the more likely consumers find value in the same or similar products and experiences.

## BRIC

Exhibit 8.4 shows a CSV scoreboard for a few select nations. Brazil, Russia, India, and China represent widely accepted emerging economies. The acronym **BRIC** refers to the collective economies of these nations. These nations are key targets for foreign investment, and the ripple effect is that consumers in these nations are becoming wealthier and better targets for all manner of goods and services. Doing business in these nations is hardly the same, though, as their CSV scores show. In this truly global marketplace, serving consumers in emerging markets can be an important route to business

**renquing** the idea that favors given to another are reciprocal and must be returned

**BRIC** acronym that refers to the collective economies of Brazil, Russia, India, and China

### EXHIBIT 8.4
### CSV Scoreboard for the United States, Australia, United Kingdom, Brazil, Russia, India, Pakistan, and China

| | Power Distance | Individualism | Masculinity | Uncertainty Avoidance | Long-Term Orientation |
|---|---|---|---|---|---|
| United States | 40 | 91 | 62 | 46 | 29 |
| Australia | 36 | 90 | 61 | 51 | 31 |
| United Kingdom | 35 | 89 | 66 | 35 | 25 |
| Brazil | 69 | 38 | 49 | 76 | 65 |
| Russia | 93 | 39 | 36 | 95 | 55a |
| India | 77 | 48 | 56 | 40 | 61 |
| Pakistan | 55 | 14 | 50 | 70 | 0 |
| China * | 80 | 20 | 66 | 30 | 118 |

a LTO score for Russia is not available. This value represents the average LTO score for these countries. Averages: PDI, 59; IDV, 44; MAS, 51; UAI, 66; LTO, 45.

success. Some are now considering where the next emerging nations will be.[19]

## CSV Leaders

Among all nations with CSV scores, Austria has the lowest power-distance scores, and Malaysia has the highest. The United States has relatively low power distance with only 15 nations reporting lower scores. For individualism, Guatemala reports the lowest score, and the United States the highest. Sweden reports the lowest masculinity score, and Japan the highest, with the exception of the Slovak nations. The United States is neither clearly masculine nor clearly feminine. Singapore reports the lowest uncertainty avoidance score and Greece the highest. The United States is relatively low on uncertainty avoidance, with only 12 nations reporting a lower score. Long-term orientation scores are available for only a few nations. But, among those with scores, Pakistan has the lowest (meaning that it is the most short-term oriented), and China has the highest.

# CULTURAL DISTANCE

More and more businesses are considering reaching out to markets outside of their own country. Certainly, the Internet has helped reduce the market separations caused by geographic distance. However, consider businesses like Carrefour, Subway, Accor Hotels, and Zara. Each already operates many stores in many countries. How should a company decide where it should expand internationally? In other words, where will it be successful?

Two approaches to this important question can be taken. First, perhaps the most intuitive response is to look to neighboring countries with which the home country shares a border. This approach is based on geographic distance. Countries are attractive because they are nearby and can be easily reached both in terms of marketing communications and physical distribution. Certainly, many U.S. businesses exist in Canada and vice versa.

The second approach looks more at how similar a target nation's consumers are to the home consumers. This approach is based more on **cultural distance**, which represents how disparate one nation is from another in terms of their CSVs. With this approach, consumers can be compared by using scores available in a CSV scoreboard. For example, Exhibit 8.5 shows the difference scores for all nations depicted in the CSV scoreboard compared to those of the United States. These are obtained simply by

*How should a company decide where it should expand internationally?*

subtracting the score for each nation on each dimension from the corresponding score for U.S. consumers.

Notice the small score differences on each dimension between Australia, the United Kingdom, and the United States compared to the other nations. A simple distance formula can summarize the cultural differences between nations. One might consider simply adding up the difference scores; however, the negative and positive scores could cancel each other out, making two nations that are really quite different appear similar. One way to correct this problem is by using the squared differences, much as would be the case in computing statistical variation. For example, the following formula is used to compute the total cultural distances from the United States for each nation shown in Exhibit 8.5:

$$CD = \sqrt{\sum_{i=1}^{5} (TCSV_i - BCSV_i)^2}$$

where CD = cultural distance, TCSV = target country value score on dimension $i$, and BCSV = baseline country value score on dimension $i$.

Thus, for example, the CD for Australia from the United States is 6.9:

$$CD = \sqrt{\begin{array}{c}(36 - 40)^2 + (90 - 91)^2 + (61 - 62)^2 +\\ (51 - 46)^2 + (31 - 29)^2\end{array}} = \sqrt{47} = 6.9$$

Among all comparisons, few would show so little difference as this. Compare these with the CD scores for the BRIC countries. The CD score between any two countries is easily computed for all nations for which CSV scores are available.

© VARIO IMAGES GMBH & CO. KG / ALAMY

Countries with relatively low CD scores are more similar and thus tend to value the same types of consumption experiences. In fact, the term **CANZUS** is sometimes used to refer to the close similarity in values between Canada, Australia, New Zealand, and the United States.[20] Additionally, the *U* could represent the United Kingdom because this nation too is very similar from a CD perspective. Not surprisingly, common consumer products, retailers, and restaurant chains that are successful in one of these countries tend to be successful in the others as well.

International expansion decisions should consider CD as well as geography.

# LO3 How Is Culture Learned?

Culture is a learned process. Consumers learn culture through one of two socialization processes discussed in this section. **Socialization** involves learning through observation and the active processing of information about lived, everyday experience. The process takes place in a sequence something like this:

Social interaction ↦ modeling ↦ reinforcement

As consumers interact they begin to model (meaning enact) behaviors learned or seen. Reinforcement occurs through the process of rewarding reactions or sanctions. Additionally, learning results in CSVs that are relatively enduring. Societal values are not easily changed, and the clash between peoples with differing CSVs has been around since the beginning of time.

## ENCULTURATION

The most basic way by which consumers learn a culture is through an enculturation process. **Enculturation** represents the way a person learns his or her native culture. In other words, enculturation represents the way in which a consumer learns and develops shared understandings of things with his or her family.

Why do some consumers like wasabi or hot peppers? The answer is enculturation. Consumers are not born liking very pungent food. But, early in life, children observe the diets of their parents and relatives and come to mimic those behaviors. When they do, they receive

**CANZUS** acronym that refers to the close similarity in values between Canada, Australia, New Zealand, and the United States

**socialization** learning through observation of and the active processing of information about lived, everyday experience

**enculturation** way a person learns his or her native culture

### EXHIBIT 8.5
## CSV Difference Scores Relative to American Consumers

|  | Power Distance | Individualism | Masculinity | Uncertainty Avoidance | Long-Term Orientation | Total Distance Score |
|---|---|---|---|---|---|---|
| Australia | −4 | −1 | −1 | 5 | 2 | 6.9 |
| United Kingdom | −5 | −2 | 4 | −11 | −4 | 13.5 |
| Brazil | 29 | −53 | −13 | 30 | 36 | 77.6 |
| Russia | 53 | −52 | −26 | 49 | 26 | 96.3 |
| India | 37 | −43 | −6 | −6 | 32 | 65.7 |
| Pakistan | 15 | −77 | −12 | 24 | −29 | 87.8 |
| China | 40 | −71 | 4 | −6 | 89 | 121.8 |

overt social rewards, thereby reinforcing their dietary choice. In Kyrgyzstan, children grow up drinking fermented mare's milk. Although *Kumis*, the Kyrg name for fermented mare's milk, has what can kindly be called a "peculiar" flavor by most standards, the fact that one grows up drinking it creates the acquired taste that makes it palatable or even tasty. The entire idea of habituation, discussed in an earlier chapter, provides a mechanism that helps make this type of enculturation possible.

## ACCULTURATION

**Acculturation** is the process by which consumers come to learn a culture other than their natural, native culture—that is, the culture to which one may adapt when exposed to a new set of CSVs. Acculturation is a learning process. When a consumer becomes acculturated, chances are that old beliefs have been replaced by new beliefs. Children generally become acculturated more quickly than adults because the old rules are not as old and thereby less resistant to change.[21] Retail managers at Sainsbury's supermarkets in the U.K. are aiming more lines of food products specifically at children. As a marketing tool, this may attract more shoppers, but as an image tool, the move positions Sainsbury's as a more healthy alternative for children.[22]

Not all consumers who are introduced into a new culture acculturate. Several factors can inhibit acculturation. For example, strong **ethnic identification**, the degree to which consumers feel a sense of belonging to the culture of their ethnic origins, can make consumers feel close-minded about adopting products from a different culture. When ethnic identification is strong,

consumers in a new land may even avoid learning the language of a new land. For instance, pockets of Chinese immigrants in Canada with strong ethnic identification choose to live the majority of their lives interacting with only other Chinese immigrants, purchasing Chinese products nearly exclusively, and paying attention to only Chinese language media.[23]

**Consumer ethnocentrism** is a belief among consumers that their ethnic group is superior to others and that the products that come from their native land are superior to other products. Consumers who are highly ethnocentric believe that it is only right to support workers in their native country by buying products from that country. Ethnocentrism is highly related to the concept of uncertainty avoidance. When ethnocentrism is very high, consumers who are in a foreign land may create their own communities within a larger enclave and display little interaction with the "outside world." Many Turkish neighborhoods exist in Germany, for instance, and many of these Turks have little contact with people outside their own neighborhoods.

Exhibit 8.6 illustrates factors that either inhibit or encourage consumer acculturation. Simply put, male consumers who have high ethnic identification, high ethnocentrism, and are relatively old, are the worst targets for adopting products of a different or new culture. Interestingly, from an international marketing perspective, CSV profiles characterized by high uncertainty avoidance and strong masculinity are likely not good targets for imported goods relative to other countries. The inhibitions that consumers have about "foreign" products distract from the value the products offer because their very meaning is inconsistent with the consumer's current belief structure.

## QUARTET OF INSTITUTIONS

Consumers *get* culture through either enculturation or acculturation. Each of these is a learning process. Consumers learn primarily through the influence of cultural institutions. Previously, consumer behavior theory suggested that a triad of institutions accounted for much of the cultural learning process. However, more recently a fourth institution has been recognized. Thus, we now recognize a **quartet of institutions** that

© ISTOCKPHOTO.COM/-KUBA-

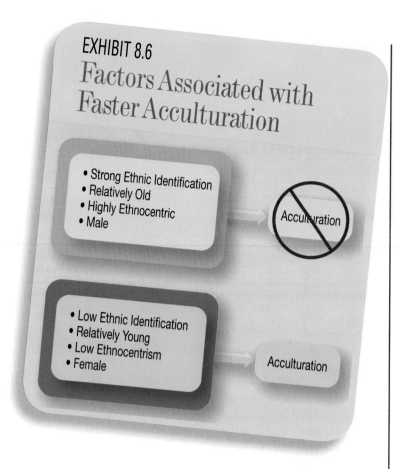

## EXHIBIT 8.6
## Factors Associated with Faster Acculturation

- Strong Ethnic Identification
- Relatively Old
- Highly Ethnocentric
- Male

→ Acculturation (prohibited)

- Low Ethnic Identification
- Relatively Young
- Low Ethnocentrism
- Female

→ Acculturation

1. **Family**
2. **School**
3. **Church**
4. **Media**

Family, school, and church have long been recognized as primary agents for acculturation and enculturation. Each of these is recognized as a vehicle for teaching values to children; therefore, they are agents of enculturation. Consumers become socialized by the behaviors that are affiliated with specific institutions.

More recently the impact of media on culture has been recognized. For instance, many nations actively limit the amount of American media that is allowed in the belief that this will protect their culture from becoming overly Americanized or Westernized. An influx of nonnative media can indeed influence the rate of acculturation.[24] In addition, children who watch more television have a more distorted view of reality, and generally presume that the typical family owns more luxury items and is better off materialistically than families in that particular culture really are. Children who watch more television become more acculturated to consumer society and are more materialistic than children who view less television.[25] Therefore, many families try to actively limit the amount of television viewed by their children.[26]

## Culture and Policy-Related Consumer Communication

Differences in CSVs may have public policy implications as well. A study of teen consumers in countries such as Italy, Austria, Slovenia, Uzbekistan, Russia, and the United States, among others, found that antismoking ads were not equally effective. The results suggest that antismoking ads targeted toward countries high in individualism should emphasize the ill effects, to individuals, of smoking. In contrast, in countries with high collectivism, antismoking ads that emphasize the negative effects of smoking to other consumers are more effective.[27]

Studies measuring CSV among consumers still show distinctions consistent with the profiles discussed earlier. Thus, beyond the teen years particularly, differences in tastes, political views, and preferences are expected to remain consistent within cultures.

are responsible for communicating the CSV through both formal and informal processes from one generation to another. The four institutions comprising the quartet are (see Exhibit 8.7):

## EXHIBIT 8.7
## The Quartet of Institutions

Church

What should I do today? What do I value?

Family

School

Media

© RAJESH JANTILAL/AFP/GETTY IMAGES

## Modeling

Modeling is an important way in which consumers are socialized into a specific culture either through acculturation or enculturation. A famous cliché says that imitation is the sincerest form of flattery. Well, **modeling** is precisely a process of imitating others' behavior.

Young children, for instance, observe their parents and model their behavior—at least until adolescence. As children become older, they may choose to model the behavior of older peers more than they model that of their parents. Adolescent children's attitudes toward smoking, as well as their actual smoking behavior, are largely influenced by the activities of peer referents.[28] In other words, adolescents will tend to model the behavior of those they aspire to be like. The 2010 World Cup created a sensation for the vuvuzela, as young soccer fans across the country modeled the behavior of World Cup attendees by seeking out the long, colorful, and obnoxious-sounding horns. A small company in Alabama cashed in by anticipating the craze and selling 30,000 vuvuzelas in a few weeks time.[29] Exhibit 8.8 displays ways that institutions facilitate modeling.

> Consumers model each other, particularly for novel products like this.

## Shaping

The instrumental conditioning process of shaping plays a key role as consumers' behavior slowly adapts to a culture through a series of rewards and sanctions. Shaping is a socialization process by which consumers' behaviors slowly adapt to a culture through a series of rewards and sanctions. Think about how one might modify his or her behavior to win acceptance from a group. A child might decide to wear different clothes to school as a way of trying to fit in. The way that other students react to the new attire can serve to shape the student's future behavior.

The CSV profile of a culture can influence the effectiveness of cultural shaping. For instance, more individualistic cultures are less susceptible to these types of normative influences.[30] Not all cultures reward complaining in the same way.[31] In collectivistic cultures, complaining can be a sign of disrespect and may be looked at as inappropriate for minor inconveniences. American consumers who complain about their hotel room being slightly too warm are not likely to risk sanction. However, in a more collectivistic culture, complaining about a room that is slightly warm can be looked down upon. The extra added value that comes from group acceptance is greater among cultures where collectivism is stronger than individualism.

## EXHIBIT 8.8
## Modeling and the Quartet

| Institution | Behavior | Description |
|---|---|---|
| School | Studying | Lower classmen follow the study habits of the upper classmen. If Thursday is party-night, chances are you don't study then. |
| Family | Table manners | Children observe parents to learn how to behave at the table. |
| Church | Prayer | People observe others in the church to learn the appropriate way to behave when in a church. |
| Media | Language | Consumers learn slang by repeating terms learned through television, movies, music, and Internet media. |

# Somebody's Watching Me.

AP IMAGES/ANDY WONG

**S**ome governments certainly believe that electronic media can affect the core societal values of consumers. Chinese officials are actively engaged in censoring Internet sites. This censorship has caused problems for companies like Google, Microsoft, and Yahoo!, all of which face U.S. scrutiny for participating in censorship. Google actually places a disclaimer along with its searches that notifies the Chinese consumer of censorship. Partly as a result, Baidu, a search engine originating in China, has grown tremendously as Chinese consumers see disclaimers from Western search engines as rebellious. Baidu also participates in the censorship but does so without resistance and with no disclaimers. The acceptance of censorship may be a clear demonstration of the high uncertainty avoidance present in Chinese culture. Baidu's revenue is approaching the $1 billion mark and they are expanding beyond China. In 2010, RIM (the makers of BlackBerry®) introduced the Torch into new markets, while at the same time facing problems with some governments such as the U.A.E. and Saudi Arabia. Both countries threaten to discontinue BlackBerry service unless RIM agrees to share with these governments the encrypted messages consumers send. Culture affects the way consumers view privacy. How do you feel?

Sources: Dvorak, P. and S. Said (2010), "Saudi Ban Rains on RIM's Party," The *Wall Street Journal* (August 4), B1; Fletcher, O. (2010), "Baidu's CEO Pursues Long-Term Growth," *The Wall Street Journal* (August 4), B8.

# LO4 Fundamental Elements of Communication

## VERBAL COMMUNICATION

**O**bviously, language can sometimes be a problem. Anyone who has ever needed directions to some location in a place where he or she doesn't know the language can appreciate this. Sometimes, even when the correct language is used, communication can still be awkward or difficult. The term *Chinglish* is used to refer to the awkward use of English traditionally common in China.[32]

In this section, **verbal communication** refers to the transfer of information through either the literal spoken or written word. Consumers will have difficulty finding value in things they cannot understand. Marketers have long wrestled with the problem of translating advertisements, research instruments, product labels, and promotional materials into foreign languages for foreign markets. This problem is only made more prevalent in today's truly international marketplace.

Verbal communication can even be difficult within a single language. Almost every language is spoken slightly differently from place to place—or with several unique **dialects**. English in the United States isn't exactly the same as English in England, which is not the same as English in Australia, which is not the same as English in Ireland. Thus, translation alone is insufficient to guarantee effective communication. Exhibit 8.9 provides some examples of difficulties in communicating even simple ideas through the spoken or written word. And, we are not even considering the complications added by slang!

### Translation Equivalence

Bilingual speakers realize that there is often more than one way to express the meaning of a word or phrase in one language when speaking in a second language. In some cases, words that exist in one language have no precise equivalent in another language. In other instances, even when the same word may exist, people in other cultures do not use the word the same way. Thus, interpretation errors and blunders occur unless one takes great care.

**metric equivalence** statistical tests used to validate the way people use numbers to represent quantities across cultures

**translational equivalence** two phrases share the same precise meaning in two different cultures

**Translational equivalence** exists when two phrases share the same precise meaning in two different cultures. Translation–back translation is a way to try to produce translational equivalence. With this process, one bilingual speaker takes the original phrase and translates it from the original language into the new language. Then, a second, independent bilingual speaker translates the phrase from the new language back into the original language. Assuming the retranslated phrase matches the first, translational equivalence exists. If not, either the phrase needs to be dropped, or more work involving other speakers fluent in both languages may be needed to determine if a common meaning can be found by changing the words in one or both languages.

## Metric Equivalence

Once a common meaning is established, things could still go wrong when consumer researchers compare consumer reactions from one country with those from another. Researchers who apply typical survey techniques, such as Likert scales or semantic differentials, may wish to compare scores from one culture with those from another. This is valid only if the two culture–languages use numbers in a somewhat similar fashion. For example, if a Chinese consumer rated a 5-foot 2-inch young woman for height, she might be rated quite tall. However, if a Norwegian rated the same person, she would be rated as quite short.

**Metric equivalence** refers to the state in which consumers are shown to use numbers to represent quantities the same way across cultures. Metric equivalence is necessary to draw basic comparisons about consumers from different countries concerning important consumer relationships. Comparing average scores for consumer attitudes from one culture to the next requires another form of equivalence known as scalar equivalence. The procedures for performing tests of metric equivalence are beyond the scope of this text, but students of consumer behavior and international marketing should be aware of these approaches because comparing quantities across cultures can be tricky.[33]

## EXHIBIT 8.9
# Example Problems with Verbal Communication

| Communication | Situation | Intended Communication | Problem |
|---|---|---|---|
| "Yo vi la Papa!" | Spanish-language slogan on t-shirts prior to Pope's visit to Mexico | "I saw the Pope!" | "La Papa" is "the potato." El (or al) Papa is the Pope. So, the t-shirts said "I saw the potato." |
| "Boy, am I stuffed!" | English-language restaurant slogan spoken by middle-aged man. | "Boy, am I full!" (meaning had a lot to eat) | Slogan works fine in the United States; however, in Australia, "stuffed" means pregnant. So, slogan depicts middle-aged, slightly overweight man saying "Boy, am I pregnant!" |
| "Strawberry Crap Dessert" | English placed on pre-prepared, refrigerated pancakes by Japanese firm intending product for Chinese market. | "Strawberry crêpe" | English can convey a quality image to products in much of Asia even if most consumers can't read the words. Here, the phonics are probably just a little off. |
| "Bite the waxed tadpole" | Chinese label for Coca-Cola | "Coca-Cola" | Coke tried to find the best phonetic way to produce something sounding like "Coca-Cola." In some Chinese dialects, but not all, strange interpretations like this resulted. |
| "Mist-stick!" | Clairol's name for a new hair care product introduced in Germany | Literally a Mist Stick that helped to tame unmanageable hair. | The English "mist stick" phonetically sounds like "miststueck" which is at best an impolite German word to use as a name for a women's product! |

小 心 滑 倒

**CAUTIOU SUIPPERY**

© JON BOWER CHINA / ALAMY

# What Do You Get When You Cross Chinese and English? Lost!

During the 2008 Olympics, thousands upon thousands of visitors flocked to China. Chinese officials launched a campaign to clean up something they felt was embarrassing, but that others felt was charming. What were they cleaning up? It was Chinglish, the awkward English translations of simple phrases, which exists throughout China. Imagine encountering signs with the following messages:

- Execution in progress!
- The slippery are very crafty.
- Dongda Hospital for Anus and Intestine Disease Beijing
- Show mercy to the Slender Grass.
- Be careful not to let skies fall.

China is not alone in slip-ups like these, and the international traveler can be both bewildered and amused. Retailers and service providers operating internationally need to take care that their translations are accurate and send the right message. Obviously, the Chinese government understands that even nonnative words can shape a consumer's image of a country or brand.

Okay, here is the intended meaning of the lines above, respectively: Caution—work in progress, Wet floor, Proctology hospital, Keep off the grass, and Hold on to your skis so they don't fall (from a chair lift)!

Sources: Xinhua (2007), "Ahead of Olympics, Beijing Says Goodbye to 'Chinglish,'" *Yahoo Sports India*, **http://in.sports.yahoo.com/070929/43/6lcge.html**, accessed February 20, 2008; Fong, Mei (2007), "Tired of Laughter, Beijing Gets Rid of Bad Translations," *The Wall Street Journal* (February 5), A1.

# NONVERBAL COMMUNICATION

A conductor at a train station in Germany is approached by an American tourist who wants to know how many stops it will be until he reaches his destination. The train is noisy and filled with people, so the conductor holds up his pointer finger in response. When the train stops, the tourist quickly exits. However, he'll soon realize he is not in the right location. Why? In Germany, one would be indicated by holding up the thumb.

**Nonverbal communication** refers to information passed through some nonverbal act—in other words, communication not involving the literal spoken or written word. This example illustrates intentional nonverbal communication; however, much communication through this means is unintentional or automatic. Many nonverbal communication cues are culturally laden so that the meaning depends on culture.

Exhibit 8.10 depicts several aspects of nonverbal communication and the way they come together to create effective communication. High-context cultures emphasize communication through nonverbal elements. In contrast, low-context cultures, such as Germany, emphasize the spoken word, and what you say is truly what you mean. The elements of nonverbal communication are touched on briefly in the following sections.

## Time

In America, the expression "time is money" is often used. Americans typically place a high value on time and timeliness. The high value placed on timeliness may be due to the importance of individualism and achievement as core values. When an American consumer plans a formal dinner meeting for 7:30 P.M., he or she expects everyone to be present at 7:30 P.M.

Consumers from some other cultures do not value timeliness in the same way. For example, in Spain, where individualism is much lower than in the United States, a formal dinner scheduled for 9:00 P.M. will certainly not begin at 9:00 P.M. The exact starting time is uncertain, but dinner will almost certainly not be served until sometime much later than 9:00 P.M.

Consistent with high long-term orientation, Asian cultures exhibit much patience. Thus, while CANZUS and many Western European salespeople will want to close a sale on the first meeting, such an approach with Asian buyers will not come across well. Asian exchange partners need time to get to know one another and are not anxious to either close a sale or be closed until *guanxi* is established.

## Mannerisms/Body Language

**Body language** refers to the nonverbal communication cues signaled by somatic (uncontrollable biological) responses. Consumers may use certain mannerisms when discussing issues with other consumers or salespeople. These cues can be more telling than the words that are spoken. The mannerisms that reveal meaning include the following characteristics:

- Facial expressions
- Posture
- Arm/leg position
- Skin conditions
- Voice

Most consumers sometimes have to pretend to be happy. This requires a fake smile. While most people can easily make their mouths produce a grin, true happiness would also be indicated by smiling eyebrows, slightly dilated pupils, and a tilted head (back). Similarly, the posture of a truly happy person generally indicates a willingness to approach the object of the emotion. Salespeople can be trained to detect if a consumer is truly experiencing pleasant emotion or if they are only pretending by close observation of facial expressions and posture.

Service providers may be successful in trying to guess which consumers will complain out of anger long before any negative words are voiced.[34] Thus, if anger is detected, intervention may actually turn the experience into something positive through proactive measures to remedy the situation causing the anger.

In today's virtual marketplace, nonverbal communication extends to virtual employees. Marketers are currently studying the mannerisms of avatars to investigate the way their messages are interpreted. In other words, how do you make an avatar seem agreeable, or disagreeable, or welcoming, or even trustful? Currently, the effects of avatars alone are small; however, the combination of verbal communication and use of an avatar may contribute to higher trust and to increased hedonic value from the shopping experience.[35] So, an interesting question for web retailers is how to get an avatar to communicate a message that will be understood by all consumers.

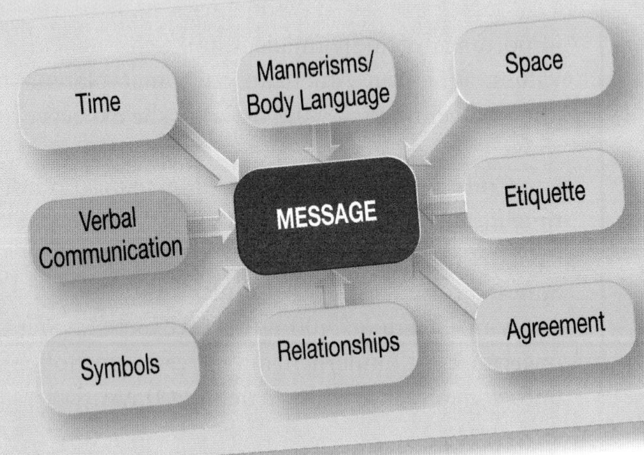

## Space

In places like the United States and Australia, there is a lot of space! Relative to many parts of the world, like Japan or Western Europe, the United States and Australia are sparsely populated. Thus, space varies in importance. The typical consumer in Seoul lives in a large high-rise condominium, in a small flat identical to that of many neighbors living in the same building. For many Americans or Australians, the fact that so many people would be packed into a tight space may make them uncomfortable. For citizens of Seoul, being very close to other people is a fact of life.

The value that consumers place on space affects communication styles. Generally, CANZUS consumers, for instance, do not like to be too close to each other. When having a conversation, they remain at "arm's length." However, Italian, Armenian, or many Arabian consumers are comfortable communicating when they are so close to each other that they are physically touching. The CANZUS consumer engaged in a conversation with an Armenian, for instance, will likely automatically try to obtain some space in the conversation by leaning backward at the waist, as if an escape were possible! The differing approaches to space have implications for sales approaches, the

**EXHIBIT 8.10**

## Nonverbal Communication Affects the Message Comprehended

Time · Mannerisms/Body Language · Space · Verbal Communication · MESSAGE · Etiquette · Symbols · Relationships · Agreement

*Body language communicates, as this message illustrates.*

way other consumers are depicted in advertising, and the design of retail environments.

## Etiquette/Manners

When Americans greet each other, the typical response, particularly if a man is involved, is a handshake. Different handshakes may communicate different impressions. However, Asian consumers would expect a bow as a greeting and show of respect. Many Europeans may plant a kiss or two on the cheek. Greeting a business client with a kiss on the cheek would be a definite no-no in the United States; however, in France, a couple of kisses to the cheek could be an appropriate greeting.

Different cultures have different etiquettes for handling various social situations. **Etiquette** represents the customary mannerisms consumers use in common social situations. Dining etiquette varies considerably from one culture to another. In the United States, a consumer cuts food with the right hand, places the knife down, then places a fork in the right hand to place food into his or her mouth. In Europe, however, good manners dictate that the knife stays in the right hand and the fork in the other. One cuts with the right hand and uses the left to efficiently scoop food into one's mouth. In any event, violating etiquette can lead to a cultural sanction.

**etiquette** customary mannerisms consumers use in common social situations

Service providers need to be sensitive to the various differences in etiquette. For example, although no formal airline passenger etiquette exists, there is an informal code, and passengers who break these unwritten rules can actually decrease the satisfaction of other passengers. This situation is exaggerated on airlines carrying multinational groups of passengers. These passengers have different rules about space, privacy, dress, and hygiene. Passengers with body odor or who dress inappropriately (for example, a man wearing a tank top is generally considered inappropriate for such close company in Western cultures) can ruin the experience for other consumers. When consumers are unaware or lack concern for the proper etiquette in a given situation, the result can be awkward and diminish the value of the experience.

## Relationships

How do consumers respond to attempts by marketers to build a personal relationship? Earlier, we discussed the Asian principle of *guanxi* and the different ways that a relationship may develop under this principle as opposed to conventional Western principles. Differing CSVs have other implications for consumer–brand or consumer–service provider relationships.

For example, with high collectivism, the idea of a relationship is no longer personal. Consumers from collectivist nations define relationships in terms of the ties between a brand or service provider and a family or relevant group of consumers. Therefore, marketing appeals aimed at building personal relationships should emphasize the collective preference of this group rather than the individual.[36]

## Agreement

How is agreement indicated and what does it mean? An Asian consumer who responds to a sales appeal with "Yes" is not indicating agreement. Instead, this "Yes" is more a way of indicating that he or she understands what is being said. Further, many Asian cultures will avoid strong affirmative or negative responses and instead use expressions like "That is possible" or "That may be difficult" to indicate agreement or lack of agreement.

Additionally, the extent to which a contract is seen as binding varies from place to place. Traditionally, South Koreans are not accustomed to signing contracts. The fact that one would be asked to sign such an agreement might be viewed as an insult. Thus, Western firms may have to adjust their practices to indicate formal agreements when doing business in these cultures.

## Symbols

The chapter began by emphasizing the link between culture and meaning. Because different cultures have different value profiles, objects and activities take on different symbolic or semiotic meaning. Perhaps nowhere is this more obvious than in the arena of religious objects. A large wooden cross is a device used to execute people in some cultures, but to Christians, a cross is an important symbol signifying everlasting life.

The symbolic meaning of objects also affects gift-giving from culture to culture. In some Western cultures, particularly among French cultures including Quebec and south Louisiana, a knife is regarded as an inappropriate gift because a knife symbolizes cutting a relationship. In China, clocks and watches are inappropriate gift items because they symbolize the finite nature of life—time is running out. Also, in Japan, the term *omiyage* refers to the custom of bringing gifts to friends from foreign trips. In particular, an omiyage gift of a famous brand can help symbolize freedom for the typical female office worker.[37] Marketers need to take care against unintentionally promoting offensive items based on cultural symbolism.

## Just over 1 billion consumers live in India. Today, the largest group of consumers in India is between 12 and 20 years old.

# Deutschland Donald

**E**ven the communication of the words, actions and symbolic meaning of cartoon characters changes with culture. Americans clearly have an affinity for Donald Duck—the ill-tempered Disney duck. But that affinity is surpassed by that of German consumers. Germans purchase over 250,000 copies of Donald Duck comic books each week. Why? In Germany, Donald Duck, who looks and sounds the same as in the United States, has a philosophical meaning over and above his free-spirited mannerisms. His popularity exceeds that of his less complex American counterpart.

Source: Bernofsky, S. (2009), "Why Donald Duck is the Jerry Lewis of Germany," *The Wall Street Journal* (May 25), **http://air.wsj.com,** accessed May 25, 2009.

© WONDERFUL WORLD OF DISNEY, THE, DONALD DUCK, 1997 / EVERETT COLLECTION

# LO5 Emerging Cultures

**m**arketing efforts are largely directed at consumers from developed nations. However, less-developed nations can offer attractive markets and many may represent emerging economies. Even low-income consumers in Third World nations can represent attractive markets to serve, particularly if low-priced, basic products can be offered. Market segments in developing nations offer tremendous opportunities, but communicating and delivering value in these segments means that the nuances of culture must be known and understood.

Exhibit 8.11 displays the most attractive national consumer markets. Countries like the United States, United Kingdom, and Germany have long been recognized as important consumer markets; however, many nations on this list are emerging, in the sense that they would not have been considered leading consumer markets a decade or two ago. Sociopolitical changes have allowed these markets to emerge.

# BRIC MARKETS

As discussed previously, the acronym BRIC stands for Brazil, Russia, India, and China. These four nations are often singled out as having economies that are growing very rapidly. In each market, large middle classes are emerging as consumers who formerly would have had little opportunity for a good job benefit from corporate capital investment. As a result, consumers in these nations have rising standards of living, and they have become attractive markets for many goods and services.

Exhibit 8.12 tracks the **purchasing power parity (PPP)** of the 10 most attractive consumer markets. The PPP gives an idea of the total size of the consumer market in each country in terms of total buying power. By 2020, China is expected to match or exceed the total purchasing power of the United States.

# CHINDIA

The term **Chindia** refers to the combined market and business potential of China and India. The consumer demographics of India today compare favorably to those of the United States in 1970. Just over one billion consumers live in India. Today, the largest group of consumers is between 12 and 20 years old. This cohort group is similar to the baby-boomer generation in the United States, which was responsible for tremendous economic growth domestically and abroad.

Over 185 million households call India home. Today, 135 million of those households are considered aspiring consumers, with equivalent household incomes under $2,500 per year. However, by 2010, expectations are that the Indian middle class will total just over 100 million households—doubling its size in less than a decade. As Indian incomes rise, the market potential of India expands as well.

The market potential for India and China is made clear in the fact that population is assessed in billions rather than millions. The key for marketers in providing to the typical Chinese or Indian consumer is to provide a functional product to consumers who are unaccustomed to elaborately designed products and who, to a large extent, are unable to read or write very well. Even inexpensive products can mean a lot of revenue for a company selling to the large Chindian populations.

# GLOCALIZATION

How should a company from another country appeal to these emerging foreign consumer markets? Certainly, these countries offer a significantly different CSV profile than

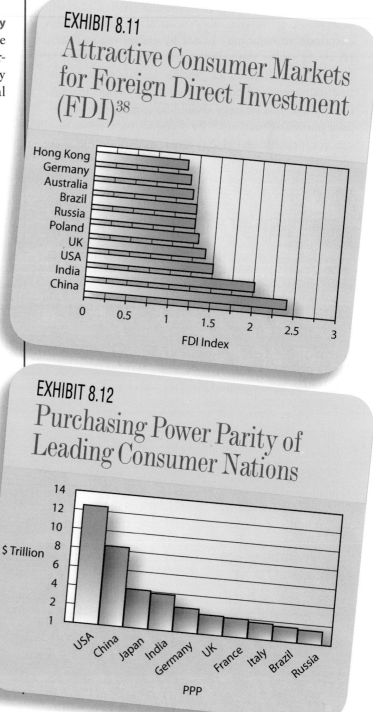

**EXHIBIT 8.11**
## Attractive Consumer Markets for Foreign Direct Investment (FDI)[38]

FDI Index

(bars for: Hong Kong, Germany, Australia, Brazil, Russia, Poland, UK, USA, India, China; axis 0 to 3)

**EXHIBIT 8.12**
## Purchasing Power Parity of Leading Consumer Nations

$ Trillion (axis 1 to 14)

PPP

(bars for: USA, China, Japan, India, Germany, UK, France, Italy, Brazil, Russia) those in the United States. The term *glocalization* represents one alternative that allows flexibility in responding to the unique value profiles of consumers. **Glocalization** represents the idea that the marketing strategy may be global, but the implementation of that strategy at the marketing tactics level should be local.

Reef Brazil beachwear (**www.reef.com**) executes a global branding strategy that appeals to the youth market by portraying a cool, carefree image.[39] This corporate strategy may be set by executives in Brazil. However, rather than dictate how this plan would be implemented, Reef could practice glocalization by letting managers and consultants in the foreign markets decide how this strategy should be carried out in their own particular markets.[40] By doing so, local consumers can comprehend the global theme and share the same meaning for the brand.

## What's Next?

During the Cold War, consumer markets like those in Russia and China were hardly seen as attractive to marketers in North America and Europe. However, times have changed. The advancement of free market economies has led to increased standards of living in many corners of the globe.

However, the fact is that half the world's consumer population remains illiterate and struggles to maintain anything more than a meager way of life. As the emerging economies advance today, so will the cost of doing business in those countries. Companies will search for cheaper places to do business and through this process, new emerging economies will develop. Much of Africa, for example, remains without the type of industrial or technological development necessary to create good jobs and the incomes that lead to a higher standard of living. Africa has a total population of nearly 800 million people. Even though parts of South Africa and northern Africa are developed, much of the rest remains destitute. Perhaps this area too will be a new emerging market later in this century.

Like other places though, the cultural barriers presented there are more than trivial. The cultural barriers go beyond dealing with consumers, but are also engrained in the sociopolitical environment. Therefore, changes in government institutions will probably be needed before many companies will feel comfortable doing business there.[41]

# 8 Study Tools

**Located at the back of the textbook**

❏ Rip-out Chapter-in-Review Card

**Located at www.cengagebrain.com**

❏ Review Key Terms Flashcards (Print or Online)

❏ Download audio summaries to review on the go

❏ Complete practice quizzes to prepare for tests

❏ Play "Beat the Clock" and "Quizbowl" to master concepts

❏ Watch Video on Method for a real company example

## what others have thought...

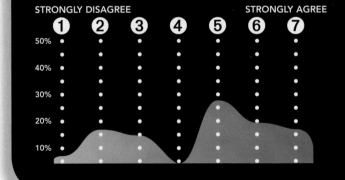

STRONGLY DISAGREE ① ② ③ ④ ⑤ STRONGLY AGREE ⑥ ⑦

50% 40% 30% 20% 10%

### Men should always pay for their date's dinner.

Opinions are almost evenly split on this question but most interestingly, nobody is neutral! Approximately 40 percent of respondents express some level of disagreement, leaving nearly 60 percent expressing some agreement. The neutral response accounts for practically no respondents!

# Microculture

membership changes the value of things.

## What do you think?

**The microcultures I belong to greatly influence the value I receive from products.**

STRONGLY DISAGREE ① ② ③ ④ ⑤ ⑥ ⑦ STRONGLY AGREE

Visit CourseMate at www.cengagebrain.com.

# 9 Microcultures

## LO1 Microculture and Consumer Behavior

the climate is remarkable in many ways. On a June day, Kevin drives westward through northern California, and in just a few minutes time the temperature indicator on the car has fluctuated from 92 to 58 degrees. The sky has gone from absolutely clear to partly cloudy to a foggy mist. East of a ridge it is hot and dry, west of a ridge, cool and damp. Drive into a valley, and it is something in between. Meteorologists explain that regional climates contain many microclimates within them. Many Americans envy Californians because of the good weather associated with California. But truly, California's weather presents many different climates. The microclimates that exist throughout central and northern California are responsible for high quality grapes that are used to make many outstanding wines.

In a similar way, we can think of a given culture containing multiple smaller and more specific microcultures. A **microculture** is indeed a culture, only smaller. We define a microculture as a group of people who share similar values and tastes that are subsumed within a larger culture. The smaller group can be quite distinct from the larger group or overall culture. The term *subculture* is often used to capture much the same idea as microculture. However, the term *microculture* is used here to portray the idea that the group is smaller but in no way less significant in terms of the potential influence on consumer behavior. You may notice that the microculture concept is similar in some ways to the group influence topic. Microcultures, however, are generally based on specific variables that we detail in this chapter. How many microcultures do you belong to? Let's take a look.

> **microculture** a group of people who share similar values and tastes that are subsumed within a larger culture

After studying this chapter, you should be able to:

**LO1** Apply the concept of microculture as it influences consumer behavior.

**LO2** Know the major U.S. microcultural groups.

**LO3** Realize that microculture is not a uniquely American phenomenon.

**LO4** Perform a demographic analysis.

**LO5** Identify major cultural and demographic trends.

# CULTURE IS HIERARCHICAL

Culture is a universal phenomenon. It is everywhere and ultimately explains the habits and idiosyncrasies of all groups of consumers. In fact, each consumer belongs to many

*Each microculture brings with it role expectations for its members.*

cultural groups – or more precisely, they move in and out of microcultures. For instance, a college student from Texas who is attending a state university in that state is likely part of American culture, Texas culture, an ethnically defined culture such as Hispanic culture, university culture, and possibly Greek culture, should he or she belong to a fraternity or sorority. In this way, culture is hierarchical. A consumer belongs to one large, overall culture and then to many smaller cultural groups—microcultures—existing and interlinking within the overall culture. Exhibit 9.1 illustrates a cultural hierarchy.

Each microculture brings with it role expectations for its members. The role provides a signal as to the behaviors that one should perform to truly belong to the group; or,

in other words, what it takes to be an authentic member of the group.[1] Obviously, some of the roles are inconsistent with each group and the consumer makes a choice to behave in ways more consistent with one group than with another. When a consumer faces a situation involving conflicting expectations based on cultural expectations, he or she is experiencing **role conflict**. For instance, when students attend a career fair for the first time they may experience some conflict over how to dress. Sorority sisters may see a certain outfit as business attire but the career-oriented woman representing a company at the event may see it as too sexy and inappropriate for the office.

The fact that the college student mentioned earlier is a Texan clearly typifies culture. Texas has a unique and identifiable culture, and this point is illustrated by the fact that by now, the reader has an image of a Texan in mind. In other words, consumers have generally consistent associations with the "Texan" social schema. A college student who wears boots, jeans, and a Stetson in Massachusetts may stand out in the crowd, but this manner of dress may help a Texan fit in. This particular consumer likely also identifies with a specific age-based or generational culture, and makes consumer choices that either reinforce this social identity or send the signal that he or she does not wish to be part of this group. Think about how these decisions explain simple things like music preferences. Polka music may be traditional in Austria, but an Austrian university student is not likely to find being a huge polka fan very gratifying among his peers. Similarly, an authentic Goth may well have to hide a liking of a country music song or two.

# MICROCULTURAL ROLES AND VALUE

Microculture membership changes the value of things. American consumers, for instance, generally find watching soccer dull, and thus consider it to be a low-value activity. In contrast, soccer is the number one spectator sport all around Europe and in other parts of the world. Cultural groups

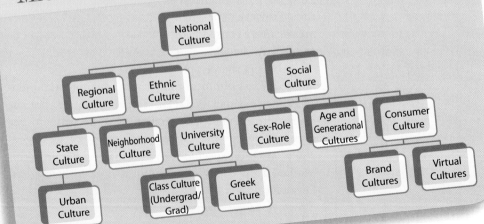

**EXHIBIT 9.1**
## The Hierarchical Nature of Culture and Microculture

In one role, this attire may be culturally acceptable, but in another role, this same attire is unacceptable and could bring sanctions.

even arise within sports fans, and an extreme soccer fan may even become a *soccer hooligan* who participates in extreme and sometimes violent behaviors as a way of creating a personally meaningful soccer experience. Anthropologists have studied this cultural phenomenon by immersing themselves within the hooligan group. Some hooligans are professional people who find involvement in soccer to be a way to escape other realities, and, thus they find hedonic value in hooligan activities. However, when soccer hooligans took up Burberry caps as preferred headwear, young, male British business professionals abandoned the caps so as not to have a preference overlapping that could identify them as a hooligan. We again see how culture is hierarchical in this example. Indeed, consumers often choose membership in microcultures in an effort to stand out or define themselves from the crowd. This phenomenon is known as **divergence**.[2]

## LO2
# Major U.S. Microcultures

**divergence** situation in which consumers choose membership in microcultures in an effort to stand out or define themselves from the crowd

**m**arketers can divide the U.S. population into consumer groups along a number of dimensions relative to market segmentation. These groupings are particularly effective when microcultures are involved because the consumers within these groups likely have very similar preferences. There are many types of microcultures in the United States. These include regional, sex role, age-based, generation, religious, ethnic, income/social class, and street microcultures.

## REGIONAL MICROCULTURE

We don't think about it much today but the U.S. Declaration of Independence declares each of the original 13 colonies "free and independent states." In much of early U.S. history, the country's name was plural. "The United States are free and independent" was a commonly used phrase, as opposed to "The United States is free and independent."[3] Using the plural form more clearly reflects the fact that lifestyles and culture vary as you travel around the United States and North America. Within America, many cultural groups can be identified. In 1981, Joel Garreau published the book *The Nine Nations of North America*.[4] The book identifies nine geographical regions that supposedly share similar value profiles and thus contain consumers with similar preferences. However, they don't neatly fit with conventional regional distinctions. For example, Florida is split with the northern part belonging to "Dixie" and the southern part belonging to "The Islands." Chicago is part of the "Breadbasket" but Indianapolis is part of Dixie. Exhibit 9.2 illustrates this concept.

The relative usefulness of the nine nation approach in segmentation is questionable, but it captures the fact that priorities among consumers do vary regionally.[5] Brand and food preferences, choices of favorite beverages, favorite sports, and even the names of things, vary by region. For example, a soda is something with ice cream in it in the South, but a soda is another term for a soft drink in much of the Northeast. Debating the best

**sex roles** societal expectations for men and women among members of a cultural group

pizza—either Chicago style or New York style—is very likely to get some consumers fighting!

One area in the United States that receives significant attention is the "Borderland" region, a region that was not included in the original *Nine Nations* approach. The Borderland covers the southwestern U.S. states that share a border with Mexico.[6] A large Hispanic population lives in this region and consumer researchers and marketers alike pay close attention to the composition and culture of the region. It is common to experience both Mexican and American culture in the area, and many marketing communications are presented in both English and Spanish.

## SEX-ROLES AND MICROCULTURE

**Sex roles** refer to the societal expectations for men and women among members of a cultural group. Sex roles are ubiquitous in society, and inconsistency with them can be a source of sanctions. The difference between societal expectations of men and women vary less in Western cultures than they do in Eastern cultures, in which sex-based divisions in roles remain more obvious.[7] Recent comparisons of brand personality tend to show greater androgyny—meaning neither clearly male nor female—among U.S. perceptions of brands relative to Korean brands.[8]

## EXHIBIT 9.2
## U.S. Regions

The Nine "Nations" of North America

### Societal Role Expectations

Even in Western cultures, certain responsibilities such as child care and household cleaning are unevenly spread among cultures. In Italy, a relatively feminine culture by Western standards, women spend a great

## EXHIBIT 9.3
## Regional Differences and Preferences among U.S. Consumers

| Actual Place | "9 Nation Region" (Garreau) | Geographical Designation | Core Societal Value Priority | Example Preference |
|---|---|---|---|---|
| Birmingham, AL | Dixie | South | Security and self-respect | Watch 24 |
| Los Angeles, CA | MexAmerica | West | Warm relationships with others and self-fulfillment | In-home cosmetics |
| Boston, MA | New England | Northeast | Sense of accomplishment | VW Rabbits |
| Chicago, IL | Breadbasket | Midwest | Security and warm relationships | Chicago pizza |

deal of time keeping their houses clean. Even an Italian woman who works outside of the home is likely to wash the floors of her home at least twice a week. Women who do not work outside the home likely wash the floors nearly every day. In addition, they tend to use stronger cleaners than their U.S. counterparts. Clearly, all of this cleaning provides utilitarian value through the result of a clean house, but Italian women also take inner gratification from the activities because they help fulfill their specific societal sex role.[9] In Western culture, men have traditionally picked up the tab during a date, but as cultures become more androgynous, this tradition may be falling by the wayside.

Marketers need to be aware of the relative sex roles within societies. Men and women may share purchasing responsibilities differently from culture to culture. In the United States, the woman in the family remains the primary purchasing agent for most things. Men are generally allowed to make purchase decisions for things such as lawn care equipment and beer. Men also play a much larger role in the purchase of big-ticket items. Women tend to purchase the majority of clothing for males in U.S. households. However, in Italy, men place great pride in their business attire and are more likely to want control of these purchase decisions. Marketers therefore need to do research to help identify these roles, or else run the risk of targeting the wrong family member with marketing communications.

## Male and Female Segments

A great deal of marketing communication is directed toward either a male or female market segment. Media are often distinguished easily based on the proportion of male and female customers. ESPN channels, for example, offer an opportunity to reach out to a predominantly male market. *Cosmopolitan* and *Harper's Bazaar* magazines offer an opportunity to reach a female market. These media clearly contain appeals geared toward the respective sex.

Although role expectations associate certain types of purchases with men or women, marketers sometimes reach out to the opposite sex. Men traditionally are the household buying agent for electronics. However,

Best Buy altered its marketing strategy in a special effort to appeal to female shoppers. Consumer research showed that women were not particularly enamored with the Big Box format, so Best Buy launched Best Buy Mobile. Best Buy Mobile units are relatively small and located in shopping centers and malls.[10] Now, female consumers are exposed to electronic gadgets in an environment more suited to their tastes. Marketers outside the United States are also taking this approach. Vespa, the world's top name in scooters, redesigned their basic model into the "Indian Vespa" by adding a foot-rest extension to the left side because Indian women, who wear relatively close-fitting foot-length garments, only ride in a side-saddle style. The effort to provide cheap transportation to relatively low-income women may pay off in a big way in the long run.

Conversely, online fashion retailers like Gilt Groupe and Rue La La have changed their marketing approach to better appeal to men.[11] Currently, only about 1 in 4 adult men regularly purchase clothing products online. These retailers seek to entice more men to their sites by offering more sports-oriented merchandise lines, such as golf apparel. The retailers believe that appealing to men will be successful based on the relatively high amount of disposable income of many middle-aged professional men.

Marketers need to keep in mind that women and men do not make consumer decisions in the same way. Perhaps the biggest difference is in the way men and women process information. Relative to women, men tend to be more heuristic/intuitive in their processing. **Cognitive structuring** is a term that refers to the reliance on schema-based heuristics in making decisions. In contrast, women tend to process information in a more piecemeal fashion.[12] Thus, men are more likely to process information based on the way it is framed and on the categories (schema, stereotypes, scripts) it evokes, rather than on a detailed breakdown of all the information. Interestingly, this doesn't mean that men make poorer choices than women, only that they make them in a different way.

**cognitive structuring**
term that refers to the reliance on schema-based heuristics in making decisions

# AGE-BASED MICROCULTURE

**Age-based microcultures** imply that people of the same age end up sharing many of the same values and develop similar consumer preferences. Perhaps no age-based group receives more attention than teens. Nearly 22,000,000 Americans are between 15 and 19 years of age.[13] Teens seem to share many similar behaviors. In fact, some argue that teen behavior is not just similar within a given country, but similar across countries. Part of the similarity in behavior allows teens to fill the role expectations for a teenager in U.S. society.

## World Teen Culture?

Consumer media involves more than just television. Radio, print publications, music, and web-based communication all can play a role in shaping culture and, therefore, the things that consumers value.[14] The Internet facilitates communication among consumers around the world, contributing to what some believe is a more universally similar **world teen culture**. Evidence of similar tastes among teenaged consumers around the world is obvious if one takes a look at teen purchase and consumption patterns. Many of these tastes are influenced by the Western media's depiction of celebrities. Thus, fashion and entertainment

# Going Retro

Consumer researchers have begun to identify an interesting response to the now dated "metrosexual" movement of men in the United States. Make room for the "retrosexual." Whereas metrosexuals, with their focus on fashion, self-indulgence, shopping, and the blurring of traditional male/female stereotypes, were all the rage in the early 2000s, retrosexuals appear to be gaining ground in today's pop culture, and they are taking a much different approach.

Although the term *retrosexual* is used in different ways, it most commonly refers to men who have returned to the ways of yesteryear by doing things like holding doors for women, paying for dates, and exhibiting chivalry in general towards women—all without a fear of chauvinism. Fashion is still important, but it is different from the trends exhibited by metrosexuals. Some retrosexuals prefer to dress in very "retro" ways, taking fashion tips from decades long past, like the 1930s or '40s. They even listen to jazz and big band music. Brands and fashion are still important for the retrosexual man, but the attitude is vastly different from the metrosexual.

Experts on culture have hypothesized that the blurring of male and female sex roles have led men to seek out the masculinity that marked the male consumer in days gone by. By adopting the retrosexual lifestyle, men draw closer to the more traditional male role. Time will tell if the retrosexual movement is a quickly passing trend or if we can expect the movement to grow. One thing is clear, however; the retrosexual microculture strongly appeals to men who long for the days when "men were men."

Sources: Based on Doll, J. (2010), "New 'Retrosexuals': Really Just Metrosexuals With a Wardrobe Change," *The Village Voice* online edition (April 7), **http://blogs.villagevoice.com/runninscared/archives/2010/04/new_retrosexual.php,** accessed August 10, 2010; Laessig, G. (2010), "Returned Male: 'Retrosexual' Trend Taps Into Desire for Manliness of Yore," (May 21), *Lawrence Journal-World online edition*, **http://www2.ljworld.com/news/2010/may/31/returned-male-retrosexual-trend-taps-desire-manlin/,** accessed August 10, 2010; "Retrosexual Revolution," *District Cut* (July 8, 2010), **http://districtcut.com/2010/07/style-report-retrosexual-revolution.html,** accessed August 10, 2010.

companies in particular may find segmenting based on age as useful as geography.

Brands listed in Exhibit 9.4 have particular appeal to teens in practically all corners of the world. Coca-Cola and McDonald's, for example, are brand names that are listed among teens' favorite brands throughout much of the world.[15] Coca-Cola takes advantage of virtual media to help stay on top. Through the website Second Life, Coke offers opportunities for consumers to build a virtual vending machine which dispenses experiences to loyal Coke drinkers.[16] Thus, Coke is

*Coca-Cola is a favorite among teens worldwide.*

attempting to use the latest media to create virtual experiences that help build loyalty among the teen market segment worldwide.

Although teens around the world may find value in many of the same types of music and clothing, research suggests that the cultural values of their home nation remain relatively distinct from nation to nation, particularly concerning personal products.[17] American teen consumers, for instance, still rate freedom as the most important CSV. In contrast, teens from Arab countries list faith as the most important CSV.[18] These differences translate into different consumption habits. For example, even though McDonald's is popular among teens practically everywhere, preferences for fast-food brands still differ between Asians and Americans.[19] Young consumers from different cultures around the world appear to have similar tastes in apparel.

## GENERATION MICROCULTURE

> **cohort** a group of people who have lived the same major experiences in their life

Age-based groups can be distinguished from generational groups. Consumers grow out of age groups. When a consumer reaches age 20, he or she no longer in the teen microculture. However, he still "belongs" to a group with his peers. Notice that people who age in the same generation still belong to the same cohort. A **cohort** is a group of people who have lived the same major experiences in their life, and the experiences end up shaping their core values. Life experiences have many different effects on a cohort. For instance, while teens tend to share some behaviors in common, such as experimenting with tobacco, their preference for music tends to be much more of a generational effect. Consumers tend to enjoy music from their own generation and each generation seems to carry its taste for music with it to a large extent. Here, we briefly introduce some of the main generational groups in the United States.

### Greatest Generation

The "greatest generation" refers to American consumers born before 1946. They represent nearly 40,000,000 consumers and their lives and values are shaped very much by World War II and their post-war experiences. These consumers tend to be more thrifty than other consumers and thus are highly price conscious. They will spend money but need to be convinced that the product is worth the money before they let go of their money.

### Baby Boomers

The Baby Boomers were born between 1946 and 1965. Over 60,000,000 Americans are Boomers. Boomers were born during a time in the United States that was marked by optimism and relative economic security. This is also a group that came of age during the very turbulent 1960s and they clearly left a mark on popular culture.

Boomers represent a major force in consumer culture and they are a substantial force in the economy. It should not be surprising, therefore, that they receive significant marketing

## EXHIBIT 9.4
## Similarities and Differences among Teen Consumers

| Favorite Brands | Similar Activities | Less Similar Choices |
|---|---|---|
| Coca-Cola | Listening to music | Religious ideas/activities |
| McDonald's | Using mobile phone | Cosmetic brands |
| Nike | Surfing the Internet | Political ideas |
| Disney | Video games | Equality of sexes |
| Cadbury | Smoking | |
| Nokia | | |

attention. Many Boomers have saved significant sums of money for retirement and plan to enjoy good times well into their elderly years. Boomers, by and large, have a huge amount of spending power and relative to other generations, they are characterized by a preference for wine and the finer things.

## Generation X

Generation X consumers were born between 1966 and 1980. They represent just over 40,000,000 consumers. Generation X consumers were long thought to be a group that was marked by alienation and cynicism. They have also been referred to as "latchkey" kids to signify the idea that many of these consumers spent a great deal of time alone due to having both parents at work. Many Generation X'ers also came from divorced households, which may explain why a good number of these consumers today focus strongly on the family and traditional family values. Although marketers often viewed Generation X'ers as slackers, many of these consumers have become successful business people and community leaders. Research also reveals that the majority of these consumers started saving money relatively early in life.[20]

## Millennials

Millennials were born between 1981 and 1995. They represent approximately 60,000,000 consumers. These consumers tend to wholeheartedly embrace technology as no other generation before them. Many of them were cocooned by protective parents when they were young and tend to view technology as a means to build community and relationships. They also tend to keep close contact with their parents.[21] They tend to be relatively impulsive and optimistic. One of the consumer behaviors that millennials enjoy is visiting coffee shops with in-store WiFi. In this way, they stay connected to their friends and to their interests. In fact, they are so technologically savvy that they may be referred to as the "always connected" generation, meaning that they are constantly in touch with other consumers through various technologies.[22]

McCafé products appeal to many consumers who once occupied the Playland out front.

© TIM BOYLE/GETTY IMAGES

## Generational Influence and Marketing

Generations provide a good basis for marketing segments because the consumer's age identifies their generation. Not every person that is age 21 right now matches the tastes of all the other millennial generation consumers, but the largest number of people within a generation are similar to some extent. McDonald's recent strategies illustrate the difference between appealing to an age group versus a cohort group. For decades, practically every McDonalds featured a playground built conspicuously at the front of each restaurant. Not only that, consumers also strongly associated the Happy Meal with McDonald's. Thus, in consumers' long- term memories, McDonald's was strongly defined by the play area, Happy Meals and children. In the past few years, McDonald's has moved away from that strategy and even removed the play areas from many of their restaurants. In some cases, they have been replaced with sections called McCafé. The Happy Meal still remains, but the shift in their marketing corresponds to the fact that they are more interested in serving the markets that grew up playing in the playgrounds and eating Happy Meals, than they are in directly appealing to children themselves. In a way, McDonald's has shifted from looking at the markets based on their age to one where they are capitalizing on a cohort group. Millennial generation consumers won't be found in the play area any longer, but you can still find them at McDonald's.

Generational effects can also explain why country music has changed so dramatically over the years. Have you ever wondered why today's country music doesn't sound like your grandpa's country? The answer lies largely in the fact that many of today's biggest stars grew up listening to classic or even alternative rock music. As you may have noticed, much of country music has a rock-edge sound to it. In some cases, it's even hard to tell the

# The New 40

**Y**ou may have heard it by now, and you'll probably hear it again: "60 is the new 40." This saying highlights the meaning of the phrase "psychological age." Life expectancies are increasing, many older consumers are living very active lifestyles, and a good portion of these consumers have significant spending power. In fact, many consumers actually begin new careers after they retire! In short, "old" isn't "old" anymore.

There is more to the "60 is the new 40" idea, however. What has really taken place is a shift in attitude for all of consumer culture. Older consumers don't only feel younger than ever, in many cases they are actually perceived to be younger by others. This is because younger consumers see their elders playing active roles in society every day. Some readers may even be able to think of certain professional athletes who have pushed age barriers to new limits.

Marketers today often use the phrase the "gray market," rather than the "elderly segment" to highlight the idea that older consumers still lead active, vibrant lives, and still have wants and needs that they seek to fill. Gone are the days when a 60-year-old was assumed to be heading for a retirement home. Today, 60 is the new 40. Tomorrow, what will 70 be?

Sources: Based on de Vries, L. (2007), "Is 60 the New 40 or is 40 the new 60?," *CBS News* online (May 2), **http://www.cbsnews.com/ stories/2007/05/02/opinion/garver/main2751907.shtml,** accessed August 10, 2010; Schreiber, L. (2007), "The New Retirement Attitude – Today's 60 is Yesterday's 40," *Ezine Articles,* **http://ezinearticles.com/?The-New-Retirement-Attitude---Todays-60-is-Yesterdays-40&id=658004,** accessed August 10, 2010; Bogert, R. (2010), "Is 60 the New 40?," *Los Angeles Times* online (January 7), **http:// www.latimes.com/sns-health-60-new-40,0,1525238.story,** accessed August 10, 2010.

religious affiliation provides a basis for microcultures within national or regional cultures. Religion affects all manner of daily life, sometimes even among those who are not devout followers of any religion. For instance, in the United States and throughout the Western world, the weekend occurs on Saturday and Sunday. In Arab lands however, where Islam is the predominant religion, Friday is the day of prayer, so the weekend occurs on Thursday and Friday. Exhibit 9.5 illustrates the proportion of consumers belonging to the main religions in the United States, other diverse nations, and the world at large.

difference between today's country and rock music. Many of today's younger country music stars were just as likely to listen to rock groups such as Van Halen, Aerosmith, or Guns N' Roses when they were growing up as to traditional country legends like Willie Nelson or Johnny Cash. Comparing today's country music star in his 30s with a country music star of the same age in 1950 clearly illustrates how generations change.

## RELIGIOUS MICROCULTURE

Recall that religion represents one of the key institutions that shapes consumer culture. Not surprisingly then,

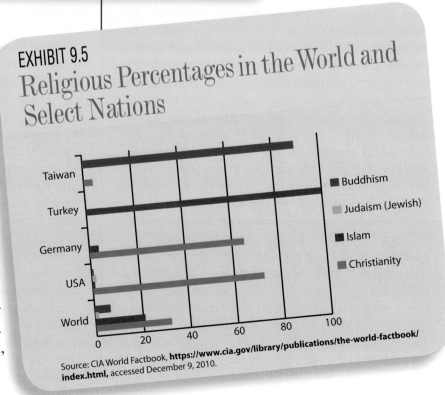

**EXHIBIT 9.5**
## Religious Percentages in the World and Select Nations

Legend: Buddhism, Judaism (Jewish), Islam, Christianity

Countries shown: Taiwan, Turkey, Germany, USA, World

Axis: 0, 20, 40, 60, 80, 100

Source: CIA World Factbook, **https://www.cia.gov/library/publications/the-world-factbook/ index.html,** accessed December 9, 2010.

Perhaps more than in other countries, U.S. Christians represent a large number of different religions. Just over half (51.3 percent) of Americans report belonging to a Protestant religion, with the remainder of Christians being Catholic (23.9 percent). One can hardly say that all Protestant denominations are the same, but generally speaking, Protestants are relatively conservative in their approach to life, and emphasize hard work and accomplishment as important goals. They also tend to be more comfortable with material acquisitions than are Catholics.[23] Some Protestant denominations are more likely than Catholics to have a moral prohibition against the consumption of beer, wine, and other forms of alcoholic beverages. In the southern United States, where large portions of the population belong to relatively conservative Protestant religions such as Southern Baptist or Pentecostal, many counties are "dry," meaning the purchase and/or possession of alcohol is prohibited by law.

Budget allocations also are associated with religion. Church organizations have not been immune from the recent economic downturn. Many Protestant denominations have tithing requirements that strongly encourage church members to give 10 percent of their gross income to the church. This is a relatively high proportion compared to other religions, even while the bad economy has hit church finances very hard.[24] The resulting strain comes at a bad time for church groups as they seek to provide assistance for the unemployed. Furthermore, many church groups provide a source of low-price and free products for lower income consumers. Groups such as St. Vincent de Paul operate stores where second-hand items and retailer overstocks are made available at a small fraction of normal retail price or even for free for the more needy consumers. The Jewish Federation also implements *tzedakah*, meaning giving assistance to the poor, which enables the poor to access products they may not otherwise be able to access.

Consumer research examines the extent to which an overt Christian appeal influences Christians.[25] For example, an advertisement containing the fish symbol (Christian fish emblem) caused Evangelical Christians to rate the perceived quality of service, and their intention to use that particular service, higher than an ad that was otherwise identical. No such effect was seen among consumers of other religious affiliations. In fact, the authors of that particular research suggest that the symbol may even backfire and have negative effects on non-Evangelicals.

Religion also affects consumers' diets and the clothing they wear. During Lent each year, fast-food restaurants heavily advertise fish offerings as a way of capitalizing on the Catholic tradition of abstaining from meat during Lent, particularly on Fridays. Jewish consumers often follow a *kosher* diet. This places a high standard on cleanliness and purity of foods. Some common Christian foods like shrimp and bacon are inconsistent with this standard. Kosher restrictions include:

- Food must be prepared with a very high degree of cleanliness. Kosher packing plants are inspected by a rabbi to certify cleanliness.
- Certain meats are prohibited, such as pork and rabbit.
- Dairy products cannot be consumed simultaneously with meat.
- Fish with scales are allowed, but shellfish are not.

In many urban areas around the United States, where relatively large Jewish populations exist, grocers dedicate entire sections of their stores to kosher goods. The Islamic religion also places dietary restrictions on its followers, and it strictly prohibits the consumption of pork. The word *halal* describes the dietary restrictions that prohibit alcohol, pork, and meats that are not slaughtered in the prescribed manner. Restaurateurs who serve these markets need to be well aware of the dietary restrictions and the sensitivity of these cultures to violations of the restrictions.

Additionally, various religions have rules and customs about public displays of the body. Muslim women often sport veils, or even cover their entire face. Although this practice is often stigmatized in the United States, some fashion retailers have offered fashionable veils that may even cross over into the secular market.[26] **Stigmatization** means that the consumer is marked in some way that indicates their place in society. Sometimes the mark is not particularly flattering. A fashionable veil can help overcome negative feelings about this stigmatized product. In 2010, France's legislature voted to make the public wearing of full veils (those covering the face as well as the head) illegal, arguing that the practice was demeaning to women. Other European countries are considering adopting similar legislation.[27] Friction is often inevitable as cultures interact and as consumers choose to follow their religious beliefs rather than laws that they perceive to clash with these beliefs. Consumers of all faiths often make decisions to follow their religious beliefs and customs. Without question, religion plays a major role in both culture and microculture.

> The fact that the American people are very diverse is undeniable.

## ETHNIC MICROCULTURE

The United States is sometimes referred to as a melting pot. The analogy tries to make the point that America is a land filled with people from a wide range of ethnic backgrounds. According to this view, these people all blend together into a single American culture. This may be an oversimplification, but the fact that the American people are very diverse is undeniable. Most Americans are aware of their heritage beyond the United States and are often proud of it. Thus, even for multigenerational Americans, their consumption is affected by their heritage. This can be much stronger for families with shorter roots in America, including recent immigrants. The previous chapter discussed the acculturation process of consumers arriving in a new land like America. Consumption in the United States, however, remains tied to ethnicity to varying extents. We choose to use the term *culture* with these groups due to the strong ties that consumers often feel to their ethnic roots. Exhibit 9.6 breaks down the major ethnic groups in the United States.

### Hispanic Culture

The largest ethnic group (aside from whites of European decent) is now Hispanic. Hispanics account for just over 15 percent of all Americans. Nearly 11 percent of Americans list Spanish as their primary language. Perhaps the most important rule to remember in dealing with any large, ethnic market segment is that the group is not homogeneous. Hispanic consumers vary a great deal from one another, based on their own personal preferences, their degree of acculturation, how many generations removed they are from their ancestral

country, what is the ancestral country (Mexico, the Dominican Republic, Cuba, etc.), and other demographic characteristics. Thus, we can only talk about general tendencies for this market.

The more generations removed from the ancestral country, the closer a consumer is likely to be to the mainstream culture. Hispanic consumers several generations removed from the ancestral country are likely to communicate in English, while first generation Hispanic immigrants may still communicate primarily in Spanish. However, care needs to be taken when trying to appeal to an ethnic group in their native language. Even if the children of American-born Hispanics (third generation or more) can speak Spanish, they may be somewhat insulted by being presented an ad in Spanish. Also, in all cultures, there is some risk of a backlash from other consumers who may resent an advertisement in something other than the native language. The safest approach is to use Spanish language ads only when dealing with immigrant Hispanic populations or Spanish language media (Spanish language radio, printed media, television). The term **bicultural** is used to describe immigrants as they face decisions and form preferences

> **bicultural** used to describe an immigrant as he or she faces decisions and form preferences based on their old or new cultures

**EXHIBIT 9.6**
**Ethnic/Racial Groups in the United States based on U.S. Census Projections[1]**

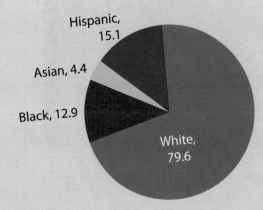

Hispanic, 15.1
Asian, 4.4
Black, 12.9
White, 79.6

Source: U.S. Census Bureau, **www.census.gov.**

[1]The percentages do not add to 100 because the U.S. Census classifies Hispanics by racial color (white or black), and reports the percentage of Hispanic people separately.

**social class** a culturally-defined group to which a consumer belongs based on resources like prestige, income, occupation, and education

based on their old or new cultures. Bicultural consumers begin to express lower ethnocentrism than their counterparts in the native country and thus are more open to products from their new country.[28]

Hispanics tend to place a high value on family-oriented values and social intimacy. Thus, products that appeal to the entire family or that somehow bring the family together tend to provide high value for Hispanic consumers. The Hispanic market cannot be ignored, as it is the fastest growing market segment in the United States.

*Care needs to be taken in using Spanish to appeal to Hispanic market segments.*

SOURCE: NIAID HIV VACCINE RESEARCH EDUCATION INITIATIVE/NIH

## African-American Culture

The African-American market segment represents about 12 percent of the total U.S. market. Like the His-

panic culture, the African-American microculture can be broken down into other more specific microcultures. Obviously, this is an important American market segment. Again, factors such as social class may have more influence in a given situation than ethnicity (such as which restaurants to patronize), but many companies have successfully capitalized on a special effort to tailor products toward the African-American consumer—McDonald's among those companies. One of the most important trends among African-American consumers is their growing affluence. The number of these Americans in professional occupations has multiplied many times over in the past few decades, as has the number of African-American owned businesses. Each of these factors contributes to an even higher buying power for this important segment.

## Asian Culture

The Asian segment also is growing rapidly. This segment represents between four and five percent of the U.S. population. Relative to other minority groups, the Asian-American culture is highly educated and highly affluent.[29] Asian-American consumers are very favorable toward luxury brands, tend to own their homes, and retain a preference for Asian foods. Asian-Americans also are concentrated in large numbers in a few areas of the United States. For example, all the major cities of California contain high proportions of Asian-Americans. The fact that they are concentrated in specific locations in the United States facilitates marketers' ability to effectively reach this market.

# INCOME AND SOCIAL CLASS MICROCULTURE

Two very important topics in consumer behavior are income and social class. The concepts permeate our everyday life and it seems that consumers are always trying to better themselves by moving up the income and class ladders. To say that income and social class are variables that marketers track closely would be a huge understatement.

Income level and social class are closely related, but distinct, concepts. Income level is truly a demographic issue, based on the amount of monetary resources a person receives. We define **social class** as a culturally-defined group to which a consumer belongs based on resources like prestige, income, occupation, and education. Income and occupation are two of the most recognizable determinants of social class.

Tastes and preferences are largely determined by social class, a finding that falls under the sociological concept of habitus. The term **habitus** refers to mental and cognitive structures through which individuals perceive the world based largely on their standing in a social class.[30] Although concrete generalizations regarding the influence of income and social class on purchase behavior are difficult, it can be said that social class tends to be a better predictor of purchases that involve value and lifestyles, as well as symbolic and highly visible products. Income tends to be a better predictor of purchases that require very substantial expenditures, while both income and social class predict purchases of symbolic, expensive products.[31]

## Social Class in the United States

Six major social classes have been identified in the United States. These include *Upper Class, Lower Upper Class, Upper Middle Class, Lower Middle Class, Upper Lower Class,* and *Lower Lower Class.*[32] Many consumers strive to move up the social ladder throughout their lifetimes, but this is not true of all consumers. Some consumers are simply content with their social standing and do not aspire to move up the social ladder. Some consumers are born into a social class (termed an *ascribed* status) while others work their way into a class (termed an *achieved* status).

Social class is an important concept because a class strongly influences lifestyles, opinions, attitudes, and behaviors. Sayings such as "birds of a feather flock together" and "keeping up with the Joneses" typify the social class conceptualization. That is to say, consumers in a particular class tend to behave similarly in the marketplace. Again, it should be emphasized that this does not mean that *every* consumer in a social class will exhibit the *exact* same behaviors, attitudes, and opinions. However, in general, it is a good rule of thumb that they will act similarly.

Two issues regarding social class that have been discussed here illustrate the difficulties with considering class in consumer behavior. The facts that not all consumers strive to move up the social ladder, and that not every consumer in a social class will act similarly, highlight the limitations of using the concept in consumer research. Nevertheless, social class is a very important societal and cultural issue that we observe in everyday life. A simple example of the influence of social class on behavior is the finding that most marriages are comprised of people from similar classes. In sociology, this is referred to as **homogamy**, or *assortative mating.*[33]

## Social Stratification

The concept of social stratification underscores the role of social class in society. **Social stratification** can be defined as the division of society into classes that have unequal access to scarce and valuable resources.[34] Of course, the finer things in life are generally enjoyed by the Upper, or Lower Upper Class. Luxury items and **status symbols** are enjoyed by these groups, while the bare essentials are relegated to the Lower Lower Class. Many of the Lower, Lower class even find themselves homeless.

The huge disparity between the Upper and Lower classes can be found in many parts of the United States. As a sad, ironic example, consider the number of homeless people that currently live in the tunnel systems under the city of Las Vegas. Under the very streets where excess is flaunted live some of the poorest and most destitute consumers in the nation.[35] The problems of poverty and homelessness are found worldwide.

## Social Class Worldwide

Social classes obviously exist throughout the world. China, with its enormous population, exhibits a range of social classes. Rapid economic development has led to recent gains in the Chinese middle class. Forecasts reveal that as many as 700 million consumers will be in the Chinese middle class by the year 2020. Middle class consumers occupy a variety of positions in the Chinese workplace, from entrepreneurs to managers of high tech companies.[36] Japan, on the other hand, has witnessed a gradual widening of the gap between the "haves" and the "have nots," along with a general shrinking middle class. India, like China, has a large middle class, estimated at approximately 170 million. Many of these consumers are young, with nearly half of its billion plus population less than 25 years old. Estimates reveal that as much as 40 percent of the population of India will be middle class in the next two decades.[37]

**habitus** mental and cognitive structures through which individuals perceive the world based largely on their standing in a social class

**homogamy** the finding that most marriages are comprised of people from similar classes

**social stratification** the division of society into classes that have unequal access to scarce and valuable resources

**status symbols** products or objects that are used to signal one's place in society

## STREET MICROCULTURE

Microcultures can grow around any number of phenomena, not just around ethnic, income/social class, generational, regional or religious differences. As we have seen, sports can provide a basis for microculture. Music can as well. One way to refer to these microcultures is using the label *street microcultures*.

The hip hop microculture illustrates one such group. Obviously, hip hop culture has influenced consumer tastes outside of its group (consider the pervasiveness of hip hop apparel). "Gothic" (or "goth") microculture represents another prevalent microculture in the United States. Gothic influence can be very strong as group members almost universally wear dark, macabre attire. The goth microculture is a great example of how strong microculture influence can be. In fact, some argue that gothic identification is even more important than gender identifications.[38] The "emo" subculture has received a lot of media attention in recent years, though its roots are thought to go back at least a few decades. Most consumers can recognize a goth or emo person easily, further evidence of how microcultures permeate our daily lives and are observed by many consumers.

Microcultures can even grow out of gaming experiences, virtual communities, and practically any other consumer activity that brings consumers with something in common together. The more easily a microculture can be reached, either physically or with various media, the better marketers can connect with them through value added communications and products.

## To Serve the Needy

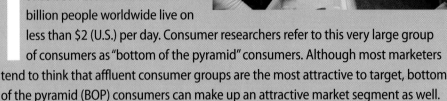

© AURORA PHOTOS /ALAMY

I t has been estimated that over 4 billion people worldwide live on less than $2 (U.S.) per day. Consumer researchers refer to this very large group of consumers as "bottom of the pyramid" consumers. Although most marketers tend to think that affluent consumer groups are the most attractive to target, bottom of the pyramid (BOP) consumers can make up an attractive market segment as well.

Of course, very poor consumers have the same basic needs as those of other consumers. The basic needs for food, shelter, belongingness, self-esteem, and actualization cut across income groups. While it is not uncommon for many consumers to intentionally seek out high-priced items (the backward sloping demand curve), marketers have succeeded by offering low-priced versions of products to BOP consumers. They have even offered re-manufactured, or used, products for the extremely poor.

Serving BOP consumers requires that the firm approaches their marketing activities from a societal viewpoint. That is, they must weigh the sometimes very small profit margins with the long-term worth of serving the starving and the needy. After all, consumers around the world seek value regardless of income level.

Sources: Based on Prahalad, C.K., *The Fortune at the Bottom of the Pyramid: Eradicating Poverty Through Profits* (Upper Saddle River, NJ: Pearson Education Inc., Wharton School Publishing, 2006); Habib, M. and L. Zurawicki (2010), "The Bottom of the Pyramid: Key Roles for Businesses," *Journal of Business & Economics Research* 8 (5), 23–32; and Rajagopal (2009), "Brand Paradigm for the Bottom of the Pyramid Markets," *Measuring Business Excellence* 13 (4), 58–68.

## LO3 Microculture Is Not Uniquely American

We often think of foreign countries with a single stereotype. A Parisian may represent all French people to some consumers. Even a country as diverse as China might be looked at very narrowly, with unfounded stereotypes. Other countries also have many bases around which microcultures are formed.

Many of the examples we've discussed transcend any specific country. Germany, Spain, and South Africa, for instance, are all countries where different languages are spoken in different regions of the country. Bavarians, from the German Alps, feel quite distinct from the typical German population. Over 1800 languages are spoken on the continent of Africa, across 53 countries. Furthermore, immigration is fast spreading through Europe, and the influx of Muslim microcultures in many European countries is adding to the diversity of these nations.

*© PETER HORREE/ALAMY*

**How many levels of culture are represented in this scene?**

Many street microcultures, including music, sports, and fashion exist around the world as well. Punk, goth, and emo microcultures are all good examples. Emo, for example, represents a popular microculture in Japan. Japanese "gothic Lolita" is another popular microculture that can best be illustrated by imagining a gothic China doll. Some Japanese girls also follow the "decora" microculture, which is marked by wearing extremely bright clothing and plastic accessories. Given the pervasiveness of microcultures throughout the world, firms' efforts to market products in virtually any part of the world need to take into account not only culture, but microculture as well.

# LO4 Demographic Analysis

Ultimately, any group or microculture has to be reached before a value proposition can be effectively delivered to them. Demographics is a term that we have used throughout this text, and it is an important concept for marketers and consumer researchers alike. **Demographics** refer to relatively tangible human characteristics that describe consumers. Demographics include characteristics such as age, ethnicity, sex, occupation, income, region, religion, and gender.

> **demographics** relatively tangible human characteristics that describe consumers
>
> **geodemographics** study of people based on the fact that people with similar demographics tend to live close to one another
>
> **demographic analysis** a profile of a consumer group based on their demographics

Demographic variables are closely related to microculture. In fact, you may have noticed from previous sections that demographic variables help one to describe microcultures. As an example, we previously discussed the fact that age distinctions can be used to describe generational microcultures. Consider the fact that consumers in the "millennial" microculture can be described as currently falling between the ages of 17 and 31. As such, the demographic variable "age" helps us to better understand and describe this microculture. The combination of demographic and microcultural information is therefore very valuable for today's marketers. This information becomes even more valuable when it is combined with **geodemographic** information, because members of many microcultures often live in close proximity to one another. Geodemographic tools such as PRIZM assist the consumer researcher with these analyses.

A **demographic analysis** develops a profile of a consumer group based on their demographics. As we have discussed, these analyses often include geodemographic approaches because marketers find it advantageous to know where targeted consumers live. These analyses become important components of a demographic segmentation strategy. If marketers can identify where their targeted consumers live, they can implement marketing campaigns much more efficiently. Newspapers, radio, television and even Internet communications can then be geared to specific regions.

One very important source for performing a demographic analysis is the U.S. Census Bureau's website (**www.census.gov**). Exhibit 9.7 shows the interface from **www.census.gov**.

The website gives a real-time estimate of the U.S. population in the upper right hand corner. The top category of options provides an entry into the search mechanisms to find details about people and households in the United States. One can find the actual counts from

EXHIBIT 9.7

## The U.S. Census Bureau's Website

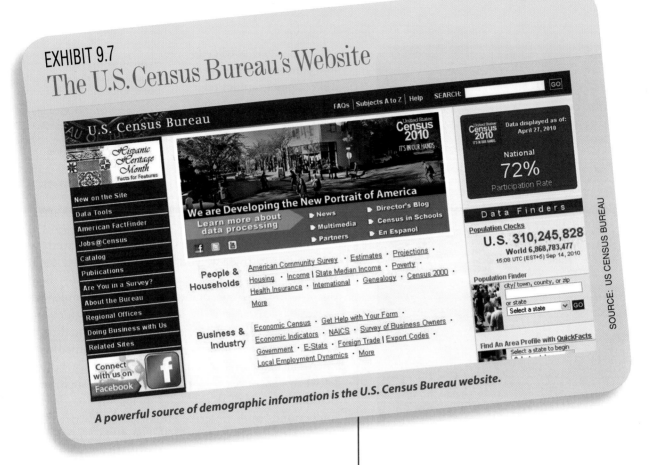

*A powerful source of demographic information is the U.S. Census Bureau website.*

SOURCE: US CENSUS BUREAU

the most recent census, or get estimates and projections of populations up to the current date. Generally, the search engine can be used to find statistics on a region of interest. Exhibit 9.8 shows the demographic profile for the state of Missouri.

This simple profile contains a great deal of useful information. For example, if a company were interested in marketing a product toward Hispanics, Missouri might not be the best target. Less than 3 percent of the population is Hispanic, which does not compare favorably to the percentage in the nation overall. In contrast, the relative proportion of white Americans versus African-Americans is quite similar to that of the national profile. In other instances, one may wish to obtain this data for a smaller region. The website makes the data available at the county level and with a bit of additional assistance, the data can be broken down by ZIP code. Also, a marketer may sometimes need a market to be at least of a certain minimum size in order for the market to be considered a viable target. A product might be targeted toward millennials and may require a market of at least 2,000,000 consumers to be viable. The target can be compared to the demographic numbers to see if the option should be pursued.

## LO5 Major Cultural and Demographic Trends

a number of cultural, microcultural, and demographic trends currently affect consumer behavior. These trends are also greatly impacting marketing practice. Notable trends include declining birth rates, increased consumer affluence, increasing life expectancy, and increasing cultural diversity worldwide.

## TRENDS AFFECTING CONSUMER BEHAVIOR

### Declining Birth Rates

One of the biggest trends in Western countries is the declining birthrate. In many European countries, the birthrate has dropped to 0.5 per person. That means that each couple is having at most one child. If this trend continues, these countries will experience declining populations. One particularly important trend in China,

EXHIBIT 9.8

# Demographic Profile for the State of Missouri

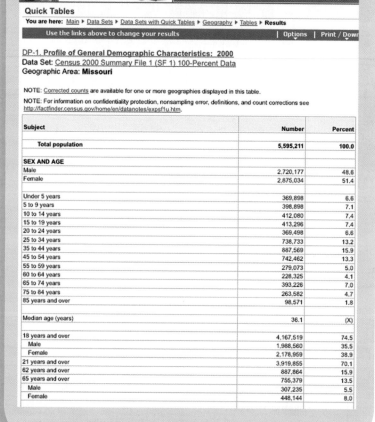

**Quick Tables**

You are here: Main ▶ Data Sets ▶ Data Sets with Quick Tables ▶ Geography ▶ Tables ▶ Results

Use the links above to change your results | Options | Print / Down

**DP-1. Profile of General Demographic Characteristics: 2000**
Data Set: Census 2000 Summary File 1 (SF 1) 100-Percent Data
Geographic Area: **Missouri**

NOTE: Corrected counts are available for one or more geographies displayed in this table.

NOTE: For information on confidentiality protection, nonsampling error, definitions, and count corrections see http://factfinder.census.gov/home/en/datanotes/expsf1u.htm.

| Subject | Number | Percent |
| --- | --- | --- |
| **Total population** | **5,595,211** | **100.0** |
| **SEX AND AGE** | | |
| Male | 2,720,177 | 48.6 |
| Female | 2,875,034 | 51.4 |
| | | |
| Under 5 years | 369,898 | 6.6 |
| 5 to 9 years | 398,898 | 7.1 |
| 10 to 14 years | 412,080 | 7.4 |
| 15 to 19 years | 413,296 | 7.4 |
| 20 to 24 years | 369,498 | 6.6 |
| 25 to 34 years | 738,733 | 13.2 |
| 35 to 44 years | 887,569 | 15.9 |
| 45 to 54 years | 742,462 | 13.3 |
| 55 to 59 years | 279,073 | 5.0 |
| 60 to 64 years | 228,325 | 4.1 |
| 65 to 74 years | 393,226 | 7.0 |
| 75 to 84 years | 263,582 | 4.7 |
| 85 years and over | 98,571 | 1.8 |
| | | |
| Median age (years) | 36.1 | (X) |
| | | |
| 18 years and over | 4,167,519 | 74.5 |
| Male | 1,988,560 | 35.5 |
| Female | 2,178,959 | 38.9 |
| 21 years and over | 3,919,855 | 70.1 |
| 62 years and over | 887,864 | 15.9 |
| 65 years and over | 755,379 | 13.5 |
| Male | 307,235 | 5.5 |
| Female | 448,144 | 8.0 |

*Information like this is very valuable.*

thought to be the result of the country's "one child" policy, is a relative imbalance in the number of men compared to women. Estimates reveal that by 2020, China could have as many as 30 million more men than women.[39] Exhibit 9.9 displays select birthrates. While birth rates are relatively low in many Western countries, notice that birth rates remain high in other countries, including Bangladesh, India, and Nigeria.

## Increasing Consumer Affluence

The combination of working couples and lower birthrates has led to greater levels of consumer affluence, particularly in the United States. As a result, many consumer segments have become targets for products once considered to be luxuries, such as cruises

and high-end automobiles. Furthermore, consumers have generally become less price sensitive in many categories. Families eat out more often and are more likely to own the latest electronic devices than consumers of the past. These trends not only affect the United States, but other countries as well. As detailed earlier, the rise in the middle class in both China and India is evidence of growing consumer affluence worldwide.

To say that consumer affluence is a trend is not to imply that poverty is not a major problem worldwide. To the contrary, poverty remains a major problem in many nations, as evidenced by the approximately 4 billion "bottom of the pyramid" consumers. Nevertheless, the growth in consumer affluence is a recognizable trend.

## Increasing Life Expectancy and the Aging Consumer

The right pane of Exhibit 9.9 displays the life expectancy for citizens of a number of different countries. Life expectancy is increasing in many, but not all, countries. The most obvious increase is found in developed nations. If we consider life expectancy as a proxy for standard of living, we can see that as the birthrate declines, the standard of living increases. Thus, unfortunately, the countries with the highest birthrates in the world are among the poorest. In developed countries, more wealth is spread over fewer consumers.

The growth trends in population, along with birth rate and life expectancy trends, all affect consumer culture in many ways. One major issue in the United States today is the aging Baby Boomer population. This segment of the consumer population is expected to dramatically affect business practices for many years to come. As discussed earlier, this segment attracts much marketing attention due to their large size and overall spending power.

## Increasing Cultural Diversity

Many societies worldwide are becoming increasingly culturally diverse. One way in which cultures become more diverse is through immigration and the growth of microcultures. There are numerous trends that could be discussed, and they range from religious to street microcultural diversity. Regarding religious microcultures, one significant trend in European countries is the growth of the Muslim faith. Islam is rapidly growing in popularity in Europe and this religious microculture is

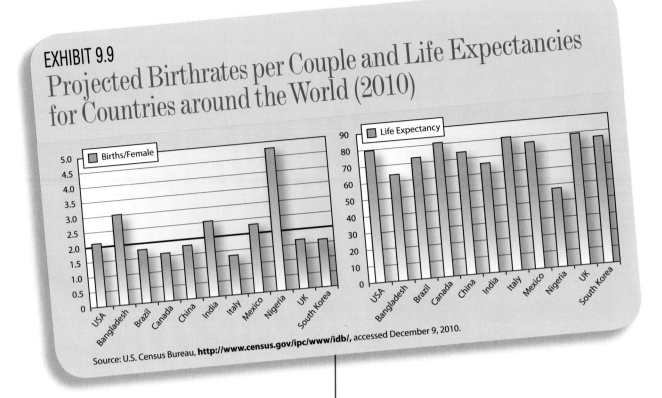

EXHIBIT 9.9

## Projected Birthrates per Couple and Life Expectancies for Countries around the World (2010)

Source: U.S. Census Bureau, **http://www.census.gov/ipc/www/idb/**, accessed December 9, 2010.

influencing consumer behavior throughout the region. In the United States, ethnic microcultures continue to become increasingly diverse due to both legal and illegal immigration. This issue is greatly impacting the Borderland region discussed earlier in this chapter.

The United Kingdom is also experiencing a general increase in immigration, with many immigrants arriving from the European Union. As such, the U.K. is realizing a growth in microcultural diversity, particularly pertaining to ethnic and religious microcultural diversity. The continued expansion of the world teen culture market is expected as many Western brands, such as Coca-Cola, McDonald's, and Starbucks, continue to succeed with foreign expansion. The influence of Western ideals and practice on the world teen culture continues. This is not to say that all young consumers will completely think and act alike. In fact, many Asian teens are carving out new and developing microcultures unlike those found in the United States. Some teens worldwide are breaking away from punk, goth, and emo microcultures to focus on more traditional clean-cut, even conservative styles.[40] As mentioned, there are many ways in which cultural diversity is increasing worldwide.

As we have seen, microcultures influence consumer behavior throughout the world, and for this reason, the study of microculture is very important for consumer researchers and marketers alike.

# 9 Study Tools

**Located at back of the textbook**

☐ Rip-out Chapter-in-Review Card

**Located at www.cengagebrain.com**

☐ Review Key Terms Flashcards (Print or Online)

☐ Download audio summaries to review on the go

☐ Complete practice quizzes to prepare for tests

☐ Play "Beat the Clock" and "Quizbowl" to master concepts

☐ Watch Video on Flight 001 for a real company example

## what others have thought...

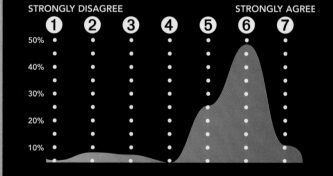

**The microcultures I belong to greatly influence the value I receive from products.**

The evidence here is very clear. Less than 10 percent of all respondents express any level of disagreement with this statement. In fact, over 3 of 4 respondents chose either agree or strongly agree. Students seem to realize that behavior is shaped by culture at all levels.

# Gaining acceptance

into a group can provide value for a consumer by satisfying needs for belonging.

## what do you think?

**The groups I belong to have a great impact on how I see myself.**

STRONGLY DISAGREE                    STRONGLY AGREE
**1**  **2**  **3**  **4**  **5**  **6**  **7**

Visit CourseMate at
www.cengagebrain.com.

# 10

# Group and Interpersonal Influence

## Introduction

the motivation to belong is an important part of human life. Consumers are social creatures who desire contact and affiliation with others. As a result, consumers often belong to (or aspire to belong to) a number of formal or informal groups. These groups can exert significant influence on consumer behavior. Other individual consumers can also influence a consumer's behavior. In this chapter, we discuss a number of issues relating to the concept of group and interpersonal influence and how these concepts apply to value. We begin by discussing the various types of reference groups that influence consumer behavior.

> **reference group**
> individuals who have significant relevance for a consumer and who have an impact on the consumer's evaluations, aspirations, and behavior

After studying this chapter, the student should be able to:

**LO1** Understand the different types of reference groups that influence consumers and how reference groups influence value perceptions.

**LO2** Describe the various types of social power that reference groups exert on members.

**LO3** Comprehend the difference between informational, utilitarian, and value-expressive reference group influence.

**LO4** Understand the importance of word-of-mouth communications in consumer behavior.

**LO5** Comprehend the role of household influence in consumer behavior.

## LO1 Reference Groups

a **reference group** is a group of individuals that has significant relevance for a consumer and that has an impact on the consumer's evaluations, aspirations, and behavior.[1] This influence affects the ways that consumers seek and receive value from consumption. Most people don't realize all the ways that reference groups influence their behavior. A good start in realizing how great the influence truly is comes when one takes inventory of all his/her reference groups. Consumers become members of many groups that either meet physically, or thanks to the Internet, meet in cyberspace. In fact, the popularity of social networking websites brings a whole new perspective on the structure and influence of personal reference groups. How many Facebook groups do you belong to? How many do you "like"? How many people or companies do you follow on Twitter? Have you followed any recommendations for new music that you've seen on Myspace? All of these examples illustrate how social media shapes group and individual behavior. To begin a discussion of these issues, we must first define what we mean by "group influence."

# GROUP INFLUENCE

**Group influence** refers to ways in which group members influence attitudes, opinions, and behaviors of others within the group. Groups are an important part of social life, and group processes profoundly affect consumer behavior by changing the perceived value of things. In fact, gaining acceptance into a group provides value for a consumer directly by satisfying his or her needs for belonging. Consider the following aspects of group life:

- Group members share common goals and interests.
- Group members communicate with, and influence, one another.
- Group members share a set of expectations, rules, and roles.
- Group members view themselves as members of a common social unit.[2]

These qualities of group membership are important. Sorority sisters share a common set of expectations that ultimately influences members' decisions about things such as activities, attire, and social involvement. A student marketing club organizes fundraisers for an end-of-the-year field trip, with all members sharing a common goal. An "over-fifty" student organization meets regularly to discuss the difficulties associated with being a nontraditional student. A Facebook group shares common interests in products and services. When you join (or like) a Facebook group or page, you share some common interest in the relevant subject.

Group influence does not just affect buying behavior. Consumer attitudes, opinions, and value perceptions also are heavily influenced by groups, even if a

specific purchase does not directly result. This is particularly the case with social networking website groups. Some groups, whether online groups or otherwise, have more influence on consumers than do others.

## Primary/Secondary Groups

A **primary group** is a group that includes members who have frequent, direct contact with one another. Primary reference groups generally have the most influence on their members, and *social ties* for these groups are very strong. A social tie is a measure of the strength of connection between group members. An example of a primary reference group is the family unit. Family members generally have much influence on one another, and many times it directly affects behavior in the marketplace. For example, studies reveal that parental influence on children's shopping and saving behavior can be quite strong.[3] Parents who openly discuss financial matters, such as developing savings accounts, can greatly influence these behaviors.

In a **secondary group**, interaction within the group is much less frequent than in a primary group. Professional organizations and social clubs are examples of secondary groups. Usually, the influence of these groups on members is not as strong as the influence of primary groups on their members. Furthermore, social ties are not as strong in secondary groups as they are in primary groups.

One special type of secondary group is a **brand community**. Brand communities are groups of consumers who develop relationships based on shared interests or product usage.[4] A popular example of a brand community is Harley-Davidson's HOG (*Harley Owners Group*). Fans of

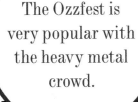

The Ozzfest is very popular with the heavy metal crowd.

© CHARLEY GALLAY/GETTY IMAGES

Harley-Davidson meet regularly at events that marketers refer to as *brandfests*. Some brand communities are found online in the form of Facebook groups for example. In the music industry, many heavy metal fans look forward to the annual Ozzfest, a concert tour that was founded by heavy metal icon Ozzy Ozbourne and his famous wife, Sharon.

In general, personal connections originating in brand communities lead to positive outcomes for consumers and companies. Consumers learn more about the products they enjoy, and they develop bonds with other users. Companies reap the rewards of positive consumer attitudes. The brand devotion that community members share helps members strongly identify with each other.[5]

## Formal/Informal Groups

A **formal group** is a group in which a consumer formally becomes a member. For example, a consumer becomes a formal member of a church congregation. Formal groups generally have a set of stated rules, accepted values, and codes of conduct that members are expected to adhere to.

An **informal group** is a group that has no membership or application requirements, and codes of conduct may be nonexistent. Examples of informal groups include groups that meet regularly to exercise, have coffee, or go to sporting events. Although informal group influence may not be as strong as formal group influence, these groups can have an impact on consumer behavior.

## Aspirational/Dissociative Groups

An **aspirational group** is a group in which a consumer desires to become a member. Aspirational group membership often appeals to the consumer's *ideal* self. The ideal self is an important part of the consumer's self-concept, and consumers often visualize themselves as belonging to certain groups. For example, a business student may desire to become a member of a professional business association once he earns his degree. Consumers frequently emulate the members of aspirational groups and perform behaviors that they believe will lead to formal acceptance into the group. Getting the first job would be the first step for joining a business organization.

A **dissociative group** is a group to which a consumer does not want to belong. For example, a Republican might want to avoid being perceived as belonging to a Democratic group (and vice-versa). Recent college graduates may want to disassociate themselves with groups from their past as they take the next step into adulthood.

# CONFORMITY

An important topic in the study of reference group influence is conformity. **Conformity** occurs when an individual yields to the attitudes and behaviors of other consumers. Conformity is very similar to the concept of persuasion. The key difference between persuasion and conformity is that with conformity, the other party does not necessarily defend its position. That is, a group may give no reason for why it expects its group members to act or think a certain way. Persuasion, on the other hand, relies on one party defending its position to another party in an explicit attempt to change attitude or behavior.[6]

> **formal group** group in which a consumer formally becomes a member
>
> **informal group** group that has no membership or application requirements and that may have no codes of conduct
>
> **aspirational group** group in which a consumer desires to become a member
>
> **dissociative group** group to which a consumer does not want to belong
>
> **conformity** result of group influence in which an individual yields to the attitudes and behaviors of others
>
> **peer pressure** extent to which group members feel pressure to behave in accordance with group expectations

Negative consumer behaviors are often heavily influenced by peer pressure.

## Peer Pressure

Peer pressure and conformity are also closely related topics. **Peer pressure** is the pressure an individual feels to behave in accordance with group expectations. Peer pressure can greatly influence behavior. In fact, peer pressure is often the strongest type of influence a consumer experiences in daily life.

Consumers of all ages feel peer pressure. In fact, very young children often desire to wear the types of clothing and brands that will allow them to feel accepted. One study found that children as young as 10 years old prefer to wear brand-name footwear (e.g., Nike) so that they will fit in with their peers.[7]

## Negative Peer Pressure

Peer pressure to wear a certain brand of clothing is not necessarily a bad thing. Unfortunately, negative consumer behaviors are often heavily influenced by peer pressure. Consumers sometimes succumb to group pressures that subtly or not so subtly encourage counterproductive or unethical—perhaps illegal—behaviors.

Experts frequently cite peer pressure as particularly persuasive among young consumers. The media direct a lot of attention to peer pressure and illegal alcohol or tobacco consumption. Binge drinking among underage consumers is a serious societal problem that can have disastrous, and sometimes fatal, effects. Peer pressure often plays a large role in this behavior. Even virtual group pressure, such as exerted through social networking sites, is sometimes accused of encouraging underage smoking.[8] Although this form of peer pressure is negative, marketers can harness the power of peer pressure in positive ways. For example, advertisements that encourage young consumers to abstain from negative behaviors (like underage drinking) can be effective when peer group members deliver the message.[9] And, consumers that stick together can change together, as illustrated by a Facebook group that encourages friending among those who want to stop smoking.

Adolescents are particularly susceptible to peer pressure and are often compelled to rebel against their families in favor of behaviors that win acceptance from their peers. Teens commonly go against family expectations and parental rules. At this stage in social development, friends begin to take on additional importance and exert greater influence in teens' lives. This can be considered a natural part of a child's develop-

> Consumers can find support for positive behaviors online.

ment; nevertheless, negative influences, including conflict within the family, can result.

Adults also feel and yield to peer pressure, and sometimes the pressure is directed toward negative behaviors. In fact, one study of adult consumers reveals that respondents reported a greater likelihood to buy an illicit product (counterfeit or stolen merchandise) if their friends did the same.[10] As with influence on children, this form of peer pressure is negative and can affect consumers, marketers, and society as a whole.

# LO2 Social Power

another important topic in the study of reference groups and group influence is social power. **Social power** refers to the ability of an individual or a group to alter the actions of others.[11] Consumers often believe that others hold a great deal of power over their own behavior. As a result, social power can greatly influence the types of products that consumers buy, the attitudes that consumers hold, and the activities in which they participate.

## TYPES OF SOCIAL POWER

Social power can be classified into five categories.[12] These categories include *referent power, legitimate power, expert power, reward power,* and *coercive power.* These forms of power can be exerted both by referent groups and by other individuals. These power bases are presented in Exhibit 10.1 and then discussed in more detail.

### Referent Power

Consumers often imitate the behaviors and attitudes of groups as a means of identifying with the group. For example, a new resident of a city might desire to join the local Rotary club, or perhaps a country club. In these cases, it is likely that the behaviors of other group members will be imitated. Belonging to such groups often allows consumers to feel as though they are fitting in.

### Legitimate Power

In many situations, social arrangements dictate that differing levels of power are dependent upon one's position in a group. Legitimate power is used

EXHIBIT 10.1

# Types of Social Power

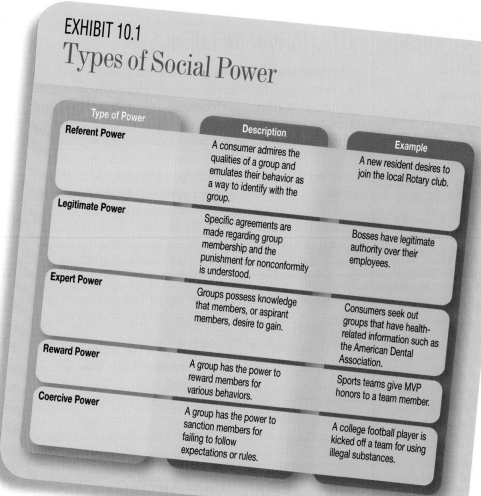

| Type of Power | Description | Example |
|---|---|---|
| Referent Power | A consumer admires the qualities of a group and emulates their behavior as a way to identify with the group. | A new resident desires to join the local Rotary club. |
| Legitimate Power | Specific agreements are made regarding group membership and the punishment for nonconformity is understood. | Bosses have legitimate authority over their employees. |
| Expert Power | Groups possess knowledge that members, or aspirant members, desire to gain. | Consumers seek out groups that have health-related information such as the American Dental Association. |
| Reward Power | A group has the power to reward members for various behaviors. | Sports teams give MVP honors to a team member. |
| Coercive Power | A group has the power to sanction members for failing to follow expectations or rules. | A college football player is kicked off a team for using illegal substances. |

to describe this type of power, and it is associated with authority. For example, bosses have legitimate power and authority over their employees. A boss has the authority to fire his or her employees. Notice that employees are usually very limited in any power that they can exert over a boss.

## Expert Power

An important motivation in consumer behavior is the motivation to understand the environment. Expert power refers to the ability of a group or individual to influence a consumer due to the group's or individual's knowledge of, or experience with, a specific subject matter. For example, consumers often find advice on health issues by consulting groups such as the American Heart Association or American Diabetes Association. Medical patients also often consult various online discussion groups for information. By consulting these groups for advice and direction relating to specific medical issues, consumers can alter their behaviors based on the perceived expertise of the source of information.

## Reward Power

Groups frequently have the power to reward members for compliance with expectations. For example, at season's end, sports teams often distribute "most valuable player" awards based on performance. The desirability of the rewards is very important. If the reward isn't valued by the group members, then the motivation to perform the desired behavior is not overly strong.

## Coercive Power

Groups may also exert coercive power over their members. When consumers fail to give in to group expectations or rules, disapproval can be harsh and may even result in loss of membership. For example, college athletes can be kicked off sports teams for using illegal substances like steroids. As mentioned earlier, groups may sanction members based on their legitimate power to do so, or they may revoke the membership of group members who do not comply with group rules.

How does social power originate? Social power actually depends upon a member's agreement to, or acceptance of, the fact that the power bases do indeed exist. That is, members must (a) *be aware that the power base exists* and (b) *desire to maintain or establish membership into the group* in order for the power base to be effective.

# LO3 Reference Group Influence

the study of reference groups requires an understanding of group influence processes. Reference group influence generally falls into one of three categories: *informational influence, utilitarian influence*, and *value-expressive influence*. These categories of influence are discussed next.[13]

# INFORMATIONAL INFLUENCE

The **informational influence** of groups refers to the ways in which consumers use the behaviors and attitudes of reference groups as information for making their own decisions. Reference groups often provide members with product- or issue-related information, and consumers often consider group-related information when purchasing products or services. Consumers desire to make informed decisions, and reference groups are often perceived as being effective sources of information.[14] Groups can be very influential in this way. Informational influence can be a result of explicit searching behavior. For example, when a consumer is seeking a doctor, friends may influence the choice by saying, "This doctor is very good."

Informational influence is also present even when the consumer is *not* explicitly searching for product-related information, but rather when he or she is observing others' behaviors. For example, a consumer may simply see another person drinking a new soft drink and decide to try one.[15]

Informational influence helps to explain why word-of-mouth communication is so persuasive. Consumers share all kinds of information about products, services, and experiences, and this information can have a significant impact on consumer behavior. Internet discussion groups, in particular, have rapidly become important sources of information for group members.

The informational influence of a group is particularly strong if the group is seen as being credible. Credibility is often associated with expertise. Professional groups are often perceived as being very credible, and for this reason, they can exert significant informational influence even if a consumer is not a member of the group. For example, a consumer may be persuaded by a message that proclaims that "four of five dentists recommend brand X." This same information obtained from the American Dental Association can affect a dentist's decisions as well, as informational influence is directly related to expert power.

# UTILITARIAN INFLUENCE

The **utilitarian influence** occurs when consumers conform to group expectations to receive a reward or avoid punishment (this is sometimes referred to as "normative" influence). Compliance with group expectations often leads to valued rewards.

As discussed earlier, young consumers often think they need to buy the correct brand of shoes or clothing to fit in. By wearing apparel approved by the reference group, a child feels accepted (the reward). If the wrong clothing is selected, the child may feel shunned by the group (a punishment). When the group is perceived as being able to give rewards and punishment based on compliance, then this influence is quite strong. Importantly, rewards can be either social (the feeling of fitting in) or economic (the attainment of direct monetary value).

Utilitarian influence of groups is not limited to any age group or demographic profile. Adult consumers often perceive a great deal of utilitarian influence from reference groups. Driving the right car, living in the right neighborhood, and belonging to the right clubs can make adults feel accepted. Here, we can see that utilitarian influence is related to reward power.

# VALUE-EXPRESSIVE INFLUENCE

Consumers often desire to seek membership into groups that hold values that are similar to their own. They also choose to adopt the values that are held by the desirable group. The **value-expressive influence** of groups refers to the ways in which consumers internalize a group's values or the extent to which consumers join groups to express their own closely held values and beliefs. This influence is related to referent power.

Consumers may also use group membership as a way to project their own self-image. Importantly, the self-image of the individual is influenced by the group, and group membership helps the individual project his or her desired image. For example, a consumer may choose to join Mothers Against Drunk Driving because she feels strongly about the drunk driving issue. Once she has joined, she can project the values of the group as well.

# VALUE AND REFERENCE GROUPS

External influences have a direct impact on the value of many activities. Reference groups and value are related in various ways.

# Valuable Groups!

The tremendous success of social networking sites like Facebook has allowed opportunities for marketers to interact with consumers in new and exciting ways. It has also allowed consumers to join and participate in groups in new ways as well. Of course, consumers have joined fan clubs for years. But rarely have these groups been able to deliver benefits like those available online. The benefits of participating online bring both utilitarian and hedonic value to consumers.

One recent trend has been the placement of coupons on social networking and media sites like Facebook and Foursquare. While these benefits are valuable for group members and users, there is more going on here than meets the eye. By using these tactics, marketers are able to encourage consumers to spread the word about the offers, thereby leading to positive WOM and increased group membership! Not only do the electronic coupons and offers cut down on the administrative costs associated with distribution, they also allow the marketer an easy opportunity to grow their fan base. Participating in these promotions is both fun and economical for group members!

Sources: Online content retrieved at *Mashable: The Social Media Guide* website, "Five Elements of a Successful Facebook Fan Page," **http://mashable.com/2009/03/30/successful-facebook-fan-page/,** accessed June 3, 2010; online content retrieved at *KMEG 46* website, **http://www.kmeg14.com/Global/story.asp?S=12266084,** accessed June 3, 2010; online content retrieved at *Couponing 101* website, **http://www.couponing101.com/2009/12/facebook-wheat-thins-and-nexxus-coupons-plus-50-advertising-credit.html,** accessed June 3, 2010.

dances can be quite enjoyable beyond any utilitarian benefits that come from membership. Simply enjoying the fun is enough! Motivations and emotions are closely related topics. The motivation to belong to, or be affiliated with, a group can bring happiness and joy. Many students join sororities and fraternities not for long-term benefits but for short-term fun!

Reference group influences affect value perceptions in other ways. Because consumers learn about products and services from referent others, the information that is obtained from groups directly affects consumer expectations about product benefits such as quality and convenience. If you hear from your friends that a product is good, you'll probably believe it! These expectations, in turn, affect value perceptions and satisfaction.

# REFERENCE GROUP INFLUENCE ON PRODUCT SELECTION

From a utilitarian value perspective, joining a campus organization (for example, Students in Free Enterprise) can be quite a valuable experience. The benefits associated with membership (networking, work experience, accomplishment) may be greater than the work that is put into the organization (work performed to complete a project, hours devoted to planning and meetings). In this way, utilitarian value is derived from belonging to the group, and group membership becomes a means to a valued end state.

Group membership also involves hedonic value perceptions. Value can be derived from simply enjoying group meetings and activities. Here, value is an end in itself. Attending functions such as sorority functions and

A number of things affect how much influence reference groups have on product selection. First, the situation in which the product is consumed must be considered. "Public" products are easily seen by others (for example, a watch). "Private" products are not (for example, an electric blanket). Second, the extent to which the product is considered to be a necessity or a luxury affects the level of reference group influence.[16] We really do need some products (for example, a refrigerator). Others aren't so necessary (for example, a hot tub). Third, reference group influence differs depending on whether a type of product or a particular brand is being selected. Obviously, a watch is a product. Rolex is a very expensive brand of watch. These elements are presented in Exhibit 10.2.

**social media** media through which communication occurs

**social networks** consumers connecting with one another based on common interests, associations, or goals

**social networking websites** websites that facilitate online social networking

For necessities, reference group influence is weak for product selection (boxes #1 and #2). Reference groups rarely influence the decision to wear blue jeans. With public necessities, however, the influence of reference groups on brand selection is strong (for example, "You should get some new Hollister jeans!" box #1). For luxuries, reference group influence is strong for product selection (boxes #2 and #4). However, group influence on brand selection is only strong for public luxuries (box #2). Reference group members could influence the choice of product (for example, "Don't you have a set of golf clubs?") and the brand used (for example, Callaway). A careful look at the exhibit reveals that group influence on brand selection is strong for all publicly viewed products!

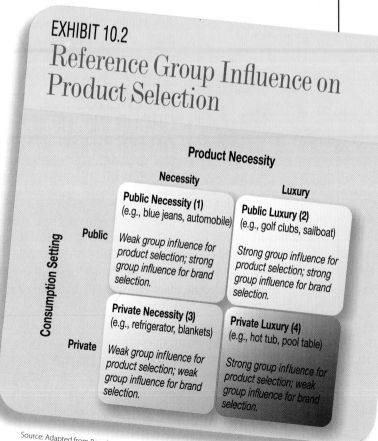

## EXHIBIT 10.2
## Reference Group Influence on Product Selection

**Product Necessity**

| | Necessity | Luxury |
|---|---|---|
| **Public** | **Public Necessity (1)** (e.g., blue jeans, automobile) Weak group influence for product selection; strong group influence for brand selection. | **Public Luxury (2)** (e.g., golf clubs, sailboat) Strong group influence for product selection; strong group influence for brand selection. |
| **Private** | **Private Necessity (3)** (e.g., refrigerator, blankets) Weak group influence for product selection; weak group influence for brand selection. | **Private Luxury (4)** (e.g., hot tub, pool table) Strong group influence for product selection; weak group influence for brand selection. |

**Consumption Setting**

Source: Adapted from Bearden, W. O. and M. J. Etzel (1982), "Reference Group Influences on Product and Brand Purchase Decisions," *Journal of Consumer Research*, 9 (2), 183–194.

# SOCIAL MEDIA AND GROUP INFLUENCE

To say that social media and the Internet are radically changing consumer behavior and group influence would be an understatement. Social media and networking now play big roles in consumer behavior. As discussed previously, consumers get both hedonic and utilitarian value from interacting through social networking websites. Because some of these sites revolve specifically around causes, interests, and activities, they also directly impact behavior in many different ways. Few groups ever meet physically, making most of them informal and secondary for group members. However, their importance shouldn't be overlooked. In fact, even when the physical proximity of other people is close, many consumers choose to connect through social media rather than face-to-face. One recent study even found that 20% of adults in the United States use digital tools to "talk" with neighbors![17]

## Social Media, Social Networks, and Social Networking Websites

It is important to distinguish between social media, social networking, and social networking websites as they pertain to group and interpersonal influence. **Social media** refers to media through which communication occurs. Essentially, social media refers to things like the Internet, television, radio and so on. **Social networks** are networks of consumers that are formed based on common interest, associations, or goals. In sociology, a social network is viewed as a group of individuals who share information and experiences. **Social networking websites** (sometimes referred to as "online social network sites") are websites that facilitate online social networking.

Social networking website activity is usually a mobile phenomenon as friends stay in virtual touch with others through laptops, iPads, BlackBerrys, cell phones, or other devices. In fact, recent statistics reveal that the majority of social media usage now originates from mobile devices rather than from desktop computers.[18] This finding illustrates the fact that not only are consumers becoming much more reliant on the Internet, but they are also relying more heavily on mobile information technologies.

## Popularity of Social Networking Websites

Current estimates regarding the use of social networking websites are striking. Three websites, in particular, highlight the popularity of online social networking: *Facebook*, *Myspace*, and *Twitter*. Although statistics change daily, according to Google's Doubleclick Adplanner service, Facebook gathered over 600 million visitors in the month of September, 2010 alone. What's more, there were nearly 700 billion page views during that time period.[19] Facebook's own statistics reveal that over 500 million users were considered "active" as of 2010, that users spent over 700 billion minutes per month on the site, and that the average user had 130 online friends![20] Clearly, Facebook has become a major player in online social networking. The site allows consumers to not only communicate daily with friends, but also to join (or like!) groups or web pages. Currently, Facebook is second only to Google in web page views, and more than one in three Internet users visit the site daily.[21]

Myspace is another popular online social networking site. According to Google's Adplanner service, Myspace gathered approximately 61 million visitors during September 2010.[22] This site remains especially popular with a younger audience. One recent study revealed that nearly 45% of Myspace users are consumers aged 24 and younger. Facebook users, however, appear to be more evenly distributed across age groups, with a slight majority being aged 35-49.[23] Twitter has also grown rapidly in popularity. The same Google service estimated that 110 million visitors visited Twitter monthly during September 2010. The amount of "tweets" sent per month also highlights the influential role of social networking in consumer behavior. Estimates reveal that as many as 2 billion tweets are sent each month.[24] Twitter also appears to be more popular with a somewhat older audience, with the majority of users over the age of 25.[25]

Social networking sites like Facebook, Myspace, and Twitter continue to grow in popularity as consumers realize the benefits of maintaining connectivity with friends and social groups. Other popular sites like *You-Tube* and *Flickr* allow users to share online video and

The mobile consumer is always in touch.

photo content. Of course, there are many more examples of popular social network and media sites. Sites such as *Linkedin*, *Classmates*, *Tagged*, *Meetup*, *Friendster*, *Ning*, *Bebo*, and *MyLife* continue to grow in popularity.

## Value, Social Media, and Social Networking

Recall from an earlier discussion that consumers derive both utilitarian and hedonic value from group membership. To illustrate, consider the website **socialvibe.com**. This site allows users to connect with brands and empowers them to share content with others to benefit a cause of their choice. By using Social Vibe, consumers can positively impact charities of their choice by completing various branded activities.[26] Although the site is not a social networking site per se, it does help consumers interact with others while supporting causes and connecting with brands, thereby offering both utilitarian and hedonic benefits. They are also able to share their activities with friends on other popular social networking sites.

Another example of value from social media sites can be found at **kaboodle.com**. Kaboodle offers both utilitarian and hedonic value by offering a social shopping community where people discover, recommend, and share products.[27] The site allows consumers to organize their shopping activities, learn about other consumers with similar styles, and enjoy discounts on popular products. Members are also able to enjoy engaging with other community members who offer suggestions for various products and services. Here, users are able to get good deals on products (a utilitarian benefit) and enjoy connections with other consumers who have similar interests (a hedonic benefit).

**Freerice.com**, sponsored by the United Nations World Food Program, invites visitors to answer a series of questions, with each correct answer leading to a donation of rice to hungry consumers throughout the world. By participating, visitors are able to help solve a world problem like hunger while enjoying a trivia game that is both fun and educational. **Foursquare.com**, a popular social networking application website that centers around geolocation and mobile technologies, not only allows users to inform friends of their location, but also allows users to earn rewards, to leave "tips" about particular destinations, and to collect coupons for various retailers.[28]

Although new online social networking sites appear nearly every day, what is most relevant for our purposes is how these sites influence group and consumer behavior. These sites offer both hedonic and utilitarian value by allowing consumers to: make connections with others, join groups, gather information, buy products, participate in social and political causes, and to spread information by word-of-mouth. We discuss word-of-mouth in more detail in a later section.

# INDIVIDUAL DIFFERENCES IN SUSCEPTIBILITY TO GROUP INFLUENCE

Although group influence plays an important role in influencing consumer behavior, not all consumers conform to group expectations equally. Individual difference variables play an important role in the extent to which consumers conform to the expectations of others. They also influence how one behaves in the presence of others. Three important variables are susceptibility to interpersonal influence, attention to social comparison information, and separateness-connectedness.

## Susceptibility to Interpersonal Influence

One individual difference variable, **susceptibility to interpersonal influence**, assesses the individual's need to enhance his or her image in terms of others by acquiring and using products, conforming to the expectations of others, and learning about products by observing others.[29]

Studies reveal that consumers who are particularly susceptible to interpersonal influence are more likely to value conspicuous items (that is, highly valued items like luxury automobiles or jewelry).[30] In the value equa-

tion (value = what you get – what you give), the benefits of quality and image would be weighted heavily in their perception of value.

Seeking approval of others through product ownership is very important to these consumers. Consumers who score highly on the susceptibility to interpersonal influence scale are also more likely to desire avoiding negative impressions in public settings.[31] For example, wearing "uncool" clothes in a shopping mall would be much more distressing to a consumer who is highly susceptible to interpersonal influence than to other consumers.

## Attention to Social Comparison Information

Another individual difference variable that affects consumer behavior related to group influence is **attention to social comparison information (ATSCI)**. Consumers who score highly on this measure are concerned about how other people react to their behavior.[32] This trait is closely related to susceptibility to interpersonal influence. Sample items from this scale are presented in Exhibit 10.3.

## EXHIBIT 10.3
### Sample Items from Attention to Social Comparison Information Scale

It's important to me to fit into the group I'm with.

At parties I usually try to behave in a manner that makes me fit in.

I tend to pay attention to what others are wearing.

I actively avoid wearing clothes that are not in style.

My behavior often depends on how I feel others wish me to behave.

Source: Adapted from Bearden, W. O. and R. L. Rose (1990), "Attention to Social Comparison Information: An Individual Difference Factor Affecting Consumer Conformity," *Journal of Consumer Research* 16 (March), 461–471.

The ATSCI trait often emerges when a consumer is shopping, as consumers with a strong degree of the trait tend to modify their purchasing behaviors when they are shopping with others. For example, a consumer who has a strong degree of ATSCI might buy an imported beer when he is shopping with others. He would buy a less expensive domestic beer when he is shopping alone. Paying attention to what others think is likely to lead consumers to conform to others' expectations, and studies have shown that consumers with a strong degree of ATSCI are more likely to conform to the expectations of others.[33]

### Separateness—Connectedness

Consumers differ in their feelings of "connectedness" to other consumers. A consumer with a **separated self-schema** perceives himself or herself as distinct and separate from others, while a consumer with a **connected self-schema** sees himself or herself as an integral part of a group.[34] Marketers are well aware of the differences in how people view their relationships with groups, and marketing messages are often based on "connected" or "separated" themes. One study found that consumers who feel connected respond more favorably to advertisements that promote group

belonging and cohesion.[35] Another study found that consumers with a high need for connection respond quite favorably to salespeople with whom they share some degree of similarity.[36]

Culture plays an important role in how separated or connected consumers feel. For example, consumers in Eastern cultures tend to feel more connected to others, while consumers in Western cultures tend to feel more separate and distinct. Advertising themes in collectivist cultures (a culture that focuses heavily on the interdependence of citizens) therefore often promote connected themes, while advertisements in the United States tend to emphasize separate themes.[37]

PRNEWSFOTO/ICONIX BRAND GROUP, INC.

*Consumers with connected self-schemas respond favorably to advertisements promoting togetherness.*

**separated self-schema** self-conceptualization of the extent to which a consumer perceives himself or herself as distinct and separate from others

**connected self-schema** self-conceptualization of the extent to which a consumer perceives himself or herself as being an integral part of a group

**word-of-mouth (WOM)** information about products, services, and experiences that is transmitted from consumer to consumer

### Social Influence and Embarrassment

The impact of groups on consumers cannot be overstated. In fact, the mere presence of others in a specific situation can make one feel uncomfortable.[38] This is especially the case when consumers are consuming or buying personal products. Consumers can feel very uneasy, or even embarrassed, by the presence of others when purchasing these items.

One study revealed that college students were particularly embarrassed with the purchase of condoms when other consumers were present.[39] This influence was affected, however, by the amount of experience the students had with buying condoms. Consumers who were familiar with the act of buying the product did not feel significantly high levels of embarrassment if others were present during the purchase. Many consumers are uncomfortable working out in a gym for fear of how they appear to others!

## LO4 Word-of-Mouth

nother important concept in the study of interpersonal influence is word-of-mouth behavior. **Word-of-mouth (WOM)** is information about products, services, and experiences that is transmitted from consumer

to consumer. WOM includes all kinds of information that can be spread about various consumer behaviors.

Two types of WOM influences can be distinguished: *organic* and *amplified*. The distinction between the concepts is highlighted by the Word of Mouth Marketing Association (WOMMA). According to WOMMA, organic WOM occurs naturally when consumers truly enjoy a product or service and they want to share their experiences with others. Amplified WOM occurs when marketers attempt to launch or accelerate WOM in existing customer circles, or when they develop entirely new forums for WOM (such as discussion boards on web pages).[40]

Consumers are heavily influenced by WOM, and its power is impressive. Consumers tell each other about products, services, and experiences all day long. If a movie is really good, moviegoers tell others. It's no wonder that word-of-mouth influences the vast majority of consumer product sales! WOM is influential because, in general, consumers tend to believe other consumers more than they believe advertisements and explicit marketing messages from companies.

# POSITIVE AND NEGATIVE WOM

The more satisfied consumers are with a company or product, the more likely they are to spread positive WOM. If consumers believe strongly in a company and its products, they are more likely to talk to others about it.[41] Terms such as *brand advocate* or *brand ambassador* are beginning to emerge in marketing to describe consumers who believe strongly in a brand and tell others about it.

Consumers are also more likely to spread WOM when a product is particularly relevant to their own self-concept and when they are highly involved with the product category.[42] For example, a motorcycle enthusiast is more likely to spread WOM about motorcycle products than a consumer who doesn't even like motorcycles.

Marketers realize that negative WOM can be extremely damaging. The reason why negative WOM is so damaging to a company is that this form of WOM is especially influential. In general, negative word-of-mouth is more influential than is positive word-of-mouth.[43] Hearing that the food at a restaurant is terrible is much more influential than hearing that it is good! Consumers also tend to tell more people about unsatisfactory experiences than pleasing ones.

> Consumers seek out other online users for advice on all kinds of issues.

## Value and Word-of-Mouth

As noted earlier, group influence processes are closely related to consumer perceptions of value. Similarly, WOM is affected in large part by the perceived value that consumers receive from products and services. One study, performed in a South Korean service setting, found that both utilitarian and hedonic value positively influence WOM intentions.[44] Customers who believed the restaurant allowed them to efficiently address their hunger received utilitarian value, and those who enjoyed the experience beyond addressing hunger received hedonic value. When this value was perceived as being particularly high, consumers were motivated to encourage their families and friends to go that restaurant as well. The more value that consumers receive, the more likely they are to tell others about their experiences with products and services!

## Word-of-Mouth in the Digital Age

Not only do social networking sites and media provide value by allowing consumers to join groups and follow others, they also represent efficient methods of spreading WOM. Consumers seek out other online users for advice on all kinds of issues, ranging from what types of products to buy, to input into health, personal, and financial decisions. In fact, recent estimates reveal that 80% of Internet users have sought online advice for health issues.[45] Consumers also regularly spread WOM through text messaging. Consider that one in three teens send more than 100 texts per day, and it's easy to see how this can impact WOM.[46] And that's just teens!

Many websites encourage the spread of information from consumer to consumer. Some sites are dedicated specifically to WOM, like **bzzagent.com**. This site not only allows consumers to spread WOM, but it also allows consumers to share web content. By becoming a "bzzagent" consumers are able to participate in a popular online WOM network.[47] **Digg.com** also focuses on sharing web content. Using this site, users submit content for others to see and then other users vote on what they like best.[48] The content comes in many forms, including other web pages, images, or videos. If the content gets enough votes, it is placed on the front page for millions of visitors to see. It also allows users to comment and share discussions about the content.

Many companies actively encourage WOM by including discussion boards on their own websites as well. This also allows companies to assist in the development and maintenance of brand communities. They may also hire their customers to blog about their products.

Although marketers can encourage the spread of positive WOM, they must also be mindful of the spread of negative WOM in the online world. Because negative is WOM is so influential, it is important for companies to monitor the content that is posted on various websites. It is becoming quite common to see what can be called *anti-brand communities*, or communities in which members spread negative information about companies and products to other users. Marketers should pay close attention to these communities.

## Measuring Online WOM

Given the importance of online WOM and how it influences consumer behavior, it is important for consumer researchers and marketers alike to be able to gather valid information on WOM statistics. Many services measure web traffic, such as the *Google Doubleclick Adplanner* site, *Quantcast*, *Alexa*, and *Comscore*. Some web traffic services allow users to focus on specific topics or trends, as would be the case with WOM. For example, the site *Trendrr* monitors the popularity of trends across social networks, blogs, and video views. Some services, such as *Tweetreach*, *Trendistic*, and *Whatthetrend* focus specifically on Twitter tweets and trends. Popular trends on any one day often include products, movies, celebrities, and news events. *Google Trends* monitors the popularity of search terms on its search engine, and *Bing* offers a similar listing. All of these services can be quite valuable for understanding popular online topics, trends, and WOM.

# Maybe Talk Isn't Cheap

**M**arketers are excited about the many opportunities that are available in cyberspace. One valuable opportunity can be found in blogging (slang for "web logging"). Blogging allow consumers to voice their opinions on a number of different topics, products, and services. Blogging has become so popular that the practice is now a part of the marketing mix for many companies!

A number of websites now allow companies to hire bloggers to write blogs about their products and services. Sites such as **payperpost.com**, **sponsoredreviews.com**, and **reviewme.com** have grown in popularity. Although the requirements for each site vary, the basic idea is that bloggers are given the opportunity to blog about products or companies for pay. Advertisers tell bloggers what products or services they want included in the blog, and the blogger agrees to write about it. The arrangement can be a win–win situation for both the blogger and advertiser. Of course, this practice may be considered to be unethical by some. Nevertheless, this form of Internet promotion is rapidly becoming an important component of buzz marketing, and given the popularity of the Internet blog, it is likely that this practice will continue to grow in popularity.

Sources: Johnson, C. Y. (2007), "Blogging for Dollars," *Knight Ridder Tribute Business News* (April 16), 1; Fernando, A. (2007), "Transparency Under Attack," *Communication World* 24 (2), 9–11; Schwartz, M. (2007), "Can Paid Blog Reviews Pay Off?," *B to B* 92 (2), 1–3; Frazier, M. (2006), "Want to Build Up Blog Buzz? Starting Writing Checks for $8," *Advertising Age* 77 (44): 3–4; Armstrong, S. (2006), "Bloggers for Hire," *New Statesman* 135 (4807), 26–27.

## BUZZ MARKETING

**buzz marketing** marketing efforts that focus on generating excitement among consumers and that are spread from consumer to consumer

**guerrilla marketing** marketing of a product using unconventional means

**viral marketing** marketing method that uses online technologies to facilitate WOM by having consumers spread messages through their online conversations

**stealth marketing** guerrilla marketing tactic in which consumers do not realize that they are being targeted for a marketing message

**opinion leader** consumer who has a great deal of influence on the behavior of others relating to product adoption and purchase

One marketing tactic that continues to evolve is called **buzz marketing**. Buzz marketing includes marketing efforts that focus on generating excitement (or buzz) that is spread among market segments. Quite often, this type of marketing utilizes some form of WOM, as is found with the BzzAgent website. Successful buzz marketing can be a powerful tool for marketers, as information about products and services can spread quickly. Buzz marketing is one form of what is called **guerrilla marketing**, or the marketing of a product using unconventional means.

Although marketers have attempted to create a buzz about their products for years, buzz marketing is currently becoming popular in large part as a response to mass media fragmentation and advertising clutter. The techniques can be quite clever. For example, automobile companies can give customers automobiles to simply ride around and be seen in. This was a tactic the Ford Motor Company utilized when it gave a handful of consumers new Ford Fiesta automobiles to drive around and be seen in. The consumers drove the Fiesta around while performing activities assigned by the company. By having consumers see the new automobile in use and receive WOM from others, Ford was able to take advantage of the power of buzz marketing.[49]

The spreading of WOM online through social networking sites can be considered another form of buzz marketing. In fact, buzz marketing uses social media tools and websites regularly. As we have discussed, companies sometimes hire consumers to spread such messages. One buzz marketing tactic that relates directly to WOM is termed viral marketing. **Viral marketing** uses online technologies to facilitate WOM by having consumers spread marketing messages through their online conversations. A great example of viral marketing can be found with **hotmail.com**, which included messages aimed at promoting their service attached to the bottom of user's emails. These messages were spread each time a consumer sent an email.

Although buzz marketing may be facilitated through online message boards and networking sites, this type of marketing is not limited to online content. The term *buzz marketing* is used much more broadly than that, with messages being delivered in many different ways to create buzz.

## STEALTH MARKETING

Another more controversial form of marketing that uses WOM is stealth marketing. **Stealth marketing** is a guerrilla marketing tactic that is similar to buzz marketing, but a key difference is that with stealth marketing consumers are completely unaware that they are being marketed to (hence, the term *stealth*). As an example of stealth marketing, imagine a camera marketer that has employees pose as tourists. These "tourists" then ask others to take their pictures with a new camera. Of course, the picture takers don't realize that the tourists are employed by the company and that they are being targeted by a marketing message.[50] Or, imagine a person who works for a beer distributor buying a round of drinks at a bar, when other customers don't know that his company markets the beer that he is buying and promoting. Some consider *product placements* in televisions shows and movies to be a type of stealth marketing because consumers generally don't realize that the companies have usually paid some fee for their product's inclusion.

The use of stealth marketing techniques, though growing, is considered questionable by many marketing professional organizations, and WOMMA is opposed to the stealth tactics. In fact, WOMMA has developed several categories of what it considers "unethical" marketing practices, including the following types of marketing techniques:[51]

- **Stealth marketing.** Deceiving consumers about the involvement of marketers in a communication
- **Shilling.** Compensating consumers to talk about, or promote, products without disclosing that they are working for the company
- **Infiltrating.** Using fake identities in online discussions to promote a product

## OPINION LEADERS

Buzz marketing techniques are especially effective when opinion leaders are used. **Opinion leaders** are consumers who have great influence on the behavior of others relating to product adoption and purchase. Opinion leaders are knowledgeable about specific products or services and have a high level of involvement with those products. Characteristics of opinion leaders depend largely on the type of product under consideration, but in general, opinion leaders are socially active and self-confident.

The launch of a perfume exemplifies the use of opinion leaders. BCBGirl, a perfume marketed by BCBG fashion, was introduced when the company sent bottles of the fragrance to teen trendsetters, along with 100 samples that each was expected to share with friends. The tactic was a success, as the perfume became the best-selling product in targeted cities the week of its full product launch.[52] By including opinion leaders in the marketing campaign for BCBGirl, BCBG fashion was able to harness the power of WOM processes. With online social networking and media sites, it's easy to find examples of a few key posters that other users tend to listen to. With Twitter, you can even track the number of followers for each user.

> Twitter users can influence a lot of people.

## Market Mavens and Surrogate Consumers

Opinion leaders are not the only influential consumers that have been identified. Market mavens and surrogate consumers also exert much influence on others. A **market maven** is a consumer who spreads information about all types of products and services that are available in the marketplace. The key difference between an opinion leader and a market maven is that the market maven's influence is not category specific. That is, market mavens spread information about numerous products and services.

Consumers can also be heavily influenced by what are termed surrogate consumers. A **surrogate consumer** is a consumer who is hired by another to provide input into a purchase decision. Interior decorators, travel consultants, and stock brokers can all be considered surrogate consumers. Surrogate consumers can be very influential, and marketers should carefully consider the level of influence of these individuals.[53] Because of their extensive product expertise, surrogate consumers can often help others derive the maximum amount of value out of their transactions by maximizing the benefits associated with product purchase.

**market maven** consumer who spreads information about all types of products and services that are available in the marketplace

**surrogate consumer** consumer who is hired by another to provide input into a purchase decision

**diffusion process** way in which new products are adopted and spread throughout a marketplace

# DIFFUSION PROCESSES

One area of interest in the study of group processes is the diffusion process. The **diffusion process** refers to the way in which new products are adopted and spread throughout a marketplace. Researchers have learned that different groups of consumers tend to adopt new products at different rates. One group may adopt a new product (for example, a hybrid automobile) very early in the product's life cycle, while another group may be very slow to adopt the product, if it adopts the product at all. A product life cycle is a description of the life of a product from the time it is introduced to the time it dies off.

In all, five categories of consumers have been identified. They include innovators, early adopters, early majority, late majority, and laggards. These

© JOCHEN TACK/ALAMY

groups are presented in Exhibit 10.4.[54]

What makes group influence relevant to the diffusion process is that each group learns about new products not only from seeing marketing messages, but also from talking with other consumers and observing their behavior. Group influence processes therefore apply to these categories.

Innovators and early adopter consumers tend to be influential when discussing products and services with members of other groups. As such, they tend to be opinion leaders for specific product categories. Innovators are often risk takers and financially well-off. Early adopter consumers are generally young and well-educated. Members of other groups, including late majority consumers, and laggards, tend to be more cautious about buying new products and wait significantly longer to buy the latest innovations. These consumers also tend to be somewhat older, with lower levels of education and spending power.

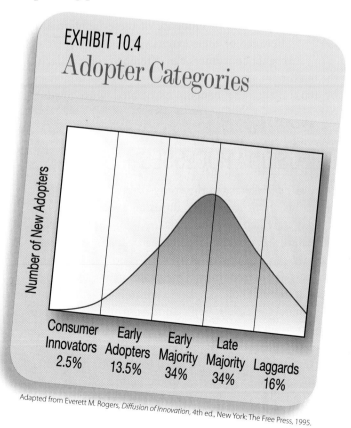

## EXHIBIT 10.4
## Adopter Categories

*Number of New Adopters*

Consumer Innovators 2.5%
Early Adopters 13.5%
Early Majority 34%
Late Majority 34%
Laggards 16%

Adapted from Everett M. Rogers, *Diffusion of Innovation*, 4th ed., New York: The Free Press, 1995.

# LO5 Household Decision Making

As we discussed previously, the family unit is an important primary reference group for consumers. Family members typically have a great deal of influence over one another's attitudes, thoughts, and behaviors. Consider the many ways that the family has an impact on consumer behavior. **Household decision making** is the process by which household units choose between alternative courses of action. To begin with, we first discuss the various conceptualizations of the term *household*.

## TRADITIONAL FAMILY STRUCTURE

The ways in which society views the family unit have changed dramatically in recent decades. Traditionally, the **family household** has been viewed as at least two people who are related by blood or marriage and who occupy a housing unit. In fact, this is how the U.S. Census Bureau defines a family unit. Other traditional family definitions include the *nuclear* family and the *extended* family.

The **nuclear family** consists of a mother, a father, and a set of siblings. The **extended family** consists of three or more generations of family members, including grandparents, parents, children, and grandchildren. In individualistic cultures like the United States, emphasis is placed on the nuclear family. However, in collectivist cultures, more focus is placed on the extended family, and it is not uncommon to see households that are comprised of extended family members living together. With this being said, the growth in multi-generational households in the United States has been significant in recent years.[55]

### Emerging Trends in Family Structure

As mentioned previously, the traditional views of the family have changed over time. Today, many nontraditional household arrangements exist throughout the United States. Societal trends toward people of opposite sex sharing living quarters (termed POSSLQ or cohabitation) and homosexual households have altered the way in which family households are conceptualized. In fact, 33% of households accounted for in the latest census information available are defined as nonfamily

Family members greatly influence one another.

of current interest is same-sex marriages. Same-sex marriages are becoming increasingly common. Marketers increasingly target same-sex couples in many of their advertisements.

Even though each of these trends offers opportunities for marketers, one clear fact remains based on the census data of households in the United States. Despite widespread attention to nontraditional households, census data reveal that the largest portion of American consumers still live in something resembling a traditional household, consisting of a married couple who either have yet to have children, have children living under the same roof, or have already raised children who no longer live at home. Also, the data reveal that the majority of American children reside in a traditional household, as is shown in Exhibit 10.5.

The prevalence of products such as SUVs and minivans as well as family-oriented movies such as *Toy Story 3* and the *Shrek* franchise, and the profitability of retailers such as Sam's Club, owe at least a portion of their success to the large numbers of traditional family units.

households (that is, consumers sharing the same living quarters who are not related by blood or marriage).[56] Of course, even if a household is categorized as a nonfamily household, members still exert significant influence on one another.

Divorce rates tend to be quite high in the United States. Nearly 50% of all marriages in the United States eventually end in divorce.[57] Divorces have dramatically altered the composition of the American family, and they have led to *blended families*. Blended families consist of previously married spouses and children from the marriages. Although the divorce rate in the United States is high, estimates reveal that the rates are currently at their lowest point in over 30 years, at approximately 3.6 divorces per 1,000 people. The highest rate recorded was in 1981, when the rate was 5.8 per 1,000 people.

Many people simply decide to never marry, even when children are present. In fact, it has been reported that more American women are now living without a husband than with one.[58] As a result of this trend and the high divorce rate, single-parent households have increased dramatically. Approximately 26% of U.S. children lived with only one parent in the year 2007,[59] and a record 41% of births in 2008 were to unmarried women.[60] Of course, not all women have children, either by choice or inability. In fact, it is estimated that the number of women aged 40-44 who were childless doubled between the years 1976-2006.[61] Another growing trend is that single men are adopting children at a rate higher than ever before.[62]

Finally, we note that the meaning of the term *nonfamily* is open to debate and interpretation. One topic

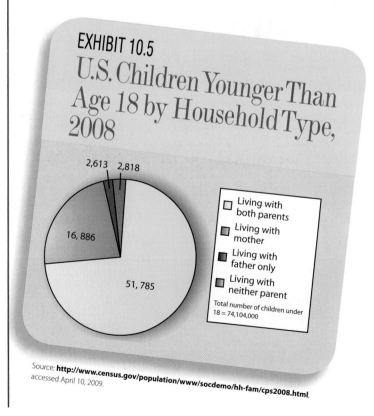

**EXHIBIT 10.5**

## U.S. Children Younger Than Age 18 by Household Type, 2008

2,613    2,818

16,886

51,785

☐ Living with both parents
◩ Living with mother
■ Living with father only
▨ Living with neither parent

Total number of children under 18 = 74,104,000

Source: **http://www.census.gov/population/www/socdemo/hh-fam/cps2008.html**, accessed April 10, 2009.

**household life cycle (HLC)** segmentation technique that acknowledges that changes in family composition and income alter household demand for products and services

## Household Life Cycle

An important concept in the study of the family unit is the **household life cycle (HLC)**. The HLC represents a segmentation technique that acknowledges that changes in family composition and income alter household demand for products and services.

The traditional HLC segments families into a number of groups based on the number of adults present and the age of the head of household. This conceptualization is presented in Exhibit 10.6. Based on this conceptualization, a number of segments are present, including consumers who never marry (Bachelor 1, 2, and 3); two-adult, childless households (Young Couple, Childless Couple, and Older Couple); two adults with children (Full Nest 1, 2, and 3 and Delayed Full Nest); and one adult with children (Single Parent 1, 2, and 3).

The categorization of the household is important for consumer researchers.[63] Product expenditures vary greatly by stage in the HLC, and at each stage, consumers often try to obtain the most value that they can from their purchases. For example, Full Nest 1 consumers often face costly expenses related to raising young children, including the cost of baby clothes, furniture, and day care. These young consumers often have to search for new living accommodations in the form of larger apartments, or a starter home, when children are born. Single parents face the same challenges as two-adult families, but they must face these challenges alone. A great strain is therefore placed on the income of single parents. Older, childless couples have more disposable income to spend on their own needs. They are much more likely to enjoy luxuries such as vacation homes, financial investments, and upscale automobiles. Couples older than 64 often enjoy their retirement years, or choose to remain employed beyond retirement age.

The categories and assumptions in the HLC are representative of general patterns of spending behavior. Not every consumer will fall neatly into one specific category. Rather, the categories help to explain the living situations and expenditures of many consumers. Obviously, each consumer faces his or her own situation.

### Middle-Aged Consumers: Boomerang Kids and the Sandwich Generation

Two important groups that are currently of interest to consumer researchers are boomerang kids and

EXHIBIT 10.6
## Traditional Household Life Cycle Categories

| | Under 35 Years | 35 – 64 Years | Older than 64 Years |
|---|---|---|---|
| One-adult household | Bachelor 1 | Bachelor 2 | Bachelor 3 |
| Two-adult household | Young Couple | Childless Couple | Older Couple |
| Two adults + children | Full Nest 1 (children < 6 years old)<br>Full Nest 2 (children > 6 years old) | Delayed Full Nest (children < 6 years old)<br>Full Nest 3 (children > 6 years old) | |
| One adult + children | Single Parent 1 (children < 6 years old)<br>Single Parent 2 (children > 6 years old) | Single Parent 3 | |

Adapted from M. C. Gilly and B. M. Enis (1982), "Recycling the Family Lifecycle: A Proposal for Redefinition," in *Advances in Consumer Research*, Vol. 9, Andrew A. Mitchell, ed., Ann Arbor, MI: Association for Consumer Research, 271–276.

members of the sandwich generation. **Boomerang kids** are young adults, aged 18 to 34, who graduate from college and move back home with their parents. Quite often, the motivation is to reduce debt that has accumulated in the college years. Some have suggested the term *adultolesence* to describe this stage. The trend is growing, and it was estimated that nearly 65% of college graduates moved back home with their parents in 2007, compared to 53% who did so in 2002.[64] More recently, the economic recession of recent years has also had an impact. In 2009, for example, 13% of adults with grown children reported having at least one child move back home, with a significant number being due to the loss of jobs.[65] This trend challenges the traditional HLC, and it greatly impacts how middle-aged consumers spend their money. A humorous view of adult children at home can be found in the movie *Failure to Launch*, starring Matthew McConaughey. The issue for parents, however, is not necessarily a laughing matter. In fact, it has been estimated that boomerang kids cost their parents $5,000 per year in disposable income.[66] The long-term implications of this trend are yet to be seen.

Financial and emotional strains on middle-aged consumers also come from belonging to the sandwich generation. The **sandwich generation** consists of those consumers who must take care of both their own children and their aging parents. An estimated 20 million consumers in the United States are members of the sandwich generation.[67] This number is also expected to increase dramatically over the next decade, as millions of Baby Boomers enter their retirement years. Taking care of both children and parents obviously affects the behavior of these consumers, as income is devoted to the needs of others. In fact, the average cost of caring for others aged 50-plus is nearly $6,000 per year. For consumers who must care for others long distance, the cost is nearly $9,000 per year.[68] Overall worker productivity is also affected, as it has been estimated that businesses lose as much as $34 billion per year due to sandwich generation employees missing work to take care of parents.[69]

## Household Purchase Roles

Each member of a household plays a specific role in product purchase. Five important roles in the household purchase process can be identified:

- *Influencer.* The person in the household who recognizes a need and provides information about a potential purchase to others

- *Gatekeeper.* The person who controls information flow into the household (for example, a mother who blocks unwanted email solicitations from her child's email account)

- *User.* The actual user of the product under consideration

- *Decision maker.* The person who makes the final decision regarding product purchase or nonpurchase

- *Purchaser.* The person who actually buys the product under consideration

Each role is important in product consideration and selection. The final purchase of the product is largely influenced by beliefs regarding the role of each person in the household.

## Gender Roles and Household Decision Making

Like many of the concepts pertaining to household composition, societal views on gender roles and family decision making have evolved over time. Traditionally, men were viewed as having the primary responsibility of providing for the family, while women were expected to meet everyday family needs and take care of the home.[70] However, changes in the education of women and the acceleration in the number of double-income families have challenged these conceptualizations.

An important concept in gender roles and family decision making is **sex role orientation (SRO)**. A family's SRO influences the ways in which household decisions are reached. Families that have a traditional SRO believe that it is the responsibility of the male head of household to make large purchase decisions, while families with a "modern" SRO believe in a more democratic approach.[71] Given the evolving nature of the typical household in the United States, it is not surprising that SROs are changing. In particular, the role of women in household decision making is more prevalent than in previous years. Indeed, studies have revealed that women are playing a bigger role in decision making in all household decision areas.[72] This, in part, reflects the fact that the percentage of women with higher education and incomes levels than their spouses has grown

**boomerang kids** young adults, between the ages of 18 and 34, who move back home with their parents after they graduate from college

**sandwich generation** consumers who must take care of both their own children and their aging parents

**sex role orientation (SRO)** family's set of beliefs regarding the ways in which household decisions are reached

significantly over the last few decades.[73]

## Kid Power

The role of children in household decision making is also evolving. Although children were once thought to have relatively little impact on purchasing decisions outside of what toy to buy, marketers are realizing that children are playing a much larger role in influencing household purchases than ever before. One recent study reveals that 36% of parents with children between the ages of 6 and 11 reported that their children significantly influence their purchasing decisions.[74]

The power of the children's market has grown substantially over the past few decades. Today, consumers between the ages of 8 and 12 spend $30 billion per year of their own money and influence another $600 billion per year in total household spending.[75] Furthermore, the teen segment frequently sees its disposable income grow at a rate that is unlike that found in any other segment. For example, the typical American 12-year-old has $1,500 per year to spend. However, this number leaps to $4,500 per year by the time the child reaches age 17.[76] Much of this income is earned income, even if it is a weekly allowance provided by parents. Obviously, older children earn much of their income from jobs outside of the home.

An important issue in the development of the child consumer is known as consumer socialization. **Consumer socialization** is defined as the process

# The Child's Role in CB

It is widely known that the child consumer of today is very different from the child consumer of yesteryear. Today's child is much more consumer savvy and has much more power in the marketplace. Children influence as much as $600 billion per year in consumer spending, and have more disposable income of their own than ever before. The influence of children on household spending ranges across spending categories, from groceries to vacation destinations to automobile purchases.

Not everyone agrees that the commercialization of children is a positive development. For many, children should be off-limits to advertisers, or at least they should be targeted less frequently. Marketers often believe that parents should play a more active role in limiting commercial exposure, while parents argue that marketers should cut back on advertisements aimed at kids. Still others believe strongly in the consumer socialization concept and that consumer education should begin early in life.

What is interesting about children today is that they are active not only as influencers, but also as gatekeepers of marketing information. Because they spend more time online than ever before, children are more likely to find marketplace information and relay the information on to the actual decision maker or purchaser: their parents! Therefore the power of children in the market-place is not only increasing from a monetary standpoint, but the roles that children play in household purchasing are evolving as well.

Sources: Schor, J. (2008), "Understanding the Child Consumer," *Journal of the American Academy of Child and Adolescent Psychiatry* 47 (5), 486 -490; "Business: Trillion Dollar Kids; Marketing to Children," *The Economist*, 381 (8506) (2006), 74; Tapscott, D. (2008), "Net Gen Transforms Marketing," *BusinessWeek* online (November 17). **http://www.businessweek.com/technology/content/nov2008/tc20081114_882532.htm,** accessed April 10, 2009.

through which young consumers develop attitudes and learn skills that help them function in the marketplace.[77] Sometimes these skills are learned at a surprisingly young age, and children have largely begun to seek products that were once considered "too old" for their age segment. This has led to the development of a well-known marketing acronym, KGOY. (Kids Growing Older, Younger).

Although many consider the issue of kid power and marketing to children controversial, it is clear that children do exert a significant influence on household decision making, and it is likely that this trend will continue.

# 10 Study Tools

**Located at back of the textbook**

❏ Rip-out Chapter-in-Review Card

**Located at www.cengagebrain.com**

❏ Review Key Terms Flashcards (Print or Online)

❏ Download audio summaries to review on the go

❏ Complete practice quizzes to prepare for tests

❏ Play "Beat the Clock" and "Quizbowl" to master concepts

❏ Watch Video on Teen Research Unlimited for a real company example

## what others have thought...

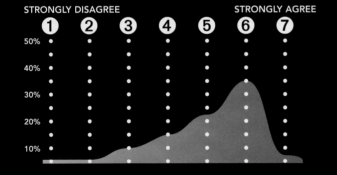

STRONGLY DISAGREE ① ② ③ ④ ⑤ ⑥ ⑦ STRONGLY AGREE

50% 40% 30% 20% 10%

**The groups I belong to have a great impact on how I see myself.**

It seems that most students agree with this statement. Our data reveals that approximately 65% of students at least somewhat agree with this. Groups do impact all of us in many ways, and they even impact how we see ourselves!

## Case 3-1

### Does Culture Affect Sales? A Hawaiian Perspective

*Written by Derrek Choy, DBA, University of Hawaii-West Oahu*

James Smith, the CEO of the Blue Water Cabinet Company, located in Minnesota, wants to bring his brand of custom cabinetry to Hawaii. He has heard the remodeling boom is now hitting the Hawaiian market and a higher quality brand of kitchen cabinetry is needed in this market. He knows that Hawaii is composed of Oahu, the capital of Hawaii, Kauai, Maui, the Big Island of Hawaii, and Molokai. Oahu has the largest population with close to 1 million people. In researching the islands, Mr. Smith's research has shown a high proportion of home ownership on Kauai, Maui, and the Big Island, by individuals from across the United States and Canada. Mr. Smith assumes that many of those residences are primarily vacation homes. He knows that those particular homes would be a good market for his higher-end cabinets. What he is not sure of is how to reach the residents that have lived on the islands for generations. He has learned Hawaii is a market that is hard to break into. Remodeling companies and contractors on the islands have a tendency to purchase cabinets from companies they've always purchased from. He has had associates trying to bring new businesses to the islands and failing in the ventures within a year. He does not want to fall into the same predicament as his associates have.

Mr. Smith sees Hawaii as any market. To Mr. Smith, Hawaii shouldn't be any different than any other part of the United States. He feels the same marketing plan he uses in his other territories should also work in the 50th state. The consumers in Hawaii have an average income of $65,000, with over half the population part of a two-income family. Therefore, with both adults in the family working, Mr. Smith believes there is more expendable income in island families. The average price of a home is over $500,000 and on the high end, over $3 million. He sees over 5,000 units on Oahu alone needing a kitchen renovation in the next decade. In evaluating the Hawaiian market, how should Mr. Smith segment each market? Is each island different in the way consumers view products?

To gain a better understanding of the Hawaiian market, he has hired Mr. Alex Ching, a long-time resident and home remodeler in the state of Hawaii, for advice on how to break into this market.

*Reprinted with permission from the author

Mr. Ching is glad that Mr. Smith has asked for his advice. He says that one of the common mistakes that mainland businesses make when entering the Hawaiian market is assuming that Hawaii is the same as any other market in the continental United States.

Mr. Ching explains that in Hawaii, building a relationship with the people you're selling to is an integral part of whether or not you will be successful. If you do not take the time to get to know the people in the company you want to sell to, and let them get to know you, there is a good chance they will not buy your product.

Mr. Ching also advises Mr. Smith to understand the diverse culture that exists in Hawaii. It is a melting pot composed of many races. Japanese, Chinese, Portuguese, Filipinos, Koreans, and Vietnamese, to name a few, have settled in Hawaii, and all have unique cultural characteristics.

Hawaii, according to Mr. Ching, is a blending of all cultures. In fact, a blending of cultures exists in all targets of the Hawaiian market. To the many potential clients of Asian ancestry, coming into a business that you are not acquainted with and pushing your product in an aggressive way is equated with rudeness and disrespect. Also, people from Hawaii are often initially quieter than business people from the Mainland are used to. Unfortunately, this quiet demeanor may be misinterpreted as weakness or a lack of interest. In reality, the local business person is often simply observing and assimilating the facts that are being given. Mr. Ching advises Mr. Smith to look at the diversity of cultures prior to entering the Hawaiian market. There is more of a blending of races in Hawaii than in other parts of the United States. In fact, Hawaii has the highest amount of interracial marriages than any other state in the union. This means that many households in Hawaii have a blending of different cultures. This blending affects the way a couple sets up their life, including the way they choose a residence, divide up household duties, manage their finances, raise their children, and how they worship. It is not unusual to see in a Hawaiian home a Buddhist shrine next to a table with pictures of Roman Catholic saints and holy candles.

Mr. Smith realizes that the Hawaiian market is more complex than he originally anticipated. Mr. Smith knew that in the continental United States there are also different cultural groups and interracial marriages. But he is beginning to realize that in Hawaii it is more prevalent, and affects the sales market more than it does on the Mainland. He is realizing the marketing plan he uses elsewhere may not work in the Hawaiian market.

If a new product such as kitchen cabinetry is introduced into the market, Mr. Ching advises Mr. Smith to look at the attitude that exists about homes. In many of the cultures in Hawaii, for example, among Chinese, Japanese, and Hawaiians, a home is not just a residence you live in for a designated time. It is often thought of as a legacy you will hand down to your children, and to many future generations. It is not unusual in Hawaii that a home will house extended families. With the high cost of living in Hawaii, and the poor economy at the present time, many people are renovating and adding to their homes, allowing their children to move back into the family homes with their children. With the cultural tradition of respecting elders, many Hawaii families are building extensions to their homes for elderly relatives. With the blending of different cultures that developed over a period of time in Hawaii, is Hawaii really unique in the way residents view products and services compared to the other 49 states?

## Questions

1. What should Mr. Smith evaluate prior to entry into the Hawaiian market?

2. Does racial diversity contribute to the consumer's view of a product?

3. If Mr. Smith plans on marketing to all of the Hawaiian Islands, what key points should he evaluate?

4. Besides evaluating the demographics and geographics of the Hawaiian market, what other considerations should be evaluated?

## Case 3-2

### Busy Being Retired

*Written by Deirdre T. Guion, PhD, North Carolina Central University*

"Lunch was delicious," said Deana.

"Sure was," replied Karen, "shopping wasn't too bad either."

Karen is Deana's shopping buddy. "When would you like to get together again?" asked Deana as she finished her lemonade. Karen quickly picked up her calendar, opened it and sighed, "Umm…this month is pretty busy." When Deana glanced over at the calendar her eyes got big and she exclaimed, "Wow! You really are busy. I work full-time and I'm not that busy." Deana thought to herself, "Boy, each and every day of the calendar has something filled in." Most days had two or three activities written in—everything from weekly bridge games, to lunches, to doctor's appointments, to fundraising events. Deana even saw some events that she figured must be for Karen's grandkids—a hay ride and apple dunking contest! Deana chuckled and thought to herself, "When I retire I will NEVER get THAT busy, no matter what!"

Who wants to be tied to a calendar when they retire? Even though retirement is a long way off, Deana was puzzled by the recognition that one of her favorite shopping buddies Karen, 67 and retired, was just as busy as Deana's own mother, Elaine, who is 68 and retired as well. To Deana, retirement meant you could do less, not more, but clearly these women did not read the book on retirement. "Well," said Deana to Karen, "I'm glad that we were able to grab lunch and do a bit of shopping today. Why don't you let me know when you have some time and we can hang out and go to lunch?"

As Deana headed home she thought about the striking similarities between her friend Karen, and her mother. Both women seemed to be in constant motion, from meetings to fundraising events, to civic, social and religious obligations. Oh, and don't forget the grandkids—picking them up from school, babysitting and even sleepovers. Deana remembered hearing about Baby Boomers and how they are

redefining what it means to grow old. They are active, physically fit, concerned with their appearance, and they like surfing the Web and traveling. She giggled as she thought about the time her friend Karen wanted to try Botox, but was too afraid to go through with it because she thought that it would permanently "freeze" her face! Deana often tells her mom that she needs to relax more and enjoy retirement—especially when her mom laments that she was up at 5:30 AM, and ran errands until 6 or 7 that evening. Deana knew that her mom was often exhausted, but only made the mistake once of voicing her concerns to her mother, "… slow down and enjoy being retired." Her mom quickly snapped back, "I am retired and I'm too busy to slow down."

While Deana is correct that the Baby Boomers (born between 1946 and 1964) have redefined what it means to grow old, it also looks as if an older population—the war babies born during World War II—are changing the way we think about what it means to be retired. This group is large and getting larger, so what we learn about them will only continue to grow as the number of people over age 65 does. In 2008 for example, persons aged 65 or older made up 12.8% of the U.S. population, or 38.9 million people. This number was an increase of 13% since 1998. The over-65 crowd is expected to reach 72.1 million by 2030, doubling the 2008 number!

It stands to reason that advances in health care are enabling people to live longer, healthier lives, but that only explains one aspect of the older folks' busy schedules. Perhaps Deana has happened upon a microculture of the older population—the busy, retired people. Some researchers suggest that in our society we embrace what's called a busy ethic, a concept related to the work ethic. This concept is based on the idea that as people transition from work to retirement they have a need to feel valued and productive. The concept is named after the question commonly asked of many retirement aged people, "What will you do to keep yourself busy when you retire?"

## Questions

1. Do you think that society expects retired people to stay busy? Explain and give examples.

*Reproduced by permission from the author

2. Do you have busy, retired people in your own family? Are these family members expected to be available to help out as needed? If so, explain what you've seen in your own family. What is the downside, if any, of expecting retired people to be busy all of the time?

3. What do you think are the marketing implications for a retired group of people that are busy all the time?

4. Look at television commercials and magazine ads that feature older consumers. What types of activities are they engaged in? Ask someone much older than you (a parent or grandparent) what types of ads they recall seeing that feature older consumers. Compare how they have changed from one period to the next.

---

## Case 3-3
### On the Cutting Edge with Fiskars

*Written by Silvia Hodges, PhD, Fordham Law School*

Somewhere in your kitchen drawer you probably have a pair of scissors with an orange handle tucked away. Launched in 1967, the Finnish craft and hand tools company, Fiskars has sold more than 1 billion of their iconic scissors worldwide. Are you enthusiastic about your scissors? Do you spend time researching scissors on the Internet?

Scissors are a low-involvement product for most consumers, unless they happen to be scrapbook enthusiasts. Scrapbooking is a method for preserving personal and family history in the form of photographs, printed media, and memorabilia in decorated albums, or scrapbooks. The idea of keeping printed materials of personal interest is not new, although scrapbooking supply stores popping up around the country might suggest otherwise.

Some say that scrapbooking dates to shortly after the invention of printing. With the advent of affordable paper, precursors to modern scrapbooks became available to a wide array of people. Friendship albums became popular in the 16th century, but in the 18th and 19th centuries friendship albums and school yearbooks afforded girls an outlet through which to share their literary skills and document their own personalized historical record. Such outlets were not previously readily available to them.

Today, scrapbooking is more popular than ever. The Craft and Hobby Association (CHA) reports that scrapbooking is the top-selling sector of the 39 craft segments in the $27 billion U.S. craft and hobby industry. There are over 3,000 independent scrapbook stores and well over 1.3 million scrapbook bloggers, thousands of scrapbooking events, and dozens of magazines dedicated to scrapbooking. Many of the major cruise lines now offer special scrapbooking cruises. Despite the widespread use of digital photography, scrapbookers enjoy the hands-on approach of "hard copy" scrapbooking to preserve memories and express their creativity.

The interest in scrapbooking across the U.S. has boomed virtually overnight. The industry doubled in size between 2001 and 2004, to

$2.55 billion. According to the CHA, about 35 percent (or 40 million) of the 113 million U.S. households scrapbook, rubber stamp, or make cards. These households spent approximately $4 billion in 2009 on scrapbook, "memory craft," and other paper crafting products.

In addition to preserving memories, the hobby is notable for the strong social network associated with it. Scrapbooking respondents have a family-oriented culture, are economically upscale, are well educated, and have an extensive communications network with others involved with the hobby. Hobbyists, known as "scrappers" or "scrapbookers," get together and scrapbook at each other's homes, local scrapbook stores, conventions, retreat centers, and on cruises. The attendees share tips and ideas, as well as enjoying a social outlet. Over 500,000 scrapbookers subscribe to a weekly newsletter on **scrapbook.com**.

All you need to begin scrapbooking are some photos, an album, adhesive, patterned paper to decorate, journal pens, and . . . a sharp pair of scissors. This is where Fiskars comes in. For many scrapbookers, Fiskars scissors are *the* scissors of choice. A household name in many countries around the world prior to the scrapbooking boom, Fiskars started its word-of-mouth (WOM) initiatives in the U.S. in 2006 and has achieved almost transformational success in building strong and supportive relationships, with a devoted following of scrapbook enthusiasts. Fiskars first recruited four part-time "ambassadors" and brought them to its U.S. headquarters in Madison, Wisconsin, for an intense educational briefing about the company, its products, and its values. The goal was to empower the ambassadors to start blogging, attend trade shows, give scrapbooking classes at retail stores, and pursue other activities on their own to spread goodwill from Fiskars. They also recruited other scrapbookers, called "Fiskateers." New Fiskateers receive welcome kits with engraved scissors, a booklet on what it means to be a Fiskateer, and tips for recruiting more to their ranks. The recruiting effort created a powerful and influential community. Fiskateers organize local gatherings for scrapbookers called "crops," where participants talk, crop, and build relationships. The events are organized online by Fiskateers, but are intended to achieve face-to-face interaction.

Engagement, online conversation, and face-to-face among scrapbookers forged strong loyalty to the Fiskars brand and strengthened its connection with customers. In 2008, online chatter in which Fiskars products were referred to by name increased by

*Reprinted by permission

600%, and visits to the company website and blog have reached 1.5+ million. Offline, there are more than 1,000 Fiskateers getting paid by craft stores to teach classes using Fiskars products. In 2009, there were more than 5,000 Fiskateers (up from 1,200 in 2007) in all 50 states and in 47 countries, compared with the company's original goal of 200. In the spring of 2010, Fiskars' official Facebook fan page had over 4,000 followers. Fans post photos of their scrapbooking projects, join discussion boards, upload videos, and share creative ideas. Avid fans of the brand and its products are seen as more trustworthy and convincing than any advertising could be.

The social media and WOM campaign not only strengthened the company's relationship with its customers, but changed the culture at Fiskars itself. Cultivating a relationship with its evangelists inspired Fiskars to change its scrapbooking product development process. Previously, new products at Fiskars were conceived and developed in a vacuum. Fiskars began to survey the Fiskateers and quickly learned from feedback that customers are a great source for product evaluations and ideas. This success, brought about by skillful use of online and offline WOM, has favorably increased brand awareness, as measured by conversation frequency and tone.

## Questions

1. How did enlisting Fiskateers help the brand?

2. How can a company like Fiskars gain the most out of a WOM program? What obstacles may have to be overcome internally?

3. How do you measure WOM success?

4. Why do people, in particular young women, want to be part of an online interest group such as Fiskars' fanpage?

---

## Case 3-4
### Spaceport America Consumers

*Written by Sarah Fischbach, New Mexico State University*

**W**hat is Spaceport America? You may be thinking to yourself, "Is that a new sci-fi movie coming to theaters soon?" Spaceport America is the new frontier in space exploration currently under construction in the "Land of Enchantment."[1] The new frontier of human space travel includes creating reusable launch vehicles to send anyone into space, and the development of the commercial space industry. The once-in-a-lifetime experience to see what Earth looks like from outer space will soon be an opportunity for every American consumer. That's right, you too could be traveling to the moon, just not quite yet. As we continue our journey into the 21st century, America's endeavor into space looks promising. How do you believe consumers will respond to this new form of space travel? What kind of marketing opportunities are open for companies wishing to participate in the space industry?

One of the latest endeavors by NASA and Virgin Galactic involves the Spaceport America site located near Truth or Consequences, New Mexico.[2] Spaceport America will be the first privately owned business, operating under NASA, to compete for space transportation. Space transportation includes partnerships with companies supporting current space operations (i.e. satellite launching) as well as human space launches. Spaceport America will be the first site to sell average Americans tickets into suborbital space.[3] The operation of this unique partnership between NASA and Virgin Galactic may open new ventures for consumers looking for a once in a lifetime experience. Existing marketing tools have been deployed to attract perspective space traveling consumers, as well as businesses.[4] The challenge will be revitalizing space exploration interest and building potential consumer relationships.

The novelty of space exploration seems to have disappeared. Since the early 1900s, thousands of prizes have been awarded for aircraft advancement. It has been estimated that over 1 million dollars in prize money was awarded through 1911. Back then, 1 million dollars was a lot of money, and still is today. So, where is all that money now? Attracting consumers in today's market is even more challenging with the amount of activities occupying our time. It is surprising in today's era of customized technology, where our best friend is our cell phone, that we are not embracing space exploration and the possibilities it brings.

Who will be competing with Spaceport America? If you were to sit down and write out your top ten places to travel before you die, would you put "space" on that list? Many consumers never thought, in their lifetime, that space travel would be on their top ten lists. Astronauts, who spend their whole career training for the opportunity to travel into space, never have been presented with this opportunity. Now that this opportunity is here, how will people react to space exploration opportunities? Marketers of destination locations have been researching their consumers to create an experience that will both attract customers and encourage them to continue spending their money at these locations. Competing with destination locations, space travel obviously has a unique selling point that no one else will be able to offer. Creative marketing experts will spend millions of research dollars creating value for consumers. When deciding to add space exploration to a to-do list, consumers

*Reprinted with permission from the author

will want to know what tangible objects they can retain from their experience. Sharing experiences with friends and family encourages others to participate. This connection may be found in a picture from outer space or a passport to space.

Space enthusiasts are already excited about space travel. Scientists, astronauts, and rocketeers have been dreaming about this day since they were born. Spaceport America does not want to limit their target market to only a few consumers. Using the excitement from these existing consumers, Spaceport America can create contagious emotions to bring in new consumers. Conducting the appropriate market research on the consumption of space travel will start with creating awareness of its possibilities. Nerdy, pocket-protector-wearing space travelers will no longer be the norm of the space community. The aim of marketers is to create a consumer relationship that will make the space travel experience accessible to all who wish to travel to an extremely unique destination.

Space marketing is a completely new avenue for companies and consumers, and comes with a fair share of ethical issues. Who will monitor the marketing of space? Is NASA ready to enter the world of business marketing and branding? Obviously, no one wants to look up in the sky and see a McDonald's logo on the moon. The potential is endless but there is a fine line of appropriateness. It will be interesting to see how it plays out as we see space exploration expand in the next generation.

Space exploration continues to grow in popularity. The current mission of NASA is to create a new heavy-lift rocket design to allow astronauts to orbit Mars somewhere near the mid-2030s.[5] It sounds like something out of a science fiction movie, but it may be possible. The current "scout mission" to Mars includes balloons and unmanned airplanes returning with samples from the planet to develop new technology. NASA is selecting proposals from the science community.[6] The government initiative to bring private industry into space travel is right on the mark. This means more competition, more brains, more savings. Marketers continue to strive to understand consumer behavior in their unique target markets. As Spaceport America enters a new realm of marketing, so does their research into consumer interest in this new endeavor.

As long as consumers have been staring up at the sky, wondering what else is out there, marketers have been studying consumer behaviors. Spaceports and suborbital travel are not a new concept. Other countries have been launching human tourists into space for quite some time. Will the opening of Spaceport America bring U.S. consumers to the doorsteps of space? How will companies respond to the commercial space industry?

Spaceport America is scheduled for completion in 2011. Judging by Spaceport America's home web page, New Mexico is excited to be part of the next chapter in space transportation.[7] In an economy where consumers and businesses are holding tight to the purse strings, companies such as Spaceport America are expanding the possibilities of the future. Marketers strive to think "outside the box" and this is exacting what they will be doing to create the new consumer consumption of space travel.

## Questions

1. What types of ethical issues about marketing space exploration might concern you as a consumer? How would you help NASA create ethical standards for marketing space? Explain.

2. After someone has traveled to space and returned, why would someone want to repeat the experience? How will Spaceport America continue to thrive on customer relationships? Explain how Spaceport America could extend the satisfaction of experienced space consumers, and create continuing relationships.

3. Go to the following website: **http://www.spaceportamerica.com/**. What type of customer relationship is Spaceport America targeting? What could they be doing differently to build interest for you as a consumer? Explain.

4. There is a video on YouTube about the development of the Spaceport to create market awareness. What type of relationship are they building with space consumers? What type of image is Spaceport America creating to appeal to consumers? Do you believe space exploration should be marketed through social media?

## Case 3-5
### Love Me Do: How The Beatles Became THE BEATLES

*Written by Aubrey R. Fowler III and K. Nathan Moates, Valdosta State University*

"**M**om, can you tell Granddad to turn down his music?" shouted 15-year old Maxwell. "I can barely concentrate on my book."

"What's wrong kid, you don't like The Beatles?" Max's granddad asked as he walked into the study, slapping his hand against his hip with the beat. "They sure don't make music like this anymore."

"It is great music," Max's mother chimed in. "There's something about those songs that just feels so comfortable and reassuring to me. I can remember listening to your granddad's old Beatles records over and over again when I was your age. I can remember going out and buying my favorite albums when they finally released them on CD."

Max put his book aside and listened to his Mom and Granddad talk about Beatles songs and albums. The more he listened, the more he found himself thinking the stuff was pretty decent music (even if he wasn't exactly sure what an "album" was). He had recently read a *Rolling Stone* article detailing the huge influence The Beatles were on popular music, even 40 years after their breakup. They were the featured music on "American Idol" just a few weeks before, and his friend Lucy had invited him over to play *The Beatles: Rock Band*™ recently on her Wii™ system. She planned for them to join an online community of Beatles fans who were devoted to the game. "All this fuss over an old band," Max thought, as his 64-year-old granddad regaled his mother with what it was like to hear *Abbey Road* for the very first time. But even though the music was old and Granddad definitely needed to invest in some ear-buds, Max found his foot tapping along with the music.

Though the group disbanded in 1970, The Beatles continue to be a cultural icon and popular selling group well into the 21st century. The success of the releases of *The Beatles: Rock Band* and remastered studio albums have resulted in a resurgence of Beatles popularity.[1] Furthermore, an appreciation of the group has transcended generations, essentially bringing multiple generations together based on their love for the music. The Beatles rank among the top four favorite bands in every age group. So, The Beatles are still "THE BEATLES," transcending their own generation to gain importance for generations introduced to their music since they last officially recorded together in 1969.[2]

Perhaps the most obvious reason for the continued success of The Beatles' brand is simply the quantity of top-selling hits over their recording career. Taking into consideration both UK and U.S. charts, The Beatles produced 27 number one singles.[3] While most "classic" bands include one transcendent songwriter, The Beatles boasted two in John Lennon and Paul McCartney, with contributions also from George Harrison. In addition to these songwriting powerhouses, the elements of the "Beatlesque" sound—impassioned lead vocals, ornate backing harmonies, chiming electric guitars, melodic bass lines, and the steady backbeat of Ringo Starr's drumming—have influenced decades of popular music. One could argue that The Beatles fusion of diverse genres of popular music (George Harrison's fascination with Eastern music, for instance) has defined Beatles music as a genre unto itself. In short, it may be the unique musicality of The

Beatles' songs and stylings that have been the major contributor to the brand's transcendence.

Others might argue that it is a multifaceted marketing campaign that has allowed The Beatles to transcend their generation. From the earliest days of the British invasion, The Beatles' brand has been carefully and deliberately shaped and marketed. From album and feature film tie-ins such *A Hard Day's Night* and *Yellow Submarine*, to lunch boxes, toys, and cartoons, The Beatles' mystique has been created from much more than their music. Like Elvis Presley before them, The Beatles embraced a diverse marketing strategy to cash in on (and further) their cross-over success. Symbols such as the classic Beatles logo, iconic album art, and the Apple Records symbol have been used for decades to keep The Beatles brand alive. The use of The Beatles' music, history, and imagery in the creation of 2009's *The Beatles: Rock Band* is an excellent example of the continued leveraging of The Beatles mythos in new, unexpected contexts.

The combination of The Beatles' musicianship with the marketing of The Beatles played a major role in introducing the Fab Four to new generations. Alternatively, the entertainment and news media play a larger role in keeping the group in the spotlight. Perhaps The Beatles are transcendent simply because the media tell consumers that they *are* transcendent. Whatever the case, The Beatles have become cultural icons and continue to have relevance far beyond the 60s generation that birthed the group. As the Baby Boomers and the surviving members of The Beatles themselves grow old, the group will remain a part of popular culture, and Max may be telling his own grandchildren one day about the first time he heard *Abbey Road*.

## Questions

1. Discuss the various reference groups that have influence over Maxwell's appreciation (or lack of appreciation as the case may be) of The Beatles and their music.

2. Discuss the importance of word-of-mouth marketing as part of what has made The Beatles into THE BEATLES.

3. What part might culture have to play in the generational transcendence of The Beatles and their music?

4. Lucy plans for the two to join an online community focused on *The Beatles: Rock Band*. How might this constitute a subculture?

5. Despite The Beatles' popularity, why is it that some consumers are turned off by the music?

*Reproduced with permission from the author

## The social environment,

referring to the other customers and employees in a service or shopping environment, cannot be ignored when explaining how "place" affects consumer behavior.

## what do you think?

**I never let anything get in the way of preparing for my consumer behavior class.**

STRONGLY DISAGREE      STRONGLY AGREE

① ② ③ ④ ⑤ ⑥ ⑦

Visit CourseMate at
www.cengagebrain.com.

# 11

# Consumers in Situations

After studying this chapter, the student should be able to:

**LO1** Understand how value varies with situations.

**LO2** Know the different ways that time affects consumer behavior.

**LO3** Analyze shopping as a consumer activity using the different categories of shopping activities.

**LO4** Distinguish the concepts of unplanned, impulse, and compulsive consumer behavior.

**LO5** Use the concept of atmospherics to create consumer value.

**LO6** Understand what is meant by antecedent conditions.

## LO1 Value in Situations?

or most American tourists, a trip to London is not complete without spending some time at Harrods of Knightsbridge. Harrods's six stories of upscale retailing present consumers with some of the most fabulously merchandised products to be found anywhere. Harrods spares no expense in creating a unique experience. For instance, most department stores have background music of some type, but Harrods entertains shoppers with a full-fledged orchestra on busy days. Certainly, the excitement created by live music helps frame purchase situations, and who could possibly leave Harrods without some souvenir that helps capture the experience in an enduring way?

While these American tourists are on their way to London, their plane may well pass a plane full of British travelers on their way to America's heartland. British travelers can take off from London and fly for a one-day shopping spree at none other than the Mall of America in Minneapolis. They leave behind Harrods and other British merchandisers such as Marks and Spencer, and spend their time, albeit limited, shopping in a different place. Certainly, after flying all the way to Minnesota, will any of these shoppers come back empty-handed? It's unlikely!

What makes these experiences different from "regular" shopping? Some of the factors involved in explaining these outcomes include:

- Exchange rates
- Time of year
- Time available for shopping
- The economic situation
- Credit policies/financing
- Who is accompanying the shopper
- The purpose of the trip—fun or work?
- Airline baggage regulations

Each of these factors and others can affect the value one experiences in exchange.

# SITUATIONS AND VALUE

This chapter focuses on precisely how the value a consumer obtains from a purchase or consumption act varies based on the context in which the act takes place. Situational influences is the term that captures these contextual effects, meaning effects independent of enduring consumer, brand, or product characteristics. As can be seen in the CVF framework, situational influences directly affect both consumer decision making and the eventual value experienced. Situational influences are enduring characteristics of neither a particular consumer nor a product or brand. Indeed, situational influences are ephemeral, meaning they are temporary conditions in a very real sense. Contexts can affect communication, shopping, brand preference, purchase, actual consumption, and the evaluation of that consumption.

> Popcorn becomes more valuable when the consumers are at the movies.

© CHUCK SAVAGE/CORBIS

> Situational influences are enduring characteristics of neither a particular consumer nor a product or brand.

The movie theater experience typifies situational influences. If the movie is a matinee, the consumer expects to pay a lower price than he or she would pay in the evening. Even though the movie hasn't changed, the number of people available to go to the movie has changed from the evening hours. Therefore, the lower demand entices the theater to offer lower prices. In contrast, far fewer people are working in the evening and thus are more likely to be able to go to a movie.

The same consumer goes to the concession stand and pays $10 for a Coke and some popcorn. For some, Coke and popcorn with a movie is a highly ritualized tradition, and the entire experience is not as good without this treat. The fact that the theater doesn't permit outside food and drink also enhances the value of the products sold at the concession stand because

competition is practically eliminated. Situational influences change the desirability of consuming things and therefore change the value of these things.

Three categories of situational influences can be described based on these influences:

- Time
- Place
- Conditions

Exhibit 11.1 provides a snapshot of examples of these influences and the way they operate. The following sections discuss each of these groups of influence in more detail with an emphasis on how value changes with each.

## EXHIBIT 11.1
# Situational Influence Categories

1. Time can influence consumers by changing the way information is processed. A consumer shopping for a computer near the store's closing time may not deliberate and consider as much information as usual. This may shift decision making to limited problem solving when the consumer would otherwise use extended problem solving and ultimately affect brand choice.

2. Place can frame any purchase, consumption, or information processing situation. Think about how the theme of a restaurant as captured by the atmosphere of the place will shape the types of foods consumed there and the value they provide. Sushi is the best in an environment with an Asian genre.

3. Conditions also can influence consumption. Beverage choices are different when a consumer is cold than when a consumer is hot. Also, social settings affect choice. Consumers in crowded restaurants and bars are more likely to choose name brand beverages than when the social condition does not involve crowds.

# LO2 Time and Consumer Behavior

**i**s time a consumer's most valuable resource? Time is truly scarce. In some ways, time is a consumer's only real resource because when we work, we convert time into economic resources. In addition, time is necessary for consumption to occur. Time-related factors also affect a consumer's thoughts, feelings, and behavior, all of which come together to create differing perceptions of value. Time can affect consumption in any of these forms:

- Time pressure
- Time of year
- Time of day

The term **temporal factor** refers to situational characteristics related to time. Thus, each of the time forms listed here represents a different temporal factor.

## TIME PRESSURE

A consumer sits down with five coworkers for lunch. Almost immediately, the waiter comes and asks, "Are you ready to order?" All the others at the table are ready. The consumer experiences a sense of urgency and hastily settles for a hamburger. Would the consumer have made a different choice if he or she had not felt rushed to make a decision rather than make the others wait?

This situation exemplifies an intense time pressure. **Time pressure** represents an urgency to act based on some real or self-imposed deadline. In the situation above, the consumer imposes a deadline of ordering at the same time as the others at the table. Therefore, she rushed to make a decision without the due deliberation that would likely take place otherwise.

Time pressure affects consumers in several ways. First, when time is scarce, consumers process less information because time is a critical resource necessary for problem solving. Consumers who experience time pressure, for instance, are able to recall less information about product choices than are consumers in the same situation who are not under the situational influence of time pressure.[1] Second, consumers experiencing time pressure are more likely to rely on simple choice heuristics than are those in less-tense situations. Thus, rather than deciding which restaurant option is more nutritious, the consumer simply chooses the fastest option.[2] Third, consumers are more likely to shop alone than with others under time pressure.[3]

Consumers who might otherwise consider many attributes in reaching a decision may simply rely on a price-quality heuristic under time pressure.[4] Time pressure shapes the value consumers perceive in products by influencing both quality and price perceptions.[5] Because consumers rely more on price-quality heuristics than they do beliefs about financial sacrifice, brands that are positioned as relatively high quality may benefit in situations characterized by high time pressure. Consumers may simply choose the well-known and potentially higher-priced brand because they don't have time to weigh different attributes against the price. Conversely, other consumers may simply choose the lowest price alternative and risk disappointment if a brand does not deliver the expected benefits.

## TIME OF YEAR

**Seasonality** refers to regularly occurring conditions that vary with the time of year. The fact is, consumers' value

**temporal factors** situational characteristics related to time

**time pressure** urgency to act based on some real or self-imposed deadline

**seasonality** regularly occurring conditions that vary with the time of year

perceptions also vary with the time of the year. A cup of hot chocolate is simply not worth as much to a consumer on a hot, sunny summer afternoon as it is on a cold, cloudy winter day.

Even though this tendency may seem as obvious as consumers purchasing more coats and sweaters during the winter, seasonality has other effects that are perhaps not so obvious.[6] Consumers tend to shop earlier in the day during winter months, and, overall, they tend to spend more during the summer months.[7] Almost all products are susceptible to some type of seasonal influence. Fashion may lead the way with traditional spring, summer, fall, and winter fashions. However, many food items vary in demand with the season. People consume champagne predominantly during the holidays. The challenge for those who sell seasonal products like champagne is to position the product more as an everyday option.

## TIME OF DAY/CIRCADIAN CYCLES

What beverage do most consumers around the world wake up to? Traditionally, Danes, Italians, and the French have been almost exclusively coffee drinkers. Consumers in the United Kingdom and in many parts of Asia wake to tea in the morning. During the 1990s, American consumers turned away from coffee toward soft drinks, particularly among young consumers. Today, however, coffee sales are on the rise, and college-aged Americans have returned to drinking coffee in the morning. Coffee sales are also increasing in the United Kingdom as coffee shops, including Starbucks, can be found in all major cities.

The increase in coffee consumption in the United States has come largely at the expense of carbonated soft drinks. Tea sales are also increasing in the United States, and although tea has largely been an afternoon and evening beverage in the past, Americans now are turning to tea, even iced tea, as a beverage to wake up to.[8]

Whether it's beverage consumption, attire, or choice of entertainment, the time of day affects the value of products and activities. Some of this influence is due to scheduled events during the day, such as one's working hours. But part is also biological. In fact, our bodies have a rhythm that varies with the time of day—or a **circadian cycle**. One aspect of the circadian cycle deals with our sleeping and waking times. Consumers would prefer to sleep between the hours of midnight and 6 A.M. and from about 1 to 3 P.M. Consumers who tend to shop during the "odd hours" will do so with less energy and efficiency and with deprived cognitive capacity.[9] However, they can also do so with less interference from other consumers.

Our circadian cycle is responsible for productivity in many activities. A host of products exist to try to aid consumers through the low-energy periods of the day, but perhaps the best fix is a quick nap! Research shows that diminished capacity will affect consumers who get less than 5 hours of sleep each day.[10] Consumers beware of late night infomercials!

## ADVERTIMING

Are you having trouble sleeping? Try Rozeram! A popular ad campaign for a Japanese pharmaceutical product used Abraham Lincoln, a beaver, and other assorted characters to convince the consumer that this product will indeed solve sleep-related problems—primarily, the lack of sleep. Rozeram runs television ads mainly from about midnight through the early morning hours. The assumption is that consumers will be most sensitive to problems with sleeping when they should be sleeping.

Companies sometimes buy advertising with a schedule that runs the advertisement primarily at times when customers will be most receptive to the message. This practice is known as **advertiming**. Advertisers practice advertiming based on seasonal patterns and even on day-to-day changes in the weather. Swimming pool marketers realize that consumers are more receptive to their ads in the spring or summer just as they are more receptive to hot chocolate sales on a cold, cloudy day.

© ISTOCKPHOTO.COM/STEPHANIE HORROCKS

# LO3 Place Shapes Shopping Activities

## INTRODUCTION

The economy depends on consumers buying things. Consumers depend on purchases to receive value. Buying is the result of the shopping process. Thus, marketers understand that shopping holds the key to value creation that stimulates economies and ultimately raises standards of living.

Many of the activities involved in the CVF and consumer behavior theory in general take place in the shopping process. What exactly is shopping? Perhaps the following questions can help put shopping in perspective:

- Do consumers have to buy to shop?
- Is a store necessary for shopping?
- What motivates consumer shopping?

Marketers naturally hope that consumers will purchase things while shopping. But not every shopping act culminates in a purchase. Sometimes a consumer goes shopping only to find out that the desired product is out of stock. Rather than buying a less desirable product, the consumer may simply pass or put off product acquisition indefinitely.

More and more, a physical store isn't necessary for shopping to take place. Consumers shop using their computers, their phones, vending machines, or more traditional "nonstore" alternatives, like catalogs. Sometimes, consumers facing an important decision like a new home or an upcoming vacation are so involved in the buying process that they can't stop thinking about their choices. In this case, they may be shopping simply from the things they hold in memory.

**shopping** set of value-producing consumer activities that directly increase the likelihood that something will be purchased

## WHAT IS SHOPPING?

**Shopping** can be defined as the set of value-producing consumer activities that directly increase the likelihood that something will be purchased. Thus, when a consumer surfs the Internet looking for a song for her iPod, she is shopping. When a consumer visits a car dealer after hours to peruse the options on new cars, he is shopping. When a consumer visits the mall as a regular weekend activity, she is shopping. Earlier, marketing was discussed as business activities that enhance the likelihood of purchase. In this sense, shopping can be looked at as the inverse of marketing. Both marketing and shopping make purchase more likely, but one involves activities of marketing people and the other involves activities of shoppers.

---

## Shopping Pals?

Is it better to shop with a shopping pal? Maybe, if the consumer has the time. Married consumers report that one of the main reasons for not shopping with a spouse is time pressure. Men in particular see an advantage in shopping together because of the reduced financial risk that comes from being able to make a joint decision. Thus, if there isn't enough time to shop together, the couple may spend more than they would otherwise, reducing the utilitarian value from the situation. However, consumers also report that shopping with a family member can reduce hedonic value. Specifically, consumers appear to have more pleasure and report greater hedonic value when shopping alone or with a friend as opposed to shopping with a family member. Family members create greater anxiety about purchase decisions and can even increase the sense of time pressure as one worries about the other family member being bored when he or she is enjoying an extended shopping period. Thus, shopping pals don't always enhance shopping value.

Sources: Lim, J. and S. E. Beatty (2010), "Factors Affecting Couples' Decisions to Jointly Shop," *Journal of Business Research*, in press. Borges, A., J. C. Chebat and B. J. Babin (2010), "Does a Companion Always Enhance the Shopping Experience?" *Journal of Retailing and Consumer Services*, 17 (July), 294–299. Grace, D. (2009), "An Examination of Consumer Embarrassment and Repatronage Intentions in the Context of Emotional Service Encounters," *Journal of Retailing and Consumer Services*, 16 (January), 1–9.

© ISTOCKPHOTO.COM/DMITRIY SHIRONOSOV

# SHOPPING ACTIVITIES

Shopping activities take place in specific places, over time, and under specific conditions or contexts. Shopping thus occurs in situations that are not easily controlled by a consumer and often not by the marketer either. The consumer may be either alone or in a crowded place, rushed or relaxed, in a good mood or a bad mood. In other words, shoppers are subjected to many situational influences that affect decision making and value. Whether the shoppers are American, European, or Asian, situational variables are at least as important

> Both marketing and shopping make purchase more likely, but one involves activities of marketing people and the other involves activities of shoppers.

in explaining eventual buying behavior as are personal characteristics or product beliefs.[11] Practically all shopping activities are influenced by contextual sources.

Four different types of shopping activities exist. At least one of these types characterizes any given shopping experience, but sometimes the shopper can combine more than one type into a single shopping trip. The four types of shopping activities are:

1. **Acquisitional shopping.** Activities oriented toward a specific, intended purchase or purchases

2. **Epistemic shopping.** Activities oriented toward acquiring knowledge about products

3. **Experiential shopping.** Recreationally oriented activities designed to provide interest, excitement, relaxation, fun, social interaction, or some other desired feeling

4. **Impulsive shopping.** Spontaneous activities characterized by a diminished regard for consequences, heightened emotional involvement, and a desire for immediate self-fulfillment

## Acquisitional Shopping

A consumer who runs out to the store on her lunch hour to buy a gift for a coworker's baby shower is strongly oriented toward getting a gift. Thus, shopping is more like a task, and this particular activity depends on high utilitarian value as an outcome.

## Epistemic Shopping

Epistemic activities include finding information on some purchase that is imminent. Alternatively, epistemic activities include shopping simply to increase an ever-growing body of knowledge about some product category of interest. In this sense, epistemic activities can be associated with either situational involvement or enduring involvement, respectively.

## Experiential Shopping

Experiential activities include things done just for the experience. Many consumers go shopping on the weekends just to do something. In other words, experiential shopping can be motivated by boredom or loneliness. On the other hand, consumers who are on vacation often take in the local shopping venues. In this way, they experience something new and possibly unique. **Outshopping** is a term used to refer to consumers who are shopping in a city or town they must travel to rather than in their own hometown. Outshopping is often motivated simply by the desire for the experience. The outshopping consumer sees this as a value opportunity and is more likely to make purchases in this less-familiar and perhaps more-intriguing place. People who live alone also go shopping to experience interacting with other people. Thus, much of the reason for shopping lies in the experience itself.

## Impulsive Shopping

Impulsive behaviors represent a unique group of shopping activities as we will see in detail later. However, impulsive activities also illustrate how a single shopping trip can result in more than one type of activity. A shopper may simply go to a big box store to acquire a gift. However, while there, the shopper may get into the environment of the store and experience strong emotions. These may also encourage the consumer to act impulsively.

## EXHIBIT 11.2
# Shopping Activities and Shopping Value

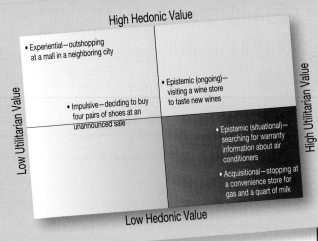

High Hedonic Value

Low Utilitarian Value

High Utilitarian Value

- Experiential—outshopping at a mall in a neighboring city
- Epistemic (ongoing)—visiting a wine store to taste new wines
- Impulsive—deciding to buy four pairs of shoes at an unannounced sale
- Epistemic (situational)—searching for warranty information about air conditioners
- Acquisitional—stopping at a convenience store for gas and a quart of milk

Low Hedonic Value

**personal shopping value (PSV)** overall subjective worth of a shopping activity considering all associated costs and benefits

**utilitarian shopping value** worth obtained because some shopping task or job is completed successfully

**hedonic shopping value** worth of an activity because the time spent doing the activity itself is personally gratifying

Exhibit 11.2 provides examples of each type of activity and ties the activities to the types of value they are more associated with.

# SHOPPING VALUE

All shopping activities are aimed at one key result—value. Consistent with the view of value from a previous chapter, **personal shopping value**, or **PSV**, is the overall subjective worth of a shopping activity considering all associated costs and benefits. Like value overall, PSV can be usefully divided into two types. **Utilitarian shopping value** represents the worth obtained because some shopping task or job is completed successfully. **Hedonic shopping value** represents the worth of an activity because the time spent doing the activity itself is personally gratifying.[12]

## Value and Shopping Activities

Thus, the activities shown in Exhibit 11.2 all provide value, but they provide value in different ways to different consumers. The old term *window shopping* illustrates this point. Some consumers window shop to find information so that an upcoming shopping trip might be more successful.

In this way, window shopping is a means to the end of a more successful future shopping task. Consumers may also window shop simply as a way of passing time in a gratifying way. Thus, window shopping can provide utilitarian and/or hedonic shopping value, respectively.

Situational influences may affect the type of shopping value desired by consumers. Time pressure, for example, may lead consumers to be more concerned with simple product acquisition than they might otherwise be. On the other hand, consumers who are in a bad mood may choose to change it by going shopping. The pleasant emotions can be personally gratifying and can potentially improve a shopper's mood.[13] Thus, hedonic shopping value becomes important. However, research suggests that utilitarian and hedonic shopping value relate to loyalty and that for department stores, hedonic value may build loyalty more strongly.[14]

## Retail Personality

Retailers specializing in things like a wide selection of

A purchase isn't needed for a consumer to get value out of shopping.

**functional quality** retail positioning that emphasizes tangible things like a wide selection of goods, low prices, guarantees, and knowledgeable employees

**affective quality** retail positioning that emphasizes a unique environment, exciting décor, friendly employees, and, in general, the feelings experienced in a retail place

**retail personality** way a retail store is defined in the mind of a shopper based on the combination of functional and affective qualities

**impulsive consumption** consumption acts characterized by spontaneity, a diminished regard for consequences, and a need for self-fulfillment

goods, low prices, guarantees, and knowledgeable employees can provide high proportions of utilitarian shopping value. This type of positioning emphasizes the **functional quality** of a retail store by facilitating the task of shopping. In contrast, retailers specializing in a unique environment, an impressive décor, friendly employees, and pleasant emotions can provide relatively high hedonic shopping value. This type of positioning emphasizes the **affective quality** of a retail store. The affective quality can be managed to create an emotionally rewarding environment capable of producing high hedonic shopping value. Together, the functional and affective qualities come together to shape retail personality. More specifically, **retail personality** is the way a retail store is defined in the mind of a shopper based on the combination of functional and affective qualities.[15]

From a strategic perspective, these two retail personality dimensions are extremely useful as perceptual map

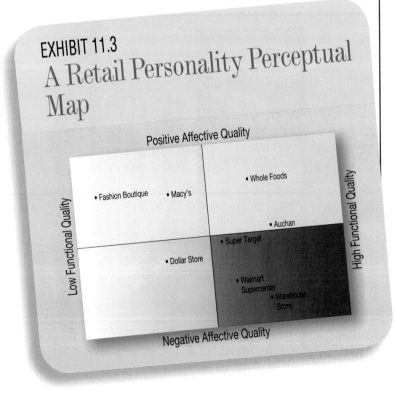

## EXHIBIT 11.3
## A Retail Personality Perceptual Map

dimensions (see Exhibit 11.3). Once again, a perceptual map of this type reveals which retail choices consumers view as most similar. As consumers' choices become more similar, they are more likely to compete with each other.

# LO4 Impulsive Shopping and Consumption

i mpulsive shopping activities take place every day. Some retailers and service providers survive largely as a result of consumers' compulsive activities. For instance, many behaviors associated with indulgence can be driven by impulsive motivations.

So, just what is an impulsive consumption act? As the definition implies, **impulsive consumption** is largely characterized by three components:

1. Impulsive acts are usually spontaneous and involve at least short-term feelings of liberation.

2. Impulsive acts are usually associated with a diminished regard for any costs or consequences (negative aspects) associated with the act.

3. Impulsive acts are usually motivated by a need for immediate self-fulfillment and are thus usually highly involving emotionally and associated with hedonic shopping value.

Activities characterized by these features are likely to be impulsive. For example, a consumer might have a bad morning at work and decide to cancel a business lunch to take a break shopping for self-gifts or "happies" via the Internet. This activity is likely characterized as impulsive and can be a way to suppress negative emotions and evoke more positive feelings.[16] The behavior can be broken down to demonstrate the impulsiveness involved as follows:

1. The act involves willingly deviating from previous plans and thus shows spontaneity and no doubt feelings of liberation from the negative events of the day.

2. The act shows diminished regard for consequences either for missing the business lunch or for any expense incurred.

3. The act fulfills the need to maintain a positive outlook on the self and thus provides hedonic value.

Internet shopping, although often viewed as utilitarian in nature, can provide hedonic value in this way.[17] Additionally, consumers who feel they have restrained their spending behavior in the past may indulge in impulsive purchases as a reward for past good behavior.[18] Thus, when the economy turns around, consumers may let loose with a lot of impulsive purchases.

## IMPULSIVE VERSUS UNPLANNED CONSUMER BEHAVIOR

Impulsive purchasing is not synonymous with unplanned purchasing behavior. **Unplanned shopping**, buying, and consuming share some, but not all, characteristics of truly impulsive consumer behavior. Exhibit 11.4 illustrates the relationship between impulsive and unplanned consumer activity. The right side of the exhibit shows that unplanned consumer acts are characterized by:

1. Situational memory
2. Utilitarian orientation
3. Spontaneity

Situational memory characterizes unplanned acts because something in the environment, such as a point-of-purchase display, usually triggers the knowledge in memory that something is needed. A consumer may enter the grocery store without Doublemint gum on her grocery list. However, the candy counter at the checkout provides a convenient reminder that her office inventory of her favorite breath freshener is depleted.

Simply put, utilitarian motivations drive many unplanned purchases. This consumer who purchases Doublemint gum is probably not very emotionally moved by the gum purchase. However, the purchase allows her to fulfill a need to replenish her supply of the product.

Unplanned acts are spontaneous and, to some extent, they share this characteristic with impulsivity. They are, by definition, unplanned and therefore done without any significant deliberation or prior decision making. The gum buyer certainly had not put a lot of thought into the decision to buy Doublemint as she planned the shopping trip.

## DISTINGUISHING IMPULSIVE AND UNPLANNED CONSUMER BEHAVIOR

The line between impulsive and unplanned purchases is not always clear because some unplanned acts are impulsive and many impulsive acts are unplanned. Las Vegas tourism for years has used a tagline that says:

*What Happens in Vegas, Stays in Vegas*

While some trips to Vegas may be completely spontaneous, most involve some degree of planning. But the tagline emphasizes the impulsive nature of consumer behavior in Las Vegas. Certainly, the campaign illustrates the high hedonic value that can be obtained and encourages consumers not to worry so much about the consequences. So perhaps an impulsive consumption act, like going to Vegas, can even be planned. Simple unplanned purchases may lack the impulsive characteristics captured so well by this campaign.

Simple unplanned purchases usually lack any real emotional involvement or significant amounts of self-gratification. Additionally, unplanned purchases often involve only minimal negative consequences and thus

> **unplanned shopping**
> shopping activity that shares some, but not all, characteristics of truly impulsive consumer behavior; being characterized by situational memory, a utilitarian orientation, and feelings of spontaneity

**EXHIBIT 11.4**
Impulsive versus Unplanned Shopping Behavior

Impulsive Behavior
Diminished Regard for Consequences
Impulse Shopping/Behavior
Emotional-Hedonic

Unplanned Behavior
MILK ???
Situational Memory
Unplanned Shopping/Behavior
Spontaneous
Utilitarian

fail to really qualify as having negative consequences. A pack of gum is not likely to cause severe financial problems for very many consumers.

# SUSCEPTIBILITY TO SITUATIONAL EFFECTS

Are all consumers susceptible to unplanned and impulsive behavior? The answer is "yes," but not all consumers are equally susceptible. Individual difference characteristics can play a role. For example, **impulsivity** is a personality trait that represents how sensitive a consumer is to immediate rewards. A consumer shopping for a gift for a friend may see shoes on sale at half off and be compelled to purchase these and obtain the *reward*.[19] Naturally, consumers with high impulsivity are more prone to impulsive acts.[20]

*The emotions and timing of online auctions just may trigger impulsive actions.*

Consumers with attention deficit disorder, for example, typically have high degrees of impulsivity, which makes them more prone to impulsive acts. One consequence is that such consumers are even less likely than others to follow step-by-step instructions for assembling or using a product.[21] Thus, they may fail to get the full value from the product because the assembly is incomplete or wrong.

Situational characteristics also influence impulse shopping.[22] For example, a consumer shopping for a purple dress for a special occasion may encounter a black dress on the 40% off rack. The low-price cue may encourage an impulse purchase in this case. Atmospheric characteristics such as the colors, music, free samples, merchandising, and salespeople also can encourage purchase. Online retailers can facilitate the actual buying process by making the transaction a simple one-step process.[23] Exhibit 11.5 summarizes things that retailers can do to encourage unplanned and impulse purchasing.

## CONSUMER SELF-REGULATION

Another key personality trait that affects a consumer's tendency to do things that are unplanned or impulsive is self-regulatory capacity. **Consumer self-regulation**, in this sense, refers to a tendency for consumers to inhibit outside, or situational, influences from interfering with shopping intentions. Consumers with a high capacity to self-regulate their behavior are sometimes referred to as **action-oriented**, whereas consumers with a low capacity to self-regulate are referred to as **state-oriented**.[24] Action-oriented consumers are affected less by emotions generated by a retail atmosphere than are state-oriented consumers. Recall the three dimensions of atmospheric emotions discussed in an earlier chapter: pleasure, arousal, and dominance. State-oriented shoppers who are emotionally aroused are far more likely to make additional purchases beyond what was planned than are action-oriented shoppers. Likewise, state-oriented shoppers' spending behavior is strongly affected by feelings of dominance in the environment. Further, feelings of dominance among state-oriented shoppers increase hedonic shopping value and decrease utilitarian shopping value. In contrast, action-oriented shoppers' purchasing and shopping value perceptions are unaffected by dominance.

New electronics can be a tempting element in a shopping environment. Self-regulation is related to a consumer's desire, and intention, to purchase such new products. A state-oriented consumer who enters an upbeat electronics store is more likely to buy a new product than an action-oriented consumer would be under the same circumstances.[25] Retailers with a high proportion of state-oriented consumers in their target market are more likely to thrive on consumers' impulse purchases.

Exhibit 11.6 lists some questions that can distinguish consumers based on self-regulatory capacity. The exhibit shows a statement and then demonstrates the way a consumer would respond to the situation. Consumers with a

## EXHIBIT 11.5
## Retail Approaches at Encouraging Impulse Purchases

| TOOL | EXAMPLE |
|---|---|
| 1. Merchandise complementary products together | Placing beer near the charcoal triggers memory so that the consumer remembers how well beer goes with barbecue. |
| 2. Encourage "add-on" purchases | Asking consumers to buy socks after they have agreed to buy shoes seems like a small request, and turning the request down risks creating negative feelings. Add-on purchases also serve as a trigger in memory. |
| 3. Create an emotionally charged atmosphere | Positive emotions, in particular excitement, are associated with larger purchases. Giving free samples can be one way of making consumers feel good. |
| 4. Make things easy to buy | Consumers have less time to think about the purchase and perhaps decide the product is not worth the price. A consumer who allows his credit card number to be automatically used by a website will be more prone to unplanned and impulse purchases. |
| 5. Provide a discount | Buy one watch, get a second for half price. The consequences become even easier to diminish. |

## EXHIBIT 11.6
## Questions Distinguishing Low from High Self-Regulatory Capacity

| STATEMENT | ACTION-ORIENTED CONSUMERS' TYPICAL RESPONSE | STATE-ORIENTED CONSUMERS' TYPICAL RESPONSE |
|---|---|---|
| If I had to work at home... | I would get started right away | I would often have problems getting started |
| When I have important things to buy... | I make a shopping plan and stick to it | I don't know how to get started |
| When I have an important assignment to finish in an afternoon... | I can easily concentrate on the assignment | It often happens that things will distract me |
| When it is absolutely necessary to do some unpleasant task... | I finish it as soon as possible | It takes a while before I can start on it |

high ability to self-regulate their behavior—in other words, the action-oriented consumers—generally form rules that they stick by to limit the extent to which situational influences determine their behavior. For example, if they know they will be tempted to overspend during a shopping trip, they may decide not to take their credit cards with them while shopping. In this way, they can resist the overspending that sometimes accompanies unplanned and impulse purchases.

Although Exhibit 11.5 lists some things retailers can do to encourage unplanned or impulse purchases, one might ask, are such actions ethical? Or, do such actions simply encourage consumers to buy things wastefully? This certainly can be the case, but unplanned purchases are often simply things consumers would indeed intend to buy if they had remembered them before they started shopping. Impulse purchases can also be a relatively harmless way that consumers control their emotions and improve their outlook on life. Impulse purchases do provide value as long as the consequences of the purchases are relatively harmless. In this way, impulse shopping can be therapeutic and emotionally uplifting. This isn't always the case though.

## IMPULSIVE VERSUS COMPULSIVE BEHAVIOR

Impulsive and compulsive consumer behavior shares many of the same characteristics. Compulsive behavior can be emotionally involving and certainly entails the possibility of negative consequences. Compulsive consumer behavior can be distinguished from impulsive consumer behavior. The three distinguishing characteristics are:

- Compulsive consumer behavior is harmful.
- Compulsive consumer behavior seems to be uncontrollable.

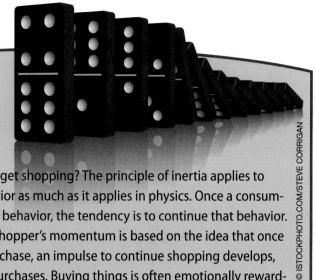

## Domino Shopping

**D**oes shopping beget shopping? The principle of inertia applies to consumer behavior as much as it applies in physics. Once a consumer initiates some behavior, the tendency is to continue that behavior. The concept of shopper's momentum is based on the idea that once a shopper makes a single purchase, an impulse to continue shopping develops, which results in even more purchases. Buying things is often emotionally rewarding. So, if one purchase creates good feelings, and perhaps hedonic shopping value, then two purchases must be even better—right?

Shoppers' momentum may also exist for nonpurchase. Inaction inertia is a term used to refer to the fact that once a consumer passes on buying a brand that he or she is used to buying, not buying that brand becomes easier. This becomes particularly apparent when a consumer misses an opportunity to buy an often-used brand on sale. That consumer is actually less likely to buy that brand again the next time the need becomes apparent. So, not buying can grow on a consumer just as buying can!

Sources: Dhar, R., J. Huber and U. Khan (2007), "The Shopping Momentum Effect," *Journal of Marketing Research*, 44 (August), 370–378; Zeelenberg, M., and V. M. Puttun (2005), "The Dark Side of Discounts: An Inaction Inertia Perspective on the Post-Promotional Dip," *Psychology & Marketing*, 22 (September), 611–622.

- Compulsive consumer behavior is driven by chronic depression.

Compulsive consumer behavior is defined and discussed in more detail in a later chapter.

## LO5 Places Have Atmospheres

**a**ll consumer behavior takes place in some physical space. This statement isn't really profound. Sometimes marketing managers easily forget that the physical environment can play a significant role in shaping buying behavior and the value a consumer receives from shopping or service. Perhaps nowhere is the true impact of place more obvious than in retail and service environments.

# RETAIL AND SERVICE ATMOSPHERICS

In consumer behavior, **atmospherics** refers to the emotional nature of an environment or, more precisely, to the feelings created by the total aura of physical attributes that comprise the physical environment. A total list of things that make up the atmosphere would be difficult to compile; however, they can be summarized by two dimensions.[26] Exhibit 11.7 provides a summary of the dimensions and what they can create.

The term **servicescape** is sometimes used to refer to the physical environment in which consumer services are performed.[27] Each servicescape has its own unique environment. Others have used terms like *e-scape* to refer to a virtual shopping environment as portrayed by a website or *festivalscape* to refer to the array of environmental characteristics a consumer encounters when attending a festival.[28] Thus, Mardi Gras in New Orleans creates an atmosphere where consumers feel uninhibited and sometimes perform extreme behaviors including acts of public nudity, which they probably would not even consider doing in another atmosphere. While consumers sometimes do things they may regret later, this feeling is a defining part of the Mardi Gras experience. No matter the "scape," atmosphere works through the same sequence:

Environment ↦ Thoughts ↦ Feelings ↦ Behavior ↦ Value

## Functional Quality

As mentioned earlier, the functional quality of an environment describes the meaning created by the total result of attributes that facilitate and make efficient the function performed there. In a shopping environment, this includes convenience in all forms: the price levels, the number and helpfulness of employees, and the breadth and depth of merchandise, along with other characteristics that facilitate the shopping task. In a service environment, the amount and expertise of service employees, the convenience of the environment, and the capability of the support staff, among other things, all contribute to the functional quality of the service environment.[29] These are often thought of as core aspects of service as some are essential for the benefits to be realized by consumers.

## Affective Quality

The affective quality represents the emotional meaning of an environment, which results from the sum effect of all ambient attributes that affect the way one feels in that place. A friendly service employee can make the environment more pleasant, cool colors can be relaxing, upbeat music can be exciting, and a crowded environment that restricts movement can be distressing. Although many managers focus more on core aspects, these more relational aspects also influence value and satisfaction.

Restaurants, for example, often go out of business despite having excellent food and a good location. A primary reason for their lack of competitiveness is a lack of attention to the environment. As a result, the restaurant lacks style or creates a distressing or boring affective quality. All consumers are susceptible to the effects of affective quality; however, female consumers appear much more demanding based on how they react to a place with a negative affective quality.[30]

So, does a retail environment with a distinctly high functional quality necessarily have an uninteresting

**atmospherics** emotional nature of an environment or the feelings created by the total aura of physical attributes that comprise a physical environment

**servicescape** physical environment in which consumer services are performed

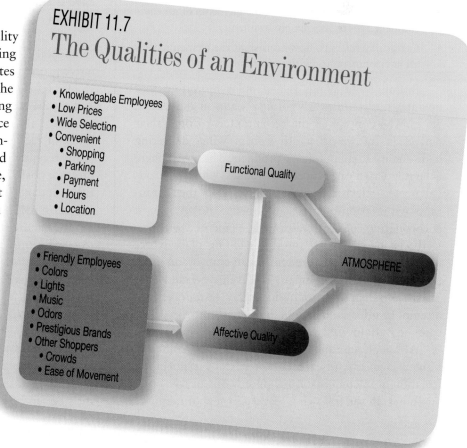

**EXHIBIT 11.7**

**The Qualities of an Environment**

- Knowledgable Employees
- Low Prices
- Wide Selection
- Convenient
  - Shopping
  - Parking
  - Payment
  - Hours
- Location

- Friendly Employees
- Colors
- Lights
- Music
- Odors
- Prestigious Brands
- Other Shoppers
  - Crowds
- Ease of Movement

Functional Quality

Affective Quality

ATMOSPHERE

or poor affective quality? Quite the contrary! If anything, the two dimensions are positively related. An environment with a favorable functional quality tends to be associated with some degree of positive affect. Adolescent girls, for example, find an environment with high levels of functional qualities like accessibility and safety features to also be more pleasing places to shop.[31] Thus, retailers should keep this in mind and realize that even things they build to create shopper safety can affect both the functional and affective meaning of a particular retailer.

# ATMOSPHERE ELEMENTS

The way an atmosphere makes a consumer feel is really determined by the consumer's perception of all the elements in a given environment working together. Therefore, naming all the elements that eventually affect the retail or service atmosphere is impossible. However, a more distinct atmosphere creates a feeling that can ultimately result in a core competitive advantage based on the unique feeling. Two factors help merchandisers and retail designers create just such an atmosphere:[32]

- **Fit** refers to how appropriate the elements of an environment are for a given environment.

- **Congruity** refers to how consistent the elements of an environment are with each other.

Buffalo Wild Wings is a popular restaurant that operates outlets in nearly all fifty states in the United States. The concept of the restaurant is to offer their patrons a fun, exciting atmosphere while delivering high-quality food and drink products. The atmosphere is largely based on a sports bar model, with numerous flat screen televisions placed throughout the restaurants with various sports games being shown. The fit and congruity of the atmospheric elements work perfectly, giving patrons a fun and exciting place where they can bring their entire families to enjoy good times and great food. The company has even won numerous "best sports bar" awards. While other restaurants can attempt to offer similar food products, none can duplicate the Buffalo Wild Wings atmosphere.

Although an atmosphere is created by a combination of elements, researchers often study elements in isolation or in combination with only one or two other attributes. In the following sections, a few of the more

AP IMAGES/J.D. POOLEY

*How would you describe the personality of this restaurant's atmosphere?*

prominent environmental elements are singled out as being particularly effective in changing or shaping an environment's atmosphere.

## Odors

Believe it or not, in Manchester, U.K., the industrial revolution museum includes a tribute to sewerage systems with a sewer museum. What should a sewer museum smell like? Well, the folks at the museum in Manchester have a sewer that smells like a sewer, and the sewer museum certainly wouldn't be authentic with the scent of roses piped in. The fact is, odors are prominent environmental elements that affect both a consumer's cognitive processing and affective reaction.

**Olfactory** is a term that refers to humans' physical and psychological processing of smells. When shoppers process ambient citrus odors, they tend to feel higher levels of pleasant emotions while shopping and to be more receptive to product information. Citrus odors produce positive responses in practically all consumers. Even more positive reactions can be obtained by matching odors with a target market. For example, women respond more favorably to floral scents while men respond more favorably to food scents like pumpkin pie. No kidding! Perhaps the way to a man's heart, or wallet, really is through his stomach.

Retailers like the Knot Shop, a chain of specialty stores for men's fashion accessories, spend considerable amounts of time and money managing the scents in their shops. In the Knot Shop, a masculine odor reminiscent of leather and tobacco is given off to help frame the shopping environment as masculine. The smell fits and helps create the store image! Retailers can also trigger greater arousal by introducing a moderately incongruent odor into an environment. In an experimental study, wine store consumers paid more attention to label information when an incongruent and slightly less pleasant odor was present and became less risk aversive and more willing to try different wines when more pleasing and consistent odors were present.[33] Odors also seem to have a greater effect when other more intrusive elements like crowding are not too strong.[34]

## Music

Fast music means fast dancing. Slow music means slow dancing. Even though consumers don't always dance through the aisles of stores, this image is fairly accurate in describing the way background music affects consumers. Both foreground and background music affect consumers, but they do so in different ways. **Foreground music** is music that becomes the focal point of attention and can have strong effects on a consumer's willingness to approach or avoid an environment. Consumers who dislike rap or country music will likely have a difficult time hanging around a place with loud rap or country music.

From a consumer behavior standpoint, **background music**, which is music played below the audible threshold that would make it the center of attention, is perhaps more interesting than foreground music. Service providers and retailers generally provide some type of background music for customers. Muzak is one of several companies whose business is providing the appropriate background music for a particular service or retail setting. Several effects are attributable to background music:

- The speed of the background music determines the speed at which consumers shop. Slower music means slower shopping. Faster music means faster shopping.
- The tempo of music affects the patience of consumers. Faster music makes consumers less patient.
- The presence of background music enhances service quality perceptions relative to an environment with no background music.
- Pop music used in the background contributes to discount store perceptions.
- Incongruent music lowers consumers' quality perceptions.

These factors are important for retail managers interested in managing quality and value perceptions. However, background music can also affect the bottom line. In restaurants, for instance, consumers who dine with slow background music are more patient and in less of a hurry to leave. As a result, they linger longer and tend to buy more beverages than consumers dining with faster background music. Thus, gross margins can actually be increased by slowing down the background music particularly in light of the higher margins realized on drink sales relative to food sales.[35]

## Color

Color is another tool that marketing managers can use to alter consumer reactions. Some colors are more liked than other colors, but liking isn't really the key to understanding consumer reactions to color. Blue is perhaps the most universally liked color. Blue presents few cultural taboos. Red, white, and black, however, all present cultural barriers associated with bad omens and death in some cultures. Red is a risky color in Japan, as is white in China and black in western cultures. Color, like other environmental elements, helps frame the shopping experience. Therefore, choosing the right color depends on how consumers react in terms of both their thoughts and their feelings.

Color, for example, affects both quality and price perceptions. Consumers who perceive a product in a predominantly blue background tend to think the product is of higher quality, and they are willing to pay more for that product.[36] In contrast, warm colors like red and orange tend to promote expectations of poor quality and low price. Exhibit 11.8 illustrates the way these effects can play out in a retail environment. Color changes behavior by framing the way one thinks about a product and also by changing the way one feels. Thus, the perceived value of an object can vary with color.

Exhibit 11.8 clearly illustrates how color can frame consumer information processing. The same product at the identical price, in this case $100, will be viewed as priced more fairly with a blue background than with an orange or red background. Consumers also express

**foreground music** music that becomes the focal point of attention and can have strong effects on a consumer's willingness to approach or avoid an environment

**background music** music played below the audible threshold that would make it the center of attention

more positive feelings when presented with blue background. Not surprisingly, consumers are also more willing to buy a product presented in a blue background than a red or orange background.

So, is blue always a good color? Like many aspects of consumer behavior, the story isn't quite that simple. Blue has drawbacks. For instance, blue is a cool color. Thus, blue does not attract attention as effectively as a warm color like red or orange does. Also, like other situational effects due to the environment, color does not work alone. Lighting can have dramatic effects on the environment and even reverse color's effect. For example, the effects above hold for bright lights. Change a store's lighting to soft lights and consumers' opinions regarding the product

© KEVIN MAZUR/WIREIMAGE/GETTY IMAGES

## Is This Going to Take Long?

**M**usic impacts consumers in many ways. As we have discussed, the tempo of music can determine the speed at which consumers shop, dine, and even browse. Tempo even affects perceptions and feelings about waiting. Fast-tempo music is generally disliked for short waits and slow tempo music is disliked for long waits. So maybe some Vivaldi would be good if the wait is short, but Green Day would be better if it's going to be a while!

Sources: Oakes, S. (2003), "Musical Tempo and Waiting Perceptions," *Psychology & Marketing*, 29 (8), 685–713; Areni, C. (2003), "Exploring Managers' Implicit Theories of Atmospheric Music: Comparing Academic Analysis to Industry Insight," *Journal of Services Marketing*, 17 (2/3), 161–184; Kellaris, J.J. and R.J. Kent (1992), "The Influence of Music on Consumers' Temporal Perceptions: Does Time Fly When You're Having Fun?," *Journal of Consumer Psychology*, 1, 365–376.

change considerably. For instance, soft lights and an orange background can eliminate the advantage for blue in that the price fairness perceptions, quality perceptions, affect, and purchase intentions are now equal to or slightly better than the combination of blue and soft lights.[37] Victoria's Secret for many years merchandised stores with predominantly warm colors; however, their soft lighting eliminated any bad effects that might be present with bright lights.

Like other elements too, a marketer must be aware of the image. If the brand is closely associated with a color, then that association may be more important than the effects discussed here. So, if you are in a bad mood, change the color of your space, and things may improve!

### Merchandising

Merchandising's point is to provide the customer with the best opportunity to purchase something. This is done by the placement of goods and store fixtures along with the use of signage. The angles or racks and the visual image of the store provide a way for consumers to view and move through a store. Signs change consumers' perceptions. For example, signs that emphasize price by using large numerals create the perception of a discount store. An up-scale store uses little signage. Increasingly, digital signage is delivered with electronic display boards. These seem to attract the attention of shoppers and can be used toward creating a specific feeling.[38] In some cases, the consumer can even interact with the display board.

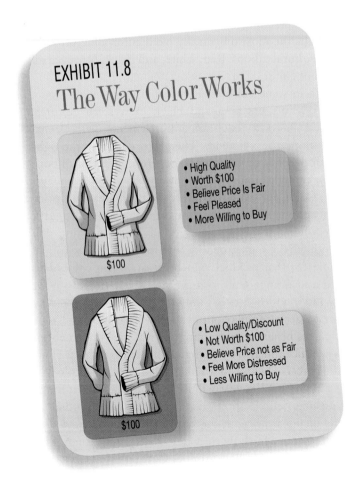

## EXHIBIT 11.8
## The Way Color Works

$100

- High Quality
- Worth $100
- Believe Price Is Fair
- Feel Pleased
- More Willing to Buy

$100

- Low Quality/Discount
- Not Worth $100
- Believe Price not as Fair
- Feel More Distressed
- Less Willing to Buy

PRNEWSFOTO/TARGETPATH LLC

*Digital signage like this attracts attention.*

## Social Settings

An old saying about Bishop Berkeley's forest goes:

*If a tree falls in the forest and nobody is there to hear it, does it make any noise?*

Well, if a consumer goes to the Magnificent Mile in Chicago and there are no other people, is there really an atmosphere? People are a huge part of the environment, and if the people are removed the atmosphere changes entirely. Thus, the social environment, referring to the other customers and employees in a service or shopping environment, cannot be ignored when explaining how atmosphere affects consumer behavior.

**Crowding** refers to the density of people and objects within a given space. A space can be crowded without any people. However, *shopper density*, meaning the number of consumers in a given space, can still exert relatively strong influences on consumer behavior. Crowding actually exerts a **nonlinear effect** on consumers, meaning that a plot of the effect by the amount of crowding does not make a straight line.

Exhibit 11.9 illustrates the way crowding works, particularly with respect to shopper density. Generally, consumers are not particularly attracted to an environment with no other consumers. The lack of consumers might signal poor quality or, in other cases, an absence of other consumers is simply awkward. For example, a consumer who enters a restaurant alone, particularly with no other diners, may well feel quite uncomfortable. In contrast, a mild degree of crowding produces the most positive outcomes in terms of shopping affect, purchase behavior, consumer satisfaction, and shopping value and high degrees of crowding lower these outcomes.[39] For instance, crowding affects utilitarian shopping value less strongly than hedonic shopping value in part because of the negative affect caused by crowding.

Hypermart chains like Carrefour, Auchan, and Walmart can unintentionally diminish the hedonic shopping value consumers experience by placing large displays on the sales floor that compound the negative affect occurring during busy shopping times. In contrast, savvy retailers can actually increase sales by decreasing the amount of merchandise on the sales floor and creating a less crowded shopping environment.

Both the number and type of salespeople can also affect shoppers. For example, the presence of more salespeople in a shopping environment can actually increase

> **crowding** density of people and objects within a given space
>
> **nonlinear effect** a plot of the effect by the amount of crowding, which does not make a straight line

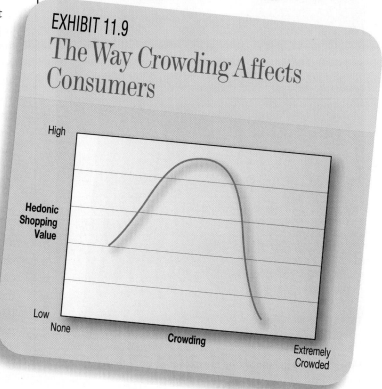

### EXHIBIT 11.9
## The Way Crowding Affects Consumers

shopper purchase intentions. However, the type of salespeople can also influence shoppers' purchasing and value perceptions. In particular, salespeople and service providers should have an appropriate appearance for the type of product sold. The salespeople should simply fit the part. At Disney theme parks, employees are referred to as "cast members" in part because their appearance is tightly controlled to fit the particular environment in which they work.

Salespeople and service providers are an important source of information and influence. **Source attractiveness** is defined as the degree to which a source's physical appearance matches a consumer's prototype (expectations) for beauty and elicits a favorable or desirous response. Intuitively, one would think that a

**How does this person shape the exchange environment?**

© BEYOND FOTO/BEYOND FOTOMEDIA/JUPITERIMAGES

more attractive person always is a good idea relative to a relatively less attractive person. This idea is known as the 'beauty is good' hypothesis.

However, a consumer who encounters an attractive salesperson may end up making an upward social comparison. **Social comparison** is a naturally occurring mental personal comparison of the self with a target individual. Simply, it's a self–other comparison that helps give the self relative meaning. An upward comparison means the target is better and a downward comparison means the target is inferior. In the case of attractiveness, an upward comparison (the salesperson perceived as more attractive than the consumer) can cause negative feelings that reduce the likelihood of purchase.[40] The presence of other attractive customers may even cause another consumer to feel embarrassed if the upward comparison is strong. This effect is more likely for same sex comparisons when the service is unrelated to beauty-related products. Think about how a very attractive appliance salesperson may come across.

Shopping buddies, meaning shopping companions, also cause consumers to react differently than when shopping alone. A shopping companion can be more fun and be a source of objective opinion. In this way, the companion can affect hedonic and utilitarian value. The shopping buddy can help reinforce positive feelings about products and thus encourage purchase. A simple statement like "those jeans look great on you" can tilt the scale toward purchase. Partly as a result, consumers who shop with a companion tend to buy more than those who shop alone. Teens' behavior is particularly affected by mall shopping companions who are members of their peer group. Research shows limits to positive effects of group shopping however. Consumers who shop with a spouse or other family member report lower hedonic value. The family members interfere or get in the way of what could otherwise be a gratifying time alone or with a friend.[41] The presence of a shopping buddy does change things.

## Virtual Shopping Situations

Shopping via the Internet is just about as commonplace as catalog shopping. Many effects seen in real "bricks and mortar" shopping environments exist in the virtual shopping world too. For example, color and sounds can work in much the same way. A website with a blue background enhances quality perceptions just as the background in a real store might. Additionally, images placed in the background of a website can produce active thoughts, particularly when consumer expertise or knowledge is low. A web-based furniture retailer using pictures of clouds in the web background, for instance, can produce thoughts of soft and comfortable furniture. Similarly, images related to money can produce thoughts related to discounts.[42]

More and more, virtual retail sites include avatars or images of real people playing the social role of a helpful salesclerk. Does a virtual salesperson have any effect on shoppers? The answer is "Yes!"[43] The advantages to these sites include increased purchase likelihood and utilitarian shopping value as the virtual people are helpful, but the additional social context particularly improves hedonic shopping value.

# LO6 Antecedent Conditions

t he term **antecedent conditions** refers to situational characteristics that a consumer brings to a particular information processing, purchase, or consumption environment. Events occurring prior to this particular point in time have created a situation. Antecedent conditions include things like economic resources, orientation, mood, and other emotional perceptions such as fear. They can shape the value in a situation by framing the events that take place. The following sections elaborate.

# ECONOMIC RESOURCES

## Buying Power

The economic resources a consumer brings to a particular purchase setting refer to the consumer's buying power. Buying power can be in the form of cash on hand, credit card spending limits, or money available by draft or debit card. Most places in the United States today accept credit cards for payment (Visa, MasterCard, Discover, American Express); however, a few businesses still insist on cash payment. Businesses not accepting "card payment" are more common in other countries. Thus, the amount of money a consumer has on hand can determine where he or she will shop or dine. For consumers short on cash, McDonald's may be a better option than Outback.

However, other issues arise. What if consumers are near their credit limits? This can also change their shopping behavior. Companies may put together special financing packages to deal with consumers whose credit is good enough to receive a major credit card even though they maintain high debt levels. Many consumers live paycheck to paycheck. If so, buying may increase

around the day that consumers are paid. Then, the awareness that they are financially better off because of payday may stimulate increased spending. Check advance services take advantage of payday timing by offering to prepay consumers in return for a portion of the total paycheck. Thus, these consumer services offer utilitarian value to consumers by providing a way for them to receive their pay before the company they work for actually issues a check.

## Consumer Budgeting

In the 1990s, consumer debt ballooned to unprecedented levels. Much of this was in the form of credit card debt. The fact is, if credit card companies can charge a high interest rate (such as 18% percent or more), then they can afford to take a few credit risks and still maintain a profitable business. Thus, credit became easy to get. As a result, the general rule is that consumers can avoid delaying gratification and have things today. However, when consumers find themselves having difficulty making payments, their spending habits must change or they run the risk of losing their credit and worse.

A mortgage crisis in the United States rippled through financial markets around the world during the late 2000s. Many consumers had taken variable rate mortgages that offered very low rates in the first few years of the loan. However, as interest rates rose, these very same consumers sometimes found themselves in a position where their home mortgage was taking 50% or more of their total income. The higher budget allocation to make a house payment lowered their buying power. Many consumers who faced foreclosure learned the hard way about the risks of a variable rate loan.

Most consumers do not perform a formal budgeting process; however, those consumers who do budget end up with different spending habits than those who do not. Generally, budgeting is associated with frugality. As the economic downturn continues in the early 2010s, American families continue to allocate resources cautiously and end up acting more frugal than they might otherwise. Occupancy rates, revenue, and profits fell dramatically at many U.S. resorts in Las Vegas, Atlantic City, Florida, and other locations as a result when compared to pre-2009 figures.[44]

Many consumers who do not prepare a formal budget do perform mental budgeting. **Mental budgeting** is simply a memory accounting for recent spending.[45] One result is that a consumer who has recently splurged on spending in one category will tend to make up for the exuberance through under consumption in another category. In other words, they buy less than they typically would. Thus, the fact that the consumer has splurged recently in one area creates an antecedent condition that affects spending in another.

## ORIENTATION

Consumers enter each exchange environment. They may have natural tendencies toward one shopping orientation or another, for instance. However, some orientations may be temporary. Consumers above may face a temporary orientation toward price consciousness as they seek to save money in uncertain times. Even a consumer with a tendency toward an experiential orientation may temporarily face a strong task-orientation. In these instances, the consumer may actually be distracted by things that might otherwise be pleasant. This effect is even true on the Internet as an aesthetically pleasing website can actually cause lower satisfaction among consumers that are highly task-oriented.[46] Employees who sense the orientation and can adjust their approach will create higher value for the consumer. Gift shopping can dramatically shift a shopper's orientation and change the shopping experience altogether.

## MOOD

Mood was defined earlier as a transient affective state. While shopping and consuming can alter a consumer's mood, each consumer brings his or her current mood to the particular consumption situation. Consumers in particularly bad moods may have a tendency to binge consume. For example, a consumer in a foul mood may down an entire pint of Ben and Jerry's ice cream. If the mood is particularly disagreeable, perhaps a quart is more likely to do the trick. The foul mood enhances the value of the ice cream temporarily because it provides the normal hedonic value from the good taste, but it is also therapeutic and, at least temporarily, helps restores a more favorable affective state.

Mood can also affect shopping. The mood that consumers bring to the shopping environment can exaggerate the actual experience. A consumer in a good mood may find even greater hedonic shopping value in a pleasant shopping experience than he or she may otherwise find.[47] Mood can also affect spending and consumer satisfaction. Shoppers who go shopping

in a bad mood are particularly likely to buy only what they absolutely need and experience lower consumer satisfaction than consumers in good moods.

## SECURITY AND FEARFULNESS

Consumers today live with ever-present reminders of vandalism, crime, and even terrorism. Large parking lots such as commonly found at Walmart stores or conventional shopping centers attract criminals who prey on seemingly defenseless consumers. Stories of abductions, muggings, assaults, car jackings, and other heinous criminal acts taking place understandably create fear among some shoppers, particularly those who view themselves as vulnerable. Shopping malls, markets, airports, and other places where large numbers of consumers gather are consistently mentioned as potential terrorist targets, providing another reason for consumers to feel less secure.

Fearfulness can affect consumers in multiple ways. A consumer who goes shopping in a fearful mood will not go about his or her shopping in the same way. A fearful consumer will tend to buy less and enjoy the experience less. Alternatively, a consumer may cope with fear of shopping by turning to non-store outlets such as the Internet as a seemingly safer way of doing business. But, even here, consumers sometimes fear providing private information often needed to complete a transaction. Thus, retailers who pay attention to making their parking and shopping environments more secure can help eliminate the feelings of fear some shoppers may have otherwise. Exhibit 11.10 lists some ways fearfulness may be reduced among consumers.

### EXHIBIT 11.10
### Enhancing Value by Making Consumers Feel More Safe

- Increase number and visibility of security personnel
- Increase number and prominence of security cameras in parking lots
- Have brightly lit parking lots
- Add carry-out service for consumers—particularly for those shopping alone
- Maintain an uncrowded, open entrance
- Clearly mark all exits
- Prevent loitering
- Discourage gangs from visiting the center

# 11

# Study Tools

**Located at back of the textbook**

☐ Rip-out Chapter-in-Review Card

**Located at www.cengagebrain.com**

☐ Review Key Terms Flashcards (Print or Online)

☐ Download audio summaries to review on the go

☐ Complete practice quizzes to prepare for tests

☐ Play "Beat the Clock" and "Quizbowl" to master concepts

☐ Watch Video on High Sierra for a real company example

## what others have thought...

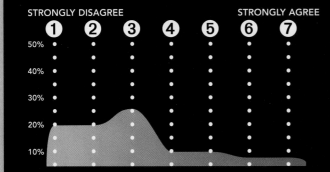

STRONGLY DISAGREE
① ② ③ ④ ⑤
STRONGLY AGREE
⑥ ⑦

50%
40%
30%
20%
10%

**I never let anything get in the way of preparing for my consumer behavior class.**

Responses to this question were given anonymously and perhaps it shows. There is strong disagreement to this statement with less than 25 percent of people expressing any level of agreement. Situational influences interfere even with the best plans.

**Both utilitarian and** hedonic value are associated with consumer decision making.

## what do you think?

**Most of the time I am a rational decision maker.**

STRONGLY DISAGREE      STRONGLY AGREE

① ② ③ ④ ⑤ ⑥ ⑦

Visit CourseMate at www.cengagebrain.com.

# 12

# Decision Making I: Need Recognition and Search

After studying this chapter, the student should be able to:

**LO1** Understand the activities involved in the consumer decision-making process.

**LO2** Describe the three major decision-making research perspectives.

**LO3** Explain the three major types of decision-making approaches.

**LO4** Understand the importance of the consideration set in the decision-making process.

**LO5** Understand the factors that influence the amount of search performed by consumers.

## LO1 Consumer Decision Making

Consumers encounter problem situations ach and every day. Most of the time there are so many situations that it's hard to recall them all. You can run out of milk, be low on gasoline, search for a new apartment, take your car to the shop, and look for an outfit for a job interview all in the same day. In each of these situations, needs are recognized. When needs occur, decision making must take place. Where should I buy milk? Who has the cheapest gasoline? Should I buy an outfit at Kohl's or Macy's?

Some situations require big decisions. For example, when a student recognizes a need for a new laptop computer, a big decision usually follows. In other situations, the decisions are relatively small. For example, when you run out of milk, the decision of which brand, or even where to shop, usually doesn't take much time or effort.

You may recall the basic consumer behavior consumption process that was presented in our opening chapter. This process is shown again in Exhibit 12.1. The process revolves around value-seeking activities that consumers perform as they go about satisfying needs. The consumer first realizes she has a particular need. She then moves through a series of steps that will help her find a desirable way to fill the need. Exchange then takes place, and she ultimately derives value from the process. As with other consumer behavior concepts, we see that value is at the heart of the process.

The decision-making process has been added to the exhibit. As you can see, decision-making processes generally include five activities: (1) need recognition, (2) search for information, (3) evaluation of alternatives, (4) choice, and (5) postchoice evaluation. In the current chapter, we focus on the first two stages of the process: need recognition and information search. The following chapter discusses evaluation of alternatives and choice.

To better visualize this process, consider Exhibit 12.2. Here, Mike is faced with a need for a new laptop as he

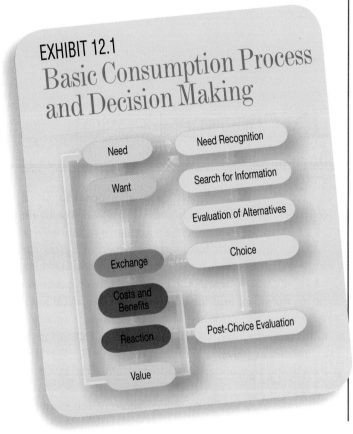

**EXHIBIT 12.1**
**Basic Consumption Process and Decision Making**

- Need — Need Recognition
- Want — Search for Information
- Evaluation of Alternatives
- Exchange — Choice
- Costs and Benefits
- Reaction — Post-Choice Evaluation
- Value

leaves for college. To learn about his options, he begins to read reports about laptops and he asks friends what type of laptop they think he should buy. After considering all of the information that he has gathered, he evaluates the alternatives that are realistically available. From there, he makes a choice and an exchange occurs. He then considers all the costs and benefits associated with the brand and the overall value that he has received from his purchase.

Note that the activities found in the decision-making process are not referred to as steps. The reason is that consumers do not always proceed through the activities in sequential fashion, nor do they always complete the process. Because consumers face numerous decision-making situations daily, they often decide to simply defer a decision until a later time. Consumers can also uncover additional problems or unmet needs as they search for information—moving them from information search to need recognition.

## DECISION MAKING AND CHOICE

Decision-making processes lead to consumer choice. The term *choice* is important. *Choice* does not

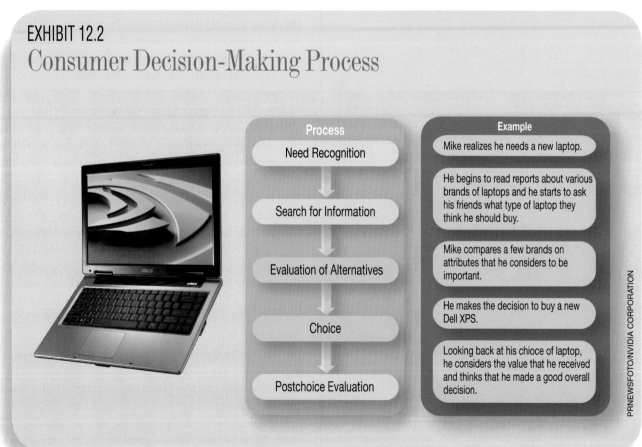

**EXHIBIT 12.2**
**Consumer Decision-Making Process**

| Process | Example |
|---------|---------|
| Need Recognition | Mike realizes he needs a new laptop. |
| Search for Information | He begins to read reports about various brands of laptops and he starts to ask his friends what type of laptop they think he should buy. |
| Evaluation of Alternatives | Mike compares a few brands on attributes that he considers to be important. |
| Choice | He makes the decision to buy a new Dell XPS. |
| Postchoice Evaluation | Looking back at his chioce of laptop, he considers the value that he received and thinks that he made a good overall decision. |

PRNEWSFOTO/NVIDIA CORPORATION

# Decision Making 101

**F**or most consumers, selecting a college is one of the biggest decisions that they face. The educational landscape has become quite competitive, and students now regularly receive information and brochures from prospective colleges while they are in their early high school years, if not sooner.

Experts in the area of college choice suggest that students pay close attention to finding the college that fits best with their personal needs and goals. Big-name colleges aren't always the best solution for students, even though the familiar names may be attractive. In fact, many times, the so-called best schools do not offer the best fit for a student. For this reason, students are encouraged to carefully search for relevant information by visiting websites, talking with guidance counselors, taking campus tours, and seeking out independent research sources. The information provided can go a long way toward helping them reach the final college decision. Although students may spend only a handful of years on a college campus, this choice can have a profound impact on the rest of their lives.

Sources: Coleman, C. (2007), "The 'Best' School Might Not Be Best for You," *Chronicle of Higher Education*, 52 (44), 66; Conboy, K. (2007), "Big-Name Schools Aren't Always Best," *Christian Science Monitor*, 99 (69), 9; Knight, M. G. (2006), "The Beginner's Guide to the College Search," *Ignite Your Faith*, 65 (3), 44–46.

necessarily mean identifying what brand of product to buy. In fact, one of the very first choices that consumers need to make when facing a decision is whether any purchase will be made at all![1] Consumers commonly either delay the purchase of a product or forgo purchases altogether.

Decision-making processes also frequently do not involve finding a tangible product. Rather, consumers make choices about behaviors not relating directly to a purchase. For example, a consumer may be trying to decide if she should volunteer at a community theater. Here, the decision involves whether time should be exchanged in return for greater involvement with the theatre. Thus, consumer decision making does not always focus on the purchase of a tangible product, but it does always involve choices linked to value.

## Decision Making and Value

Both utilitarian value and hedonic value are associated with consumer decision making. As we have discussed previously, the car-buying experience involves both value types. First, a car is in itself a means to an end. That is, owning a car enables the consumer to transport himself or herself from place to place. As such, an automobile delivers utilitarian value. Second, much of the car-buying (and car-owning) experience is based on hedonic value. The image associated with a particular model of car and the feelings that go with sporty handling are hedonic benefits. Many other consumption activities also provide both hedonic value and utilitarian value. For example, a $400 Coach purse may provide the same utilitarian value as an $8 purse from Target. However, the hedonic value of each would differ based on the feelings involved with consumption.

Value perceptions also influence the activities found in the decision-making process itself. For example, consumers generally continue searching for information about products only as long as the perceived benefits that come from searching exceed the perceived costs associated with the process.

## Decision Making and Motivation

As discussed in our motivation chapter, motivations are the inner reasons or driving forces behind human actions as consumers are driven to address needs. It isn't surprising, therefore, that decision making and motivation are closely related concepts.[2] For example, a student may notice that the ink in his printer is low and perceive a need to fix the problem (a utilitarian motivation). Or, the same student may be bored on a Saturday afternoon and decide to play paintball (a hedonic motivation). The relationship between decision making and motivation is well-known and almost all consumer decisions revolve around goal-pursuit.[3]

> The assumption that consumers are "rational" is also debatable. Of course, what is rational to some may be irrational to others.

## Decision Making and Emotion

Consumer decision making is also closely related to emotion. The decision-making process can be very emotional depending on the type of product being considered or the need that has arisen. Because the decision-making process can be draining, consumers frequently have feelings of frustration, irritation, or even anger as they attempt to satisfy needs. This is especially true when consumers must make difficult decisions, cannot find acceptable solutions to problems, or must make tradeoffs by giving up one alternative for another.[4] As a college student, you may soon face the difficult task of deciding which job offer to take. Perhaps there will be a job offer many miles away, or one that is closer to your family. Decisions like these can be quite emotional.

## LO2 Decision-Making Perspectives

onsumer researchers view the decision-making process from three perspectives: the rational decision-making perspective, the experiential decision-making perspective, and the behavioral influence decision-making perspective.[5] These perspectives are similar to the attitude hierarchies that we discussed in our attitude chapter.

It is important to remember two important aspects of these perspectives. First, each perspective serves as a theoretical framework from which decision making can be viewed. That is, the perspectives pertain to how consumer researchers view the decision-making process, and they are not consumer decision-making strategies. Second, most consumer decisions can be analyzed from a combination of these perspectives. The perspectives are presented in Exhibit 12.3.

## RATIONAL DECISION-MAKING PERSPECTIVE

The early study of consumer decision making centered upon what is referred to as the rational decision-making perspective. This perspective is considered by many to be the traditional approach to studying decision making. The **rational decision-making perspective** assumes that consumers diligently gather information about purchases, carefully compare various brands of products on salient attributes, and make informed decisions regarding what brand to buy. This approach centers on the assumption that human beings are rational creatures who carefully consider their decisions

### EXHIBIT 12.3
### Perspectives on Consumer Decision Making

| Perspective | Description | Example |
|---|---|---|
| Rational Perspective | Consumers are rational and they carefully arrive at decisions. | Aubrey carefully considers the attributes included with various car stereos. |
| Experiential Perspective | Decision making is often influenced by the feelings associated with consumption. | Devin goes rock climbing simply for the fun of it. |
| Behavioral Influence Perspective | Decisions are responses to environmental influences. | The soothing music in the store encourages Shelby to browse longer. |

and that they can identify the expected value associated with a purchase. The act of selecting either cable or satellite television often follows a rational process. Consumers will often compare service, features, and prices carefully when making these purchases. The rational perspective fits very well with the concept of utilitarian value.

Even though the rational perspective makes sense, we cannot assume that consumers follow this process in all situations. In fact, consumers often make purchases and satisfy needs with very little cognitive effort or rationality. We simply don't want to think extensively about every single product choice that we make. Nor could we!

The assumption that consumers are "rational" is also debatable. Of course, what is rational to some may be irrational to others. Paying over $1,000 for a single season ticket to a sporting event could hardly be considered rational to some, but sports fans do it every single year! Although researchers focused on the rational perspective for several years, the experiential and behavioral influence perspectives have recently gained significant attention.

decisions based on the affect, or feeling, attached to the product or behavior under consideration. Recall from the discussion in our attitude chapter that consumers sometimes follow a "feel-do-think" hierarchy. That is, behaviors are based largely on the sheer enjoyment involved with consumption rather than on extensive cognitive effort.

Experiential decision processes often focus on hedonic value. For example, a consumer may decide to spend time at a day spa as the result of an experiential decision-making process. Here, decisions are based on feeling—not on a drawn-out decision-making process. That is, the value comes from the experience, not from an end result.

> **experiential decision-making perspective** assumes consumers often make purchases and reach decisions based on the affect, or feeling, attached to the product or behavior under consideration

> **behavioral influence decision-making perspective** assumes many consumer decisions are actually learned responses to environmental influences

© CJ GUNTHER/EPA/LANDOV

Hedonic value often results from experiential decision making.

## EXPERIENTIAL DECISION-MAKING PERSPECTIVE

The **experiential decision-making perspective** assumes that consumers often make purchases and reach

## BEHAVIORAL INFLUENCE DECISION-MAKING PERSPECTIVE

The **behavioral influence decision-making perspective** assumes that many decisions are actually learned responses to environmental influences. For example, soft music and dim lighting can have a strong influence on consumer behavior in a restaurant. These influences generally lead consumers to slow down, stay in the restaurant for a longer time, and buy more drinks and dessert. Here, behavior is influenced by environmental forces rather than by cognitive decision making.

The behavioral influence perspective also helps to explain how consumers react to store layout, store design, and POP (point-of-purchase) displays. Traffic flows in a grocery store greatly influence grocery shopping behavior. In fact, consumers often buy products that are placed on display simply because they are on display! Retailers use the "brand-lift index" to measure the incremental sales that occur when a product is on display. Lift indices can be impressive. In fact, one study indicated that POP displays in convenience stores can increase product sales by nearly 10%. This

**perceived risk** perception of the negative consequences that are likely to result from a course of action and the uncertainty of which course of action is best to take

**extended decision making** assumes consumers move diligently through various problem-solving activities in search of the best information that will help them reach a decision

is a sizable amount. Considering that incremental sales opportunities for POP materials in grocery stores can be in the billions of dollars, retailers should pay close attention to the behavioral influence perspective![6]

# LO3 Decision-Making Approaches

Consumers reach decisions in a number of different ways. The decision-making approach that is used depends heavily on the amount of involvement a consumer has with a product category or purchase and the amount of purchase risk involved with the decision. Note that involvement can be associated with the product, the purchase situation, or both. In general, as involvement and risk increase, consumers are motivated to move more carefully through the decision-making process.

You may remember from an earlier chapter that consumer involvement represents the degree of personal relevance that a consumer finds in pursuing value from a given act. **Perceived risk** refers to the perception of the negative consequences that are likely to result from a course of action and the uncertainty of which course of action is best to take. Consumers face several types of risk, including:[7]

- **Financial risk.** Risk associated with the cost of the product
- **Social risk.** Risk associated with how other consumers will view the purchase
- **Performance risk.** Risk associated with the likelihood of a product performing as expected
- **Physical risk.** Risk associated with the safety of the product and the likelihood that physical harm will result from its consumption
- **Time risk.** Risk associated with the time required to search for the product

and the time necessary for the product to be serviced or maintained

Risk varies across consumers and situations. For example, signing a year-long apartment lease is a financially risky process for most consumers. For the very wealthy, this may not be the case at all. Likewise, buying a new dress shirt is usually not perceived as being risky, unless one is making the purchase to wear on a first date!

Decision-making approaches can be classified into three categories: extended decision making, limited decision making, and habitual (or "routine") decision making. Remember, these are approaches that consumers use, and they differ from the researcher perspectives discussed previously. Exhibit 12.4 presents these categories in the form of a continuum based on involvement and risk.

## EXTENDED DECISION MAKING

When consumers engage in **extended decision making**, they tend to search diligently for information that will help them reach a satisfactory decision. This information can come from both internal sources (for example, previous experiences) and external sources (for example, websites such as shopping.com). Consumers carefully assimilate the information they have gathered and evaluate each alternative based on its potential to satisfy their need. This process is generally rather lengthy. Extended decision making occurs when involvement is high and when there is a significant amount of purchase risk involved with the decision. Expensive products such as houses, automobiles, and televisions are usually purchased only after an extended decision-making process has occurred.

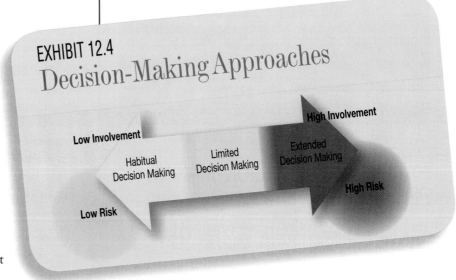

**EXHIBIT 12.4**
*Decision-Making Approaches*

High Involvement

Low Involvement

Habitual Decision Making

Limited Decision Making

Extended Decision Making

High Risk

Low Risk

# LIMITED DECISION MAKING

With limited decision making, consumers search very little for information and often reach decisions based on prior beliefs about products and their attributes. There is little comparison between brands. Given the time constraints that consumers often feel, this type of decision making occurs with great frequency.

**Limited decision making** usually occurs when there are relatively low amounts of purchase risk and product involvement. For example, a consumer may need to buy a new a roll of adhesive tape, and there may be very few attributes that are considered in the process. Perhaps the consumer will want to find a roll that is designed to be "invisible." Any brand that offers this feature would likely be selected.

# HABITUAL DECISION MAKING

With **habitual decision making** (sometimes referred to as "routine" decision making), consumers generally do not seek information at all when a problem is recognized. Choice is often based on habit. Here, consumers generally have a specific brand in mind that will solve the problem, and they believe that the consumption of the product will deliver value. For example, most consumers have a favorite type of soft drink that they habitually buy when they are thirsty.

Two topics are of special importance concerning habitual decision making: *brand loyalty* and *brand inertia*. **Brand loyalty** may be defined as a deeply held commitment to rebuy a product or service regardless of situational influences that could lead to switching behavior.[8] For a consumer to truly be brand loyal, he or she must have a bond with the product and believe that

the consumption activity delivers value. Companies often attempt to reward loyalty with rewards programs as found in frequent flier miles, hotel reward points, and credit card cash-back deals. However, in order for these tactics to be successful, consumers must ultimately value both the product and the incentives offered.[9] This leads to a key difference between loyalty and what is referred to as brand inertia. **Brand inertia** is present when a consumer simply buys a product repeatedly without any real attachment. Loyalty, on the other hand, includes an attitudinal component that reflects a true affection for the product.[10] Strictly speaking, a consumer is not considered loyal if she simply buys the same product habitually.

Brand loyalty affects consumption value in a number of ways. First, loyalty enables consumers to reduce searching time drastically by insisting on the brand to which they are loyal. This leads to a benefit of convenience. Second, loyalty creates value for a consumer through the benefits associated with brand image. Ford trucks are well-known for their ruggedness and durability, and the Ford image is one benefit of owning the product. Finally, loyalty enables consumers to enjoy the benefits that come from long-term relationships with companies. For example, a consumer might enjoy special incentives that are offered to long-time Ford purchasers.

Brand loyalty also has an impact on the value of the brand to the firm. As branding expert David Aaker asserts, consumer brand loyalty influences the value of a product to a firm because (a) it costs much less to retain current customers than to attract new ones, and (b) highly loyal customers generate predictable revenue streams.[11] As can be seen, brand loyalty has benefits for both the consumer and the marketer. Brand loyalty is discussed in more detail in a subsequent chapter.

*Reward cards can be a successful method of rewarding loyalty if consumers value both the product and the incentives offered.*

PRNEWSFOTO/BEST WESTERN INTERNATIONAL

## Final Thought on Decision-Making Approaches

Consumers go through decision-making processes, but these processes do not guarantee maximum value from a consumption experience. Consumers often make mistakes or settle for alternatives that they are really unsure about. In reality, many consumer purchases are made with very little prepurchase decision effort.[12] Most purchases made on a daily basis are low-involvement purchases that do not entail significant risk. Also, consumers are not always motivated to make the "best" decision. In fact, in many situations, consumers engage in what is called satisficing. **Satisficing** is the practice of using decision-making shortcuts to arrive at satisfactory, rather than optimal, decisions.[13] When a consumer says to herself "this is good enough," satisficing has occurred. Time pressures, search fatigue, and budgetary constraints often lead consumers to engage in satisficing.

## LO4 Need Recognition, Internal Search, and the Consideration Set

As we have discussed, the recognition of a need leads the consumer to begin searching for information. Several important issues are relevant here.

## NEED RECOGNITION

The decision-making process begins with the recognition of a need. Simply put, a need is recognized when a consumer perceives a difference between an actual state and a desired state. A consumer's **actual state** is his or her perceived current state, while the **desired state** is the perceived state for which the consumer strives. A consumer recognizes a need when there is a gap between these two. Note that either the actual state or the desired state can change, leading to a perceptual imbalance between the two. When the actual state begins to drop, for example when a consumer runs out of deodorant, a need is recognized. Obviously, needs like this are recognized many times each day. Importantly, however, marketers also focus on what they term *opportunity recognition*. Here, a consumer's actual state doesn't change, but his or her desired state changes in some significant way.

To illustrate how a desired state can be changed, consider how happy consumers once were with their cell phones—that is, before the iPhone was released. After the iPhone was introduced, the desired state for many consumers changed dramatically. Phones became much more than just phones. Apple then introduced the iPad, and some have suggested that the iPad may signal the end of the PC!

## Isn't Variety a Good Thing?

It is easy to think that a little bit of variety is a good thing. A common problem for consumers today is that in many situations there are simply *too many alternatives* from which to choose. A simple walk down any grocery store aisle will confirm that the average consumer is bombarded with hundreds—if not thousands—of product varieties every day. Whereas previous generations often faced the problem of not having enough products to choose from, today there are often too many!

When should a shopper stop looking for information? Frequently, the answer comes when one finds an acceptable, rather than optimal, solution. This is what satisficing is all about. Shoppers often simply focus on finding the first alternative that meets their minimum requirements. So, instead of finding the best paper towel available, they'll simply look for the one that delivers an acceptable level of value and move on. The decision-making process becomes much easier for consumers who "satisfice."

© RAGNAROCK /SHUTTERSTOCK.COM

Sources: Douglas, K., and D. Jones (2007), "How to Make Better Choices," *New Scientist*, 194 (2602), 35–43; Pelusi, N. (2007), "When to Choose is to Lose," *Psychology Today*, 40 (5), 69–70; Moyer, D. (2007), "Satisficing," *Harvard Business Review*, (April), 144; Wright, P. (1975), "Consumer Choice Strategies: Simplifying Vs. Optimizing," *Journal of Marketing Research*, 12 (February), 60–67.

*Desired states changed with the introduction of the iPad.*

Desired states can be affected by many factors, including reference group information, consumer novelty seeking, and cognitive thought processes.[14] As we discussed in our group influence chapter, reference groups are important sources of information for consumers and the information that is gathered from others directly affects what consumers think they should do and what types of products they think they should buy. Desired states are also influenced by novelty. Many times consumers desire to try a new product simply because of boredom or because of a motivation to engage in variety-seeking. Finally, consumers have the ability to cognitively plan their actions by anticipating future needs. For example, college graduates realize after graduation that they face the need for all types of insurance they may not have considered before, including life, health, and homeowner's insurance.

Not all needs are satisfied quickly nor does the recognition of a need always trigger the other activities found in the decision-making process. Value is again important here. If the end goal is not highly valued, consumers may simply put off a decision. For example, a consumer may realize that the leather on the seat of her bicycle has ripped, but this does not necessarily mean that she will begin to search for information on where to buy a new seat. She may simply realize that there is a problem that eventually needs to be fixed. In fact, she may have to be reminded of this need several times before she does anything about it. Or, she may decide to do nothing at all about it. For instance, she may simply sell her bike and buy a new one. From this example, we are again reminded of why we don't refer to the activities found in decision making as steps. That is, the sequential ordering of the activities is not concrete.

We should once again clarify the distinction between a want and a need. Both of these terms have been discussed in a previous chapter. As you many remember, a want is the way in which a consumer goes about addressing a need. It's quite common for marketers to be criticized for attempting to turn wants into needs. For example, a consumer may want to fulfill a need for transporting personal items by buying an expensive purse like Dooney & Bourke or Coach, even though a much less expensive purse would suffice.

*Luxury brands appeal to customers' desired states.*

## SEARCH BEHAVIOR

When consumers perceive a difference between an actual state (an empty gas tank) and a desired state (a full tank), the decision-making process is triggered.[15] **Consumer search behavior** refers to the behaviors that consumers engage in as they seek information that can be used to satisfy needs. Consumers seek all types of information about potential solutions to needs, including:

**ongoing search** search effort that is not necessarily focused on an upcoming purchase or decision but rather on staying up to date on the topic

**prepurchase search** search effort aimed at finding information to solve an immediate problem

**information overload** situation in which consumers are presented with so much information that they cannot assimilate the variety of information presented

**internal search** retrieval of knowledge stored in memory about products, services, and experiences

**consideration set** alternatives that are considered acceptable for further consideration in decision making

(1) the number of alternatives available, (2) the price of various alternatives, (3) the relevant attributes that should be considered and their importance, and (4) the performance of each alternative on the attributes.[16] Consumer search behaviors can be categorized in a number of ways, including ongoing search, prepurchase search, internal search, and external search.

## Ongoing and Prepurchase Search

A consumer performs an **ongoing search** when she seeks information simply because she is interested in a particular topic (such as a product or an organization). Here, the search effort is not necessarily focused on an upcoming purchase or decision; rather the effort is focused on simply staying up to date on a topic of interest. Consumers who perform ongoing searches are usually highly involved with the product category and seek information simply for enjoyment. They also tend to spend more in the relevant product category than do consumers who do not regularly search for information.[17]

**Prepurchase search** activities are focused on locating information that will enable the consumer to reach a decision for a specific problem. These searches are purchase-specific. Prepurchase search can also be exhibited in browsing behavior. When consumers browse, they are simply gathering information that can be used in decisions that involve a longer time frame. Note that browsing and ongoing searches are similar. The difference between ongoing searches and browsing behavior is that an ongoing search is performed when consumers have an enduring interest or involvement with the product, not simply when information is being gathered for a specific purchase.

The concept of information search has changed dramatically in recent years due to the mass adoption of the Internet as well as the proliferation of mobile information technologies like cell phones and personal data assistants. In today's environment, finding

*Consumers are able to learn about new developments with products by following them online.*

information generally isn't a problem. The problem is that there is simply too much information out there![18] Information overload is therefore a more important topic than ever before. **Information overload** refers to the situation in which consumers are presented with so much information that they cannot assimilate it all. One way that consumers can try to minimize information overload in the online environment is by joining a specific group for a product or brand on a site like Facebook. The search engine Bing.com has recently utilized an advertising campaign aimed at highlighting the downside of what they term "search overload." By focusing specifically on a group or fan page, consumers are able to look for relevant information in one place and can gain a sense of what other posters they can and cannot trust for information. Information search on social network sites can either ongoing or prepurchase.

# THE CONSIDERATION SET

**Internal search** includes the retrieval of knowledge about products, services, and experiences that is stored in memory. This type of knowledge is related directly to consumers' experiences with products and services. When confronted with a need, consumers begin to scan their memories for available solutions to the problem that can aid in decision making. As such, consumers most often perform internal searches before any other type of search begins.

Marketers find it valuable to understand the **consideration set** of their customers in order to learn about the total number of brands, or alternatives, that are considered in consumer decision making.[19] The conceptualization of a consideration set is presented in Exhibit 12.5.

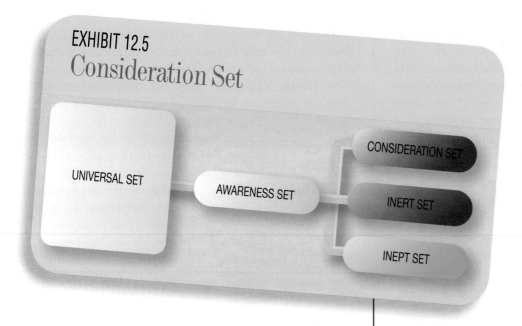

**EXHIBIT 12.5**
## Consideration Set

UNIVERSAL SET

AWARENESS SET

CONSIDERATION SET

INERT SET

INEPT SET

**universal set** total collection of all possible solutions to a consumer problem

**awareness set** set of alternatives of which a consumer is aware

**inept set** alternatives in the awareness set that are deemed to be unacceptable for further consideration

**inert set** alternatives in the awareness set about which consumers are indifferent or do not hold strong feelings

**external search** gathering of information from sources external to the consumer such as friends, family, salespeople, advertising, independent research reports, and the Internet

The total collection of all possible solutions to a recognized need (for example, the total number of brands of deodorant available on the market) is referred to as the **universal set** of alternatives. Although the universal set may be quite large, consumers generally do not realize how many solutions are potentially available when a need arises. In fact, decision making is limited by what is referred to as the awareness set. The **awareness set** includes, quite simply, the set of brands or alternatives of which a consumer is aware. Alternatives that have been previously selected are included in this set,[20] and the size of the awareness set increases as external search proceeds.

Within the awareness set, three categories of alternatives are found. The first is the consideration set (or the "evoked set"). The consideration set includes the brands, or alternatives, that are considered acceptable for further consideration in decision making. There are also alternatives in the awareness set that are deemed to be unacceptable for further consideration. These alternatives comprise the **inept set**. The **inert set** includes those alternatives to which consumers are indifferent, or for which strong feelings are not held.

Exhibit 12.5 demonstrates how the size of both the awareness set and consideration set is smaller than the universal set. This is because, for most decisions, these sets are much smaller than the universal set. Research confirms that consumers generally consider only a small fraction of the actual number of problem solutions that are available.[21] Note that although the consideration set is held internally in a consumer's memory, alternatives that are found in external search can be added to the set as the decision-making process continues. Of course, good marketers ensure that their brands are placed in consumers' consideration sets.

## LO5
# External Search

**f**requently, consumers do not have stored in their memories enough information that will lead to adequate problem solving. For this reason, external search efforts are often necessary. **External search** includes the gathering of information from sources external to the consumer, including friends, family, salespeople, advertising, independent research reports (such as *Consumer Reports*), or the Internet. In selecting the best information source, consumers consider factors such as:

- The ease of obtaining information from the source
- The objectivity of the source
- The trustworthiness of the source
- The speed with which the information can be obtained

In general, consumers find that information from family and friends is dependable but that information from commercial sources (like advertising or salespeople) is less credible for input into decision making.[22]

## THE ROLE OF PRICE AND QUALITY IN THE SEARCH PROCESS

The term *evaluative criteria* is used to refer to the attributes of a product that consumers consider when reviewing possible solutions to a problem. Many things can become evaluative criteria. However, two evaluative criteria are used across almost all consumer decisions: price and quality. Consumers tend to seek out information about these concepts early in the search process, and they play important roles in external search.

**Price** represents an important type of information that consumers generally seek. But what is a price? A price is really a piece of information. More specifically, price is information signaling how much potential value may be derived from consuming something. In this sense, price is like the physical concept of potential energy.

> ### Price and quality perceptions are related as consumers generally assume that higher prices mean higher quality.

Generally, we think of a high price as being a bad thing. In other words, a higher price means greater sacrifice to obtain some product. This view of price is referred to as the negative role of price. From this view, needless to say, a lower price is more desirable. Some consumers are very sensitive to the negative role of price. They tend to be very bargain conscious and do things like collect and redeem coupons.

However, a positive role of price also exists. In this sense, price signals how desirable a product is and how much prestige may be associated with owning the product. Some consumers are more sensitive to the positive role of price and tend to desire things with high prices as a way of signaling prestige and desirability to others.[23] You may remember from an earlier discussion that a backward sloping demand curve is not necessarily rare.

Consider a consumer shopping for a new outfit to wear "out on the town." She may find a cute outfit at Target, but this outfit may not offer enough value given that it will be worn in a socially sensitive situation. Therefore, she may opt for a higher-priced outfit that may be somewhat similar. The higher price will signal more prestige. Thus, she may feel more comfortable shopping at Banana Republic or some other more prestigious fashion retailer.

Consumers also commonly search for information about a product's quality. Consumers nearly always consider quality as an important evaluative criterion. Although quality can mean many things to many people, from a consumer perspective, **quality** represents the perceived overall goodness or badness of some product. In other words, consumers generally use the word *quality* as a synonym for relative goodness. A high-quality hotel room is a good hotel room and a low-quality hotel room is a bad hotel room.

Quality perceptions take place both before and after purchase. However, consumers do not always seek high quality because many times, consumers do not need the "best" product available. Although Fairfield Inns may not offer as high quality of an experience as does a Hyatt Regency hotel, it does adequately address the need for a place to sleep on a cross-country drive.

Consumers almost always use price and quality when making decisions. Indeed, price and quality perceptions are related as consumers generally assume that higher prices mean higher quality. This issue is discussed in more detail in our next chapter.

## EXTERNAL SEARCH AND THE INTERNET

As discussed previously, in today's fast-paced information-rich environment, a tremendous amount of information is at our fingertips. There's no denying that the Internet has quickly become a popular consumer search tool.[24] Due to the popularity of various search engines like Google and Bing as well as social networking sites like Facebook, consumers can find solutions to all sorts of problems online. Of course, this has simplified search processes to a large extent.

The Internet improves consumer search activities in several ways. First, the Internet can lower the costs associated with search and can also make the process more productive.[25] Second, the search process itself can be enjoyable and deliver hedonic value to the consumer.[26] Third, consumers have the ability to control information flow much more efficiently than if they are viewing product information on a television commercial or hearing about a product from radio ads. In general, the ability to control information flow increases the value of information and increases the consumers' ability to remember information that is gathered.[27] Of course, consumers may also buy products directly from companies that place sponsored advertisements on search engines and social media sites. This greatly impacts the ease of consumer online shopping behavior.

Studies have indicated that Internet search behavior depends heavily on website construction. For example, one recent study found that consumers spend more time searching in three-dimensional, interactive web environments than in two-dimensional web spaces. However, the study also revealed that the number of brands examined was actually higher for two-dimensional web pages than for three-dimensional sites.[28] Of course, website design is very important! We can expect consumers to use the Internet for search activities even more as computer availability becomes more widespread and as mobile technologies continue to be embraced.

# AMOUNT OF SEARCH

The amount of search that a consumer performs related to decision making can be measured in a number of ways including the number of stores visited, the number of Internet sites visited, the number of personal sources (friends, family, salespeople) used, the number of alternatives considered, and the number of advertisements studied.

Many factors influence information search effort, including previous experience with a product, involvement, perceived risk, value of search effort, time availability, attitudes toward shopping, personal factors, and situational influencers.[29]

**Product Experience.** Prior product experience with a product has been shown to influence how much a consumer searches. A number of researchers have examined this issue, sometimes with conflicting results. As a general statement, evidence shows that moderately experienced consumers search for purchase-related information more than do either experienced or inexperienced consumers. This finding is shown in Exhibit 12.6.[30]

One explanation for the finding that moderately experienced consumers search more than other

consumers is that individuals with little experience are unable to make fine distinctions between product differences and will likely see product alternatives as being similar. As such, they find little value in extensive information search. Highly experienced consumers can make fine distinctions between products and may know so much about products that they do not need to search at all. Moderately experienced consumers, on the other hand, perceive some differences among brands and are more likely to value information about these distinctions.[31]

**Involvement.** As noted earlier, purchase involvement is positively associated with search activities, especially for ongoing searches. Because involvement represents a level of arousal and interest in a product, search tends to increase when a consumer possesses a high level of purchase involvement.[32]

**Perceived Risk.** As perceived risk increases, search effort increases.[33] As discussed earlier in the chapter, a number of risks can be associated with the consumption act including financial, social, performance, physical, and time risks. Consumers are usually motivated to reduce these risks as much as possible and will therefore expend considerable time and effort in searching for information.

**Value of Search Effort.** Value can be obtained from the search process itself. When the benefits received from searching exceed the associated costs, consumers derive value. When searching costs are greater than the benefits of the search process, consumers no longer value the activity and search stops.[34] Costs associated with

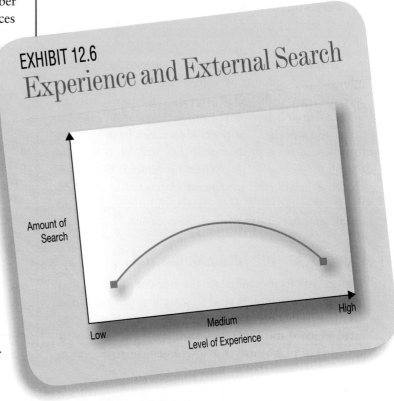

EXHIBIT 12.6
Experience and External Search

Amount of Search

Low    Medium    High
Level of Experience

search can be either monetary (for example, the cost of driving around town looking for a new bedroom dresser) or nonmonetary (for example, psychological or physical exhaustion or stress). Even online searching brings about certain mental costs.[35]

**Time Availability.** All other things being equal, more time to spend on search usually results in increased search activity.[36] Because time is valued so highly by most consumers, search will decrease when time constraints are present.

**Attitude toward Shopping.** Consumers who value shopping and who possess positive attitudes toward shopping generally spend more time searching for product infor-mation.[37]

**Personal Factors.** Search tends to increase as a consumer's level of education and income increases. Search also tends to decrease as consumers become older.[38]

**Situational Influencers.** Situational factors also influence the amount of search that takes place. Perceived urgency, financial pressure, and mood can all impact search behavior. The purchase occasion can also affect the search. Consumers sometimes have such an urgent need for a product that they will select the first option they come across. When a product is being purchased as a gift, the amount of search will depend on the relationship between the giver and the receiver and on the amount of time before the occasion.

## External Search Often Minimized

While many factors influence the amount of search that takes place, consumers tend to search surprisingly little for most products.[39] This is true for both high- and low-involvement products. Consumers may already have a stored rule in memory for low-involvement products

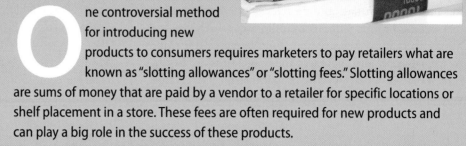

# Pay to Play

One controversial method for introducing new products to consumers requires marketers to pay retailers what are known as "slotting allowances" or "slotting fees." Slotting allowances are sums of money that are paid by a vendor to a retailer for specific locations or shelf placement in a store. These fees are often required for new products and can play a big role in the success of these products.

One advantage of slotting allowances is that they help to balance the risk of new products between both vendors and retailers. They also signal how valuable a new product is for a vendor. Vendors often have better information about the likely success of a new product than do retailers. Accordingly, the amount paid by a vendor can be a signal of the attractiveness of the product.

Critics often charge that these allowances represent a type of extortion on the part of retailers. Retailers, on the other hand, recognize the value of prime retail location in supporting product success. While these allowances are generally legal, they can violate anti-trust laws. Regardless of the views of vendors or retailers, consumers are often unaware that slotting fees have often been paid in an effort to introduce new products. New products enter the consumer's consideration set . . . at a cost!

Sources: Adapted from: Sudhir, K. and V. Rao (2006), "Do Slotting Allowances Enhance Efficiency or Hinder Competition?" *Journal of Marketing Research*, 43 (May): 137–155; Davis, R. W. (2001), "Slotting Allowances and Antitrust," *Antitrust* 15 (2), Spring, 69–76; Anonymous (2005), "Slotting Allowances – A Good Thing," *Chain Store Age*, (May), 43.

and may engage in extensive ongoing search activities and have acceptable alternative solutions in mind for high-involvement categories.[40]

# SEARCH REGRET

As we have discussed, emotions and decision making are closely related topics. The search process can lead directly to emotional responses for consumers as well. The term **search regret** refers to the negative emotions that come from failed search processes. Many times, consumers are simply not able to find an acceptable solution to their problems. As a result, the decision-making process stops. In these situations, consumers may feel as if the entire search process was a waste of time, and they will start to feel search regret. Regret is related to the amount of search effort, the emotions felt during the process, and the use of unfamiliar search techniques.[41]

Many issues relate to the topics of need recognition and search. Our next chapter discusses evaluation of alternatives and choice.

## 12 Study Tools

**Located at back of the textbook**

☐ Rip-Out Chapter-in-Review Card

**Located at www.cengagebrain.com**

☐ Review Key Terms Flashcards (Print or Online)

☐ Download audio summaries to review on the go

☐ Complete practice quizzes to prepare for tests

☐ Play "Beat the Clock" and "Quizbowl" to master concepts

☐ Watch Video on Scholfield Honda for a real company example

## what others have thought...

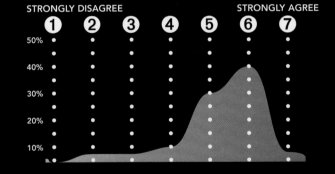

STRONGLY DISAGREE — ① ② ③ ④ ⑤ ⑥ ⑦ — STRONGLY AGREE

50% 40% 30% 20% 10%

### Most of the time I am a rational decision maker.

We can see that most students claim to be rational decision makers. A strong majority of students have indicated at least some level of agreement with our survey question. There's a pretty good chance that this doesn't apply to all purchases, however. We can all be a bit irrational some of the time!

# The value that
consumers believe they will receive from a product directly impacts their evaluation of that product.

## what do you think?
**Getting a hair style for under $10 is a very good thing.**

STRONGLY DISAGREE ① ② ③ ④ ⑤ ⑥ ⑦ STRONGLY AGREE

Visit CourseMate at
www.cengagebrain.com

# 13

# Decision Making II: Alternative Evaluation and Choice

## Introduction

Selecting a new apartment is obviously a big decision. There are many issues to consider. Which location is best? How much rent will I have to pay? Is this apartment complex safe? Are utilities included in the rent? What kind of lease do I have to sign? Making a final decision can be draining. Thankfully, not every decision we face is this difficult.

As you will remember from our first decision-making chapter, the decision-making process includes need recognition, search for information, alternative evaluation, choice, and postchoice evaluation. The decision-making model is shown once again in Exhibit 13.1.

After studying this chapter, the student should be able to:

**LO1** Understand the difference between evaluative criteria and determinant criteria.

**LO2** Comprehend how value affects the evaluation of alternatives.

**LO3** Explain the importance of product categorization in the evaluation of alternatives process.

**LO4** Distinguish between compensatory and noncompensatory rules that guide consumer choice.

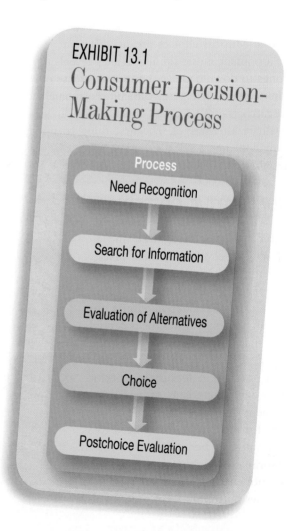

**EXHIBIT 13.1**
**Consumer Decision-Making Process**

Process

Need Recognition

↓

Search for Information

↓

Evaluation of Alternatives

↓

Choice

↓

Postchoice Evaluation

**evaluative criteria** attributes that consumers consider when reviewing alternative solutions to a problem

**feature** performance characteristic of an object

**benefit** perceived favorable results derived from a particular feature

**determinant criteria** criteria that are most carefully considered and directly related to the actual choice that is made

In the current chapter, we focus on evaluation of alternatives and choice.

# LO1
# Evaluation of Alternatives: Criteria

a very important part of decision making is evaluating alternative solutions to problems. As we have discussed throughout this text, consumers are bombarded daily by a blistering array of product varieties, brands, and experiences from which to choose. For example, consumers can select from hundreds of varieties of breakfast cereals, snack foods, and athletic shoes. Musical choices are no different. A quick look at a popular music site like iTunes reveals thousands of songs to download! Trying to make sense out of all the alternatives can be very difficult. Fortunately, consumer researchers have learned much about how consumers evaluate alternatives. The first thing to understand is how consumers select criteria that can be used in differentiating one alternative from another.

## EVALUATIVE CRITERIA

After a need is recognized and a search process has taken place, consumers begin to examine the criteria that will be used for making a choice. **Evaluative criteria** are the attributes, features, or potential benefits that consumers consider when reviewing possible solutions to a problem. A **feature** is a performance characteristic of an object. Remember from our attitude chapter that features are often referred to as attributes. A **benefit** is a perceived favorable result that is derived from the presence of a particular feature.[1] A timer button on a coffee maker is a

feature. A benefit of the button is that it keeps consumers from having to wait for hot coffee in the morning. These concepts are illustrated in Exhibit 13.2.

Benefits play an important role in the value equation. A consumer doesn't really buy a coffee maker because of a timer button. What they really want is hot coffee as soon as possible! If there was some other way to deliver this benefit without the button, consumers would be quick to buy this other solution. You may remember that benefits represent "what you get" in the value equation.

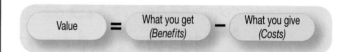

## DETERMINANT CRITERIA

Not all evaluative criteria are equally important. **Determinant criteria** (sometimes called determinant attributes) are the evaluative criteria that are related to the actual choice that is made.[2] Consumers don't always reveal, or may not even know, the criteria that truly are determinant. This is true even when several attributes are considered to be important. For example, airline safety is definitely an important feature of an airline, and consumers would quickly voice this opinion. But, because consumers do not perceive a difference in safety among major airlines, safety does not actually determine the airline that is eventually selected. For this reason, statistical tools are often needed to establish determinance.

**EXHIBIT 13.2**
## Product, Feature, and Benefit

| Product | Feature | Benefit |
|---------|---------|---------|
| Coffee Maker | Timer button | Hot coffee ready to go |
| HDTV | LED display | Better picture quality |
| Laptop | Wireless Card | Freedom to connect from anywhere |

When the MacBook Air was introduced, the product was promoted largely on thinness and portability.

Which criteria are determinant can depend largely on the situation in which a product is consumed. For example, a consumer might consider gas mileage as a determinant criterion when buying a car for himself. However, the safety of a car would likely be a determinant factor if he is buying a car for his daughter. Marketers therefore position products on the determinant criteria that apply to a specific situation.

## LO2 Value and Alternative Evaluation

o understand how alternatives are evaluated and how final choices are made, we must again highlight the key role that value plays in decision making. The value that consumers believe they will receive from a product has a direct impact on their evaluation of that product. In fact, the word

*evaluate* literally means to set a value or worth to an object. Remember that benefits are at the heart of the value equation, and value is a function of both benefits and costs.

## HEDONIC AND UTILITARIAN VALUE

It should be clear that consumers seek both hedonic and utilitarian value. The criteria that consumers use when evaluating a product can also often be classified as either hedonic or utilitarian.[3] Hedonic criteria include emotional, symbolic, and subjective attributes or benefits that are associated with an alternative. For example, the prestige that one associates with owning a BMW is a hedonic criterion. These criteria are largely experiential. Utilitarian criteria pertain to functional or economic aspects associated with an alternative. For example, safety of a BMW is a utilitarian criterion.

Marketers often promote both utilitarian and hedonic potential of a product. For example, the advertisements presented in Exhibit 13.3 promote utilitarian and hedonic automobile attributes. Consumers often use both categories of criteria when evaluating alternatives and making a final choice.

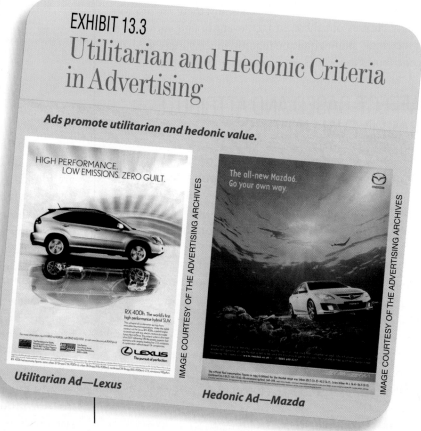

**EXHIBIT 13.3**
## Utilitarian and Hedonic Criteria in Advertising

Ads promote utilitarian and hedonic value.

HIGH PERFORMANCE. LOW EMISSIONS. ZERO GUILT.

RX 400h. The world's first high performance hybrid SUV.

LEXUS
The pursuit of perfection.

Utilitarian Ad—Lexus

The all-new Mazda6.
Go your own way.

Hedonic Ad—Mazda

## Rationality, Effort, and Variety

As discussed previously, consumers are not always rational when they are evaluating and choosing from possible solutions to a problem. What's more, consumers often have limited ability to process all the information that's available in the environment. The term **bounded rationality** describes the idea that perfectly rational decisions are not always feasible due to constraints found in information processing.

Even when consumers have the ability to consider all possible solutions to a problem, they do not always do so. Quite simply, sometimes the task just isn't worth it. In fact, consumers often minimize the effort that they put into alternative evaluation and choice. As we discussed in our need recognition and information search chapter, consumers often settle for a solution that is simply good enough to solve a problem. Realistically, there are just too many choices out there. In fact, even though variety is a good thing, studies indicate that too much variety actually contributes to feelings of discontent and unhappiness![4]

## AFFECT-BASED AND ATTRIBUTE-BASED EVALUATIONS

We can distinguish between two major types of evaluation processes: affect-based and attribute-based. With **affect-based evaluation**, consumers evaluate products based on the overall feeling that is evoked by the alternative.[5] When consumers say something like, "I'm not even sure why I bought this sweater, I just liked it," an affect-based process is reflected. Emotions play a big role in affect-based evaluation, as do mood states.[6]

When you are in a good mood, you may evaluate a product more positively even if there is not a lot of information given.

In general, positive mood states lead to positive evaluations while negative mood states lead to negative evaluations. Mood is also influential when limited information is found about an alternative.[7] For example, when you are in a good mood, you may evaluate a product positively even if there is not a lot of information given about the product.

Strong feelings also motivate consumers to seek variety as a means of escaping boredom. Beverage marketers like Coca-Cola and Pepsi-Cola frequently update their offerings in order to combat consumer boredom. Snacks are also updated frequently in an attempt to keep things new and exciting. It's common to see new flavors of Doritos or Pringles on the grocery store shelf.

With **attribute-based evaluation**, alternatives are evaluated across a set of attributes that are considered relevant to the purchase situation. As we have noted, the rational decision-making process assumes that consumers carefully integrate information about product attributes and make careful comparisons between products. This process illustrates attribute-based evaluation.

## LO3 Product Categorization and Criteria Selection

One of the first things that a consumer does when she receives information from the environment is attempt to make sense of the information by placing it in the context of a familiar category. Existing schemas, as discussed in our comprehension chapter, allow consumers to provide meaning to objects. Within these schemas, both product categories and brand categories are found.

**Product categories** are mental representations of stored knowledge about groups of products. When considering a new product, consumers rely on the knowledge that they have regarding the relevant product category. Knowledge about the existing category is then transferred to the novel item. For example, when consumers view a slide phone for the first time, they start to compare it with existing cell phone categories and draw from their knowledge of phones. Even if a product is very different from products that are currently available, consumers still draw on existing category knowledge to guide their expectations and attitudes toward the new product.[8] The successful launch of the iPhone years back is a good example of this.

# May I Help You?

**A** fundamental challenge for consumers when they shop online is that they can't always reach their final choice without some help. Because more information is now available online than ever before, many websites have incorporated the use of interactive decision aids.[1] Decision aids allow consumers to make more informed decisions and, hopefully, to be more satisfied with the outcome.

Consumers, of course, can decide whether they want to use the online aids or not. One study found that those consumers who decide not to seek online help tend to have less complex search behaviors than those who do. As such, they end up viewing fewer options and re-visiting web pages less frequently.[2] They instead rely on themselves rather than relying on others.

Of course, it is often to the company's advantage to have consumers browse in more depth. By doing so, consumers are able to consider options that they would not have otherwise. Many times, these products are more profitable for the company than the ones that the consumer would have originally sought to purchase. The consumer benefits because they are able to make better decisions while expending much less effort.[3] Online decision aids can therefore be a win-win for everybody.

Sources: 1. Bechwati, N. N., and L. Xia (2003), "Do Computers Sweat? The Impact of Perceived Effort of Online Decision Aids on Consumers' Satisfaction with the Decision Process," *Journal of Consumer Psychology*, 13 (1–2): 139–148; 2. Senecal, S., P. J. Kalczynski, and J. Nantel (2005), "Consumer's Decision-Making Process and Their Online Shopping Behavior: A Clickstream Analysis," *Journal of Business Research*, 58: 1599–1608; 3. Haubl, G. and V. Trifts (2000), "Consumer Decision Making in Online Shopping Environments: The Effects of Interactive Decision Aids," *Marketing Science*, 19 (1): 4–21.

© ISTOCKPHOTO.COM/ALEX SLOBODKIN

## CATEGORY LEVELS

Consumers possess different levels of product categories. The number of levels and details within each level is influenced by familiarity and expertise with products.[9] Consumers know the differences between snacks, breakfast, and dinner. Further distinctions can be made within any of these categories. For example, within the "snack" category, distinctions can be made between salty snacks, sweet snacks, fruits, and vegetables. Even finer distinctions can be made at yet a third level. Salty snacks may be broken down into crackers, chips, snack mix, and so on. Therefore, distinctions at basic levels are generally made across product categories (for example, snacks, breakfast foods, dinner foods). Distinctions at subsequent levels increase in specificity, ultimately to the brand and attribute level.[10] Expertise and familiarity play important roles in this process.

## Superordinate and Subordinate Categories

The different levels of product categories are referred to as being either superordinate or subordinate.[11] *Superordinate categories* are abstract in nature and represent the highest level of categorization. An example of a superordinate category would be "beverages." *Subordinate categories* are more detailed. Here, the consumer examines the knowledge that he has stored about various options. For example, a consumer would proceed through the beverage superordinate category to the subordinate categories of "colas," "sports drinks," and "juices." As a hypothetical example, assume that a consumer visited the web pages for sports drinks and found the information listed in Exhibit 13.4.

We should note that evaluations are generally more relevant and meaningful at subordinate levels.[12] For example, assume that the consumer who is looking at the information in Exhibit 13.4 notices specific differences in the brands at the subordinate level. Hypothetically, he may notice that G-O2 has fewer calories than the other products. Or, he may notice that All-Sport has less sodium than the competitors. Or, he may notice that Powerade ION4 has less potassium than the others. This information would then guide his final decision for which sports drink to buy.

Recall from our memory chapter that exemplars are first thought of within any category. An exemplar for sports drinks may be G. New alternatives will be compared to exemplars first and then to other brands that are found in the brand category. For example, when our consumer sees an advertisement for a new brand of sports drink, he will quickly move through the beverage and sports drinks categories and arrive at

**perceptual attributes** attributes that are visually apparent and easily recognizable

**underlying attributes** attributes that are not readily apparent and can be learned only through experience or contact with the product

**signal** attribute that consumers use to infer something about another attribute

ing attributes. **Perceptual attributes** are visually apparent and easily recognizable. Size, shape, color, and price are perceptual attributes. These attributes are sometimes referred to as search qualities because they can easily be evaluated prior to actual purchase.

**Underlying attributes** are not readily apparent and can only be learned through experience with the product. These attributes are sometimes referred to as experience qualities because they are often perceived only during consumption. An example of an underlying attribute is product quality. The distinction between the two types is important because consumers most often infer the existence of underlying attributes through perceptual attributes. As we discussed in our search chapter, the price of a product often tells the consumer something about its quality. In this way, price is used as a signal of quality. A **signal** is a characteristic that allows a consumer to diagnose something distinctive about an alternative. When a retailer offers a price-matching guarantee, meaning that they will match any competitor's advertised price, they give off a signal that consumers will enjoy low prices when they shop at this particular store.

Signals such as brand name, price, appearance, and retailer reputation often infer information about product quality. This is particularly so in the following situations:

G. G will then be used as the first benchmark. Other brand comparisons will then occur.

## Perceptual and Underlying Attributes

When evaluating products, consumers also distinguish between perceptual and underlying attributes.

- When the consumer is trying to reduce risk
- When purchase involvement is low
- When the consumer lacks product expertise[13]

Interestingly, young and inexperienced consumers rely more heavily on perceptual attributes than do older consumers.[14]

# CRITERIA SELECTION

## What Determines the Type of Evaluative Criteria That Consumers Use?

A number of factors influence the type of criteria that consumers use when evaluating alternatives. Situational influences, product knowledge, social influences, expert opinions, online sources, and marketing communications all influence the type of criteria that are used.

1. **Situational Influences.** As discussed earlier in this chapter, the type of criteria that are considered depends heavily on situational influences. If a product is being purchased as a gift, the buyer may pay close attention to hedonic attributes such as the image of the product and its reputation. For example, when buying perfume for a loved one, brand name and imagery can be very important. These criteria would therefore be weighted

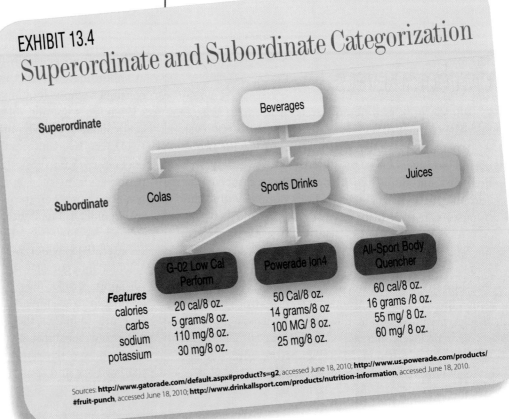

**EXHIBIT 13.4**
## Superordinate and Subordinate Categorization

Superordinate — Beverages

Subordinate — Colas — Sports Drinks — Juices

G-02 Low Cal Perform — Powerade Ion4 — All-Sport Body Quencher

**Features**
calories
carbs
sodium
potassium

| | G-02 Low Cal Perform | Powerade Ion4 | All-Sport Body Quencher |
|---|---|---|---|
| calories | 20 cal/8 oz. | 50 Cal/8 oz. | 60 cal/8 oz. |
| carbs | 5 grams/8 oz. | 14 grams/8 oz | 16 grams /8 oz. |
| sodium | 110 mg/8 oz. | 100 MG/ 8 oz. | 55 mg/ 8 oz. |
| potassium | 30 mg/8 oz. | 25 mg/8 oz. | 60 mg/ 8 oz. |

Sources: **http://www.gatorade.com/default.aspx#product?s=g2**, accessed June 18, 2010; **http://www.us.powerade.com/products/** **#fruit-punch**, accessed June 18, 2010; **http://www.drinkallsport.com/products/nutrition-information**, accessed June 18, 2010.

# Seeing Green

Green marketing is a method of marketing that focuses on offering products that satisfy both the needs of consumers and society in a sustainable way.[1] The practice has slowly grown to become a major movement in the marketing world. Early on, consumer researchers focused their efforts on the "green" segment and how this segment made purchase decisions. Today, however, it is clear that there are really several segments to consider,[2] ranging from consumers who are die-hard greens to those who buy only when it is economically advantageous to do so.

One barrier to green marketing reaching its potential, however, is that when it comes to decision making for the majority of consumers, there is often a belief that green products are actually inferior to their mainstream alternatives. The attribute correlation between "green" and "effective" is therefore often negative. For example, consumers may think that an environmentally friendly glass cleaner just isn't as good as a regular glass cleaner. Or, a green fabric softener just isn't as good as a traditional one. Marketers must therefore clearly communicate the effectiveness of their green products.[3] For many consumers, it is not enough for a product to be green; it still has to do the job!

Sources: 1. Peattie, K. and M. Charter (1997), *Green Marketing*. In: P. McDonaugh and A. Prothero (eds.) *Green Management*. New York: The Dryden Press: 388 – 412; 2. Banikarim, M. (2010), "Seeing Shades in Green Consumers," *AdWeek*, 51 (16), 18; 3. Pickett-Baker, J., and R. Ozaki (2008), "Pro-Environmental Products: Marketing Influence on Consumer Purchase Decision," *Journal of Consumer Marketing*, 25 (5): 281 – 293.

heavily in the evaluation process. Perhaps a consumer buying perfume for personal consumption may rely more heavily on other criteria such as price and convenience.

2. **Product Knowledge.** As a consumer's level of knowledge increases, he or she is able to focus on criteria that are most important in making a selection and to discount irrelevant information.[15] As such, an expert would be expected to be able to quickly discern what information is important and what is not.

3. **Expert Opinions.** Because brand experts have well-developed knowledge banks for products, they can be used to help others determine what types of information to pay attention to when evaluating products. For example, a computer science professor would be able to guide students in selecting the most important criteria to consider when buying a new computer. Market mavens are also trusted sources who can guide consumers in focusing on various product attributes.

4. **Social Influences.** Friends, family members, and reference groups also have an impact on the type of criteria that are used for decision making. This is especially true for socially visible products like automobiles or clothing.[16] Friends and families are considered to be trustworthy sources of information, and guidance that they give into what type of attributes to consider is usually closely followed.

5. **Online Sources.** Numerous websites can assist consumers with information on product attributes and brand differences. **Consumerreports.com** explains what types of criteria to consider when buying products. Popular retail sites like **bestbuy.com** also explain what attributes consumers should consider.

6. **Marketing Communications.** Marketing communications also assist consumers in deciding what features to consider when buying a particular product. Marketers generally promote the attributes that their products excel on and attempt to convince consumers that these are the most important. For example, Papa John's Pizza is well known for advertising "Better Ingredients, Better Pizza." While the company claims that their pizza contains better ingredients than that of their competitors, they also attempt to convince consumers that ingredients are important criteria to consider when buying pizza.

© MIKE KEMP/RUBBERBALL/JUPITERIMAGES

**judgments** mental assessments of the presence of attributes and the consequences associated with those attributes

**attribute correlation** perceived relationship between product features

## Are Consumers Accurate in Their Assessment of Evaluative Criteria?

The accuracy of a consumer's evaluation depends heavily on the quality of judgments that they make. **Judgments** are mental assessments of the presence of attributes and the benefits associated with those attributes. Consumer judgments are affected by the amount of knowledge or experience a consumer has with a particular object. During the evaluation process, consumers make judgments about the following:

- **Presence of features.** Does this MP3 player play videos?

- **Feature levels.** How many videos can be stored?

- **Benefits associated with features.** I'd be able to watch a movie on a long trip.

- **Value associated with the benefit.** That would be nice.

- **How objects differ from each other.** The other one doesn't have this.

There are several issues that affect consumer judgments. We review a few of these issues here.

1. **Just Noticeable Difference.** The ability of a consumer to make accurate judgments when evaluating alternatives is influenced by his or her ability to perceive differences in levels of stimuli between two options. As was discussed in our perception chapter, the just noticeable difference (JND) represents how much stronger one stimulus must be compared to another if someone is to notice that the two are not the same. For example, when judging sound quality, a consumer may not be able to discern the difference between speakers that have a frequency range between 47 Hz and 20 kHz and those that have a range between 50 Hz and 20 kHz. If consumers cannot tell the difference, then their judgments about the products may not be accurate.

Sometimes, the same manufacturer offers different brands or models that are very similar to each other. The term *branded variants* is used to describe the practice of offering essentially identi-

> Waiting time can be correlated with perceptions of quality.

cal products with different model numbers or names.[17] Even if differences are perceived, the differences might not be very meaningful. As we discussed earlier, the JND concept is also important.

The impact of the JND on consumer judgments applies to how consumers react to counterfeit products. Some counterfeits are so much like the original that consumers simply can't perceive the difference between them. This is, of course, a bad situation for marketers of the original.

2. **Attribute Correlation.** Consumers often make judgments about features based on their perceived relationship with other features. For example, earlier we stated that price is often used as a signal for quality. Here, consumers rely on **attribute correlation** to describe the perceived relationship between attributes of products.[18] Recall from our consumer search chapter that price and quality are often assumed to be positively correlated. That is, when a product has a high price, consumers often assume it will be high quality.

Attributes can also be negatively correlated. For example, if a consumer's wait time at a bank is long, he or she might think that the bank offers poor service. Here, the consumer assumes that as wait time goes up, service quality goes down (hence, a negative correlation). This can be a faulty assumption because a long wait time may simply mean that consumers get individualized attention and really good service. Some things are worth waiting for!

3. **Quality Perceptions.** Marketers have long realized that consumer perception is critical to marketing success. As we have discussed, percep-

tions are not always in line with reality. One issue that pertains to consumer judgments is the difference between objective quality and perceived quality. *Objective quality* refers to the actual quality of a product that can be assessed through industry specification or expert rating. For example, a cell phone provider may advertise that its service has been proven to have the fewest dropped calls in the industry. *Perceived quality* is based on consumer perceptions. Even if the cell phone has objectively been shown to have the best coverage in the industry, consumers may still perceive poor quality if the coverage in their immediate area is not good.

Companies spend a great deal of time and money on improving the objective quality of their products. These efforts are limited, however, by consumer perceptions of quality. In fact, a recent study revealed that improvements in objective quality may take as many as six years to be fully recognized by consumers![19] You may remember from our discussion in the comprehension chapter that consumers act on declarative knowledge even if the knowledge is incorrect. So if a company invests in improving the quality of its products, consumers may still act on the assumption that the product's quality is not good.

4. **Brand Name Associations.** Brand names also have an impact on consumer judgments. Much like price, brand names can be used as signals of quality. In fact, studies have found that brand names are even stronger signals of quality than is price.[20] For example, Energizer batteries are assumed to last a long time and Gillette razors are believed to be the best a man can get.

Unusual product names also influence consumer judgments. One technique that marketers have used for several years is coming up with unexpected, even humorous, names for products. This is especially true in the snack food industry. Hot sauce brands are known for their funny names. Names like Arizona Gunslinger and Java Hot Sauce are quite common. Research indicates that unexpected names can lead to increased product preference and choice.[21]

What can a brand name tell you about a product?

## How Many Criteria Are Necessary to Evaluate Alternatives Effectively?

As we have discussed, too many alternatives can be draining for consumers. However, research suggests that consumers can handle a surprisingly high number of comparisons before overload sets in. One study revealed that consumers can evaluate as many as ten product alternatives and fifteen attributes before overload occurs.[22] Even though consumers can handle this much information, they rarely like to do so. And they generally do not consider this many alternatives. In fact, consumers are often able to make good choices when considering only a single attribute.[23]

## What If Information Is Missing?

Consumers may have a good understanding of the types of attributes that they would like to use for alternative evaluation, but sometimes attribute information is not available. This actually happens quite frequently in the marketplace. For example, consider the information given in Exhibit 13.5. Here, information is given for two televisions that a consumer collects from print advertisements. Assume that both televisions cost roughly the same amount, say $1,000. As you can see, the information for television A lacks the details for picture quality while the information given for television B lacks the details regarding the product's warranty. Consumer satisfaction ratings are available for both products.

Consumers are often able to make good choices when considering only a single attribute.

**conjoint analysis**
technique used to develop an understanding of the attributes that guide consumer preferences by having consumers compare product preferences across varying levels of evaluative criteria and expected utility

# "Real" Estate Downsize

It's well known that the housing market played a major role in the worldwide economic tailspin of the last few years. Lenders lent money to risky borrowers and the subprime mortgage business boomed. Housing prices escalated to unrealistic levels and adjustable rate mortgage payments eventually began to climb. The market finally burst as many consumers began to default on their mortgages. Obviously, severe economic ramifications resulted.

One of the direct results of the housing market collapse is that many consumers today are intentionally "downsizing" their home purchases. Granted, mortgages are harder to come by than in recent years, but for those home buyers who can qualify for mortgages, many are deciding to buy well below their means. This has actually put an increased demand on smaller, rather than larger homes. Whereas a very large home with all the bells and whistles has long been considered a status symbol, many consumers are readjusting their ways of thinking and this is dramatically affecting decision making.

Sources: Gopal, P. (2009), "Even Once-Strong Housing Markets Stumble," *Business Week (online)*, January 28, 2009; Gardner, D. (2008), "The Incredible Shrinking House," *Northeast Pennsylvania Business Journal*, 23 (10). 77; Farrell, C. (2998), "Choosing Where to Grow Old," *Business Week*, July 14, 2008 (4092), 44; Gandel, S. (2008), "Real Estate's Next Evolution," *Money*, June, 37 (6), 98; Evans, K. (2007), "Size of New Homes Starts Shrinking as Builders Battle Housing Slump," *The Wall Street Journal*, September 12, 2007, A1.

To help solve this dilemma, consumers tend to weigh the criteria that are common to both alternatives quite heavily in the evaluation. They also tend to discount information that is missing for the option that performs better on the common criteria. For example, satisfaction ratings are given for both sets in this exhibit. Consumers would likely discount the missing warranty information for television B because this alternative performs better on the common criterion of consumer satisfaction ratings.[24]

## How Do Marketers Determine Which Criteria Consumers Use?

Marketers can use several techniques to determine the criteria that consumers use when judging products. They can directly ask consumers through surveys. They can also gather information from warranty registrations that ask consumers to indicate the specific criteria that were used in arriving at a purchase decision.

Marketers also use techniques such as perceptual mapping and conjoint analysis to assess choice criteria. Perceptual mapping was discussed in a previous chapter. **Conjoint analysis** is used to understand

## EXHIBIT 13.5
## Missing Information

| Features | Television A | Television B |
|---|---|---|
| Consumer satisfaction ratings | Good | Excellent |
| Warranty | 2 years parts & labor | Not given |
| Picture quality | Not given | Good |

Source: Kivetz, R., and I. Simonson (2000), "The Effects of Incomplete Information on Consumer Choice," *Journal of Marketing Research*, 37 (4), 427–448.

the attributes that guide preferences by having consumers compare products across levels of evaluative criteria and the expected utility associated with the alternatives.[25]

# LO4 Consumer Choice: Decision Rules

Once consumers have evaluated alternative solutions to a problem, they begin to make a choice. "Choice" does not mean that a particular alternative will be chosen. Rather, consumers may simply choose to delay a choice until a future date or to forgo a selection indefinitely.

There are two major types of rules that consumers use when selecting products: compensatory rules and noncompensatory rules. **Compensatory rules** allow consumers to select products that may perform poorly on one attribute by compensating for the poor performance by good performance on another attribute. A consumer using a compensatory rule might say something like "It's OK that this car isn't very stylish; it gets good gas mileage. I'll buy it."

Noncompensatory models do not allow for this process to take place. Rather, when **noncompensatory rules** are used, strict guidelines are set prior to selection, and any option that does not meet the specifications is eliminated from consideration. For example, a consumer might say "I'll only choose a car that gets good gas mileage. I am not budging on that."

## COMPENSATORY MODELS

The attitude-toward-the-object model (Fishbein model) that was presented in our attitude chapter represents a compensatory approach. The formula $[A_o + \Sigma(b_i)(e_i)]$ allows for poor scores on one attribute to be compensated for by good scores on another.

Our example from that chapter is again shown in Exhibit 13.6. This example revealed that Lifestyles fitness center was selected even though it scored highest on the attribute that Brooke rated most poorly, high fees. The high ratings on other attributes compensated for Brooke's belief that Lifestyles has high fees.

**compensatory rule** decision-making rule that allows consumers to select products that may perform poorly on one criterion by compensating for the poor performance on one attribute by good performance on another

**noncompensatory rule** decision-making rule in which strict guidelines are set prior to selection and any option that does not meet the guidelines is eliminated from consideration

**conjunctive rule** noncompensatory decision rule where the option selected must surpass a minimum cutoff across all relevant attributes

## NONCOMPENSATORY MODELS

Consumer researchers have identified four major categories of noncompensatory rules.[26] They include the conjunctive rule, the disjunctive rule, the lexicographic rule, and the elimination-by-aspects (EBA) rule.

1. Following the **conjunctive rule**, the consumer sets a minimum mental cutoff point for various features and rejects any product that fails to meet or exceed this cutoff point across all features.

## EXHIBIT 13.6
## A Compensatory Approach

| Attribute | e | LIFESTYLE b | LIFESTYLE (b)(e) | CURVES b | CURVES (b)(e) | SHAPES b | SHAPES (b)(e) |
|---|---|---|---|---|---|---|---|
| Circuit training | −1 | 1 | −1 | 10 | −10 | 9 | −9 |
| Class variety | 2 | 10 | 20 | 2 | 4 | 3 | 6 |
| Amenities | 1 | 9 | 9 | 5 | 5 | 5 | 5 |
| Fees | −3 | 6 | −18 | 4 | −12 | 5 | −15 |
| Location | 3 | 6 | 18 | 8 | 24 | 9 | 27 |
| $A_o$ | | | 28 | | 11 | | 14 |

Note: "e" + evaluative ratings. These ratings are generally scaled from −3 to +3, with −3 being very negative and +3 being very positive. "b" + strength of belief that the object possesses the attribute in question. Beliefs are generally scaled from 1 to 10, with 1 meaning "highly unlikely" and 10 meaning "highly likely." "(b)(e)" is the product term that is derived by multiplying the evaluative ratings (e) by belief strength (b). $A_o$ is the overall attitude toward the object. This is determined by adding the (b)(e) product terms for each object.

2. Following the **disjunctive rule**, the consumer sets a minimum mental cutoff for various features. This is similar to the conjunctive rule. However, with the disjunctive rule, the cutoff point is usually high. The product that meets or exceeds this cutoff on any feature is selected.

3. Following the **lexicographic rule**, the consumer selects the product that he or she believes performs best on the most important feature.

4. Following the **elimination-by-aspects rule (EBA)**, the consumer sets minimum cutoff points for the attributes. Beginning with the most important feature, he or she then eliminates options that don't meet or surpass the cutoff point on this important feature. The consumer then moves on to the next most important feature and repeats the process and does this until only one option remains and a choice is made.

To illustrate these rules, consider the information that is presented in Exhibit 13.7. Here, the consumer is evaluating different makes and models of cars.

The process involved with each decision rule would be as follows:

1. **Conjunctive Rule.** Assume that all features must meet or surpass a mental cutoff of 5 in order for the car to be selected. Looking across the various features for the cars, we see that only the Ford Focus has performance ratings at or above 5 on all features. Using this rule, the Ford Focus would therefore be selected. Its performance ratings are, respectively: 7, 6, 8, 8, 6, 5. Notice that at least one of the performance ratings for the attributes of the other cars falls below the cutoff of 5.

2. **Disjunctive Rule.** Assume that the consumer wants a car that excels at any of the features. Here, he would set a high cutoff of, say, 10. The only car that offers a performance rating of 10 on any attribute is the Hyundai Accent. The "low price" criterion is particularly strong for this car, and the consumer rates this feature as a 10. Using the disjunctive rule, the Hyundai Accent would be selected. He is considering performance ratings, and not the importance of the attributes.

3. **Lexicographic Rule.** Here, the product that is thought to perform best on the most important attribute is selected. In this example, the Honda Fit would be selected because it scores highest (9) on the most important attribute, gas mileage.

## EXHIBIT 13.7
## Noncompensatory Decision Approaches

| Attribute | Importance | Chevy Aveo Belief Ratings | Ford Focus Belief Ratings | Honda Fit Belief Ratings | Hyundai Accent Belief Ratings |
|---|---|---|---|---|---|
| Gas mileage | 10 | 5 | 7 | 9 | 8 |
| Low price | 9 | 8 | 6 | 7 | 10 |
| Styling | 8 | 9 | 8 | 4 | 4 |
| Warranty | 5 | 4 | 8 | 9 | 8 |
| Service | 6 | 5 | 8 | 7 | 3 |
| Handling | 7 | 6 | 6 | 3 | 3 |
|  |  |  | 5 | 3 |  |

Note: Belief ratings are performance judgments scaled from 1 = very poor to 10 = very good. Importance ratings are scaled so that 10 = most important, 9 = next most important, and so on.
Source: Wright, P. (1975), "Consumer Choice Strategies: Simplifying Vs. Optimizing," *Journal of Marketing Research*, 12 (1), 60–67.

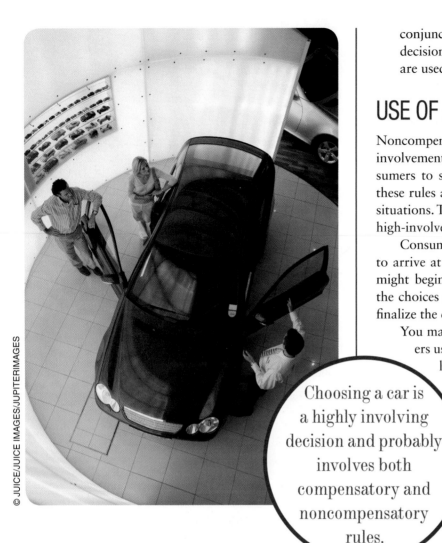

© JUICE/JUICE IMAGES/JUPITERIMAGES

Choosing a car is a highly involving decision and probably involves both compensatory and noncompensatory rules.

conjunctive and eba rules can result in the same decision. This will occur if the same cutoff points are used for both rules.

## USE OF DECISION RULES

Noncompensatory rules are often used in low-involvement situations because these rules allow consumers to simplify their thought processes. However, these rules are also used in high-involvement purchase situations. The decision of what car to buy is certainly a high-involvement decision for most people.

Consumers can combine decision rules in order to arrive at a final solution. For example, a consumer might begin with a conjunctive rule to narrow down the choices and then use a compensatory approach to finalize the decision.

You may be wondering what type of rule consumers use most often. Studies have revealed that the lexicographic rule is very common. This is because consumers usually know what features are most important, and they simply select the product that offers the best performance on that feature.

You may also wonder how often consumers use these rules. Actually, the rules are used quite frequently. We should emphasize, however, that the processes are indeed mental. That is, the comparisons are almost always made mentally, without the strict use of a mathematical formula. Nevertheless, by considering issues such as cutoff points, researchers are able to gain a better understanding of the processes behind consumer choice.

## RETAIL OUTLET SELECTION

Up to this point, we have emphasized the processes that consumers use when selecting from alternative solutions to a problem. Consumers must also choose where they will buy the product. Sometimes, consumers will decide *where* they will buy before they determine *what* they will buy. One consumer says to another: "I'm going to the store; what do we need?" The other replies, "Where are you going?" Here, the decision of what product to buy hinges on where you are shopping.

As we have noted earlier in this text, consumers have gradually become less brand-loyal and more store-loyal. This underscores the importance of store choice in consumer behavior research. Several factors influence

4. **EBA Rule.** Assuming a minimum cutoff point of 5 once again, the consumer begins with the most important attribute, gas mileage. Any product that does not meet or surpass the cutoff of 5 on this attribute would be eliminated. All options meet or surpass 5 on the gas mileage attribute and no products are eliminated. Next, the consumer looks at the next most important attribute, low price. Again, all options meet the 5 criterion and no options are eliminated.

On the next most important attribute, styling, two options are eliminated because they don't reach the 5 cutoff—the Honda Fit and the Hyundai Accent. The consumer continues on with the next most important attribute, handling. Both the Aveo and the Focus surpass the 5 cutoff on this attribute. The same is true for the next most important attribute, service. Finally, on the final attribute, warranty, the Aveo is eliminated from consideration because it does not reach the cutoff and the Ford Focus is ultimately selected. Notice that the

the choice of retail outlet including objective and subjective criteria such as product variety, store image, location, service, and product quality.[27] Of course, consumers may also decide to make their purchases on the Internet. The Internet has quickly become the channel of choice for many consumers. The actual decision of which website to use is based on several factors including the availability of product variety and information, customer service, security, and navigational ease.[28] Of course, many large retailers have both physical presence (a bricks-and-mortar store) and an online presence (website).

As you can tell, evaluating alternatives and making final purchase decisions are part of an involved process. Our next chapter will consider the processes that occur after a choice has been made.

© RICHARD LEVINE/ALAMY

*Online retailers have to thoroughly describe the evaluative criteria that consumers may use.*

# 13
## Study Tools

**Located at back of the textbook**
- ☐ Rip-out Chapter-in-Review Card

**Located at www.cengagebrain.com**
- ☐ Review Key Terms Flashcards (Print or Online)
- ☐ Download audio summaries to review on the go
- ☐ Complete practice quizzes to prepare for tests
- ☐ Play "Beat the Clock" and "Quizbowl" to master concepts
- ☐ Watch Video on Ford for a real company example

## what others have thought...

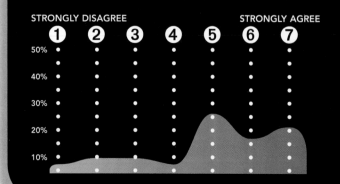

STRONGLY DISAGREE
① ② ③ ④ ⑤ ⑥ ⑦
STRONGLY AGREE

50%
40%
30%
20%
10%

### Getting a hair style for under $10 is a very good thing.

Most students seem to feel like getting an inexpensive haircut is a good thing. The majority have agreed with this statement. However, some students do not agree. Of course, price and quality are related. No one wants a bad haircut and you get what you pay for!

# MORE BANG FOR YOUR BUCK!

**CB3** has it all, and so can you! Between the text and online resources, **CB3** offers everything you need to study:

- Interactive eBook
- Chapter In Review Cards
- Auto-Graded Quizzes
- Crossword Puzzles
- Videos
- PowerPoint® Slides
- And More!

**Visit CourseMate to see all that CB3 has to offer! Access at www.cengagebrain.com.**

# Case 4-1

## Consumer Decision Making with Compensatory, Non-Compensatory Models

*Written by: Lindsey M. Hudson, Rhode Island College Student (Lindsey is a student of Dr. Stephen P. Ramocki, a professor of marketing at Rhode Island College.)*

Palm trees, soft sand, sun-soaked women in bikinis sipping on an exotic drink portrays a typical scenario for alcohol advertising. On the flip side, alcohol can take on prestigious roles with certain target markets. Alcohol advertising relies heavily on peripheral cues to get consumers to take an interest in their products. Every customer views his or her decision as rational, but realistically there are implications of status that can play a role in the process. In many situations, friends' social influences can also play a significant role in a consumer's decision-making process. This year, four vodka brands launched advertising campaigns and three friends viewed the ads as part of a class assignment. The brands were Grey Goose, Smirnoff, Belvedere, and Absolut.

The advertisers of these brands employ brand personality to differentiate themselves from other brands in addition to claiming that their brands each have desirable and distinguishing attributes. Grey Goose reflects the personality of a reliable and dependable alcohol brand. This brand is viewed as stately and has a certain status quality associated with it to attract affluent and successful consumers. Smirnoff casts the image of being both daring and spirited. The positioning is towards a more experiential and youthful target market. Belvedere's personality revolves around luxury and glamour in addition to quality. The brand image is geared towards those who live extravagantly and have discretionary purchasing power. Absolut is represented as honest and genuine. It is viewed as high-quality vodka with an indisputable taste.

The three college students see the ads in different ways based on their personal lifestyles and personalities. Thus, both hedonic and utilitarian factors influence their decision-making processes. Greg is aspiring to be a CPA after graduating from college. His personality is relatively meticulous and directed with rational considerations. He relentlessly looks for quality in all the purchases he makes to preserve his image of practical opulence.

Angelina is a logical shopper who is going to be hosting a dinner party at her house this weekend with friends. She is rational with many of her higher-involvement purchases and considers a number

*Reprinted with permission from the author*

of attributes in her decisions. However, she really wants to impress her guests, so perceived quality becomes the most important attribute. She generally follows a compensatory approach.

Bella is getting ready to go on vacation in Miami with her roommates. Her relationship with her friends is a huge part of her life and she relies on them for decision-making inputs. Significant portions of her life are spent developing strong social ties and establishing more acquaintances. She is not illogical by any means, as she does have her own preferences and considers multiple attributes when making purchase decisions. She is drawn to many advertisements by peripheral cues and she remains quite susceptible to influence from the social sphere captured by these cues. Even though she may be fully aware that her friends don't consider the attributes at all or in the same way she might, she accommodates their suggestions.

Bella is aware of all the ads for Grey Goose, Belvedere, Smirnoff, and Absolut. Although she doesn't really care too much about vodka, her beliefs and evaluations regarding these attributes are well established. However, she is influenced significantly by her friends' opinions. She has a relatively clear idea of the attributes and their advantages, however, when she gets to the store she begins to reflect on previous conversations and the attitudes of her peers. As she approaches the vodka display in the store, she takes into consideration the full array of evaluative characteristics shown in Table C.

As the above discussion implies, for purchases of this nature, consumers may or may not have distinct assessments of various attributes and the beliefs that these attributes are contained in the products they buy. What is fascinating, and at the same time challenging for marketers, concerning such purchases, is that what may begin as a totally rational process may not exactly pan out that way. As the text clearly states, for purchases of this nature various consumers are apt to use compensatory or non-compensatory models, or even combinations of the two. What can be frustrating in understanding decision-making approaches is that consumers may be inclined to start with one model and then switch to another or even blend different approaches. In this situation, both Greg's and Angelina's decision models are intended to be relatively straightforward. Greg is prone to applying the lexicographic model, while Angelina will likely use the compensatory model. Bella's choice revolves highly around brand personality and social influence, but she simply seeks a brand that is good enough because she doesn't really care too much about vodka.

Advertisers obviously have to consider the approaches that they are taking in terms of the elaborative likelihood model discussed in the text. They need to consider the directness of the advertising in terms of attributes versus the more peripheral approach that draws people in by focusing on personality and lifestyle. In a product such as vodka, companies want consumers to consider taste and utilitarian attributes. However, they also realize that brand personalities can play significant roles in the final decision process, and in establishing brand loyalty.

As each of these purchasers is settling on the actual purchase decisions, they will be employing different cognitive and affective strategies. Although the questions below suggest an answer or an outcome in each of these three students' buying situations, there still is reasonable room for discussion concerning why different choices may result. Each of these college students is led to select a different brand of vodka based on his/her individual decision-making preferences. Your task is to assess each student's decision-making approach along with the likely brand of choice.

## Questions

1. Do you believe brand personality plays a major part in decision making? Explain.

2. After evaluating Table A, which alcohol brand will Greg be most likely to purchase?

3. Using Table B and taking Angelina's shopping habits into consideration, which brand of alcohol will she buy?

4. Looking at Table C and considering what you know about Bella's decision-making style, which brand is she likely to purchase?

5. How might the decision-making processes for each consumer change if shopping for the product at a warehouse store like Costco as opposed to an upscale wine shop in Florida?

### TABLE A: (LEXICOGRAPHIC MODEL)

| Attributes | IMPORTANCE | GREY GOOSE BELIEF RATINGS | SMIRNOFF BELIEF RATINGS | BELVEDERE BELIEF RATINGS | ABSOLUT BELIEF RATINGS |
|---|---|---|---|---|---|
| Perceived Quality | 9 | 8 | 5 | 9 | 6 |
| Price | 8 | 6 | 8 | 7 | 8 |
| Quantity | 1 | 8 | 4 | 9 | 8 |
| Bottle Design | 1 | 5 | 4 | 7 | 5 |

Note: Belief ratings are measured on a 1–10 scale with 1 as very unlikely and 10 as very likely. The importance ratings are based on a scale from 1 = not at all important to 10 = very important.

### TABLE B: (COMPENSATORY MODEL)

| Attributes | E | GREY GOOSE B | GREY GOOSE (B)(E) | SMIRNOFF B | SMIRNOFF (B)(E) | BELVEDERE B | BELVEDERE (B)(E) | ABSOLUT B | ABSOLUT (B)(E) |
|---|---|---|---|---|---|---|---|---|---|
| Perceived Quality | 3 | 8 | 24 | 1 | 3 | 7 | 21 | 2 | 6 |
| Price | -3 | 4 | -12 | 8 | -24 | 5 | -15 | 8 | -24 |
| Quantity | 2 | 7 | 14 | 7 | 14 | 6 | 12 | 7 | 14 |
| Bottle Design | -1 | 2 | -2 | 2 | -2 | 6 | -6 | 3 | -3 |
| $A_O$ | | | 24 | | -9 | | 12 | | -7 |

Note: Belief ratings (belief that the attribute is present) are measured on a 1-10 scale with 1 as very unlikely and 10 as very likely. Attribute evaluations (E) are based on a -3 to +3 scale with 3 being good and -3 implying bad.

### TABLE C: (CONJUNCTIVE APPROACH)

| Attributes | E | GREY GOOSE B | GREY GOOSE (B)(E) | SMIRNOFF B | SMIRNOFF (B)(E) | BELVEDERE B | BELVEDERE (B)(E) | ABSOLUT B | ABSOLUT (B)(E) |
|---|---|---|---|---|---|---|---|---|---|
| Imagery | 3 | 4 | 12 | 6 | 18 | 5 | 15 | 9 | 27 |
| Attractiveness of spokesperson | 1 | 4 | 4 | 4 | 4 | 6 | 6 | 9 | 9 |
| Brand personality | 3 | 3 | 9 | 6 | 18 | 2 | 6 | 7 | 21 |
| Friends' opinions/subjective norm | 3 | 1 | 3 | 7 | 21 | 1 | 3 | 5 | 3 |
| $A_O$ | | | 28 | | 61 | | 30 | | 60 |

Note: Belief ratings are measured on a 1–10 scale with 1 as very unlikely and 10 as very likely. Attribute evaluations are based on a -3 to +3 scale with 3 being good and -3 implying bad. Conjunctive approach method is used with "5" as the cutoff.

*Reprinted with permission from the author

## Case 4-2
### Redefining Good Cleaning Products

*Written by Nancy Artz, Ph.D., University of Southern Maine and Dudley Greeley, USM Sustainability Coordinator*

Jill thinks all dishwashing soaps are alike, so she buys the cheapest brand. Jack buys the brand of laundry detergent his mom always bought. Consumers typically have low involvement with the decision to buy household cleaning products, and make quick choices. But Elena researches nontoxic cleaning supplies in detail before her baby is born.

The market for green cleaning products was pioneered by small firms like Seventh Generation, Inc., which, in 1988, started selling environmentally friendly household products in health food stores and specialty stores. Two decades later, in 2007, green cleaners still accounted for less than 1% of cleaning product sales,[1] even though surveys found that 60% of consumers were "concerned about the impact cleaning products have on the environment."[2] Only truly committed green consumers will make an extra trip to a specialty store to pay more for utilitarian-looking products that are perceived to be less effective because they are environmentally safer.

Even though mainstream consumers aren't willing to sacrifice price, convenience, quality, and other product benefits for the sake of greener products, they will use green features to break a tie between otherwise comparable brands. Marketers have used this knowledge to introduce a host of new green cleaners.

Two young entrepreneurs launched, Method®, an environmentally friendly line of cleaning products that differentiates itself from other brands—green and nongreen alike—by innovative, stylish packaging. For example, Method's Le Scrub bathroom cleaner has a built-in sponge holder. Method is sold at specialty stores and mass-market retailers like Target, at about twice the price of traditional brands. The cofounders believe that style "creates mass market relevance for a green product"[3] and that consumers discover Method because of its trendy designer look, find that they love the fragrance and then "discover it's good for you—it's that third piece that drives loyalty."[4] Perhaps that explains the company's sales growth from about $90,000 in 2001 to $77 million in 2006.[5]

The market for green cleaners took off in 2008, when the Clorox Company launched its Green Works® line of cleaners. Green Works became the market leader the next year, with $200 million

*Reprinted with permission from the author

in sales (42% share of the green cleaner market).[6] Interestingly, Green Works' success didn't come at the expense of Seventh Generation and Method—sales of those products didn't drop— Green Works attracted consumers from mass market brands. This is consistent with Green Work's strategy to target "Chemical Avoiding Naturalists," who want a greener cleaner, but view existing options as not working well, not coming from brands they know or trust, and not generally available where they shop.[7]

The Green Works line launched with five products: an all-purpose cleaner, a glass cleaner, a toilet bowl cleaner, a dilutable cleaner, and a bathroom cleaner. The line was quickly expanded to include dishwashing liquid, laundry products, and biodegradable wipes. The products were priced 20% higher than typical cleaners, considerably less than Seventh Generation or Method's 100% higher price.[8] As a large company, Clorox was able to launch Green Works with a substantial advertising campaign (e.g., 30-second television spots and use of social media) and broad retail distribution (e.g., Walmart agreed to provide prominent shelf space and other forms of in-store promotion).

Green Works cleaners are green-tinted liquids sold in recyclable bottles with a prominent yellow flower on the label. The products have been promoted as made from natural, plant-based ingredients with no harsh chemical fumes or residues. One claim, for example, was that "clothes washed in Green Works are gentle on skin."[9] Consumers who read the label or the website find the product is made from ingredients such as coconuts and lemon oil and is biodegradable, non-allergenic, and not tested on animals. The products are formulated to have a pleasant fragrance rather than a strong "cleaner" odor.

Rather than downplaying the connection between Green Works and Clorox, the company emphasized the link to promote the new brand as dependable and effective. Likewise, the Green Works brand name was chosen to counter consumer beliefs that natural cleaners don't work.[10] Green Works was initially promoted in ads and on the package as working just as well as traditional cleaners. A competitor complained to the National Advertising Division (NAD) of the Council of Better Business Bureaus. NAD determined that Green Works was not as effective as traditional cleaners in grease removal and that consumers might incorrectly assume the product to be a disinfectant. Green Works agreed to stop claiming "works as well" as other cleaners.[11]

Because Clorox is known for bleach and "chemical" cleaners, Green Works has used third-party endorsements to reassure consumers about the legitimacy of its environmental and health features:

- From its inception, Green Works packaging has displayed the Design for Environment (DfE) logo. DfE certification means a product only contains ingredients that pose the least concern among chemicals in their class. Few consumers recognize or understand the DfE criteria, but the logo indicates that DfE is sponsored by the well-respected U.S. Environmental Protection Agency.

- Four months after product launch, packaging displayed the Sierra Club logo. This well-known nonprofit agreed to the use of its logo to help "move" the market to offer more environmentally-preferred products and, in return for a percentage of sales ($470,000 in 2008).[12] Although not widely known among mainstream consumers, this arrangement was criticized by some as a conflict of interest and inappropriate because the Club's expertise is public policy, not consumer product chemistry.

- Almost two years after product launch, Green Works added Good Housekeeping's new green label to its bathroom cleaner. This "green" certification is not particularly rigorous, but the Good Housekeeping seal is widely recognized.[13]

Green Works is not the only firm pursuing third-party endorsements. Method now carries significant sustainability certifications such as Cradle-to-Cradle, DfE, and B-Corp. Do eco-labels add value for the consumer? Credible labels relating to the product's most important ecological and social attributes can help consumers distinguish truly green products from products engaged in greenwashing. Unfortunately, a proliferation of new eco-labels—including in-house labels without independent verification—has caused consumer doubt about the relevance, rigor, and credibility of labels.

Green Works' success demonstrates that environmentally preferred products appeal to mainstream consumers—in one year, Green Works doubled sales in the green cleaner market.

Sales in this market are expected to grow rapidly as other established firms introduce their own green lines and the price premium for green drops. Mintel, a prominent research firm, predicts the green share of the cleaning market will grow from 3% in 2008 to 30% by 2013.[14] The green cleaner market contributes to a paradigm shift that is redefining what it means for a product to provide good value. Price, efficacy and availability are still desired attributes—but a good product today is increasingly one that is also safe for people and the planet. How much longer will Jill continue to view all cleaners as alike?

## Questions

1. What temporary situations, or changes in life circumstances, might influence a consumer to recognize a need for a cleaning product, in general, or a green cleaner, in particular? How might a marketer leverage this knowledge?

2. What types of purchase decisions were made by Jack, Jill and Elena: A) extended decision making, b) limited decision making, c) habitual decision making: brand inertia vs. brand loyalty? Explain.

3. How do perceptual attributes and packaging characteristics of the brands in this case study signal product quality in terms of the underlying environmental and health benefits?

4. How are consumers who shop at Whole Foods (a natural food store) and those who shop at Walmart likely to differ in terms of their consideration sets, determinant criteria, and use of a compensatory or noncompensatory rule when factoring environmentally preferred attributes? How does product categorization explain Method's decision to initially deemphasize green features when the product was launched?

| | WHOLE FOODS | WALMART |
|---|---|---|
| consideration set | | |
| determinant criteria | | |
| (non) compensatory rule | | |

*Reprinted with permission from the author

**Marketers can be** extremely successful by focusing on value. In fact, Walmart's success is more about value than satisfaction.

## what do you think?

**When I'm treated unfairly by a business, dissatisfaction describes my feelings well.**

STRONGLY DISAGREE                    STRONGLY AGREE

① ② ③ ④ ⑤ ⑥ ⑦

Visit CourseMate at www.cengagebrain.com.

# 14

# Consumption to Satisfaction

## LO1 Consumption, Value, and Satisfaction

**C**onsumption is at the heart of all consumer behavior. Obviously, a consumer *consumes*! In fact, one might say that all human activity focuses on some form of consumption. Even when we work, we consume time so that we can earn money to consume other things! In the **consumption process**, consumers use the product, service, or experience that has been selected. Ultimately, consumers consume products and receive value in return.

**consumption process** process in which consumers use the product, service, or experience that has been selected

**durable goods** goods that are usually consumed over a long period of time

**nondurable goods** goods that are usually consumed quickly

After studying this chapter, the student should be able to:

**LO1** Gain an appreciation of the link from consumption to value to satisfaction.

**LO2** Discuss the relative importance of satisfaction and value in consumer behavior.

**LO3** Know that emotions other than satisfaction can affect postconsumption behavior.

**LO4** Use expectancy disconfirmation, equity, and attribution theory approaches to explain consumers' postconsumption reactions.

**LO5** Understand problems with commonly applied satisfaction measures.

**LO6** Describe some ways that consumers dispose of products.

## CONSUMPTION LEADS TO VALUE

The important role of consumption becomes apparent when one considers that without consumption, there is no value. Accordingly, consumer value is directly derived from product consumption.[1] Earlier, we defined consumption as the process that converts time, goods, ideas or service into value. Consumption experiences potentially produce utilitarian and/or hedonic value.

The basic consumption process that is at the heart of the CVF is shown again in Exhibit 14.1.

## CONSUMPTION AND PRODUCT CLASSIFICATION

Many issues go along with the consumption of goods, services, and experiences. Important differences exist for the consumption of durable and nondurable goods. **Durable goods** are goods that are consumed over long periods of time. A dishwasher is a durable good. **Nondurable goods** are consumed quickly. Soft drinks are nondurable goods.

**consumption frequency** number of times a product is consumed

For nondurable goods especially, marketers try to increase consumption frequency as much as possible. **Consumption frequency** refers to the number of times a product or service is consumed in a given time period. Credit card companies have made it easier and easier for consumers to use their cards on routine shopping trips. Visa and MasterCard were once thought of as inappropriate for routine purchases like groceries. Today, however, consumers often use these for all manner of everyday purchases.

Marketers also attempt to increase the amount of product consumed per occasion. For example, soft drink marketers gradually increased the average size of soft drinks over time. Many students may be surprised to find out that the traditional Coke bottle was much smaller than today—weighing in at a mere 6½ ounces. Pepsi's selling point was a 10-ounce bottle at the same

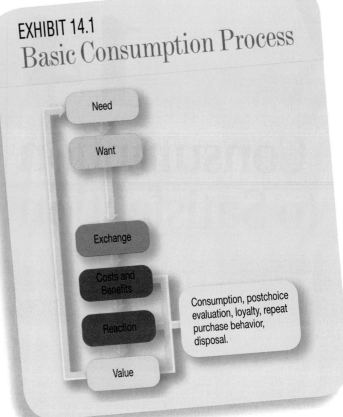

## EXHIBIT 14.1
## Basic Consumption Process

Need

Want

Exchange

Costs and Benefits

Reaction

Value

Consumption, postchoice evaluation, loyalty, repeat purchase behavior, disposal.

*The original Pepsi strategy encouraged a larger serving size at the same price as Coke's 6½ ounce bottle.*

© PAULVIDLER/ALAMY

price. Today consumers often consume 20-ounce or even 1-liter bottles a number of times per day! The soft drink industry has slowly facilitated an increase in the average soft drink serving size.

Services and experiences are usually classified as "nondurable" by default. However, some services are more clearly consumed over extended time periods. For example, we consume insurance daily even though consumers may pay premiums only periodically. Experiences are complete when consumption stops. However, marketers of these products encourage repeat consumption of their products by offering season tickets, club memberships, and special invitations to events. By encouraging increased consumption, these marketers are able to foster customer relationships.

## SITUATIONS AND CONSUMER REACTIONS

As discussed previously, consumption situations and settings have a significant impact on the consumer experience. The temporal factors, antecedent conditions, and physical environment are particularly influential on the consumption experience. How, what, and when we consume is largely dependent upon the environment that we are in.

# For Better or For Worse

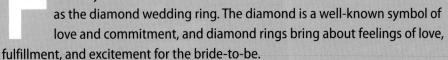

**F**ew material items are as symbolic as the diamond wedding ring. The diamond is a well-known symbol of love and commitment, and diamond rings bring about feelings of love, fulfillment, and excitement for the bride-to-be.

Consumer researchers carefully observed diamond ring sales during the recent economic downturn. What they found was that although the demand for diamonds did fall, the symbolism of the diamond ring ensured that wedding rings would still sell. Of course, people continue to marry whether the economy is good or bad. Many consumers simply turned away from high-end diamonds to less-pricey alternatives.

The demand for diamond rings highlights the importance of product symbolism and the strong impact that emotions have on consumption even during economic hard times. Economic conditions can sour, but diamonds still hold their symbolic meaning. When it comes to marriage, diamonds are still a girl's best friend!

Sources: Barbee, J. (2009), "Diamonds Are Forever?" *GlobalPost,* May 13, 2009, online content found at **www.globalpost.com/dispatch/ aftrica/090512/diamonds-are-forever.htm**. Mortished, C. (2009), "Now Cheaper, Are Diamonds Still a Girl's Best Friend," *The Times,* April 11, 2009, 49; Greene, J. (2008), "Blue Nile: A Guy's Best Friend," *BusinessWeek,* June 09, 2008, 39.

For example, football fans enjoy tailgating and numerous products are essential to convert the occasion into value. Beer, burgers, and brats are standard fare at typical Midwestern tailgates. In Louisiana, jambalaya, gumbo, gator tail, and perhaps even a Cajun band may accompany the beer. The products become artifacts in part of a tailgating ritual. Without these, the experience is less than authentic. **Authenticity** means something is real and genuine and has a history or tradition.[2] The consumption of authentic things adds value over the consumption of synthetic experiences particularly when the consumption environment contains high degrees of symbolism or consumers are highly involved in some activity. The very same products, like fried gator tail, offer less value when they are not contributing to an authentic consumer experience.

The environment plays a large role in influencing consumption and consumer satisfaction. When golfers play a crowded golf course, other golfers determine how fast one can play. Although proper etiquette is to allow faster players to pass slower golfers on the course, the interference with one's usual pace of play distracts from the enjoyment of the experience. Some courses have employees who will even require a group that is playing too slowly to skip a hole. Environmental factors like this influence how much value consumers receive and how satisfied they are with the experience.

## CONSUMPTION, MEANING, AND TRANSFERENCE

Consumers' lives are very much intertwined with consumption. Value depends on a process called **meaning transference**. From a utilitarian standpoint, the meaning of consumption is straightforward. Consumers buy shoe polish to polish their shoes. That's easy. What is not as straightforward is the hedonic component of consumption. Here, inner meanings, including cultural meaning, must be considered.

Meaning transference begins with culture. Value is affected largely by the meaning of goods, services, and experiences. Marketers work to transfer important cultural ideals or values into products via advertising and word-of-mouth that occurs between consumers. If they can attach a freedom theme to a product—for example, a motorcycle—then a consumer not only consumes the motorcycle itself, but also the meaning attached to the bike. Ultimately, the meaning of the product becomes an important part of the consumption experience.[3] The transfer of meaning in the consumption process is illustrated in Exhibit 14.2.

## CONSUMPTION OUTCOMES AND EMOTION

Consumers choose products, services, and experiences that they believe will deliver value by addressing their wants and needs. They anticipate good outcomes from

**hope** a fundamental emotion evoked by positive, anticipatory appraisals

their choices or else they would have made another choice. In previous chapters, we've stressed how emotions play key roles before and during consumption. Fantasies, fun, and feelings all are associated with consumption, and these elements of consumption are closely tied to perceived value.[4]

In this portion of the CVF, we stress how consumer emotions end up influencing consumption outcomes. This process begins with anticipation. **Hope**, for example, is a fundamental emotion evoked by positive, anticipatory appraisals. The consumer anticipates an outcome that could bring about a better situation in some way, and he or she feels the emotion hope in return. In this way, hope is the opposite of fear, which involves anticipation of a negative outcome.[5] Feelings like hope are linked with expectations and in this way they play a role in creating consumption outcomes.

> The consumer anticipates an outcome that he or she imagines could bring about a better situation in some way, and he or she feels the emotion hope in return.

Consumption, value, and satisfaction are tied closely together. Not surprisingly, consumers tend to be more satisfied with exchanges they find valuable, as value is at the heart of marketing transactions. Value

*Cause-related efforts like the Wounded Warriors Project rely on feelings of hope. In this case, hope that involvement will mean they are not forgotten.*

© BOBBY BANK/WIREIMAGE/GETTY IMAGES

**EXHIBIT 14.2**
**Transfer of Meaning in Consumption**

- Culturally defined meaning
- Product, service, experience
- Consumer

Source: McCracken, G. (1986), "Culture and Consumption: A Theoretical Account of the Structure and Movement of the Cultural Meaning of Consumer Goods," *Journal of Consumer Research*, 13 (1), 71–84.

perceptions, therefore, directly influence consumer satisfaction.[6] The relationship between consumption, value, and satisfaction is shown in Exhibit 14.3. However, the link between value and satisfaction is nowhere near perfect, as will be seen later.

## LO2 Value and Satisfaction

Satisfaction is a key variable, and certainly most companies try hard to satisfy customers. However, is satisfaction *the* key outcome variable for marketers and consumers? Consider Exhibit 14.4. It plots scores from the ACSI, which is the American Consumer Satisfaction Index.[7] This index plots satisfaction scores for many major companies. This particular chart plots satisfaction for retail companies operating in the United States.

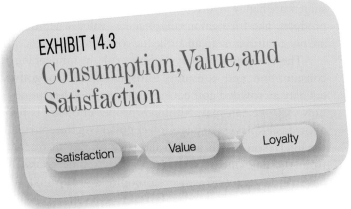

**EXHIBIT 14.3**
**Consumption, Value, and Satisfaction**

Satisfaction → Value → Loyalty

EXHIBIT 14.4

# The ACSI Scores for U.S. Retailers

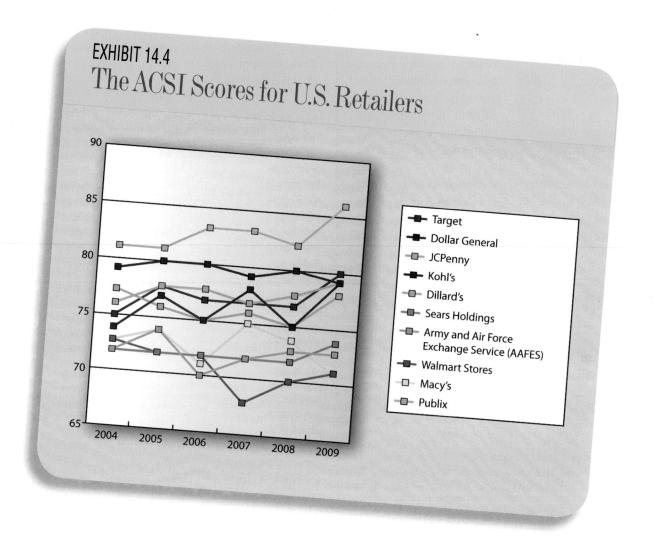

Legend:
- Target
- Dollar General
- JCPenny
- Kohl's
- Dillard's
- Sears Holdings
- Army and Air Force Exchange Service (AAFES)
- Walmart Stores
- Macy's
- Publix

## Is satisfaction the key outcome variable for marketers and consumers?

Notice that Publix (a large supermarket chain based in Florida) has the highest customer satisfaction rating over the entire period with Kohl's also scoring higher on the ACSI than most of the retailers. JCPenney, Dillard's, Target, and Dollar General all have higher satisfaction ratings than Walmart. What does this mean? Has any retailer enjoyed more success than Walmart in recent years? But, as the ACSI shows, Walmart is hardly a leader in satisfaction. In fact, Walmart's satisfaction ratings are the lowest of all retailers listed according to the ACSI. What can explain this? The answer lies in value. Even if Walmart does not provide high customer satisfaction, it does provide value leadership, particularly the perception that high utilitarian value results from shopping at Walmart. Thus, the track record says

COURTESY OF AMERICAN CUSTOMER SATISFACTION INDEX (ASCI)

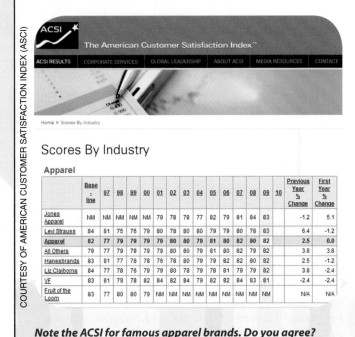

## Scores By Industry

### Apparel

| | Base-line | 97 | 98 | 99 | 00 | 01 | 02 | 03 | 04 | 05 | 06 | 07 | 08 | 09 | 10 | Previous Year % Change | First Year % Change |
|---|---|---|---|---|---|---|---|---|---|---|---|---|---|---|---|---|---|
| Jones Apparel | NM | NM | NM | NM | NM | NM | 79 | 78 | 78 | 77 | 82 | 79 | 81 | 84 | 83 | | -1.2 | 5.1 |
| Levi Strauss | 84 | 81 | 75 | 76 | 79 | 80 | 78 | 80 | 80 | 79 | 79 | 80 | 78 | 83 | | 6.4 | -1.2 |
| Apparel | 82 | 77 | 79 | 79 | 79 | 79 | 80 | 80 | 79 | 81 | 80 | 82 | 80 | 82 | | 2.5 | 0.0 |
| All Others | 79 | 77 | 79 | 79 | 79 | 79 | 80 | 80 | 79 | 81 | 80 | 82 | 79 | 82 | | 3.8 | 3.8 |
| Hanesbrands | 83 | 81 | 77 | 78 | 78 | 76 | 78 | 80 | 79 | 79 | 82 | 82 | 80 | 82 | | 2.5 | -1.2 |
| Liz Claiborne | 84 | 77 | 78 | 76 | 79 | 79 | 80 | 78 | 79 | 78 | 81 | 79 | 79 | 82 | | 3.8 | -2.4 |
| VF | 83 | 81 | 79 | 78 | 82 | 84 | 82 | 84 | 79 | 82 | 82 | 84 | 83 | 81 | | -2.4 | -2.4 |
| Fruit of the Loom | 83 | 77 | 80 | 80 | 79 | NM | NM | NM | NM | NM | NM | NM | NM | NM | | N/A | N/A |

**Note the ACSI for famous apparel brands. Do you agree?**

Walmart should continue to prioritize value over satisfaction.

The importance of value in the consumption experience cannot be overstated. In fact, the reason a firm exists at all is to create value.[8] Exhibit 14.3 shows how value comes from the consumption process, and that value, in turn, influences customer satisfaction. As stated in a previous chapter and suggested by the ACSI scores, value is the heart of consumer behavior, and value therefore can be thought of as the key outcome variable in the consumption experience.[9] If marketers ever face the decision of providing value or satisfaction, value should be prioritized because, as illustrated by the ACSI, firms can do well even when they do not enjoy the highest industry satisfaction scores, but the firm that does not provide value in some form can't succeed for long.

## WHAT IS CONSUMER SATISFACTION?

Customer satisfaction has received much attention from consumer researchers and marketing managers. However, different people define satisfaction differently and as a result it often is confused with numerous closely related concepts like quality and cognitive dissonance. However, satisfaction is distinct from these concepts.

**Consumer satisfaction** is a mild, positive emotional state resulting from a favorable appraisal of a consumption outcome. Several points distinguish consumer satisfaction from other important consumer behavior concepts:

- Consumer satisfaction is a postconsumption phenomenon because it is a reaction to an outcome.

- Like other emotions, satisfaction results from a cognitive appraisal. Some refer to this appraisal as the satisfaction judgment.

- Satisfaction is a relatively mild emotion that does not create strong behavioral reactions.

Other key consumer variables like expectations, quality, or attitude are generally more relevant preconsumption or even prepurchase in explaining consumer behavior.[10] Nevertheless, managers consider consumer satisfaction to be important because consumer's word-of-mouth, repeat purchase, and ultimately, consumer

loyalty correlate with consumer satisfaction scores. These relationships are discussed in detail in the next chapter.

## WHAT IS CONSUMER DISSATISFACTION?

Recall from the material on consumer information processing (CIP) that consumers react quite differently when responding to losses than when responding to gains. Additionally, some debate exists over whether or not low satisfaction necessarily means a consumer has high dissatisfaction. For reasons like these, consumer behavior theory distinguishes consumer dissatisfaction from consumer satisfaction. Therefore, **consumer dissatisfaction** can be defined as a mild, negative affective reaction resulting from an unfavorable appraisal of a consumption outcome.[11] Even though conceptually dissatisfaction is an opposite concept to satisfaction, the fact that consumers react differently to negative contexts means that dissatisfaction will explain behaviors that satisfaction cannot.

## LO3 Other Postconsumption Reactions

 lthough people often use *satisfaction* as a colloquialism for everything that happens after a consumer buys something, many other things, including other emotions, may also occur post consumption. This view can cause other important postconsumption reactions to be overlooked. Among these are specific emotions, including delight, disgust, surprise, exhilaration, and even anger. These particular emotions are often much more strongly linked to behavior because although they are also emotional reactions to appraisals, they are often much stronger.

An angry consumer exhibits much more noticeable and persistent behavior than does a consumer with low satisfaction. The angry consumer likely complains and sometimes shouts and, in extreme cases, begins boycott initiatives against a company that is the target of anger. A consumer with low satisfaction would not likely exhibit any visible signs of irritation. The particular emotion experienced by consumers will do much to determine the behavioral reaction as we will see in the

# I Hope It's Real, Really!

**M**arketers often claim to offer an authentic experience as a way of creating more value. That means the experience has to be the real thing! A restaurant that promises an authentic Parisian café experience needs to offer a menu and décor that is true to the promise. The consumer enters this experience hoping to experience something special—not a warmed over (no pun intended) roadside dinner house. Paté, Tavel (a French rosé wine) and crusty bread may just fulfill the hope and replace it with delight. In contrast, many Internet companies offer "authentic" designer products from Gucci, Prada, Louis Vuitton, Rolex, etc. Evidence suggests, however, that a large portion of designer products sold through the Internet is actually counterfeit. Imagine the post-purchase reactions from a consumer who recently got a good deal on a Louis Vuitton backpack for his fiancé—claimed to be 60% off! He can fill the bag with expectations. Before giving it to her, a friend jokes, "Hey, is that thing real?" After a few seconds of silence, he adds in a comforting tone, "Don't worry, it still works even if it isn't real!" Will the hope turn to anxiety or fear? How will his satisfaction be affected by the thought that it just might not be authentic?

Sources: Boss, D.L. (2008), "Providing Authentic Customer Experiences Yields Real Results," *Nation's Restaurant News*, (February 25), 40; Stumpf, S.A. and P. Chaudry (2010), "Country Matters: Executives Weigh In on the Causes and Counter Measures of Counterfeit Trade," *Business Horizons*, 53, 305–314.

---

following chapter when we discuss complaining in more detail. We will see more on this in the next chapter but any model of what happens after purchase would be remiss not to include possibilities beyond satisfaction.

# LO4 Theories of Postconsumption Reactions

## EXPECTANCY/DISCONFIRMATION

The most commonly accepted theory of consumer satisfaction is the **expectancy/disconfirmation theory**. The basic disconfirmation model proposes that consumers enter into a consumption experience with predetermined cognitive expectations of a product's performance. These expectations are used as a type of benchmark against which actual performance perceptions are judged.

**expectancy/disconfirmation theory** proposes that consumers use expectations as a benchmark against which performance perceptions are judged and this comparison is a primary basis for satisfaction/dissatisfaction

**positive disconfirmation** according to the expectancy/disconfirmation approach, a perceived state wherein performance perceptions exceed expectations

**negative disconfirmation** according to the expectancy/disconfirmation approach, a perceived state wherein performance perceptions fall short of expectations

Disconfirmation becomes central in explaining consumer satisfaction. When performance perceptions are more positive than what was expected, **positive disconfirmation** occurs. Positive disconfirmation leads to consumer satisfaction. When performance perceptions do not meet expectations, meaning performance is less than expected, **negative disconfirmation** occurs. Negative disconfirmation leads to dissatisfaction. Finally, if performance perceptions exactly match what was expected, confirmation (sometimes simply referred to as *neutral disconfirmation*) is said to occur.

The expectancy disconfirmation approach is shown in Exhibit 14.5. Taken together, disconfirmation represents the cognitive appraisal that produces postconsumption emotions like consumer satisfaction. Using different terminology, disconfirmation is the satisfaction judgment. The blue boxes represent cognitive postconsumption reactions, whereas the green box represents an affective or emotional postconsumption reaction. The relationships between the concepts are explained in the section that follows.

### Expectations

Expectations may be thought of as preconsumption beliefs of what will occur during an exchange and/or consumption of a product. Consumer expectations have two components: (1) The probability that something will occur and (2) an evaluation of that potential occurrence.[12] Exhibit 14.5 reveals that expectations also can have a direct impact on satisfaction (by the dotted line), independent of their role in the disconfirmation process.[13] This can occur when the consumer has very little involvement. In these cases, little effort is put into either expectation or performance appraisal, and satisfaction formation is largely impacted by consumer expectations alone. In other words, with low involvement, high expectations will be associated directly with increased satisfaction, and low expectations will be associated directly with increased dissatisfaction.

The same sort of effect can be found with very high involvement. In these cases, balance theory kicks in and consumers may adjust their reactions automatically as a way of protecting themselves from the realization that they may have made a poor choice. When consumers go on spring break they may anticipate the event so highly that they block out some of the bad things that happen so that their satisfaction reaction adjusts to their preconsumption expectations. Thus, under conditions of very low or very high involvement, expectations can influence satisfaction directly.

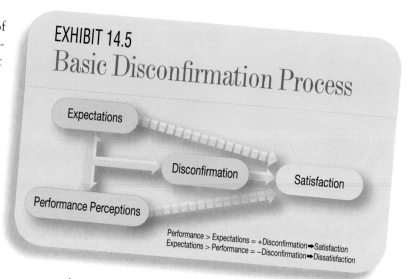

## EXHIBIT 14.5
## Basic Disconfirmation Process

Performance > Expectations = +Disconfirmation→Satisfaction
Expectations > Performance = −Disconfirmation→Dissatisfaction

**How will expectations influence the spring break experience?**

## Types of Expectations

Consumers bring different types of expectations into a consumption situation.

- **Predictive Expectations.** Expectations that form about what a consumer thinks will actually occur during an experience.

- **Normative Expectations.** Expectations of what a consumer thinks should happen given past experiences with a product or service.

- **Ideal Expectations.** Expectations about what a consumer really wants to happen during an experience if everything were ideal.

- **Equitable Expectations.** Expectations that a consumer forms regarding what he or she thinks should happen given the level of work that he or she has put into the experience.

## Source of Expectations

How do consumers form expectations? In other words, what are the sources of information that allow consumers to form expectations? In reality, consumers form expectations based on a number of different sources.[14] Word-of-mouth communication from other consumers is an important source of information. When a close friend tells you that a new television show is good, you'll probably hope that this is to be the case if you plan on watching it. A consumer's experience also influences expectations. If you've gone to a dentist who was caring and respectful of your feelings on the first visit, then you would expect the same kind of treatment during the next visit. Explicit promises such as advertisements and promotions create consumer expectations as well. If a company promises that it will deliver a package within two days, a 2-day delivery is what you probably expect! Personal factors also influence expectations. Some people simply expect more out of products and services than do others. Perhaps you know people who expect restaurant meals to be perfect or flights to arrive on time in any conditions. Here, personal factors influence the expectations that they have about the service.

© ANDRES RODRIGUEZ/ALAMY

## Expectation Confidence and Performance Perceptions

The disconfirmation approach seems to be relatively straightforward; however, the processes behind the approach can be complex. This is especially true given the roles of performance perceptions, expectation confidence, and the "confirmatory bias."

### Performance Perceptions

Recall that perception plays a very important role in consumer behavior. "Perception *is* reality!" Marketers are well aware of this. Perception directly influences how a consumer interacts with the world.

Perception is also very important for the consumption and postconsumption processes. As is the case with expectations, performance perceptions can also directly influence consumer satisfaction formation independent of the disconfirmation process (dotted line in Exhibit 14.5). This is particularly the case when expectations are low. For example, if a consumer buys a brand of product that he or she knows will be bad, expectations are likely to be low. Even if these low expectations are met by performance perceptions, the consumer is likely to be dissatisfied. Also, if a consumer has no previous experience or expectation regarding a product (for example, a new product), then perception can directly influence satisfaction.[15]

Marketers may think twice about setting expectations too firmly among consumers. Domino's Pizza once emphasized the 30-minute delivery guarantee for their pizzas. Consumers then began to expect this performance so strongly that they became very dissatisfied when the expectation was not met, so much so that the drivers became hazards on the road in an effort to meet the 30-minute deadline. In the end, Domino's had to back off the guarantee to avoid legal liability for accidents incurred by drivers who could easily be accused of driving recklessly in an effort to meet the 30-minute promise.

### Confidence in Expectations and the Confirmatory Bias

Another issue that is important in satisfaction theory is the degree to which consumers are confident in their expectations. For example, if a complete stranger tells a consumer that a movie is good, the consumer may not be very confident in his or her expectations. However, if a family member tells the consumer that a movie is good, then the consumer might feel much more confident in expecting the movie to be good. Research has indicated that when expectations are held with a strong degree of confidence,

both disconfirmation and performance perceptions affect satisfaction. However, when expectations lack a strong degree of confidence, perceived performance more strongly influences satisfaction.[16]

Not only do expectations play a key role in satisfaction formation, they also can affect how consumers see things. That is, expectations can affect performance perceptions.[17] Imagine a student who goes into a class thinking, "This class is going to be really bad!" There is a tendency for an expectation like this to actually alter his or her perception of the class experience. If the student thinks it's going to be bad, he or she may very well look for evidence to support this expectation! The term to explain this phenomenon is **confirmatory bias**. The confirmatory bias works in conjunction with self-perception theory. **Self-perception theory** states that consumers are motivated to act in accordance with their attitudes and behaviors. Here, consumers are motivated to perceive their environment through the lens of their expectations. The confirmatory influence of expectations on perceptions is especially strong when consumers are quite confident in what to expect.

### Expectations and Service Quality

**Service quality** can be thought of as the overall goodness or badness of a service provided. Service quality is often discussed as the difference between consumer expectations of different service aspects and the actual service that is delivered. When a gap exists, for example, when a dental hygienist is not as empathetic as a consumer expected, then quality perceptions are diminished. In fact, the **SERVQUAL** scale, a commonly applied approach for measuring service quality, takes this approach. From this perspective, service quality is really a disconfirmation approach.[18] Perhaps it goes without saying, but service quality then becomes a key driver of consumer satisfaction or dissatisfaction.

### Desires and Satisfaction

Although expectations play a major role in satisfaction formation, consumer desires are also very important.

**confirmatory bias** tendency for expectations to guide performance perceptions

**self-perception theory** theory that states that consumers are motivated to act in accordance with their attitudes and behaviors

**service quality** overall goodness or badness of a service experience, which is often measured by SERVQUAL

**SERVQUAL** way of measuring service quality that captures consumers' disconfirmation of service expectations

**Desires** are the level of a particular benefit that will lead to a valued end state. Studies have shown that desires directly impact satisfaction, beyond the influence of disconfirmation alone.[19] What consumers truly desire, rather than expect, from a product, service, or experience is therefore very important.

## Emotions, Meaning, and Satisfaction

As discussed earlier, emotions and meaning play important roles in consumption. These elements are also an important part of satisfaction formation. An experience producing positive emotions is logically likely to be satisfying as well. Conversely, if a consumer is in a bad mood when he or she goes to a restaurant, overall satisfaction with the experience will likely be affected in a mood-congruent direction. In other words, a bad mood tends to create dissatisfaction. Furthermore, the meaning behind the meal contributes to satisfaction as well. For example, perhaps that meal is one with a loved one, or a business meal that will be used to seal an important business agreement. Here, the meaning of the consumption experience affects the overall satisfaction with the meal independently of prior expectations or perceptions. An interpretive study of river-rafting consumers revealed that the emotions that consumers felt while consuming the experience related strongly to the value they experienced during the trip.[20]

© THINKSTOCK IMAGES/JUPITERIMAGES

*How are the emotions of river rafting consumers related to the value they experience during the trip?*

## EQUITY THEORY AND CONSUMER SATISFACTION

Perceptions of fairness can also have an impact on consumer satisfaction. **Equity theory** proposes that consumers cognitively compare their own level of inputs and outcomes to those of another party in an exchange.[21] Equitable exchanges occur when these ratios are equal. In equation form:

$$outcomes_A/inputs_A \approx outcomes_B/inputs_B$$

The equation states that as long as comparisons of outcomes to inputs for consumer A are approximately the same as the same ratio for another party (for example, a company or another consumer), then satisfaction will be positively affected. So, an inequitable exchange can occur when a consumer believes that he or she has been taken advantage of by a company or when another customer has been treated more favorably.

When a consumer sets out to buy a computer, she will put quite a bit of effort into finding just the right one. She will take time to visit a store such as Best Buy, talk with friends about what brand to buy, visit websites such as **Dell.com**, and try to figure out the best way to finance the computer. She considers all these inputs before conducting the transaction. What will the consumer get when she buys the computer? Of course, she will get a computer, but she will also get a warranty, service contract, and maybe even in-home installation. These things represent her outcomes.

The computer salesperson should put time into understanding the consumer's desires and the way she will use the computer and then try to match these with a good arrangement of product features. Perhaps the salesperson will show effort by listening and physically searching store inventory for the most appropriate product. These are inputs for the salesperson. Salesperson outcomes include a salary and any commission tied directly to the sale. When consumers put a lot into an important purchase, they don't like to be shortchanged by an apathetic employee. That wouldn't be fair, and the output-to-input ratios would reflect this. Fairness perceptions affect satisfaction in addition to any influence of disconfirmation. In fact, consumers sometimes feel over rewarded, sometimes in a service recovery effort, and these consumers pay the business back with very high satisfaction.[22]

*The idea of "no charge" could increase a consumer's perception of equity by creating the perception of getting something for nothing.*

## Inequitable Treatment

Perhaps more often, equity perceptions involve inequitable treatment of customers. A single customer enters a restaurant for lunch and puts in an order. A few minutes later, a couple enters and sits beside the first customer at the next table. They place their order. After ten minutes, the couple receives their food and the original customer is still waiting. To the original customer, this may seem unfair and be a source of dissatisfaction. Thus, service providers need to be keenly aware of how customers are treated in public to maintain perceptions that all customers are treated in much the same way—or at least treated in a fair way.

## Inequitable Consumers

Some consumers will try to take advantage of situations. Even though treatment is inequitable, if the inequity is in the consumers' favor, these particular customers may be very satisfied. For example, some consumers may take a minor mishap and complain so fiercely that managers feel compelled to offer something overly generous as a way of calming the consumer down. Other consumers may realize that a cashier has made a significant error and given them significantly too much change and not correct the mistake. These consumers may be satisfied because the equity balance

favors them. However, their actions can sometimes disadvantage other consumers.

> **attribution theory** theory that proposes that consumers look for the cause of particular consumption experiences when arriving at satisfaction judgments

## ATTRIBUTION THEORY AND CONSUMER SATISFACTION

Another approach to satisfaction can be found in attribution theory. **Attribution theory** focuses on explaining why a certain event has occurred. When consumers select and consume products, they are motivated to make attributions as to why good or bad things happen. Humans are innately curious. There are three key elements to the attribution theory approach: *locus*, *control*, and *stability*.[23]

- **Locus.** Judgments of who is responsible for an event. Consumers can assign the locus to themselves or to an external entity like a service provider. A self-ascribed event occurs when a consumer blames himself or herself for a bad event. For example, a consumer might say to himself, "I took way too long between oil changes; it's no wonder that my engine blew up!" Self-ascribed causes are referred to as internal attributions. If an event is attributed to a product or company, an external attribution is made. For example, a consumer might say, "I changed my oil regularly! It's not my fault that the engine blew up! Chrysler is still turning out junk!" This type of attribution of blame toward a marketing entity increases consumer dissatisfaction.

- **Control.** The extent to which an outcome was controllable or not. Here, consumers ask themselves, "Should this company have been able to control this event?" Two consumers are stranded in the Frankfurt, Germany airport overnight because their destination airport, Dallas/Fort Worth, is iced over. One consumer is irate (beyond dissatisfaction) with the airline because he believes the airline should have equipment to clear the ice off the runway—even in the southern part of the country. Another consumer who is booked on the same flight is not happy about the situation but does not blame the airline because she understands that weather events are uncontrollable. Therefore, the situation does not significantly affect her satisfaction process.

- **Stability.** The likelihood that an event will occur again in the future. Here, consumers ask themselves, "If I buy this product again, is another bad outcome likely to happen?" Let's briefly return to the Frankfurt airport example. If a customer has recently been stranded because of weather problems in Dallas on occasions other than the recent ice storm, he naturally comes to believe that this is a stable situation and his satisfaction with the airline will be diminished. On the other hand, if the other consumer has never before been stranded due to problems at the Dallas airport, her satisfaction with the airline is not likely to be affected by the current situation.

*Dissonance has also been responsible for more than a few cold feet in the days before a wedding day.*

## COGNITIVE DISSONANCE

Consumers also can experience what is known as cognitive dissonance following a purchase or a big decision. As was discussed with the balance theory approach, consumers prefer consistency among their beliefs. When faced with the knowledge that a bad decision may have been made, consumers experience dissonance (literally meaning "lack of agreement") between the thought that they are a good decision maker and that they made a bad decision. **Cognitive dissonance** refers to lingering doubts about a decision that has already been made.[24] Dissonance is sometimes known as buyer's regret. For example, a consumer may reach a decision to buy one house and then experience discomfort due to doubt that creeps in when the consumer realizes there were many other attractive houses available in addition to the one purchased.

Cognitive dissonance does not occur for all decisions. For high ticket items like automobiles or homes, though, dissonance is a real possibility if not a probability. Dissonance has also been responsible for more than a few cold feet in the days before a wedding day. These are situations that naturally lend themselves to the experience of dissonance. A consumer is more likely to experience true dissonance following a purchase when the following conditions exist:

1. The consumer is aware that there are many attractive alternatives that may offer comparable value relative to the product/brand purchased.
2. The decision is difficult to reverse.
3. The decision is important and involves risk.
4. The consumer has low self-confidence.

The dissonance among consumers' beliefs following a consumption experience can be very discomforting and be a source of negative postconsumption emotions. Consumers may therefore be motivated to lessen this discomfort. Furthermore, effective marketing can target consumers after purchase to take steps to reinforce their customers' decisions to select a brand. Many universities automatically send graduates university-sponsored magazines in order to maintain relationships and to reinforce the idea that choosing the school was indeed a good idea.

To lessen feelings of discomfort following purchase, consumers may engage in any, or all, of the activities listed in Exhibit 14.6.

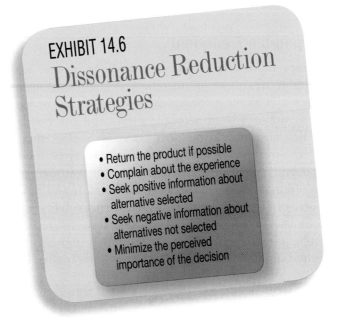

**EXHIBIT 14.6**
**Dissonance Reduction Strategies**

- Return the product if possible
- Complain about the experience
- Seek positive information about alternative selected
- Seek negative information about alternatives not selected
- Minimize the perceived importance of the decision

### Cognitive Dissonance and Satisfaction

Satisfaction and cognitive dissonance are closely related topics. The major difference between the two concepts is that satisfaction is generally felt *after* a consumption experience but dissonance may be experienced even *before* consumption begins. For example, after a decision has been made, a consumer might immediately think, "I should have bought the other one!" The uncertainty of events that might occur provides the basis for dissonance.[25]

# LO5 Consumer Satisfaction/Dissatisfaction Measurement Issues

here are many ways that marketers can measure consumer satisfaction. Three popular ways are through direct measures, difference scores, and disconfirmation.

- **Direct, Global Measure.** Simply asks consumers to assess their satisfaction on a scale such as:

  *How do you rate your overall satisfaction with your television?*

  | completely dissatisfied | dissatisfied | satisfied | completely satisfied |
  |---|---|---|---|
  | ☐ | ☐ | ☐ | ☐ |

- **Attribute-Specific.** Assesses a consumer's satisfaction with various components, or attributes, of a product, service, or experience, such as:

  *How satisfied are you with the following attribute of your television?*

  Picture Quality

  | completely dissatisfied | | | | completely satisfied |
  |---|---|---|---|---|
  | 1 | 2 | 3 | 4 | 5 |

- **Disconfirmation.** Compares the difference between expectations and performance perceptions. This measure can be taken in a direct, subjective fashion, such as:[26]

  *Compared to my expectations, this television performs . . .*

  | much worse than I expected | | | | much better than I expected |
  |---|---|---|---|---|
  | 1 | 2 | 3 | 4 | 5 |

## IMPROVING SATISFACTION MEASURES

Satisfaction is one of the most commonly measured concepts in consumer behavior but is also one of the most difficult to measure accurately. For example, the typical four-choice satisfaction approach as shown in the direct global measure example actually proves quite problematic in practice. The problems can be severe and limit the ability to use satisfaction ratings to explain or predict other outcomes including whether or not the consumer will return.

Consider that marketers measure satisfaction among existing customers most frequently. These customers have already decided to patronize a business. So, a web pop-up for **Amazon.com** may ask a consumer to rate satisfaction with a simple measure of this type. This consumer should already be favorable because he or she has decided to purposefully visit **Amazon.com** and shop using this site. Thus, he or she already feels favorable toward **Amazon.com**. Therefore, we would expect even without knowing what happened during the visit that the customer would report some degree of satisfaction. In fact, typical consumer responses to this type of measure show that the vast majority of consumers, 80% or more, choose "satisfied" or "completely satisfied." Statistically speaking, these data are **left skewed,** in this instance meaning that the bulk of consumers have indicated that they are satisfied or completely satisfied with the product or service.

Does this reflect reality, or is the scale simply inadequate in truly differentiating consumers experiencing different levels of satisfaction? The truth is that both possibilities are likely true to some extent. From a measurement perspective, giving consumers more choices to respond to may increase the amount of variance displayed in the satisfaction measure and thereby increase its usefulness in trying to use satisfaction to predict and explain other behaviors. An alternative would be to have consumers score their satisfaction on a 0 (no satisfaction) to 100 (complete satisfaction) point scale. The results will still typically show an average satisfaction score above 50 points; however, the statistical properties are much improved, making for a more useful measure. Even better, a researcher might have a respondent rate his or her satisfaction with multiple scale items.

Exhibit 14.7 displays an improved way of measuring consumer satisfaction using multiple scale items.[27] The scale mitigates problems with skewness and/or bias by providing scales with more response points and by using different response formats for each response item. The scale also focuses only on satisfaction. Although a marketer may choose to measure only satisfaction, this scale suggests that dissatisfaction should be measured with its own scale. A dissatisfaction scale can be formed by substituting the word *dissatisfaction* for satisfaction in each of the four items. Even if a total of eight items are used (four satisfaction and four dissatisfaction items), a

**consumer refuse** any packaging that is no longer necessary for consumption to take place or, in some cases, the actual good that is no longer providing value to the consumer

consumer can typically respond to these items in less than one minute. The question of whether or not dissatisfaction is more than just low satisfaction can be sorted out statistically. That topic is left for another course.

# LO6 Disposing of Refuse

## DISPOSAL DECISIONS

A final step in consumption is disposal of any consumer refuse. **Consumer refuse** is any packaging that is no longer necessary for consumption to take place or, in some cases, the actual good that is no longer providing value to the consumer. Many consumers have old computers that they no longer use but have not yet disposed of because of various concerns including security issues. At first, this may seem like a straightforward process wherein the consumer simply throws away their trash. However, a number of disposal alternatives are available. These include trashing, recycling, converting to another use, trading, donating, or reselling.[28]

- **Trashing.** One alternative that a consumer has is to simply throw away waste material including unused products, packaging, and by-products. Of course, there are environmental concerns with this alternative. According to the Environmental Protection Agency (EPA), approximately 254 million tons of municipal garbage is generated each year, or an average of 4.6 pounds of garbage per person, per day![29] Many marketers have turned to so-called green marketing initiatives, which aim to use packaging materials that cut down on the environmental impact of waste.

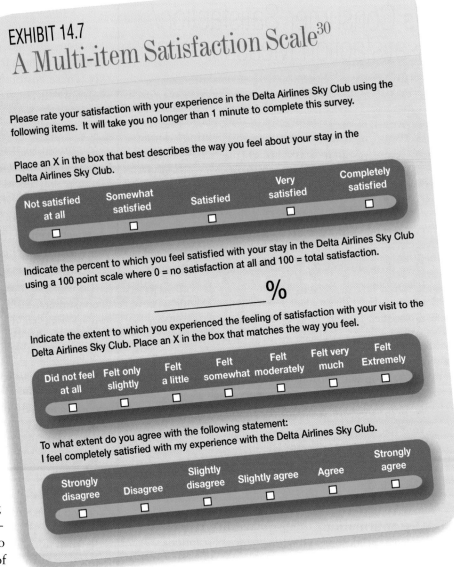

**EXHIBIT 14.7**
**A Multi-item Satisfaction Scale**[30]

Please rate your satisfaction with your experience in the Delta Airlines Sky Club using the following items. It will take you no longer than 1 minute to complete this survey.

Place an X in the box that best describes the way you feel about your stay in the Delta Airlines Sky Club.

| Not satisfied at all | Somewhat satisfied | Satisfied | Very satisfied | Completely satisfied |

Indicate the percent to which you feel satisfied with your stay in the Delta Airlines Sky Club using a 100 point scale where 0 = no satisfaction at all and 100 = total satisfaction.

_____ %

Indicate the extent to which you experienced the feeling of satisfaction with your visit to the Delta Airlines Sky Club. Place an X in the box that matches the way you feel.

| Did not feel at all | Felt only slightly | Felt a little | Felt somewhat | Felt moderately | Felt very much | Felt Extremely |

To what extent do you agree with the following statement:
I feel completely satisfied with my experience with the Delta Airlines Sky Club.

| Strongly disagree | Disagree | Slightly disagree | Slightly agree | Agree | Strongly agree |

- **Recycling.** Another alternative for consumers is to recycle used products or packaging. Recycling cuts down on garbage while providing raw materials for other new products. Consumers can then buy new products made of recycled materials.

- **Converting.** Consumers can convert products, or product packaging, into new products in a number of creative ways. For example, consumers often use old t-shirts and socks as car-wash rags. Of course, consumers know many uses for old products!

- **Trading.** Another alternative for consumers is to trade in old products for new products. The automotive industry has encouraged this practice for years. Consumers can often get thousands of dollars off of a new automobile purchase by trading in an old model. Even a car that doesn't run has some value in the form of spare parts.

- **Donating.** Consumers also have the ability to donate used products to various causes. Eyeglasses, clothing, and (surprisingly) automobiles are often donated in order to help other consumers who may not be able to afford new products.

- **Reselling.** One of the most popular methods for permanently disposing of used products is to simply sell them. Garage sales and swap meets are popular means of disposing of products in this way. Of course, online methods such as eBay and Craigslist are also quite popular with consumers.

## DISPOSAL, EMOTIONS, AND PRODUCT SYMBOLISM

Consumers often develop emotional bonds with their possessions. As discussed in an earlier chapter, possessions can help express a consumer's self-concept. The decision to part with belongings can therefore be very emotional, especially for older consumers who place much symbolic value on many products.[31] Strong feelings of attachment may be placed on many goods, especially those goods that are considered to be family heirlooms. Selling, giving away, or donating these goods can lead consumers to feel as if they have lost a part of themselves. In other situations, consumers can be quite ready to dispose of products that bring back bad memories, or that lead the consumers to have uneasy feelings about themselves or their past.[32]

Some consumers are very reluctant to part ways with their possessions. The term *packrat* is used to describe a person who keeps possessions that fulfill no utilitarian or hedonic need and who have a difficult time disposing of products. Packrats are likely to visit garage sales, swap meets, and flea markets to purchase products that serve no immediate need.[33] Even though the term *packrat* is often used loosely, the packrat behavior can be associated with various psychological conditions including obsessive–compulsive disorder.

# Buy, Sell, and Trade the Online Way

From **eBay.com** to **Craigslist.com** to **Kijiji.com**, online buying, selling, and trading have become a huge business. Whereas consumers once only had a few options if they wanted to buy, sell, or trade used items, the Internet has made the process much easier.

Of course, the Internet phenomenon eBay has long been the benchmark in the online trading world. The Internet giant that is well known for allowing consumers to auction off their belongings in an online marketplace has been wildly successful for several years. Rival **Craigslist.com**, which focuses on online classified advertising, has also experienced rapid growth, and the site currently accounts for over 90% of online classified listing traffic. Not to be outdone, eBay's **Kijiji.com**, which also focuses on online classified advertising, is becoming a major player in the growing industry.

Thanks to sites such as these, consumers can now auction their products, place classified ads online, or simply browse local pages for good deals. The ease and availability of these sites are rapidly changing how consumers buy and sell goods and, ultimately, how consumers interact with one another.

Sources: Fowler, G. A. (2009), "Auctions Fade in eBay's Bid for Growth," *The Wall Street Journal* (online), May 26, 2009, A1, accessed June 15, 2009; MacMilliam, D. (2009), "Craigslist Fuels Online Classified-Ad Surge," *BusinessWeek* (online), New York: May 25, 2009, accessed June 15, 2009; Dell, K. (2008), "eBay Bids for Revitalization," *Time* (online), 172 (25), December 22, 2008, G1, accessed June 15, 2009.

# 14
## Study Tools

**Located at back of the textbook**
- ☐ Rip-Out Chapter-in-Review Card

**Located at www.cengagebrain.com**
- ☐ Review Key Terms Flashcards (Print or Online)
- ☐ Download audio summaries to review on the go
- ☐ Complete practice quizzes to prepare for tests
- ☐ Play "Beat the Clock" and "Quizbowl" to master concepts
- ☐ Watch Video on Sephora for a real company example

# what others have thought...

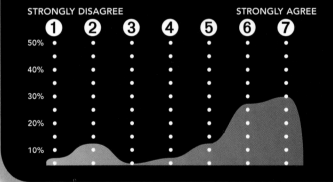

STRONGLY DISAGREE ① ② ③ ④ ⑤ ⑥ ⑦ STRONGLY AGREE

50% 40% 30% 20% 10%

### When I'm treated unfairly by a business, dissatisfaction describes my feelings well.

Most respondents agree. Nearly sixty percent either agree or strongly agree with this statement. However, 15 percent either disagree or strongly disagree. Perhaps these respondents feel hurt or angry more than dissatisfied.

# REVIEW! HE DID

**CB3** puts a multitude of study aids at your fingertips. After reading the chapters, check out these resources for further help:

• **Review Cards,** found in the back of your book, include all learning outcomes, key terms and definitions, and visual summaries for each chapter.

• **Online Printable Flashcards** give you additional ways to check your comprehension of key Consumer Behavior concepts.

• Other great tools to help you review include **interactive games, videos, and auto-graded quizzes.**

**Go to CourseMate for CB3 to find plenty of resources to help you *Review!* Access at www.cengagebrain.com.**

**Truly loyal**

customers are like gold to a company.

what do you think?

**When I have a good experience with a brand, I reward it by telling my friends how great it is.**

STRONGLY DISAGREE ① ② ③ ④ ⑤ ⑥ ⑦ STRONGLY AGREE

Visit CourseMate at www.cengagebrain.com.

# 15

# Consumer Relationships

## LO1 Outcomes of Consumption

t he previous chapter focused significantly on customer satisfaction/dissatisfaction. Many companies have satisfaction guarantees:

*100% Satisfaction or Your Money Back!*

Assuming that marketers' motivations for such guarantees are well intentioned, are companies really interested in satisfaction? If consumers could not return to do business again, the pursuit of satisfaction would be relegated to a purely altruistic exercise. Many firms might lose interest in serving customers well if this were the case. However, firms are interested in what happens

> **procedural justice** the extent that consumers believe the processes involved in processing a transaction and handling any complaints is fair

after a consumer is satisfied or dissatisfied because they would like customers to return to do business again. Thus, this chapter picks up where the previous chapter left off. Here, the focus is squarely on postconsumption reactions—the things that happen after a consumer has received most consumption benefits.

Exhibit 15.1 expands the disconfirmation framework traditionally used to explain consumer satisfaction. This particular chart divides up the different concepts into three groups. The green color variables represent things that are predominantly cognitive. These include the actual disconfirmation formation process that results from comparing actual performance with expected performance. Additionally, consumer's attribution and equity cognitions are also included among cognitions. Perceptions of justice are included within the equity cognitions. **Procedural justice**, in particular, refers to the extent that consumers believe the processes involved in processing a transaction and handling any complaints is fair.

Postconsumption cognitions lead to an affective reaction most conventionally represented by consumer satisfaction/dissatisfaction (CS/D). This particular model recognizes that the evaluation process could lead to any

After studying this chapter, the student should be able to:

**LO1** List and define the behavioral outcomes of consumption.

**LO2** Know why consumers complain and the ramifications of complaining behavior for a marketing firm.

**LO3** Use the concept of switching costs to understand why consumers do or do not repeat purchase behavior.

**LO4** Describe each component of true consumer loyalty.

**LO5** Understand the role that value plays in shaping loyalty and building consumer relationships.

number of varying affective outcomes, many of which have stronger behavioral reactions than CS/D. The blue sections in Exhibit 15.1 show the affective variables.

Finally, the exhibit shows behavioral outcomes of the postconsumption process in red boxes. Indeed, this is why marketers are interested in pursuing satisfaction. The behaviors that complete this process do much to determine the success or failure of competitive enterprises. Never has this been truer than in today's relationship marketing era. While the negative behaviors like complaining perhaps receive more attention as reactions to consumption, positive outcomes, including positive word-of-mouth behavior and ultimately the development of a strong relationship, are essential elements to success.

We begin this chapter by looking at some common behaviors that follow consumption. Exhibit 15.1 lists the behaviors; and although all but the last, loyalty, may seem negative, if properly managed the firm can turn these negative behaviors into positive value experiences. When this is done, customers are more likely to become loyal, and loyalty is the positive outcome relationship-oriented firms seek.

# LO2 Complaining and Spreading WOM

## COMPLAINING BEHAVIOR

**Complaining behavior** occurs when a consumer actively seeks out someone to share an opinion with regarding a negative consumption event. The person may be a service provider, a supervisor, or someone designated by a company to take complaints. Think about this question:

*How long should a consumer have to wait for service before complaining?*

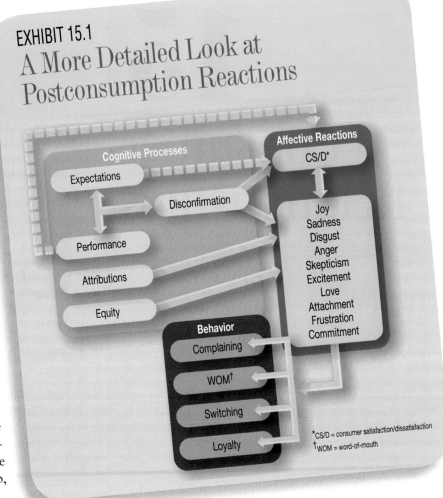

EXHIBIT 15.1
A More Detailed Look at Postconsumption Reactions

Cognitive Processes

Expectations

Disconfirmation

Performance

Attributions

Equity

Affective Reactions

CS/D*

Joy
Sadness
Disgust
Anger
Skepticism
Excitement
Love
Attachment
Frustration
Commitment

Behavior

Complaining

WOM†

Switching

Loyalty

*CS/D = consumer satisfaction/dissatisfaction
†WOM = word-of-mouth

The answer to this may depend on several factors, including the type of service involved. A 30-minute wait may be unacceptable and evoke negative disconfirmation, a negative affective consequence, and an active complaint if a consumer is waiting to be served for lunch. However, a consumer waiting to see a doctor for 30 minutes may not experience the same reaction because the expectation is that one will wait for 30 minutes or more. Even if one waits longer than expected to see a doctor, the consumer still may not complain for other reasons.

## Complainers

Generally, we think of dissatisfied customers as complainers. Not all customers reporting dissatisfaction complain. In fact, far less than half of customers experiencing some dissatisfaction complain to management. Only 17% of healthcare consumers complain upon experiencing some problem with the service or care they are receiving, and a recent survey among restaurant consumers suggests that no more than 5% of consumers with a problem complain.[1] What makes a *complainer* different? Consumers who do complain experience different emotions than do those who do not complain. In contrast to consumers who are merely dissatisfied, angry consumers are very likely to complain and at times, the anger becomes very strong and reaches the stage of rage.[2] These consumers complain and more.

A potentially worse outcome for a business occurs when a consumer has a negative experience, realizes this, and then reacts more with disgust than anger. Compared to the angry customer, a disgusted or hopeless consumer is not likely to complain.[3] Consumers' behavioral reactions can be understood by considering whether the

emotions they experience evoke approach or avoidance reactions. Negative approach emotions like anger are most likely to precede complaining behavior. Complaining is a relatively mild way of coping with anger.

The consumer who reacts with disgust is unlikely to complain. Disgust evokes an avoidance response, and as a result, a disgusted consumer avoids a potential confrontation and simply goes away. When the disgusted consumer simply goes away, the information about what caused the problem in the first place also goes away. Complainers, although sometimes unpleasant to deal with, are valuable sources of feedback about potential problems in service quality, product performance, or system malfunction. Unfortunately, the disgusted consumer copes by going away.

When a consumer complains, the marketer has a chance to rectify the negative situation. A consumer that sulks away takes the valuable information with him or her. A truly consumer-oriented company should encourage customers to complain when things go wrong. If "100% satisfaction" is not just a slogan, the company must encourage its customers to act like whistle blowers when something goes wrong. In this sense, an angry customer is a valuable asset for a business!

> Complainers, although sometimes unpleasant to deal with, are valuable sources of feedback about potential problems in service quality, product performance, or system malfunction.

### The Result of Complaining

Exhibit 15.2 provides a summary of what happens when consumers do or do not complain. The fact of the matter is that for consumers as well as marketers, complaining pays off. When consumers complain, more often than not, some corrective action is taken that culminates with the consumer feeling satisfied when he or she reevaluates the situation. A consumer

> Actively listening to the complaints of annoyed customers can lead to greatly improved service.

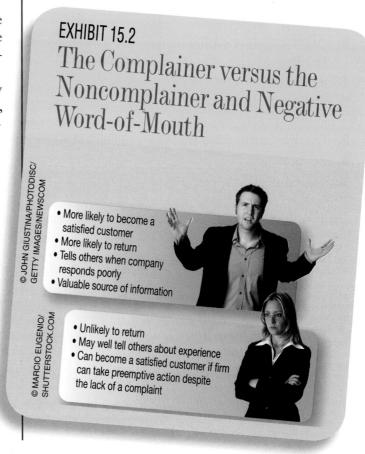

**EXHIBIT 15.2**
## The Complainer versus the Noncomplainer and Negative Word-of-Mouth

- More likely to become a satisfied customer
- More likely to return
- Tells others when company responds poorly
- Valuable source of information

- Unlikely to return
- May well tell others about experience
- Can become a satisfied customer if firm can take preemptive action despite the lack of a complaint

who complains about a noisy hotel room gets moved to another room, perhaps a suite! In such a case, the customer is likely to believe that he or she was treated fairly after complaining, and these thoughts evoke a more positive outcome. This positive outcome can represent a win–win situation.

Earlier, we mentioned that only about 5% of restaurant customers with a service problem actually complained to management. However, among those who complained, 95% were likely to remain customers of the restaurant when their complaint was handled quickly and responsively. The following list gives service providers advice for handling consumer complaints effectively:[4]

1. Thank the guest for providing the information.

2. Ask questions to clarify the issue.

3. Apologize sincerely.

4. Show empathy for the customer's situation.

5. Explain the corrective action that will take place.

6. Act quickly.

7. Follow up with the customer after the corrective action.

Today it's easier than ever for consumers to complain publicly. Check out websites like these:

- www.complaints.com
- http://esupport.fcc.gov/complaints.htm
- http://www.bbb.org/

These websites allow consumers to lodge formal complaints, make their complaints public, and get advice on the proper steps to follow should the consumer need to take further official action.

# Payback Can Be Swell!

All too often, the news contains stories of customers gone wild. An angry McDonald's customer tried to run over two customers with her car in a parking lot in a situation that started with a long line to place the order. Another woman was enraged because McDonald's was out of chicken nuggets and went berserk and attacked the person working at the drive-thru window. Sometimes, complaining behavior becomes extreme and takes the form of revenge. Web resources even offer assistance (for a small fee) in taking out revenge on companies (**www.consumer-revenge.com**). Every consumer has a critical boiling point and once this is reached, the likelihood of retaliatory actions becomes real. One key trigger is procedural justice, or the lack thereof. The consumer thinks they have been treated unfairly and that the business is responsible. When this happens, they become prone to all manner of complaints including negative word-of-mouth and even potentially unethical or even illegal action such as vandalism or battery. These types of revenge behaviors help consumers cope with their feelings and create an opportunity for them to reduce or eliminate their own negative mood state. In that way, revenge is swell.

Sources: Rio-Lanza, A. B., R. Vazquez-Casielles and A. M. Diaz-Martin (2009), "Satisfaction with Service Recovery: Perceived Justice and Emotional Responses," *Journal of Business Research*, 62, 775–781; Zourrig, H., J.C. Chebat and R. Tofoli (2009), "Consumer Revenge Behavior: A Cross-Cultural Perspective," *Journal of Business Research*, 62, 995–1001; Kalamas, M., M. Laroche and L. Makdessian (2008), "Reaching the Boiling Point: Consumers' Negative Affective Reactions to Firm-Attributed Service Failures," *Journal of Business Research*, 61, 813–824; **www.breitbart.com/article.php?id=08JGINJG18show_article=1,** accessed August 10, 2010.

## The Result of Not Complaining

So, what happens when the consumer does not complain? Let's return to the noisy hotel room. A customer may simply put up with the inconvenience and end up leaving miserable after a poor night's sleep. Is this the end of the story? Not really! The consumer may well remember this incident and be less likely to do business with this hotel again. He or she may also complain to others about the episode. Interestingly, though, when marketers can take action to address a negative situation before a consumer complains, a very positive outcome can result. So, imagine that a bell clerk reports the noise in one of the halls of the hotel to management. Management then takes action by calling the adjacent rooms to suggest that they move to a better room. These customers are likely to be very appreciative and become more likely to return again.[5]

## Revenge

On occasion, consumers' verbal complaints to the marketing company do not eliminate the negative emotions they are experiencing. In these instances, consumers may retaliate in the form of revenge-oriented behaviors. These could be as simple as trying to prevent others from using the business by spreading the word about how bad the business is but the behaviors can become more aggressive. **Rancorous revenge** is when a consumer yells, insults, and makes a public scene in an effort to harm the business.[6] However, in extreme cases the furious consumer can become violent or try to vandalize the business. **Retaliatory revenge** is a term that captures these extreme types of behavior.

# WORD-OF-MOUTH

Just because a consumer doesn't complain to the offending company doesn't mean he or she just keeps the episode inside. **Negative word-of-mouth** (negative WOM) takes place when consumers pass on negative information about a company from one to another. As can be seen from Exhibit 15.2, both the complainer and the noncomplainer may well participate in this kind of potentially destructive behavior. Some estimates suggest that a consumer who fails to achieve a valuable consumption experience is likely to tell his or her story to more than ten other consumers.[7] Recall that as a source of information, WOM is powerful because of relatively high source credibility. The fact that most consumers who participate in WOM do so to multiple consumers makes the matter all the more important.

WOM is not always negative. In fact, **positive WOM** occurs when consumers spread information from one to another about positive consumption experiences with companies. Conventionally, negative WOM is seen as more common than positive WOM. However, in the television industry, consumers appear more likely to spread the word about shows they find valuable rather than those they do not.[8] Whether positive or negative, WOM exerts very strong influences on other consumers. As we will see later, a consumer spreading positive WOM is likely to be an asset to a business.

## Negative Public Publicity

When negative WOM spreads to a relatively large scale, it can result in **negative public publicity**. Negative public publicity could even involve media coverage. Thus, most large companies have employees whose job it is to try to quell or respond to negative public publicity. A Delta Air Lines customer had a camera stolen from a checked bag. After personally investigating the situation, he was able to track down the culprit, a Delta baggage handler. Eventually, the media picked up the story, at which point a Delta Air Lines official contacted the customer and refunded him the price of the original flight.[9] In this case, the negative publicity paid off for the customer.

Today, consumers can easily make their complaints public using the World Wide Web. Numerous websites that facilitate just this sort of behavior exist. One such site is **www.consumeraffairs.com**. Consumers who are considering a purchase can go to this site and search for complaints on brands and products that are being considered. The consumer complains that a brand of pet food made his pets very sick including giving them chronic digestive problems. In the complaint, he tosses blame on the brand, the retailer and particularly on his vet who recommended the brand. However, he came across information on the Internet where other consumers had complained about the pet food previous at this website. Needless to say, he is trying to stop others from using the product.

Negative publicity can do considerable harm to a brand. In an earlier chapter, we discussed how Toyota received a lot of negative publicity about "unintended acceleration." Interestingly, in the 1980s Audi's U.S. market share was virtually wiped out within a short period after the news show *60 Minutes* ran a segment claiming that Audis were susceptible to sudden acceleration syndrome. In reality, *60 Minutes* producers had rigged an Audi sedan to appear to be driving in circles with no driver in the car as a way of trying to convince viewers that Audis were indeed dangerous.[10] After over a decade of study, the FTA actually cleared Audi of this charge with the cases

**rancorous revenge** is when a consumer yells, insults, and makes a public scene in an effort to harm the business in response to an unsatisfactory experience

**retaliatory revenge** consumer becomes violent with employees and/or tries to vandalize a business in response to an unsatisfactory experience

**negative word-of-mouth** (negative WOM) action that takes place when consumers pass on negative information about a company from one to another

**positive WOM** action that occurs when consumers spread information from one to another about positive consumption experiences with companies

**negative public publicity** action that occurs when negative WOM spreads on a relatively large scale, possibly even involving media coverage

**Marketers understand that switching is a barrier to new business.**

being attributed to driver error—hitting the accelerator when meaning to press the brake. While the negative publicity hit Audi hard, the impact on Toyota seems to be much less.

How should a firm handle negative public publicity? Here are some alternative courses of action:

1. Do nothing; the news will eventually go away.

2. Deny responsibility for any negative event.

3. Take responsibility for any negative events and be visible in the public eye.

4. Release information allowing the public to draw its own conclusion.
   What is the best approach?

## Doing Nothing or Denying Responsibility

Doing nothing is neither the best nor the worst option. Taking action seems to be a responsible thing to do, but the action can backfire. Even when the basis for the negative publicity is simply rumor, denying any responsibility can be a very bad idea.

Common sense should suggest that McDonald's would never substitute worms for ground beef simply on the basis of cost alone (worms would have to be more expensive than ground beef). Enough consumers believed this rumor at one point in time that McDonald's market share suffered. McDonald's reacted with a 100% beef ad campaign; and even Ray Croc, the founder of McDonald's, did interviews suggesting the idea had no basis in common sense or reality.[11] In essence, this was a denial response. Claiming the burgers were 100% beef was much the same as saying they are 0% worm! Denying a ridiculous claim only gives it credibility and results in negative effects for the brand.

## Taking Responsibility

One might easily see that attribution theory plays a role in dealing with negative publicity. If consumers blame the company for the event surrounding the negative publicity, then the potential repercussions appear serious. However, public action to deal with any consequences of a negative event can mollify any negative effects.

One of the most famous negative publicity cases of all time involves Tylenol pain medicine. In the fall of 1982, over half a dozen consumer deaths in the Chicago area were attributed to cyanide traces in Tylenol capsules. Tylenol executives considered their options, including plausible deniability, and decided to take action by immediately having all Tylenol removed from shelves all around the country immediately. In addition, they agreed to take steps to make sure they discovered what had happened and to make sure it could not happen again. The dramatic action helped convince consumers that Tylenol truly cared about the welfare of customers and wanted to make sure this never happened again. Even though they were quite certain they had no culpability in what appears to be senseless murder, they acted in a way that led to a huge short-term loss. However, this action saved Tylenol's reputation. In fact, many younger consumers may wonder how we came to have tamper-proof packaging for over-the-counter medications and now practically all food products. While today government mandates require such packaging in many instances, the beginning of tamper-proof packaging goes back to Tylenol's response to this potentially damaging negative publicity associated with these murders.

## Releasing Information

Sometimes, a company may be able to release some counter-PR to media that allows consumers to make up their own minds about the potential source of any negative PR. If this is done properly, the company does not publicly deny any allegation about the event and instead insists that actions are being taken to get to the bottom of the event.

In the mid-1990s, a consumer made the news by claiming that he was simply drinking a Pepsi when a hypodermic needle began to flow out of the can and stuck his lip. Within two days of this story going public, dozens of consumers from all around the country made the same claim. Pepsi, rather than denying any responsibility, opened the doors of canning operations around North America. Film crews were allowed to come in and videotape cans streaming down an assembly line at high speed. Pepsi released information about the number of canning plants that exist and how they are spread around the country. This action worked to prevent any negative fallout for Pepsi. The media coverage allowed consumers to draw their own conclusions. Obviously, if a needle would get into some Pepsi cans, the chances that this would happen at multiple canning plants all around the country seemed unlikely. Thus, how could this be happening all over? Also, watching the canning operations made clear the fact that nobody could possibly slip a needle into a can at the speeds the assembly line operates. This entire incident was over in just a couple of weeks. All of the alleged needle victims confessed to making up the stories with the hope of getting some part of any settlement that Pepsi might be forced to pay. Thus, this appears to be a textbook way to deal with negative publicity for an implausible event.

## Participating in Negative WOM

One of the factors that helps determine negative word-of-mouth returns to the issue of equity. Consumers who believe they have not been treated with fairness or justice become particularly likely to tell others and, in some cases, report the incident to the media.[12]

*The media are a vehicle for both spreading negative publicity and for managing the implications of negative publicity.*

Consumers can be angry when they believe they have been wronged in this way, and these actions are a small way of trying to get revenge. Consumers who spread negative WOM without complaining to the company itself are particularly likely not to ever do business with that company again.[13] This tendency provides all the more reason for companies to make consumers feel comfortable about complaining and creating the impression of genuine concern for the consumer's situation.

## Implications of Negative WOM

One reason consumers share negative WOM is as a way of preventing other consumers from falling victim to a company. Thus, negative WOM can hurt sales. However, this is not the only potential negative effect. Negative WOM also can damage the image of the firm. When a consumer hears the negative WOM from a credible source, that information is very likely to become strongly attached to the schema for that brand. Thus, not only is the consumer's attitude toward the brand lowered but the consumer will also find the firm's advertising harder to believe.[14]

In extreme cases, the negative WOM attached to one company can have effects that spill over to an entire industry. For instance, news attributing accidents at one amusement park to a lack of maintenance will certainly damage the image of that particular amusement park. However, a consumer hearing this news may end up not feeling very comfortable about any similar amusement park. Thus, firms must be wary of negative WOM not just for their own brand, but for the industry as well.[15]

Negative WOM does not affect all consumers in the same way. Consumers who have very strong, positive feelings about a brand may have a difficult time accepting negative WOM. Once again, this can be due to balance theory as consumers try to maintain their existing belief systems. If the relationship with the brand is strong, accepting negative information also diminishes the consumer's self-concept. Thus, a consumer who holds strong convictions about a brand is less likely to be affected by negative WOM or negative publicity. Brands whose images are strongly linked to positive emotions such that the emotions help provide meaning can also insulate themselves from negative WOM to some degree.[16]

# LO3 Switching Behavior

exhibit 15.1 suggests that a consumer evaluates a consumption experience, reacts emotionally, and then, perhaps, practices switching behavior. **Switching** in a consumer behavior context refers to the times when a consumer chooses a competing choice, rather than the previously purchased choice, on the next purchase occasion. If a consumer visited Dunkin' Donuts for breakfast last Tuesday, and chooses Krispy Kreme on Saturday, the next time she goes out for breakfast, the consumer has practiced switching behavior. This could be due to any number of reasons, but perhaps the last experience at Dunkin' Donuts was less than satisfying.

All things considered, consumers prefer the status quo. Change brings about, well … change, and this can mean costs that diminish the value of an experience. If the consumer has been a regular Dunkin' Donuts customer, she now has to learn the new assortment of doughnuts available at Krispy Kreme, may lose the benefits of any accumulated loyalty card from Dunkin' Donuts, and cannot refill her Dunkin' Donuts insulated coffee mug.

Thus, the consumer will incur some **switching costs**, or the costs associated with changing from one choice (brand/retailer/service provider) to another. Switching costs are one reason why a consumer may be dissatisfied with a service provider but will continue to do business with them. Switching costs can be divided into three categories:[17]

1. Procedural
2. Financial
3. Relational

## PROCEDURAL SWITCHING COSTS

**Procedural switching costs** involve lost time and effort. Although Apple computers have a stellar reputation for being easy to use, most computer users stick with PC models. Why? Even if an Apple is easy to use, a consumer familiar with a PC-based Windows operating platform would have to forgo this knowledge to learn how to use an Apple. Thus, the effort that went into learning the PC system is lost and replaced by effort that would be needed to learn how to use an Apple. Most consumers would not want to invest the time and effort needed to learn a new system that would, in their minds, produce similar benefits. Thus, when consumers master a technologically complex product, they become very resistant to switching.

Similarly, Apple received a great deal of negative publicity when problems surfaced soon after the release of the iPhone 4.[18] The problems included dropped calls due to reception problems. *Consumer Reports* gave the iPhone 4 a bad rating, and suggested several other brands as better alternatives. That said, most iPhone customers would like to trade up to the iPhone 4. Part of the love-hate relationship with a product is due to procedural switching costs that would be experienced if the consumer switched to another brand.

© ISTOCKPHOTO.COM/MICHAEL FLIPPO

How do procedural switching costs influence loyalty to computer brands?

# FINANCIAL SWITCHING COSTS

**Financial switching costs** consist of the total economic resources that must be spent or invested as a consumer learns how to obtain value from a new product choice. A consumer in Rivel, France, plans a summer vacation to the Mexican Riviera. A few weeks later, the consumer hears friends discussing their upcoming vacation in Florida and suffers cognitive dissonance. Even though the vacation to Florida now seems better, he has already purchased airfare for his family and the airlines would impose a €50 penalty on each ticket. This financial cost of switching does much to influence the final decision to go to Mexico. On some occasions, consumers receive services with bundled prices (cable, Internet and phone in one bill). The consumer could potentially perceive, and may actually realize, an increased price if they were to replace only one of the services in the bundle.[19] A financial switching cost would be incurred in this situation.

# RELATIONAL SWITCHING COSTS

The **relational switching cost** refers to the emotional and psychological consequences of changing from one brand/retailer/service provider to another. Imagine a consumer who has used the same hairstylist for five years. When she goes to college, however, she finds another hair salon that is more convenient. She is greeted by a stylist named Karla just after entering the salon. Although Karla seems nice, the consumer is very uneasy during the entire salon visit. In fact, she even feels a bit guilty for letting Karla do her hair. This uneasiness is an example of a typical relational switching cost.

# UNDERSTANDING SWITCHING COSTS

Exhibit 15.3 demonstrates conventional consumer behavior theory that explains switching costs. Consumers become dissatisfied for any number of reasons, and these reasons and dissatisfaction together determine how likely a consumer is to return on the next purchase occasion.[20] Equity judgments, in particular perceptions of unfair treatment, are particularly prone to lead consumers to switch. Perceptions of unfair prices may make consumers temporarily angry, but they also create lasting memories. When coastal building centers raise plywood prices immediately before a hurricane's landfall, they may enjoy a short-term profit, but consumers will probably remember this and switch to a different retailer the next time they need a building center. Retailers like Home Depot make a point of advertising policies that they maintain prices during weather crises like hurricanes.

Furthermore, even though all types of functional costs can prevent switching, evidence suggests that relational barriers may be the most resistant to influence. Retailers who build up procedural switching costs, particularly through the use of loyalty cards and other similar programs, may gain temporary repeat purchase behavior, but they fail to establish the connection with the customer that wins them true loyalty.[21] Additionally, the inability of web-based retailers to build in anything other than procedural loyalty may be responsible for the low levels of loyalty observed for pure play (Internet only) retailers.[22]

**financial switching costs** total economic resources that must be spent or invested as a consumer learns how to obtain value from a new product choice

**relational switching cost** emotional and psychological consequences of changing from one brand/retailer/service provider to another

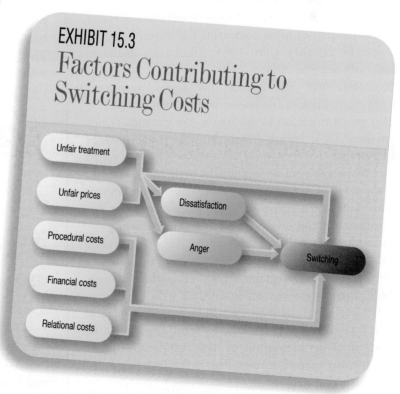

**EXHIBIT 15.3**
## Factors Contributing to Switching Costs

- Unfair treatment
- Unfair prices
- Procedural costs
- Financial costs
- Relational costs
- Dissatisfaction
- Anger
- Switching

## SATISFACTION AND SWITCHING

The intermingling of consumer satisfaction/dissatisfaction and switching costs has received considerable attention. In fact, in addition to the measurement difficulties associated with CS/D, switching costs are another important reason why CS/D results often fail to predict future purchasing behavior. Exhibit 15.4 summarizes how vulnerable a company is to consumer defections based on the interaction between switching costs, competitive intensity, and consumer satisfaction.

As can be seen in Exhibit 15.4, dissatisfaction does not always mean that the consumer is going to switch. Before reaching a conclusion on vulnerability to losing a customer, one also has to take into account at least two other factors. For instance, the amount of competition and the competitive intensity also play a role in determining who switches. **Competitive intensity** refers to the number of firms competing for business within a specific category. Until 1984, American consumers had only one choice for telephone service—"Ma Bell." So, competitive intensity was low. Today, consumers have many choices for phone service. Bell Telephone, as it was known, no longer exists, but consumers can choose AT&T, Sprint, Alltel, or an Internet provider like Skype.

When competitive intensity is high and switching costs are low, a company is vulnerable to consumers who will switch providers even when customers are satisfied. The consumer has many companies vying for the business and changing presents little barrier. Today, a consumer has many choices for getting the car's oil changed, and the switching costs are virtually negligible. Even if a consumer is satisfied with the corner Jiffy Lube, he or she may try 5-Minute Oil Change the next time if the location is slightly more convenient. In contrast, under conditions of high competitive intensity and low switching costs, dissatisfied consumers are almost certain to switch.

### EXHIBIT 15.4
## Vulnerability to Defections Based on CS/D

| CUSTOMERS | HIGH COMPETITIVE INTENSITY | | LOW COMPETITIVE INTENSITY | |
|---|---|---|---|---|
| | SWITCHING COSTS | | SWITCHING COSTS | |
| | Low | High | Low | High |
| Satisfied | Vulnerable | Low vulnerability | Low vulnerability | No vulnerability |
| Dissatisfied | Highly vulnerable | Vulnerable | Vulnerable | Low vulnerability |

In contrast, Exhibit 15.4 suggests that even when consumers are dissatisfied, consumers may not switch. Consider the case when competitive intensity is low, meaning there are few alternatives for the consumer and switching costs are high. In this case, even dissatisfied consumers may return time and time again. In many small- to medium-size markets in the United States, Walmart Supercenters dominate the mass merchandising landscape. Many conventional grocery stores were unable to compete in these markets; as a result, the Walmart Supercenter becomes practically the only choice for buying groceries on any large scale. Thus, although consumers may experience dissatisfaction, the fact that there are few places to turn to and the costs of switching might involve a long drive to the next larger city in the area makes Walmart only slightly vulnerable to defections due to low consumer satisfaction.

## LO4 Consumer Loyalty

### CUSTOMER SHARE

marketing managers have come to accept the fact that getting business from a customer who has already done business with the company before is easier and less expensive than getting a new customer. This basic belief motivates much of relationship marketing. The rubrics that determine marketing success then switch from pure sales and margin toward indicators that take into account marketing efficiencies. One important concept is **customer share**, which is the portion of resources allocated to one brand from among the set of competing brands. Here, *brand* is used loosely to capture any type of consumer alternative including a retailer, service provider, or actual product brand. Some managers use the term **share of wallet** to refer to customer share.

Exhibit 15.5 illustrates customer share. The exhibit shows the choices made by two consumers who each make daily coffee shop visits. On July 1, Bill goes to Starbucks (SB) and spends $5 and Erin does the same thing. On July 2, Bill returns to Starbucks and spends $10. Erin however, goes to CC's (CC) and spends $15. In ten days, Bill choses Starbucks (SB) eight out of ten times and spent $60 out of the $80 total at Starbucks. Erin choses Starbucks only three times out ten visits and spent $20 out of the $70 total at Starbucks. Thus, Starbucks gets considerably greater customer share from Bill than from Erin. The tenet of relationship marketing is that a company's marketing is much more efficient when most of the business comes from repeat customers. In this sense, Bill is a more valuable consumer to Starbucks than Erin. Starbucks gets a greater share of Bill's coffee business than they do out of Erin.

Customer share represents a behavioral component that is indicative of customer loyalty. Behaviorally, Bill is more loyal than Erin. When customers don't switch, they repeat their purchase behavior over again. At times, they repeat the behavior over and over and over again. We examine the question of whether or not a consumer is truly loyal by examining why a consumer is repeating behavior. This brings us to the concept of consumer inertia.

## Consumer Inertia

In physics, inertia refers to the fact that a mass that is in motion (at rest) will stay in motion (at rest) unless the mass is acted upon by a greater force. The concept of consumer inertia presents an analogy. **Consumer inertia** means that a consumer will tend to continue a pattern of behavior until some stronger force motivates him or her to change. In fact, resistance to change is one of the biggest reasons why new products fail in the

*At this store, you can drive up and collect a regular order of groceries without leaving your car. Will this create loyalty?*

© SIMON ISABELLE/SIPA/NEWSCOM

---

## EXHIBIT 15.5
## Customer Share Information for Two Coffee Shop Customers

| | Date of Visit | | | | | | | | | | Total Spent |
|---|---|---|---|---|---|---|---|---|---|---|---|
| | 7-1 | 7-2 | 7-3 | 7-4 | 7-5 | 7-6 | 7-7 | 7-8 | 7-9 | 7-10 | |
| Bill Choice | SB | SB | CC | SB | SB | CC | SB | SB | SB | SB | |
| $$ Spent | 5 | 10 | 10 | 5 | 15 | 10 | 5 | 5 | 10 | 5 | $80 |
| Erin Choice | SB | CC | M | M | SB | M | CC | SB | CC | M | |
| $$ Spent | 5 | 15 | 5 | 5 | 5 | 5 | 10 | 10 | 5 | 5 | $70 |

SB = Starbucks
CC = CC's
M = McDonald's

marketplace.[23] Change often means consumers must give something up. For example, many grocers try to take advantage of technology to increase the utilitarian value of getting groceries. The latest approach involves a regular grocery purchase that the customer simply drives up, pays for using a credit card, and drives away with in a matter of minutes. This seems like a great value-added service. However, it comes at the price of the value that a customer gets by actually entering in the store and getting to see, touch, and smell the products beforehand. Remember that losses loom larger than gains and a potential loss motivates consumers more to continue with their current consumer behavior.

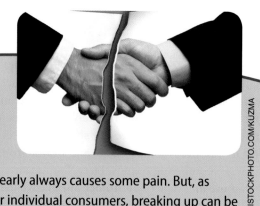

# Breaking Up Is Hard to Do!

Breaking up a relationship nearly always causes some pain. But, as painful as breaking up is for individual consumers, breaking up can be devastating for an entire company when a business switches service providers. At times, businesses may even try to build in switching costs to their products as a way of making it more difficult for competitors to compete successfully for business. Think about all the computer systems necessary to manage a large organization. SAP is a provider of software for businesses, including Customer Relationship Management (CRM) software programs and even more generalized systems known as enterprise suites. Many firms that implement CRM programs are dissatisfied with their decision. However, even though they are dissatisfied, they often stick with the software systems because changing would mean significant procedural and financial switching costs as well as facing the trauma that goes along with sunk costs incurred from implementing the system. As a result, these employees, who are consumers of the software, must cope with the consequences. Thus, breaking up the relationship, in this case between a firm and a software systems provider, really is hard to do. In much the same way, many consumers who are less than satisfied with things like digital entertainment and communication services also hang in there and try to reconcile because of the financial costs involved with breaking a service contract and the procedural costs involved in learning a new system.

Sources: Porter, M. E. (2008), "The Five Competitive Forces that Shape Strategy," *Harvard Business Review*, 86 (January), 78–93; Whitten, D., and K. W. Green, Jr. (2005), "The Effect of Switching Costs on Intent to Switch: An Application in IS Service Provision Markets," *International Journal of Mobile Communication*, 3 (4), 1.

## In fact, resistance to change is one of the biggest reasons why new products fail in the marketplace.

## Loyalty Programs

Many marketers have experimented with loyalty cards or programs as a way of increasing customer share. Loyalty cards also allow marketers to learn more about customer groups' demographics and shopping patterns. A **loyalty card/program** is a device that keeps track of the amount of purchasing a consumer has had with a given marketer (as well as a list of actual items purchased by the consumer) and once some level is reached, a reward is offered usually in terms of future purchase incentives. Loyalty programs differ somewhat based on the firms offering them. Today, European firms typically offer the standard reward in terms of a future purchase incentive, but in the United States, loyalty programs more often work by offering on-the-spot discounts on selected items. One result is a two-tiered pricing system where there is one price for customers who comply with the card program, and a higher price for those who do not use the card on those selected items.

*Good airline customers get to wait in a comfortable area and enjoy a snack and a glass of wine on the house—but this area is not for just anybody!*

However, the results are mixed with respect to the effectiveness of loyalty cards. In fact, they can sometimes even backfire by appealing too strongly to consumers who are bargain shoppers. Consumers with a strong economic orientation display lower customer share with all competitors, instead choosing to shop in the place with the current best offer.[24]

While these programs are referred to as "loyalty" programs, the question occurs as to exactly what constitutes loyalty. Customer share reflects a behavioral component of loyalty by reflecting repeated behavior. In Exhibit 15.5, Bill repeats similar behavior over again and appears to be loyal to Starbucks, but is he really? This question is the focus of the next section.

## CUSTOMER COMMITMENT

Bill does appear at least partially loyal to Starbucks. However, repeated behavior alone cannot answer the loyalty question. True consumer loyalty consists of both a pattern of repeated behavior as evidenced by high customer share and a strong feeling of attachment, dedication, and sense of identification with a brand. **Customer commitment** captures this sense of attachment, dedication, and identification. Exhibit 15.6 depicts the components of loyalty. Customer share is behavioral, and commitment is an affective component of loyalty.

Highly committed customers are true assets to a company. They are willing to sacrifice to continue doing business with the brand and serve as a source of promotion by spreading positive WOM. If we look at a consumer with a pattern of consistent behavior like Bill in Exhibit 15.5, the question becomes whether the behavior is simply inertia or motivated by true commitment. Perhaps this particular customer just happens to live next door to a Starbucks and thus getting coffee there is merely the easiest thing to do. If a CC's Coffee Shop were to take over the current Starbucks location, the customer would then buy his coffee there. However, if Bill were truly committed, he would seek out another Starbucks location even if the one next to his place were to close or get leased to a different coffee competitor. This distinguishes inertia from a truly loyal customer. Even if Starbucks is not convenient or the least-expensive alternative, the truly loyal consumer will still seek out Starbucks!

The CLV (Customer Lifetime Value equation from Chapter 2) concept demonstrates why high customer commitment is so beneficial to a company. The certainty of a lengthy stream of revenues is much less for a customer acting only on inertia. In addition, the customer acting on inertia alone is likely not contributing on the equity side of the equation as is the truly committed customer. A firm that concentrates on repeated behavior alone, perhaps by always being convenient, can do well but remains more vulnerable to competitors. The reason for the vulnerability is that competitors easily duplicate tangible assets like convenience; but the intangible assets, like the feel associated with a choice or place, like the feelings consumers have for visiting Starbucks or drinking a Coke, are very hard to duplicate.

**customer commitment**
sense of attachment, dedication, and identification

**EXHIBIT 15.6**
**True Loyalty Requires Customer Commitment**

Customer share

Customer commitment

# ANTILOYALTY

Loyalty is almost always discussed from a positive perspective. However, at times consumers act in an antiloyal way. **Antiloyal consumers** are those who will do everything possible to avoid doing business with a particular marketer. These consumers generally are driven by a severe dislike of this particular company and the negative emotions that go along with the aversion. Antiloyalty is often motivated by a bad experience between a consumer and the marketer in which the marketer could not redress the problem.

Attributes a marketer build into a product to create procedural switching costs are one source of frustration. These attributes include parts that are incompatible with widely available replacements or a mobile phone contract that locks a consumer into a specific service set for a lengthy time period. Consumers may wonder if their mobile phone number is transferable. In fact, many consumers may be frustrated with their mobile phone carrier but feel locked in particularly if the phone number is not transferable or difficult to transfer.[25]

Antiloyal customers are often consumers who have switched and treat the former marketing partner as a jilted partner. They obviously have no net positive lifetime value for the target firm. Moreover, these antiloyal consumers who are former customers become perhaps the most frequent source for negative word-of-mouth.[26] Thus, antiloyal consumers can be a major force to reckon with.

# VALUE AND SWITCHING

Exhibit 15.7 reproduces the center portion of the CVF. The exhibit clearly shows that value plays a role in the postconsumption process. During an exchange, the consumer goes through the consumption process, and the result produces some amount and type of value. The value, in turn, shapes what happens next. Thus, the CVF makes up for a shortcoming of the disconfirmation theory approach (as displayed in Exhibit 15.1) by explicitly accounting for value.

For a host of reasons, consumers may end up maintaining a relationship even if they experience dissatisfaction. However, consumers do not maintain relationships in which they find no value. Even if consumers do not enjoy shopping at Walmart, they tend to repeat the behavior because of high utilitarian value. Also, even though a consumer may be able to bank at a more convenient location, he might continue doing business with his original bank because he enjoys the personal relationships he has developed with bank personnel. Thus, both utilitarian and hedonic value can be a key in preventing consumers from switching to a competitor and creating true loyalty among consumers.

Is one type of value more important in preventing switching behavior? The answer to this question depends on the nature of the goods or services being consumed. For functional types of services, such as banking, utilitarian value is more strongly related to customer share (and therefore preventing switching) than is hedonic value.[27] However, for more experiential types of services, such as mall shopping, hedonic value is more strongly related to customer share.[28]

Value also is linked to the affective side of loyalty, customer commitment. Again, both value dimensions relate positively to commitment. Hedonic value, however, plays a larger role in creating commitment. In particular, customers who have switched service providers are more likely to become loyal customers when they experience increased hedonic value compared to the previous service provider. Exhibit 15.8 suggests ways that value plays a role in shaping loyalty and preventing switching behavior for different types of businesses.

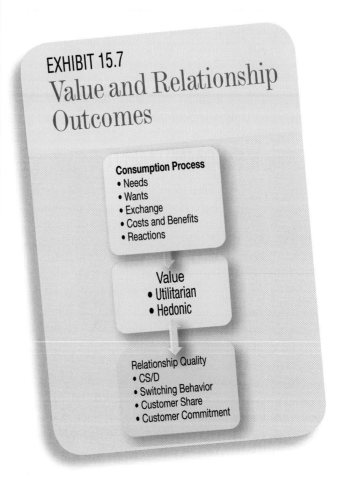

**EXHIBIT 15.7**
## Value and Relationship Outcomes

**Consumption Process**
- Needs
- Wants
- Exchange
- Costs and Benefits
- Reactions

**Value**
- Utilitarian
- Hedonic

**Relationship Quality**
- CS/D
- Switching Behavior
- Customer Share
- Customer Commitment

## EXHIBIT 15.8
## Value Types and Loyalty

**Functional**
- Banking
- Pharmacies
- Fast-food (adults)
- Internet services

→ Utilitarian value brings them back a bit more than hedonic value

**Experiential**
- Mall shopping
- Spa/salon services
- Fine dining
- Resort hotels

→ Hedonic value brings them back a bit more than utilitarian value

# LO5 Value, Relationships, and Consumers

## RELATIONSHIPS AND THE MARKETING FIRM

Marketers have come to realize that the exchange between a business and a consumer comprise a relationship. Two factors help make this clear:

1. Customers have a lifetime value to the firm.

2. True loyalty involves both a continuing series of interactions and feelings of attachment between the customer and the firm.

In return, many firms that truly adopt a relationship marketing approach with customers enjoy improved performance.[29] This is particularly the case as the relationship between customer and seller becomes very personal and involves trust.

Taken together, CS/D, complaining behavior, switching, customer share, and commitment all indicate relationship quality. Generally, **relationship quality** represents the degree of connectedness between a consumer and a retailer. When relationship quality is high, the prospects for a continued series of mutually valuable exchanges exist. Relationship quality represents the health of the relationship so that, in all likelihood, healthy relationships continue. When consumers are truly loyal, and this loyalty is returned by the marketer, relationship quality is high.

## VALUE AND RELATIONSHIP QUALITY

A healthy relationship between a consumer and a marketer enhances value both for the consumer and the marketer.[30] For the consumer, decision-making becomes simpler, enhancing utilitarian value, and relational exchanges often involve pleasant relational and experiential elements, enhancing hedonic value. For the marketer, the regular consumer does not have to be resold and thus much of the selling effort required to convert a new customer is not necessary.

> In fact, when relationship quality is very strong, the marketer and the customer act as partners.

In fact, when relationship quality is very strong, the marketer and the customer act as partners. When something bad happens to the marketer, the customer is affected. When something bad happens to the customer, the marketer is affected. Customers and sellers often act very closely as partners in business-to-business contexts. However, relationship quality can be very important in business-to-consumer contexts, too.

Universities hope a high-value experience leads graduates to continue a life-long relationship with the school.

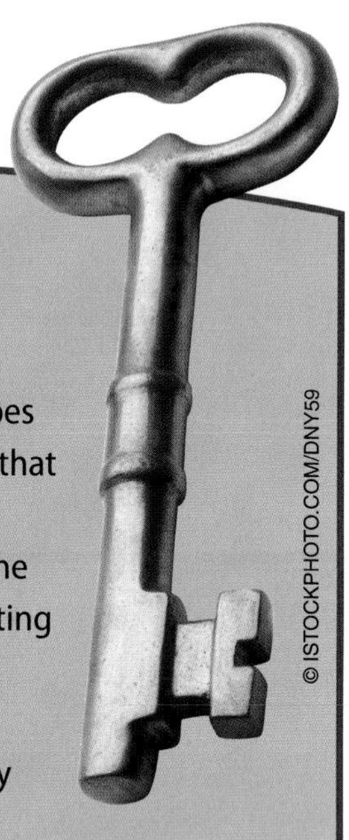

# Takes Three to Tango!

Consumers and salespeople have many different types of relationships. Marketing managers often realize that salespeople hold the key to building effective relationships with customers. In fact, salespeople are the critical link in successfully implementing a relationship marketing strategy. When customers like the salespeople they deal with, they often turn to this person first when they need assistance from the company. Even though the salesperson's first job may be to sell, a relationship-marketing-oriented firm will encourage its salespeople to spend the time necessary to satisfactorily address a good customer's problem. In this way, the salesperson returns the loyalty shown by the customer, and as a result, the customer develops loyalty to the company. The same sort of three-way relationship can exist with service providers where the customer becomes loyal to a particular service provider who shows loyalty to the customer, and as a result, the customer and firm develop a lasting bond.

the agent monitors the flight status. If there is a delay, she phones the customer to exchange information and begins rebooking any connecting flights, hotel reservations, or car rentals in case the delay disrupts the original plans. In this case, we can see that many of the characteristics displayed in Exhibit 15.9 are illustrated. This agent is customer oriented, has a personal relationship with the customer, communicates well, and is competent; the relationship is characterized by trust. Chances are that this customer will be loyal for quite some time.

Sources: Palmatier, R.W., L.K. Scheer, M.B. Houston, K.R. Evans and S. Gopalakrishna (2007), "Use of Relationship Marketing Programs in Building Customer-Salesperson and Customer-Firm Relationships: Differential Influences on Financial Outcomes," *International Journal of Research in Marketing*, 24, 210–223; Macintosh, G. (2007), "Customer Orientation, Relationship Quality, and Relational Benefits to the Firm," *Journal of Services Marketing*, 21 (3), 150–157.

When a parent sends a child off to college, chances are that a strong relationship exists or will soon exist between the family and the college. The family will don school colors on game day and become a prime target for fund-raising campaigns. The strong relationship quality means that the family and the university share many common goals.

Exhibit 15.9 displays some of the characteristics of a marketing relationship that is very healthy. Consider this example. A consumer uses the same travel agent for practically all travel. When the consumer calls the agent, the agent does not have to ask the customer for preferences or personal information, not even a credit card number, because she has all the information about the customer. She knows the customer is a Delta SkyMiles member so she books on Delta whenever possible. She knows the customer doesn't like close connections (under an hour), so she tries to always allow at least an hour and a half between connecting flights. Whenever the customer flies,

## EXHIBIT 15.9
## The Characteristics of Relationship Quality

- **Competence** Consumer views company and service providers as knowledgeable and capable
- **Communication** Consumer and firm understand each other and "speak the same language"
- **Trust** Buyer and seller can depend on each other
- **Equity** Both buyer and seller see equity in exchange and are able to equitably resolve conflicts
- **Personalization** Buyer treats the customer as an individual with unique desires and requirements
- **Customer oriented** Strong relationships are more likely to develop when a firm practices a marketing orientation, and this filters down to service providers and salespeople

# 15

## Study Tools

**Located at back of the textbook**

☐ Rip-out Chapter-in-Review Card

**Located at www.cengagebrain.com**

☐ Review Key Terms Flashcards (Print or Online)

☐ Download audio summaries to review on the go

☐ Complete practice quizzes to prepare for tests

☐ Play "Beat the Clock" and "Quizbowl" to master concepts

☐ Watch Video on 1–800–FLOWERS for a real company example

## what others have thought...

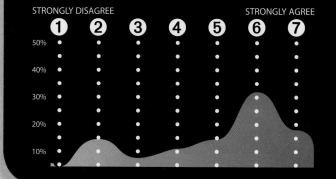

STRONGLY DISAGREE ① ② ③ ④ ⑤ ⑥ ⑦ STRONGLY AGREE

**When I have a good experience with a brand, I reward it by telling my friends how great it is.**

More than two out of three respondents express some level of agreement with the greatest number (1/3) indicating "agree." This goes to show the power of word-of-mouth. Loyal customers make good publicity!

**In order for exchanges** to occur in an orderly fashion, the expectations of the consumer, the marketer, and even other consumers must coincide with one another.

what do you think?

**Consumers are generally more ethical than the typical businessperson.**

STRONGLY DISAGREE

① ② ③ ④ ⑤ ⑥ ⑦

STRONGLY AGREE

Visit CourseMate at www.cengagebrain.com

# 16

# Consumer and Marketing Misbehavior

## Introduction

**m**ost of the behaviors that we have discussed so far are generally considered "acceptable" or "normal" by societal standards. A number of important topics, however, fall outside of what would be considered acceptable. In this chapter, we focus on what is referred to as consumer and marketer misbehavior. The term *misbehavior* is used cautiously because opinions regarding what is acceptable or normal depend on our ethical beliefs, ideologies, and even culture. For consumers, examples include shoplifting, downloading music illegally, drinking and driving, and engaging in fraud. Marketers sometimes engage in unethical activities as well. For example, they mislead consumers through deceptive advertising, state that regular prices are "sale" prices, and artificially limit the availability of products in order to increase prices. As we discuss, a fair marketplace depends on ethical behavior by *both* consumers and marketers.

> **consumer misbehavior**
> behaviors that are in some way unethical and that potentially harm the self or others

After studying this chapter, the student should be able to:

**LO1** Understand the consumer misbehavior phenomenon and how it affects the exchange process.

**LO2** Distinguish between consumer misbehavior and consumer problem behavior.

**LO3** Discuss marketing ethics and how marketing ethics guide the development of marketing programs.

**LO4** Comprehend the role of corporate social responsibility in the field of marketing.

**LO5** Understand the various forms of regulation that affect marketing practice.

**LO6** Comprehend the major areas of criticism to which marketers are subjected.

## LO1 Consumer Misbehavior and Exchange

**c**onsumer misbehavior may be viewed as a subset of the *human deviance* topic. This topic has a long history of research in the fields of sociology and social psychology. We consider misbehavior a subset in part because the term covers only negative or destructive deviance and does not consider positive deviance.

Consumer misbehavior can be defined in numerous ways. We define it as behaviors that are in some way unethical and that potentially harm the self or others.[1]

Misbehavior violates norms and also disrupts the flow of consumption activities. For example, a consumer screaming loudly at a waiter because his order is wrong makes other consumers feel uncomfortable. His actions disrupt others' meals and may ruin the entire evening. Chances are that a waiter who endures such scolding will perform poorly during the rest of the evening as well. This single consumer's actions potentially affect all the other customers in the restaurant.

Consumer misbehavior is sometimes called the "dark side" of consumer behavior, and words such as *aberrant*, *illicit*, *dysfunctional*, and *deviant* have been used to describe it. Some behaviors are clearly illegal, while others are simply immoral. There's a difference. For example, shoplifting is illegal and almost always considered immoral. Speeding, however, is illegal but not necessarily immoral. Not returning excess change that is mistakenly given at a store is immoral but not illegal.[2] A consumer might purchase a product one day, use it, and then return it for a refund. This may be immoral but not illegal. This practice is called *retail borrowing* and it costs the retail sector billions of dollars annually.

> Consumer misbehavior is, quite simply, selfish!

In order for exchanges to occur in an orderly fashion, the expectations of the consumer, the marketer, and even other consumers must coincide with one another.[3] When we see consumers becoming abusive, cutting in line at a movie theatre, or making other people uncomfortable, the exchange process is disrupted. Consumers who shoplift disrupt the exchange process and increase costs for all consumers. Consumers who make fraudulent insurance claims increase insurance costs.

Belligerent sports fans turn otherwise joyous occasions into annoying events for everybody. All sorts of misbehaviors affect exchange.

## THE FOCUS OF MISBEHAVIOR: VALUE

As we have discussed throughout this text, a central component for understanding consumer behavior is value. It shouldn't be surprising then that the focal motivation for consumer misbehavior is value.[4] However, *how* consumers obtain value is the key issue. Rowdy sports fans think that the best way to obtain value is to be obnoxious. Identity thieves believe that the best way to obtain value is to steal from others. In each instance, consumers seek to maximize the benefits they receive from an action while minimizing, or eliminating, their own costs. Ultimately, others' costs increase. In this way consumer misbehavior is, quite simply, selfish!

## CONSUMER MISBEHAVIOR AND ETHICS

Moral beliefs and evaluations influence decisions pertaining to marketplace behaviors.[5]

### Moral Beliefs

**Moral beliefs**, or beliefs about the perceived ethicality or morality of behaviors, play a very important role. The effect of moral beliefs on ethical decision making and consumer misbehavior is shown in Exhibit 16.1.

Notice that a consumer's moral beliefs are comprised of three components: moral equity, contractualism, and relativism.[6]

- **Moral equity** represents beliefs regarding an act's fairness or justness. Do I consider this action to be fair? Is it fair for me to shoplift this item?

- **Contractualism** refers to beliefs about the violation of written (or unwritten) laws. Does this action break a law? Does it break an unwritten promise of how I should act? Is shoplifting illegal?

- **Relativism** represents beliefs about the social acceptability of an act. Is this action culturally acceptable? Is shoplifting acceptable in this culture?

© ISTOCKPHOTO.COM/ JAMES STEIDL

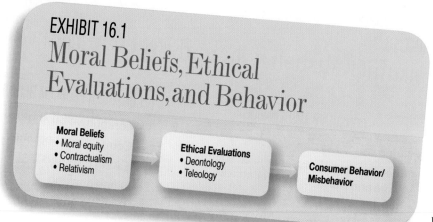

## EXHIBIT 16.1
# Moral Beliefs, Ethical Evaluations, and Behavior

**Moral Beliefs**
- Moral equity
- Contractualism
- Relativism

**Ethical Evaluations**
- Deontology
- Teleology

**Consumer Behavior/ Misbehavior**

**deontological evaluations** evaluations regarding the inherent rightness or wrongness of specific actions

**teleological evaluations** consumers' assessment of the goodness or badness of the consequences of actions

## Ethical Evaluations

Consumers bring their moral beliefs into all decision-making settings. Once a consumer enters into a situation that calls for an ethical decision (*Should I steal these sunglasses?*), he or she considers the various alternative courses of action. Here, two sets of ethical evaluations occur: deontological evaluations and teleological evaluations.[7]

**Deontological evaluations** focus on specific *actions*. Is this action "right"? As such, deontology focuses on *how* people accomplish their goals. The deontological perspective is, in large part, attributed to the work of Immanuel Kant. Kant's *Categorical Imperative* suggests that one should act in a way that would be considered a universal law for all people facing the same situation.

**Teleological evaluations** focus on the *consequences* of the behaviors and the individual's assessment of those consequences. How much "good" will result from this decision? With teleological evaluations, consumers consider the perceived consequences of the actions for various stakeholders, the probability that the consequence will occur, the desirability of the consequences for the stakeholders, and the importance of the stakeholder groups to the consumer.[8]

# MOTIVATIONS OF MISBEHAVIOR

Moral beliefs and behavioral evaluations indeed play important roles in consumer misbehavior. However, the question remains: why do consumers misbehave? Researchers Ronald Fullerton and Girish Punj offer the following motivations of consumer misbehavior:[9]

- **Unfulfilled Aspirations.** Many consumers have unfulfilled aspirations that influence their misbehavior. An important concept here is *anomie*. Anomie has been conceptualized as both a response to rapid cultural change and an explanation for deviance. To understand anomie as an explanation for deviance, consider the goals that are generally accepted in a culture. The U.S. culture places a great deal of emphasis on attaining material possessions and "getting ahead." However, not all members of the society have the necessary resources to be able to get ahead and enjoy the things that society deems important. As a result, some consumers turn to deviant actions or actions deemed inappropriate by society, in order to acquire these things. It's when societal goals are out of reach given the accepted means of achieving them that deviance occurs.[10]

- **Thrill-seeking.** The thrill of the action may lead consumers to misbehave. For example, breaking the speed limit can be exciting for some consumers.

- **Lack of Moral Constraints.** Some consumers simply don't have a set of moral beliefs that are in agreement with society's expectations and see no problem with their behavior. For example, some consumers who scare others by driving aggressively don't see a problem with the behavior.

- **Differential Association.** Differential association explains why groups of people replace one set of acceptable norms with another set that others view as unacceptable. By acting in opposition to acceptable standards, group members forge their own identities and strengthen group cohesion.[11] For example, gangs often accept behaviors that society finds unacceptable.

- **Pathological Socialization.** Consumers may view misbehavior as a way of getting revenge against companies. Stealing from large corporations may seem less severe than stealing from a family-owned retailer, and consumers may believe that big companies "deserve it."

- **Provocative Situational Factors.** Factors like crowding, wait times, excessive heat, and noise can contribute to consumer misbehavior. A well-mannered, quiet person may erupt and misbehave after waiting in line for 20 minutes at a drive-through restaurant.

- **Opportunism.** Misbehavior can also be the outcome of a deliberate decision-making process that weighs the risks and rewards of the behavior. For example, consumers may believe that the rewards associated with stealing outweigh the risks of getting caught.

## EXHIBIT 16.2
## Consumer Misbehavior and Problem Behavior

| CONSUMER MISBEHAVIOR | CONSUMER PROBLEM BEHAVIOR |
|---|---|
| • Shoplifting<br>• Computer-mediated behaviors: illicit sharing of software and music, computer attacks, cyberbullying<br>• Fraud<br>• Abusive consumer behavior<br>• Dysfunctional sports behaviors<br>• Illegitimate complaining<br>• Product misuse: aggressive driving, drunk driving, cell phone use | • Compulsive buying<br>• Compulsive shopping<br>• Eating disorders<br>• Binge drinking<br>• Problem gambling<br>• Drug abuse |

# LO2 Distinguish Consumer Misbehavior and Problem Behavior

Consumer misbehavior can be distinguished from what we refer to as consumer "problem behavior." The misbehavior term is used to describe behavior deliberately harmful to the self or another party during an exchange. **Consumer problem behavior** refers to behaviors that are seemingly outside of a consumer's control. For example, some people compulsively shop. Some people are addicted to drugs or alcohol. In cases like these, consumers may express a desire to stop the behaviors but simply find quitting too difficult.

Although the line between consumer misbehavior and problem behaviors can be blurred, we distinguish between the two areas by considering the issue of self-control. Exhibit 16.2 presents examples of consumer misbehaviors and problem behaviors, but again the line is blurry. Drug addiction is listed as a problem behavior, but when someone drives under the influence of drugs, the individual risks injuring or killing someone else. Shoplifting could also be considered either a problem behavior or misbehavior, as the behavior can sometimes be clinically diagnosed as *kleptomania*.

# CONSUMER MISBEHAVIOR

Many of the behaviors that are listed in Exhibit 16.2 are discussed frequently in the popular press. For example, you may have heard stories in the news media about the devastating effects of binge drinking or problem gambling. Although there are many different types of consumer misbehavior, we limit our discussion to behaviors that have gathered significant attention.

## Shoplifting

Did you know that consumers steal more than $35 million of products from retailers every day? That's over $13 billion per year! In fact, more than 10 million people have been caught shoplifting in the last 5 years.[12] How could this number be so high? Consumers' motivations for shoplifting are similar to motivations for other forms of misbehavior. Specifically, consumers shoplift because the temptation can be very strong, they believe that retailers can afford the monetary loss, they believe they probably won't get caught, they seek acceptance into a group, and the act can be exciting.[13]

As we have mentioned, shoplifting can sometimes be diagnosed as kleptomania. Although there are many differences between the behavior and the illness, as a general statement the shoplifting behavior is usually premeditated whereas kleptomania is generally triggered by compulsion with little or no rationale for the items that are stolen.

**Emotions and Shoplifting.** Emotions play a large role in shoplifting. Fear of being caught plays a role in predicting shoplifting intentions, especially among young consumers. Interestingly, the shoplifting intentions of adolescents appear to be more heavily influenced by emotions than by moral beliefs. The opposite occurs in older consumers. Research also shows that consumers who shoplift are sometimes motivated by repressed feelings of stress and anger.[14]

**Age and Shoplifting.** Shoplifting behavior appears to peak during the adolescent years. This may be because adolescents are yet to fully mature and often find themselves in the stressful transition from childhood to adulthood. Adolescents also tend to consider shoplifting as being more ethical than do adult shoppers.[15]

## Computer-Mediated Behaviors: Illegal Sharing of Software and Music

Due to improvements in technology, consumers often have the ability to illicitly download electronic material from a number of sources. Major problems here include the pirating of computer software, video games, and music.

The software industry loses billions of dollars annually due to illegal copying. In fact, the Business Software Alliance estimates that as much as 41% of software loaded on PCs worldwide is obtained illegally and that $53 billion is lost globally due to the illegal use of software products.[16] The music industry has also been hit hard by these actions. The U.S. Digital Millennium Copyright Act deems the sharing of copyrighted music as illegal. Although there are numerous legal download services such as **itunes.com, napster.com, zune.com,** and **rhapsody.com,** consumers continue to share music in illegal ways.

Interestingly, research reveals that how consumers view illegal downloading depends on the motivation for the behavior. That is, if the motivation is primarily based on utilitarian value (that is, for personal gain), then the act is viewed as less morally ethical and socially acceptable than if the behavior occurs based on hedonic value (that is, for "fun").[17]

## Computer-Mediated Behaviors: Attacks

Computers present other opportunities for misbehavior. Did you know that consumers in the United States send more spam than do consumers in any other nation? Losses from clogging up computers and slowing Internet connectivity result in losses of up to $17 billion annually in business productivity![18] Computer viruses

*Fraud is growing due to the popularity of the Internet.*

are another major problem. Today there are thousands of computer viruses being circulated from computer to computer, and the effects range from being mildly annoying to devastating. In fact, it has been estimated that viruses cost U.S. businesses over $55 billion annually.[19]

Another form of computer misbehavior is *cyberbullying.* Cyberbullying, the attack of innocent people on the Internet, is especially a problem for young consumers. Current research indicates that girls tend to be targeted by, and instigate, cyberattacks more often than boys.[20] However, cyberbullying is a serious issue for both genders. Recent statistics reveal that as many as 32% of online teens have been victim of some type of cyberbullying.[21]

## Consumer Fraud

There are many types of consumer fraud. For instance, consumers fraudulently obtain credit cards, open bank accounts, and turn in insurance claims. Although it is difficult to estimate exactly how much consumer fraud ends up costing consumers, the Coalition Against Insurance Fraud estimates that insurance fraud alone costs Americans at least $80 billion per year.[22]

Identity theft is another major public concern. The Federal Trade Commission estimates that as many as 9 million consumers have their identities stolen each year, and this number appears to be growing.[23] Laws such as the Identity Theft and Assumption Deterrence Act of 1998 and the Identity Theft Penalty Enhancement Act of 2004 have been passed in efforts to curb the crime. The increased reliance on computer technology for transactions has contributed to the spread of identity theft. It is no wonder that information privacy and security concerns are becoming hot topics for consumers.

## Abusive Consumer Behavior

As we have discussed, abusive consumers can be a real problem. Consumers who are aggressive or rude to employees and other consumers are considered to be abusive.[24] One early study in the area of problem customers suggested that four categories of customers can be identified: verbally or physically abusive customers, uncooperative customers, drunken customers, and customers who break company policy.[25] Needless to say, employees don't like to deal with customers who act this way, and abusive behaviors can have negative effects on other consumers as well.[26]

One area of abusive behavior that has gained attention is dysfunctional fan behavior. *Dysfunctional fan behavior* is abnormal functioning relating to sporting event consumption. Several college towns have seen riots that have occurred after big losses (or wins) of the home team. Unfortunately, riots can get out of hand quickly. While there are many explanations for such behavior, some think that dysfunctional fan behavior is simply a result of an increasingly violent society.[27]

Another controversial issue today is culture jamming. *Culture jamming* refers to attempts to disrupt marketing

© MUSKOPF PHOTOGRAPHY, LLC / ALAMY

# Consumer Misbehavior: "Sexting"

One growing form of consumer misbehavior is "sexting." Sexting is taking nude photos of oneself and sending them to another person via cell phone. It seems to occur most frequently among teen-aged consumers and it is becoming increasingly common.

Multiple media reports indicate that many teens feel like sexting isn't harmful. Parents and school administrators don't feel the same way. Parents are concerned that the images can be passed from person to person, and even onto the Internet. Sexting also raises moral, ethical, and legal issues.

One major concern with sexting is that it can lead to child pornography charges. If a minor is charged with possession or distribution of child pornography, he or she may have to register as a sex offender. There are many legal issues that surround sexting, and it's often unclear exactly who should be charged in these cases.

Should the person taking the photo be charged or the person receiving the photo? What about people to whom the images are forwarded? While legal authorities wrestle with questions such as these, it is clear that the cell phone was never meant to be used for sending or receiving pornography.

Sources: Searcy, D. (2009), "Currents: A Lawyer, Some Teens and a Fight Over Sexting," *Wall Street Journal*, April 21, 2009, A17; Kingston, A. (2009), "The Sexting Scare," *Maclean's*, March 16, 2009, 52; Koch, W. (2009), "Teens Caught 'Sexting' Face Porn Charges," *USA Today* (online edition), March 11, 2009, online content retrieved at: **http://www.usatoday.com/tech/wireless/2009-03-11-sexting_N.htm**, accessed June 18, 2009.

campaigns by altering the messages in some meaningful way. For example, billboards are often altered in a way that delivers messages that conflict with those originally intended. Also, websites that attempt to disrupt marketing efforts are often created. Sites like **amexsux.com** have popped up in the online world. Of course, calling culture jamming an abusive behavior depends on your own perspective. Proponents believe that their behaviors are good for society.

## Illegitimate Complaining

Consumers also complain about products and services even when there really isn't a problem. To date, the research on illegitimate complaining remains relatively scarce. However, one study did find that illegitimate complaining is motivated by a desire for monetary gain, a desire to evade personal responsibility for product misuse, a desire to enhance the consumer's ego and look good to others, or a desire to harm a service provider or company.[28]

## Product Misuse

Consumers also sometimes use products in ways that were clearly not intended. For example, some consumers will sniff glue or household cleaners to get "high." Marketers therefore work hard to ensure that consumers understand the ways in which products should be used. However, even when warnings and instructions are provided, consumers still misuse products. Injuries that result can be very costly. In fact, statistics from the Consumer Product Safety Commission reveal that deaths and injuries resulting from product consumption cost the United States over $800 billion annually.[29]

Why do consumers use products in unsafe ways? A number of explanations have been offered. Consumers may simply not pay attention to what they are doing, may feel as though they generally get away with risky behaviors, may have a tendency to be error prone, or may focus more on the thrill of misuse rather than the actual risk of the behavior.[30] Here, we discuss three major issues regarding the misuse of a highly visible product: the automobile.

**Aggressive Driving.** Aggressive driving may range from mild displays of anger to seriously violent acts while driving. Although aggressive driving is often thought of as an act by a solitary consumer, aggressive driving problems often involve multiple drivers, as victims often retaliate with their own aggression.[31] Younger, less-educated males have been shown to be more likely to engage in aggressive driving behavior.[32] Situational factors, such as intense traffic congestion and driver stress, and personality traits also play a part. Traits like instability and competitiveness have been found among aggressive drivers.[33]

**Drunk Driving.** Statistics reveal that approximately 13,000 people die from alcohol-related traffic accidents per year and that nearly three out of every ten Americans will be involved in an alcohol-related crash at some point in their lives.[34] Sadly, approximately one out of every six fatalities among children aged 14 and younger are due to alcohol-related accidents.[35] Furthermore, one study found that nearly 64% of all drivers aged 15–20 who were involved in fatal accidents had blood alcohol levels above .08.[36] Of course, this group is under the legal drinking age! Not surprisingly, drunk driving is often related to binge drinking. In fact, one study indicated that over 80% of respondents who reported alcohol-impaired driving also reported engaging in binge drinking behaviors.[37]

**Cell Phone Use in Cars.** As we have stated previously, there are currently nearly 4 billion cell phones worldwide,[38] and over 270 million U.S. consumers now have mobile phone service.[39] A growing area of public concern involves the use of cell phones while driving. Like drinking and driving, neither behavior in isolation is considered to be a problem but the use of the two products at the same time is a problem. Studies reveal that consumers who use cell phones while driving are four times as likely to get into serious accidents, and the problem is particularly serious for teens. One study found that 26% of teens surveyed aged 16–17 have texted while driving and 43% have talked on a cell phone while driving.[40]

Currently, eight states ban driving while talking on a cell phone, and texting while driving is banned in 28 states. This issue is likely to remain under intense public scrutiny and laws change frequently. The problem is not confined to the United States, however, as 40 countries worldwide currently restrict or ban the use of cell phones while driving.[41]

© ISTOCKPHOTO.COM/SEAN LOCKE

*Texting while driving is extremely dangerous.*

# CONSUMER PROBLEM BEHAVIOR

Consumer problem behaviors include other acts that do not necessarily break any specific laws or societal norms. For example, consumers shop too much, rack up large amounts of debt, and sometimes harm their own bodies in desperate attempts to look thin. Psychological problems can cause or influence these behaviors.

**compulsive consumption** repetitive, excessive, and purposeful consumer behaviors that are performed as a response to tension, anxiety, or obtrusive thoughts

**addictive consumption** physiological dependency on the consumption of a consumer product

**compulsive buying** chronic, repetitive purchasing that is a response to negative events or feelings

**compulsive shopping** repetitive shopping behaviors that are a response to negative events or feelings

**binge eating** consumption of large amounts of food while feeling a general loss of control over food intake

## Compulsive Consumption

**Compulsive consumption** refers to repetitive, excessive, and purposeful consumer behaviors that are performed as a response to tension, anxiety, or obtrusive thoughts.[42] The term *compulsive consumption* is often used broadly and consists of a number of specific behaviors related to the purchase and use of consumer products and services.[43] Compulsive consumption should not be confused with *addictive consumption*. **Addictive consumption** refers to a physiological dependency on the consumption of a product. The word *dependency* is important, and in the strictest sense, addictions are characterized by the physical inability to discontinue a behavior, or a physical reliance. A person who is addicted to a product physically needs it. Compulsive consumption often takes two forms: *compulsive buying* and *compulsive shopping*.

**Compulsive Buying.** **Compulsive buying** may be defined as chronic, repetitive *purchasing* behaviors that are a response to negative events or feelings.[44] This behavior can have harmful results including the accumulation of debt, domestic problems, and feelings of frustration. Influencers of this form of buying include feelings of low self-esteem, obsessive–compulsive tendencies, fantasy-seeking motivations, and materialism,[45] as well as a focus on the short term rather than the long term.[46] Among adolescents, the behavior can be a response to family problems like divorce.[47] The same negative feelings that influence compulsive buying can also result from the behavior itself so that a consumer who buys compulsively as a reaction to negative feelings often experiences even more negative feelings after going on buying binges.[48] In this way, compulsive buying can be a vicious circle.

**Compulsive Shopping.** **Compulsive shopping** refers to repetitive *shopping* behaviors. The word *oniomania* is sometimes used to describe this behavior. Compulsive shoppers often feel preoccupied with shopping, exhibit uncontrollable shopping tendencies, and experience guilt from their behaviors.[49] The key difference between compulsive shopping and buying is the buying process itself. Compulsive shoppers tend to focus on the mental highs associated with "the hunt,"[50] whereas compulsive buyers feel the need to buy. Although early research on this issue revealed that compulsive shopping was predominately a problem for women, more recent evidence suggests that both women and men engage in compulsive shopping. One study confirmed that equal proportions of men and women are compulsive shoppers (6% of women, 5.5% of men).[51]

## Eating Disorders

**Binge eating** refers to the consumption of large amounts of food while feeling a general loss of control over intake. Binge eating may result in medical complications, including high cholesterol, high blood pressure, and heart disease. Exhibit 16.3 presents a description of the binge eating disorder.

Binge eating has been shown to be associated with compulsive buying. This is particularly the case for obese consumers. In fact, obese consumers who engage in binge eating are likely to have other psychiatric disorders that require treatment.[52] Unfortunately, many consumers who binge eat fail to seek treatment. Binge eating is also often associated with *bulimia*, a disorder that includes binge eating episodes followed by self-induced vomiting. *Anorexia*, or the starving of one's body in the pursuit of thinness, is another consumer eating disorder.

### EXHIBIT 16.3
### Binge Eating Disorder

Binge eating disorder consists of:

- Frequent eating episodes that include large quantities of food in short time periods.
- A felt loss of control over eating behavior.
- Feelings of shame, guilt, and/or disgust about the amount of food consumed.
- The consumption of food when one is not hungry.
- The consumption of food in secret.

Source: Based on National Eating Disorders Association, **www.nationaleatingdisorders.org**.

## Binge Drinking

**Binge drinking** is defined as the consumption of five or more drinks in a single drinking session for men and four or more drinks for women,[53] and the behavior is particularly prevalent among full-time college students. In fact, estimates reveal that binge drinking rates among full-time college students are over 45%, compared to 38% for students who are not enrolled full-time.[54] Binge drinking occurs globally. In fact, one study revealed that students in the United Kingdom binge drink for the sole purpose of getting drunk and feel that getting drunk is a key part of college life.[55]

Binge drinking has been linked to suicide attempts, unsafe sexual practices, legal problems, academic disruptions, and even death.[56] Sadly, over 1,700 college students between the ages of 18 and 24 die each year from alcohol-related unintentional injuries.[57] College students who have higher self-actualization values generally have lower attitudes toward binge drinking, whereas students who value social affiliation tend to have more positive attitudes toward the behavior.[58]

Binge drinking is not confined only to the traditional college crowd. Rather, the behavior cuts across demographic groups. One alarming trend is the occurrence of binge drinking among underage consumers, with one study indicating that nearly half of the alcohol consumed on four-year college campuses is consumed by underage consumers.[59]

## Problem Gambling

**Problem gambling** is another serious issue. This behavior may be described as an obsession with gambling and the loss of control over gambling behavior and its consequences.[60] Consumers who are problem gamblers frequently gamble longer than planned, borrow money to finance their gambling, and feel major depression due to their gambling behaviors. Although casino and online gambling receive much research attention, lottery-ticket and scratch-ticket purchases can also be considered problem gambling behaviors.[61]

Estimates reveal that as many as two million consumers meet the criteria of pathological gambling and another four to six million could be considered problem gamblers.[62] Problem gamblers exhibit at least some of the criteria for pathological gambling. Although problem gambling is often thought of as being primarily an issue for middle-aged consumers, approximately 8% of college students gamble problematically.[63] What's more, a recent study revealed that nearly 70% of seniors older

than 65 had gambled at least once in the previous year and nearly 11% were considered at "at risk" for problem gambling.[64] Research indicates that problem gambling is often associated with compulsive buying and drug abuse.[65]

> **binge drinking** consumption of five or more drinks in a single drinking session for men and four or more drinks for women
>
> **problem gambling** obsession over the thought of gambling and the loss of control over gambling behavior and its consequences

## Drug Abuse

Both illegal and legal drugs (such as over-the-counter medications) can become problematic for consumers. A recent study by the Partnership for a Drug Free America revealed that nearly one in five teenagers report using prescription drugs to get high, and nearly one in ten report abusing cough medicine. Even more troubling is the finding that nearly 40% of teenagers sampled believe that abusing prescription drugs is safer than abusing illegal drugs.[66]

The abuse of illegal drugs (including marijuana, cocaine, and hallucinogens) has been a major problem for years and is particularly serious for young consumers. One study in 2008 revealed that over 14% of eighth graders in the U.S. reported using illicit drugs in the previous year.[67] The number is much higher for older teens. In fact, one estimate reveals that over 40% of high school seniors have tried marijuana.[68]

We've discussed only a handful of behaviors that may be considered consumer problem areas here. Space prohibits a complete discussion of several other consumer problem areas.

# LO3 Marketing Ethics and Misbehavior

**a**s we have stated, a fair marketplace depends on each party in an exchange acting fairly and with due respect for each other. Whenever anyone acts unethically, inefficiencies result and chances are that somebody will suffer. Marketers, like consumers, can act unethically. Media reports all too often describe company actions that are at best questionable, at times immoral, and at worst illegal. Unscrupulous actions of companies directly impact the marketplace because they upset the

## "Too Much Is Too Much"

Some consumer behavior texts have suggested that overconsumption in and of itself is a form of misbehavior. When is too much simply too much?

The advertising world sends all kinds of messages wrapped around promises to make consumers younger looking, sexier, more popular, better loved, and more successful. As a result, consumers often buy many more products and services than are really necessary. What's more, the value that the advertising world attempts to place on possessions, money, physical appearance, and success actually leads to overconsumption, which can lead to unhappiness, anxiety, financial problems, or even mental disorders.

Some consumers have actually fought back on the temptation to overconsume by voluntarily simplifying their lives. This has been noted by consumer researchers during the current turbulent economic times. Many consumers have adjusted their perspectives by moving their focus away from overconsumption to "voluntary simplicity." Attitudes towards buying, credit, and saving have changed for many consumers.

Even though attitudes towards overconsumption appear to have changed for some, the issue remains important. The impact of overconsumption on personal finance, pollution, and personal happiness continues to be noted. Sometimes enough is simply enough!

Sources: Ives, N. (2009), "Marketers Fear Frugality May Just Be Here to Stay," *Advertising Age*, June 1, 2009, 80 (21), 1–2; Evans, K. (2009), "The Outlook: Frugality Forged in Today's Recession Has Potential to Outlast It," *Wall Street Journal*, April 6, 2009, A2; James, O. (2008), "It's More than Enough to Make You Sick," *Marketing*, January 23, 2008, 26–28.

value equation associated with a given exchange. When a company misrepresents a product, consumers are led to expect more than is actually delivered.

Not everyone will agree on what behaviors should be considered marketing "misbehaviors." The topic again centers on ethics. The term **ethics** refers to standards or moral codes of conduct to which a person, group, or organization adheres. **Marketing ethics** consist of societal and professional standards of right and fair practices that are expected of marketing managers as they develop and implement marketing strategies.[69] More simply, ethics determines how much tolerance one has for actions that take advantage of others.

Many organizations have explicitly stated rules or codes of conduct for their employees. Exhibit 16.4 presents the Code of Conduct for the American Marketing Association.

Like consumer misbehavior, marketer misbehavior can be viewed as a subset of *deviance*. For a marketer to misbehave, he or she must be aware that an action will be considered unethical and act with deviance to cover intent. Sometimes, marketers don't intend to misbehave but mistakes are made in marketing execution. As in a court of law, proving intent is rarely an easy thing to do.

## CONSUMERISM

The **marketing concept** proposes that all the functions of the organization should work together in satisfying its customers' wants and needs. This is important for any business. When businesses begin taking advantage of consumers, consumers lose, businesses lose, and society as a whole eventually loses. In fact, it can be said that the ethical treatment of consumers is a cornerstone of a fair marketplace.[70]

Much of the pressure that has been placed on marketers comes directly from consumer groups. **Consumerism** is used to describe the activities of various groups to protect basic consumer rights. Many years ago, the voice of the consumer simply didn't garner much attention. In the early days of mass production, much

# EXHIBIT 16.4
# American Marketing Association Code of Ethics

**Preamble** The American Marketing Association commits itself to promoting the highest standard of professional ethical norms and values for its members. Norms are established standards of conduct that are expected and maintained by society and/or professional organizations. Values represent the collective conception of what people find desirable, important and morally proper. Values serve as the criteria for evaluating the actions of others. Marketing practitioners must recognize that they not only serve their enterprises but also act as stewards of society in creating, facilitating and executing the efficient and effective transactions that are part of the greater economy. In this role, marketers should embrace the highest ethical *norms* of practicing professionals and the ethical *values* implied by their responsibility toward stakeholders (e.g., customers, employees, investors, channel members, regulators and the host community).

## General Norms:

1. Marketers must do no harm. This means doing work for which they are appropriately trained or experienced so that they can actively add value to their organizations and customers. It also means adhering to all applicable laws and regulations and embodying high ethical standards in the choices they make.

2. Marketers must foster trust in the marketing system. This means that products are appropriate for their intended and promoted uses. It requires that marketing communications about goods and services are not intentionally deceptive or misleading. It suggests building relationships that provide for the equitable adjustment and/or redress of customer grievances. It implies striving for good faith and fair dealing so as to contribute toward the efficacy of the exchange process.

3. Marketers must embrace, communicate and practice the fundamental ethical values that will improve consumer confidence in the integrity of the marketing exchange system. These basic *values* are intentionally aspirational and include honesty, responsibility, fairness, respect, openness and citizenship.

## Ethical Values

**Honesty**—to be truthful and forthright in our dealings with customers and stakeholders. We will tell the truth in all situations and at all times. We will offer products of value that do what we claim in our communications. We will stand behind our products if they fail to deliver their claimed benefits. We will honor our explicit and implicit commitments and promises.

**Responsibility**—to accept the consequences of our marketing decisions and strategies. We will make strenuous efforts to serve the needs of our customers. We will avoid using coercion with all stakeholders. We will acknowledge the social obligations to stakeholders that come with increased marketing and economic power. We will recognize our special commitments to economically vulnerable segments of the market such as children, the elderly and others who may be substantially disadvantaged.

**Fairness**—to try to balance justly the needs of the buyer with the interests of the seller. We will represent our products in a clear way in selling, advertising and other forms of communication; this includes the avoidance of false, misleading and deceptive promotion. We will reject manipulations and sales tactics that harm customer trust. We will not engage in price fixing, predatory pricing, price gouging or "bait-and-switch" tactics. We will not knowingly participate in material conflicts of interest.

**Respect**—to acknowledge the basic human dignity of all stakeholders. We will value individual differences even as we avoid stereotyping customers or depicting demographic groups (e.g., gender, race, sexual orientation) in a negative or dehumanizing way in our promotions. We will listen to the needs of our customers and make all reasonable efforts to monitor and improve their satisfaction on an ongoing basis. We will make a special effort to understand suppliers, intermediaries and distributors from other cultures. We will appropriately acknowledge the contributions of others, such as consultants, employees and coworkers, to our marketing endeavors.

**Openness**—to create transparency in our marketing operations. We will strive to communicate clearly with all our constituencies. We will accept constructive criticism from our customers and other stakeholders. We will explain significant product or service risks, component substitutions or other foreseeable eventualities that could affect customers or their perception of the purchase decision. We will fully disclose list prices and terms of financing as well as available price deals and adjustments.

**Citizenship**—to fulfill the economic, legal, philanthropic and societal responsibilities that serve stakeholders in a strategic manner. We will strive to protect the natural environment in the execution of marketing campaigns. We will give back to the community through volunteerism and charitable donations. We will work to contribute to the overall betterment of marketing and its reputation. We will encourage supply chain members to ensure that trade is fair for all participants, including producers in developing countries.

**Implementation** Finally, we recognize that every industry sector and marketing subdiscipline (e.g., marketing research, e-commerce, direct selling, direct marketing, advertising) has its own specific ethical issues that require policies and commentary. An array of such codes can be accessed through links on the AMA website. We encourage all such groups to develop and/or refine their industry and discipline-specific codes of ethics to supplement these general norms and values.

of the focus was on production efficiencies rather than on the consumer. This changed gradually throughout the 20th century as the marketplace became more competitive. The voice of the consumer grew steadily. The **Consumer Bill of Rights,** which today stands as a foundation of the consumerism movement, was introduced in 1962, and included:

1. The right to safety
2. The right to be informed
3. The right to redress and to be heard
4. The right to choice

© BETTMANN/CORBIS

*The Consumer Bill of Rights dramatically changed how businesses viewed the consumer.*

# THE MARKETING CONCEPT AND THE CONSUMER

The marketing concept developed greatly in the 1960s. It was early in this time period that Theodore Levitt published the article "Marketing Myopia." Among other things, Levitt's work brought about a new perspective that argued that businesses should define themselves in terms of the consumer needs that they satisfy rather than in terms of the products they make. He argued that a firm's long-term health depends on its ability to exist as a consumer-satisfying entity rather than a goods-producing entity. As we have discussed in this text,

companies should focus on the *total value concept* and remember that products provide value in multiple ways.

While many companies today adhere to the marketing concept, numerous questions arise regarding actual marketing practice. For example, companies often come under criticism for marketing products that some consider harmful. In particular, the fast-food, cereal, tobacco, and alcohol industries are often under fire from various groups. Even though freedom of choice is a central tenet of the U.S. economic system, these products are among the many that society often considers harmful.

## The Marketing Mix and the Consumer

Marketers should use the tools found in the marketing mix carefully as they target consumers. When consumers question the way in which they are treated, they are likely to spread negative information through word-of-mouth and seek some form of remedy.

One of the most visible elements of the marketing mix is pricing. When consumers believe that a firm's prices are unfair, they are likely to leave the firm and spread negative information about it.[71] Consumers also complain that marketing efforts lead to overall higher prices. Marketers counter by explaining that marketing expenditures allow for increased economies of scale that contribute to lower overall production costs. Pricing issues are certainly debatable. Exhibit 16.5 presents the four P's of marketing as well as their ethical and unethical uses.

The product portion of the marketing mix also commonly comes under fire. Consumers question the extent to which products are actually harmful to themselves or society in the long run. Many products can lead to short-term satisfaction, but they can also lead to long-term consumer and/or societal problems. Consider the following categories of products originally discussed by Philip Kotler:[72]

- **Deficient products** are products that have little to no potential to create value of any type (for example, faulty appliances).
- **Salutary products** are products that are good for both consumers and society in the long run (for example, air bags). These products offer high utilitarian value, but do not provide hedonic value.
- **Pleasing products** are products that provide hedonic value to consumers but may be harmful in the long run (for example, cigarettes).
- **Desirable products** are products that deliver high utilitarian and hedonic value and that benefit both consumers and society in the long run (for example, pleasant-tasting weight-loss products).

## EXHIBIT 16.5
## The Marketing Mix and Business Ethics

| TOOL | COMMON USE | UNETHICAL USE |
|------|-----------|---------------|
| Product | The development of a good, service, or experience that will satisfy consumers' needs. | Failure to disclose that product won't function properly without necessary component parts. |
| Place | The distribution of a marketing offer through various channels of delivery. | Limiting product availability in certain markets as a means of raising prices. |
| Price | The marketer's statement of value received from an offering that may be monetary or non-monetary. | Stating that a regular price is really a "sales" price. This practice is prohibited by law. |
| Promotion | Communicating an offering's value through techniques such as advertising, sales promotion, and word-of-mouth. | Promoting one item as being on sale and then informing the customer that the product is out of stock and that a more expensive item should be bought. This practice, known as "bait and switch," is illegal. |

to major events being made available in only a few very select channels. As a result, consumers often feel like they are being treated unfairly. In 2009, Bruce Springsteen fans were enraged when they tried to buy tickets to his New Jersey concerts through **ticketmaster.com**. After logging in at the appropriate time, fans were given a website error message and re-directed to the Ticketmaster-owned site **ticketsnow. com**. The problem was that the ticket prices were much higher than face value on **ticketsnow.com**. Springsteen condemned the practice and Ticketmaster later apologized.[73]

Marketers clearly want to avoid offering *deficient* products. The difficult issue comes with the marketing of *pleasing* products. Many consumers know that the products they enjoy are harmful, but they buy them anyway! Needless to say, the tobacco industry has been under criticism for years for marketing products that many think are unsafe. Individual responsibility and freedom are important factors in consumer decisions to use these products. Most of the time, these companies deliver both customer satisfaction and value.

## Many products can lead to short-term satisfaction, but they can also lead to long-term consumer and/or societal problems.

The promotion and place elements of the marketing mix can also be questioned. Consumers often believe that products are promoted in ways that are simply too good to be true. Consumers also question distribution tactics used by marketers. For example, they complain about tickets

© RONEN/SHUTTERSTOCK.COM

*Restricting tickets to popular events can ultimately harm consumers.*

## Consumer Vulnerability and Product Harmfulness

Two important issues to consider when discussing marketing ethics are product harmfulness and consumer vulnerability.[74] A classification of product harmfulness/consumer vulnerability applied to marketing decision making is presented in Exhibit 16.6. Public criticism of marketing strategies tends to be most intense when a marketer targets vulnerable consumer groups with harmful products, as is the case when a marketer targets high-alcohol-content beverages to segments that have a large proportion of alcohol problems.

Of course, what constitutes a "harmful" product is a question of interpretation, as is the definition of a "vulnerable" consumer. What is a harmful product? What is a vulnerable consumer? One issue that is currently a hot topic is the growth of obesity in the United States. Both media attention and public pressure have led fast-food marketers to rethink their menu offerings.

## EXHIBIT 16.6
## Product Harmfulness and Consumer Vulnerability

**Product Harmfulness**

|  | Less Harmful | More Harmful |
|---|---|---|
| **Less Vulnerable** | Low-fat fast-food item promoted to above-average income segment consumers | High-interest-rate credit cards marketed to above-average income segment consumers |
| **More Vulnerable** | Low-nicotine cigarette promoted to undereducated consumers | High-alcohol-content drink marketed to consumer groups known to have disproportionate levels of alcohol problems |

**Consumer Vulnerability**

Source: Adapted from Smith, N. C., and E. Cooper-Martin (1997), "Ethics and Target Marketing: The Role of Product Harm and Consumer Vulnerability," *Journal of Marketing*, 61 (3), 1–20.

## Employee Behavior

Individual employees play an important part in the execution of marketing programs. Although consumers hope that a firm's employees are acting in good faith, this is not always the case. When a used car salesperson sets the odometer back on automobiles, the salesperson should know that the act is unethical and illegal. Some situations, however, are not as straightforward. Consider a salesperson facing the temptation to use bribery as a means of obtaining a sale. In some cultures, this practice is commonplace and acceptable; however, the practice is prohibited in the United States. But what if the salesperson is dealing with a customer who is living in the United States but is from a country where bribes are commonplace?

Individual behavior is guided largely by morals. **Morals** are personal standards and beliefs that are used to guide individual action. Certainly, each individual must answer to his or her own belief system.

# LO4 Corporate Social Responsibility

**C**orporate social responsibility may be defined as an organization's activities and status related to its societal obligations.[75] Due to increased pressure from consumer groups, companies are finding that they must be socially responsible. In fact, a popular catchphrase for socially responsible businesses is "doing well by doing good."

There are many ways in which companies can be responsible. Activities such as making donations to causes, supporting minority programs, ensuring responsible manufacturing processes and environmental protectionism, acting quickly when product defects are detected, focusing on employee safety, and encouraging employees to volunteer for local causes are some of the many ways in which companies can exhibit their social responsibility.[76] Basically, the actions described fall into one of three categories:

- *Ethical duties* include acting within expected ethical boundaries.
- *Altruistic duties* include giving back to communities through philanthropic activities.

# "All Shades of Green"

The growth in consumer demand for green products has produced all kinds of opportunities for marketers. Green products continue to gain in popularity and there is much money to be made while helping to save the environment. One emerging problem with green marketing, however, is when products are promoted as being green or environmentally friendly when they really aren't. The practice has become so common that the phrase "greenwashing" was introduced.

Greenwashing is exactly that: misleading consumers into believing that either a product or the processes used to make the product are green. For example, some products might be promoted as certified green when they really aren't, or they may be promoted as including all natural ingredients when the natural ingredients are actually harmful. Although research in this area is scarce, it is safe to say that consumers are turned off by the practice and this is a form of marketer misbehavior.

Sources: Brent, P. (2008), "Greenwashing: It's a Sin," *Marketing*, April 28, 2008, 7 (27), 1.; Schaefer, P. (2007), "The Six Sins of Greenwashing-Misleading Claims Found in Many Products," online content retrieved at *Environmental News Network* website, **http://www.enn.com/green_building/article/26388**, accessed July 1, 2010; online content retrieved at Organic Consumers website, "Whole Foods Market Imposes One-Year Deadline on Brands to Drop Bogus Organic Label Claims and Calls for Federal Regulation of Personal Care Products," **http://www.organicconsumers.org/bodycare/index.cfm**, accessed July 1, 2010.

**societal marketing concept** marketing concept that states that marketers should consider not only the wants and needs of consumers but also the needs of society

## THE SOCIETAL MARKETING CONCEPT

Part of being socially responsible is adopting the **societal marketing concept.** This concept considers the needs of society along with the wants and needs of individual consumers.[79] All firms have many stakeholders, and the effects of marketing actions on all these stakeholder groups should be considered. Some argue that if a product promotion achieves profitability at the expense of the general good, then the effort should not be undertaken. All of the stakeholders of a firm should be considered when marketing programs are initiated. Exhibit 16.7 presents prescriptions for improved marketing ethics.

- *Strategic initiatives* include strategically engaging in socially responsible activities in order to increase the value of the firm.[77]

Socially responsible marketing is associated with favorable consumer evaluations, increased customer satisfaction, and the likelihood of increased sales. This is particularly the case when an individual consumer identifies with the company and the causes to which it contributes.[78]

## EXHIBIT 16.7
## Prescriptions for Improved Marketing Ethics

- Marketers must put people first and consider the effects of their actions on all stakeholders.
- Actions must be based on standards that go beyond laws and regulations.
- Marketers must be held responsible for the means they use to achieve their desired ends. Focusing on profit motivations is not enough.
- Marketing organizations should focus on training employees in ethical decision making.
- Marketing organizations should embrace and disseminate a core set of ethical principles.
- Decision makers must adopt a stakeholder orientation that leads to an appreciation of how marketing decisions affect all relevant parties.
- Marketing organizations should specify ethical decision-making protocols.

Source: Laczniak, G. R., and P. E. Murphy (2006), "Normative Perspectives for Ethical and Socially Responsible Marketing," *Journal of Macromarketing*, 26 (2), 154–177.

# LO5 Regulation of Marketing Activities

many federal, state, and local laws were established in order to protect consumers from marketer misbehavior. Federal regulatory bodies such as the Federal Trade Commission (FTC) and the Food and Drug Administration (FDA) monitor exchanges that take place between consumers and marketers. Other groups, such as the Better Business Bureau (BBB) and the American Association of Advertising Agencies (AAAA), also play important roles in monitoring marketing activities. Although these groups attempt to bring fairness to the marketplace, it is ultimately up to managers to ensure that the actions of their firms fall within generally accepted business guidelines.

## MARKETING AND THE LAW

Exhibit 16.8 presents legislation that has been enacted in an effort to regulate commerce and ensure free trade. Many of these acts are aimed at maintaining or improving the general welfare of consumers in a free marketplace. They also protect the value that consumers receive from exchanges by prohibiting acts such as deceptive advertising and the selling of defective or unreasonably dangerous products.

## EXHIBIT 16.8
### Major Acts Affecting Commerce and Consumer Safety

| | |
|---|---|
| Sherman Antitrust Act (1890) | Prohibits restraint of free trade |
| Federal Food and Drug Act (1906) | Prohibits misleading practices associated with food and drug marketing |
| Clayton Act (1914) | Restricts price discrimination, exclusive dealing, and tying contracts |
| Wheeler Lea Act (1938) | Provides FTC with jurisdiction over misleading or false advertising |
| Fair Packaging and Labeling Act (1966) | Marketers must present proper packaging and content information about products |
| Child Protection Act (1966) | Prohibits the marketing of dangerous toys |
| Truth In Lending Act (1968) | Lenders required to disclose complete costs associated with loans |
| Consumer Product Safety Act (1972) | Created Consumer Product Safety Commission |
| Children's Online Privacy Protection Act (1998) | Establishes rules governing online marketing practices aimed at children |
| Anticybersquatting Consumer Protection Act (1999) | Prohibits the act of cybersquatting |
| Consumer Telephone Records Act (2006) | Prohibits the sale of consumer cell phone records |
| Consumer Product Safety Improvement Act of 2008 | Establishes product safety standards and other requirements for children's products |
| Credit Card Accountability, Responsibility, and Disclosure Act (2009) | Amends Truth in Lending Act to establish fair and transparent practices relating to consumer credit |
| Helping Families Save Their Homes Act (2009) | Prevents mortgage foreclosures and enhances mortgage availability |

# LO6 Public Criticism of Marketing

**U**nethical marketers intend to do harm in some way, act negligently, and/or manipulate consumers. As we have stated, however, marketers can simply make innocent mistakes. For example, a company may not discover a product defect until it has been released for public consumption. It would then issue a product recall. At issue is the *intent* and *knowledge* of the firm. Consumer perception is also important, as bad events can mean disaster for the firm in terms of lost business, customer boycotts, and bad publicity. We could discuss any number of different issues regarding public criticism of marketing; however, we focus on only a handful of issues here.

## DECEPTIVE ADVERTISING

Deceptive advertising (sometimes called false or misleading advertising) is an important issue for marketers. Deceptive advertising is covered under the Wheeler Lea Act (1938). This act was amended by the Federal Trade Commission Act by including false advertising issues. The FTC protects consumers from acts of fraud, deception, and unfair business practices, and the Wheeler Lea Amendment plays an important role in regulating advertising. The FTC has power to issue cease-and-desist orders and to issue fines against firms that are found guilty of deceptive advertising.

According to the FTC, **deceptive advertising** is advertising that (a) contains or omits information that is important in influencing a consumer's buying behavior and (b) is likely to mislead consumers who are acting "reasonably."[80] The extent to which advertisers *intentionally* misrepresent their products is crucial. Although the FTC defines what deceptive advertising is, actual deception can be difficult to prove.

An important distinction in practice is the difference between deceptive advertising and *puffery*. The term **puffery** describes making exaggerated claims about a product's superiority. Puffery differs from deceptive advertising in that there is no overt attempt to deceive a targeted consumer. In general, objective claims must be substantiated. In fact, the American Advertising Federation promotes the idea that advertising claims must be, among other things, truthful and substantiated.[14] The line between puffery and deception can be blurry.

Although regulatory mechanisms are in place to protect consumers from deceptive advertising, most businesses prefer forms of self-regulation over governmental regulation. For this reason, self-regulatory bodies, such as the National Advertising Review Council (NARC), work to ensure that advertisements are truthful. The NARC provides guidelines and sets standards for truth and accuracy for national advertisers.[81] National organizations such as the American Association of Advertising Agencies and the American Advertising Federation also monitor the advertising practices of their members.

> **deceptive advertising** message that omits information that is important in influencing a consumer's buying behavior and is likely to mislead consumers acting "reasonably"
>
> **puffery** practice of making exaggerated claims about a product and its superiority

## MARKETING TO CHILDREN

Children typify a vulnerable group because they often lack the knowledge of how to behave as responsible consumers. Two important issues arise with marketing to children. First, there is the question of whether children can understand that some marketing messages do not offer literal interpretations of the real world. For example, many toys are shown in unrealistic settings. Second, the quantity of marketing messages to which children are exposed can be called into question. It has been estimated that the average American child sees more than 40,000 television commercials per year—or an average of over 100 commercials per day.[82] The Children's Television Act was put into effect to limit the amount of advertising to which children are exposed, with a limit of 10.5 minutes of commercials per hour on weekends and 12 minutes on weekdays.

The Children's Advertising Review Unit (CARU) of the Better Business Bureau is a self-regulatory body that examines marketing activities that are aimed at children.

*Marketing to children is a controversial issue.*

Among other things, the CARU guidelines state that advertisers should into account the limited knowledge and comprehension that children have regarding marketing issues. Furthermore, the CARU maintains that advertisers should pay close attention to the educational role that advertising plays in a child's development and that advertising should stress positive behaviors.[83]

Internet marketing aimed at children is another important issue. The *Children's Online Privacy Protection Act* focuses on the online collection of personal information from children who are 13 years or younger. It specifies what marketers must include in privacy policies, when and how to seek consent from parents, and the responsibilities that marketers have to protect children's privacy and safety online.[84] The act places strict restrictions on the collection and dissemination of information about or from children.

# POLLUTION

The process of marketing a product often leads to pollution and marketers are often criticized for harming the environment. Of course, consumption also leads to pollution.[85] Ultimately, both marketers and consumers play important roles in environmental protection.

Environmental protection continues to grow in importance, and several popular movies and events highlight consumer pressure on businesses and government to increase environmental protectionism. The "Live Earth" concert of 2007 was formed to bring attention to global warming and the importance of climate change issues. The event is an example of millions of consumers coming together to support a cause. Although experts disagree on the severity and causes of climate change, the issue continues to gain attention.

# PLANNED OBSOLESCENCE

Marketers are also criticized for intentionally phasing out products before their usefulness wears out. For example, video game manufacturers are criticized for releasing new and seemingly "improved" gaming consoles even when older models haven't been on the market very long. The practice of managing and intentionally setting discontinue dates for products, is known as **planned obsolescence**. Critics charge that it is both wasteful and greedy for marketers to engage in planned obsolescence. Marketers counter by arguing that by continually offering improved products, consumers are able to enjoy improved standards of living and innovation.

# ARTIFICIAL NEEDS

Marketers are also criticized for imposing what might be called "artificial" needs on consumers. You may recall that a want represents the way in which a consumer goes about addressing a need. A consumer might have a need for food and sustenance, but have the want to fulfill that need with an expensive steak dinner. Do consumers really need a 60-inch LED HDTV? Do consumers really need whiter teeth or luxury cars? Wants and needs can easily become confused, and some argue that marketers only fuel the fire. By confusing wants and needs, consumers often give in to overconsumption.

Consumers also complain that advertisers create unrealistic expectations in their advertisements. For example, marketers of weight-loss products often promote lofty expectations. Advertisers include disclaimers such as "results vary" or "results are not typical" in their advertisements, but consumers rarely notice them.

# MANIPULATIVE SALES TACTICS

High-pressure and manipulative sales pitches are often the cause of consumer dissatisfaction. For example, a realtor might tell a client that several other people have looked at a particular house when they actually haven't. Or a salesperson might tell a customer that a product is in short supply when it really isn't.

Salespeople who adhere to a **sales orientation** are often guilty of these types of high-pressure tactics. To have a sales orientation means that the salesperson is more focused on the immediate sale and short-term results than on long-term customer satisfaction and relationship development. A more appropriate way to approach a sale is to adhere to what is referred to as a customer orientation. When using a **customer orientation**, the salesperson focuses on customer needs. Several studies have shown that having a customer orientation leads to favorable results for salespeople.

*Ingratiation* tactics are sometimes used by salespeople in order to get a sale. These techniques are often viewed as being manipulative.[86] Techniques such as the foot-in-the-door technique, the door-in-the-face technique, the even-a-penny-will-help technique, and the "I'm working for you!" technique can be called into question. These methods are considered unethical to the extent to which they are used for manipulation.

- A salesperson using the **foot-in-the-door technique** focuses on simply getting a "foot in the door." When consumers realize that they have opened themselves up to a sales pitch they are more likely to listen to the pitch and they are also more likely to buy a product. The salesperson first makes a small request such as "May I have a few minutes of your time?" and follows with larger request such as "May I show you how this works?" and finally by the largest request of "May I have your order?" The foot-in-the-door technique is based on *self-perception theory*, which proposes that consumers use perceptions of their own actions when forming attitudes. The consumer realizes that he has "let the salesperson in" and has given in to a small request; therefore, he must be the type of person who would give in to larger requests and ultimately buy the product. Of course, salespeople could argue that this is simply good salesmanship.

- With the **door-in-the-face technique**, a salesperson begins by making a really large request such as "Can I get you to buy this car today?" Realizing that very few, if any, customers would say "Yes!" the salesperson prepares for the dreaded "No!" Showing that her feelings are hurt, she follows with a guilt-ridden statement like "Well, can I show you its features?" Many consumers would feel bad about responding negatively to the first request and would allow the salesperson to explain the car's features. This tactic relies on the *reciprocity norm*, which states that individuals are motivated to give back to those who have given them something. By feeling that he just rejected a salesperson, the customer feels that he at least owes the salesperson the courtesy of listening.

- Using the **even-a-penny-will-help technique**, cause-related marketers suggest to potential donors that even the smallest donation will go a long way toward reaching the desired goal, such as ending child abuse, feeding the hungry, or sheltering the homeless.[87] The idea is to make the donor feel ashamed to give such a small amount. Instead of giving the penny, they may give a dollar. This technique is considered unethical to the extent that it relies on feelings of guilt.

- Using the **"I'm working for you!" technique**, salespeople attempt to lead customers into believing that they are working as hard as possible to give them the best deal when in reality they are following a script or routine. A salesperson walks away from his office during a negotiation to "go check with the manager" when he is really going to get coffee. The salesperson returns and says something like "I'm really working for you and here's a good deal!" This technique relies on *equity theory*. Here, the consumer would think that the salesperson is working hard, thereby raising the denominator in the equity theory comparison equation and leading to higher levels of satisfaction, and potentially purchase likelihood. Of course, salespeople often do consult with managers and work as hard as possible to give their customers the best deal.

**foot-in-the-door technique** ingratiation technique used in personal selling in which a salesperson begins with a small request and slowly leads up to one major request

**door-in-the-face technique** ingratiation technique used in personal selling in which a salesperson begins with a major request and then follows with a series of smaller requests

**even-a-penny-will-help technique** ingratiation technique in which a marketing message is sent that suggests that even the smallest donation, such as a penny or a dollar, will help a cause

**"I'm working for you!" technique** technique used by salespeople to create the perception that they are working as hard as possible to close a sale when they really are not doing so

## STEALTH MARKETING

One area of marketing that is currently receiving increased attention is the use of stealth marketing. This type of marketing was discussed earlier. Is it ethical for businesses to market products to consumers when the consumers do not realize that they are being targeted by marketing messages? As you may remember from our earlier discussion, with *stealth marketing*, consumers are completely unaware that they are being marketed to (hence, the term stealth). Again, WOMMA (Word of Mouth Marketing Association) is opposed to such tactics and considers their use to be unethical.[88]

*Salespeople can manipulate consumers in many ways.*

# PRODUCTS LIABILITY

Big business is often criticized for marketing unsafe products. The Consumer Product Safety Commission is the main body that monitors product safety, and the right to be safe is a basic consumer right listed in the Consumer Bill of Rights. Deaths, injuries, and/or property damage from consumer products in the United States cost the nation more than $800 billion annually.[89] Another organization with which consumers are familiar is the Insurance Institute for Highway Safety. This organization focuses on deaths, injuries, and property damage from automobile accidents on the nation's highways.

Product safety is governed in different ways around the world. American consumers are largely protected by regulations resulting from tort law. When a consumer is harmed by a product, he has the right to sue the party believed to be responsible. The issue of **products liability**, which is the extent to which businesses are held responsible for product-related injuries, is determined through this process. At one extreme, the consumer could live by the "buyer beware" principle and face responsibility for all injuries. At the other, firms could be responsible for any consumer injury. In the latter case, the marketplace would be so restricted that few firms could afford to operate.

The primary legal doctrine governing products liability in the U.S. today is strict liability. With **strict liability**, consumers can win a legal action against a firm if it can be demonstrated in court that an injury occurred and that the product associated with the injury was faulty in some way. This doctrine has become more prominent recently than the former guiding doctrine of negligence. With **negligence**, an injured consumer would have to show that the firm could foresee a potential injury that might occur and then decided not to act on that knowledge. The doctrine of strict liability means that firms face increased exposure to costs associated with product injury lawsuits.

A famous consumer incident involved McDonald's and a customer in the U.S. who spilled coffee onto her legs, burning herself. She obtained counsel and sued McDonald's. Under negligence, the plaintiff would have to prove that McDonald's knew such an injury could occur and did nothing to prevent such a mishap, but under strict liability, the consumer needed to demonstrate that an injury occurred and that the product was faulty. In this case, an action under strict liability was pursued on the basis that the consumer was burned and the coffee, being hot, was faulty. The woman ended up winning the lawsuit. A similar action led to Wendy's discontinuing the sale of hot chocolate because if "being hot" made the chocolate faulty, there was little need in offering the product for sale! Warning labels are now commonplace.

The costs of products liability are high in many industries. Physicians in the United States face huge costs due to the cost of liability insurance they must carry. Some claim that one of the biggest cost elements to an automobile is the cost of liability exposure, and companies have little choice but to pass these costs on to consumers. So, when a consumer purchases a ladder, a big part of the price covers liability exposure. A potentially bigger cost comes from stifled innovation as firms fear introducing products that are novel because they could be considered faulty. Companies like Cessna, Piper, and Beechcraft produce piston engine aircraft using the same basic technology that existed in 1950. More innovative aircraft are produced in the "kit plane" industry where the consumer has the responsibility of manufacturing the airplane himself or herself, limiting company liability.

Generally, firms face higher liability costs in the United States than in most other countries. One reason is because liability lawsuits that actually reach a courtroom often involve jury trials. In Europe, most liability actions would be overseen by a magistrate rather than a jury. Juries tend to be more sympathetic and are much more likely to award substantial punitive damages as well as compensatory damages. **Punitive damages** are intended to punish a company

*Finding the balance between consumer protection and market freedom is difficult.*

for injuries and **compensatory damages** are intended to cover costs incurred by a consumer due to an injury.

The issue of products liability is a good way to illustrate the importance of public policy to consumer behavior. However, the issue can be complicated and emotional. But, while tilting the balance of bearing the burden of product injuries toward firms may, at times, seem reasonable, such tilting actually restricts the market by driving businesses out of certain industries and restricting the choices of consumers. If pharmaceutical firms face costs that are too high and regulations that are too stringent, they may simply stop producing potentially life-saving medications because of product risk. The key to effective public policy is finding the proper balance, which offers consumers protection but still provides a high degree of freedom in the marketplace. This, of course, is no easy task.

**compensatory damages** damages that are intended to cover costs incurred by a consumer due to an injury

# 16
## Study Tools

**Located at the back of the textbook**
- ☐ Rip-out Chapter-in-Review Card

**Located at www.cengagebrain.com**
- ☐ Review Key Terms Flashcards (Print or Online)
- ☐ Download audio summaries to review on the go
- ☐ Complete practice quizzes to prepare for tests
- ☐ Play "Beat the Clock" and "Quizbowl" to master concepts
- ☐ Watch Video on Organic Valley for a real company example

## what others have thought...

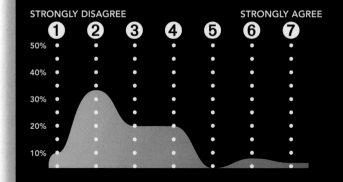

STRONGLY DISAGREE ① ② ③ ④ ⑤ STRONGLY AGREE ⑥ ⑦

50% 40% 30% 20% 10%

**Consumers are generally more ethical than the typical businessperson.**

Interestingly, it seems that the slight majority of students at least somewhat disagree with this statement. With all the media attention given to marketer misbehavior, this is surprising. However, it suggests that consumers are suspicious of each other and that they may often view others doing things in the marketplace that they shouldn't!

## Case 5-1

### Bullying Behavior: It's Not Just on the Playground Anymore

*Written by Allyn White, Mississippi State University*

October 17, 2006, is a day that Tina Meier will unfortunately never forget. It was on this day that Tina's daughter, Megan Meier, took her own life as the result of "cyberbullying," an increasingly prevalent consumer misbehavior. Cyberbullying, defined by the National Crime Prevention Council (NCPC) as "when the Internet, cell phones or other devices are used to send or post text or images intended to hurt or embarrass another person,"[1] presents multiple problems to society today. In fact, cyberbullying can be blamed for the suicides of at least three students between the ages of 12 and 13, according to popular news reports (e.g., *USA Today*). In the case of Megan Meier, the incident led to the identification and federal investigation of the perpetrator, Lori Drew, the mother of Megan's fellow student. However, Drew was ultimately acquitted of the crime.[2]

While physical bullying behavior has been a well-documented phenomenon among secondary school populations, technology provides a much larger arena for the posting of gossip. Indeed, negative information in the form of written gossip and photographs can be communicated via virtual social networks such as **Myspace .com**, or through the proliferation of cellular phones owned by the preteen and teenage population. What was once a behavior limited to physical interaction is now a much larger problem, primarily because of the wide reach of virtual interactive media. Cyberbullying occurs in many forms. The NCPC provides examples of cyberbullying methods, including (but not limited to) pretending to be someone other than one's self, spreading lies and rumors about someone, sending or forwarding cruel text messages, and posting pictures of a person without his or her consent. Research suggests that around 32% of all Internet-using teens have reported experiences with cyberbullying,[3] and sadly, the number of unreported virtual bullying is likely much larger, particularly for preteen and teenage individuals. Not surprisingly, cyberbullying is most often committed by members of the same age groups. Furthermore, a 2007 poll conducted by Pew Internet and American Life Project suggests that girls tend to be the victims of the majority of cyberbullying cases. Finally, the NCPC finds that 81% of teenagers report thinking cyberbullying is funny, while the remainder of the respondents do not consider the magnitude of the

consequences, do not think they will get caught, or simply assume that everyone participates in cyberbullying. Many researchers suggest that, because the bullying doesn't occur in person, the perpetrators feel more detached from the situation, and are less likely to realize the magnitude of the consequences of this behavior.[4]

Not surprisingly, preteens and teenage cyberbullying victims are often reluctant to report their experiences. While, as in the case of Megan Meier and others, lethal consequences can result, cyberbullying leads to other very critical problems for victims. Recent research suggests that victims of cyberbullying tend to be associated with school problems, assaultive behavior, and issues with substance abuse.[5] In response to cyberbullying, local, state, and federal organizations have instituted punishment guidelines related to the crimes of slander and defamation of character. No laws specific to cyberbullying behavior, however, currently exist. Private sector firms are also joining the effort to reduced cyberbullying incidents. For example, Sony Creative Software collaborated with the National Crime Prevention and Ad Councils to sponsor a contest for public service announcements addressing cyberbullying. One winner, "In the Kitchen with Megan," stresses to consumers the importance of the information being communicated, and not necessarily the message medium.[6] The theme of the message states that, "If you wouldn't say it in person, don't say it online," which focuses on always using good judgment when communicating with others. At this point in time, cyberbullying is widely considered outrageous and rude, but not necessarily criminal. The controversy over cyberbullying legislation continues, though, and the potentially lethal consequences of this behavior cannot be underestimated.

## Questions

1. Have you ever experienced or observed cyberbullying? If so, think about the incident and how it affected members of the situation.

2. Many times, cyberbullying occurs on social networks such as **Myspace.com**. In light of this, are these networks good for preteen and teenage consumers? Consumers of all ages?

3. Why would marketers, such as Sony Creative Software, become involved with the effort to reduce cyberbullying?

---

*Reprinted with permission from the author.

## Case 5-2

### Green Attitude Leads to Green Action

*Written by Mohan K. Menon, University of South Alabama*

**M**adhu was a conscientious housewife who, like others, tried to economize her purchases in order to manage her family's finances in a prudent manner. Recently, she had to take on more familial duties in the form of being green and eco-friendly. Being an avid reader of newspaper and magazine articles and having been exposed to news reports about ecological damage caused by human actions, she had developed an environmentally concerned attitude but never acted on it in a diligent manner. Now was the time to act.

After consultation with her family, she decided that she was going to lead by example and make hers a "green family." She began greening her family by pledging to methodically alter their food consumption patterns. She visited various websites such as **planetgreen.com, gogreeninitiative.com, thegreenguide.com**, etc., and gathered information about the first steps to get started on this epic journey.

She knew she was organized to begin this process. Madhu always kept her purchase receipts from cash, credit card, and check transactions for about a year after she diligently entered them in Quicken, the personal finance software. She had been using the software for over five years. Armed with a record of purchases, she was able to track her grocery purchases. It took her a few weeks but she was able to analyze the frequency of purchases, the quantity purchased and consumed, prices paid, and so on for most of the food items. She created graphs in Quicken to better understand and analyze the information.

She was indeed surprised by some of the purchases. An example of this was the frequency of bulk purchases of bottled water for which she paid about $200 during the previous 12-month period. This one seemed especially illogical since she has a refrigerator with a water filtration system and a water filter attached to her kitchen faucet. Madhu realized that she and her family were not only spending the money but also polluting the earth with more plastic in the landfills. As a result, she bought metal water bottles for each member of her household and bottled water purchases were limited to certain situations such as traveling.

She found similar "wasteful" spending with buying groceries in large quantities while also having three to four family meals per week in restaurants. As a result of her preliminary analysis, she calculated overspending at about 20% in food and drinks.

With the quantities of groceries she bought, she had accumulated and discarded plastic grocery bags without much thought. Her friend advised her to switch to paper bags. But her 'research' indicated that it might not make much difference since less energy is used to produce plastic bags compared to paper bags.[1] Fortunately, she found that these bags could be reused as garbage bags. Although she realized that she would still be sending some of these non-degradable bags to the local landfill, she took comfort in the fact that she could eliminate spending on store-bought plastic trash bags and also switch to cloth bags to reduce dependence on plastic bags. Of course, she had to buy smaller metal trash cans to use with the grocery bags.

The next step was to reduce household waste sent to the landfills. Her city, although not proactive in curb-side recycling, had a central recycling center about eight miles from her residence. She visited the center and obtained a list of items accepted for recycling. Madhu decided to actively recycle. But how could she get her young children involved? They are more likely to throw things in the trash sight unseen. She decided to make a game of it. She placed cardboard boxes in the garage and affixed labels with their names on them. Madhu discussed with her children the benefits of recycling and educated them on what can and cannot be recycled. Just as she had learned, she advised her children to look for the recycling symbol or phrases such as "please recycle" on the packages and bottles. She decided to provide a combination of monetary and non-monetary (favorite food) incentives to get her children to recycle.

Soon, the recycling boxes were filling up and the children were doing their part. She would take the items to the recycling center on a bi-weekly basis. Although she spent more time and effort for this, she valued the additional time she got to spend with her children. As a result, her curbside garbage can filled up once in three weeks and thus the garbage truck could make less frequent visits to her house. As a consequence, she saved significantly in garbage collection fees.

As these post-consumption activities became routine, Madhu realized that what she has managed to do thus far is just a first step. There are other ways she and her family can make a difference in greening the planet. She hopes to steadily continue on this journey to accomplish her new mission in life, a comprehensive, earth-friendly, green living existence.

Yet, in the process of greening her household, Madhu recognized that some eco-friendly claims on products were deceptive. One might get "greenwashed" into paying more for nothing more than a nice green label.

*Reprinted with permission.

Madhu, like many others, hoped that soon there would be a way to verify these claims, making her decision making less complex. She wondered, why is there no "Good Housekeeping"-type seal of approval for green household items?

## Questions

1. Why do consumers such as Madhu think green but not really act green? What are some of the impediments to acting green?

2. Are incentives necessary to alter consumer behavior related to reusing and recycling? Provide both pros and cons to this strategy.

3. As a green living consultant, what other courses of action would you recommend to Madhu and her family in their quest to reduce their impact on the planet?

4. Can you help Madhu find agencies and organizations that provide an eco-friendly seal of approval for household items such as grocery purchases?

## Case 5-3

### The Ethics of Selling Home Improvement Services

*Written by Paul Christensen, Saint Mary's University of Minnesota*

Don is a retired accountant who resides in the same four-bedroom house in which he and his late wife raised their family. Although Don has acquired many home improvement skills over the past forty years, he also knows when to hire the experts. Such was the case three years ago; the roof of Don's house needed replacing. He therefore hired a reputable contractor who installed new roof shingles that have a twenty-five year life expectancy. The new roof looks great and has already weathered several major storms. Don is passionate about his house and all of the memories associated with it, and he spares no expense with home maintenance.

One Saturday afternoon, a representative from a local roofing company with whom Don was not familiar knocked on the door. Introducing himself as Joel, he stated that he was offering homeowners in the neighborhood a free roof inspection to determine whether any damage from a hail storm had been incurred. Don asked which hail storm Joel was referring to; Joel stated "the one last July 23rd" (which was nine months ago). Don responded that he had not noticed any damage or leaking, although he admitted that the shingles had not been inspected. Don also questioned whether the hail storm had been severe enough to even cause damage ("I don't recall it being a bad storm," Don commented). Joel began unloading the ladder from his truck while responding to Don's questions.

"Well, let me climb up on your roof and take a quick look," replied Joel. "And no charge, Don," Joel added. "Let's just make sure you don't have any serious damage." Less than a minute had passed from the time Joel introduced himself to the moment he started climbing a ladder up to Don's roof. Joel's outgoing demeanor sharply contrasted Don's analytical, soft-spoken personality.

After ten minutes, Joel climbed down the ladder. "Well, Don, the south side of your roof looks just fine, but I see some damage on the north side." Joel continued, "Some of the shingles have lost some of their granules, which is common with hail damage." Suddenly, Don became concerned that his roof was seriously damaged.

"So how many shingles have lost granules? Is my roof going to leak? What do I need to do?" Don inquired. Joel responded to Don's questions, although with considerably less detail than Don had hoped for.

"Well, I'm not going to tell you that your roof will leak in the next five years, Don," replied Joel. "But if one shingle needs to be replaced, then the insurance companies tend to want the entire roof reshingled. And you can't really replace even a few damaged shingles without replacing them all." Joel followed up by asking, "So which insurance company do you use, Don?" Don gave him the answer; Joel then stated that he had worked with this insurance company on several other hail-damaged roofs in the area. "I would be happy to contact your insurance provider and work out all of the details, Don," Joel continued. Caught up in the emotion of the moment, Don's next thought was to give Joel the go-ahead to call the insurance company and start the reshingling process. Don paused, however, and reflected on Joel's responses to his questions.

"Thank you for taking a look at my roof, Joel," Don replied. "However, my nephew is a commercial construction contractor. I'm going to ask him to stop by when he's in town next week and give me a second opinion."

---

*Reproduced with permission from the author.

Joel was taken aback for a second, but then responded, "I see. But keep in mind that I'm an expert in my field. Roofing is all that I do, and while I mean no disrespect to your nephew, I have to believe that I have a higher level of expertise to assess hail-damaged roofing shingles." Joel had made his point.

"Thank you for your time, Joel," replied Don. "I will keep your business card and call you if my nephew thinks that replacing my shingles is a good idea."

## Questions

1. Which sales technique discussed in Chapter 16 best describes the one used by Joel? Explain.

2. Why might Joel's sales technique be considered manipulative?

3. In the context of this marketing situation, can the argument be made that Don is a "vulnerable" consumer? Explain.

4. Does Don have a "true" need? Or is Joel creating an artificial one?

# ENDNOTES

## Chapter 1

1. Roberts, D. (2010), "Mania on the Mainland," BusinessWeek, (January 11), 30–34.
2. Lahart, J. and J. Bater (2010), "Home Builders' Confidence Drops," *The Wall Street Journal*, (June 16), A2.
3. See Walters, C. Glenn, and Gordon W. Paul (1970), *Consumer Behavior: An Integrated Approach*, 3rd Edition. Irwin, Homewood, IL; Howard, John L., and Jagdish Sheth (1969), *The Theory of Buyer Behavior*, Wiley, New York.
4. See **http://dictionary.laborlawtalk.com/ Economics** for different perspectives on economics; accessed January 8, 2007.
5. Pan, Suwen, Cheng Fang, and Jaime Malaga (2006), "Alcoholic Beverage Consumption in China: a Censored Demand System Approach," *Applied Economics Letters*, 13 (12/15), 975–979.
6. Christie, Jennifer, Dan Fisher, John C. Kozup, Scott Smith, Scott Burton, and Elizabeth H. Creyer (2001), "The Effects of Bar-Sponsored Alcohol Beverage Promotions Across Binge and Nonbinge Drinkers," *Journal of Public Policy & Marketing*, 20 (Fall), 240–253.
7. Tyler, Leona E. (1981), "More Stately Mansions—Psychology Extends Its Boundaries," *Annual Review of Psychology*, 32, 1–20.
8. Yoon, Carolyn, Gilles Laurent, Helen H. Fung, Richard Gonzales, Angela H. Gutchess, Trey Hedden, Raphaelle Lambert-Pandraud, Mara Mather, Denise C. Park, Ellen Peters, and Ian Skurnik (2005), "Cognition, Persuasion and Decision Making in Older Consumers," *Marketing Letters*, 16 (3), 429–441.
9. Darroch, Jenny, Morgan P. Miles, Andrew Jardine, and Ernest F. Cooke (2004), "The 2004 AMA Definition of Marketing and Its Relationship to a Market Orientation: An Extension of Cooke, Rayburn, & Abercrombie (1992)," *Journal of Marketing Theory & Practice*, 12 (Fall), 29–38.
10. Mittelstaedt, Robert A. (1990), "Economics, Psychology, and the Literature of the Subdiscipline of Consumer Behavior," *Journal of the Academy of Marketing Science*, 18 (4), 303–311.
11. Zinkhan, George M., Martin S. Roth, and Mary Jane Saxton (1992), "Knowledge Development and Scientific Status in Consumer-Behavior Research: A Social Exchange Perspective," *Journal of Consumer Research*, 19 (September), 282–291.
12. Ibid.
13. Henry, G. T., and Theodore Poister (1994), "Citizen Ratings of Public and Private Service Quality: A Comparative Perspective," *Public Administration Review*, 54, 11a; Winkler, C. (2003), "When Yanking the Mainframe Isn't an Option," *Computerworld*, 37, 35–36.
14. Bello, M. (2009), "DMVs Hit by Budget Cutbacks: Drivers face Higher Fees, Longer Waits," *USA Today*, (November 23), 3A.
15. Weiss, E.M. (2002), "DMV Waits Irk Customers; Holiday, New Closings Aggravate End-of-Month Crunch," *The Washington Post*, (December 1, 2002), p. C03. Kinney, M.Y. (2009), "Speeding Welcome Behind the Counter at License Bureaus," *The Philadelphia Inquirer*, (May 17), p. B01.
16. Narver, J. C., and S. F. Slater (1990), "The Effect of a Market Orientation on Business Profitability," *Journal of Marketing*, 54 (October), 20–35. Narver, J. C., S. Slater, and B. Tietje (1998), "Creating a Market Orientation," *Journal of Market-Focused Management*, 2 (3), 241–55.
17. Voss, G. B., and Z. G. Voss (2000), "Strategic Orientation and Firm Performance in an Artistic Environment," *Journal of Marketing*, 64, 67–83. Auh, Seigyoung, and B. Menguc (2006), "Diversity at the Executive Suite: A Resource-Based Approach to the Customer Orientation–Organizational Performance Relationship," *Journal of Business Research*, 59, 564–572.
18. Skogland, I., and J. A. Siguaw (2004), "Are Your Satisfied Customers Loyal?" *Cornell Hotel and Restaurant Administration Quarterly*, 45, 221–234. Berger, P. D., N. Eechambadi, G. Morris, D. R. Lehmann, R. Rizley, and R. Venkatesan (2006), "From Customer Lifetime Value to Shareholder Value: Theory, Empirical Evidence and Issues for Future Research," *Journal of Services Research*, 9, 156–167.
19. Neslin, S. A., D. Grewal, R. Leghorn, V. Shankar, M. L. Teerling, J. S. Thomas, and P. C. Verhoef (2006), "Challenges and Opportunities in Multichannel Customer Management," *Journal of Services Research*, 9, 95–112.
20. Hunt, S. D. (1997), "Competing Through Relationships; Grounding Relationship Marketing in Resource Advantage Theory," *Journal of Marketing Management* 13 (5), 431–445.
21. All dates taken from company websites. Samsung was originally founded in 1938 but as a Korean food exporter. In 1969, Samsung Electronics was created.
22. Christenson, C. M., S. Cook, and T. Hall (2005), "Marketing Malpractice: The Cause and the Cure," *Harvard Business Review*, 83, 74–83.
22a. Tryhorn, C., (2009), "Mobile Phone Use Passes a Milestone," *The Guardian*, (March 06), p. 9.
23. U.S. Federal Reserve Statistics, **http://www .federalreserve.gov**, accessed June 19, 2010.
24. *Market Europe* (2006), "UK Consumers Carry a Heavy Load of Debt," 17 (October), 3.
25. Pinto, M. B., P. M. Mansfield, and D. H. Parente (2004), "Relationship of Credit Attitude and Debt to Self-Esteem, and Locus of Control in College-Age Consumers," *Psychological Reports*, 94, 1405–1418.
26. Zikmund, W.G. and B.J. Babin (2010), *Exploring Marketing Research*, Cengage/ Southwestern, Mason, OH.
27. Bode, Mathias (2006), "Now That's What I Call Music! An Interpretive Approach to Music in Advertising," *Advances in Consumer Research*, 33, 580–585.
28. Tadajewski, M. (2006), "Remembering Motivation Research: Toward an Alternative Genealogy of Interpretive Consumer Research," *Marketing Theory*, 6, 429–466.
29. Moe, W., and P. Fader (2001), "Measuring Hedonic Portfolio Products: A Joint Segmentation Analysis of Music Compact Disc Sales," *Journal of Marketing Research*, 38, 376–385.
30. Chiou, J. S., C. Y. Huang, and H. H. Lee (2005), "The Antecedents of Music Piracy Attitudes and Intentions," *Journal of Business Ethics*, 57, 161–174.
31. Zikmund and Babin (2007), p. 131.
32. **http://assets.starbucks.com/assets/company-profile-feb10.pdf**, accessed June 19, 2010.
33. **http://academic.emporia.edu/smithwil/ 00spmg456/eja/pieschl.html#Sears**.
34. **http://www.census.gov/retail/mrts/www/ data/html/10Q1.html**, accessed June 20, 2010.
35. **http://www.alexa.com/topsites**, accessed June 19, 2010.
36. **http://online.wsj.com/article/SB100014 2405274870485200457525835124532 1016.html?KEYWORDS=unemployment**, accessed June 20, 2010.
37. Rohwedder, C. (2009), "U.K. Grocers in Price Fight, and It's Drawing Customers," *The Wall Street Journal*, (August 10), A1. Benning, T. (2009), "Slump Strains Church Finances as Need Grows," *The Wall Street Journal*, (August 11), A13.

## Chapter 2

1. Seattle Post-Intelligencer News Services (2003), "Rock Still the Most Popular Music Genre," SeattlePI.com (May 13), **http:// seattlepi.nwsource.com/pop/122353_ tf217.html**, accessed February 26, 2006.
2. Grégoire, Yany, T.M. Tripp and R. Legoux (2009), "When Customer Love Turns into Lasting Hate: the Effects of Relationship Strength and Time on Customer Revenge and Avoidance," *Journal of Marketing* 73 (November), 18–32. Grégoire, Yany and Robert Fisher (2006), "The Effects of Relationship Quality on Customer Retaliation," *Marketing Letters* 17 (1), 31-46. Kressmann, Frank, M. Joseph Sirgy, Andreas Herrmann, Frank Huber, Stephanie Huber and Dong-Jin Lee (2006), "Direct and Indirect Effects of Self-image Congruence on Brand Loyalty," *Journal of Business Research* 59 (September), 955–964.
3. "Extra Care Delivers Value to Customers," *Chain Drug Review* 32 (April 26, 2010), 106.
4. Crosby, L.A., W. Marks, and S. L. Johnson (2007), "On Their Behalf," *Marketing Management* 16 (2), 12–13. Treacy, Michael and Fred Wiersema (1993), "Customer Intimacy and Other Value Disciplines," *Harvard Business Review* 71 (January/February), 84–93.
5. Babin, B. J., W. R. Darden, and M. Griffin (1994), "Work and/or Fun: Measuring Hedonic and Utilitarian Shopping Value," *Journal of Consumer Research*, 20 (March), 644–656.
6. Levitt, T. (1960), "Marketing Myopia," *Harvard Business Review* 38 (July-August), 57–66.
7. "Coca-Cola Gains Market Share Over Pepsi; Soft Drink Industry Shows Modest Growth," *Food and Drink Weekly* (March 3, 2003), **http://www.findarticles.com/p/ articles/mi_m0EUY/is_8_9/ai_98594588**, accessed June 30, 2010.
8. **www.ferrari.com**, accessed June 30, 2010.

9. Halliday, Jean (2005), "Total Value Promise a Total Mess for GM Sales," *Advertising Age*, 76, 3.

10. Adner, R. (2006), "Match Your Innovation Strategy to Your Innovation Ecosystem," *Harvard Business Review*, 84 (April), 98–108.

11. Vargo, S. L. and R. F. Lusch (2008), "Service-Dominant Logic: Continuing the Evolution," *Journal of the Academy of Marketing Science* 36 (March), 1–10.

12. Dickson, P. R., and J. L. Ginter (1987), "Market Segmentation, Product Differentiation and Marketing Strategy," *Journal of Marketing*, 51, 1–10.

13. More precisely, in economics, price elasticity represents the proportionate change in demand associated with a proportionate change in price. The slope coefficient represents the parameter of the line showing how demand responds to price. The slope of the line is constant over the range while the elasticity changes at any point on the line. To calculate the actual total quantity demanded, the total size of the population would have to be included in the equation. For simplicity of illustration, this is omitted here.

14. Orth, U.R., M. McDaniel, T. Shellhamer, and K. Lopetcharat (2004), "Promoting Brand Benefits: The Role of Consumer Psychographics and Lifestyle," *Journal of Consumer Marketing* 21, 97–108.

15. Swinyard, William R. and Scott M. Smith (2003), "Why People (Don't) Shop Online: A Lifestyle Study of the Internet Consumer," *Psychology & Marketing* 20, 567–597. Martin, C. (2009), "Consumption Motivation and Perceptions of Malls: A Comparison of Mothers and Daughters," *Journal of Marketing, Theory and Practice* 17 (Winter), 49–61.

16. Rust, R. and N. Donthu (1994), "Positioning a Radio Station," *Journal of Applied Business Research* 10, 21–27.

17. Sunil, G., D. Hanssens, B. Hardie, W. Kahn, V. Kumar, L. Nathaniel and N.R. Sriram (2006), "Modeling Customer Lifetime Value," *Journal of Service Research* 9 (November), 139–155.

18. Kumar, V., D. Shah and R. Venkatesan (2006), "Managing Retailer Profitability—One Customer at a Time!" *Journal of Retailing* 82, 277–294.

19. Kumar et al. (2006)

Case 1-1

1. Ranking measured by sales in 2009. http://www.forbes.com/lists/2009/18/global-09_The-Global-2000_Sales.html.

Case 1-2

1. Natural Marketing Institute, "NMI's LOHAS Segmentation Model," http://www.nmisolutions.com/lohasd_segment.html (accessed May 1, 2010).

2. Organic Trade Association, "OTA's 2009 Organic Industry Survey," http://www.ota.com/pics/documents/01a_OTAExecutiveSummary.pdf (accessed May 1, 2010).

3. Dugan, Emily (October 29, 2007), "Organic Food is Healthier and Safer, Four-year EU Investigation Shows," *The Independent* (London), http://www.independent.co.uk/environment/green-living/organic-food-is-healthier-and-safer-fouryear-eu-investigation-shows-395483.html (accessed May 1, 2010).

4. Magkos F, F. Arvaniti, and A. Zampelas (2003), "Organic Food: Nutritious Food or Food for Thought? A Review of the Evidence," *International Journal of Food Sciences and Nutrition* 54(5): 357–371, http://informahealthcare.com/doi/abs/10.1080/09637480120092071 (accessed 5/1/10).

5. World Health Organization, "Toxic Hazards," http://www.who.int/heli/risks/toxics/chemicals/en/index.html (accessed May 1, 2010).

6. Kramer, Sasha B., John P. Reganold, Jerry D. Glover, Brendan J. M. Bohannan, and Harold A. Mooney (March 21, 2006), "Reduced Nitrate Leaching and Enhanced Dentrifer Activity and Efficiency in Organically Fertilized Soils," *Proceedings of the National Academy of Sciences*, http://www.pnas.org/cgi/content/full/103/12/4522#B2 (accessed May 1, 2010).

7. Ottman, Jacquelyn A., Edwin R. Stafford, and Cathy L. Hartman (2006), "Avoiding Green Marketing Myopia," *Environment* 48 (5): 22-36.

Case 1-3

1. Coca-Cola Annual Report, 2008.

2. Klassen, Abbey (2010), "New Coke: One of Marketing's Biggest Blunders Turns 25 and You Think You'd Like to Forget Your Birthday," *Advertising Age*, April 23, http://adage.com/adages/post?article_id=143470. Accessed August 31, 2010.

3. Hartley, Robert F. (2004), *Marketing Mistakes and Successes*, 9th edition, John Wiley & Sons, Inc., New York, p. 26.

4. Zyman, Sergio (2000), "The End of Marketing as We Know It," *Marketing Is Science*, Harper Business, New York, pp. 47-49.

# Chapter 3

1. Levinsky, D. L., and T. Youm (2004), "The More Food Young Adults Are Served, the More they Overeat," *Journal of Nutrition*, 134, 2546–2549; Rolls, B. J., L. S. Roe, and J. S. Meengs (2006), "Reductions in Portion Size and Energy Density of Foods Are Addictive and Lead to Sustained Decreases in Energy Intake," *American Journal of Clinical Nutrition*, 83, 11–17.

2. Antonides, G., P.C. Verhoef and M. van Aalst (2002), "Consumer Perception and Evaluation of Waiting Time: A Field Experiment," *Journal of Consumer Psychology* 12 (3), 193-202.

3. Argo, J.J., M. Popa and M.C. Smith (2010), "The Sound of Brands," *Journal of Marketing* 74 (July), 97-109.

4. Raghunathan, Rajagopal and Julie R. Irwin (2010), "Walking the Hedonic Product Tread-mill: Default Contrast and Mood-Based Assimilation in Judgments of Predicted Happiness with a Target Product," *Journal of Consumer Research* 28, 355-368.

5. Meyers-Levy, Joan, and Alice M. Tybout (1989), "Schema Congruity as a Basis for Product Evaluation," *Journal of Consumer Research* 16 (1), 39-54.

6. Sylvie, M., L. Dubè, and J.C. Chebat (2007), "The Role of Pleasant Music in Service-scapes: A Test of the Dual Model of Environmental Perception," *Journal of Retailing* 83, 115-130.

7. Kim, J., A.M. Flore, and H.H. Lee (2006), "Influences of Online Store Perception, Shopping Enjoyment, and Shopping Involvement on Consumer Patronage Behavior Towards an Online Retailer," *Journal of Retailing and Consumer Services* 14, 95-107.

8. Merkile, P.M. (2000), "Subliminal Perception," *Encyclopedia of Psychology* 7, 497-499.

9. Gable, M., H. Wilkens, L. Harris, and R. Feinbert (1987), "An Evaluation of Subliminally Embedded Sexual Stimuli in Graphics," *Journal of Advertising* 16, 26-31.

10. Broyles, S.J. (2006), "Misplaced Paranoia over Subliminal Advertising: What's the Big Uproar?" *Journal of Consumer Marketing* 23, 312-313.

11. Broyles, S.J. (2006), "Subliminal Advertising and the Perceptual Popularity of Playing to People's Paranoia," *Journal of Consumer Affairs* 40, 392-406.

12. Lantos, G. (1996), "Ice Cube Sex: the Truth about Subliminal Advertising: Book Review," *Journal of Consumer Marketing* 13, 62-64.

13. Key, W.B. (1974), *Subliminal Seduction: Ad Media's Manipulation of a Not so Innocent America*, Signet, New York; Packard, V. (1957), *The Hidden Persuaders*, D. McKay Co., New York.

14. Cook, W.A. (1993), "Looking Behind Ice Cubes," *Journal of Advertising Research* 33 (March/April), 7-8.

15. Garfield, Bob (2000), "Subliminal Seduction and Other Urban Myths," *Advertising Age* 71 (September 18), 104-105.

16. Vroomen, J., and M. Keetels (2006), "The Spatial Constraint in Intersensory Pairing: No Role in Temporal Ventriloquism," *Journal of Experimental Psychology* 32, 1063-1071.

17. Miller, Richard L. (1962), "Dr. Weber and the Consumer," *Journal of Marketing*, 57-67.

18. Hoffman, K.D., L.W. Turley and S.W. Kelley (2002), "Pricing Retail Services," *Journal of Business Research* 55 (December), 1015-1023.

19. Kalyanam, K., and T.S. Shively (1998), "Estimating Irregular Pricing Effects: A Stochastic Spline Regression Approach," *Journal of Marketing Research*, 35, 16-29.

20. Miller, "Dr. Weber and the Consumer."

21. Yoo, C.Y. (2008), "Unconscious Processing of Web Advertising: Effects on Implicit Memory, Attitude toward the Brand and Consideration Set," *Journal of Interactive Marketing* 22 (Spring), 2-18.

22. Janiszewski, Chris (1993), "Preattentive Mere Exposure Effects," *Journal of Consumer Research* 20 (3), 376-392.

23. Smith, Gene F. (1982), "Further Evidence of the Mediating Effect of Learning in the 'Mere Exposure' Phenomenon," *Journal of General Psychology* 197, 175-178; Stang, D.J. (1975), "Effects of 'Mere Exposure' on Learning and Affect," *Journal of Personality and Social Psychology* 31, 7-12.

24. Gustav, K., and Z. Dienes (2005), "Implicit Learning of Nonlocal Musical Rules: Implicitly Learning More than Chucks," *Journal of Experimental Psychology/Learning, Memory & Cognition* 31 (November), 1417-1432; Chakraborty, G., V. Lala, and D. Warran (2003), "What Do Customers Consider Important in B2B Websites?" *Journal of Advertising Research* (March), 50.

25. Bulik, B.S. (2007), "Media Morph: People Search," *Advertising Age* 78 (March 28), 18. Ballenson, J.N., S. Iyengar, N. Yee and N.A. Collins (2008), "Facial Similarity between Voters and Candidates Causes Influence," *Public Opinion Quarterly* 72 (5), 935-961.

26. Yang, M., D. Roskos-Ewoldson, L. Dinu, and L.M. Arpan (2006), "The Effectiveness of 'In-Game' Advertising," *Journal of Advertising* 35 (Winter), 143-152.

27. Auty, S., and C. Lewis (2004), "Exploring Children's Choice: The Reminder Effect

of Product Placement," *Psychology & Marketing* 21 (9), 697-713.

28. Ang, S.H., S.M. Leong, and W. Yeo (1999), "When Silence Is Golden: Effects of Silence on Consumer Ad Responses," *Advances in Consumer Research* 26, 295-299.

29. David, B., D.W. Wooten (2006), "From Labeling Possessions to Possessing Labels: Ridicule and Socialization Among Adoles-cents," *Journal of Consumer Research* 33, 188-198.

30. Skinner, B.F. (1989), "The Origins of Cognitive Thought," *American Psychologist* 44 (1): 13-18.

31. Ibid.

32. Malone, John C., Jr., and Natalie M. Cruchon (2001), "Radical Behaviorism and the Rest of the Psychology: A Review/Precis of Skinner's About Behaviorism," *Behavior and Philosophy* 29, 31-57.

33. http://www.simplypsychology.pwp .blueyonder.co.uk/behaviourism.html, accessed July 9, 2010.

## Chapter 4

1. Lepkowska-White, E. and A. Parsons (2001), "Comprehension of Warnings and Resulting Attitudes," *Journal of Consumer Affairs* 35, 278-294. Cox, A.D., D. Cox and S. Powell Mantel (2010), "Consumer Response to Drug Risk Information: The Role of Positive Affect," *Journal of Marketing* 74 (July), 31-44.

2. Argo, J. J., and K. J. Main (2004), "Meta-Analysis of the Effectiveness of Warning Labels," *Journal of Public Policy and Marketing*, 23 (Fall), 193-208.

3. Borges, A. (2009), "Price Matching Guarantees: The Effect of Refund Size and the Moderating Role of Retail Price Strategy," *Recherche et Applications en Marketing* 24 (1), 29-39. Kukar-Kinney, M. and R. G. Walters (2007), "Comparison of Consumers to PMGs in Internet and Bricks-and-Mortar Retail Environments," *Journal of the Academy of Marketing Science* 35 (Summer), 197-207.

4. Doyle, J.R. and P.A. Bottemly (2006), "Dressed for the Occasion: Font-Product Congruity in the Perception of Logotype," *Journal of Consumer Psychology* 16 (2), 112-123.

5. Noel, H. and B. Vallen (2009), "The Spacing Effect in Marketing: A Review of Extant Findings and Directions for Future Research," *Psychology & Marketing* 26 (November), 951-969.

6. Madhubalan, V., and M. Hastak (2002), "The Role of Summary Information in Facilitating Consumers' Comprehension of Nutrition Information," *Journal of Public Policy & Marketing*, 21, 305-318.

7. Shen, Y. C., and T. C. Chen (2006), "When East Meets West: The Effect of Cultural Tone Congruity in Ad Music and Message on Consumer Ad Memory and Attitude," *International Journal of Advertising*, 25, 51-70.

8. See Kellaris, J. J., A. D. Cox, and D. Cox (1993), "The Effects of Background Music on Ad Processing: A Contingency Explanation," *Journal of Marketing*, 57, 114-125.

9. Burke, R.R., and T. K. Srull (1988), "Competitive Interference and Consumer Memory for Advertisements," *Journal of Consumer Research*, 15 (June), 55-68.

10. Dholokia, R. R., and B. Sternthal (1997), "Highly Credible Sources Persuasive

Facilitator or Persuasive Liabilities?" *Journal of Consumer Research*, 3, 223-232.

11. http://goinglikesixty.com/2010/03/ boomer-favorite-icons-m-ms-are-most-beloved-characters-in-the-whole-universe/, accessed July 7, 2010. LeBel, J.L. and N. Cooke (2008), "Branded Food Spokescharacters: Consumers' Contributions to the Narrative of Commerce," *Journal of Product & Brand Management* 17 (3), 143-153.

12. Taylor, V. A., and A. B. Bower (2004), "Improving Product Instruction Compliance: If You Tell Me Why, I Might Comply," *Psychology & Marketing*, 21, 229-245.

13. Block, L. and T. Kramer (2009), "The Effect of Superstitious Beliefs on Performance Expectations," *Journal of the Academy of Marketing Science* 37, 161-169.

14. Celsi, Richard L., and Jerry C. Olson (1988), "The Role of Involvement in Attention and Comprehension Processes," *Journal of Consumer Research*, 15 (2): 210-224.

15. Menon, S., and D. Soman (2004) "Managing the Power of Curiosity for Effective Web Advertising Strategies," *Journal of Advertising* 31, 1-14.

16. Moorman, C. (1996), "A Quasi-Experiment to Access the Consumer and Informational Determinants of Nutrition Information Processing Activities: The Case of Nutrition Labeling and Education Act," *Journal of Public Policy and Marketing* 15, 28-44. See also Nalor, R.W., C.M. Droms and K.L. Haws (2009), "Eating with a Purpose: Consumer Response to Functional Food Health Claims in Conflicting Versus Complementary Information Environments," *Journal of Public Policy and Marketing* 28 (Fall), 221-233.

17. Redden, J.P. (2008), "Reducing Satiation: The Role of Categorization Level," *Journal of Consumer Research* 34 (February), 624-634. Nordhielm, C.L. (2002), "The Influence of Levels of Processing on Advertising Repetition Levels," *Journal of Consumer Research*, 29 (December), 371-382.

18. Griffin, M., B.J. Babin, and D. Modianos (2000), "Shopping Values of Russian Consumers: The Impact of Habituation in a Developing Economy," *Journal of Retailing* 76, 33-52.

19. Allison, Ralph I., and Kenneth P. Uhl (1964), "Influence of Beer Brand Identification on Taste Perception," *Journal of Marketing Research*, August (1): 36-39.

20. Kaufman-Scarborough, C. (2000), "Seeing through the Eyes of the Color-Deficient Shopper: Consumer Issues for Public Policy," *Journal of Consumer Policy*, 23, 461-492.

21. Bapna, Ravi, P. Goes, A. Gupta, and G. Karuga (2002), "Optimal Design of the Online Auction Channel: Empirical and Computational Insights," *Decision Sciences*, 33, 557-577.

22. Cox, A. D., D. Cox, and G. Zimet (2006), "Understanding Consumer Responses to Product Risk Information," *Journal of Marketing*, 70 (January), 79-91.

23. Tversky, A., and D. Kahneman (1981), "The Framing of Decisions and the Psychology of Choice," *Science*, 211, 453-458.

24. Rick, S. (2010), "Losses, Gains, and Brains: Neuroeconomics can Help to Answer Open Questions about Loss Aversion," *Journal of Consumer Psychology* (in press).

25. Fitzsimons, G.M., T.L. Chartrand and G.J. Fitzsimons (2008), "Automatic Effects of Brand Exposure on Motivated Behavior:

How Apple Makes you Think Different," *Journal of Consumer Research* 35 (1), 21-35.

26. Saini, R., R.S. Rao and A. Monga (2010), "Is That Deal Worth My Time? The Interactive Effect of Relative and Referent Thinking on Willingness to Seek a Bargain," *Journal of Marketing*, 74 (January), 34-48.

27. Luna, D. and H.M. Kim (2009), "How Much was your Shopping Basket? Working Memory Processes in Total Basket Price Estimation," *Journal of Consumer Psychology*, 19, 346-355.

28. Vanhuele, M., and X. Drèze (2002), "Measuring the Price Knowledge Consumers Bring to the Store," *Journal of Marketing*, 66, 72-85.

29. Krishna, A., M.Q. Lwin and M. Morrin (2010), "Product Scent and Memory," *Journal of Consumer Research* 37 (June), 57-67.

30. Dawson, B. (2005), "Jingles' Best Days May Be Behind Them," *Minneapolis Star Tribune*, April 13, http://www.ocregister .com/ocr/sections/life/lf_trends/article _478162.php, accessed April 4, 2007.

31. Vanhuele, M., G. Laurent, and X. Drèze (2006), "Consumers Immediate Memory for Prices," *Journal of Consumer Research*, 33, 153-172.

32. Cline, T. W., and J. J. Kellaris (2007), "The Influence of Humor Strength and Humor-Message Relatedness and Ad Memorability," *Journal of Advertising*, 36, 55-67.

33. Chan, J.C.K., K.B. McDermott, J.M. Watson, and D.A. Gallo (2005), "The Importance of Material-Processing Interactions in Inducing False Memories," *Memory & Cognition* 33, 389-395.

34. Debenedetti, A. and P. Gomez (2010), "Mental Rumination: How Unwanted and Recurrent Thoughts Can Perturbate the Purchasing Behavior," *Advances in Consumer Research* 37, 1-6.

35. Lee, A. Y., and B. Sternthal (1999), "The Effects of Positive Mood on Memory," *Journal of Consumer Research*, 26, 115-127.

36. McFerran, B., D. W. Dahl, G. J. Fitzsimons and A. C. Morales (2010), "Might an Overweight Waitress Make You Eat More? How the Body Type of Others is Sufficient to Alter our Food Consumption," *Journal of Consumer Psychology* 20, 146-151.

37. Fisher, R.J. and L. Dubé, (2005), "Gender Differences in Responses to Emotional Advertising: A Social Desirability Perspective," *Journal of Consumer Research*, 31, 850-858.

38. Chaplin, L.N. and T.M. Lowrey (2009), "The Development of Consumer-Based Consumption Constellations in Children," *Journal of Consumer Research*, 36 (February), 757-777.

39. Moore, R.S. (2005), "The Sociological Impact of Attitudes Toward Smoking: Secondary Effects of the Demarketing of Smoking," *The Journal of Social Psychology*, 145, 703-718.

40. Celsi and Olson (1988), "The Role of Involvement in Attention and Comprehension Processes," *Journal of Consumer Research* 15 (September), 210-224.

41. Saegert, J. (1979), "A Demonstration of Levels of Processing Theory in Memory for Advertisements," *Advances in Consumer Research* 6, 82-84.

## Chapter 5

1. Childers, T.L., C.L. Carr, J. Peck, and S. Carson (2001), "Hedonic and Utilitarian Motivations for Online Retail Shopping

Behavior," *Journal of Retailing* 77 (Winter), 511–535.

2. Laurent, G., and J.N. Kapferer (1985), "Measuring Consumer Involvement Profiles," *Journal of Marketing Research* 22 (February), 41–53.

3. Howard, D.J., and R.A. Kerin (2006), "Broadening the Scope of Reference Price Advertising Research: A Field Study of Shopping Involvement," *Journal of Marketing* 70 (October), 185–204.

4. Kim, H., K. Park, and N. Schwarz (2010), "Will This Trip Be Exciting? The Role of Incidental Emotions in Product Evaluations," *Journal of Consumer Research* 36 (April), 983–991.

5. Plutchik, R. (2003), *Emotions and Life: Perspectives from Psychology, Biology and Evolution*, Washington DC: American Psychological Association.

6. Fonberg, E. (1986), "Amygdala: Emotions, Motivation, and Depressive States," in *Emotion: Theory, Research, and Experience*, R. Plutchik et al., eds., New York: Kluwer Press, 302.

7. Babin, B. J., W. R. Darden, and L. A. Babin (1998), "Negative Emotions in Marketing Research: Affect of Artifact?" *Journal of Business Research* 42, 271–285. Russell, J. A., and J. Snodgrass (1987), "Emotion and the Environment," in *Environment and Psychology*, D. Stokols and I. Altman, eds., New York: John Wiley and Sons, 245–280.

8. Saini, R. and S. C. Thota (2010), "The Psychological Underpinnings of Relative Thinking in Price Comparisons," *Journal of Consumer Psychology* 20, 185–192.

9. Watson, L., and M. Spencer (2007), "Causes and Consequences of Emotions on Consumer Behaviour: A Review and Integrative Cognitive Appraisal Theory," *European Journal of Marketing* 41, 487–511; Stephens, N., and K. Gwinner (1998), "Why Don't Some People Complain: A Cognitive-Emotive Process Model of Consumer Behavior," *Journal of the Academy of Marketing Science* 26, 172–189.

10. Brennan, L. and W. Binney (2010), "Fear, Guilt and Shame Appeals in Social Marketing," *Journal of Business Research* 62, 140–146.

11. Zourrig, H., J.C. Chebat and R. Toffoli (2009), "Consumer Revenge Behavior: A Cross-Cultural Perspective," *Journal of Business Research* 62, 995–1001.

12. Babin, B.J., and W.R. Darden (1996), "Good and Bad Shopping Vibes: Spending and Patronage Satisfaction," *Journal of Business Research* 35, 201–206.

13. Pucinelli, N.M. (2006), "Putting Your Best Foot Forward: The Impact of Customer Mood on Salesperson Evaluation," *Journal of Consumer Psychology* 16, 156–162.

14. Raghunathan, R., and J.R. Irwin (2001), "Walking the Hedonic Product Treadmill: Default Contrast and Mood-Based Assimilation in Judgments of Predicted Happiness with a Target Product," *Journal of Consumer Research* 28 (December), 355–368.

15. Cialdini, R. B. and D. T. Kenrick (1976), "Altruism as Hedonism: A Social Development Perspective on the Relationship of Negative Mood State and Helping," *Journal of Personality and Social Psychology* 34, 907–914.

16. Raghubir, P. (2006)"An Information Processing View of the Subjective Value of Money and Prices," *Journal of Business Research* 59, 1053–1062.

17. See Karolein, P., and S. Dewitte (2006), "How to Capture the Heart? Twenty Years of Emotion Measurement in Advertisement," *Journal of Advertising* 46, 18–37.

18. For an overview, see Drake, R.A., and L.R. Myers (2006), "Visual Attention, Emotion, and Action Tendency: Feeling Active or Passive," *Cognition and Emotion* 20, 608–622.

19. Russell, J.A., and G. Pratt (1979), "Affect Space is Bipolar," *Journal of Personality and Social Psychology* 37, 1161–1178; Babin et al. (1998).

20. Havlena, W.J., and M.B. Holbrook (1986), "The Varieties of Consumption Experience: Comparing Two Typologies of Emotion in Consumer Behavior," *Journal of Consumer Research* 13, 97–112. Kottasz, R. (2006), "Understanding the Influences of Atmospheric Cues on the Emotional Responses and Behaviours of Museum Visitors," *Journal of Nonprofit & Public Sector Marketing* 16, 95-121.

21. White, C., and Y. Yi-Ting (2005), "Satisfaction Emotions and Consumer Behavioral Intentions," *Journal of Services Marketing* 19, 411–420; Chebat, J.C., and W. Sluszrczyk (2005), "How Emotions Mediate the Effects of Perceived Justice on Loyalty in Service Recovery Situation: An Empirical Study," *Journal of Business Research* 56, 664–673.

22. Moorradian, T.A., and J.M. Oliver (1997), "I Can't Get No Satisfaction: The Impact of Personality and Emotion on Postpurchase Processes," *Psychology & Marketing* 14, 379–393.

23. Mascarenhas, O., R. Kesavan, and M. Bernacchi (2006), "Lasting Customer Loyalty: A Total Customer Experience Approach," *Journal of Consumer Marketing* 23, 397–405.

24. Hiam, A. (2000), "Match Premiums to Marketing Strategies," *Marketing News,* 34 (20), 12.

25. Hoffman, D. L. and T. P. Novak (2009), "Flow Online: Lessons Learned and Future Prospects," *Journal of Interactive Marketing* 23, 23–24.

26. Chou, T.J., and C.C. Ting (2003), "The Role of *Flow* Experience in Cyber-Game Addiction," *Cyber Psychology & Behavior* 6, 663–675.

27. Cohen, E. (2009), "Five Clues That You Are Addicted to Facebook," cnnhealth. com, **http://www.cnn.com/2009/ HEALTH/04/23/ep.facebook.addict/ index.html,** accessed July 28, 2010.

28. Sénécal, Sylvain, J.E. Gharbi, and J. Nantel (2002), "The Influence of Flow on Utilitarian and Hedonic Shopping Values," *Advances in Consumer Research* 29, 483–484.

29. Smith, Donnavieve N., and K. Sivakumar (2004), "Flow and Internet Shopping Behavior," *Journal of Business Research* 57, 1199–1208.

30. Dailey, L. (2004), "Navigational Web Atmospherics: Explaining the Influence of Restrictive Navigation Cues," *Journal of Business Research* 57, 795–803.

31. Gottman J.M., and R.W. Leveson (1992), "Emotional Suppression: Physiology, Self-Report, and Expressive Behavior," *Journal of Personality and Social Psychology* 64 (April), 970–986.

32. Gross, J.J., and O.P. John (1997), "Revealing Feelings: Facets of Emotional Expressivity in Self-Reports, Peer Ratings, and Behavior," *Journal of Personality and Social Psychology* 72 (February), 435–448.

33. Particularly when the emotions are consistent with the sex-role expectations of the female social schema. Social schemata are discussed in a later chapter.

34. Taute, H.A., B.A. Huhmann, R. Thakur (2010), "Emotional Information Management: Concept Development and Measurement in Public Service Announcements," *Psychology & Marketing* 27 (May), 417–444.

35. Rozell, E.J., C.E. Pettijohn, and R.S. Parker (2006), "Emotional Intelligence and Dispositional Affectivity as Predictors of Performance in Salespeople," *Journal of Marketing Theory and Practice* 14, 113–124.

36. Chang, J. (2003), "Born to Sell?" *Sales & Marketing Management* 155, 34–39.

37. Ferré, P. (2003), "Effects of Level of Processing on Memory for Affectively Valenced Words," *Cognition and Emotion* 17, 859–880, quotation taken from p. 859.

38. Baird, Thomas R., R.G. Wahlers, and C.K. Cooper (2007), "Non Recognition of Print Advertising: Emotion Arousal and Gender Effects," *Journal of Marketing Communications* 13, 39–57.

39. White, K. and C. McFarland (2009), "When Are Moods Likely to Influence Consumers' Product Preferences? The Role of Mood Focus and Perceived Relevance of Moods," *Journal of Consumer Psychology* 19, 526–536. Merchant. A., J.B.Ford and G. Rose (2010), "How Personal Nostalgia Influences Giving to Charity," *Journal of Business Research*, in press, doi.10.1016/j.busres2010.06.013.

40. Forgas, J.P., and J. Ciarrochi (2001), "On Being Happy and Possessive: The Interactive Effects of Mood and Personality on Consumer Judgments, *Psychology & Marketing*, 239–260.

41. Sierra, J.J., and S. McQuitty (2007), "Attitudes and Emotions as Determinants of Nostalgic Purchases: An Application of Social Identity Theory, *Journal of Marketing Theory and Practice* 15, 99–112.

42. Schema adapted from Babin, B.J., J.S. Boles, and W.R. Darden (1995), "Salesperson Stereotypes, Consumer Emotions, and Their Impact on Information Processing," *Journal of the Academy of Marketing Science* 23, 94–105.

43. Proyer, R.T., T. Platt, W. Ruch (2010), "Self-Conscious Emotions and Ridicule: Shameful Gelotophobes and Guilt Free Katagelasticists," *Personality and Individual Differences* 49, 54–58. Brennan and Binney (2010). Lau-Gesk, L. and A. Drolet (2008), "The Publicly Self-Conscious Consumer: Prepared to be Embarrassed," *Journal of Consumer Psychology* 18, 127–136.

44. Gountas, S.M., T. Ewing and J.L. Gountas (2007), "Testing Airline Passengers' Responses to Flight Attendants' Expressive Displays: The Effects of Positive Affect," *Journal of Business Research* 60, 81–83. Hennig-Thurau, T., M. Groth, P. Michael and D.D. Gremier (2006), "Are All Smiles Created Equal? How Emotional Contagion and Emotional Labor Affect Service Relationships," *Journal of Marketing* 70, 58–73.

45. Argo, J.L., D.W. Dahl and A.C. Morales (2008), "Positive Consumer Contagion: Responses to Attractive Others in a Retail Context," *Journal of Marketing Research* 45 (December), 690–701.

## Chapter 6

1. For a discussion of individual difference variables in consumer research and marketing practice, see Mowen, John C. (2000), *The 3M Model of Motivation and Personality: Theory and Empirical Applications to Consumer Behavior*, Boston, Kluwer Academic Publishers.

2. This definition is based on a number of different sources in personality psychology literature, including Allport, G. W. (1961), *Pattern and Growth in Personality*, New York, Holt, Rinehart, and Winston; Pervin, L. A., and O. P. John (1977), *Personality Theory and Research*, New York, John Wiley & Sons; Brody, Nathan, and Howard Ehrlichman (1998), *Personality Psychology: The Science of Individuality*, Upper Saddle River, NJ, Prentice Hall; Mowen (2000).

3. Angleitner, Alois (1991), "Personality Psychology: Trends and Developments," *European Journal of Personality* 5, 185–197.

4. A discussion of the debate regarding personality and behavioral consistency across situations may be found in Mischel, W., and P. K. Peake (1983), "Some Facets of Consistency: Replies to Epstein, Funder, and Bem," *Psychological Review* 89, 394–402; Epstein, S. (1983), "The Stability of Confusion: A Reply to Mischel and Peake," *Psychological Review* 90, 179–194; Buss, David (1989), "Personality as Traits," *American Psychologist* 44, 1378–1388.

5. For a discussion of psychoanalytical theory and applications to marketing, see Kassarjian, Harold H. (1971), "Personality and Consumer Behavior: A Review," *Journal of Marketing Research* 8 (November), 409–418. Also see Kassarjian, Harold H., and Mary Jane Sheffet (1991), "Personality and Consumer Behavior: An Update," in *Perspectives in Consumer Behavior,* 4th ed., Harold H. Kassarjian and Thomas S. Robertson, eds., Upper Saddle River NJ, Prentice Hall, 81–303. For a general description of the psychoanalytical approach in psychology, see Brody, Nathan, and Ehrlichman (1998).

6. Interesting examples of the early use of these motivational techniques can be found in Gustafson, Philip (1958), "You Can Gauge Customers' Wants," *Nation's Business* 49 (April), 76–84.

7. Kassarjian, Harold H. (1971), "Personality and Consumer Behavior," *Journal of Marketing Research* 8 (November), 409–418.

8. Brody, Nathan, and Ehrlichman (1998).

9. Buss, David (1989).

10. Allport, G. W., and H. S. Odbert (1936), "Trait Names," *Psychological Monographs* 47 (211), 1–37.

11. Lichtenstein, Donald R., Richard G. Netemeyer, and Scot Burton (1990), "Distinguishing Coupon Proneness from Value Consciousness: An Acquisition-Transaction Utility Theory Perspective," *Journal of Marketing* 54 (3), 54–67.

12. Belk, Russell W. (1985), "Materialism: Trait Aspects of Living in the Material World," *Journal of Consumer Research*, 12 (3) (December), 265–280.

13. Richins, Marsha L. (1994), "Special Possessions and the Expression of Material Values," *Journal of Consumer Research*, 21 (3) (December), 522–533; Belk (1985).

14. Rindfleisch, Aric, James E. Burroughs, and Nancy Wong (2009), "The Safety of Objects: Materialism, Existential Insecurity, and Brand Connection," *Journal of Consumer Research* 36 (June), 1–16.

15. Tian, Kelly, and Russell W. Belk (2005), "Extended Self and Possessions in the Workplace," *Journal of Consumer Research* 32 (2) (September), 297–310.

16. Wallendorf, Melanie, and Eric J. Arnould (1988), "My Favorite Things: A Cross-Cultural Inquiry into Object Attachment, Possessiveness, and Social Linkage," *Journal of Consumer Research*, 14 (4) (March), 531–547.

17. Belk (1985).

18. Graham, Judy F. (1999), "Materialism and Consumer Behavior: Toward a Clearer Understanding," *Journal of Social Behavior & Personality* 14 (2) (June), 241–259; Loftus, Mary (2004), "Till Debt Do Us Part," *Psychology Today* 37 (6) (November/December), 42–50.

19. Lastovicka, John L., Lance A. Bettencourt, Renee Shaw Hughner, and Ronald J. Kuntze (1999), "Lifestyle of the Tight and Frugal: Theory and Measurement," *Journal of Consumer Research* 26 (1) (June), 85–98.

20. This definition is based on the works of Midgley, David F., and Grahame R. Dowling (1978), "Innovativeness: The Concept and Its Measurement," *Journal of Consumer Research*, 229–242; Rogers, Everett M., and Floyd F. Shoemaker (1971), *Communication of Innovations*, New York, The Free Press.

21. Hartman, Jonathan B., Kenneth C. Gerht, and Kittichai Watchravesringkan (2004), "Re-Examination of the Concept of Innovativeness in the Context of the Adolescent Segment: Development of a Measurement Scale," *Journal of Targeting, Measurement and Analysis for Marketing* 12, 353–366; Wood, Stacy L., and Joffre Swait (2002), "Psychological Indicators of Innovation Adoption: Cross-Classification Based on Need for Cognition and Need for Change," *Journal of Consumer Psychology* 12, 1–13; Goldsmith, Ronald E., and Charles E. Hofacker (1991), "Measuring Consumer Innovativeness," *Journal of the Academy of Marketing Science* 19, 209–221; Venkatraman, Meera A. (1991), "The Impact of Innovativeness and Innovation Type on Product Adoption," *Journal of Retailing* 67, 51–67.

22. Hirunyawipada, Tanawat, and Audhesh K. Paswan (2006), "Consumer Innovativeness and Perceived Risk: Implications for High Technology Product Adoption," *Journal of Consumer Marketing* 23/24, 182–198; Hirschman, Elizabeth C. (1980), "Innovativeness, Novelty Seeking, and Consumer Creativity," *Journal of Consumer Research* 7, 283–295; Manning, Kenneth C., William O. Bearden, and Thomas J. Madden (1995), "Consumer Innovativeness and the Adoption Process," *Journal of Consumer Psychology* 4, 329–345; Citrin, A. V., D. E. Sprott, S. N. Silverman, and D. E. Stem (2000), "Adoption of Internet Shopping: The Role of Consumer Innovativeness," *Industrial Management & Data Systems* 100, 294–300.

23. Cacioppo, John and Richard Petty (1982), "The Need for Cognition," *Journal of Personality and Social Psychology* 42 (January), 116–131.

24. Haugtvedt, Curt, Richard Petty, John Cacioppo, and Theresa Steidley (1988), "Personality and Ad Effectiveness: Exploring the Utility of Need for Cognition," in *Advances in Consumer Research*, Vol. 15, Michael Houston, ed., (Provo, UT: Association for Consumer Research), 209–212.

25. Zhang, Yong (1996), "Responses to Humorous Advertising: The Moderating Effect of Need for Cognition," *Journal of Advertising* 25 (1), 15–31.

26. Putrevu, Sanjay (2008), "Consumer Responses Toward Sexual and Nonsexual Appeals: The Influence of Involvement, Need for Cognition, and Gender," *Journal of Advertising* 37 (2), 57–70.

27. Mowen, John C., (2004), "Exploring the Trait of Competitiveness and Its Consumer Behavior Consequences," *Journal of Consumer Psychology* 14, 52–63.

28. Cialdini, Robert B., Richard J. Borden, Avril Thorne, Marcus R. Walker, Stephen Freeman, and Lloyd R. Sloan (1976), "Basking in Reflected Glory: Three (Football) Field Studies," *Journal of Personality and Social Psychology* 34 (3), 366–375.

29. Pons, Frank, and Mehdi Mourali (2006), "Consumer Orientation Toward Sporting Events," *Journal of Service Research* 8 (3) (February), 276–287.

30. A number of researchers have contributed to the development of the Five-Factor Model. For example, see Costa, P. T., and R. R. McCrae (1985), *The NEO Personality Inventory Manual*, Odessa, FL, Psychological Assessment Resources; Goldberg, L. R. (1992), "The Development of Matters for the Big-Five Factor Structure," *Psychological Assessment* 4, 26–42; Wiggins, J. S. (1996), *The Five-Factor Model of Personality*, New York, Guilford Press.

31. Harris, Eric G., and John C. Mowen (2001), "The Influence of Cardinal, Central-, and Surface-Level Personality Traits on Consumers' Bargaining and Complaining Behaviors," *Psychology & Marketing*, (November), 18 (11) (November), 1150–1185; Harris, Eric G., and David E. Fleming (2005), "Assessing the Human Element in Service Personality Formation: Personality Congruency and the Five Factor Model," *Journal of Services Marketing* 19 (4), 187–198; Mowen, John C., and Nancy Spears (1999), "Understanding Compulsive Buying Among College Students," *Journal of Consumer Psychology* 8 (4), 407–430; Finn, Seth (1997), "Origins of Media Exposure: Linking Personality Traits to TV, Radio, Print, and Film Use," *Communication Research* 24 (5) (October), 507–530; Fraj, Elena, and Eva Martinez (2006), "Influence of Personality on Ecological Consumer Behaviour," *Journal of Consumer Behaviour* 5, 167–181.

32. Notable works in this area include Eysenck, H. J. (1947), *Dimensions of Personality*, London, Routledge & Kegan Paul; Allport, G. W. (1961), *Pattern and Growth in Personality*, New York, Holt, Rinehart, and Winston; Paunonen, S. V. (1998), "Hierarchical Organization of Personality and Prediction of Behavior," *Journal of Personality and Social Psychology* 74, 538–556; Mowen (2000).

33. This section is based on a number of sources that have discussed problems with the trait approach in consumer behavior including Kassarjian, Harold H. (1971), "Personality and Consumer Behavior: A Review," *Journal of Marketing Research* 8 (November), 409–418; Kassarjian and Sheffet (1991); Lastovicka, John L., and Eric A. Joachimsthaler (1988), "Improving the Detection of Personality-Behavior Relationships," *Journal of Consumer Research* 14 (4) (March): 583–587; Mowen (2000).

34. Baumgartner, Hans (2002), "Toward a Personology of the Consumer," *Journal of Consumer Research* 29 (2) (September), 286–292; also McAdams, Dan P. (1996), "Personality, Modernity, and the Storied Self: A Contemporary Framework for Studying Persons," *Psychological Inquiry* 7 (4), 295–321.

35. Aaker, Jennifer (1997), "Dimensions of Brand Personality," *Journal of Marketing Research* 34 (3) (August), 347–356.

36. Gwinner, K. P., and J. Eaton (1999), "Building Brand Image Through Event Sponsorship: The Role of Image Transfer, *Journal of Advertising* 38, 47–57.

37. Swaminathan, Vanitha, Karen M. Stilley, and Rohini Ahluwalia (2009), "When

Brand Personality Matters: The Moderating Role of Attachment Styles," *Journal of Consumer Research* 35 (April), 985–1002.

38. Aaker, David A. (1996), *Building Strong Brands*, New York, Free Press; also online content retrieved at: **http://www.gsb.standford.edu/news/research/mktg_good-brands.shtml,** accessed May 24, 2010.

39. This section based on Aaker (1996).

40. Fournier, Susan (1998), "Consumers and Their Brands: Developing Relationship Theory in Consumer Research," *Journal of Consumer Research* (March), 343–373; Aaker, Jennifer, Susan Fournier, and S. Adam Brasel (2004), "When Good Brands Do Bad," *Journal of Consumer Research* (June), 1–16.

41. Fournier (1998).

42. Harris, Eric G., and David E. Fleming (2005), "Assessing the Human Element in Services Personality Formation: Personality Congruency and The Five-Factor Model," *Journal of Services Marketing* 19, 187–198.

43. This information from: **www.harleydavidson.com,** accessed February 25, 2008.

44. Aaker, Fournier, and Brasel (2004).

45. Darden, W. R., and D. Ashton (1974), "Psychographics Profiles of Patronage Preference Groups," *Journal of Retailing* 50 (Winter), 99–112.

46. Lazer, W. (1963), "Lifestyle Concepts and Marketing," in S. Greyer (ed.), *Towards Scientific Marketing*, Chicago, American Marketing Association.

47. Lawson, Rob, and Sarah Todd (2002), "Consumer Lifestyles: A Social Stratification Perspective," *Marketing Theory* 2, 295–307.

48. Gonzalez, Ana M., and Laurentino Bello (2002), "The Construct 'Lifestyle' in Market Segmentation: The Behaviour of Tourist Consumers," *European Journal of Marketing* 36, 51–85.

49. Benezra, Karen (1998), "The Fragging of the American Mind," *Brandweek* (June), S12–S19.

50. Johnson, Trent, and Johan Bruwer (2003), "An Empirical Confirmation of Win-Related Lifestyle Segments in the Australian Wine Market," *International Journal of Wine Marketing* 15, 5–33.

51. Taylor, A. (1995), "Porsche Slices Up its Buyers," *Fortune* (January 16), 24.

52. Online content retrieved at Natural Marketing Institute website, **www.nmisolutions.com/lohasd_segment.html,** accessed May 24, 2010.

53. This section based on information obtained on the SBI International website, **http://www.strategicbusinessinsights.com/vals/presurvey.shtml,** accessed May 25, 2010.

54. This information based on materials found at **http://enus.nielsen.com/tab/product_families/nielsen_claritas/prizm,** accessed May 25, 2010.

55. Ridgeway, Cecilia L., and Henry A. Walker (1995), "Status Structures," in *Sociological Perspectives on Social Psychology,* Karen S. Cook, Gary A. Fine, and James S. House, eds., Boston, Allyn and Bacon, 281–310.

56. Mead, George H. (1934), *Mind, Self and Society*, Chicago, University of Chicago Press; Mick, David Glen (1986), "Consumer Research and Semiotics: Exploring the Morphology of Signs, Symbols, and Significance," *Journal of Consumer Research* 13 (2) (September), 196–213; Holbrook, Morris B. (2001), "The Millennial Consumer in the Texts of Our Times: Exhibitionism," *Journal of Macromarketing* 21, 81–95; Chaudhuri, Himadri Roy, and Sitanath Majumdar (2006), "Of Diamonds and Desires: Understanding Conspicuous

Consumption from a Contemporary Marketing Perspective," *Academy of Marketing Science Review,* (2006), 1.

57. See also Schau, Hope Jensen, and Mary Gilly (2003), "We Are What We Post? Self-Presentation in Personal Web Space," *Journal of Consumer Research* 30 (3) (December), 385–404; Trammell, Kaye D., and Ana Keshelashvili (2005), "Examining the New Influencers: A Self-Presentation Study of A-List Blogs," *Journalism and Mass Communication Quarterly* 82 (4) (Winter), 82, (4), 968–983.

58. Aaker, Jennifer (1999), "The Malleable Self: The Role of Self-Expression in Persuasion," *Journal of Marketing Research* 36 (1) (February), 45–57.

59. These concepts based on Sirgy, M. Joseph (1982), "Self-Concept in Consumer Behavior: A Critical Review," *Journal of Consumer Research* 9 (3) (December), 287–300; Belk, Russell (1988), "Possessions and the Extended Self," *Journal of Consumer Research* 15 (2) (September), 15 (2), 139–168.

60. Ahuvia, Aaron C. (2005), "Beyond the Extended Self: Loved Objects and Consumers' Identity Narratives," *Journal of Consumer Research* 32 (1) (June), 171–184; Escalas, Jennifer, and James R. Bettman (2005), "Self-Construal, Reference Groups, and Brand Meaning," *Journal of Consumer Research* 32 (3) (December), 378–389.

61. Chaplin, Lon Nguyen, and Debrah Roedder John (2005), "The Development of Self-Brand Connections in Children and Adolescents," *Journal of Consumer Research* 32 (1) (June), 119–130.

62. Smeesters, Dirk, and Naomi Mandel (2006), "Positive and Negative Media Image Effects on the Self," *Journal of Consumer Research* 32 (4) (March), 576–582; Richins, Marsha (1991), "Social Comparison and the Idealized Images of Advertising," *Journal of Consumer Research* 18 (1) (June), 71–83; Grogan, Sarah (1999), *Understanding Body Dissatisfaction in Men, Women, and Children*, London, Routledge.

63. Tan, Cheryl Lu-Lien (2007), "Fashion Group Sets Guides to Rein in Ultra-Thin Models," *The Wall Street Journal* (January 8), B4.

64. Keim, Brandon (2006), "Media Messes with Mens' Minds Too," *Psychology Today* 39 (5) (September/October), 26.

65. Hafner, Michael (2004), "How Dissimilar Others May Still Resemble the Self: Assimilation and Contrast After Social Comparison," *Journal of Consumer Psychology* 14, 187–196.

66. Online content retrieved at The American Society for Aesthetic Plastic Surgery website, **http://www.surgery.org/media/news-releases/despite-recession-overall-plastic-surgery-demand-drops-only-2-percent-from-last-year,** accessed May 25, 2010.

67. Bui, Eric, Rachel Rodgers, Lionel Cailhol, Phillippe Birmes, Henri Chabrol, and Laurent Schmitt (2010), "Body Piercing and Psychopathology: A Review of the Literature," *Psychotherapy and Psychosomatics* 79: 125–129.

68. Brumberg, Joan Jacobs (2006), "Are We Facing an Epidemic of Self-Injury?" *Chronicle of Higher Education* 53, B6–B8.

69. Braithwaite, R., A. Robillard, T. Woodring, T. Stephens, and K. J. Arriola (2001), "Tattooing and Body Piercing Among Adolescent Detainees: Relationship to Alcohol and Other Drug Use," *Journal of Substance Abuse* 13, 5–16; Grief, J., and W. Hewitt (1998), "The Living Canvas: Health Issues in Tattooing, Body Piercing, and Branding,"

*Advances for Nurse Practitioners* 12, 26–31; Roberti, Jonathon W., and Eric A. Storch (2005), "Psychosocial Adjustment of College Students With Tattoos and Piercings," *Journal of College Counseling* 8 (1) (Spring), 14–19.

70. Totten, Jeff W., Thomas J. Lipscomb, and Michael A. Jones (2009), "Attitudes Toward and Stereotypes of Persons With Body Art: Implications for Marketing Management," *Academy of Marketing Studies Journal* 13 (2): 77–96.

71. Sirgy, M. Joseph, Dhruv Grewal, Tamara Mangleburg, and Jae-ok Park (1997), "Assessing the Predictive Validity of Two Methods of Measuring Self-Image Congruence," *Journal of the Academy of Marketing Science* 25 (3) (Summer), 229–241.

72. Sirgy, M. Joseph, and A. Coskun Samli (1985), "A Path Analytic Model of Store Loyalty Involving Self-Concept, Store Image, Geographic Loyalty, and Socioeconomic Status," *Journal of the Academy of Marketing Science* 13 (3) (Summer), 13 (3), 265–291.

73. Aaker (1999), 47.

74. Landon, E. Laird (1974), "Self Concept, Ideal Self Concept, and Consumer Purchase Intentions," *Journal of Consumer Research* 1 (2) (September), 44–51.

Chapter 7

1. This definition is based on a summary of several works in the social psychology and consumer behavior literatures, including Eagly, Alice, and Shelly Chaiken (1993), *The Psychology of Attitudes*, New York, Harcourt Brace; Cacioppo, John, Stephen Harkins, and Richard Petty (1981), "The Nature of Attitudes and Cognitive Responses and Their Relations to Behavior," in *Cognitive Responses in Persuasion*, Richard Petty, Thomas Ostrom, and Timothy C. Brock, eds., Hillsdale, NJ: Lawrence Erlbaum; Thurstone L. L. (1931), "The Measurement of Social Attitudes," in *Readings in Attitude Theory and Measurement*, M. Fishbein ed., New York, Wiley.

2. The information in this section is based on Katz, Daniel (1960), "The Functional Approach to the Study of Attitudes," *Public Opinion Quarterly* 24 (2), 163–204.

3. Gibson, Heather, Cynthia Willming, and Andrew Holdnak (2003), "We're Gators... Not Just Gator Fans: Serious Leisure and University of Florida Football," *Journal of Leisure Research* 34 (4), 397–425.

4. Ray, Michael (1973), "Marketing Communications and the Hierarchy-of-Effects," in *New Models for Mass Communications*, P. Clarke, ed., Beverly Hills, CA, Sage, 147–176.

5. Krugman, Herbert (1965), "The Impact of Television Advertising: Learning Without Involvement," *Public Opinion Quarterly* 29 (Fall), 349–356.

6. A recent example of the experiential nature of consumption may be found in Belk, Russell, Guliz Ger, and Soren Askegaard (2003), "The Fire of Desire: A Multisited Inquiry into Consumer Passion," *Journal of Consumer Research* 30 (3), 326–351.

7. Fishbein, Martin, and Icek Ajzen (1975). *Belief, Attitude, Intention, and Behavior: An Introduction to Theory and Research*, Reading, MA, Addison-Wesley.

8. A number of researchers have addressed this issue, including Alwitt, Linda F., and Ida E. Berger (1992), "Understanding the Link Between Environmental Attitudes and Consumer Product Usage: Measuring the

Moderating Role of Attitude Strength," in *Advances in Consumer Research*, vol. 20, Leigh McAlister and Michael Rothschild, ed., Provo, UT, Association for Consumer Research, 189–194; Wicker, Allan (1969), "Attitudes versus Actions: The Relationship of Verbal and Overt Behavioral Responses to Attitude Objects," *Journal of Social Issues* 25 (Autumn), 41–78.

9. Ajzen, Icek, and Martin Fishbein (1977), "Attitude–Behavior Relations: A Theoretical Analysis and Review of Empirical Research," *Psychological Bulletin* 84 (5) (September), 888–918.

10. Ryan, Michael J., and E. H. Bonfield (1980), "Fishbein's Intentions Model: A Test of External and Pragmatic Validity," *Journal of Marketing* 44 (2), 82–95.

11. More on this model may be found in Notani, Art Sahni (1998), "Moderators of Perceived Behavioral Control's Predictiveness in the Theory of Reasoned Action," *Journal of Consumer Psychology* 7 (3), 247–271. Also, an interesting presentation of the planned behavior model applied to food choice may be found in Conner, Mark T. (1993), "Understanding Determinants of Food Choice: Contributions from Attitude Research," *British Food Journal* 95 (9), 27–32.

12. Mitchell, Andrew A. and Jerry Olson (1981), "Are Product Attribute Beliefs the Only Mediator of Advertising Effects on Brand Attitude?" *Journal of Marketing Research* 18, 318–332.

13. Several studies have approached this issue including Scott MacKenzie and Richard Lutz (1989), "An Empirical Examination of the Structural Antecedents of Attitude towards the Ad in an Advertising Pretesting Context," *Journal of Marketing* 53 (April), 48–65; Burton, Scot, and Donald Lichtenstein (1988), "The Effect of Ad Claims and Ad Context on Attitude towards the Advertisement," *Journal of Advertising* 17 (1), 3–11.

14. Brown, Tom J., and Peter A. Dacin (1997), "The Company and the Product: Corporate Associations and Consumer Product Responses," *Journal of Marketing* 61 (January), 68–84.

15. Sen, Sankar, and C.B. Bhattacharya (2001), "Does Doing Good Always Lead to Doing Better? Consumer Reactions to Corporate Social Responsibility," *Journal of Marketing Research* 38 (May), 225–243.

16. Petty, Richard E., John T. Cacioppo, and David Schuman (1983), "Central and Peripheral Routes to Advertising Effectiveness: The Moderating Role of Involvement," *Journal of Consumer Research* 10 (2), 135–146.

17. Celsi, Richard L., and Jerry C. Olson (1988), "The Role of Involvement in Attention and Comprehension Processes," *Journal of Consumer Research* 15 (2) (September), 210–224; MacInnis, Deborah J., and C. Whan Park (1991), "The Differential Role of Characteristics of Music on High- and Low-Involvement Consumers' Processing of Ads," *Journal of Consumer Research* 18 (2) (September), 161–173.

18. Heider, Fritz (1958), *The Psychology of Interpersonal Relations*, New York, John Wiley.

19. Russell, Cristel, and Barbara B. Stern (2006), "Consumers, Characters, and Products: A Balance Model of Sitcom Product Placement Effects," *Journal of Advertising* 35 (1), 7–21.

20. Woodside, Arch (2004), "Advancing Means-End Chains by Incorporating Heider's Balance Theory and Fournier's Consumer-Brand Relationship Typology," *Psychology & Marketing* 21 (4), 279–294.

21. Escalas, Jennifer Edson, and James R. Bettman (2005), "Self-Construal, Reference Groups, and Brand Meaning," *Journal of Consumer Research* 32 (3), 378–389.

22. Sherif, Muzafer, and Carl Hovland (1961), *Social Judgment: Assimilation and Contrast Effects in Communication and Attitude Change*, New Haven, CT, Yale University Press.

23. Hoffman, Donna L., and Thomas P. Novak (1996), "Marketing in Hypermedia Computer-Mediated Environments: Conceptual Foundations," *Journal of Marketing* 60 (3), 50–68.

24. This estimate based on information retrieved at **http://www.internetworldstats.com/stats.htm**, accessed May 28, 2010; also online content retrieved at **http://www.qwasi.com/news/tag/text-message-statistics**, accessed June 1, 2010; also online content retrieved at *New York Times* online edition, December 28, 2008, **http://www.nytimes.com/2008/12/28/technology/28iht-digi.1.18953204.html?_r=1**, accessed June 1, 2010.

25. Hoffman and Novak (1996).

26. Dudley, Sid C. (1999), "Consumer Attitudes Toward Nudity in Advertising," *Journal of Marketing Theory and Practice* 7 (4), 89–96.

27. LaTour, Michael S. (1990), "Female Nudity in Print Advertising: An Analysis of Gender Differences in Arousal and Ad Response," *Psychology & Marketing* 7 (1), 65–81.

28. Simpson, Penny M., Steve Horton, and Gene Brown (1996), "Male Nudity in Advertisements: A Modified Replication and Extension of Gender and Product Effects," *Journal of the Academy of Marketing Science* 24 (3), 257–262.

29. Huang, Ming-Hui (2004), "Romantic Love and Sex: Their Relationship and Impacts on Ad Attitudes," *Psychology & Marketing* 21 (1), 53–73.

30. Eisend, Martin (2009), "A Meta-Analysis of Humor in Advertising," *Journal of the Academy of Marketing Science* 37 (Summer), 191–203.

31. Krishnan, H. S., and D. Chakravarti (2003), "A Process Analysis of the Effects of Humorous Advertising Executions on Brand Claims Memory," *Journal of Consumer Psychology* 13 (3), 230–245.

32. Zhang, Yong (1996), "The Effect of Humor in Advertising: An Individual-Difference Perspective," *Psychology & Marketing* 13 (6), 531–545.

33. Cline, Thomas W., Moses B. Altsech, and James J. Kellaris (2003), "When Does Humor Enhance or Inhibit Ad Responses?" *Journal of Advertising* 32 (3), 31–46.

34. Chattopadhyay, Amitava (1990), "Humor in Advertising: The Moderating Role of Prior Brand Evaluations," *Journal of Marketing Research* 29 (November), 466–476.

35. Smith, Stephen M. (1993), "Does Humor in Advertising Enhance Systematic Processing," in *Advances in Consumer Research*, vol. 20, L. McAlister and M. Rothschild, eds., Provo, UT, Association of Consumer Research, 155–158.

36. LaTour, Michael S., and Herbert J. Rotfeld (1997), "There Are Threats and (Maybe) Fear-Caused Arousal: Theory and Confusions of Appeals to Fear and Fear Arousal Itself," *Journal of Advertising* 3 (Fall), 45–59.

37. Keller, Punam Anand, and Lauren Goldberg Block (1996), "Increasing the Persuasiveness of Fear Appeals: The Effect of Arousal and Elaboration," *Journal of Consumer Research* 22 (4), 448–459.

38. Mowen, John C., Eric G. Harris, and Sterling A. Bone (2004), "Personality Traits and Fear Response to Print Advertisements: Theory and an Empirical Study," *Psychology & Marketing* 21 (11), 927–943.

39. Potter, Robert F., Michael S. LaTour, Kathryn A. Braun-LaTour, and Tom Reichert (2006), "The Impact of Program Context on Motivational System Activation and Subsequent Effects on Processing a Fear Appeal," *Journal of Advertising* 35 (3): 67–80.

40. Tanner, John F., James B. Hunt, and David R. Eppright (1991), "The Protection Motivation Model: A Normative Model of Fear Appeals," *Journal of Marketing* 55 (3), 36–45.

41. Duke, Charles R., Gregory M. Pickett, Les Carlson, and Stephen J. Grove (1993), "A Method for Evaluating the Ethics of Fear Appeals," *Journal of Public Policy & Marketing* 1 (Spring), 120–130.

42. Sawyer, Alan G., and Daniel J. Howard (1991), "Effects of Omitting Conclusions in Advertisements to Involved and Uninvolved Audiences," *Journal of Marketing Research* 28 (November), 467–474.

43. Wilkie, William L., and Paul W. Ferris (1973), "Comparison Advertising: Problems and Potential," *Journal of Marketing* 39 (October), 7–15.

44. Miniard, Paul W., Michael J. Barone, Randall L. Rose, and Kenneth C. Manning (2006), "A Further Assessment of Indirect Advertising Claims of Superiority Overall All Competitors," *Journal of Advertising* 35 (4), 53–64.

45. Stewart, Dennis D., Cheryl B. Stewart, Clare Tyson, Vinci Gail, and Tom Fioti (2004), "Serial Position Effects and the Picture-Superiority Effect in the Group Recall of Unshared Information," *Group Dynamics: Theory, Research, and Practice* 8 (3): 166–181.

46. Haugtvedt, Curtis P., and Duance T. Wegener (1994), "Message Order Effects in Persuasion: An Attitude Strength Perspective," *Journal of Consumer Research* 21 (June), 205–218.

47. Unnava, H. Rao, Robert E. Burnkrant, and Sunil Erevelles (1994), "Effects of Presentation Order and Communication Modality on Recall and Attitude," *Journal of Consumer Research* 21 (December), 481–490.

48. Li, Cong (2009), "Primacy Effect or Recency Effect? A Long-Term Memory Test of Super Bowl Commercials," *Journal of Consumer Behaviour* 9 (October): 32–44.

49. Jain, S. P., and S. S. Posavac (2001), "Prepurchase Attribute Verifiability, Source Credibility, and Persuasion," *Journal of Consumer Psychology* 11 (3), 169–180.

50. Homer, Pamela M., and Lynn R. Kahle (1990), "Source Expertise, Time of Source Identification, and Involvement in Persuasion," *Journal of Advertising* 19 (1), 30–39.

51. Nan, Xiaoli (2009), "The Influence of Source Credibility on Attitude Certainty: Exploring the Moderating Effects of Time of Source Identification and Individual Need for Cognition," *Psychology & Marketing* 26 (4): 321–332.

52. Wilson, Elizabeth, and Daniel L. Sherrell (1993), "Source Effects in Communication and Persuasion Research: A Meta-Analysis of Effect Size," *Journal of the Academy of Marketing Science* 21 (2), 101–112.

53. Wiener, Josh, and John C. Mowen (1985), "The Impact of Product Recalls on Consumer Perceptions," *The Journal of the Society of Consumer Affairs Professionals in Business* (Spring), 18–21.

54. Lafferty, Barbara A., Ronald E. Goldsmith, and Stephen J. Newell (2002), "The Dual Credibility Model: The Influence of Corporate and Endorser Credibility on Attitudes and Purchase Intention," *Journal of Marketing Theory & Practice* 10 (3), 1–12.

55. Till, Brian D., and Michael Busler (2000), "The Match-Up Hypothesis: Physical Attractiveness, Expertise, and the Role of Fit on Brand Attitude, Purchase Intent, and Brand Beliefs," *Journal of Advertising* 3 (Fall), 1–13; Chaiken, Shelly (1979), "Communicator Physical Attractiveness and Persuasion," *Journal of Personality and Social Psychology* 37 (August), 1387–1397.

56. Baker, Michael, and Gilbert Churchill (1977), "The Impact of Physically Attractive Models on Advertising Effectiveness," *Journal of Marketing Research* 14 (November), 538–555.

57. Kang, Yoon-Soon and Paul M. Herr (2006), "Beauty and the Beholder: Toward an Integrative Model of Communication Source Effects," *Journal of Consumer Research* 33 (1): 123–130.

58. Information gathered from Marketing Evaluations, Inc. website at: **http://www .qscores.com,** accessed May 28, 2010.

59. Reinhard, Marc-Andre and Matthias Messner (2009), "The Effects of Source Likeability and Need for Cognition on Advertising Effectiveness Under Explicit Persuasion," *Journal of Consumer Behaviour* 8 (4): 179–191.

60. Lynch, James and Drue Schuler (1994), "The Matchup Effect of Spokespersons and Product Congruency: A Schema Theory Interpretation," *Psychology & Marketing* 11 (September–October): 417–445; Kamins, Michael A. (1990), "An Investigation into the 'Match-Up' Hypothesis in Celebrity Advertising: When Beauty May Be Only Skin Deep," *Journal of Advertising* 19 (1): 4–13.

Case 2-1
1. "The First Can-Am Spyder Roadster Rolls Off the Assembly Line in Valcourt, Quebec" (2007), *Canadian Corporate News* (September 14), p. NA.

2. George, P. E. (2009),"How 3-Wheel Cars Work" **http://auto.howstuffworks.com/ three-wheel-car.htm/printable,** accessed October 3, 2010.

3. "The First Can-Am Spyder Roadster Rolls Off the Assembly Line in Valcourt, Quebec" (2007). **http://corp.brp.com/en-CA/ Media.Center/Press.Releases/1/20070914 .htm,** accessed October 3, 2010.

4. Thompson, S. (2007). "Another Spyder Spins an Intriguing Web," *Autoweek* 57 (13), 10.

5. Balona, Denise-Marie. (2008), "Three-wheel Bike: Can-Am Spyder Makes Waves at Daytona's Bike Week," *The Orlando Sentinel,* Fla., distributed by McClatchy-Tribune Information Services, (February 29), **http://articles.orlandosentinel.com/2008-02-29/news/spyder29_1_spyder-two-wheels-schmidt,** accessed October 8, 2010.

6. "An Intriguing Industry Question" (2007), *Powersports Business,* (March 12), 50–51.

7. Balona, Denise-Marie (2008).

8. "BRP Adds a Touring Model to its Can-Am Spyder Roadster Line-up" (2009), *PR Newswire* (September 2), p. NA.

9. "BRP Adds a Touring Model to its Can-Am Spyder Roadster Line-up" (2009).

Case 2-2
1. Belk, Russell (1996), "Hyperreality and Globalization: Culture in the Age of Ronald McDonald," in *Global Perspectives in Cross-Cultural and Cross-National Consumer Research,* L.A. Manrai and A.K. Manrai ed., Binghamton, NY: International Business Press, 23–28.

2. Lee, B (2004), "Plastic Surgery and Attitudes of Beauty and Success," *China Daily* (July 5), Retrieved from **http://www .chinadaily.com.cn,** accessed Sept. 8, 2010.

3. Dong, L and Kelly Tian (2009), "The Use of Western Brands in Asserting Chinese National Identity," *Journal of Consumer Research* 36 (October), 504–523.

4. McNeal, J. U and M. F. Ji. (1999), "Chinese Children as Consumers: An Analysis of Their New Product Information Resources," *Journal of Consumer Marketing* 16 (4), 345–365.

Case 2-3
1. For more information, go to the U.S. Department of Housing and Urban Development website at: **http://www.hud.gov/ offices/hsg/sfh/hecm/rmtopten.cfm).**

2. Stats taken from **http://www.hud.gov/ offices/hsg/sfh/hecm/rmtopten.cfm,** accessed September 20, 2010.

Case 2-4
1. Nielsen Three Screen Report. (Q4 2009).

2. Flint, Joe (2005), "Marketers Should Learn to Stop Worrying and Love the DVR," *The Wall Street Journal,* October 26, 2005.

3. Neff, Jack (2003), "TiVo Less of a Threat? Surprising P&G Findings," *AdAge.com,* March 17, 2003.

4. Rouwenhorst, Robert (2009) "Zipped Commercials, Zapped Memory? The Impact of Zipping on Attitude and Memory for Commercials," Unpublished PhD dissertation. University of Iowa.

5. Ang, Wee Hoon, Siew Meng Leong, and Wendy Yeo (1999), "When Silence is Golden: Effects of Silence on Consumer Ad Response," *Advances in Consumer Research* 26, 295–299.

6. Schacter, Daniel (1987), "Implicit Memory: History and Current Status," *Journal of Experimental Psychology: Learning, Memory, and Cognition* 13, 501–518.

7. Shapiro, Stewart and H. Shanker Krishnan (2001), "Memory-Based Measures for Assessing Advertising Effects: A Comparison of Explicit and Implicit Memory Effects," *Journal of Advertising* 30 (3), 1–13.

8. Tulving, Endel and Daniel L. Schacter (1990), "Priming and Human Memory Systems," *Science* 247, 301–306.

9. Bornstein, R.F., Leone, D.R., & Falley, D.J. (1987), "The Generalizability of Subliminal Mere Exposure Effects." *Journal of Personality and Social Psychology* 53, 1070–1079.

10. Fang, Xiang, Surendra Singh, and Rohini Ahluwalia (2007) "An Examination of Different Explanations for the Mere Exposure Effect," *Journal of Consumer Research* 34 (1), 97–103.

11. Grinne M. Fitzsimons, Tanya L. Chartrand and Gavan J. Fitzsimons (2008), "Automatic Effects of Brand Exposure on Motivated Behavior: How Apple Makes You 'Think Different'," *Journal of Consumer Research* 35 (1), 21–35.

12. See note 4 above.

## Chapter 8

1. McCracken, G. (1986), "Culture and Consumption: A Theoretical Account of the Structure and Movement of the Cultural Meaning of Consumer Goods," *Journal of Consumer Research* 13, 71–84.

2. Lenartowicz, T., and K. Roth (1999), "A Framework for Culture Assessment," *Journal of International Business Studies* 30, 781–798; Lenartowicz, T., and K. Roth (2001), "Culture Assessment Revisited: The Selection of Key Informants in IB Cross-Cultural Studies," 2001 Annual Meeting of the Academy of International Business.

3. Overby, J.W., R.B. Woodruff, and S.F. Gardial (2005), "The Influence of Culture on Consumers' Desired Value Perceptions: A Research Agenda," *Marketing Theory* 5 (June), 139–163.

4. See Hofstede, Geert (2010), **http://www.geert-hofstede.com/geert_hofstede_resources.shtml** for an overview, accessed August 3, 2010.

5. For a concise review of Hofstede's value dimensions, see Soares, A.M., M. Farhangmehr, and A. Shoham (2007), "Hofstede's Dimensions of Culture in International Marketing Studies," *Journal of Business Research* 60, 277–284.

6. Hirschman, E.C. (2003), "Men, Dogs, Guns and Cars," *Journal of Advertising* 32 (Spring), 9–22.

7. Petrova, P. K., R. B. Cialdini and S.J. Sills (2007), "Consistency-Based Compliance Across Cultures," *Journal of Experimental and Cosial Psychology* 43, 104–111.

8. Hofstede (2010).

9. Jung, J.M., and J.J. Kellaris (2006), "Responsiveness to Authority Appeals Among Young French and American Consumers," *Journal of Business Research* 59 (June), 735–744.

10. Jung, J.M., and J.J. Kellaris (2004), "Cross-National Difference in Proneness to Scarcity Effects: The Moderating Roles of Familiarity, Uncertainty Avoidance and Need for Cognitive Closure," *Psychology & Marketing* 21 (September), 739–753.

11. Erevelles, S., R. Abhik, and L. Yip (2001), "The Universality of the Signal Theory for Products and Services," *Journal of Business Research* 52 (May), 175–187.

12. Martin, D. (2010), "Uncovering Unconscious Memories and Myths for Understanding International Tourism Behavior," *Journal of Business Research* 63, 372–383. Mowen, J.C., X. Fang and K. Scott (2009), "A Hierarchical Model Approach for Identifying the Trait Antecedents of General Gambling Propensity and of Four Gambling-Related Genres," *Journal of Business Research* 62, 1262–1268.

13. Hofstede, G. (2001), *Culture's Consequences,* Thousand Oaks, CA: Sage Publications.

14. Keysuk, K., and C. Oh (2002), "On Distributor Commitment in Marketing Channels for Industrial Products: Contrast Between the United States and Japan," *Journal of International Marketing* 10, 72–107; Ryu, S., S. Kabadavi, and C. Chung (2007), "The Relationship Between Unilateral and Bilateral Control Mechanisms: The Contextual Effect of Long-Term Orientation," *Journal of Business Research* 60 (July), 681–689.

15. Hofstede (2001).

16. Wang, C.L. (2007), "Guanxi vs. Relationship Marketing: Exploring Underlying Differences," *Industrial Marketing Management* 36, 81–86.

17. Worthington, S. (2005), "Entering the Market for Financial Services in Transitional Economies," *International Journal of Bank Marketing* 23, 381–396.

18. Ren, X., S. Oh, and J. Noh (2010), "Managing Supplier-Retailer Relationships: From Institutional and Task Environment Perspectives," *Industrial Marketing Management* 39, 593–604.

19. Byrne, P.M. (2007), "Thinking Beyond BRIC," *Logistics Management* 46, 24–26.

20. For example, see Muller, T.E. (2000), "Targeting the CANZUS Baby-Boomer Explorer and Adventurer Market," *Journal of Vacation Marketing* 6, 154–169.

21. Laroche, M., Z. Yang, C. Kim, and M.O. Richard (2007), "How Culture Matters in Children's Purchase Influence: A Multi-Level Investigation," *Journal of the Academy of Marketing Science* 35 (Winter), 113–126.

22. Bokale, J. (2008), "Supermarkets Bolster Focus on Children's Ranges," *Marketing* (February 6), 1.
23. Chankon, K., M. Laroche, and M. Tomiuk (2004), "The Chinese in Canada: A Study of Ethnic Change with Emphasis on Gender Roles," *Journal of Social Psychology* 144 (February), 5–27.
24. Laroche, M., K. Chankon, M. Tomiuk, and D. Belisle (2005), "Similarities in Italian and Greek Multidimensional Ethnic Identity: Some Implications for Food Consumption," *Canadian Journal of Administrative Science* 22, 143–167.
25. Bristol, T., and T.F. Mangleburg (2005), "Not Telling the Whole Story: Teen Deception in Purchasing," *Journal of the Academy of Marketing Science* 33 (Winter), 79–95.
26. Bakir, A., G.M. Rose, and A. Shoham (2005), "Consumption Communication and Parental Control of Children's Viewing: A Multi-Rater Approach," *Journal of Marketing Theory and Practice* 13 (Spring), 47–58; Carlson, L., and S. Grossbart (1988), "Parental Style and consumer Socialization in Children," *Journal of Consumer Research* 15 (June), 77–94.
27. Miller, C., F. Bram, J. Reardon, and I. Vida (2006), "Teenagers' Response to Self- and Other-Directed Anti-Smoking Messages," *International Journal of Market Research* 49, 515–533.
28. Clark, A.E., and Y. Loheac (2007), "It Wasn't Me, It Was Them! Social Influence in Risky Behavior by Adolescents," *Journal of Health Economics* 26, 763–784; Kelly, K.J., M.D. Slater, and D. Karan (2002), "Image Advertisements' Influence on Adolescents' Perceptions of the Desirability of Beer and Cigarettes," *Journal of Public Policy & Marketing* 21 (Fall), 295–304.
29. Neeleman, S.E. (2010), "Firm Toots Horn Via Search," *The Wall Street Journal* (July 1), B1.
30. Mourali, M., M. Laroche, and F. Pons (2005), "Individual Orientation and Consumer Susceptibility to Interpersonal Influence," *Journal of Services Marketing* 19, 164–173.
31. Matilla, A.S., and P.G. Patterson (2004), "The Impact of Culture on Consumers' Perceptions of Service Recovery Efforts," *Journal of Retailing* 80, 196–207.
32. Fong, Mei (2007), "Tired of Laughter, Beijing Gets Rid of Bad Translations," *The Wall Street Journal* (February 5), A1.
33. See Griffin, Babin, and Modianas (2000).
34. Dallimore, K.S., B.A. Sparks, and K. Butcher (2007), "The Influence of Angry Customer Outbursts on Service Providers' Facial Displays and Affective States," *Journal of Services Marketing* 10 (August), 78–92.
35. Wang, L.A., J. Baker, J.A. Wagner, and K. Wakefield (2007), "Can a Retail Website Be Social?" *Journal of Marketing* 71 (July), 143–157; Qiu, L., and I. Bernbasat (2005), "Online Consumer Trust and Live Help Interfaces: The Effects of Text-to-Speech Voice and Three-Dimensional Avatars," *Journal of Human-Computer-Interaction* 19, 75–94.
36. Kramer, T., S. Spolter-Weisfeld, and M. Thakker (2007), "The Effect of Cultural Orientation on Consumer Responses to Personalization," *Marketing Science* 26 (March/April), 246–258.
37. Pigliasco, G.C. (2005), "Lost in Translation: From Omiyage to Souvenir: Beyond Aesthetics of the Japanese Ladies' Gaze in Hawaii," *Journal of Material Culture* 10 (July), 177–196.

38. Sheth, J.N. (2007) "Rise of Chindia and Its Impact on World Marketing," presented at the 2007 Academy of Marketing Science World Marketing Congress, Verona, Italy, July 13.
39. Strizhakova, Y., R.A. Coulter and L. Price (2008), "Branded Products as a Passport to Global Citizenship: Perspectives from Developed and Developing Countries," *Journal of International Marketing* 16 (4), 57–85.
40. Sheth (2007).
41. See www.transparency.org for an overview of culture and corruption around the world.

## Chapter 9

1. Beverland, M.B., F. Farrelly and P. G. Quester (2010), "Authentic Subcultural Membership: Antecedents and Consequences of Authenticating Acts and Authoritative Performances," *Psychology & Marketing* 27 (July), 608–716.
2. Berger, J. and C. Heath (2008), "Who Drives Divergence? Identity Signaling, Outgroup Similarity, and the Abandonment of Cultural Tastes," *Journal of Personality and Social Psychology* 95, 593–607.
3. http://itre.cis.upenn.edu/~myl/languagelog/archives/002663.html, accessed August 6, 2010.
4. Garreau, J. (1981), *The Nine Nations of North America*. New York: Avon.
5. Kahle, L.R. (1986), "The Nine Nations of North America and the Value Basis of Geographic Segmentation," *Journal of Marketing* 50 (April), 37–47.
6. Cutler, Blayne (1991), "Welcome to the Borderlands," *American Demographics* (February), 44–49, 57.
7. Guimond, S., S. Brunot, A. Chatard, D.M. Garcia, D. Martinot, N.R. Branscombe, M. Desert, S. Haque and V. Yzerbyt (2007), "Culture, Gender, and the Self: Variations and Impact of Social Comparison Processes," *Journal of Personality and Social Psychology* 92 (June), 1118–1134.
8. Sung, Y. and S.F. Tinkham (2005), "Brand Personality Structures in the United States and Korea: Common and Culture-Specific Factors," *Journal of Consumer Psychology* 15 (4), 334–350.
9. Ball, D. (2006), "Women in Italy Like to Clean but Shun the Quick and Easy," *The Wall Street Journal* (April 25), A1.
10. Bustillo, M. and M. E. Lloyd (2010), "Best Buy Seeks Female Shoppers," *The Wall Street Journal* (June 16), B5.
11. Smith, R. A. (2010), "Wanted: Guy Shoppes for Fashion Sites," *The Wall Street Journal* (July 22), B1.
12. Yoram, B.T. and M. Jarymowicz (2010), "The Effect of Gender on Cognitive Structuring: Who are more Biased, Men or Women?" *Psychology* 1, 80–87.
13. Statistics in this chapter are taken from the U.S. Census Bureau (www.census.gov) or the CIA Factbook (www.cia.com).
14. Lueg, J.E., and R.Z. Finney (2007), "Interpersonal Communication in the Consumer Socialization Process: Scale Development and Validation," *Journal of marketing Theory and Practice* 15 (Winter), 25–39.
15. Business Wire (1999), "International Survey Shows That Coca-Cola and McDonald's are Teenagers' Favorite Brands," (February 8), www.encyclopedia.com/printable.aspx?id=1G1:53724844, accessed August 18, 2007.
16. Devaney, P. (2007), "Coca-Cola to Launch on Virtual World Second Life," *Marketing Week* (February 19), 6.

17. Muk, A., and B.J. Babin (2006), "U.S. Consumers Adoption-Non-Adoption of Mobile SMS Advertising," *Journal of Mobile Marketing* 1 (June), 21–29.
18. "Global Teen Culture - Does It Exist?" *Brand Strategy* 167 (January, 2003), 37–38.
19. Parker, R.S., A.D. Schaefer, and C.M. Hermans (2006), "An Investigation Into Teens' Attitudes Towards Fast-Food Brands in General: A Cross-Culture Analysis," *Journal of Foodservice Business Research* 9 (4), 25–40.
20. Siskos, Catherine (1998), "Generation X Socks it Away," *Kiplinger's Personal Finance Magazine* 52 (5), 20.
21. This information based on Gibbs, Nancy (2010), "Generation Next," *Time* online edition (March 11), http://www.time.com/time/magazine/article/0,9171,1971433-2,00.html, accessed August 10, 2010.
22. Kohut, Andrew, *et al.* (2010), "Millennials: A Portrait of Generation Next," *Pew Research Center*, http://pewsocialtrends.org/assets/pdf/millennials-confident-connected-open-to-change.pdf, accessed August 10, 2010.
23. Boski, P., "Humanism-materialism: Centuries-long Polish Cultural Origins and 20 Years of Research." In Kim, U., Yang, K.S., & Hwang, K.-K. (Eds.). *Indigenous and Cultural Psychology: Understanding People in Context* (2006): 373–402, New York: Springer.
24. Benning, T. (2009), "Slump Strains Church Finances as Need Grows," *The Wall Street Journal* (August 11), A13.
25. Taylor, V.A., D. Halstead and P.J. Haynes (2010), "Consumer Advertising to Christian Religious Symbols in Advertising," *Journal of Advertising* 39 (2), 79–92.
26. Sandikci, O. and G. Ger (2010), "Veiling in Style: How Does a Stigmatized Practice Become Fashionable?" *Journal of Consumer Research* 37 (June), 15–36.
27. Online content retrieved at BBC News online edition, "French MPs Vote to Ban Islamic Full Veil in Public," *BBC News Online*, http://www.bbc.co.uk/news/10611398, accessed August 9, 2010.
28. Zolfagharian, M.A. and Q. Sun (2010), "Country of Origin, Ethnocentrism and Bicultural Consumers: The Case of Mexican Americans," *The Journal of Consumer Marketing* 27, 345.
29. Online content retrieved at "Marketing to Asian Americans," *AdWeek Media* online edition, May 26, 2008, http://www.adweekmedia.com/aw/content_display/custom-reports/mtaa/e3i70fa56666e6c5bc-cfb3fe3b2dc4c015b, accessed August 8, 2010.
30. This definition based on Ritzer, George (1996), *Sociological Theory*, Fourth edition, New York: McGraw-Hill.
31. Schaninger, Charles M. (1981), "Social Class Versus Income Revisited: An Empirical Investigation," *Journal of Marketing Research* (May), 192–208.
32. Warner, Lloyd W. and Paul S. Hunt, eds., (1941), *The Social Life of a Modern Community*, New Haven: CT: Yale University Press.
33. Schwartz, C.R. and R.D. Mare (2005), "Trends in Educational Assortative Marriage from 1940 to 2003," *Demography* 42 (4), 621–646; Snyder, E.C. (1964), "Attitudes: A Study of Homogamy and Marital Selectivity," *Journal of Marriage and Family* 26 (3), 332–336.
34. This definition based on Eller, Jack (2009), *Cultural Anthropology: Global Forces, Local Lives*, New York: Routledge, and Jonothon Turner H. Turner (1981), *Sociology: Studying the Human System*, Santa Monica: Goodyear Publishing.

35. Ling, Lisa and Katie Hinman (2009), "Under Las Vegas: Tunnels Stretch for Miles," *ABC News* online (September 23), **http://abcnews.go.com/Nightline/las-vegas-strip-home-homeless/story?id=8652139**, accessed August 11, 2010; also Powers, Ashley (2009), "A Life Saved From the Shadows," *Los Angeles Times* online (December 22), **http://articles.latimes.com/2009/dec/22/nation/la-na-tunnel22-2009dec22**, accessed August 11, 2010.

36. Hodgson, An (2007), "China's Middle Class Reaches 80 Million," *Euromonitor* online (July 25), **http://www.euromonitor.com/Chinas_middle_class_reaches_80_million**, accessed August 11, 2010.

37. This section based on Fernando, Vincent (2010), "Faber: India's Middle Class Will Soon Be Larger than America's," *Business Insider*, **http://www.businessinsider.com/faber-dont-ignore-india-2010-2**, accessed August 11, 2010; also Beinhocker, Eric, Diana Ferrell, and Adil Zainulbhai (2007), "Tracking the Growth of India's Middle Class," *McKinsey Quarterly* online, **http://www.mckinseyquarterly.com/Tracking_the_growth_of_Indias_middle_class_2032**, accessed August 11, 2010.

38. Goulding, C. and M. Saren (2009), "Performing Identity: An Analysis of Gender Expressions at the Whitby Goth Festival," *Consumption Markets & Culture* 12 (March), 27–46.

39. Martin, Bob (2007), "Wife Shortage Looms in China," *Culture Briefings*, **http://www.culturebriefings.com/articles/chwifesh.html**, accessed August 12, 2010; also "Study: China Faces 24M Bride Shortage by 2020," *CNN* online (2010), **http://www.cnn.com/2010/WORLD/asiapcf/01/11/china.bride.shortage/index.html**, accessed August 12, 2010.

40. "Asian Youth Trends," *American Demographics* 26 (8) (2004), 14.

## Chapter 10

1. Park, C. Whan, and V. Parker Lessig (1977), "Students and Housewives: Differences in Susceptibility to Reference Group Influence," *Journal of Consumer Research* 4 (September), 102–110.

2. Michener, H. Andrew, and Michelle P. Wasserman (1995), "Group Decision Making," in *Sociological Perspectives on Social Psychology*, Karen S. Cook, Gary Alan Fine, and James S. House, eds., Boston: Allyn and Bacon, 336–361.

3. Webley, Paul, and Ellen K. Nyhus (2006), "Parent's Influence on Children's Future Orientation and Saving," *Journal of Economic Psychology* 27 (1), 140–149.

4. Muniz, Albert M., Jr., and Thomas C. O'Guinn (2001), "Brand Community," *Journal of Consumer Research*, 27 (4), 412–432.

5. Alexander, James H., John W. Schouten, and Harold F. Koening (2002), "Building Brand Community," *Journal of Marketing* 66 (1), 38–54.

6. Lascu, Dana-Nicoleta, and George Zinkhan (1999), "Consumer Conformity: Review and Applications for Marketing Theory and Practice," *Journal of Marketing Theory and Practice* 7 (3), 1–12.

7. Ross, Jill, and Ross Harradine (2004), "I'm Not Wearing That! Branding and Young Children," *Journal of Fashion Marketing and Management* 8 (1), 11–26.

8. Online content retrieved at *Suite101* website, **http://public-healthcare-issues.suite101.com/article.cfm/tobacco-company-undermines-global-treaty-on-facebook**, accessed June 17, 2010.

9. Smith, Karen H., and Mary Ann Stutts (2006), "The Influence of Individual Factors on the Effectiveness of Message Content in Antismoking Advertisements Aimed at Adolescents," *Journal of Consumer Affairs* 40 (2), 261–293; Rosenberg, Merri (2002), "Anti-Smoking Ads Aimed at Peers," *The Wall Street Journal* (February 17), **http://query.nytimes.com/gst/fullpage.html?sec=health&res=9D06E5D8163FF934A25751C0A9649C8B63**.

10. Albers-Miller, Nancy (1999), "Consumer Misbehavior: Why People Buy Illicit Goods," *The Journal of Consumer Marketing* 16 (3), 273–287.

11. Gergen, Kenneth J., and Mary Gergen (1981), *Social Psychology*, New York: Harcourt Brace Jovanovich.

12. French, J. R. P., and B. Raven (1959), "The Bases of Social Power," in D. Cartwright, ed., *Studies in Social Power*, Ann Arbor, MI: Institute for Social Research.

13. Park and Lessig (1977).

14. Bearden, William O., and Michael J. Etzel (1982), "Reference Group Influence on Product and Brand Purchase Decisions," *Journal of Consumer Research* 9 (2), 183–194.

15. Park and Lessig (1977).

16. Bearden and Etzel (1982).

17. Online content retrieved at *Pew Research Center* website, "Neighbors Online," **http://pewresearch.org/pubs/1620/neighbors-online-using-digital-tools-to-communicate-monitor-community-developments**, accessed June 11, 2010.

18. Online content retrieved at *Read Write* website, **www.readwriteweb.com/archives/social_networking_now_more_popular_on_mobile_than_desktop_php**, accessed June 12, 2010.

19. Online content retrieved at *Google Doubleclick Adplanner* website **www.google.com/adplanner/static/top1000/**, accessed November 23, 2010.

20. Online content retrieved at *Facebook* website, **http://www.facebook.com/press/info.php?statistics**, accessed November 23, 2010.

21. Online content retrieved at *Alexa* website, **http://www.alexa.com/topsites**, accessed June 17, 2010

22. Online content retrieved at *Google Doubleclick Adplanner* website, **www.google.com/adplanner/static/top1000/**, accessed November 23, 2010.

23. Online content retrieved at *Comscore* website, "Comscore 2009 U.S. Digital Year in Review," **http://www.comscore.com/Press_Events/Presentations_Whitepapers/2010/The_2009_U.S._Digital_Year_in_Review/(language)/eng-US**, accessed June 10, 2010.

24. Online content retrieved at *Mashable* .com website, **http://mashable.com/2010/06/08/twitter-hits-2-billion-tweets-per-month/**, accessed June 8, 2010.

25. Online content retrieved at *Comscore* website, "Comscore 2009 U.S. Digital Year in Review," **http://www.comscore.com/Press_Events/Presentations_Whitepapers/2010/The_2009_U.S._Digital_Year_in_Review/(language)/eng-US**, accessed June 10, 2010.

26. Online content retrieved at *SocialVibe* website, **http://www.socialvibe.com/info/faq.html**, accessed June 10, 2010.

27. Online content retrieved at *Kaboodle* website, **http://www.kaboodle.com/zm/about**, accessed June 10, 2010.

28. Online content retrieved *Foursquare* website, **www.foursquare.com**, accessed June 10, 2010.

29. Bearden, William O., Richard G. Netemeyer, and Jesse E. Teel (1989), "Measurement of Consumer Susceptibility to Interpersonal Influence," *Journal of Consumer Research* 15 (4): 473–481.

30. Batra, Rajeev, Pamela M. Homer, and Lynn R. Kahle (2001), "Values, Susceptibility to Normative Influence, and Attribute Importance Weights: A Nomological Perspective," *Journal of Consumer Research* 11 (2), 115–128.

31. Wooten, David B., and Americus Reed II (2004), "Playing it Safe: Susceptibility to Normative Influence and Protective Self-Presentation," *Journal of Consumer Research* 31 (3), 551–556.

32. Wooten, David B., and Randall L. Rose (1990), "Attention to Social Comparison Information: An Individual Difference Variable Affecting Consumer Conformity," *Journal of Consumer Research* 16 (4), 461–471.

33. Clark, Ronald A., and Ronald E. Goldsmith (2006), "Global Innovativeness and Consumer Susceptibility to Interpersonal Influence," *Journal of Marketing Theory and Practice* 14 (4), 275–285.

34. Wang, Cheng Lu, and Allan K. K. Chan (2001), "A Content Analysis of Connectedness vs. Separateness Themes Used in U.S. and P.R.C. Print Advertisements," *International Marketing Review* 18 (2), 145–157; Wang, Cheng Lu, and John C. Mowen (1997), "The Separateness-Connectedness Self-Schema: Scale Development and Application to Message Construction," *Psychology & Marketing* 14 (March), 185–207.

35. Wang and Mowen (1997).

36. Lan, Jiang, Joandrea Hoegg, Darren W. Dahl, and Amitava Chattopadhyay (2010), "The Persuasive Role of Incidental Similarity on Attitudes and Purchase Intentions in a Sales Context," *Journal of Consumer Research* 36 (5), 778–791.

37. Wang and Chan (2001).

38. Argo, Jennifer J., Darren W. Dahl, and Rajesh V. Manchanda (2005), "The Influence of a Mere Social Presence in a Retail Context," *Journal of Consumer Research* 32 (2), 207–212.

39. Dahl, Darren W., Rajesh V. Manchanda, and Jennifer J. Argo (2001), "Embarrassment in Consumer Purchase: The Roles of Social Presence and Purchase Familiarity," *Journal of Consumer Research* 28 (3), 473–481.

40. Online content retrieved at *Word of Mouth Marketing Association* (WOMMA) website: **http://www.womma.org/wom101/04/**.

41. Brown, Tom J., Thomas E. Berry, Peter A. Dacin, and Richard F. Gunst (2005), "Spreading the Word: Investigating Antecedents of Consumers' Positive Word-of-Mouth Intentions and Behaviors in a Retailing Context," *Journal of the Academy of Marketing Science* 33 (2), 123–138.

42. Chung, Cindy M. Y. (2006), "The Consumer as Advocate: Self-Relevance, Culture, and Word-of-Mouth," *Marketing Letters* 17 (4), 269–284; Wangenheim, Florian v. (2005), "Postswitching Negative Word-of-Mouth," *Journal of Service Research* 8 (1), 67–78.

43. Bone, Paula (1995), "Word-of-Mouth Effects on Short-Term and Long-Term Product Judgments," *Journal of Business Research* 32 (3), 213–223.

44. Babin, Barry J., Yong-Ki Lee, Eun-Ju Kim, and Mitch Griffin (2005), "Modeling Consumer Satisfaction and Word-of-Mouth:

Restaurant Patronage in Korea," *Journal of Services Marketing* 19 (3), 133–139.

45. Online content retrieved at *Pew Internet Net and American Life Project* website, **http://www.pewinternet.org/topics/Health.aspx**, accessed June 11, 2010.

46. Online content retrieved at *Pew Research Center* website, "Teens and Mobile Phones," **http://www.pewinternet.org/Reports/2010/Teens-and-Mobile-Phones.aspx?r=1**, accessed June 12, 2010.

47. Online content retrieved at *Bzzagent*.com website, **www.bzzagent.com,** accessed June 17, 2010.

48. Online content retrieved at *Digg* website, **www.digg.com,** accessed June 10, 2010.

49. Online content retrieved at *BusinessWeek* website, "How Ford Got Social Marketing Right," **http://www.businessweek.com/managing/content/jan2010/ca2010018_445530.htm**, accessed June 12, 2010.

50. Kaikati, Andrew M., and Jack G. Kaikati (2004), "Stealth Marketing: How to Reach Consumers Surreptitiously," *California Management Review* 46 (4), 6–22.

51. Online content retrieved at *Word of Mouth Marketing Association* (WOMMA), "Unethical Word-of-Mouth Marketing Strategies," **http://www.womma.org/ wom101/06/**.

52. Johnson, Mark (2005), "Target the Few to Reach the Many," *PR Week* (October 4), S8–S11.

53. Solomon, Michael (1986), "The Missing Link: Surrogate Consumers in the Marketing Chain," *Journal of Marketing* 50 (October), 208–218.

54. Rogers, Everett M. (1995), *Diffusion of Innovations*, 4th ed., New York: The Free Press.

55. Online content retrieved at *Pew Research Center* website, "The Return of the Multi-Generational Household," **http://pewresearch.org/pubs/1528/multi-generational-family-household**, accessed June 11, 2010.

56. Data retrieved from *U.S. Census Bureau* website, **www.factfinder.census.gov**, June 12, 2010.

57. Online content retrieved at *DivorceRate* website, **http://www.divorcerate.org/,** accessed June 11, 2010.

58. Roberts, Sam (2007), "51% of Women are Now Living Without Spouse," *The New York Times* (January 16), 1.

59. "50 Million Children Lived With Married Parents in 2007," U.S. Census Bureau News, **http:// http://www.census.gov/newsroom/releases/archives/marital_status_living_arrangements/cb08-115.html** accessed April 3, 2009.

60. Online content retrieved at *Pew Research Center* website, "The New Demography of American Motherhood," **http://pewsocialtrends.org/pubs/754/new-demography-of-american-motherhood,** retrieved June 11, 2010.

61. Dye, Jane Lawler (2008), "Current Population Reports: Fertility of American Women 2006," *U.S. Census Bureau* (August), **http://www.census.gov/prod/2008pubs/p20-558.pdf**, accessed April 3, 2009.

62. Koch, Wendy (2007), "Number of Single Men Adopting Fosters Kids Doubles; Historic Shift From When Kids Went Only to Married Couples," *USA Today* (June 15), 5A.

63. Wilkes, Robert E. (1995), "Household Life-Cycle Stages, Transitions, and Product Expenditures," *Journal of Consumer Research*, 22 (1), 27–41.

64. Chatzky, John (2007), "Your Adult Kids are Back. Now What?" *Money* 36 (1), 32–35.

65. Online content retrieved at *Pew Research Center* website, "Home for the Holidays…And Every Other Day," **http://pewsocialtrends.org/assets/pdf/home-for-the-holidays.pdf**, accessed June 11, 2010.

66. Chatzky, John (2007).

67. "A Generation Caught Between Two Others," *MSNBC*, February 13, 2007, online content retrieved at **http://www.msnbc.msn.com/id/17134636/**, accessed April 3, 2009.

68. "Valuing The Invaluable: The Economic Value of Family Caregiving, 2008 Update," AARP Public Policy Institute, online content retrieve at: **http://assets.aarp.org/rgcenter/il/i13_caregiving.pdf**, accessed April 3, 2009.

69. Online content retrieved at *New Jersey Newsroom* website, "The Sandwich Generation: Modern Dilemma of Elder Care," **http://www.newjerseynewsroom.com/healthquest/the-sandwich-generation-the-modern-dilemma-of-elder-care**, accessed June 11, 2010.

70. Gentry, James W., Suraj Commuri, and Sunkyu Jun (2003), "Review of Literature on Gender in the Family," *Academy of Marketing Science Review*, 1.

71. Lee, Christina K. C., and Sharon E. Beatty (2002), "Family Structure and Influence in Family Decision Making," *Journal of Consumer Marketing* 19 (1), 24–41.

72. Belch, Michael A., and Laura A. Willis (2002), "Family Decisions at the Turn of the Century: Has the Changing Structure of Households Impacted the Family Decision-Making Process?" *Journal of Consumer Behaviour* 2 (2), 111–125.

73. Online content retrieved at *Pew Research Center* website, **http://pewresearch.org/pubs/1466/economics-marriage-rise-of-wives?src=prc-latest&proj=peoplepress**, accessed June 11, 2010.

74. "Kid Power," *Chain Store Age*, 83 (3) (2007), 20.

75. Koetters, Michelle (2007), "Tweeners' Money Talks," *Knight Ridder Tribune Business News* (May 14), 1.

76. Maich, Steve (2006), "The Little Kings and Queens of the Mall," *Maclean's* 119 (25), 37.

77. This definition based on Scott Ward (1980), "Consumer Socialization," in Harold H. Kassarjian and Thomas S. Robertson, eds., *Perspectives in Consumer Behavior*, Glenview, IL: Scott, Foresman, 380.

**Case 3-4**

1. Visit the Spaceport America website **http://www.spaceportamerica.com/ http://www.youtube.com/watch?v=PIuzf9gcEiU** for further information on the upcoming endeavors.

2. Visit the Virgin Galactic website **http://www.virgingalactic.com/overview/spaceport/** for a detailed analysis of Spaceport America endeavors.

3. See the Spaceport America website **http://www.spaceportamerica.com/http://www.youtube.com/watch?v=PIuzf9gcEiU** for further information on marketing endeavors.

4. See the Virgin Galactic website **http://www.virgingalactic.com/overview/spaceport/** for a detailed analysis of Spaceport America endeavors.

5. Peter Gwyne (2010), "Obama Sets Mission to Mars," *Physics World* (April 16), **http://physicsworld.com/cws/article/news/42348**, accessed May 5, 2010.

6. Visit the NASA Web site **http://marsprogram.jpl.nasa.gov/missions/future/futureMissions.html** for further information about the NASA science community.

7. See the Spaceport America website **http://www.spaceportamerica.com/ http://www.youtube.com/watch?v=PIuzf9gcEiU** for further information on the upcoming flight schedule.

**Case 3-5**

1. Hiatt, Brian (2009), "Meet the Beatles, Again," *Rolling Stone*, issue 1086 (September 3), 53–54.

2. Spitz, Bob (2005), *The Beatles: A Biography*, New York: Back Bay Books.

3. Whitburn, Joel (2008), *The Billboard Book of Top 40 Hits*, 8th Edition, New York: Billboard Books.

## Chapter 11

1. Dhar, R., and S.M. Nowlis (1999), "The Effect of Time Pressure on Consumer Choice Deferral," *Journal of Consumer Research* 25 (March), 369–384.

2. Bublitz, M. G., L. A. Peracchio and L. G. Block (2010), "Why Did I Eat That? Perspectives on Food Decision Making and Dietary Restraint," *Journal of Consumer Psychology*, in press.

3. Lim, J. and S. E. Beatty (2010), "Factors Affecting Couples' Decisions to Jointly Shop," *Journal of Business Research*, in press.

4. Nowlis, S.M. (1995), "The Effect of Time Pressure on the Choice Between Brands that Differ in Quality, Price and Product Features," *Marketing Letters* 6 (October), 287–296.

5. Suri, R., and K.B. Monroe (2003), "The Effects of Time Constraints on Consumers' Judgments of Prices and Products," *Journal of Consumer Research* 30 (June), 92–104.

6. Wagner, J., and M. Mokhtari (2000), "the Moderating Effect on Household Apparel Expenditure," *Journal of Consumer Affairs*, 34 (2), 22–78.

7. Roslow, S., T. Li, and J.A.F. Nicholls (2000), "Impact of Situational Variables and Demographic Attributes in Two Seasons on Purchase Behavior," *European Journal of Marketing* 34 (9), 1167–1180.

8. *Prepared Foods* (2007), "Tea Totally," 176 (May), 33.

9. Yoon, C., C. Cole and M.P. Lee (2009), "Consumer Decision Making and Aging: Current Knowledge and Future Decisions," *Journal of Consumer Psychology*, 19, 2–16. Bublitz et al. (2010).

10. Okamura, H., A. Tsuda, J. Yajima, H. Mark, S. Horiuchi, N. Troyoshima and T. Matsuishi (2010), "Short Sleeping Time and Psychological Responses to Acute Stress," *International Journal of Psychophysiology,* doi 10.1016/j.ijpsycho.2010.0/.010.

11. Zhuang, G., A.S. Tsang, N. Zhou, F. Li, and J.A. Nicholls (2006), "Impacts of Situational Factors on Buying Decisions in Shopping Malls," *European Journal of Marketing*, 40, 17–43.

12. Babin, B.J., W.R. Darden, and M. Griffin (1994), "Work and/or Fun: Measuring Hedonic and Utilitarian Shopping Value," *Journal of Consumer Research*, 20 (4), 644–656.

13. Babin et al. (1994).

14. Babin, B.J., and J.S. Attaway (2000), "Atmospheric Affect as a Tool for Creating Value and Gaining Share of Customer," *Journal of Business Research*, 49, 91–99.

15. Darden, W.R., and B.J. Babin (1994), "Exploring the Concept of Affective Quality: Expanding the Concept of Retail Personality," *Journal of Business Research*, 29 (February), 101–109.

16. Ramanathan, S., and P. Williams (2007), "Immediate and Delayed Emotional consequences of Indulgence: The Moderating Influence of Personality Type on Mixed Emotions," *Journal of Consumer Research*, 34, 212–223.

17. Childers, T.L., C.L. Carr, J. Peck, and S. Carson (2001), "Hedonic and Utilitarian Motivations for Online Shopping Behavior," *Journal of Retailing*, 77, 511–535.

18. Mukhopadhyay, A. and Johar, G.V. (2009), "Indulgence as Self-Reward for Prior Shopping-Restraint: A Justification Based Mechanism," *Journal of Consumer Psychology*, 19 (July), 334–345.

19. Franken, I.H.A., and P. Muris (2006), "Gray's Impulsivity Dimension: A Distinction Between Reward Sensitivity and Rash Impulsiveness," *Personality & Individual Differences*, 40 (July), 1337–1347; Ramanathan and Williams (2007).

20. Dholakia, U.M. (2000), "Temptation and Resistance: An Integrated Model of Consumption Impulse Formation and Enactment," *Psychology & Marketing*, 17 (November), 955–982.

21. Kaufman-Scarborough, C., and J. Cohen (2004), "Unfolding Consumer Impulsivity: An Existential-Phenomenological Study of Consumers with Attention Deficit Disorder," *Psychology & Marketing*, 21 (August), 637–669.

22. Beatty, S.E., and E.M. Ferrell (1998), "Impulse Buying: Modeling its Precursors," *Journal of Retailing*, 74, 161–191.

23. Zhang, X., V.R. Prybutok, and D. Strutton (2007), "Modeling Influences on Impulse Purchasing Behaviors During Online Marketing Transactions," *Journal of Marketing Theory and Practice* 15 (Winter), 79–89.

24. Babin, B. J. and W. R. Darden (1995), "Consumer Self-Regulation in a Retail Environment," 71 (Spring), 47–70.

25. Herzenstein, M., S.S. Posavac, and J.J. Brakus (2007), "Adoption of New and Really New Products: The Effects of Self-Regulation Systems and Risk Salience," *Journal of Marketing Research* 44 (May), 251–260.

26. Darden and Babin (1994); Russell, J.A. and G. Pratt (1980), "A Description of the Affective Quality Attributable to Environments," *Journal of Personality and Social Psychology* 38, 311–322.

27. Bitner, M.J. (1992), "Servicescapes: The Impact of the Physical Environment on Customers and Employees," *Journal of Marketing* 56 (April), 57–71.

28. Koernig, S.K. (2003), "E-Scapes: The Electronic Physical Environment and Service Tangibility," *Psychology & Marketing* 20, 151–167; Lee, Y.K., C.K. Lee, S.K. Lee, and B.J. Babin (2008), "Festivalscapes and Patrons' Emotions, Satisfaction, and Loyalty," *Journal of Business Research*, (in press).

29. Brady, M.K., C.M. Voorhees, J.J. Cronin, and B.L. Boudreau (2006), "The Good Guys Don't Always Win: The Effect of Valence on Service Perceptions and Consequences," *Journal of Services Marketing* 20, 83–91.

30. Williams, G. (2004), "It's a Style Thing," *Entrepreneur* 32 (March), 34; Iacbucci, D., and A. Ostrom (1993), "Gender Differences in the Impact of Core and Relational Aspects of Services on the Evaluation of Service Encounters," *Journal of Consumer Psychology* 2, 257–286.

31. Haytko, D.L., and J. Baker (2004), "It's All at the Mall: Exploring Adolescent Girls' Experiences," *Journal of Retailing* 80 (Spring), 67–83.

32. Babin, B.J., and J.C. Chebat (2004), "Perceived Appropriateness and Its Effect on Quality, Affect and Behavior," *Journal of Retailing and Consumer Services* 11 (September): 287–298; Michon, R., J.C. Chebat, and L.W. Turley (2005), "Mall Atmospherics: the Interaction Effects of the Mall Environment on Shopping Behavior," *Journal of Business Research* 58 (May), 576–583.

33. Orth, O.R., and A. Bourrain (2005), "Ambient Scent and Consumer Exploratory Behavior: A Causal Analysis," *Journal of Wine Research* 16, 137–150.

34. Michon et al, 2005.

35. Turley, L.W., and J.C. Chebat (2002), "Linking Retail Strategy, Atmospheric Design and Shopping Behavior," *Journal of Marketing Management* 18, 125–144; Milliman, R.E. (1986), "The Influence of Background Music on the Behavior of Restaurant Patrons," *Journal of Consumer Research* 13 (September), 286–289; Babin and Chebat (2003).

36. Crowley, A.E. (1993), "The Two-Dimensional Impact of Color on Shopping," *Marketing Letters* 4, 59–69; Bellizi, J., and R.E. Hite (1992), "Environmental Color, Consumer Feelings and Purchase Likelihood," *Psychology & Marketing* 59 (Spring), 347–363; Babin, B.J., D.M. Hardesty, and T.A. Suter (2003), "Color and Shopping Intentions: The Intervening Effect of Price Fairness and Affect," *Journal of Business Research* 56, 541–551.

37. Babin, Hardesty, and Suter (2003).

38. Dennis, C., A. Newman, R. Michon, J.J. Brakus and L.T. Wright (2010), "The Mediating Effects of Perception and Emotion: Digital Signage in Mall Atmospherics," *Journal of Consumer and Retail Services* 17, 205–215.

39. Cotlet, P., M.C. Lichtlè, and V. Plichon (2006), "The Role of Value in a Services: A Study in a Retail Environment," *Journal of Consumer Marketing*, 23, 219–227; Eroglu, S.A., K. Machleit, and T.F. Barr (2005), "Perceived Retail Crowding and Shopper Satisfaction: The Role of Shopping Values," *Journal of Business Research* 58 (August), 1146–1153.

40. Price, B. and D. Murray (2010), "Match-Up Revisited: The Effect of Staff Attractiveness on Purchase Intentions in Younger Adult Females: Social Comparative and Produce Relevance Effects," *Journal of International Business and Economics* 9, 55–76. Koering, S. K. and A. L. Page (2002), "What if your Dentist Looked Like Tom Cruise? Applying the Match-up Hypothesis to a Service Encounter," *Psychology & Marketing* 19 (January), 91–110. Grace, D. (2009), "An Examination of Consumer Embarrassment and Repatronage Intentions in the Context of Emotional Service Encounters," *Journal of Retailing and Consumer Services* 16 (January), 1–9.

41. Borges, A., J.C. Chebat and B.J. Babin (2010), "Does a Companion always Enhance the Shopping Experience?" *Journal of Retailing and Consumer Services*, 17 (July), 294–299. Lim, J. and S. E. Beatty (2010), "Factors Affecting Couples' Decisions to Jointly Shop," *Journal of Business Research*, in press.

42. Mande, N., and E.J. Johnson (2002), "When Web Pages Influence Choice: Effects of Visual Primes on Experts and Novices," *Journal of Consumer Research* 20 (September), 235–245.

43. Wang, L.C., J. Baker, J. Wagner, and K. Wakefield (2007), "Can a Web Site be Social?" *Journal of Marketing* 71 (July), 143–157.

44. http://www.nj.com/news/index.ssf/ 2010/04/atlantic_city_casinos_struggli .html, accessed August 10, 2010.

45. Heath, C., and J.B. Soll (1996), "Mental Budgeting and Consumer Decisions," *Journal of Consumer Research* 23 (June), 40–52.

46. Wang, Y.J., M. D. Hernandez and M.S. Minor (2010), "Web Aesthetics Effects on Perceived Online Service Quality and Satisfaction in an e-tail Environment: The Moderating Role of Purchase Task," *Journal of Business Research* 53, 935–942.

47. Michon, R., H. Yu, D. Smith, and J.C. Chebat (2007), "The Shopping Experience of Female Fashion Leaders," *International Journal of Retail and Distribution Management* 35 (6), 488–501; Swinyard, W.R. (1992), "The Effects of Mood, Involvement, and Quality of Store Experience on Shopping Intentions," *Journal of Consumer Research* 20 (September), 271–280.

## Chapter 12

1. Xu, Alison Jing, and Robert W. Wyer, Jr. (2008), "The Effect of Mind-Sets on Consumer Decision Strategies," *Journal of Consumer Research*, forthcoming.

2. Bagozzi, Richard P., and Utpal Dholakia (1999), "Goal Setting and Goal Striving in Consumer Behavior," *Journal of Marketing* 63 (Special Issue), 19–32.

3. Lawson, Robert (1997), "Consumer Decision Making Within a Goal-Driven Framework," *Psychology & Marketing* 14 (5), 427–449.

4. Luce, Mary Frances, James R. Bettman, and John W. Payne (2001), "Tradeoff Difficulty: Determinants and Consequences for Consumer Decisions," *Monographs of the Journal of Consumer Research Series* 1 (Spring); Menon, Kalyani, and Laurette Dube (2000), "Ensuring Satisfaction by Engineering Salesperson Response to Customer Emotions," *Journal of Retailing* 76 (3), 285–307.

5. Mowen, John C. (1988), "Beyond Consumer Decision Making," *Journal of Consumer Marketing* 5 (1), 15–25.

6. Anonymous (2003), "POP Sharpens Its Focus," *Brandweek* 44 (24), 31–36.

7. Prasad, V. Kanti (1975), "Socioeconomic Product Risk and Patronage Preferences of Retail Shoppers," *Journal of Marketing* 39 (July), 42–47; Dowling, Grahame R., and Richard Staelin (1994), "A Model of Perceived Risk and Intended Risk-Handling Activity," *Journal of Consumer Research* 21 (1), 119–134.

8. This definition is based on Oliver, Richard (1997), *Satisfaction: A Behavioral Perspective on the Consumer*, New York: McGraw-Hill.

9. O'Brien, Louise, and Charles Jones (1995), "Do Rewards Really Create Loyalty?" *Harvard Business Review* 73 (May/June), 75–82.

10. Keller, Kevin Lane (1998), *Strategic Brand Management: Building, Measuring, and*

*Managing Brand Equity*. Upper Saddle River, NJ: Prentice Hall.

11. Aaker, David A. (1997), *Building Strong Brands*, New York: The Free Press, 21.

12. Olshavsky, Richard W., and Donald H. Granbois (1979), "Consumer Decision Making—Fact or Fiction?" *Journal of Consumer Research* 6 (2), 93–100.

13. Moyer, Don (2007), "Satisficing," *Harvard Business Review* 85 (4), 144; Schwartz, Barry, Andrew Ward, John Monterosso, Sonja Lyubomirsky, Katherine White, and Darrin R. Lehman (2002), "Maximizing versus Satisficing: Happiness Is a Matter of Choice," *Journal of Personality and Social Psychology* 83 (5), 1178–1197.

14. Bruner, Gordon C., III, and Richard J. Pomazal (1988), "Problem Recognition: The Crucial First Stage of the Consumer Decision Process," *Journal of Consumer Marketing* 5 (1), 51–63.

15. Sirgy, Jospeh M. (1983), *Social Cognition and Consumer Behavior*, New York: Praeger.

16. Beatty, Sharon, and Scott M. Smith (1987), "External Search Effort: An Investigation Across Several Product Categories," *Journal of Consumer Research* 14 (1), 83–95.

17. Bloch, Peter H., Daniel L. Sherrell, and Nancy M. Ridgway (1986), "Consumer Search: An Extended Framework," *Journal of Consumer Research* 13 (1), 119–126.

18. Lurie, Nicholas H. (2004), "Decision Making in Information-Rich Environments: The Role of Information Structure," *Journal of Consumer Research* 30 (4), 473–487.

19. Punj, Girish, and Richard Brookes (2004), "Decision Constraints and Consideration Set Formation in Consumer Durables," *Psychology & Marketing* 18 (8), 843–864; Shocker, Allan D., Moshe Ben-Akiva, Bruno Boccara, and Prakash Nedungadi (1991), "Consideration Set Influences on Consumer Decision Making and Choice: Issues, Models, and Suggestions," *Marketing Letters* 2 (3), 181–197.

20. Donkers, Bas (2002), "Modeling Consideration Sets Across Time: The Relevance of Past Consideration," in American Marketing Association Conference Proceedings, vol. 13, Chicago: American Marketing Association, 322.

21. Hauser, John R., and Birger Wernerfelt (1990), "An Evaluation Cost Model of Consideration Sets," *Journal of Consumer Research* 16 (4), 393–408.

22. Jarvis, Cheryl Burke (1998), "An Exploratory Investigation of Consumers' Evaluations of External Information Sources in Prepurchase Search," in *Advances in Consumer Research*, vol. 25, Joseph W. Alba and J. Wesley Hutchinson. eds. Provo, UT: Association for Consumer Research.

23. Lichtenstein, D. R., N. M. Ridgway, and R. P. Netemeyer (1993), "Price Perceptions and Consumer Shopping Behavior," *Journal of Marketing Research* 30, 234–245.

24. Bickart, Barbara, and Robert M. Schindler (2001), "Internet Forums as Influential Sources of Consumer Information," *Journal of Interactive Marketing* 15 (3), 31–40.

25. Ratchford, Brian T., Myung-Soo Lee, and Debabrata Talukdar (2003), "The Impact of the Internet on Information Search for Automobiles," *Journal of Marketing Research* 40 (2), 193–209.

26. Mathwick, Charla, and Edward Rigdon (2004), "Play, Flow, and the Online Search Experience," *Journal of Consumer Research* 31 (2), 324–332.

27. Ariely, Dan (2000), "Controlling the Information Flow: Effects on Consumers' Decision Making and Preferences," *Journal of Consumer Research* 27 (2), 233–248.

28. Mazursky, David, and Gideon Vinitzky (2005), "Modifying Consumer Search Processes in Enhanced On-Line Interfaces," *Journal of Business Research* 58 (10), 1299–1309.

29. Beatty and Smith (1987).

30. Srinivasan, Narasimhan, and Brian T. Ratchford (1991), "An Empirical Test of a Model of External Search for Automobiles," *Journal of Consumer Research* 18, 233–242; Johnson, Eric J., and Edward J. Russo (1984), "Product Familiarity and Learning New Information," *Journal of Consumer Research* 11, 542–550; Moore, William L., and Donald R. Lehmann (1980), "Individual Differences in Search Behavior for a Nondurable," *Journal of Consumer Research* 7, 296–307.

31. Moorthy, Sridhar, Brian T. Ratchford, and Debabrata Talukdar (1997), "Consumer Information Search Revisited: Theory and Empirical Analysis," *Journal of Consumer Research* 23 (4), 263–277; also see Alba, Joseph W., and J. Wesley Hutchinson (1987), "Dimensions of Consumer Expertise," *Journal of Consumer Research* 13 (4), 411–454.

32. Beatty and Smith (1987).

33. Dowling, G. R., and R. Staelin (1994), "A Model of Perceived Risk and Intended Risk-Handling Activity," *Journal of Consumer Research* 21 (1), 119–134; Dedler, Konrad, I. Gottschalk, and K. G. Grunert (1981), "Perceived Risk as a Hint for Better Information and Better Products," in *Advances in Consumer Research*, vol. 8, Kent Monroe, ed., Ann Arbor, MI: *Association for Consumer Research*, 391–397.

34. Mehta, Nitin, Surendra Rajiv, and Kannan Srinivasan (2003), "Price Uncertainty and Consumer Search: A Structural Model of Consideration Set Formation," *Marketing Science* 22 (1), 58–84.

35. Hofacker, Charles F. and Jamie Murphy (2009), "Consumer Web Page Search, Clicking Behavior, and Reaction Time," *Direct Marketing: An International Journal* 3 (2): 88 – 96.

36. Beatty and Smith (1987).

37. Ibid.

38. Capon, Noel, and Mariane Burke (1980), "Individual, Product Class, and Task-Related Factors in Consumer Information Processing," *Journal of Consumer Research* 7 (3), 314–326; Newman, Joseph, and Richard Staelin (1972), "Prepurchase Information Seeking for New Cars and Major Household Appliances," *Journal of Marketing Research* 7 (August): 249–257.

39. Cobb, Cathy J., and Wayne D. Hoyer (1988), "Direct Observation of Search Behavior in the Purchase of Two Nondurable Products," *Psychology & Marketing* 2 (3), 161–179; Newman and Staelin (1972).

40. Punj, Girish (1987), "Presearch Decision Making in Consumer Durable Purchases," *Journal of Consumer Marketing* 4 (1): 71–83.

41. Reynolds, Kristy E., Judith Anne Garretson Folse, and Michael A. Jones (2006), "Search Regret: Antecedents and Consequences," *Journal of Retailing* 82 (4), 339–348.

## Chapter 13

1. Futrell, Charles M. (2003), *ABCs of Relationship Selling*, 7th ed., Boston: McGraw-Hill.

2. Myers, James H., and Mark Alpert (1968), "Determinant Buying Attitudes: Meaning and Measurement," *Journal of Marketing*, (October), 13–20.

3. Williams, Terrell G. (2002), "Social Class Influences on Purchase Evaluation Criteria," *Journal of Consumer Marketing* 19 (2/3), 249–276; Dhar, Ravi, and Klaus Wertenbroch (2000), "Consumer Choice Between Hedonic and Utilitarian Goods," *Journal of Marketing Research* 37 (February), 60–71; Hirschman, Elizabeth C., and S. Krishnan (1981), "Subjective and Objective Criteria in Consumer Choice: An Examination of Retail Store Choice," *Journal of Consumer Affairs* 15 (1), 115–127.

4. Schwartz, Barry (2004), "The Tyranny of Choice," *Scientific American* 290 (4), 70–75.

5. Pham, Michel T., Joel B. Cohen, John W. Pracejus, and G. David Hughes (2001), "Affect Monitoring and the Primacy of Feelings in Judgment," *Journal of Consumer Research* 28 (2), 167–188.

6. Gorn, Gerald, J., Marvin E. Goldberg, and Kunal Basu (1993), "Mood, Awareness, and Product Evaluation," *Journal of Consumer Psychology* 2 (3): 237–256.

7. Bakamitsos, Georgios A. (2006), "A Cue Alone or a Probe to Think? The Dual Role of Affect in Product Evaluations," *Journal of Consumer Research* 33 (December), 403–412.

8. Moreau, C. Page, Arthur B. Markman, and Donald R. Lehmann (2001), "What Is It? Categorization Flexibility and Consumers' Responses to Really New Products," *Journal of Consumer Research* 27 (4), 489–498.

9. This discussion based on Alba, Joseph W., and J. Wesley Hutchinson (1987), "Dimensions of Consumer Expertise," *Journal of Consumer Research* 13 (4), 411–454.

10. Johnson, Michael D., and Claes Fornell (1987), "The Nature and Methodological Implications of the Cognitive Representation of Products," *Journal of Consumer Research* 14 (2), 214–228.

11. Viswanathan, Madhubalan, and Terry L. Childers (1999), "Understanding How Product Attributes Influence Product Categorization: Development and Validation of Fuzzy Set-Based Measures of Gradedness in Product Categories," *Journal of Marketing Research* 36 (1), 75–94.

12. Sujan, Mita, and Christine Dekleva (1987), "Product Categorization and Inference Making: Some Implications for Comparative Advertising," *Journal of Consumer Research* 14 (3), 372–378.

13. Dawar, Niraj, and Philip Parker (1994), "Marketing Universals: Consumers' Use

of Brand Name, Price, Physical Appearance, and Retailer Reputation as Signals of Product Quality," *Journal of Marketing* 58 (2), 81–95.

14. John, Deborah Roedder, and Mita Sujan (1990), "Age Differences in Product Categorization," *Journal of Consumer Research* 16 (4), 452–460.
15. Alba and Hutchinson (1987).
16. Williams (2002).
17. Bergen, Mark, Shantanu Dutta, and Steven M. Shugan (1996), "Branded Variants: A Retail Perspective," *Journal of Marketing Research* 33 (1), 9–19.
18. Fasolo, Barbara, Gary H. McClelland, and Peter M. Todd (2007), "Escaping the Tyranny of Choice: When Fewer Attributes Make Choice Easier," *Marketing Theory* 7 (1), 13–26.
19. Mitra, Debanjan, and Peter N. Golder (2006), "How Does Objective Quality Affect Perceived Quality?" *Marketing Science* 25 (3), 230–247.
20. Dawar and Parker (1994).
21. Miller, Elizabeth G., and Barbara E. Kahn (2006), "Shades of Meaning: The Effect of Color and Flavor Names on Consumer Choice," *Journal of Consumer Research* 32 (1), 86–92.
22. Jacoby, J., D. E. Speller, and C. A. Kohn (1974), "Brand Choice Behavior as a Function of Information Load: Replication and Extension," *Journal of Consumer Research* 1, 33–41; Malhotra, Naresh K. (1982), "Information Load and Consumer Decision Making," *Journal of Consumer Research* 8, 419–430.
23. Fasolo et al. (2007).
24. Kivetz, Ran, and Itamar Simonson (2000), "The Effects of Incomplete Information on Consumer Choice," *Journal of Marketing Research* 37 (4), 427–448.
25. Hair, Joseph F., Jr., Rolph Anderson, Ronald L. Tatham, and William C. Black, *Multivariate Data Analysis*, 5th ed., Upper Saddle River, NJ: Prentice Hall.
26. Wright, Peter (1975), "Consumer Choice Strategies: Simplifying vs. Optimizing," *Journal of Marketing Research*, 12 (February), 60–67.
27. Hirschman and Krishnan (1981); Baker, Julie, A. Parasuraman, Dhruv Grewal, and Glenn B. Voss (2002), "The Influence of Multiple Store Environmental Cues on Perceived Merchandise Value and Purchase Intentions," *Journal of Retailing* 66 (2), 120–142.
28. Seock, Yoo-Kyoung, and Jessie H. Chen-Yu (2007), "Website Evaluation Criteria Among U.S. College Student Consumers with Different Shopping Orientations and Internet Channel Usage," *International Journal of Consumer Studies* 31 (3), 204–212; Kim, Soyoung, Reginald Williams, and Yulee Lee (2003), "Attitude Toward Online Shopping and Retail Website Quality: A Comparison of U.S. and Korean Consumers," *Journal of International Consumer Marketing* 16 (1), 89–111.

Case 4-2
1. http://www.npr.org/templates/story/story.php?storyId=18751684
2. http://www.usatoday.com/money/advertising/adtrack/2007-11-25-green-mop_N.htm
3. http://www.grist.org/article/fighting-dirty/

4. http://www.sfgate.com/cgi-bin/article.cgi?f=/c/a/2006/10/08/BUGRMLJPJB1.DTL
5. http://www.usatoday.com/money/advertising/adtrack/2007-11-25-green-mop_N.htm
6. http://www.environmentalleader.com/2010/03/10/method-green-household-cleaners-try-to-take-market-share-from-clorox/
7. http://makower.typepad.com/joel_makower/2008/01/clorox-aims-to.html
8. http://www.bnet.com/2403-13241_23-253321.html
9. http://www.youtube.com/watch?v=N-gGAe8Ltsw&feature=related
10. http://www.npr.org/templates/transcript/transcript.php?storyId=18751684
11. http://www.greenbiz.com/news/2008/08/19/clorox-told-modify-green-works-claims#ixzz0nNemoTRa
12. http://www.greenbiz.com/news/2009/01/19/clorox-expands-green-works-line-gives-470k-sierra-club#ixzz0nMI0Y9eq
13. http://www.greenbiz.com/news/2009/09/25/aveeno-green-works-natures-source-products-get-green-good-housekeeping-seal#ixzz0nMJHj4Rv
14. http://www.environmentalleader.com/2010/03/10/method-green-household-cleaners-try-to-take-market-share-from-clorox/

## Chapter 14

1. Woodruff, Robert B. (1997), "Customer Value: The Next source for Competitive Advantage," *Journal of the Academy of Marketing Science* 25 (2), 139–153.
2. Beverland, M.B. and F. Farrelly (2010), "The Quest for Authenticity in Consumption: Consumers' Purposive Choice of Authentic Cues to Shape Experienced Outcomes," *Journal of Consumer Research* 36 (February), 838–856.
3. McCracken, Grant (1986), "Culture and Consumption: A Theoretical Account of the Structure and Movement of the Cultural Meaning of Consumer Goods," *Journal of Consumer Research* 13 (1), 71–84.
4. Holbrook, Morris B. (2006), "Consumption Experience, Customer Value, and Subjective Personal Introspection: An Illustrative Photographic Essay," *Journal of Business Research* 59, 714–725; Hirschman, Elizabeth C., and Morris B. Holbrook (1983), "Hedonic Consumption: Emerging Concepts, Methods, and Propositions," *Journal of Marketing* 46, 92–101.
5. MacInnis, D. and G.E. deMello (2005), "The Concept of Hope and its Relevance to Product Evaluations and Choice," *Journal of Marketing* 69 (January), 1–14.
6. Patterson, Paul G., and Richard G. Spreng (1997), "Modeling the Relationship Between Perceived Value, Satisfaction, and Repurchase Intentions in a Business-to-Business, Services Context: An Empirical Investigation," *International Journal of Industry Management* 8 (5), 414-434.
7. www.theacsi.org, accessed August 12, 2010.
8. Slater, Stanley (1997), "Developing a Customer Value-Based Theory of the Firm," *Journal of the Academy of Marketing Science* 25 (2), 162-167.

9. Holbrook, Morris B. (1986), "Emotion in the Consumption Experience: toward a Model of the Human Consumer," in *The Role of Affect in Consumer Behavior: Emerging Theories and Applications*, Robert A. Peterson et al., eds., Lexington, MA: Heath, 17–52.
10. This definition based in part on Westbrook, Robert A., and Richard L. Oliver (1991), "The Dimensionality of Consumption Emotion Patterns and Consumer Satisfaction," *Journal of Consumer Research* 18 (1), 84-91.
11. Babin, Barry J., and Mitch Griffin (1998), "The Nature of Satisfaction: An Updated Examination and Analysis," *Journal of Business Research* 41, 127–136.
12. Oliver, Richard L. (1983), "Measurement and Evaluation of Satisfaction Processes in Retail Settings," *Journal of Retailing* 57 (Fall), 25–48.
13. Churchill, Gilbert A., J., and Carol Surprenant (1982), "An Investigation into the Determinants of Consumer Satisfaction," *Journal of Marketing Research* 19 (4), 491–504.
14. Zeithaml, Valarie A., Leonard L. Berry, and A. Parasuraman (1993), "The Nature and Determinants of Customer Expectations of Service," *Journal of the Academy of Marketing Science* 21 (1), 1–12.
15. Tse, David K., and Peter C. Wilton (1988), "Models of Consumer Satisfaction Formation: An Extension," *Journal of Marketing Research* 24 (2), 204–212; LaTour, Stephen A., and Nancy C. Peat (1979), "Conceptual and Methodological Issues in Consumer Satisfaction Research," in *Advances in Consumer Research*, vol. 6, William L. Wilkie, ed., Ann Arbor, MI: Association of Consumer Research.
16. Spreng, Richard A., and Thomas J. Page, Jr. (2001), "The Impact of Confidence in Expectations on Consumer Satisfaction," *Psychology & Marketing* 18 (11), 1187–1204.
17. Hoch, Stephen J., and John Deighton (1989), "Managing What Consumers Learn from Experience," *Journal of Marketing* 53 (2), 1–20.
18. For a discussion of this topic, see Carrilat, F.A., J. Fernando, and J.P. Mulki (2007), "The Validity of the SERVQUAL and SERVPREF Scales," *International Journal of Service Industry Management* 18 (May), 472–490. Also see, Bebko, C., L. M. Sciulli, and R.K. Garg (2006), "Consumers' Level of Expectations for Services and the Role of Implicit Service Promises," *Services Marketing Quarterly* 28, 1–23.
19. Spreng, Richard A., Scott B. MacKenzie, and Richard W. Olshavsky (1996), "A Reexamination of the Determinants of Consumer Satisfaction," *Journal of Marketing* 60 (3), 15–32.
20. Price, Linda L., Eric J. Arnould, and Patrick Tierney (1995), "Going to Extremes: Managing Service Encounters and Assessing Provider Performance," *Journal of Marketing* 59 (April), 83–97.
21. Adams, J. Stacey (1965), "Inequity in Social Exchange," in *Advances in Experimental Social Psychology*, vol. 2, Richard Berkowitz, ed., New York: Academic Press, 267-299.
22. Barnes, D.C., M. B. Beauchamp and C. Webster (2010), "To Delight, or Not to Delight? This Is the Question Service

Firms Must Address," *Journal of Marketing, Theory and Practice* 18 (Summer), 275-283.

23. Wiener, Bernard (2000), "Attributional Thoughts About Consumer Behavior," *Journal of Consumer Research* 27 (3), 382-387.

24. Festinger, L. (1957), *A Theory of Cognitive Dissonance*, Standford, CA: Stanford University Press.

25. Sweeney, Jillian C., Douglas Hausknecht, and Geoffrey N. Soutar (2000), "Cognitive Dissonance After Purchase: A Multidimensional Scale," *Psychology & Marketing* 17 (5), 369-387.

26. Peter, J. Paul, Gilbert A. Churchill, Jr., and Tom J. Brown (1993), "Caution in the Use of Difference Scores in Consumer Research," *Journal of Consumer Research*, 19 (4), 655-662.

27. Babin and Griffin (1998).

28. Jacoby, Jacob, Carol K. Berning, and Thomas F. Dietvorst (1977), "What About Disposition?" *Journal of Marketing* 41 (2), 22-28.

29. Online content retrieved May 13, 2009, "Municipal Solid Waste in the United States: 2007 Facts and Figures," Environmental protection Agency, website: **http://www.epa.gov/epawaste/nonhaz/municipal/pubs/msw07-rpt.pdf**.

30. Adapted from Babin and Griffin (1998).

31. Price, Linda L., Eric J. Arnould, and Carolyn Folkman Curasi (2000), "Older Consumers' Disposition of Special Possessions," *Journal of Consumer Research* 27 (2), 179-182.

32. Lastovicka, John L., and Karen V. Fernandez (2005), "Three Paths to Disposition: The Movement of Meaningful Possessions to Strangers," *Journal of Consumer Research* 31 (4), 813-823.

33. Coulter, Robin A., and Mark Ligas (2003), "To Retain or to Relinquish: Exploring the Disposition Practices of Packrats and Purgers," *Advances in Consumer Research* 30, 38-43.

## Chapter 15

1. Consumer Policy (2007), "Complain? Why Bother, It's the NHS," *Consumer Policy Review* 17 (September/October), 221; Simos, P. (2005), "Seven Steps to Handle Complaints," *Restaurant Hospitality* 89 (August), 36; Blodgett, J.G., D.H. Granbois, and R.G. Walters (1993), "The Effects of Perceived Justice on Complainants' Negative Word-of-Mouth Behavior and Repatronage Intentions," *Journal of Retailing* 69 (Winter), 399-428.

2. Kalamas, M., M. Laroche and L. Makdessian (2008), "Reaching the Boiling Point: Consumers' Negative Affective Reactions to Firm-Attributed Service Failures," *Journal of Business Research* 61, 813-824.

3. Voorhees, C.M., M.K. Brady, and D.M. Horowitz (2006), "A Voice from the Silent Masses: An Exploratory and Comparative Analysis of Non-Complaining," *Journal of the Academy of Marketing Science* 34 (September), 513-527.

4. Simos, P. (2005).

5. Voorhees et al. (2006).

6. McColl-Kennedy, J. R., P. G. Patterson, A. K. Smith and M. K. Brady (2009), "Customer Rage Episodes: Emotions, Expressions and Behaviors," *Journal of Retailing* 85, 222-237.

7. Hart, C.A., J.L. Heskett, and E.W. Sasser (1990), "The Profitable Art of Service Recovery," *Harvard Business Review* 68 (4), 148-156.

8. Romaniuk, J. (2007), "Word of Mouth and the Viewing of Television Programs," *Journal of Advertising Research* 47 (December), 462-470.

9. **www.consumerist.com/consumer/complaints**, accessed October 25, 2007.

10. Crain, K. (2004), "At CBS, Shades of Audi Debate," *Automotive News* 79 (9/20), 12; Flint, J. (1988), "Hot Seat," *Forbes* 142 (June), 199.

11. See **www.snopes.com** for more on this story, accessed October 26, 2007.

12. Blodgett, J.G., D.H. Granbois, and R.G. Walters (1993), "The Effects of Perceived Justice on Complainants' Negative Word-of-Mouth Behavior and Repatronage Intentions," *Journal of Retailing* 69 (Winter), 399--428.

13. Nyer, P.M., and M. Gopinath (2005), "Effects of Complaining Versus Negative WOM on Subsequent Changes in Satisfaction: The Role of Public Commitment," *Psychology & Marketing* 22 (December), 937-953.

14. Lange, F., and M. Dahlen (2006), "Too Much Bad PR Can Make Ads Ineffective," *Journal of Advertising Research* 46 (December), 528-542; Aaker, J., S. Fournier, and B.S. Adam (2004), "When Good Brands Go Bad," *Journal of Consumer Research* 31 (June), 1-16.

15. Lange and Dahlen (2006).

16. Pullig, C., R.C. Netemeyer, and A. Biswas (2006), "Attitude Basis Certainty and Challenge Alignment: A Case of Negative Publicity," *Journal of the Academy of Marketing Science* 34 (Fall), 528-542.

17. Burnham, T.A., J.K. Frels, and V. Mahajan (2003), "Consumer Switching Costs: A Typology, Antecedents and Consequences," *Journal of the Academy of Marketing Science* 31 (Spring), 109-126.

18. Yukari, I. K. (2010), "Apple, Under Fire, to Discuss iPhone Friday," *The Wall Street Journal*, (July 13), A1. Yukai, I.K. and N. Sheth (2010), "Consumer Reports Slams New iPhone," *The Wall Street Journal*, (July 12), B3.

19. Andrews, M.L., R. L. Benedicktus, and M.K. Brady (2010), "The Effect of Incentives on Customer Evaluations of Service Bundles," *Journal of Business Research* 63, 71-76.

20. Antón, C., C. Camarero, and M. Carrero (2007), "The Mediating Effect of Satisfaction on Consumers' Switching Intention," *Psychology & Marketing* 24 (June), 511-538.

21. Jones, M.A., K.E. Reynolds, D.L. Mothersbaugh, and S.E. Beatty (2007), "The Positive and Negative Effects of Switching Costs on Relational Outcomes," *Journal of Services Research* 9 (May), 335-355.

22. Balabanis, G., N. Reynolds, and A. Simintiras (2006), "Base of E-Store Loyalty: Perceived Switching Barriers and Satisfaction," *Journal of Business Research* 59 (February), 214-224.

23. Gourville, J.T. (2006), "Eager Sellers & Stony: Understanding the Psychology of New-Product Adoption," *Harvard Business Review* 84 (June), 99-106.

24. Magi, A.W. (2003), "Share of Wallet in Retailing: The Effects of Consumer Satisfaction, Loyalty Cards and Shopper Characteristics," *Journal of Retailing* 79 (Summer), 97-106.

25. Shin, Dong H., and Won Y. Kim (2007), "Mobile Number Portability on Customer Switching Behavior: In the Case of the Korean Mobile Market," *Info* 9, 38-54.

26. Wangenheim, F.V. (2005), "Postswitching Negative Word of Mouth," *Journal of Services Research* 8, 67-78.

27. Chiu, H.C., Y.C. Hsieh, Y.C. Li, and L. Monle (2005), "Relationship Marketing and Consumer Switching Behavior," *Journal of Business Research* 58 (December), 1681-1689.

28. Babin, B. J. and J. P. Attaway (2000), "Atmospheric Affect as a Tool for Creating Value and Gaining Share of Customer," *Journal of Business Research* 49 (August), 91-99.

29. Palmatier, R.W., R.P. Dant, D. Grewal, and K.R. Evans (2006), "Factors Influencing the Effectiveness of Relationship Marketing: A Meta-Analysis," *Journal of Marketing* 70 (October), 136-153.

30. Palmatier, R.W., L.K. Scheer, M.B. Houston, K.R. Evans and S. Gopalakrishna (2007), "Use of Relationship Marketing Programs in Building Customer-Salesperson and Customer-Firm Relationships: Differential Influences on Financial Outcomes," *International Journal of Research in Marketing* 24, 210-223.

## Chapter 16

1. Fullerton, R. A., and G. Punj (2004), "Repercussions of Promoting an Ideology of Consumption: Consumer Misbehavior," *Journal of Business Research*, (57), 1239-1249.

2. Fowler III, Aubry R., Barry J. Babin, and Amy K. Este (2005), "Burning for Fun or Money: Illicit Consumer Behavior in a Contemporary Context," paper presented at the Academy of Marketing Science Annual Conference, presented May 27, 2005, Tampa, FL.

3. Fullterton and Punj (2004).

4. Fowler et al. (2005).

5. Vitell, Scott J. (2003), "Consumer Ethics Research: Review, Synthesis and Suggestions for the Future," *Journal of Business Ethics* 43 (1/2) (March), 33-47.

6. Babin, Barry J., and Laurie A. Babin (1996), "Effects of Moral Cognitions and Consumer Emotions on Shoplifting Intentions," *Psychology & Marketing* 13 (December), 785-802.

7. Vitell, Scott (2003).

8. Hunt, Shelby, and Scott Vitell (1986), "A General Theory of Marketing Ethics," *Journal of Macromarketing* 6 (1) Spring, 5-16.

9. This section is based on Fullerton and Punj (2004).

10. Merton, Robert (1968), *Social Theory and Social Structure*. New York: Free Press.

11. Hamilton, V. Lee, and David Rauma (1995), "Social Psychology of Deviance and Law," in Karen S. Cook, Gary A. Fine, and James S. House, eds., *Sociological Perspectives on Social Psychology*, Boston: Allyn and Bacon, 524-547.

12. Information and statistics provided by the National Association for Shoplifting Prevention (**NASP**), a non-profit organization; **www.shopliftingprevention.org**, accessed June 29, 2010.

13. Cox, Dena, Anthony D. Cox, and George P, Moschis (1990), "When Consumer Behavior Goes Bad: An Investigation of Adolescent Shoplifting," *Journal of Consumer Research* 17 (2) (September), 149–159.

14. Babin and Babin (1996); Webster, Cynthia (2000), "Exploring the Psychodynamics of Consumer Shoplifting Behavior," *American Marketing Association Conference Proceedings* (11), 360–365.

15. Babin, Barry J., and Mitch Griffin (1995), "A Closer Look at the Influence of Age on Consumer Ethics," *Advances in Consumer Research*, (22), 668–673.

16. Information obtained from Business Software Alliance website, **http://global .bsa.org/internetreport2009/2009internet piracyreport.pdf** , accessed June 30, 2010.

17. Fowler et al. (2005).

18. Shropshire, Corilyn (2007), "Spam Floods Inboxes," *Knight Ridder Tribune Business News*, (Jan 23, 2007), 1; Anonymous (2007), "U.S. Branded 'Biggest Spam and Virus Host," *Precision Marketing* (January 26), 9.

19. online content by Mark Smail (2010), "Are We Risking Our Digital Lives?" Technewsworld.com, **http://www .technewsworld.com/story/69145.html**, accessed June 30, 2010.

20. Herskovits, Beth (2006), "APA Shows Public How Psychology Fits Into Their Lives," *PR Week* (January 2), 19.

21. Lenhart, Amanda (2010), online presentation "Cyberbullying: What the Research is Telling Us…" Pew Internet & American Life Project, online content retrieved at **http://www.pewinternet.org/ Presentations/2010/May/Cyberbullying-2010.aspx**, accessed June 30, 2010.

22. Information obtained from Coalition Against Insurance Fraud website: **http:// www.insurancefraud.org**, accessed June 9, 2009.

23. Information obtained from **http://www .ftc.gov/bcp/edu/microsites/idtheft/ consumers/about-identity-theft.html**, accessed June 30, 2010.

24. Dupre, Kathryne, Tim Jones, and Shirley Taylor (2001), "Dealing With the Difficult: Understanding Difficult Behaviors in a Service Encounter," *American Marketing Association Proceedings*, 173–180.

25. Bitner, Mary J., Bernard H. Booms, and Lois Mohr (1994), "Critical Service Encounters: The Employee's Viewpoint," *Journal of Marketing* 58 (4), 95–106.

26. Harris, Lloyd, and Kate L. Reynolds (2003), "The Consequences of Dysfunctional Customer Behavior," *Journal of Service Research* 6 (2) November, 144–161.

27. Based on Thorne, Scott (2006), "An Exploratory Investigation of the Characteristics of Consumer Fanaticism," *Qualitative Market Research* 9, 51–72; Pimentel, Robert W., and Kristy E. Reynolds (2004), "A Model for Consumer Devotion: Affective Commitment with Proactive Sustaining Behaviors," *Academy of Marketing Science Review*, 1–45; Wakefield, Kirk L., and Daniel L. Wann (2006), "An Examination of Dysfunctional Sports Fans: Method of Classification and Relationships with Problem Behaviors," *Journal of Leisure Research* 38, 168–186; Hunt, Kenneth A., Terry Bristol, and R. Edward Bashaw (1999), "A Conceptual Approach to Classifying Sports Fans," *Journal of Services Market-*

*ing* 13, 439–449; Saporito, Bill (2004), "Why Fans and Players are Playing So Rough," *Time* (December 6), 30–35.

28. Reynolds, Kate L., and Lloyd C. Harris (2005), "When Service Failure Is Not Service Failure: An Exploration of the Forms and Motives of 'Illegitimate' Customer Complaining," *Journal of Services Marketing* 19, 321–335.

29. Information obtained from Consumer Products Safety Commission website, **http://www.cpsc.gov**, accessed March 17, 2008.

30. Stoltman, Jeffrey, and Fed Morgan (1993), "Psychological Dimensions of Unsafe Product Usage," in Rajan Varadarajan and Bernard Jaworski, eds., *Marketing Theory and Applications*, 4th ed., Chicago: American Marketing Association.

31. National Safety Commission (2006), "Road Rage Leads to More Road Rage" (December 6), **http://www.nationalsafe-tycommisson.com**, accessed March 17, 2008.

32. Crimmins, Jim, and Chris Callahan (2003), "Reducing Road Rage: The Role of Target Insight in Advertising for Social Change," *Journal of Advertising Research*, (December), 381–390.

33. Bone, Sterling A., and John C. Mowen (2006), "Identifying the Traits of Aggressive and Distracted Drivers: A Hierarchical Trait Model Approach," *Journal of Consumer Behaviour* 5 (5), September–October, 454–465; also Hennessy, D. A., and D. L. Wiesenthal (1997), "The Relationship Between Traffic Congestion, Driver Stress, and Direct versus Indirect Coping Behaviors," *Ergonomics* (40), 348–361.

34. Information obtained from Mothers Against Drunk Drivers website: **http:// www.madd.org/**, accessed June 17, 2009.

35. Information obtained from Centers for Disease Control website, **http://www.cdc .gov/MotorVehicleSafety/Impaired_ Driving/impaired-drv_factsheet.html**, accessed June 17, 2009.

36. Information obtained from the "Under Your Influence" website, supported by the National Highway Traffic Safety Administration, **www.underyourinfluence .org/UnderageDrinkingFact.html**, accessed June 17, 2009.

37. Quinlan, Kyran P., Robert D. Brewer, Paul Siegel, David A. Sleet, Ali H. Mokdad, Ruth A. Shults, and Nicole Flowers (2005), "Alcohol Impaired Driving Among U.S. Adults 1993–2003," *American Journal of Preventive Medicine*, (May), 346–350.

38. Online content retrieved at **https://www .cia.gov/library/publications/the-world-factbook**, accessed June 19, 2010.

39. Online content retrieved at CTIA-The Wireless Association website, **http:// files.ctia.org/pdf/CTIA_Survey_ Midyear_2009_Graphics.pdf,** accessed June 30, 2010.

40. Statistics in this section are based on online content retrieved at Insurance Institute website, **http://www.iii.org/media/ hottopics/insurance/cellphones/**, accessed July 1, 2010.

41. This information based on online content retrieved at **http://www.iihs.org/laws/ cellphonelaws.aspx**, accessed June 30, 2010.

42. This definition based on O'Guinn, Thomas C., and Ronald J. Faber (1989),

"Compulsive Buying: A Phenomenological Exploration," *Journal of Consumer Research* 16 (2) September, 147–157.

43. Nataraajan, Rajan, and Brent G. Goff (1992), "Manifestations of Compulsiveness in the Consumer-Marketplace Domain," *Psychology & Marketing* 9, 31–44.

44. This definition based on Faber, Ronald, and Thomas O'Guinn (1992), "A Clinical Screener for Compulsive Buying," *Journal of Consumer Research* 19 (3) December, 459–469.

45. Hirschman, Elizabeth C. (1992), "The Consciousness of Addiction: Toward a General Theory of Compulsive Consumption," *Journal of Consumer Research*, (September), 155–179; O'Guinn and Faber (1989); Dittmar, Helga (2005), "A New Look at Compulsive Buying: Self-Discrepancies and Materialistic Values as Predictors of Compulsive Buying Tendencies," *Journal of Social and Clinical Psychology*, (September), 832–859.

46. Joireman, Jeff, Jeremy Kees, and David Sprott (2010), "Concern with Immediate Consequences Magnifies the Impact of Compulsive Buying Tendencies on College Students' Credit Card Debt," *Journal of Consumer Affairs* 44 (1), 155–178.

47. Roberts, James A., Chris Manolis, and John F. Tanner, Jr. (2006), "Adolescent Autonomy and the Impact of Family Structure on Materialism and Compulsive Buying," *Journal of Marketing Theory and Practice* 14 (4) Fall, 301–314.

48. Roberts, James A. (1998), "Compulsive Buying Among College Students: An Investigation of its Antecedents, Consequences, and Implications for Public Policy," *Journal of Consumer Affairs* 32 (2) Winter, 295–319; O'Guinn and Faber (1989).

49. Black DW (2000). "Assessment of compulsive buying," In: Benson AL, ed. *I Shop, Therefore I Am: Compulsive Buying and the Search for Self*. Northvale, NJ: Jason Aronson, 191–216.

50. Parker-Pope, Jessica (2005), "This is Your Brand at the Mall: Why Shopping Makes You Feel So Good," *The Wall Street Journal* (December 6), D1.

51. Koran, Lorrin M., Ronald J. Faber, Elias Aboujauode, Michael D. Large, and Richard T. Serpe (2006), "Estimated Prevalence of Compulsive Buying Behavior in the United States," *The American Journal of Psychiatry*, (October), 1806–1812.

52. Yanovski, Susan, and Billinda K. Dubbert (1993), "Association of Binge Eating Disorder and Psychiatric Comorbidity in Obese Subjects," *The American Journal of Psychiatry*, (October), 1472–1479.

53. National Institute for Alcohol Abuse and Alcoholism website, **http://www.niaaa .nih.gov**, accessed March 17, 2008.

54. Information obtained from Mothers Against Drunk Drivers website: **http:// www.madd.org/Under-21/College/ Statistics/AllStats.aspx#STAT_1800**, accessed July 2, 1010.

55. Piacentini, Maira G., and Emma N. Banister (2006), "Getting Hammered? . . . Students Coping with Alcohol," *Journal of Consumer Behaviour* 5 (2) March–April, 145–156.

56. Wechsler H., J. E. Lee, M. Kuo, M. Seibring, T. F. Nelson, and H. P. Lee

(2002), "Trends in College Binge Drinking During a Period of Increased Prevention Efforts: Findings from Four Harvard School of Public Health Study Surveys," *Journal of American College Health* 50, 203–217; Presley, C. A., M. A. Leichliter, and P. W. Meilman (1998), *Alcohol and Drugs on American College Campuses: A Report to College Presidents: Third in a Series*, 1995, 1996, 1997, Carbondale, IL: Core Institute, Southern Illinois University.

57. Online content retrieved at College Drinking – Changing the Culture website, **http://www.collegedrinkingprevention .gov/StatsSummaries/snapshot.aspx**, accessed June 30, 2010.

58. Shim, Soyeon, and Jennifer Maggs (2005), "A Cognitive and Behavioral Hierarchical Decision-Making Model of College Students' Alcohol Consumption," *Psychology & Marketing* 22 (8), August, 649–668.

59. Information obtained from Mothers Against Drunk Drivers website: **http:// www.madd.org/Under-21/College/ Statistics.aspx**, accessed July 2, 2010.

60. This definition based on Netemeyer, Richard G., Scot Burton, Leslie K. Cole, Donald A. Williamson, Nancy Zucker, Lisa Bertman, and Gretchen Diefenbach (1998), "Characteristics and Beliefs Associated with Probable Pathological Gambling: A Pilot Study with Implications for the National Gambling Impact and Policy Commission," *Journal of Public Policy & Marketing* 17 (2) Fall, 147–160.

61. Balabanis, George (2002), "The Relationship Between Lottery-Ticket and Scratch-Card Buying Behaviour, Personality and Other Compulsive Behaviors," *Journal of Consumer Behaviour* 2 (1) September, 7–22.

62. Statistics based on information found at National Council on Problem Gambling, **http://www.ncpgambling.org/i4a/pages/ Index.cfm?pageID=3315#widespread**, accessed June 30, 2010.

63. McComb, J.L., and Hanson W.E. (2009), "Problem Gambling on College Campuses," *NASPA Journal* 46 (1), 1–29.

64. Levens, Suzi, Anne-Marie Dyer, Cynthia Zubritsky, Kathryn Knott, and David W. Oslin (2005), "Gambling Among Older, Primary Care Patients," *American Journal of Geriatric Psychiatry* **13**, 69–76; Loroz, Peggy Sue (2004), "Golden-Age Gambling: Psychological Benefits and Self-Concept Dynamics in Aging Consumers' Consumption Experiences," *Psychology & Marketing* 25 (1) May, 323–350.

65. Kwak, Hyokjin, George M. Zinkhan, and Elizabeth P. Lester Roushanzamir (2004), "Compulsive Comorbidity and its Psychological Antecedents: A Cross-Cultural Comparison Between the U.S. and South Korea," *The Journal of Consumer Marketing* 21, 418–434; Netemeyer, Richard G., Scot Burton, Leslie K. Cole, Donald A. Williamson, Nancy Zucker, Lisa Bertman, and Gretchen Diefenbach (1998), "Characteristics and Beliefs Associated with Probable Pathological Gambling: A Pilot Study with Implications for the National Gambling Impact and Policy Commission," *Journal of Public Policy & Marketing* 17 (2) Fall, 147–160.

66. Partnership for a Drug Free America (2006), "Generation Rx: National Study Confirms Abuse of Prescription and Over-the-Counter Drugs," Partnership for a Drug Free America website, **http://www .drugfree.org**, accessed March 17, 2008.

67. The National Institute on Drug Abuse "Monitoring the Future" Study, 2008, online content retrieved at: **www .drugabuse.gov/pdf/infofacts/HSYouth-Trends08.pdf**, accessed June 18, 2009.

68. Online content retrieved at **http://www .drugabuse.gov/MarijBroch/Marijpar-entsN.html**, accessed June 30, 2010.

69. This definition based on Lacyniak, Gene R., and Patrick E. Murphy (2006), "Normative Perspectives for Ethical and Socially Responsible Marketing," *Journal of Macromarketing* 26 (2), 154–177.

70. Karpatkin, Rhoda H. (1999), "Toward a Fair and Just Marketplace for All Consumers: The Responsibilities of Marketing Professionals," *Journal of Public Policy & Marketing* 18 (1), 118–122.

71. Xia, Lan, Kent B. Monroe, and Jennifer L. Cox (2004), "The Price is Unfair! A Conceptual Framework of Price Fairness Perceptions," *Journal of Marketing* 68 (October), 1–15; Campbell, Margaret C. (1999), "Perceptions of Price Fairness: Antecedents and Consequences," *Journal of Marketing Research* 36 (May), 187–199.

72. Kotler, Philip (1972), "What Consumerism Means for Marketers," *Harvard Business Review* 50 (May–June), 48–57.

73. McShane, Larry (2009), "Bruce Springsteen Slams Tickmaster Over Working on a Dream Ticket Sales," *New York Daily News* (online), online content retrieved at: **http://www.nydailynews.com/ gossip/2009/02/04/2009-02-04_bruce_ springsteen_slams_ticketmaster_ove.html**, accessed June 19, 2009.

74. Smith, N. Craig, and Elizabeth Cooper-Martin (1997), "Ethics and Target Marketing: The Role of Product Harm and Consumer Vulnerability," *Journal of Marketing* 61 (3), 1–20.

75. This definition based on Brown, Tom J., and Peter A. Dacin (1997), "The Company and the Product: Corporate Associations and Consumer Product Responses," *Journal of Marketing* 61 (1), 68–84.

76. Sen, Sankar, and C. B. Bhattacharya (2001), "Does Doing Good Always Lead to Doing Better? Consumer Reactions to Corporate Social Responsibility," *Journal of Marketing Research* 38 (2), 225–243.

77. Lantos, Geoffrey P. (2001), "The Boundaries of Strategic Corporate Social Responsibility," *Journal of Consumer Marketing* 18 (7), 595–630.

78. These assertions based on several works including Luo, Xueming, and C. B. Bhattacharya (2006), "Corporate Social Responsibility, Customer Satisfaction, and Market Value," *Journal of Marketing* 70 (4): 1–18; Lichenstein, Donald R., Minette E. Drumwright, and Bridgette M. Braig (2004), "The Effect of Corporate Social Responsibility on Customer Donations to Corporate-Supported Nonprofits," *Journal of Marketing* 68 (4), 16–32; Sen, Sankar, and C. B. Bhattacharya (2001), "Does Doing Good Always Lead to Doing Better Consumer Reactions to Corporate Social Responsibility," *Journal of Marketing Research* 38 (2), 225–243; Brown, Tom J., and Peter A. Dacin (1997), "The Company and the Product: Corporate Associations and Consumer Product Responses," *Journal of Marketing* 61 (1), 68–84.

79. Kotler (1972).

80. Federal Trade Commission website, **http://www.ftc.gov/bcp/conline/pubs/ buspubs/ad-faqs.shtm**, accessed March 17, 2008.

81. National Advertising Review Council website, **http://www.narcpartners.org/**, accessed March 17, 2008.

82. American Psychological Association (2004), "Television Advertising Leads to Unhealthy Habits in Children; Says APA Task Force" (February 23), **http:// www.apa.org/releases/childrenads.html**, accessed August 2007.

83. Online content retrieved at the CARU website, **http://www.caru.org/guidelines/ index.aspx**, accessed July 2, 2010.

84. On-line information obtained from the Federal Trade Commission website: **http://www.ftc.gov/bcp/conline/pubs/ buspubs/coppa.shtm, accessed March 17, 2008**.

85. Fry, Marie-Louis, and Michael Jay Polonsky (2004), "Examining the Unintended Consequences of Marketing," *Journal of Business Research* 57, 1303–1306.

86. Tybout, Alice M., Brian Sternthal, and Bobby J. Calder (1988), "Information Availability as a Determinant of Multiple-Request Effectiveness," *Journal of Marketing Research* 20 (August), 280–290; Mowen, John C. Mowen, and Robert Cialdini (1980), "On Implementing the Door-in-the-Face Compliance Strategy in a Marketing Context," *Journal of Marketing Research* 17 (May), 253–258; Freedman, Jonathon L., and Scott C. Fraher (1966), "Compliance Without Pressure: The Foot-in-the-Door Technique," *Journal of Personality and Social Psychology* 4 (August), 195–202.

87. Cialdini, Robert, and David Schroeder (1976), "Increasing Compliance by Legitimizing Paltry Contributions: When Even a Penny Helps," *Journal of Personality and Social Psychology* 34 (October), 599–604.

88. WOMMA, "Unethical Word-of-Mouth Marketing Strategies," **http://www .womma.org/wom101/06/**, accessed March 17, 2008.

89. Consumer Product Safety Commission website, **http://www.cpsc.gov/about/ about.html**, accessed March 17, 2008.

Case 5-1

1. **www.ncpc.org**
2. Maag, Christopher, "A Hoax Turned Fatal Draws Anger but No Charges," *The New York Times*, November 28, 2007.
3. "Virtual Bullying, Real Consequences," *Virtue in Action*, January 2008, **http:// www.virtueinaction.com/2008/VIA_ Meier.pdf**.
4. "Virtual Bullying, Real Consequences," *Virtue in Action*, January 2008, **http:// www.virtueinaction.com/2008/VIA_ Meier.pdf**.
5. Hinduja, S. & Patchin, J. (2008). "Cyberbullying: An exploratory analysis of factors related to offending and victimization," *Deviant Behavior*, 29(2), 1-29.
6. **http://www.ncpc.org/media/audio/ megan.mp3**

Case 5-2

1. **http://www.enviroliteracy.org/article .php/1268.html**

## A

**ABC approach to attitudes** approach that suggests that attitudes encompass one's affect, behavior, and cognitions (or "beliefs") toward an object

**absolute threshold** level over which the strength of a stimulus must be greater so that it can be perceived

**accommodation** state that results when a stimulus shares some but not all of the characteristics that would lead it to fit neatly in an existing category, and consumers must process exceptions to rules about the category

**acculturation** process by which consumers come to learn a culture other than their natural, native culture

**acquisitional shopping** activities oriented toward a specific, intended purchase or purchases

**action-oriented** consumers with a high capacity to self-regulate their behavior

**actual state** consumer's perceived current state

**adaptation level** level of a stimulus to which a consumer has become accustomed

**addictive consumption** physiological dependency on the consumption of a consumer product

**advertiming** ad buys that include a schedule that runs the advertisement primarily at times when customers will be most receptive to the message

**aesthetic labor** effort put forth by employees in carefully managing their appearance as a requisite for performing their job well

**affect** feelings associated with objects or experienced during events

**affect-based evaluation** evaluative process wherein consumers evaluate products based on the overall feeling that is evoked by the alternative

**affective quality** retail positioning that emphasizes a unique environment, exciting décor, friendly employees, and, in general, the feelings experienced in a retail place

**age-based microculture** term that describes the finding that people of the same age end up sharing many of the same values and develop similar consumer preferences

**aggregation approach** approach to studying personality in which behavior is assessed at a number of points in time

**AIO statements** activity, interest, and opinion statements that are used in lifestyle studies

**antecedent conditions** situational characteristics that a consumer brings to information processing

**anthropology** study in which researchers interpret relationships between consumers and the things they purchase, the products they own, and the activities in which they participate

**antiloyal consumers** consumers who will do everything possible to avoid doing business with a particular marketer

**aspirational group** group in which a consumer desires to become a member

**assimilation** state that results when a stimulus has characteristics such that consumers readily recognize it as belonging to some specific category

**associative network** network of mental pathways linking all knowledge within memory; sometimes referred to as a semantic network

**atmospherics** emotional nature of an environment or the feelings created by the total aura

of physical attributes that comprise a physical environment

**attention** purposeful allocation of information-processing capacity toward developing an understanding of some stimulus

**attention to social comparison information (ATSCI)** individual difference variable that assesses the extent to which a consumer is concerned about how other people react to his or her behavior

**attitude tracking** effort of a marketer or researcher to track changes in consumer attitudes over time

**attitude-behavior consistency** extent to which a strong relationship exists between attitudes and actual behavior

**attitudes** relatively enduring overall evaluations of objects, products, services, issues, or people

**attitude-toward-the-object (ATO) model** attitude model that considers three key elements including beliefs consumers have about salient attributes, the strength of the belief that an object possesses the attribute, and evaluation of the particular attribute

**attribute** a product feature that delivers a desired consumer benefit

**attribute correlation** perceived relationship between product features

**attribute-based evaluation** evaluative process wherein alternatives are evaluated across a set of attributes that are considered relevant to the purchase situation

**attribution theory** theory that proposes that consumers look for the cause of particular consumption experiences when arriving at satisfaction judgments

**augmented product** actual physical product purchased plus any services such as installation and warranties necessary to use the product and obtain its benefits

**authenticity** something that is real, genuine, and has a history or tradition

**autobiographical memories** cognitive representation of meaningful events in one's life

**autonomic measures** responses that are automatically recorded based on either automatic visceral reactions or neurological brain activity

**awareness set** set of alternatives of which a consumer is aware

## B

**background music** music played below the audible threshold that would make it the center of attention

**balance theory** theory that states that consumers are motivated to maintain perceived consistency in the relations found in a system

**behavioral influence decision-making perspective** assumes many consumer decisions are actually learned responses to environmental influences

**behavioral intentions model** model, developed to improve on the ATO model, that focuses on behavioral intentions, subjective norms, and attitude toward a particular behavior

**behaviorist approach to learning** theory of learning that focuses on changes in behavior due to association without great concern for the cognitive mechanics of the learning process

**benefit** perceived favorable results derived from a particular feature

**benefits** positive results of consumption

**bicultural** used to describe an immigrant as he or she faces decisions and form preferences based on their old or new cultures

**binge drinking** consumption of five or more drinks in a single drinking session for men and four or more drinks for women

**binge eating** consumption of large amounts of food while feeling a general loss of control over food intake

**bipolar** situation wherein if one feels joy he or she cannot also experience sadness

**body language** nonverbal communication cues signaled by somatic responses

**boomerang kids** young adults, between the ages of 18 and 34, who move back home with their parents after they graduate from college

**bounded rationality** idea that consumers attempt to act rationally within their information processing constraints

**brand community** groups of consumers who develop relationships based on shared interests or product usage

**brand inertia** what occurs when a consumer simply buys a product repeatedly without any real attachment

**brand loyalty** deeply held commitment to rebuy a product or service regardless of situational influences that could lead to switching behavior

**brand personality** collection of human characteristics that can be associated with a brand

**BRIC** acronym that refers to the collective economies of Brazil, Russia, India, and China

**buzz marketing** marketing efforts that focus on generating excitement among consumers and that are spread from consumer to consumer

## C

**CANZUS** acronym that refers to the close similarity in values between Canada, Australia, New Zealand, and the United States

**central cues** information presented in a message about the product itself, its attributes, or the consequences of its use

**central route to persuasion** path to persuasion found in ELM where the consumer has high involvement, motivation, and/or ability to process a message

**Chindia** combined market and business potential of China and India

**chunking** process of grouping stimuli by meaning so that multiple stimuli can become one memory unit

**circadian cycle** rhythm (level of energy) of the human body that varies with the time of day

**classical conditioning** change in behavior that occurs simply through associating some stimulus with another stimulus that naturally causes some reaction; a type of unintentional learning

**cognition** thinking or mental processes that go on as we process and store things that can become knowledge

**cognitive appraisal theory** school of thought proposing that specific types of appraisal thoughts can be linked to specific types of emotions

**cognitive dissonance** an uncomfortable feeling that occurs when a consumer has lingering doubts about a decision that has occurred

**cognitive interference** notion that everything else that the consumer is exposed to while trying to remember something is also vying for processing capacity and thus interfering with memory and comprehension

**cognitive organization** process by which the human brain assembles sensory evidence into something recognizable

**cognitive psychology** study of the intricacies of mental reactions involved in information processing

**cognitive structuring** term that refers to the reliance on schema-based heuristics in making decisions

**cohort** a group of people who have lived the same major experiences in their life

**collectivism** extent to which an individual's life is intertwined with a large cohesive group

**compensatory damages** damages that are intended to cover costs incurred by a consumer due to an injury

**compensatory model** attitudinal model wherein low ratings for one attribute are compensated for by higher ratings on another

**compensatory rule** decision-making rule that allows consumers to select products that may perform poorly on one criterion by compensating for the poor performance on one attribute by good performance on another

**competitive intensity** number of firms competing for business within a specific category

**competitiveness** enduring tendency to strive to be better than others

**complaining behavior** action that occurs when a consumer actively seeks out someone to share an opinion with regarding a negative consumption event

**comprehension** the way people cognitively assign meaning to (i.e., understand) things they encounter

**compulsive buying** chronic, repetitive purchasing that is a response to negative events or feelings

**compulsive consumption** repetitive, excessive, and purposeful consumer behaviors that are performed as a response to tension, anxiety, or obtrusive thoughts

**compulsive shopping** repetitive shopping behaviors that are a response to negative events or feelings

**conditioned response** response that results from exposure to a conditioned stimulus that was originally associated with the unconditioned stimulus

**conditioned stimulus** object or event that does not cause the desired response naturally but that can be conditioned to do so by pairing with an unconditioned stimulus

**confirmatory bias** tendency for expectations to guide performance perceptions

**conformity** result of group influence in which an individual yields to the attitudes and behaviors or others

**congruity** how consistent the elements of an environment are with one another

**conjoint analysis** technique used to develop an understanding of the attributes that guide consumer preferences by having consumers compare product preferences across varying levels of evaluative criteria and expected utility

**conjunctive rule** noncompensatory decision rule where the option selected must surpass a minimum cutoff across all relevant attributes

**connected self-schema** self conceptualization of the extent to which a consumer perceives himself or herself as being an integral part of a group

**consideration set** alternatives that are considered acceptable for further consideration in decision making

**consistency principle** principle that states that human beings prefer consistency among their beliefs, attitudes, and behaviors

**consumer (customer) orientation** way of doing business in which the actions and decision making of the institution prioritize consumer value and satisfaction above all other concerns

**consumer affect** feelings a consumer has about a particular product or activity

**consumer behavior** set of value-seeking activities that take place as people go about addressing realized needs

**consumer behavior as a field of study** study of consumers as they go about the consumption process; the science of studying how consumers seek value in an effort to address real needs

**Consumer Bill of Rights** introduced by President John F. Kennedy in 1962, list of rights that includes the right to safety, the right to be informed, the right to redress and to be heard, and the right to choice

**consumer culture** commonly held societal beliefs that define what is socially gratifying

**consumer dissatisfaction** mild, negative affective reaction resulting from an unfavorable appraisal of a consumption outcome

**consumer ethnocentrism** belief among consumers that their ethnic group is superior to others and that the products that come from their native land are superior to other products

**consumer inertia** situation in which a consumer tends to continue a pattern of behavior until some stronger force motivates him or her to change

**consumer involvement** degree of personal relevance a consumer finds in pursuing value from a particular category of consumption

**consumer misbehavior** behaviors that are in some way unethical and that potentially harm the self or others

**consumer problem behavior** consumer behavior that is deemed to be unacceptable but that is seemingly beyond the control of the consumer

**consumer refuse** any packaging that is no longer necessary for consumption to take place or, in some cases, the actual good that is no longer providing value to the consumer

**consumer satisfaction** mild, positive emotion resulting from a favorable appraisal of a consumption outcome

**consumer search behavior** behaviors that consumers engage in as they seek information that can be used to resolve a problem

**consumer self-regulation** tendency for consumers to inhibit outside, or situational, influences from interfering with shopping intentions

**consumer socialization** the process through which young consumers develop attitudes and learn skills that help them function in the marketplace

**Consumer Value Framework (CVF)** consumer behavior theory that illustrates factors that shape consumption-related behaviors and ultimately determine the value associated with consumption

**consumerism** activities of various groups to voice concern for, and to protect, basic consumer rights

**consumption** process by which goods, services, or ideas are used and transformed into value

**consumption frequency** number of times a product is consumed

**consumption process** process in which consumers use the product, service, or experience that has been selected

**contractualism** beliefs about the violation of written (or unwritten) laws

**contrast** state that results when a stimulus does not share enough in common with existing categories to allow categorization

**core societal values (CSV), or cultural values** commonly agreed-upon consensus about the most preferable ways of living within a society

**corporate social responsibility** organization's activities and status related to its societal obligations

**corporate strategy** way a firm is defined and its general goals

**costs** negative results of consumption

**counterarguments** thoughts that contradict a message

**credibility** extent to which a source is considered to be both an expert in a given area and trustworthy

**crowding** density of people and objects within a given space

**cultural distance** representation of how disparate one nation is from another in terms of their CSV

**cultural norm** rule that specifies the appropriate consumer behavior in a given situation within a specific culture

**cultural sanction** penalty associated with performing a nongratifying or culturally inconsistent behavior

**customer commitment** sense of attachment, dedication, and identification

**customer lifetime value (CLV)** approximate worth of a customer to a company in economic terms; overall profitability of an individual consumer

**customer orientation** practice of using sales techniques that focus on customer needs

**Customer Relationship Management (CRM)** systematic management information system that collects, maintains, and reports detailed information about customers to enable a more customer-oriented managerial approach

**customer share** portion of resources allocated to one brand from among the set of competing brands

# D

**deceptive advertising** message that omits information that is important in influencing a consumer's buying behavior and is likely to mislead consumers acting "reasonably"

**declarative knowledge** cognitive components that represent facts

**deficient products** products that have little or no potential to create value of any type

**demographic analysis** a profile of a consumer group based on their demographics

**demographics** observable, statistical aspects of populations such as age, gender, or income

**demographics** relatively tangible human characteristics that describe consumers

**deontological evaluations** evaluations regarding the inherent rightness or wrongness of specific actions

**desirable products** products that deliver high utilitarian and hedonic value and that benefit both consumers and society in the long run

**desired state** perceived state for which a consumer strives

**desires** level of a particular benefit that will lead to a valued end state

**determinant criteria** criteria that are most carefully considered and directly related to the actual choice that is made

**dialects** variations of a common language

**differentiated marketers** firms that serve multiple market segments each with a unique product offering

**diffusion process** way in which new products are adopted and spread throughout a marketplace

**discriminative stimuli** stimuli that occur solely in the presence of a reinforcer

**disjunctive rule** noncompensatory decision rule where the option selected surpasses a relatively high cutoff point on any attribute

**dissociative group** group to which a consumer does not want to belong

**divergence** situation in which consumers choose membership in microcultures in an effort to stand out or define themselves from the crowd

**door-in-the-face technique** ingratiation technique used in personal selling in which a salesperson begins with a major request and then follows with a series of smaller requests

**dostats** Russian word that can be roughly translated as "acquiring things with great difficulty"

**dual coding** coding that occurs when two different sensory traces are available to remember something

**durable goods** goods that are usually consumed over a long period of time

## E

**echoic storage** storage of auditory information in sensory memory

**ecological factors** physical characteristics that describe the physical environment and habitat of a particular place

**economics** study of production and consumption

**ego** component in psychoanalytic theory that attempts to balance the struggle between the superego and the id

**ego-defensive function of attitudes** function of attitudes whereby attitudes work as defense mechanisms for consumers

**elaboration** extent to which a consumer continues processing a message even after an initial understanding is achieved

**elaboration likelihood model** attitudinal change model that shows attitudes are changed based on differing levels of consumer involvement through either central or peripheral processing

**elasticity** reflects how sensitive a consumer is to changes in some product characteristic

**elimination-by-aspects rule** noncompensatory decision rule where the consumer begins evaluating options by first looking at the most important attribute and eliminating any option that does not meet a minimum cutoff point for that attribute and where subsequent evaluations proceed in order of importance until only one option remains

**emotion** a specific psychobiological reaction to a human appraisal

**emotional contagion** extent to which an emotional display by one person influences the emotional state of a bystander

**emotional effect on memory** relatively superior recall for information presented with mild affective content compared to similar information presented in an affectively neutral way

**emotional expressiveness** extent to which a consumer shows outward behavioral signs and otherwise reacts obviously to emotional experiences

**emotional intelligence** awareness of the emotions experienced in a given situation and the ability to control reactions to these emotions

**emotional involvement** type of deep personal interest that evokes strongly felt feelings simply from the thoughts or behavior associated with some object or activity

**emotional labor** effort put forth by service workers who have to overtly manage their own emotional displays as part of the requirements of the job

**encoding** process by which information is transferred from workbench memory to long-term memory for permanent storage

**enculturation** way a person learns his or her native culture

**enduring involvement** ongoing interest in some product or opportunity

**episodic memory** memory for past events in one's life

**epistemic shopping** activities oriented toward acquiring knowledge about products

**equity theory** theory that proposes that people compare their own level of inputs and outcomes to those of another party in an exchange

**ethics** standards or moral codes of conduct to which a person, group, or organization adheres

**ethnic identification** degree to which consumers feel a sense of belonging to the culture of their ethnic origins

**ethnography** qualitative approach to studying consumers that relies on interpretation of artifacts to draw conclusions about consumption

**etiquette** customary mannerisms consumers use in common social situations

**evaluative criteria** attributes that consumers consider when reviewing alternative solutions to a problem

**even-a-penny-will-help technique** ingratiation technique in which a marketing message is sent that suggests that even the smallest donation, such as a penny or a dollar, will help a cause

**exchange** acting out of the decision to give something up in return for something of greater value

**exemplar** concept within a schema that is the single best representative of some category; schema for something that really exists

**expectancy/disconfirmation theory** proposes that consumers use expectations as a benchmark against which performance perceptions are judged and this comparison is a primary basis for satisfaction/dissatisfaction

**expectations** beliefs of what will happen in some future situation

**experiential decision-making perspective** assumes consumers often make purchases and reach decisions based on the affect, or feeling, attached to the product or behavior under consideration

**experiential shopping** recreationally oriented activities designed to provide interest, excitement, relaxation, fun, social interaction, or some other desired feeling

**expertise** amount of knowledge that a source is perceived to have about a subject

**explicit memory** memory that developed when the person was trying to remember the stimulus

**exposure** process of bringing some stimulus within proximity of a consumer so that the consumer can sense it with one of the five human senses

**extended decision making** consumers move diligently through various problem-solving activi-

ties in search of the best information that will help them reach a decision

**extended family** three or more generations of family members

**external influences** social and cultural aspects of life as a consumer

**external search** gathering of information from sources external to the consumer such as friends, family, salespeople, advertising, independent research reports, and the Internet

**extinction** process through which behaviors cease because of lack of reinforcement

## F

**family household** at least two people who are related by blood or marriage

**feature** performance characteristic of an object

**femininity** sex role distinction within a group that emphasizes the prioritization of relational variables such as caring, conciliation, and community; CSV opposite of masculinity

**figure** object that is intended to capture a person's attention; the focal part of any message

**figure–ground distinction** notion that each message can be separated into the focal point (figure) and the background (ground)

**financial switching costs** total economic resources that must be spent or invested as a consumer learns how to obtain value from a new product choice

**fit** how appropriate the elements of a given environment are

**five-factor model** multiple-trait perspective that proposes that the human personality consists of five traits: agreeableness, extroversion, openness to experience (or creativity), conscientiousness, and neuroticism (or stability)

**flow** extremely high emotional involvement in which a consumer is engrossed in an activity

**foot-in-the-door technique** ingratiation technique used in personal selling in which a salesperson begins with a small request and slowly leads up to one major request

**foreground music** music that becomes the focal point of attention and can have strong effects on a consumer's willingness to approach or avoid an environment

**formal group** group in which a consumer formally becomes a member

**framing** a phenomenon in which the meaning of something is influenced (perceived differently) by the information environment

**functional quality** retail positioning that emphasizes tangible things like a wide selection of goods, low prices, guarantees, and knowledgeable employees

**functional theory of attitudes** theory of attitudes that suggests that attitudes perform four basic functions

## G

**geodemographic techniques** techniques that combine data on consumer expenditures and socioeconomic variables with geographic information in order to identify commonalities in consumption patterns of households in various regions

**geodemographics** study of people based on the fact that people with similar demographics tend to live close to one another

**glocalization** idea that marketing strategy may be global but the implementation of that strategy at the marketing tactics level should be local

**ground** background in a message

**group influence** ways in which group members influence attitudes, behaviors, and opinions of others within the group

**guanxi** (pronounced gawn-shi) Chinese term for a way of doing business in which parties must first invest time and resources in getting to know one another before consummating any important deal

**guerrilla marketing** marketing of a product using unconventional means

## H

**habitual decision making** consumers generally do not seek information at all when a problem is recognized and select a product based on habit

**habituation** process by which continuous exposure to a stimulus affects the comprehension of, and response to, the stimulus

**habitus** mental and cognitive structures through which individuals perceive the world based largely on their standing in a social class

**hedonic motivation** drive to experience something emotionally gratifying

**hedonic shopping value** worth of an activity because the time spent doing the activity itself is personally gratifying

**hedonic value** value derived from the immediate gratification that comes from some activity

**hierarchical approaches to personality** approaches to personality inquiry that assume that personality traits exist at varying levels of abstraction

**hierarchy of effects** attitude approach that suggests that affect, behavior, and cognitions form in a sequential order

**homeostasis** state of equilibrium wherein the body naturally reacts in a way so as to maintain a constant, normal bloodstream

**homogamy** the finding that most marriages are comprised of people from similar classes

**hope** a fundamental emotion evoked by positive, anticipatory appraisals

**household decision making** process by which decisions are made in household units

**household life cycle (HLC)** segmentation technique that acknowledges that changes in family composition and income alter household demand for products and services

## I

**iconic storage** storage of visual information in sensory memory and the idea that things are stored with a one-to-one representation with reality

**id** the personality component in psychoanalytic theory that focuses on pleasure-seeking motives and immediate gratification

**ideal points** combination of product characteristics that provide the most value to an individual consumer or market segment

**idiographic perspective** approach to personality that focuses on understanding the complexity of each individual consumer

**implicit memory** memory for things that a person did not try to remember

**impulsive consumption** consumption acts characterized by spontaneity, a diminished regard for consequences, and a need for self-fulfillment

**impulsive shopping** spontaneous activities characterized by a diminished regard for consequences, spontaneity, and a desire for immediate self-fulfillment

**impulsivity** personality trait that represents how sensitive a consumer is to immediate rewards

**"I'm working for you!" technique** technique used by salespeople to create the perception that they are working as hard as possible to close a sale when they really are not doing so

**individual difference variables** descriptions of how individual consumers differ according to specific trait patterns of behavior

**individual differences** characteristic traits of individuals, including personality and lifestyle

**individualism** extent to which people are expected to take care of themselves and their immediate families

**inept set** alternatives in the awareness set that are deemed to be unacceptable for further consideration

**inert set** alternatives in the awareness set about which consumers are indifferent or do not hold strong feelings

**informal group** group that has no membership or application requirements and that may have no codes of conduct

**information intensity** amount of information available for a consumer to process within a given environment

**information overload** situation in which consumers are presented with so much information that they cannot assimilate the variety of information presented

**information processing perspective** approach that focuses on changes in thought and knowledge and how these precipitate behavioral changes

**informational influence** ways in which a consumer uses the behaviors and attitudes of reference groups as information for making his or her own decisions

**innovativeness** degree to which an individual is open to new ideas and tends to be relatively early in adopting new products, services, or experiences

**instrumental conditioning** type of learning in which a behavioral response can be conditioned through reinforcement—either punishment or rewards associated with undesirable or desirable behavior

**intentional learning** process by which consumers set out to specifically learn information devoted to a certain subject

**internal influences** things that go on inside of the mind and heart of the consumer

**internal search** retrieval of knowledge stored in memory about products, services, and experiences

**interpretive research** approach that seeks to explain the inner meanings and motivations associated with specific consumption experiences

**involuntary attention** attention that is beyond the conscious control of a consumer

**involvement** the personal relevance toward, or interest in, a particular product

## J

**JMD** just meaningful difference; smallest amount of change in a stimulus that would influence consumer consumption and choice

**JND** just noticeable difference; condition in which one stimulus is sufficiently stronger than another so that someone can actually notice that the two are not the same

**judgments** mental assessments of the presence of attributes and the consequences associated with those attributes

## K

**knowledge function of attitudes** function of attitudes whereby attitudes allow consumers to simplify decision-making processes

## L

**learning** change in behavior resulting from some interaction between a person and a stimulus

**left skewed** occurs when a disproportionate number of observations cluster toward the right end of a scale as when most people report satisfied or very satisfied

**lexicographic rule** noncompensatory decision rule where the option selected is thought to perform best on the most important attribute

**lifestyles** distinctive modes of living, including how people spend their time and money

**limited decision making** decision-making approach wherein consumers search very little for information and often reach decisions based largely on prior beliefs about products and their attributes

**long-term memory** repository for all information that a person has encountered

**long-term orientation** values consistent with Confucian philosophy and a prioritization of future rewards over short-term benefits

**loyalty card/program** device that keeps track of the amount of purchasing a consumer has had with a given marketer once some level is reached

## M

**market maven** consumer who spreads information about all types of products and services that are available in the marketplace

**market orientation** organizational culture that embodies the importance of creating value for customers among all employees

**market segmentation** separation of a market into groups based on the different demand curves associated with each group

**marketing** multitude of value-producing seller activities that facilitate exchanges between buyers and sellers

**marketing concept** concept that states a firm should focus on consumer needs as a means of achieving long-term success

**marketing ethics** societal and professional standards of right and fair practices that are expected of marketing managers as they develop and implement marketing strategies

**marketing mix** combination of product, pricing, promotion, and distribution strategies used to implement a marketing strategy

**marketing myopia** a common condition in which a company views itself in a product business rather than in a value, or benefits producing, business. In this way, it is shortsighted.

**marketing strategy** way a company goes about creating value for customers

**marketing tactics** ways marketing management is implemented; involves price, promotion, product, and distribution decisions

**masculinity** role distinction within a group that values assertiveness and control; CSV opposite of femininity

**Maslow's hierarchy of needs** a theory of human motivation which describes consumers as addressing a finite set of prioritized needs

**matchup hypothesis** hypothesis that states that a source feature is most effective when it is matched with relevant products

**materialism** extent to which material goods have importance in a consumer's life

**meaning transference** process through which cultural meaning is transferred to a product and onto the consumer

**meaningful encoding** coding that occurs when information from long-term memory is placed on the workbench and attached to the information on the workbench in a way that the information can be recalled and used later

**memory** psychological process by which knowledge is recorded

**memory trace** mental path by which some thought becomes active

**mental budgeting** memory accounting for recent spending

**mere exposure effect** that which leads consumers to prefer a stimulus to which they've previously been exposed

**message congruity** extent to which a message is internally consistent and fits surrounding information

**message effects** how the appeal of a message and its construction affects persuasiveness

**metric equivalence** statistical tests used to validate the way people use numbers to represent quantities across cultures

**microculture** a group of people who share similar values and tastes that are subsumed within a larger culture

**modeling** process of imitating others' behavior; a form of observational learning

**moderating variable** variable that changes the nature of the relationship between two other variables

**mood** transient and general affective state

**mood-congruent judgments** evaluations in which the value of a target is influenced in a consistent way by one's mood

**mood-congruent recall** consumers will remember information better when the mood they are currently in matches the mood they were in when originally exposed to the information

**moral beliefs** beliefs about the perceived ethicality or morality of behaviors

**moral equity** beliefs regarding an act's fairness or justness

**morals** personal standards and beliefs used to guide individual action

**motivational research era** era in consumer research that focused heavily on psychoanalytic approaches

**motivations** inner reasons or driving forces behind human actions as consumers are driven to address real needs

**multiple store theory of memory** theory that explains memory as utilizing three different storage areas within the human brain: sensory, workbench, and long-term

**multiple-trait approach** approach in trait research wherein the focus remains on combinations of traits

## N

**need for cognition** refers to the degree to which consumers enjoy engaging in effortful cognitive information processing

**negative disconfirmation** according to the expectancy/disconfirmation approach, a perceived state wherein performance perceptions fall short of expectations

**negative public publicity** action that occurs when

negative WOM spreads on a relatively large scale, possibly even involving media coverage

**negative reinforcement** removal of harmful stimuli as a way of encouraging behavior

**negative word-of-mouth** (negative WOM) action that takes place when consumers pass on negative information about a company from one to another

**negligence** situation whereby an injured consumer attempts to show that a firm could foresee a potential injury might occur and then decided not to act on that knowledge

**niche marketing** plan wherein a firm specializes in serving one market segment with particularly unique demand characteristics

**nodes** concepts found in an associative network

**nomothetic perspective** variable-centered approach to personality that focuses on particular traits that exist across a number of people

**noncompensatory rule** decision-making rule in which strict guidelines are set prior to selection and any option that does not meet the guidelines is eliminated from consideration

**nondurable goods** goods that are usually consumed quickly

**nonlinear effect** a plot of the effect by the amount of crowding, which does not make a straight line

**nonverbal communication** information passed through some nonverbal act

**nostalgia** a mental yearning to relive the past associated with emotions related to longing

**nuclear family** a mother, a father, and a set of siblings

## O

**olfactory** refers to humans' physical and psychological processing of smells

**one-to-one marketing** plan wherein a different product is offered for each individual customer so that each customer is treated as a segment of one

**ongoing search** search effort that is not necessarily focused on an upcoming purchase or decision but rather on staying up-to-date on the topic

**opinion leader** consumer who has a great deal of influence on the behavior of others relating to product adoption and purchase

**orientation reflex** natural reflex that occurs as a response to something threatening

**outshopping** shopping in a city or town to which consumers must travel rather than in their own hometowns

## P

**PAD** self-report measure that asks respondents to rate feelings using semantic differential items; acronym stands for pleasure–arousal–dominance

**paths** representations of the association between nodes in an associative network

**peer pressure** extent to which group members feel pressure to behave in accordance with group expectations

**perceived risk** perception of the negative consequences that are likely to result from a course of action and the uncertainty of which course of action is best to take

**perception** consumer's awareness and interpretation of reality

**perceptual attributes** attributes that are visually apparent and easily recognizable

**perceptual map** tool used to depict graphically the positioning of competing products

**peripheral cues** nonproduct-related information presented in a message

**peripheral route to persuasion** path to persuasion found in ELM where the consumer has low involvement, motivation, and/or ability to process a message

**personal elaboration** process by which a person imagines himself or herself somehow associating with a stimulus that is being processed

**personal shopping value (PSV)** overall subjective worth of a shopping activity considering all associated costs and benefits

**personality** totality of thoughts, emotions, intentions, and behaviors that a person exhibits consistently as he or she adapts to the environment

**persuasion** attempt to change attitudes

**phenomenology** qualitative approach to studying consumers that relies on interpretation of the lived experience associated with some aspect of consumption

**physical characteristics** tangible elements or the parts of a message that can be sensed

**planned obsolescence** act of planning the premature obsolescence of product models that perform adequately

**pleasing products** products that provide hedonic value for consumers but may be harmful in the long run

**pleasure principle** principle found in psychoanalytic theory that describes the factor that motivates pleasure-seeking behavior within the id

**positive disconfirmation** according to the expectancy/disconfirmation approach, a perceived state wherein performance perceptions exceed expectations

**positive reinforcers** reinforcers that take the form of a reward

**positive WOM** action that occurs when consumers spread information from one to another about positive consumption experiences with companies

**power distance** extent to which authority and privileges are divided among different groups within society and the extent to which these facts of life are accepted by the people within the society

**preattentive effects** learning that occurs without attention

**prepurchase search** search effort aimed at finding information to solve an immediate problem

**price** information that signals the amount of potential value contained in a product price, promotion, product, and distribution decisions

**primacy effect** occurs when the information placed early in a message has the most impact

**primary group** group that includes members who have frequent, direct contact with one another

**priming** cognitive process in which context or environment activates concepts and frames thoughts and therefore both value and meaning

**PRIZM** popular geodemographic technique that stands for Potential Ratings Index by ZIP Market

**problem gambling** obsession over the thought of gambling and the loss of control over gambling behavior and its consequences

**procedural justice** the extent that consumers believe the processes involved in processing a transaction and handling any complaints is fair

**procedural switching costs** lost time and extended effort spent in learning ways of using some product offering

**product** potentially valuable bundle of benefits

**product categories** mental representations of stored knowledge about groups of products

**product contamination** refers to the diminished positive feelings someone has about a product because another consumer has handled the product

**product differentiation** marketplace condition in which consumers do not view all competing products as identical to one another

**product enthusiasts** consumers with very high involvement in some product category

**product involvement** the personal relevance of a particular product category

**product placements** products that have been placed conspicuously in movies or television shows

**product positioning** way a product is perceived by a consumer

**production orientation** approach where innovation is geared primarily toward making the production process as efficient and economic as possible

**products liability** extent to which businesses are held responsible for product-related injuries

**prospect theory** theory that suggests that a decision, or argument, can be framed in different ways and that the framing affects risk assessments consumers make

**prototype** schema that is the best representative of some category but that is not represented by an existing entity; conglomeration of the most associated characteristics of a category

**psychoanalytic approach to personality** approach to personality research, advocated by Sigmund Freud, that suggests personality results from a struggle between inner motives and societal pressures to follow rules and expectations

**psychobiological** a response involving both psychological and physical human responses

**psychographics** quantitative investigation of consumer lifestyles

**psychology** study of human reactions to environments including behavior and mental processes

**puffery** practice of making exaggerated claims about a product and its superiority

**punishers** stimuli that decrease the likelihood that a behavior will persist

**purchasing power parity (PPP)** total size of the consumer market in each country in terms of total buying power

## Q

**qualitative research tools** means for gathering data in a relatively unstructured way, including case analysis, clinical interviews, and focus group interviews

**quality** perceived overall goodness or badness of some product

**quantitative research** approach that addresses questions about consumer behavior using numerical measurement and analysis tools

**quartet of institutions** four groups responsible for communicating the CSV through both formal and informal processes from one generation to another: family, school, church, and media

## R

**rancorous revenge** is when a consumer yells, insults, and makes a public scene in an effort to harm the business in response to an unsatisfactory experience

**rational decision-making perspective** assumes consumers diligently gather information about purchases, carefully compare various brands of products on salient attributes, and make informed decisions regarding what brand to buy

**reality principle** the principle in psychoanalytic theory under which the ego attempts to satisfy the id within societal constraints

**recency effect** occurs when the information placed late in a message has the most impact

**reference group** individuals who have significant relevance for a consumer and who have an impact on the consumer's evaluations, aspirations, and behavior

**relational switching cost** emotional and psychological consequences of changing from one brand/retailer/service provider to another

**relationship marketing** activities based on the belief that the firm's performance is enhanced through repeat business

**relationship quality** degree of connectedness between a consumer and a retailer, brand, or service provider

**renqing** the idea that favors given to another are reciprocal and must be returned

**repetition** simple mechanism in which a thought is kept alive in short-term memory by mentally repeating the thought

**researcher dependent** subjective data that requires a researcher to interpret the meaning

**resource-advantage theory** theory that explains why companies succeed or fail; the firm goes about obtaining resources from consumers in return for the value the resources create

**response generation** reconstruction of memory traces into a formed recollection of information

**retail personality** way a retail store is defined in the mind of a shopper based on the combination of functional and affective qualities

**retaliatory revenge** consumer becomes violent with employees and/or tries to vandalize a business in response to an unsatisfactory experience

**retrieval** process by which information is transferred back into workbench memory for additional processing when needed

**role conflict** a situation involving conflicting expectations based on cultural role expectations

**role expectations** the specific expectations that are associated with each type of person within a culture or society

**rumination** unintentional but recurrent memory of long-ago events that are spontaneously (not evoked by the environment) triggered

## S

**sandwich generation** consumers who must take care of both their own children and their aging parents

**satisficing** practice of using decision-making shortcuts to arrive at satisfactory, rather than optimal, decisions

**schema** cognitive representation of a phenomenon that provides meaning to that entity

**schema-based affect** emotions that become stored as part of the meaning for a category (a schema)

**script** schema representing an event

**search regret** negative emotions that come from failed search processes

**seasonality** regularly occurring conditions that vary with the time of year

**secondary group** group to which a consumer belongs whose contact is less frequent than that found in a primary group

**selective attention** process of paying attention to only certain stimuli

**selective distortion** process by which consumers interpret information in ways that are biased by their previously held beliefs

**selective exposure** process of screening out

certain stimuli and purposely exposing oneself to other stimuli

**self-concept** totality of thoughts and feelings that an individual has about himself or herself

**self-congruency theory** theory that proposes that much of consumer behavior can be explained by the congruence of a consumer's self-concept with the image of typical users of a focal product

**self-conscious emotions** specific emotions that result from some evaluation or reflection of one's own behavior, including pride, shame, guilt, and embarrassment

**self-esteem** positivity of the self-concept that one holds

**self-improvement motivation** motivations aimed at changing the current state to a level that is more ideal, not at simply maintaining the current state

**self-perception theory** theory that states that consumers are motivated to act in accordance with their attitudes and behaviors

**semantic coding** type of coding wherein stimuli are converted to meaning that can be expressed verbally

**semiotics** study of symbols and their meanings

**sensation** consumer's immediate response to a stimulus

**sensory memory** area in memory where a consumer stores things exposed to one of the five senses

**separated self-schema** self conceptualization of the extent to which a consumer perceives himself or herself as distinct and separate from others

**serial position effect** occurs when the placement of information in a message impacts recall of the information

**service quality** overall goodness or badness of a service experience, which is often measured by SERVQUAL

**servicescape** physical environment in which consumer services are performed

**SERVQUAL** way of measuring service quality that captures consumers' disconfirmation of service expectations

**sex role orientation (SRO)** family's set of beliefs regarding the ways in which household decisions are reached

**sex roles** societal expectations for men and women among members of a cultural group

**shaping** process through which a desired behavior is altered over time, in small increments

**share of wallet** customer share

**shopping involvement** personal relevance of shopping activities

**shopping** set of value-producing consumer activities that directly increase the likelihood that something will be purchased

**signal** attribute that consumer uses to infer something about another attribute

**signal theory** explains ways in which communications convey meaning beyond the explicit or obvious interpretation

**single-trait approach** approach in trait research wherein the focus is on one particular trait

**situational influences** things unique to a time or place that can affect consumer decision making and the value received from consumption

**situational involvement** temporary interest in some imminent purchase situation

**social comparison** is a naturally occurring mental personal comparison of the self with a target individual within the environment

**social environment** elements that specifically deal with the way other people influence consumer decision making and value

**social judgment theory** theory that proposes that consumers compare incoming information to their existing attitudes about a particular object or issue and that attitude change depends upon how consistent the information is with the initial attitude

**social media** media through which communication occurs

**social networking** consumers connecting with each other based on interests, associations, or goals

**social networking website** website that facilitates online social networking

**social power** ability of an individual or a group to alter the actions of others

**social psychology** study that focuses on the thoughts, feelings, and behaviors that people have as they interact with other people

**social schema** cognitive representation that gives a specific type of person meaning

**social stereotype** another word for social schema

**social stratification** the division of society into classes that have unequal access to scarce and valuable resources

**socialization** learning through observation of and the active processing of information about lived, everyday experience

**societal marketing concept** marketing concept that states that marketers should consider not only the wants and needs of consumers but also the needs of society

**sociology** the study of groups of people within a society, with relevance for consumer behavior because a great deal of consumption takes place within group settings or is affected by group behavior

**source attractiveness** the degree to which a source's physical appearance matches a prototype for beauty and elicits a favorable or desirous response

**source effects** characteristics of a source that impact the persuasiveness of a message

**spreading activation** way cognitive activation spreads from one concept (or node) to another

**state-oriented** consumers with a low capacity to self-regulate their behavior

**status symbols** products or objects that are used to signal one's place in society

**stealth marketing** guerrilla marketing tactic in which consumers do not realize that they are being targeted for a marketing message

**stigmatization** a situation in which a consumer is marked in some way that indicates their place in society

**strategy** a planned way of doing something

**strict liability** legal action against a firm whereby a consumer demonstrates in court that an injury occurred and that the product associated with the injury was faulty in some way

**subliminal processing** way that the human brain deals with very low-strength stimuli, so low that the person has no conscious awareness

**superego** component in psychoanalytic theory that works against the id by motivating behavior that matches the expectations and norms of society

**support arguments** thoughts that further support a message

**surrogate consumer** consumer who is hired by another to provide input into a purchase decision

**susceptibility to interpersonal influence** individual difference variable that assesses a consumer's need to enhance his or her image with others by acquiring and using products, conforming to the expectations of others, and learning about products by observing others

**switching costs** costs associated with changing from one choice (brand/ retailer/service provider) to another

**switching** times when a consumer chooses a competing choice, rather than the previously purchased choice, on the next purchase occasion

**symbolic interactionism** perspective that proposes that consumers live in a symbolic environment and interpret the myriad of symbols around them, and that members of a society agree on the meanings of symbols

# T

**tag** small piece of coded information that helps with the retrieval of knowledge

**target market** identified segment or segments of a market that a company serves

**teleological evaluations** consumers' assessment of the goodness or badness of the consequences of actions

**temporal factors** situational characteristics related to time

**theory of planned action** attitudinal measurement approach that expands upon the behavioral intentions model by including a perceived control component

**theory** theory that explains why companies succeed or fail; the firm goes about obtaining resources from consumers in return for the value the resources create

**time pressure** urgency to act based on some real or self-imposed deadline

**total value concept** business practice wherein companies operate with the understanding that products provide value in multiple ways

**touchpoints** direct contacts between the firm and a customer

**tradition** customs and accepted ways of everyday behavior in a given culture

**trait approach to personality** approaches in personality research that focus on specific consumer traits as motivators of various consumer behaviors

**trait** distinguishable characteristic that describes one's tendency to act in a relatively consistent manner

**translational equivalence** two phrases share the same precise meaning in two different cultures

**trustworthiness** how honest and unbiased the source is perceived to be

# U

**uncertainty avoidance** extent to which a culture is uncomfortable with things that are ambiguous or unknown

**unconditioned response** response that occurs naturally as a result of exposure to an unconditioned stimulus

**unconditioned stimulus** stimulus with which a behavioral response is already associated

**underlying attributes** attributes that are not readily apparent and can be learned only through experience or contact with the product

**undifferentiated marketing** plan wherein the same basic product is offered to all customers

**unintentional learning** learning that occurs when behavior is modified through a consumer–stimulus interaction without any effortful allocation of cognitive processing capacity toward that stimulus

**universal set** total collection of all possible solutions to a consumer problem

**unplanned shopping** shopping activity that shares some, but not all, characteristics of truly impulsive consumer behavior; being characterized by situational memory, a utilitarian orientation, and feelings of spontaneity

**utilitarian function of attitudes** function of attitudes in which consumers use attitudes as ways to maximize rewards and minimize punishment

**utilitarian influence** ways in which a consumer conforms to group expectations in order to receive a reward or avoid punishment

**utilitarian motivation** drive to acquire products that can be used to accomplish something

**utilitarian shopping value** worth obtained because some shopping task or job is completed successfully

**utilitarian value** value derived from a product that helps the consumer with some task

# V

**VALS** popular psychographic method in consumer research that divides consumers into groups based on resources and consumer behavior motivations

**value** a personal assessment of the net worth obtained from an activity

**value co-creation** the realization that a consumer is necessary and must play a part in order to produce value

**value consciousness** the extent to which consumers tend to maximize what they receive from a transaction as compared to what they give

**value-expressive function of attitudes** function of attitudes whereby attitudes allow consumers to express their core values, self-concept, and beliefs to others

**value-expressive influence** ways in which a consumer internalizes a group's values or the extent to which a consumer joins groups in order to express his or her own closely held values and beliefs

**verbal communication** transfer of information through either the literal spoken or written word

**viral marketing** marketing method that uses online technologies to facilitate WOM by having consumers spread messages through their online conversations

**visceral responses** certain feeling states that are tied to physical reactions/behavior in a very direct way

# W

**want** way a consumer goes about addressing a recognized need

**Weber's Law** law stating that a consumer's ability to detect differences between two levels of the stimulus decreases as the intensity of the initial stimulus increases

**word-of-mouth (WOM)** information about products, services, and experiences that is transmitted from consumer to consumer

**workbench memory** storage area in the memory system where information is stored while it is being processed and encoded for later recall

**world teen culture** speculation that teenagers around the world are more similar to each other than to people from other generations in the same culture

# INDEX

**NEW** Chapter 9 in Part 3 is a new chapter focusing on cultures within cultures. In Part 5, Chapters 15 & 16 from the second edition have been combined into one new chapter on consumer and marketing misbehavior, with a focus on marketing ethics.

- NEW: Glossary
- NEW: End of Part Cases
- NEW: Study Tools
- NEW: What Others Have Thought Polling Results

Visit **login.cengage.com** for additional materials to enhance your lectures!

What's New in This Edition?

# CHAPTER 1

## What Is CB, and Why Should I Care?

- New information about how consumer behavior ties into the struggling economy.
- New example of Apple's iPad.
- Updated material on bad service at state DMVs.
- Updated Exhibit 1.3: How Old Are These Companies?
- New company example of Curtis Mathes not surviving in contrast to Exhibit 1.3.
- New Stride Rite example of niche marketing.
- Updated information in *Hold the Phone* box feature.
- Updated statistics on consumer debt.
- New box feature *The Face of the Consumer? Do You Like It?* replaces *Credit Card Crazy* box feature.
- Updated Starbucks statistics.
- Updated Internet retailing statistics.
- New section Changing Communication that explains the impact of social networking media on consumer communications.
- New section Changing Economy that explains this as a consumer behavior trend.

# CHAPTER 2

## Value and the Consumer Behavior Value Framework

- New song example "California Gurls."
- Updated Exhibit 2.1: The Consumer Value Framework.
- New example of CVS, illustrating its successful loyalty program.
- Revised box feature *Stuck on Me!*
- New example of *Toy Story 3*, a product that accomplishes utilitarian and hedonic value.
- New example of an Apple iPad as an augmented product.
- New section on value co-creation.
- New eBay example about product differentiation.
- New box feature *Is It The Real Cheese? Does Anyone Care?* replaces *E-segments* box feature.
- New key terms: **marketing myopia** and **value co-creation.**

## CHAPTER 3

### Consumer Learning Starts Here: Perception

- Revised learning objectives.

- Updated webvan.com example.

- Revised text surrounding Exhibit 3.3: Sensing, Organizing, and Reacting.

- New box feature *What's the Best Time to Buy* replaces *Haven't I Seen You Before?* box feature.

- New example of cognitive organization with new research on how consumers categorize sounds.

- Revised box feature *Subliminal Groovin'?* to include reference to the Judas Priest trial.

- Rearranged the material on mere exposure to appear within the implicit memory section.

- Revised definitions of explicit and implicit memory.

- New section: Familiarity.

## CHAPTER 4

### Comprehension, Memory, and Cognitive Learning

- New concept of signal theory.

- New font ACME brick example to demonstrate font meanings.

- New spacing concept and how it can influence memory.

- New Exhibit 4.4: The Figure and Ground Distinction.

- New example of likeability with the Geico Gecko.

- New section on Prior Knowledge.

- New box feature *Healthiness Can Be Bad for Your Brain?* replaces *The V's and G's* box feature.

- Revised definition of framing.

- New research about the way syllables influence recall.

- New Exhibit 4.7: Dual Coding Illustrated.

- New concept rumination.

- New example about the origins of the Smart brand as a combination of Swatch and Mercedes.

- Explicitly recognized consumer usage knowledge as associated with scripts and episodic memory. New example about younger people knowing how to facebook or tweet each other because that information is stored and ready to use relative to some other more experienced consumers.

- New box feature *Value is Meaning: The Small and Big of It!* replaces *To Tell the Truth?* box feature.

- New key terms: **signal theory** and **rumination.**

Visit **login.cengage.com** for additional materials to enhance your lectures!

What's New in Each Chapter?

# CHAPTER 5

## Motivation and Emotion: Driving Consumer Behavior

- New example of utilitarian motivation with Crest toothpaste.

- New example about price discounts that create emotion and drive consumer behavior.

- Revised explanation of the four appraisal types within cognitive appraisal theory.

- New example of how consumers do things like reward themselves with a gift to manage their moods.

- New example of Facebook addiction signs within the flow section.

- New box feature *Bad Hair Days – Bad Times!* replaces *To Know It Really Is to Feel It!* box feature.

- New aesthetic labor section.

- New self-conscious emotions section.

- New product contamination section.

- New key terms: **aesthetic labor, self-conscious emotions** and **product contamination.**

# CHAPTER 6

## Personality, Lifestyles, and the Self-Concept

- New example of band, The Black Eyed Peas, to illustrate a particular behavior adds value.

- New example within personality qualities #3.

- New questions a researcher might use while studying a consumer.

- New nomothetic example about Tia being conscientious.

- New example about materialism and mortality.

- Removed Complaint Proneness section and key term.

- New section Need for Cognition.

- New example of fantasy sports within competitiveness section.

- New box feature *Trait Superstition* replaces *Ultimate Frisbee* box feature.

- New examples of brand personality products to include MTV, Fox Apparel, and PacSun.

- New brand personality examples LG and Hallmark cards.

- Removed four lifestyle segment examples.

- New examples about lifestyle of health and sustainability.

- New box feature *The Cyber Self* replaces *The Presentation of Self in Cyberspace* box feature.

- Updated statistics on cosmetic surgery and body piercings.

- New example Built Ford Tough for the ideal self-concept.

- New pull quote.

- New key term: **need for cognition.**

# CHAPTER 7

## Attitudes and Attitude Change

- New iPad example of the ABC approach to attitudes.

- New description of the functional theory of attitudes has been added. The Utilitarian Function is described more in terms of product benefits as presenting rewards for consumers, and consumer loyalty is described as an outcome of the Knowledge Function. The Value Expressive Function has been described to include the satisfaction that one gets from expressing attitudes that reflect his/her self-image, and a new example has been provided.

- New Brawny example for the Low-Involvement Hierarchy.

- Revised *Change the Station* box feature with a new title *I Like This Store!*

- New box feature *It's Not Worth It* replaces *Who's Setting the Table?* box feature.

- New box feature *The 2010 Census – Moving Forward* replaces *Digital TV Transition* box feature.

- New Exhibit 7.6: Balance Theory includes Dale Earnhardt, Jr. and Nationwide Insurance.

- New estimate of Internet usage worldwide based on latest information and estimates of text messaging. A discussion of how this applies to the communication model is included.

- New research on Humor Effects is cited.

- References to the serial position effect have been added, and recent findings regarding the placement of Super Bowl ads have been added.

- Recent findings on the impact of source credibility on attitude certainty have been highlighted.

- Recent findings regarding source likeability and need for cognition have been added.

- New pull quote.

- New key term: **serial position effect.**

# CHAPTER 8

## Consumer Culture

- Updated Starbucks statistics in *The World Is Their Cup* box feature.

- New section about societal role expectations replaced "sex role" section.

- New Exhibit 8.2: Societal Role Expectations Vary.

- New discussion of renquing as part of Eastern cultures and long-term orientation in particular.

- Added Pakistan to Exhibits 8.4 and 8.5.

- New Exhibit 8.8: Modeling and the Quartet.

- New vuvuzela example within the modeling section.

- New box feature *Somebody's Watching Me* replaces *What Consumers Do Know Can Hurt Them?* box feature.

- Revised German meaning of miststueck.

- Moved the World Teen Culture section to chapter 9.

- New key terms: **role expectations** and **renquing.**

Visit **login.cengage.com** for additional materials to enhance your lectures!

What's New in Each Chapter?

# CHAPTER 9

## Microcultures

- This is an entirely new chapter for CB 3e.

# CHAPTER 10

## Group and Interpersonal Influence

- New chapter title.

- New information about how social media like Facebook, Twitter, YouTube, and MySpace play a role in group influence.

- New example of Ozzfest as a brand community.

- New box feature *Valuable Groups!* replaces *We've Got Connections* box feature.

- New example of Hollister jeans.

- New section entitled Social Media and Group Influence that covers the popularity of social networking and social media on group and consumer behavior.

- New section entitled Popularity of Social Networking Sites, which includes current statistics for Facebook, MySpace, and Twitter.

- New section entitled Value, Social Media, and Social Networking, which discusses how hedonic and utilitarian value are related to online social activities.

- New Exhibit 10.3: Sample Items from Attention to Social Comparison Information Scale.

- New example of recent studies regarding the need for connection and salesperson effectiveness.

- Updated section Word-of-Mouth in the Digital Age to include discussion of how WOM is influenced by online.

- New section entitled Measuring Online WOM, which includes examples of companies and websites that focus on this area.

- New example of buzz marketing—Ford Fiesta campaign.

- New example of stealth marketing tactic.

- New reference of how Twitter allows the consumer to track the popularity of various posters.

- New statistic about children being born to unmarried mothers.

- New family-oriented movie examples.

- New information about how the economic slowdown affected boomerang kids, with reference to the movie *Failure to Launch*.

- New information about the billions of dollars lost in productivity due to sandwich generation issues.

- New information about the growing trend of married women having more education and income than their spouses.

- New pull quotes.

- New key terms: **social media, social networking,** and **social networking website.**

## CHAPTER 11

### Consumers in Situations

- New bullet point about the economic situation on list of things that influence shopping behaviors.

- New box feature *Shopping Pals* replaces *Let the Madness Begin* box feature.

- Added more information about the role of social interactions in experiential shopping.

- New example of indulgence as a reward for previous constraint as a reason for impulse shopping.

- New section on Merchandising.

- New information about source attractiveness and social comparison.

- New section on how consumer orientations can shift and represent an antecedent condition that one brings to the environment.

- New key terms: **source attractiveness** and **social comparison.**

## CHAPTER 12

### Decision Making I: Need Recognition and Search

- New examples in Exhibit 12.3: Perspectives on Consumer Decision Making.

- New example of desired state, Apple's iPad.

- New example of Facebook groups as source of information for search.

- New example of "search overload" campaign of Bing.com.

- New examples of search engines, Bing and Facebook.

- New information about consumers being able to buy directly at sponsored links.

- New information about mobile technologies in addition to the Internet.

- New box feature *Pay to Play* replaces *Get In, Get Out!* box feature.

- New pull quote.

## CHAPTER 13

### Decision Making II: Alternative Evaluation and Choice

- New example for coffee maker and timer button for evaluative criteria.

- Updated Exhibit 13.2: Product, Feature, and Benefit and surrounding text.

- New snack examples of updated products.

- New box feature *Seeing Green* replaces *Something New* box feature.

- New Exhibit 13.4: Superordinate and Subordinate Categorization and surrounding text.

- New box feature *May I Help You?* replaces *Get Real!* box feature.

- New pull quote.

Visit **login.cengage.com** for additional materials to enhance your lectures!

What's New in Each Chapter?

# CHAPTER 14

## Consumption to Satisfaction

- New information about ritualized consumption and how authenticity adds value.

- New information about hope includes consumption expectations that are part of the disconfirmation model.

- Updated Exhibit 14.4: The ACSI Scores for U.S. Retailers.

- New box feature *I Hope It's Real, Really!* replaces *Tailgate 101* box feature.

- New concept of over-rewarding consumers to the equity theory section.

- New key terms: **authenticity, hope,** and **consumer dissatisfaction.**

# CHAPTER 15

## Consumer Relationships

- New box feature *Payback is Swell!* replaces *Complaining Made Easy!* box feature.

- New section on revenge as a type of complaining behavior.

- New example of complaints consumers post online about Nutro dog food.

- New example about procedural switching costs with the Apple iPhone 4 problems.

- New information about recent research relating bundled pricing to financial switching costs.

- Revised Exhibit 15.5: Customer Share Information for Two Coffee Shop Customers.

- New key terms: **procedural justice, rancorous revenge,** and **retaliatory revenge.**

# CHAPTER 16

## Consumer and Marketing Misbehavior

*This chapter has been re-written, combining chapters 15 (Consumer Misbehavior) and chapter 16 (Marketing Ethics, Misbehavior, and Value) from the second edition of *CB*. Concepts and references have been updated for both chapters.

- Revised section on Product Misuse.

- Revised section for Aggressive Driving.

- Updated statistics for drinking and driving and cell phone use in vehicles.

- Revised section on compulsive consumption, compulsive buying, and compulsive shopping.

- Updated statistics for binge drinking, problem gambling, and drug abuse.

- New box feature *All Shades of Green.*

- Revised section under Marketing Ethics.

- Revised section about Public Criticisms of Marketing.

What's New in Each Chapter?

Visit **login.cengage.com** for additional materials to enhance your lectures!

**WHAT'S INSIDE** Key topics in this chapter: how consumers get treated in different exchange environments, the role of consumer behavior in business and society, different approaches to studying consumer behavior, and why consumer behavior is so dramatic along with recent trends affecting consumers.

# CHAPTER 1 PREP CARD

## What Is CB, and Why Should I Care?

## Learning Outcomes

**LO1** Understand the meaning of *consumption* and *consumer* behavior.

**LO2** Describe how consumers get treated differently in various types of exchange environments.

**LO3** Explain the role of consumer behavior in business and society.

**LO4** Be familiar with basic approaches to studying consumer behavior.

**LO5** Describe why consumer behavior is so dynamic and how recent trends affect consumers.

## Chapter 1 Outline

## Multimedia

### PPT—THE HIGHLIGHTS
- Slide 4     Consumer Behavior Perspectives
- Slide 6     Exhibit 1.1: The Basic Consumption Process
- Slide 12    Questions to Consider
- Slide 15    Why Study CB?
- Slide 25    Exhibit 1.5: Comparing Quantitative and Qualitative Research

### VIDEO

**PowerPoint Clip from *Netflix***

Run time: 1:24 minutes

Netflix is a subscription service that provides streaming video over the Internet and delivers DVDs via mail. Netflix changed the way people rent movies and TV shows by cutting out the "shop front." For a monthly fee, consumers have increased selections, no late fees, the ability to rent as many times as they like, and no need to leave their homes. Headquartered in Silicon Valley, CA, Netflix maintains distribution centers all over the country, including remote places like Hawaii and Alaska, in order to maintain the company's business model of speedy delivery and catering to consumers' convenience needs.

**Ask your students:**
1. How has Netflix's business model successfully tapped into consumer behavior?
2. How does Netflix use consumer behavior and the Internet to avoid becoming obsolete as technology changes?

### CHAPTER VIDEO SUMMARY

**ReadyMade–Do it Yourself**

Run time: 8:00 minutes

*ReadyMade* magazine is for do-it-yourselfers who want eco-friendly home improvement ideas. More *Trading Spaces* than *This Old House,* the niche magazine offers interviews with interior designers, articles on sustainable living, and tips on repurposing home items for clever new uses. According to co-founders Grace Hawthorne and Shoshana Berger, urban living and DIY trends of the past decade have contributed to *ReadyMade's* popularity with environmentally conscious readers.

**Ask your students:**
1. While *ReadyMade* magazine was still in the design stages, very little research was done to determine whether an interested market existed. Did this adversely affect the magazine as it moved forward to publication? Explain.
2. How does the cover of *ReadyMade* magazine reflect the principles of packaging design as influenced by the known behavior of its consumers?

Visit **login.cengage.com** for additional materials to enhance your lectures!

# Key Terms

# Lecture Example

Consumer behavior is driven by many things, including the weather. If your sprinkler breaks down during a dry, hot spell, you are likely to replace it quickly. However, you might have to travel to the back of the store before you get to the product you need, passing by fans, bathing suits, and air conditioners along the way. Savvy marketers use consumer's seasonal needs to drive sales and promote other products. However, because retailers must order inventory months in advance, this strategy can backfire. In New York, ordering huge stocks of air conditioners for a predictably hot July of 2009 turned out to be just such a mistake. It was the coolest July in 115 years and retailers were stuck with merchandise they couldn't move.

Source: Jennifer Waters, "Retailers Use Weather To Anticipate Consumers' Behavior," *The Wall Street Journal*, July 29, 2010, **http://online.wsj.com**.

# Discussion Questions

1. What is consumption? Provide three examples of something you have "consumed" recently, and illustrate the concept of consumption with each example.

2. What two basic approaches to studying (i.e., researching) consumer behavior are discussed in this chapter? How do they differ?

3. How is the fact that communication media preferences are changing affecting consumer behavior and the effective use of consumer behavior in business?

# Group Activity

Use the Internet to do a brief research paper on a current public policy issue in which consumer behavior plays an important role. Develop an opinion on whether some type of new regulation or restriction might actually address the issue and create a better societal outcome. Prepare a brief skit to enact your issue, and summarize the ways in which knowledge of consumer behavior can contribute to understanding the issue.

Have some fun with this. Relate the consumer behaviors to the amount of competition involved and the fact that public policy has both advantages and disadvantages for consumers.

# Assignments

Ethics is an important aspect of consumer behavior. Later chapters will focus on ethics in more detail. However, given that consumer behavior is useful from a business, societal, and personal viewpoint, in which area are ethics and consumer behavior most closely related? Explain your choice.

# Beyond the Class

A selection of materials is in the Instructor's Manual.

Visit **login.cengage.com** for additional materials to enhance your lectures!

WHAT'S INSIDE   Key topics in this chapter: the consumer value framework, consumer value (utilitarian and hedonic value), how firms create value for their consumers, the psychology of the consumer, perceptual maps, and consumer's lifetime value for a long-term orientation.

# CHAPTER 2   PREP CARD

## Value and the Consumer Behavior Value Framework

## Learning Outcomes

**LO1**   Describe the consumer value framework, including its basic components.

**LO2**   Define consumer value and compare and contrast two key types of value.

**LO3**   Apply the concepts of marketing strategy and marketing tactics to describe the way firms go about creating value for consumers.

**LO4**   Explain the way market characteristics like market segmentation and product differentiation affect marketing strategy.

**LO5**   Analyze consumer markets using elementary perceptual maps.

**LO6**   Justify consumers' lifetime value as an effective focus for long-term business success.

## Chapter 2 Outline

Visit **login.cengage.com** for additional materials to enhance your lectures!

## Multimedia

### PPT—THE HIGHLIGHTS
- Slide 6      Exhibit 2.1: The Consumer Value Framework (CVF)
- Slide 19    Exhibit 2.4: Business Strategy Exists at Different Levels
- Slide 23:   Market Segmentation and Product Differentiation
- Slide 27    Exhibit 2.7: A Perceptual Map
- Slide 31:   Customer Lifetime Value (CLV)

### VIDEO

**PowerPoint Clip from *The Toledo Mud Hens***

Run time:   1:12 minutes

The Toledo Mud Hens is a minor league baseball team inspired by the poem *Casey at the Bat*. The baseball team is positioned as a family entertainment brand. Although the team has had historically strong players and performs well during the baseball season, the major focus of the positioning strategy is actually to brand an experience all fans can count on: a fun, affordable, family or group outing. This strategy has worked successfully for the team in both athletic performance and marketing performance arenas.

**Ask your students:**
1. How does the business model of the Mud Hens provide a different value to minor league fans than it would to major league fans?
2. How does attending a Mud Hens' event provide value beyond a baseball game?

### CHAPTER VIDEO SUMMARY

**E-business at Evo**

Run time: 7:49 minutes

When ski enthusiast Bryce Phillips launched Evo from his garage in 2001, the sports-equipment company consisted of an Internet connection, used ski gear, and a single employee. Today the Seattle-based ski-and-snowboard retailer is the premier online destination for closeout-model equipment and apparel. Consumers of ski and water sport products choose Evo for its online shopping experience, discounted brand name merchandise, and no-haggle customer service. The retailer's website also delivers value through detailed product reviews and Evo-hosted travel opportunities.

**Ask your students:**
1. Aside from offering good prices, how does **evogear.com** offer value to the consumer?
2. Evo has opened a large brick-and-mortar store/community art space in Seattle, Washington. Go to **http://culture.evogear. com/category/seattle/** to learn more about what the store offers. Do you think this store will distract or enhance the website? Consider potential channel conflicts, pricing strategy, convenience, and consumer behavior in your answer.

# Key Terms

# Lecture Example

Consumer segments play a vital and sometimes surprising role in marketing. Consider the wine industry. The image that likely comes to mind is of an older crowd composed mostly of Baby Boomers. While this image isn't completely wrong, the demographics of wine consumption have changed dramatically in the last decade. According to the Wine Market Council, under-35 consumers have increased by almost 40% over the last year alone. This means more and more of the consumers who are buying and drinking wine are Millennials—a target segment almost as large as the Boomers and one marketers are already eager to reach.

Source: Jessica Yadegaran, "Millennials: The Next Generation of Wine Judges," *San Jose Mercury News*, July 28, 2010, **http://www.mercurynews.com**.

# Discussion Questions

1. What is the total value concept? Can you use the total value concept to explain why Callaway Golf or Starbucks are such successful companies?

2. What is marketing myopia? How does it relate to the total value concept?

3. What is a perceptual map? What are the dimensions of a perceptual map?

# Group Activity

Have students interview other students in class to determine whether some students are members of a club, fraternity, or sorority; are working part time; or are engaged in other extracurricular activities. Then, have students pair up in groups to analyze how members of their organization are following Maslow's hierarchy in regard to their purchases or activities outside of school.

You may also want to incorporate a homework assignment in which each group finds a print ad that appeals to each of the levels of Maslow's hierarchy. Is there overlap between levels? Is this good or bad?

# Assignments

Interview three consumers from your town. Ask them how they believe the following companies provide value to consumers:

- Home Depot
- Apple
- Barnes and Noble
- John Deere

# Beyond the Class

A selection of materials is in the Instructor's Manual.

Visit **login.cengage.com** for additional materials to enhance your lectures!

WHAT'S INSIDE   Key topics in this chapter: preliminary stages of consumer perception, phases in the consumer perception process, concept of Just Noticeable Difference (JND), implicit and explicit memory, enhancing a consumer's attention, and differences in unintentional and intentional learning.

# CHAPTER 3   PREP CARD
## Consumer Learning Starts Here: Perception

## Learning Outcomes

**LO1**  Define learning and perception and how the two are connected.

**LO2**  List and define phases of the consumer perception process.

**LO3**  Apply the concept of the JND.

**LO4**  Contrast the concepts of implicit and explicit memory.

**LO5**  Know ways to help get a consumer's attention.

**LO6**  Understand key differences between intentional and unintentional learning

## Chapter 3 Outline

## Multimedia

### PPT—THE HIGHLIGHTS

- Slide 6    Elements of Consumer Perception
- Slide 8    Exhibit 3.3: Consumer Perception Phases
- Slide 14   JND (Just Noticeable Difference)
- Slide 22   Ways to Enhance Attention
- Slide 25   Intentional vs. Unintentional Learning

### VIDEO

**PowerPoint Clip from *Culver's Restaurants***
Run time:  1:22 minutes

Culver's is an American style hamburger and ice cream family-owned restaurant, with a strong focus on the positive interactions between customers, staff, and high-quality food. Founded in 1984, Culver's is famous for their friendly and quick service as well as their fresh never frozen Butterburger. CEO Craig Culver founded the business with his wife and parents after working for McDonald's and realizing there was a niche for providing fresh, quality food in a fast-paced environment.

**Ask your students:**
1. Why does Culver's use a phrase like "quick service" rather than "fast food" to describe their food service?
2. Why is a high-level of customer service such an important part of Culver's business model?

### CHAPTER VIDEO SUMMARY

**Advertising and PR at Ogden Publications**
Run time: 7:45 minutes

Readers of *Mother Earth News* have a unique profile: they care deeply about the natural environment and are willing to pay more for eco-friendly products. Ogden Publications, the magazine's publisher, shares those perspectives. Ogden's marketing efforts condition audiences to buy authentically green products, and businesses that advertise in *Mother Earth News* must demonstrate support for the magazine's message of sustainability. Ogden's environmentally choosy readers repel some advertisers, however, creating challenges for the Topeka-based publisher.

**Ask your students:**
1. Given that most of a magazine's revenue comes from ads, would you be willing to turn down a large consumer advertiser because your readers may disagree with their product or business practices? Discuss the ethical, PR, and financial implications of your decision.
2. What challenges do specialized magazines such as *Mother Earth News* face when trying to entice advertisers? Create a pitch to a potential green-product advertiser stating the benefits of advertising in *Mother Earth News*.

Visit **login.cengage.com** for additional materials to enhance your lectures!

CHAPTER 3 CONSUMER LEARNING STARTS HERE: PERCEPTION

# Key Terms

# Lecture Example

Consumer perception and reality are not always the same thing—a point that Gulf of Mexico fish and seafood retailers are well acquainted with after the BP oil spill of 2010. Although aggressive marketing messages were immediately used to communicate to consumers that products from the Gulf fishing areas that remained open were safe to eat, public confidence continued to erode. Even with extra funding from BP and the government, some estimate it may take up to five years and many millions of dollars to regain consumer confidence.

Source: Kari Huus, "Is BP On the Hook for Fish's Sullied Reputation?" MSNBC, July 30, 2010, **http://fieldnotes.msnbc.msn. com/_news/2010/07/30/4785891-is-bp-on-the-hook-for-fishs-sullied-reputation**.

# Discussion Questions

1. Define learning within a consumer context. Provide an example of something you have learned as a consumer.

2. Provide three examples each of how consumers might learn through explicit and implicit memory.

3. How does the JND differ from the absolute threshold?

# Group Activity

Get together with at least two other students from the class. Have one of the students play beat the clock for Chapter 3 while the others reserve. Then, have another student try beat the clock for Chapter 1 and the third try beat the clock for Chapter 2. Is there a winner (did one do better than another)? Are there any CEOs? Explain what is going on perceptually when playing beat the clock. How is explicit memory involved? Is there a way for implicit memory to play a role?

# Assignments

Ask a friend who has never studied marketing or consumer behavior to flip through a popular magazine, such as *Sports Illustrated* or *People*. Ask them to find examples of attempted subliminal persuasion. Have them discuss the ads and explain their choices. What do you think of their opinions?

# Beyond the Class

A selection of materials is in the Instructor's Manual.

Visit **login.cengage.com** for additional
materials to enhance your lectures!

**WHAT'S INSIDE** Key topics in this chapter: theory and evidence addressing how consumers learn when they are trying to learn something, factors that affect what gets comprehended in a marketing message, how consumers form memory and how that memory is represented, knowledge is stored and relies upon categories captured with concepts like schema, social schema and exemplar.

# CHAPTER 4 PREP CARD

## Comprehension, Memory, and Cognitive Learning

## Learning Outcomes

**LO1** Identify factors that influence consumer comprehension.

**LO2** Explain how knowledge, meaning, and value are inseparable using the multiple stores memory theory.

**LO3** Understand how the mental associations that consumers develop are a key to learning.

**LO4** Use the concept of associative networks to map relevant consumer knowledge.

**LO5** Apply the cognitive schema concept in understanding how consumers react to products, brands and marketing agents.

## Chapter 4 Outline

## Multimedia

### PPT—THE HIGHLIGHTS

### VIDEO

**PowerPoint Clip from *RJ Julia Booksellers***
Run time: 1:19 minutes

RJ Julia Booksellers is an independent bookstore with a focus on direct customer interaction. Owner Roxanne Coady has found that in order to really connect people with the right book, you must get involved in their lives to a certain degree. She also feels strongly that a book recommendation should be annotated based on a consumer's needs or even mood and works to draw high-interest authors to the store for readings and discussions. This level of customer relationship management is difficult for big-box stores and online-only stores to provide.

**Ask your students:**
1. What can an RJ Julia Booksellers recommendation provide that an online bookseller might not?
2. How else does RJ Julia Booksellers create meaning and value in the minds of consumers?

### CHAPTER VIDEO SUMMARY

**Cold Stone Creamery**
Run time: 6:35 minutes

Cold Stone Creamery has a mission to create the ultimate ice cream experience. Success at Cold Stone begins with the official goal to "make people happy," and employees deliver pure bliss to customers in the form of delectable ice cream treats and toppings. But careful planning and goal setting are critical to achieving any corporate mission, and Cold Stone's Pyramid of Success 2010 campaign communicates important messages that are memorable and comprehensible to workers and consumers alike.

**Ask your students:**
1. During one's experience at Cold Stone Creamery, what type of memory is drawn on?
2. How does Cold Stone Creamery cater to different ethnic groups?

Visit **login.cengage.com** for additional materials to enhance your lectures!

# Key Terms

adaptation level   72
associative network   80
chunking   78
cognitive interference   77
comprehension   66
counterarguments   70
credibility   70
declarative knowledge   80
dostats   72
dual coding   77
echoic storage   75
elaboration   84
encoding   76
episodic memory   83
exemplar   81
expectations   73
expertise   70
figure   70
figure-ground distinction   70
framing   73
ground   70
habituation   72
iconic storage   75
information intensity   73
long-term memory   79
meaningful encoding   77
memory   74
memory trace   79
message congruity   68
multiple store theory of
    memory   75
nodes   80
nostalgia   80
paths   80
personal elaboration   84
physical characteristics   67
priming   73
prospect theory   73
prototype   82
repetition   77
response generation   78
retrieval   76
rumination   79
schema   81
script   82
semantic coding   79
sensory memory   75
signal theory   66
social schema   83
social stereotype   83
spreading activation   79
support arguments   70
tag   79
trustworthiness   70
workbench memory   76

# Lecture Example

Social media is quickly becoming a popular method for marketers looking to deliver influential, lasting, and targeted messages. General Motors launched a social media advertising campaign to market the 2011 Buick Regal. Using cell phone messaging via Twitter and Internet sites like Facebook, Flickr, and YouTube provides a highly interactive forum for consumers to receive and deliver messages. These types of media allow marketers to develop dynamic and memorable message characteristics. This format can also lend an air of credibility to message receivers because they are able to communicate with the brand as well as with other consumers.

Source: Suzanne Ashe, "Buick Drives Regal Message Through Social Media," CNet Reviews, July 29, 2010, **http://reviews.cnet.com/8301-13746_7-20011997-48.html**

# Discussion Questions

1. What advice would you have for a marketing company that is considering the use of avatars (animated people-like images) on their website? Lead this exercise in the context of trying to help consumers to comprehend the content of the site.

2. What three storage areas are responsible for memory? Describe each in terms of its duration and capacity. Where is meaning attached to stimuli?

3. What is an associative network? Why do you believe it is sometimes called a semantic network? Where are associative networks located?

# Group Activity

Look for marketing messages in either print advertisements or on the Internet. Find one that you believe illustrates a successful way in which to get consumers to chunk information for better recall later. Explain your reasons.

# Assignments

Ask a few consumers from among your acquaintance if they know what a torrent is and what it is used for. If you are unfamiliar with this term, search a torrent site on the Internet to find out what it is. How do new product concepts come to be defined? Are there times when the script associated with using some product might include questionably ethical associations? What is your knowledge? Is the use of a torrent unethical?

# Beyond the Class

A selection of materials is in the Instructor's Manual.

Visit **login.cengage.com** for additional materials to enhance your lectures!

**WHAT'S INSIDE** Key topics in this chapter: human behavior and what drives it, basic consumer motivations and a general hierarchy of motivations, consumer emotions, and the schema-based affect.

# CHAPTER 5 PREP CARD

## Motivation and Emotion: Driving Consumer Behavior

# Learning Outcomes

**LO1** Understand what initiates human behavior.

**LO2** Classify basic consumer motivations.

**LO3** Describe consumer emotions and demonstrate how they help shape value.

**LO4** Apply different approaches to measuring consumer emotions.

**LO5** Understand how different consumers express emotions in different ways.

**LO6** Define and apply the concepts of schema-based affect and emotional contagion.

# Chapter 5 Outline

# Multimedia

## PPT—THE HIGHLIGHTS

- Slide 4     Motivations
- Slide 6     Exhibit 5.1: An Illustration of Consumer Motivations According to Maslow's Hierarchy
- Slide 12   Emotions
- Slide 22   Difference in Emotional Behavior
- Slide 26   Schema-Based Affect

## VIDEO

### PowerPoint Clip from *The Putting Lot*

Run time:  2:02 minutes

The Putting Lot is a community mini-golf course on a former vacant lot founded with the intention of sustaining an existing community while helping it to transition toward new developments. The nine-hole course is designed around themes of urban sustainability. The one-summer project quickly drew attention from local volunteers, interested artists and architects, as well as press from around the world. The project was developed with the hope of inspiring discussions of and actions toward urban sustainability.

**Ask your students:**

1. Why was it so easy, if surprising, for The Putting Lot to find neighborhood volunteers during the development and building stages?
2. Why do you think this project received so much "free" word-of-mouth press on such a large scale?

## CHAPTER VIDEO SUMMARY

### jetBlue

Run time:  6:05 minutes

The airline industry has long been plagued by high prices and low customer satisfaction. But jetBlue is finding ways to transform industry failings into market opportunities. The budget airline offers new planes, leather seats, video, and dependable service—at affordable fares. Flying jetBlue also has important emotional benefits: the sense of comfort and luxury, the feeling of safety, and the personal satisfaction of getting a good bargain.

**Ask your students:**

1. What are the key consumer factors that influence the decision to fly? How does jetBlue address these factors?
2. How are emotional factors important in this situation? How does jetBlue address these factors?

Visit **login.cengage.com** for additional materials to enhance your lectures!

CHAPTER 5 MOTIVATION AND EMOTION: DRIVING CONSUMER BEHAVIOR

# Key Terms

# Lecture Example

During an economic downturn consumers tighten their belts and more carefully watch their spending habits. Marketers must keep up with the economic situation by understanding consumer's priorities. During a recession many marketers avoid promoting "convenience" products and packaging, for which most consumers are no longer willing to a pay a premium. Name-brand marketers turn to discount strategies such as coupons, incentives, and volume discounts to keep up with consumers who are trading down to non-premium brands.

Source: "Consumer Thriftiness Signals Need to New Marketing Approach," July 23, 2010, **http://www.rbr.com/media-news/research/26135.html**

# Discussion Questions

1. Explain the difference between hedonic and utilitarian motivation. Provide examples of each.

2. How are emotions and value linked together?

3. What advantage do marketers have when dealing with consumers who are highly expressive emotionally?

# Group Activity

Conduct an interview with at least 10 consumers asking them to respond to the PANAS scale to rate their current mood. Then, have them evaluate the faculty at your particular university using a 10-point scale with 1 being "lousy" to 10 being "terrific." Do you think there is a relationship between mood and their ratings of faculty?

# Assignments

While visiting a grocery or clothing store, try to observe and document evidence of things from this chapter, like emotional contagion or product contamination. Describe the events and explain how they capture the idea.

# Beyond the Class

A selection of materials is in the Instructor's Manual.

Visit **login.cengage.com** for additional materials to enhance your lectures!

**WHAT'S INSIDE** Key topics in this chapter: personality and consumer behavior, major traits in consumer research, lifestyle and demographics, self-concept as it relates to consumer behavior, and issue of self-congruency.

# CHAPTER 6 PREP CARD

## Personality, Lifestyles, and the Self-Concept

## Learning Outcomes

**LO1** Define personality and know how various approaches to studying personality can be applied to consumer behavior.

**LO2** Discuss major traits that have been examined in consumer research.

**LO3** Understand why lifestyles and psychographics are important to the study of consumer behavior.

**LO4** Comprehend the role of the self-concept in consumer behavior.

**LO5** Understand the concept of self-congruency and how it applies to consumer behavior issues.

## Chapter 6 Outline

## Multimedia

### PPT—THE HIGHLIGHTS

### VIDEO

**PowerPoint Clip from *Smart, USA***

Run time:  0:56 minutes

The Smart Car was originally developed for the European car market, where small, fuel-efficient cars are more common. Before the company could introduce the Smart Car to American consumers, marketers needed to understand how they could help a U.S. audience see beyond the car's unusual appearance and size in order to appreciate its benefits as many Europeans already do. The marketers also needed to know who their target consumers would be and what would inspire them to buy a car like this. Smart, USA quickly learned that this car would be sold not based on age or socio-economic status, but on consumers' attitudes and lifestyles.

**Ask your students:**

1. How would you describe the Smart Car's brand personality?
2. Why does it make the most sense to define the Smart Car's target market by attitude and lifestyle?

### CHAPTER VIDEO SUMMARY

**Wheelworks**

Run time:  9:30 minutes

Since 1977, Wheelworks has been a hub of the East Coast cycling community. The Boston-based bicycle shop has earned both national and consumer's choice awards for its selection and service. Because cycling is a lifestyle pursuit that generates excitement among recreational enthusiasts and professional competitors alike, sales personnel at Wheelworks bypass hard selling and focus instead on educating consumers, promoting bicycle clubs, and sharing their passion for riding.

**Ask your students:**

1. What is the key to Wheelworks' success?
2. How does Wheelworks motivate the sales force to provide excellent customer service?

Visit **login.cengage.com** for additional materials to enhance your lectures!

# Key Terms

# Lecture Example

Self-concept and consumerism seems to be an ever important, ever hot topic in the world of business and marketing. While many advertising campaigns rely on an appeal to one's sense of beauty and glamour, both consumers and marketers alike are concerned about the ethics of promoting body modification services, such as cosmetic surgery. But where a service is offered, and a consumer desire exists, marketing will be there to fill the communication gap. Now, credit card companies are even offering charge cards specifically for cosmetic surgery. Is this type of long-term, interest-rated spending any different from buying a car or other big-ticket item? Or is there an ethical question about providing money for an elective procedure?

Source: Zelevansky, Nora. "Plastic Makes Perfect: Cosmetic Surgery Charge Cards," *The Huffington Post*, July 20, 2010, **http://www.huffingtonpost.com**.

# Discussion Questions

1. Compare and contrast psychoanalytical personality theory approaches with the trait factor theory of personality. Which is more appropriate when studying consumer behavior?

2. Do you believe that superstition can be considered to be a trait? Do you consider yourself to be superstitious? Do you know of anyone who you think is very superstitious? Have any superstitions affected your behavior as a consumer?

3. What are the various dimensions of self-concept? Describe each of these dimensions as they pertain to you personally.

# Group Activity

Go to the following website address **www.trappedinspace/brands.** Complete a few comparisons of the brands listed. What do you think about this information? Do you agree with it?

# Assignments

Visit a couple of retail outlets that you tend to regularly shop at (for example, Hollister, PacSun, American Eagle, etc.). How do self-congruency principles apply to your decision to shop at these stores?

# Beyond the Class

A selection of materials is in the Instructor's Manual.

Visit **login.cengage.com** for additional materials to enhance your lectures!

**WHAT'S INSIDE** Key topics in this chapter: attitude and attitude components, functions of attitudes, hierarchy of effects, consumer attitude models, attitude change theories, message, and source effects to influence persuasion.

# CHAPTER 7 PREP CARD

## Attitudes and Attitude Change

## Learning Outcomes

**LO1** Define attitudes and describe attitude components.

**LO2** Describe the functions of attitudes.

**LO3** Understand how the hierarchy of effects concept applies to attitude theory.

**LO4** Comprehend the major consumer attitude models.

**LO5** Describe attitude change theories and their role in persuasion.

**LO6** Understand how message and source effects influence persuasion.

## Chapter 7 Outline

## Multimedia

### PPT—THE HIGHLIGHTS

- Slide 4     Attitudes
- Slide 5     ABC Approach to Attitudes
- Slide 7     Exhibit 7.1: Functions of Consumer Attitudes
- Slide 9     Exhibit 7.2: Hierarchy of Effects
- Slide 11    Attitude-Toward-the-Object Model
- Slide 17    Persuasion
- Slide 28    Message Appeal and Construction

### VIDEO

**PowerPoint Clip from *Southwest Airlines***

Run time:  1:41 minutes

Founded on the basic principle of simple, no-fuss flying with a high-level of staff with positive attitudes, Southwest Airlines (SWA) remains one of this country's highest rated businesses in terms of both work culture and customer service. However, in the current economic downturn, and the particularly negative effect it has had on the commuter industry, SWA has to carefully consider the implications of its marketing and pricing efforts. While most airlines are increasing fees and cutting services in order to protect revenues, SWA has responded by keeping a one-price per flight experience policy. This concept is intended to reinforce consumer's positive attitudes toward the airline's customer service and product delivery.

**Ask your students:**

1. How does SWA's approach to no-fee flying (offering the entire flight experience for one price) reinforce consumers' positive attitudes toward the airline?

2. How does the Business Select option specifically accomplish this goal?

### CHAPTER VIDEO SUMMARY

**Targeting and Positioning at Numi Tea**

Run time:  6:46 minutes

Demand for natural products has exploded in recent years, giving a boost to companies like Numi Organic Teas. Getting consumers to try Numi products often involves addressing attitudes on health, sustainability issues, and the value of premium products. Although sampling is Numi's most successful tactic for attracting new customers, the company also uses advertising to educate consumers on fair trade issues and the health benefits of tea drinking.

**Ask your students:**

1. Which of the bases for segmenting consumer markets does Numi use to divide up the overall market of tea products?

2. Would you classify Numi Tea's marketing strategy as "concentrated"? If so, what are the plusses and minuses of using such a strategy in today's market?

Visit **login.cengage.com** for additional materials to enhance your lectures!

CHAPTER 7 ATTITUDES AND ATTITUDE CHANGE

# Key Terms

# Lecture Example

Marketers know that consumers' attitudes and beliefs can play a strong role in their buying behaviors. In this country, one of the most powerful of these is the ever elusive American Dream. While difficult to define, most people would include owning their own home as part of their idea of "making it." And this seems to be holding true, even in this current economic downturn. What developers and marketers need to respond to here, is not the belief that home ownership is a powerful testament to success, but to Americans' changing attitudes about what they need and are willing to spend when purchasing a home. The years of maxing out qualification budgets and flipping houses into luxury palaces are no longer present. According to a recent Coldwell Banker Real Estate survey, 68% of buyers paid less for a home than the amount for which they qualified, while 53% reported that they purchased a home because it was more economical than renting.

Source: Michael Lerner. "Buying Home Still American Dream," *The Washington Times*, July 22, 2010, **http://www.washingtontimes.com.**

# Discussion Questions

1. What are the various components to attitude? How are they different from each other?

2. What are the components of the attitude-toward-the-object model?  What are the components of the theory of reasoned action?

3. Q-score ratings are used to describe the favorableness of celebrity endorsers. Who are your favorite celebrities? What products do you think they would be most effective in endorsing? What source characteristics do they possess?

# Group Activity

Based on the opening vignette of the chapter, conduct a discussion about attitudes toward brands. In the opening story, Keiton purchased an Apple iPad. This is a discussion that tends to appeal to both sexes in the class. Visit **www.google.com**, and copy the images of the top ten brands. (I've used Sean John, GE, my university logo, Baskin Robbins, KFC, McDonalds, Tony the Tiger, Betty Crocker, Marlboro, and Pillsbury Doughboy.) Put the images on a PowerPoint slide show, and project them to the class. This activity can also be completed on a sheet of paper. See how many students can name all ten of the top brands. The first student to name all ten correctly can be awarded extra credit points for participation or on an exam. This activity can then prompt a discussion about how we shape attitudes and the role that marketers play. You can refer back to Keiton and his iPad. Why did he buy it? Did his parents own iPads? Did he do research about it? Did he get advice from family and friends?

# Assignments

Consider all of the Facebook groups that you belong to, or the tweets that you follow on Twitter. How do/does this behavior(s) say anything about your attitudes towards brands or products?

# Beyond the Class

A selection of materials is in the Instructor's Manual.

Visit **login.cengage.com** for additional materials to enhance your lectures!

**WHAT'S INSIDE** Key topics in this chapter: culture and the meaning of objects and activities, key dimensions of core societal values, acculturation and enculturation, elements of verbal and nonverbal communication, and current emerging markets and opportunities.

# CHAPTER 8 PREP CARD

## Consumer Culture

# Learning Outcomes

**LO1** Understand how culture provides the true meaning of objects and activities.

**LO2** Use the key dimensions of core societal values to apply the concept of cultural distance.

**LO3** Define acculturation and enculturation.

**LO4** List fundamental elements of verbal and nonverbal communication.

**LO5** Discuss current emerging consumer markets and scan for opportunities.

# Chapter 8 Outline

# Multimedia

## PPT—THE HIGHLIGHTS
- Slide 4   What is Culture?
- Slide 11   Dimensions of Cultural Values
- Slide 13   Cultural Distance
- Slide 16   How is Culture Learned?
- Slide 22   Verbal and Nonverbal Communication
- Slide 34   Emerging Cultures

## VIDEO

**PowerPoint Clip from *Raleigh America***

Run time: 1:33 minutes

Raleigh Bicycle is a bicycle manufacturing company founded in 1887 in Nottingham, England. When the "Lance Armstrong effect" toward lighter, faster bikes began to dominate the cycling market, Raleigh needed a way to differentiate its products. Historically Raleigh is known for producing a sturdy, all-steel frame bicycle. To compete in today's market, Raleigh relied on the culture of its European consumers as well as the messenger cyclists here in the states. The result is a return to the steel-frame lifestyle bicycle for the U.S. market that stands out in a sea of training cycles and meets the needs of an emerging market.

### Ask your students:
1. How does Raleigh use its knowledge of existing consumer cultures to adapt and market a competitive product?
2. How does Raleigh's steel-frame bicycle translate into value for their target consumer?

## CHAPTER VIDEO SUMMARY

**Method Global Beginnings**

Run time: 8:00 minutes

Method believes cleaning should be a happy, healthy experience. While the company's non-toxic home cleaners and personal care products have earned the trust of moms and eco-consumers in the U.S., Method aims to take its vision of "a cleaner clean" to countries around the world. But while Method co-founder Eric Ryan celebrates his company's success in domestic markets, creating a global brand presents many challenges arising from international differences in language and culture.

### Ask your students:
1. Is Method a multinational company? Explain.
2. Which environmental factors facing all global markets is Method confronting as it begins to expand into foreign markets?

Visit **login.cengage.com** for additional materials to enhance your lectures!

CHAPTER 8 CONSUMER CULTURE

# Key Terms

# Lecture Example

In order to tap into one of the hottest emerging consumer markets, Western marketers must tap into the culture of China. One question marketers must consider is whether companies should try to localize their brands in Chinese consumers' minds, or if brands should maintain their Western messaging. The answer for now seems to be "both." Companies should adjust brand messages in order to gain access to the Chinese consumer culture while holding on to the positive associations that are often linked to western products, such as quality and safety.

Source: Joel Backaler. "Inside China's Consumer Culture," *Forbes.com*, August 12, 2010, **http://blogs.forbes.com.**

# Discussion Questions

1. In what 3 ways does culture shape value for consumers?

2. List and briefly describe each of the five dimensions of CSVs.

3. What is meant by glocalization?

# Group Activity

Design an advertisement that intends to communicate the benefits of a facial cream to family skin care for each of the following consumer markets. Consider the relative role of verbal and nonverbal communication in doing so.

- Germany
- Egypt
- Japan
- Israel
- New Zealand

# Assignments

Interview a fellow student who is from a culture other than your own. How does this student view the dimensions of CSV (individualism, masculinity, power distance, uncertainty avoidance, long-term avoidance)? How have these dimensions affected the student's behavior since arriving in your country? Were you aware of the importance of these dimensions in the student's life? What major cultural differences has the student noticed since arriving in your country?

# Beyond the Class

A selection of materials is in the Instructor's Manual.

Visit **login.cengage.com** for additional
materials to enhance your lectures!

WHAT'S INSIDE   Key topics in this chapter: how microcultures affect consumer behavior, how culture is hierarchical, major U.S. microcultures including regional, sex role, age-based, generational, religious, ethnic, income/social class, and street, the role of microcultures worldwide, demographic analysis, and trends in culture and demographics.

CHAPTER 9 PREP CARD

**Microcultures**

## Learning Outcomes

**LO1** Apply the concept of microculture as it influences consumer behavior.

**LO2** Know the major U.S. microcultural groups.

**LO3** Realize that microculture is not a uniquely American phenomenon.

**LO4** Perform a demographic analysis.

**LO5** Identify major cultural and demographic trends.

## Chapter 9 Outline

## Multimedia

### PPT—THE HIGHLIGHTS

- Slide 4   Microculture and Consumer Culture
- Slide 10   Exhibit 9.3: Regional Differences and Preferences Among U.S. Consumers
- Slide 14   Generation Microculture
- Slide 17   Ethnic Microculture
- Slide 28   Cultural and Demographic Trends Affecting Consumer Behavior

### VIDEO

**PowerPoint Clip from *Ben & Jerry's***
Run time:  1:29 minutes

Ben & Jerry's premium ice cream was founded in 1978 with little more than $12,000 and an old-fashioned rock-salt ice cream maker. Today it is one of the most successful brands on the market. Part of the company's success lies in its clearly defined brand image as a super-premium product with a fun, counter-cultural edge.

**Ask your students:**
1. Describe a typical Ben & Jerry's consumer.
2. Which microcultures does the Ben & Jerry's brand appeal to?

### CHAPTER VIDEO SUMMARY

**Flight 001**
Run time:  6:55 minutes

The video features Brad John and John Sencion, co-founders of Flight 001, talking about their business venture, the products they sell, and their unique approach to reaching their target market. The focus of the video is on the operations of the firm's Greenwich Village store in New York City. Some Flight 001 employees also offer observations regarding how the company seeks to connect with and provide various types of products that travelers—particularly air travelers—need for their journeys.

**Ask your students:**
1. Describe the microcultures that Flight 001 is targeting with the product lines that it sells.
2. How does Flight 001 reach customers in these microcultures?

Visit **login.cengage.com** for additional materials to enhance your lectures!

CHAPTER 9 MICROCULTURES

# Key Terms

# Lecture Example

Researching microcultures isn't something marketers do just for fun. It's an important method of staying on top of trends in order to develop and promote goods, products, and services that will appeal to consumers. One hot microculture businesses are cashing in on is the "retrosexual" male. Consider the hot barbershops cropping up in major cities across the United States, particularly in Los Angeles. These barbershops borrow the traditional male elements of London's historic barbershop, while updating them with mod influences popular on TV shows such as "Mad Men." Today's man can get the clean-cut and well turned-out appearance of a gentleman all while playing Xbox and having a beer.

Source: Jim Shi, "Hip Barbershops in Los Angeles," *The Financial Times,* August 6, 2010, **http://www.ft.com.**

# Discussion Questions

1. What is meant by the term "the nine nations of North America"?

2. What is meant by the term demographic analysis?

3. What are some major cultural and demographic trends?

# Group Activity

Using the six class distinctions detailed in this chapter, how would you describe the social classes present at your university?

# Assignments

Ask fellow students what occupations they hope to one day secure. How would you describe the social class that applies to these occupations? Also, ask your classmates if one reason for going to college is to achieve a higher social class.

# Beyond the Class

A selection of materials is in the Instructor's Manual.

Visit **login.cengage.com** for additional materials to enhance your lectures!

**WHAT'S INSIDE** Key topics in this chapter: different types of reference groups that influence consumers and value perceptions; social power that reference groups have on perceptions; differences between utilitarian, informational, and value-expressive group influence; the importance of word-of-mouth communications; household influence on consumer behavior, and the role of social media and networking in influencing groups.

# CHAPTER 10 PREP CARD
## Group and Interpersonal Influence

## Learning Outcomes

**LO1** Understand the different types of reference groups that influence consumers and how reference groups influence value perceptions.

**LO2** Describe the various types of social power that reference groups exert on members.

**LO3** Comprehend the difference between informational, utilitarian, and value-expressive reference group influence.

**LO4** Understand the importance of word-of-mouth communications in consumer behavior.

**LO5** Comprehend the role of household influence in consumer behavior.

## Chapter 10 Outline

## Multimedia

### PPT—THE HIGHLIGHTS

- Slide 4    Reference Group
- Slide 6    Types of Groups
- Slide 17   Word-of-Mouth (WOM)
- Slide 26   Traditional Family Households
- Slide 28   Household Purchase Roles

### VIDEO

**PowerPoint Clip from *Peet's Coffee and Tea***

Run time: 1:30 minutes

Peet's Coffee and Tea has focused on building relationships and founding a community since its founding. In 1966 Alfred Peet opened a coffee shop in Berkley, California where he roasted coffee beans using techniques he learned in his native Holland. The shop soon became a place for the community to gather as well as a place for consumers to purchase and learn about Peet's products. Now a large-scale chain, Peet's developed the Peetniks member program to develop and maintain a sense of community that will enhance consumers' experiences as well as bolster sales.

**Ask your students:**

1. How does the Peetniks program create a sense of group influence?
2. What hard benefits do members get from belonging to the Peetniks program?

### CHAPTER VIDEO SUMMARY

**Teen Research Unlimited**

Run time: 8:10 minutes

Gathering information is key to marketing success. For businesses interested in selling products to teens, Teenage Research Unlimited (TRU) is an invaluable research partner. The marketing research firm has been studying teen habits since the 1980s, and data gleaned from TRU's focus groups and surveys reveals the ways in which teens are influenced by reference groups and each other. According to analysts, the teenage consumer segment will continue to grow in importance, especially in the age of cell phones, iPods, and social networking.

**Ask your students:**

1. What makes TRU's research so important?
2. In what way is the company unique?

Visit **login.cengage.com** for additional materials to enhance your lectures!

# Key Terms

# Lecture Example

When we hear the term peer-pressure we tend to think of the negative effects group behavior can have on young adults. Well, try this on for size—billionaires using peer-pressure to increase philanthropic giving. The intent of the "giving pledge," founded in the summer of 2010, is to encourage giving from America's wealthiest citizens in order to address some of America's most pressing social issues. With an impressive list of names like Warren Buffet, Bill and Melinda Gates, Michael Bloomberg, Barron Hilton, Ted Turner, and George Lucas, the hope is to generate peer-pressure among billionaires, encouraging them toward a large-scale approach to philanthropy.

Source: Andrew Clark, "U.S. Billionaires Club Together—To Give Away Half Their Fortunes to Good Causes," *The Guardian*, August 4, 2010, **http://www.guardian.co.uk.**

# Discussion Questions

1.  What are the differences between formal and informal reference groups? What formal and informal groups do you belong to?

2.  How do the various power bases emerge in an online social networking setting? Or, do they?

3.  How does WOM influence consumers? Why isn't all WOM equally influential? What type of WOM has the greatest impact on consumers?

# Group Activity

Discuss with students the issue of sex role orientation as it pertains to household decision making. What differences emerge in student feelings about sex role orientation? How does this affect their behavior?

# Assignments

Ask a group of classmates if they belong to any Facebook groups. How many do they belong to? Which groups are they? Are any of them for a company or a brand? Do you belong to any? What benefits do you (or your classmates) get from participating in these groups?

# Beyond the Class

A selection of materials is in the Instructor's Manual.

Visit **login.cengage.com** for additional
materials to enhance your lectures!

**WHAT'S INSIDE**   Key topics in this chapter: how values vary in situations; how time affects consumer behavior; shopping as a consumer activity; types of purchases: unplanned, impulsive and compulsive shopping; atmospherics; and antecedent conditions.

# CHAPTER 11 | PREP CARD

## Consumers in Situations

## Learning Outcomes

**LO1**   Understand how value varies with situations.

**LO2**   Know the different ways that time affects consumer behavior.

**LO3**   Analyze shopping as a consumer activity using the different categories of shopping activities.

**LO4**   Distinguish the concepts of unplanned, impulse, and compulsive consumer behavior.

**LO5**   Use the concept of atmospherics to create consumer value.

**LO6**   Understand how antecedent conditions can alter consumer outcomes.

## Chapter 11 Outline

## Multimedia

### PPT—THE HIGHLIGHTS

- Slide 4    Situational Influences
- Slide 8    Time and Consumer Behavior
- Slide 17    Exhibit 11.4: Impulsive vs. Unplanned Shopping Behavior
- Slide 24    Exhibit 11.7: The Qualities of an Environment
- Slide 28    Antecedent Conditions

### VIDEO

**PowerPoint Clip from *Murray's Cheese***

Run time: 1:43 minutes

Murray's Cheese is a dairy retailer that has grown in recent years from a single counter to a multi-store, wholesale business with a partnership with a large chain of grocery stores. One of the keys to Murray's success lies in its employees who do more than just sell cheese. Counter mongers walk customers through an experience helping them to learn and choose the cheese that is right for their taste and occasion. Part of the experience involves tasting the cheese. This helps customers make informed decisions and also provides Murray with immediate product feedback. This strategy also involves providing promotional cheeses for sampling at the counter to increase sales from a single cheese to a multi-cheese sale.

**Ask your students:**

1. What type of shopping value does Murray's provide for its customers?
2. Why does at-counter tasting help promote Murray's Cheese sales?

### CHAPTER VIDEO SUMMARY

**High Sierra Climbs to New Heights**

Run time: 6:30 minutes

High Sierra Sport Company is a leading manufacturer of bags for sports, travel, business, and personal use. For over 30 years the brand has been associated with rugged design and quality. Although High Sierra sells to retailers and not directly to consumers, its marketers are aware of how seasons, situations, and retail settings impact the demand for its bags. Skiers, students, professionals, and institutional buyers are all purchasers of High Sierra bags, but the situations in which each group makes purchase decisions are markedly different, requiring different marketing approaches.

**Ask your students:**

1. How would you classify High Sierra's products? Explain your choice.
2. Describe the factors that contribute to High Sierra's brand equity.

Visit **login.cengage.com** for additional materials to enhance your lectures!

# Key Terms

# Lecture Example

Using coupons to encourage consumer purchasing is nothing new. Using a cell phone to deliver and personalize those coupons is definitely new. This application allows marketers to instantly provide targeted incentives to consumers. Consumers benefit by receiving deals on items they are potentially already out shopping for, and the coupons are instantly redeemable.

Source: Sarah Haughey, "Coupons? There's an App for That," *The San Francisco Examiner,* August 15, 2010, **http://www.sfexaminer.com.**

# Discussion Questions

1. How does time pressure affect consumer behavior? Name at least two businesses or industries whose survival depends on consumer segments that experience high amounts of time pressure.

2. What are the different types of shopping activities in which consumers participate? What types of value would you associate with each? Can a retail website be designed to cater specifically to each type of orientation? Explain.

3. What is the sequence of events through which atmosphere might encourage a purchase? Use an example to illustrate your answer.

# Group Activity

Have students pair up to work on this group activity. Have each group describe a woman's level of involvement with purchasing a designer item (e.g., shoes or outfit); another option is for students to determine a man's level of involvement with his car. In both cases, the group should determine the different marketing stimuli. For the women, determine how you might design a strategy for consumers who like to purchase items at discounters, such as Marshall's or DSW Footwear. For the men, determine a strategy that fits the DIY (do-it-yourself) market for those who are very involved in working on their cars.

# Assignments

Take a look at 3–5 Internet retail sites for multichannel retailers (meaning those with both physical stores and virtual shores), such as **www.harrods.com.** Is the real shopping environment or the virtual shopping environment likely to have a greater impact on consumer behavior? Explain your choice.

# Beyond the Class

A selection of materials is in the Instructor's Manual.

Visit **login.cengage.com** for additional materials to enhance your lectures!

**WHAT'S INSIDE** Key topics in this chapter: activities involved in the consumer decision-making process, three major decision research perspectives, consideration set in the decision-making process, and factors that influence the amount of consumer search.

# CHAPTER 12 PREP CARD

## Decision Making I: Need Recognition and Search

# Learning Outcomes

**LO1** Understand the activities involved in the consumer decision-making process.

**LO2** Describe the three major decision-making research perspectives.

**LO3** Explain the three major types of decision-making approaches.

**LO4** Understand the importance of the consideration set in the decision-making process.

**LO5** Understand the factors that influence the amount of search performed by consumers.

# Chapter 12 Outline

# Multimedia

## PPT—THE HIGHLIGHTS

- Slide 5    Exhibit 12.2: Consumer Decision-Making Process
- Slide 9    Exhibit 12.3: Perspectives on Consumer Decision Making
- Slide 13   Exhibit 12.4: Decision-Making Approaches
- Slide 22   Exhibit 12.5: Consideration Set
- Slide 27   Factors Influencing the Amount of Search

## VIDEO

### PowerPoint Clip from *Manifest Digital*

Run time:  1:49 minutes

Manifest Digital is a marketing and design firm with a focus in website development. Manifest Digital focuses on making their client's sites customer-oriented and easy to use. This company relies on user-centered principles to meet the needs of both their clients—those producing and marketing goods, as well as the website's users—potential consumers. For Manifest Digital the end goal is providing users with a rewarding experience.

**Ask your students:**

1. What does Manifest Digital mean when it says its philosophy is based on "user-centered principles"?
2. How has this philosophy contributed to the company's success?

## CHAPTER VIDEO SUMMARY

### Consumer Behavior at Scholfield Honda

Run time:  5:49 minutes

Buying an automobile is a lengthy process, and the sales associates at Scholfield Honda are experts at identifying how different shoppers arrive at different purchase decisions. Though some drivers are habitual Honda buyers, most consumers research brands and models before driving a vehicle off the lot. Whether an individual is shopping for a sports car, SUV, hybrid, or convertible, the issues of fuel efficiency, size, quality, and price are important considerations in the decision-making process.

**Ask your students:**

1. Name the top influence(s) impacting a consumer's decision to buy a car from Scholfield Honda.
2. Go to **www.honda.com** and view the different Hondas to select the car you would be most likely to purchase.

Visit **login.cengage.com** for additional materials to enhance your lectures!

# Key Terms

# Lecture Example

Anticipating and predicting how and why consumers make purchasing decisions is a vital part of marketing. The closer one's product or service is to what a customer wants, the more likely a sale is to be made. Companies need not only to provide information, but the right kind of information. Sometimes what companies want to represent and what consumers want can differ. For example, demand for calorie labels has seen a recent spike, particularly in the fast-food industry, but some restaurateurs are reluctant to make this move. In a recent survey conducted by Aramark, a food services company, 83% of consumers want nutritional information available in restaurants. However, the question remains if providing this information will really affect food choices toward healthier options—some studies have shown that only 10-20% of diners make a lower-calorie choice based on nutritional information.

Source: Roni Caryn Rabin, "Calorie Labels May Clarify Options, Not Actions," *The New York Times,* July 17, 2010, **http://www.nytimes.com.**

# Discussion Questions

1. Describe how social networking sites relate to each of the steps in consumer decision making.

2. What types of products are generally purchased after an extended decision-making process has occurred? What types of products are purchased after a habitual decision-making process?

3. What are the differences between the awareness set, consideration set, inert set, and inept set?

# Group Activity

Compare a number of automobile-buying websites, such as **www.autobytel.com** and **www.carsdirect.com.** What types of information are shown? What site features do you find to be most valuable?

# Assignments

Visit a Facebook fan page, like Honda, for example. What types of information about the product can you find on the site? What types of topics are discussed on the site?

# Beyond the Class

A selection of materials is in the Instructor's Manual.

Visit **login.cengage.com** for additional materials to enhance your lectures!

WHAT'S INSIDE  Key topics in this chapter: difference between evaluative criteria and determinant criteria, how values affect the evaluation of alternatives, importance of product categorization in the evaluation of alternatives process, and compensatory and noncompensatory rules that guide consumer choice.

CHAPTER 13 | PREP CARD

## Decision Making II: Alternative Evaluation and Choice

# Learning Outcomes

**LO1** Understand the difference between evaluative criteria and determinant criteria.

**LO2** Comprehend how value affects the evaluation of alternatives.

**LO3** Explain the importance of product categorization in the evaluation of alternatives process.

**LO4** Distinguish between compensatory and noncompensatory rules that guide consumer choice.

# Chapter 13 Outline

# Multimedia

## PPT—THE HIGHLIGHTS

- Slide 5   Evaluative Criteria
- Slide 8   Determinant Criteria
- Slide 11   Value and Alternative Evaluation
- Slide 14   Product Categories
- Slide 25   Consumer Choice: Decision Rules

## VIDEO

**PowerPoint Clip *from Kodak***

Run time:  0:42 minutes

To maintain sales, even an old, highly successful company such as Kodak must invest in product development and management. Consumers will not continue to buy products that are outdated, particularly in the realm of electronics. To stay on the cutting edge, Kodak has paid close attention to consumer's needs, even if consumers aren't yet aware of them. This means occasionally introducing a product that may have low sales because it is ahead of its time. At Kodak, consumer confidence is linked to trusting Kodak's technical abilities, product usability, and up-to-date merchandise.

**Ask your students:**

1. What attributes of consumers' decision-making process does Kodak rely on?
2. What other attributes are necessary for a customer to actually make a purchase?

## CHAPTER VIDEO SUMMARY

**Ford Motor Company**

Run time:  8:00 minutes

Shopping for a fuel-efficient SUV was easy in 2005 when Ford introduced the Escape, the first and only hybrid on the market. But today there are dozens of alternative energy models on the road, and consumers looking for the most environmentally friendly SUV have many options from which to choose. The Ford brand continues to benefit from its association with historic firsts in auto manufacturing, but some consumers ignore brand history and simply choose the vehicle that performs best on a single important feature, such as fuel economy.

**Ask your students**

1. Why would Ford create a hybrid SUV? What makes the Escape attractive to consumers?
2. How did Ford approach the pricing of the Escape? What effect does this have on consumers' decisions?

Visit **login.cengage.com** for additional materials to enhance your lectures!

CHAPTER 13 DECISION MAKING II: ALTERNATIVE EVALUATION AND CHOICE

# Key Terms

# Lecture Example

Product categorization and criteria selection play an important role in consumer behavior. If consumers perceive benefits beyond their own lives, a "feel-good" effect can come into play. This can happen when proceeds from a purchase go to support charities, the local economy, or particularly hot now, environmental or "green" causes. However, while demand for green products and services remains on the rise, the economic downturn has negatively affected spending in this category. This is according to the Green Confidence Index which measures Americans' attitudes toward and confidence in the green movement according to three components: responsibility (of companies or institutions, and leaders); information provided; and purchasing rates of consumers.

Source: "Flagging Economy Sinks Green Consumer Confidence," *GreenBiz.com*, August 2, 2010, **http://www.greenbiz.com.**

# Discussion Questions

1. What is the difference between features and benefits? Do consumers pay more attention to features or benefits? How can benefits be utilitarian or hedonic?

2. How does product categorization theory apply to snack foods like potato chips? How does this categorization help you as a consumer?

3. Do consumers rely on one type of decision rule or another? Can the rules be used together?

# Group Activity

Assign students to groups and have them visit Facebook. Within Facebook, ask them to look up various fan pages for products of their choice. Examples would be cereals, snack food, ice cream, colas, etc. Within each of these group pages (e.g., Special K group for cereal), ask the students to share how many times competing products are mentioned and have them present how the other products are discussed. How would these discussions on fan pages influence their decision making? Are all of the discussions about competing products negative? Does the sponsor of the website (the company) provide comparative information about competing brands? If so, how does this influence consumers? Ask students to compare their findings across groups. What differences in information are found for various product categories?

# Assignments

The next time you go shopping, look for green products in the cleaning aisle of the grocery/department store. Do you think that these products are as effective as other cleaning products? Why or why not? What can marketers do to improve the promotion of these products?

# Beyond the Class

A selection of materials is in the Instructor's Manual.

Visit **login.cengage.com** for additional
materials to enhance your lectures!

**WHAT'S INSIDE** Key topics in this chapter: the link from consumption value to satisfaction, importance of satisfaction in consumer behavior, emotions that can affect postconsumption behavior, expectancy disconfirmation, equity, and attribution theory approaches, problems with commonly applied satisfaction measures and how consumers dispose of products.

# CHAPTER 14 PREP CARD

## Consumption to Satisfaction

# Learning Outcomes

**LO1** Gain an appreciation of the link from consumption to value to satisfaction.

**LO2** Discuss the relative importance of satisfaction and value in consumer behavior.

**LO3** Know that emotions other than satisfaction can affect postconsumption behavior.

**LO4** Use expectancy disconfirmation, equity, and attribution theory approaches to explain consumers' postconsumption reactions.

**LO5** Understand problems with commonly applied satisfaction measures.

**LO6** Describe some ways that consumers dispose of products.

# Chapter 14 Outline

# Multimedia

## PPT—THE HIGHLIGHTS

- Slide 9   Exhibit 14.3: Consumption, Value, and Satisfaction
- Slide 17   Exhibit 14.5: Basic Disconfirmation Process
- Slide 20   Equity Theory
- Slide 21   Attribution Theory
- Slide 28   Disposing of Refuse

## VIDEO

### PowerPoint Clip from *Boyne Resorts*

Run time:  0:54 minutes

Boyne USA Resorts has built on its customer base of sport and leisure enthusiasts to grow from a single outpost to a multi-resort, nationwide company. Because much of Boyne's success depends on the weather, Boyne leadership, managers, and employees must be resourceful and adaptable in order to keep consumer satisfaction high. In some cases this has meant heavy investment in snowmaking technology, while in others it involves building large-scale, indoor water parks. In any situation, Boyne reinforces consumer satisfaction through a program called "Boyne Basics". This company-wide program is designed to build excellence in customer service.

**Ask your students:**

1. In what ways does the "Boyne Basics" program enhance customer satisfaction?
2. How does the Boyne company structure reinforce the goal of consumer satisfaction?

## CHAPTER VIDEO SUMMARY

### Sephora Retailing for Success

Run time:  8:00 minutes

At Sephora, shopping is all about experiencing products. When the French cosmetics retailer came to America in the late 1990s, it immediately opened its counters to free trials of makeup, fragrances, and skin care items. The try-before-you-buy concept is a hit with female customers, and sales associates at Sephora are always on hand to facilitate and educate. The company's loyalty program ensures that satisfied customers keep coming back for more.

**Ask your students:**

1. Visit **www.sephora.com** and browse the online store. How does Sephora use the online environment to promote its products without the advantage of letting customers try before they buy?
2. Sephora is working out the details of a new loyalty program and they have asked you to give your input and advice. What do you tell them? How should they integrate this new program with the retailing mix they have already adopted?

Visit **login.cengage.com** for additional materials to enhance your lectures!

# Key Terms

# Lecture Example

When we think about consumer satisfaction and the consumption process, the link seems clear. Businesses with high levels of consumer satisfaction succeed, and those with low levels fail. However, this isn't always the case. According to a major recent survey, the social networking website Facebook ranks in the bottom five percent of consumer satisfaction with privately held companies in the United States. Respondents had no shortage of complaints about the site's performance and user-friendliness. Yet, Facebook continues to grow at an explosive rate. How is this? Consumers who want to participate in social networking and want access to the largest possible community have little choice but to use the Facebook system. This means that the value of access outweighs the value of performance satisfaction.

Source: Matthew Shaer, "Why Facebook Enjoys Explosive Growth—Despite Its Many Stumbles," *The Christian Science Monitor,* August 19, 2010, **http://www.csmonitor.com.**

# Discussion Questions

1. What determines a product's authenticity? How and when does authenticity contribute to increased value?

2. How does the expectancy/disconfirmation process work?

3. List different sources of consumer satisfaction.

# Group Activity

In class, have students brainstorm a list of their favorite brands and/or products. This activity is directly related to the consumption process (reaction). During class, have students individually write a letter to the customer service department expressing why they like that particular brand. Have 2-3 students share their letters with the class. Students should be encouraged to send their letters to the particular companies.

# Assignments

What role does hope play in creating satisfaction or dissatisfaction? Can you think of an instance when you felt a lot of hope prior to trying some product? How did it turn out?

# Beyond the Class

A selection of materials is in the Instructor's Manual.

Visit **login.cengage.com** for additional materials to enhance your lectures!

**WHAT'S INSIDE** Key topics in this chapter: outcomes of consumption including why consumers complain and take out revenge for bad experiences; in addition, switching costs and how they affect future customer behavior, customer loyalty and the role value plays in shaping true loyalty and building relationships.

# CHAPTER 15 | PREP CARD

### Consumer Relationships

## Learning Outcomes

**LO1** List and define the behavioral outcomes of consumption.

**LO2** Know why consumers complain and the ramifications of complaining behavior for a marketing firm.

**LO3** Use the concept of switching costs to understand why consumers do or do not repeat purchase behavior.

**LO4** Describe each component of true consumer loyalty.

**LO5** Understand the role that value plays in shaping loyalty and building consumer relationships.

## Chapter 15 Outline

## Multimedia

### PPT—THE HIGHLIGHTS

- Slide 4    Exhibit 15.1: A More Detailed Look at Postconsumption Reactions
- Slide 6    Complaining Behavior
- Slide 8    Exhibit 15.2: The Complainer vs. the Noncomplainer
- Slide 15   Exhibit 15.3: Factors Contributing to Switching
- Slide 29   Exhibit 15.9: Characteristics of Relationship Quality

### VIDEO

**PowerPoint Clip from *Travelocity***

Run time: 1:42 minutes

Travelocity is a pioneering brand in the world of Internet travel businesses. Travelocity has maintained its brand leadership by embracing a stance of traveler advocacy. The Travelocity Guarantee promotes the idea that what you book will be right, or Travelocity will work with their partners to make it right.

**Ask your students:**

1. How does the Travelocity Guarantee reinforce brand loyalty?
2. What kind of response has Travelocity gotten from the launch of the guarantee program?

### CHAPTER VIDEO SUMMARY

**Success Blooms at 1-800-FLOWERS**

Run time: 6:56 minutes

The floral industry changed forever when 1-800-FLOWERS began offering same-day delivery of fresh cut flowers anywhere in the United States. But delivering flowers nationwide in a timely manner requires Web-based technologies and careful coordination with local florists and couriers. In all, 1-800-FLOWERS uses approximately 35,000 supply chain partners to deliver its fast, reliable service. The result of this behind-the-scenes effort is unprecedented convenience at a level that only e-commerce can deliver.

**Ask your students:**

1. Describe the unique challenges faced by companies that sell highly perishable products.
2. How does 1-800-FLOWERS meet and address those challenges?

Visit **login.cengage.com** for additional materials to enhance your lectures!

CHAPTER 15 CONSUMER RELATIONSHIPS

# Key Terms

# Lecture Example

During an economic downturn, one of the first consumer relationships to take a hit is brand loyalty. When customers are feeling the pressures of cost, they are more likely to turn to low-priced, bargain products rather than stick with their favorite brands. However, prices can only go so low and downturns don't last forever. Retailers need to consider how they can earn long-term, loyal consumers now. Recent research indicates that one powerful way to do this is through social networking. Consumers are increasingly using the Web to collect and put out information related to products, goods, and services. Building a social community around a brand helps promote awareness and allows marketers to keep brands relevant and targeted.

Source: Helen Leggatt, "Rebuild Brand Loyalty with Social Media," *Biz Report,* August 19, 2010, **http://www.bizreport.com.**

# Discussion Questions

1. Describe an instance when you complained about poor service. Using Exhibit 15.1, explain how you complained to the establishment. Was your complaint acted upon by the service-providing firm?

2. What are the different types of switching costs that a consumer faces? Provide examples of each from your own consumer experiences.

3. What is relationship quality, and how does a relationship create value?

# Group Activity

A similar exercise performed in Chapter 14 would also apply to this chapter under the category "dissatisfied customers." Have a few students share negative experiences (cognitive dissonance) with a brand or establishment and write letters expressing their dissatisfaction. Students should be encouraged in the "proper" way to complain so that they can distinguish the difference between complainers and dissatisfied customers. This important exercise emphasizes the point that relatively few customers actually complain. Have students share their experiences in class, and assess which groups would be considered "angered complainers" and "disgusted or hopeless" customers. Complainers, although sometimes unpleasant to deal with, are valuable sources of feedback about potential problems in service quality, product performance, or system malfunction.

# Assignments

What switching costs are built into doing business with mobile phone providers, healthcare providers, Internet music services, and health clubs? Are all switching costs ethical?

# Beyond the Class

A selection of materials is in the Instructor's Manual.

Visit **login.cengage.com** for additional materials to enhance your lectures!

**WHAT'S INSIDE** Key topics in this chapter: consumer misbehavior and marketing ethics, consumer misbehavior and exchange, the difference between consumer misbehavior and consumer problem behavior, specific examples of consumer misbehavior and problem behavior, marketing ethics, corporate social responsibility, regulation in the marketing practice, major areas of public criticism of marketing.

# CHAPTER 16 PREP CARD

## Consumer and Marketing Misbehavior

# Learning Outcomes

**LO1** Understand the consumer misbehavior phenomenon and how it affects the exchange process.

**LO2** Distinguish between consumer misbehavior and consumer problem behavior.

**LO3** Discuss marketing ethics and how marketing ethics guide the development of marketing programs.

**LO4** Comprehend the role of corporate social responsibility in the field of marketing.

**LO5** Understand the various forms of regulation that affect marketing practice.

**LO6** Comprehend the major areas of criticism to which marketers are subjected.

# Chapter 16 Outline

Visit **login.cengage.com** for additional materials to enhance your lectures!

# Multimedia

## PPT—THE HIGHLIGHTS

- Slide 4     Consumer Misbehavior and Exchange
- Slide 6     Exhibit 16.1: Moral Beliefs, Ethical Decision Making, and Behavior
- Slide 11   Consumer Misbehavior and Problem Behavior
- Slide 10   The Marketing Concept and the Consumer
- Slide 28   Public Criticism of Marketing
- Slide 30   Products Liability

## VIDEO

### PowerPoint Clip from *Recycline*

Run time: 1:23 minutes

For an environmentally conscious consumer-product company like Recycline, it is essential that the customer understands and believes the "green story" behind their products. This means marketing both to retail partners in order to get the products on store shelves as well as marketing directly to consumers to make product sales. Recycline wants consumers to know that participating in the green marketplace doesn't mean that customers have to make sacrifices.

### Ask your students:

1. What does Recycline feel is essential to making green products mainstream?
2. What are consumers wary of when it comes to green marketing and green companies?

## CHAPTER VIDEO SUMMARY

### Organic Valley

Run time: 10:35 minutes

Organic Valley is a Wisconsin-based farming cooperative that produces dairy, vegetable, and meat products without pesticides or synthetic hormones. The co-op is part of a larger social responsibility trend in which businesses create products without depleting natural resources, harming animals, or polluting the environment. Organic Valley formed two decades ago when a group of farmers banded together to share organic farming techniques, and today the cooperative generates $200 million in annual revenue and boasts 600 members.

### Ask your students:

1. Describe at least one ethical challenge faced by organic farmers, such as Paul Deustche, or by Organic Valley.
2. How have consumers' perceptions of and attitudes toward organic foods changed over time?

# Key Terms

# Lecture Example

Every year *Fortune* magazine publishes a list of the world's most admired companies. While this list celebrates companies' positive behavior, many might not realize that this edition of the magazine also functions as a watchdog against companies' misbehavior. The magazine lists the top ten best and the top ten worst performers in each of the following categories:

- Innovation
- Use of assets
- Management quality
- Long-term investment
- Global competitiveness
- People management
- Social responsibility
- Financial soundness
- Product quality

Source: "World's Most Admired Companies," *Fortune*, March 22, 2010, **http://money.cnn.com/magazines/fortune.**

# Discussion Questions

1. How is value related to consumer misbehavior?

2. How do marketing ethics guide marketing decision making?

3. How does deceptive advertising differ from "puffery"?

# Group Activity

Have students get into groups. Have them discuss the oil spill that devastated the Gulf of Mexico in 2010. As them to discuss the following questions amongst themselves and then to compare answers across the groups. Encourage them to debate across groups what the company did well, what they did not do well, and what they should have done?

* In what ways did BP exhibit corporate social responsibility?

* In what ways did the company practice the societal marketing concept?

* How did they live up to their altruistic duties, ethical duties, and strategic initiatives?

* What should they have done differently?

* How would your group handle the situation if you were in control at BP?

# Assignments

In your opinion, which is a bigger problem area for society, consumer misbehavior or consumer problem behavior? Why? Ask consumers from an older demographic segment, like your parents, what they think are the biggest problem areas. Do you agree? Do you disagree? In what ways?

# Beyond the Class

A selection of materials is in the Instructor's Manual.

Visit **login.cengage.com** for additional materials to enhance your lectures!